Farewell to Maine Road

Gary James

POLAR PUBLISHING

Farewell to Maine Road

First published in Great Britain in 2003
by Polar Group Ltd, 9-17 Tuxford Road,
Leicester LE4 9WE, England.

Text copyright © Gary James 2003

Design copyright © Polar Print Group Ltd 2003

ISBN 0 1899538 19 4

Edited by Julian Baskcomb

Assistant Editor Julia Byrne

Designed by Trevor Hartley

Printed by Polar Print Group Ltd, 9-17 Tuxford Road,
Leicester LE4 9WE, England.
Tel: 0116 274 4700

Maine Road's most successful manager wraps up as he leaves the ground during 1968. As well as tremendous success as a manager Joe Mercer was also Arsenal's captain when the record League attendance was set, and played in England's 8-0 demolition of Scotland at the ground.

Contents

Introduction   *page* 6

1 END OF AN ERA   14
City v Manchester United, 2002   21
David Bernstein & Chris Bird   24
City v Southampton, 2003   25

**2 CONSTRUCTION OF
    MAINE ROAD**   34
Charles Swain   43
The Story of a Gypsy's Curse   44
Ernest Mangnall   46
City v Sheffield United, 1923   53
Going to the Game   60

3 THE FIRST DECADE   66
City v Cardiff City (FAC), 1924   69
Max Woosnam   71
Billy Meredith Benefit Match, 1925   72
City v Crystal Palace (FAC), 1926   74
Huddersfield v Sheff United (FACsf), 1928   76
FA Cup Semi-Finals at Maine Road   78
The Ground Committee   80
The Alexander Family   84
Cult Heroes   86

4 RECORD BREAKING YEARS   88
Wilf Wild   91
City v Stoke City (FAC), 1934   95
City v Arsenal, 1935   102
City v Arsenal, 1937   103
England v Scotland, 1943   109
Chants & Songs   113

**5 YOU'RE SUPPOSED TO
    BE AT HOME**   116
Birmingham v Derby (FACsf), 1946   121
United at Maine Road   124
City v Newport County, 1947   127
City v Manchester United, 1947   129
Roy & Kath Clarke   130
City v Hearts (Floodlit Friendly)   132
Rugby at Maine Road   133
Internationals at Maine Road   134

6 BIRTH OF THE KIPPAX   136
City v Everton (FAC), 1966   140
City v Newcastle United, 1957   144
Royal Blues   146
City v Swindon Town, 1965   151
Stan Gibson   154

7 THE NORTH STAND   158
City v Everton (FAC), 1966   162
North Stand Design   166
The Social Club   169
City v Tottenham Hotspur, 1967   174
City in Europe   178
Fanzines   180
Maine Road on Film   183

**8 UNDERSOIL AND OFF
    THE PITCH**   186
Rose's Room   191
Bernard Halford   192
City v Newcastle United, 1977   194
Crowd Control   198
Junior Blues   202
Rock the Stadium   204

9 ECLECTIC BLUES   208
City v Luton Town, 1983   214
Liverpool v Everton (Lge Cp Final), 1984   215
City v Charlton Athletic, 1985   217
City v Huddersfield Town, 1987   220
City v Manchester United, 1989   223
City v Queens Park Rangers, 1992   226
City v Tottenham Hotspur (FAC), 1993   229
Demonstrations   231

10 ALL SEATER   234
Peter Swales   238
City v Chelsea, 1994   239
The Flag   242
City v Tottenham Hotspur, 1994   246
Fans Committee   247
City v Newcastle United, 1996   247
City v Liverpool, 1996   248
The Great Queue of '99   250
City v Stoke City, 1998   250
Francis Lee   251
City v Birmingham City, 2000   252
City v Portsmouth, 2002   254
Supporters' Organisations   256
Helen Turner: Lady with the Bell   257

11 CITY ARE BACK   258
Ardwick FC v Bootle, 1892   261
Jimmy Broad   266
City v Burton Wanderers, 1894   263
Lawrence Furniss   267
John Chapman   268
Hyde Road Milestones   271
Turnstiles   272
City of Manchester Stadium Milestones   276
City v TNS (UEFA Cup), 2003   277
A First Time for Everything   281
Programmes   282

12 STATISTICS AND RECORDS   284
Hyde Road Facts & Figures   286
Maine Road Facts & Figures   287
The Maine Road Record   288
Selected Maine Road Milestones   288
Attendances Records   290

**A SPECIAL PLACE IN
  OUR HEARTS**   294
Subscribers   297

Introduction

Football grounds hardly ever feature in architectural histories. The people who compile such publications rarely investigate the background to some of the most attended buildings in the nation. Even Manchester publications have largely ignored the sports grounds which have helped to give this city its unique position. Of course, this is starting to change as City's award winning new home, The City of Manchester Stadium, appears in major works on the city and on English architecture, but Maine Road, and indeed United's and Lancashire's grounds, should also feature in any major work on Greater Manchester's buildings. The fact they don't says a great deal about perceptions of sports grounds. Clearly these grounds may not be as architecturally beautiful as the Town Hall or Central Library, but in terms of their history and importance they do deserve at least a mention.

To me, Maine Road is the most important sports building in Manchester. It holds many, many records and firsts. First English venue to stage European football; first to host a World Cup qualifying match; highest provincial crowd; highest League crowd... the list goes on. This book aims to do what all architectural works have failed to do and that is to recognise the stadium's importance to Manchester and to consider the development of Maine Road throughout the last eighty or so years.

I've attended Maine Road since I was a baby in the 1960s and have always felt I understood what the place meant, however over the last couple of years Maine Road has taken on a different significance for me as I have researched this book. I've seen areas of the ground I didn't know existed; I've met and interviewed some wonderful people; and I've re-discovered some excellent historical photographs and information.

Maine Road means different things to different people. A few - and it is only a few - believe it's simply a stadium. Nothing more, nothing less. Fortunately to most, Maine Road means a great deal more as I hope this book demonstrates.

I originally planned to write a book on the stadium back in 1986 - this would have been my first publication - but fortunately circumstances prevented its development from progressing. I say fortunately because I know now I was ill-equipped to compile something of the quality Maine Road deserves back then.

I did not stop my research into the grounds of Manchester City though. At every opportunity I would interview supporters hoping to capture specific ground details, or locate newspaper articles from the earliest years of the club and of Maine Road. I found I became obsessed with multi-span roofs at Hyde Road, or the development of the old Platt Lane Stand in the 1930s. As time wore on I realised these were not the actions of a sane man, and turned my attention back to the first team struggles of Alan Ball's time!

In 1998 I started to consider the possibility of a book on the stadium when I rediscovered my old Maine Road book plans from 1986 - I had chapters marked 'Rugby at Maine Road', 'United at Maine Road, 'Cassidy & Queen', and a couple (only a couple!) on City. I soon realised these plans needed considerable work and I started to discuss my ideas with publishers, the club, and

supporters. While this was happening I was also co-writing a novel, 'Atkinson For England', and updating 'Manchester – The Greatest City'. It was a busy time, but I knew I just had to research and write about Maine Road.

By 2001 the club had already decided to produce a couple of books tied in with the move from Maine Road and myself, Noel Bayley, Kevin Cummins and Phil Noble met with Chris Bird to discuss ideas. Over the course of the following months plans were devised with the club making the decision to have two official publications – a photographic record of the last season (to be produced by photographer Kevin Cummins), and the history of the stadium (this book) written by me.

Since that time my life has been as frenetic as it always is when I throw myself into a project. Any writing project requires dedication, enthusiasm, and a determination to make it worthy of its subject, but this book required much more. I had put so much effort into 'Manchester – The Greatest City' I was worried this would simply repeat what I had previously written. Therefore, I deliberately set out to find completely new material and different angles for my writing. It was not easy.

While carrying out my research specifically for this book I have interviewed fans from varying backgrounds and ages. I've also interviewed local residents, former players, club personnel, three former Chairmen, and many others with an interest in the ground. I have also consulted my earlier research and interviews - including my interviews and discussions with supporters and club personnel since deceased such as Joe Mercer, Peter Swales and Hyde Road attendee Harry Hughes - and tried to look for material to develop.

The question I have always asked during my research is 'what does Maine Road mean to you?' Naturally, I've received a variety of answers, although most were along the lines of 'Maine Road means everything', 'it's my home', or 'I can't imagine life without it'. All of this made me question what it means to me.

For much of Maine Road's final year I've been working with the club managing the development of the 'Manchester City Experience' – City's new museum – and so have been based at the ground more or less on a daily basis. This has tainted my view to some extent. The shabbier parts of the stadium are more visible when it's empty and I guess I've become a little too familiar with the present day Maine Road.

What hasn't changed though is the feeling of excitement and anticipation I always feel when I enter the ground. Sports grounds have always held a fascination for me, but Maine Road remains the most powerful and passionate ground of all. I enjoy simply being there. Sometimes I try to imagine what true City fans feel when they get to play in the first team for the Blues. Can you imagine what it must have been like for loyal Blues Paul Lake and Mike Doyle the first time they ran down the tunnel? Or when they faced a packed ground on derby day? – and won in style!

Many feel it is the supporters that make a place special. They create the colours, the chants, the general

Below: In 1994 the whole dynamic of watching football at Maine Road changed as the Kippax terracing was demolished. These fans were among the last to soak up the unique atmosphere of the old stand.

ambience. Clearly, this is true in many ways, but if this was totally true why would so many fans want to see the place when it's empty? Why do we all still get a feeling in our stomach when we catch sight of a roof or, between the fifties and nineties, see a floodlight pylon?

In the final few days of June I decided to walk into the ground for a last proper look around. I passed Mike Corbett, the security man on main reception, walked up the staircase, through the International Lounge, and into the Directors' Box. The moment I saw the blue of the Kippax and the green of the pitch I felt the rush of excitement I have always felt. The place was empty. The pitch was damaged. The temporary stands almost completely removed. Seats were missing. It should have been a sorry sight, but to me it was still a more gratifying experience than anything any other League ground or building could offer.

Walking around Maine Road for that last time before this book was published I couldn't help but reminisce. Every turn made me remember a past moment or wonderful experience. It wasn't necessarily great games. It was more like watching myself at different ages and reliving those experiences. I turned right from the Directors' Box and headed towards the Platt Lane Stand. As I walked I remembered the 1986 FA Youth Cup Final and the Simod Cup game against Plymouth in 1987 - only because I sat in this area of the Main Stand and in those days this was a rarity.

When I reached the Family Stand I stopped and dozens of wonderful moments returned. My first visits were always in the old Platt Lane Stand and this stand was always special. In those days I came to the games with my Dad and brother and we used to set off from our home in Hattersley hours before the match. As a five year old it seemed to take forever to get there. I used to search for a glimpse of the floodlight towers, in the same way you'd search for Blackpool Tower. From Belle Vue it was possible, just, to catch sight of the top of a couple of floodlights and if the game was at night you would

certainly notice the glow. I loved searching for that first sight of the ground.

In those days we would park our car somewhere close to Hart Road and walk the last fifteen minutes for what seemed an eternity, cutting through all the numbered passageways in between the old Platt Lane Stand and the streets around Platt Lane itself. You had to dodge the puddles and the excrement left by dogs and police horses, and then, if you were lucky you'd stop at one of the chip shops. Usually the one on Yew Tree Road, but sometimes the City Chippy on Claremont Road.

Then we'd walk down the passage between the houses on Thornton Road and the exterior wall of, first, the Kippax then the Platt Lane. Always dark, even on a sunny day, this passageway felt sinister, especially the section between the Platt Lane Stand and the car park. In later years I learned of the crowd disorder and ambushes that took place there, but as a boy I had no concept of crowd trouble.

Once we escaped from the passage we would be on the Maine Road forecourt. It always seemed packed and everyone seemed to be in a rush to get in. I don't know if people got into the ground earlier then, but no matter how early we were it felt as if we were late. What seemed like almost the entire population of Manchester was rushing to get in, although there were always a couple of men, with placards proclaiming "Jesus Saves" or "The World Ends Tomorrow", who were never in a rush.

The front of the ground looked tall, dark and typical of industrial Manchester. It wasn't that beautiful to look at but that was perhaps part of the charm. It was grim, gritty, and Mancunian in the same way as Coronation Street was at the time. Time has changed the look and feel of both, but back then Manchester was far from the modern, vibrant, cosmopolitan city it is today.

Once we entered via the Platt Lane turnstiles I then felt I was part of the club. Even as a child I felt the fans were part of the all round experience and, for me, there was no better sight than the one that greeted me every time I walked down the large corner tunnel. The anticipation would increase with every step and as you moved further the view of the pitch and of the Kippax Stand was breathtaking. The lush green surface was like nothing I'd seen before, especially when lit by the floodlights, and the colour and brightness of the turf contrasted perfectly with the darkness of the Kippax Stand in the distance.

To me the Kippax in those days was a complete and utter mystery. It was difficult to make out the faces and the size and scale of it all was lost on me. It seemed huge, but how huge? Every so often a small glow would appear in the darkness of the stand as a fan would light a cigarette, and even that sight was entertaining.

The Platt Lane Stand also felt enormous. In front of the tunnel a large blue gate separated the tunnel from the pitch. To the left the Platt Lane corner carried around to the Main Stand, to the right the stand continued to the Kippax corner. We always turned right and usually walked a little towards the goal. The stand was higher in the corner than behind the goal. I found out while researching this book that the corner had been rebuilt in 1931 with a steeper rake. This meant that those seated in the corner in the early seventies actually had a better viewing position than the rest of the stand. That is if we disregard the number of stanchions developed to hold the roof in place.

In June 2003 I stood at the white perimeter wall where the blue gate used to be and remembered how I felt as a young boy. Every game used to start with the Kippax demanding City to come on to the field. "Bring on the Champions!" would be chanted over and over again until the team eventually took to the pitch. Presumably this chant began in 1968 and I know it continued into the eighties as I remember chanting it when I stood in the Kippax myself during the mid-80s.

Once the team were on the pitch the excitement seemed to intensify and the kick off was one of the most magical moments. Nowadays it can seem rather dull, but back in the early seventies you always felt as if something major was going to happen from the start. Once play was under way the atmosphere in the Platt Lane was very entertaining. The stand seemed to be full of almost every type of City fan and there was always someone with an opinion.

Of course every time the action came to the Platt Lane end of the ground everybody would stand up. I must have missed so many goals because of this as a boy, but in a strange way even the jumping up added to the excitement of the moment.

At half-time we would nip to the front of the stand to get a drink and a packet of Chipmunk Crisps or a Wagon Wheel. I have a vague recollection that Wagon Wheels were launched at Maine Road although I am probably mistaken about that. I do know I first tasted one at Maine Road but I also know I stopped liking them after a couple of games. Perhaps it had something to do with results, or more likely it was the arrival of Jaffa Cakes at the ground.

In those days a tea urn would be pushed around the perimeter track selling drinks, crisps and Wagon Wheel/ Jaffa Cake style snacks and almost every boy in the stand would rush to the front when either the tea urn trolley arrived near the steps closest, or at half-time.

Towards the end of the second half my Dad would always make us leave. Some games this was not popular, while at other times it felt a relief, but on each occasion the decision to leave was only ever a half-hearted one as my Dad would take us to the bottom of the stand – perversely we would never leave by the steps at the back even if they were closer.

At the pitch side, we would walk to the Platt Lane tunnel and then wait in the tunnel near the gate. We would stand there watching a few further minutes of action. The ground felt entirely different from this angle. In fact it felt as if two sides of the ground – the Platt Lane and Main Stands – were watching you. I would stare across towards the Main Stand when there was a break in the action and watch the crowd. It sounds as if I'm talking about another world now, but back then I do remember groups of older supporters wearing flat caps. It wasn't exactly a Lowry scene, but it certainly wasn't a 'Madchester' scene.

When we eventually did decide to leave the race began to get back to the car. We'd be rushing through each of the passages and streets to get back to the Hart Road area as soon as we could. If the game was on we'd sometimes hear a roar – 'was that a City goal or a save?' Often we'd only know the truth about those final minutes play when we got home because, as with the cars of most of my friends, ours did not have a radio.

The memory of those days remains very clear, and as I wandered from Platt Lane towards the new Kippax I started to think about my days on the terracing. Whereas the old Platt Lane always brings back memories of attending games with my Dad and brother, the Kippax signifies independence. I first stood here in 1983 with Paul Alexander and Cros Ward, friends from school, and the general buzz of the place was incredible.

I started working in 1984 and immediately bought my first Kippax season ticket - with my own money! - for £27. I could stand where I wanted to and create my own Maine Road routine. That's independence.

As I walked around the ground in 2003 I couldn't help but nip behind the modern Kippax and have a look at the turnstiles and perimeter wall, and remember the pre-match scene. Fans sunbathing on the old steps, or huddled in the tunnels drinking on rainy days. Everything about the Kippax was basic, but it was also the most fantastic part of the ground. The feeling of standing there with your friends for the first time is like a rite of passage, and sadly is something future generations will never experience. No matter how it's described, it is impossible to get over the feeling of the Kippax to those that have never stood there.

Incidentally, some of these turnstiles have been in use at City venues since the 1890s. Back in 1985 I first became aware that some turnstiles had been brought to Maine Road from Hyde Road in 1923 and ever since I have been trying to piece together exact details of the turnstiles' history and of how many were brought across. I have been surprised at what I've discovered, and have included the key details within this book.

The North Stand reminds me of the excitement I felt when I sat here during the late Seventies, but it is also the place where I sat when David Pleat did his jig in 1983. I remember the old supporter sat a couple of seats away was in tears. He mentioned the desolate days of 1964-5 and dreaded the future. Clearly a lot's happened since then, but relegation in 1983 was the saddest I had ever felt at Maine Road at the time, and so the North Stand will always be linked with that day for me.

I walked in front of the North Stand, passed 'J' Block - I sat here when Bobby McDonald went in nets for the injured Joe Corrigan and played a blinder in 1982 - and in front of the Main Stand. I sat there when we beat United 5-1 in 1989, so even though I have always felt like an impostor in the stand, it will always be linked with that magical moment. As I made my way to the Directors' Box I paused and took a final look around the modern ground. Even today's stands hold magical memories. Clearly, recent successes have helped, but I've also brought my own children to games. They will never understand what it was like to sit on benches, or stand on the Kippax - they weren't even born when its last game was played. They won't feel what I've felt but, hopefully, their memories of Maine Road and of the new stadium will mean as much to them as my memories do to me.

I feel fortunate to have attended Maine Road on a regular basis from the early seventies, through to its demise. I believe I have witnessed Maine Road's greatest years. To me Maine Road will always be best remembered the way it looked in the mid-1970s. That period typifies the ground to me but every supporter will have their own views and special memories.

I hope this book enables you to relive your favourite Maine Road days, while also providing enough information on the stadium's development to satisfy your interest. As I mentioned earlier this book has been very difficult to write. I have tried to avoid falling into the trap of simply concentrating on architectural issues, and have considered activities that have taken place at the ground.

Below: Weeds grow on a pitch declared the best in the League only a few weeks earlier. This was the sorry sight at Maine Road in September 2003. The Kippax Stand in the background had the shortest life of all the permanent stands ever erected at the ground. The stand was only eight years old when City moved out in 2003.

For example, I have included features on the Junior Blues and on Demonstrations. The link with Maine Road's history may not immediately be apparent, but I feel these features, and many others, are important as they do have an indirect link with the ground's development. The Junior Blues, for example, helped to increase interest and encouraged young supporters to attend, while demonstrations sometimes led to regime changes but also helped to challenge perceptions of all-seater stadia.

Other features cover the shocking story of merger discussions with United in the mid-Sixties; crowd control; fanzines; Royal visits etc. I have also considered the use of Maine Road for pop concerts, rugby matches, international football games, United's use of the ground, tennis competitions, and religious festivals. I know I have not covered every non-City event, but I hope I have included enough to entertain and inform.

During the course of the last few years I have learned a great deal about the ground and have also been desperately keen to challenge my own perceptions. I know I'm biased - Maine Road's such a special place - but I've been determined to look objectively at the ground. I have been prepared to criticise the place where necessary but what has surprised me the more I've researched is exactly how impressive the ground was when first built. Not only that but the club still wanted to

achieve more with the site, and within eight years of the ground opening the Blues had already embarked on phase two of Maine Road's development plan. By the end of 1935 Maine Road had been extended to hold somewhere in the region of 90,000, and had World War Two not intervened I firmly believe the stadium would have had a fully roofed 100,000 plus capacity by 1950.

I know that sounds like an amazing suggestion but the planning and foresight of men like architect Charles Swain, builders Sir Robert McAlpine & Sons, directors Lawrence Furniss and Albert Alexander snr, manager Ernest Mangnall, and secretary Wilf Wild was such that this could have been achieved. They all wanted Maine Road to be the greatest stadium in the country and when it opened it was certainly the best League ground.

Incidentally, year after year many writers and historians have claimed that Maine Road was designed as the Wembley of the north. As this book hopes to prove, this was far from the case, and I personally hope that comment is never made again. Clearly, there are comparisons to be made as Wembley was built by the same builders as Maine Road and the two stadia were planned at the same time. However Wembley did not have any kind of reputation when the Maine Road foundations were being laid, and by the time City's ground opened Wembley had a very bad reputation for crowd control and safety. In fact City's architect and builders learnt from Wembley's mistakes as *All Sports Weekly* mentioned in 1923: "The lessons of Wembley have been taken to heart, and a feature of the ground will be six tunnels communicating with the terraces, giving easy access to all parts."

City aimed for the best, but they did not aim to copy Wembley, nor did they aim for a new Old Trafford as some have also claimed. Far from it! Inspiration did come from Hampden Park, but it should be stressed that Maine Road was never based on any other English ground. Its aims were higher.

As well as including my own research and interview material within this book I have tried to ensure I have incorporated a wide selection of other supporters' memories. I have been sent a considerable number and have tried to include as many as possible. Sadly, I have only been able to include about half of what I received but I hope you agree the memories I have chosen give a rounded view of Maine Road through the ages.

Finally, I've had some exceptionally good times at Maine Road and some absolutely depressing days, but no matter how good or how bad I've felt the stadium has always made me feel welcome and at home. We all feel that Maine Road is our place. It's a symbol of what we believe in. It's enormously difficult to convey in words exactly what Maine Road means and I certainly don't expect to capture how you feel about the place. I know how I feel, and I hope I've conveyed enough to keep you interested.

I hope you enjoy this book and that it brings back many happy memories. In the future, when Maine Road has long since been demolished I hope this is a publication you pick up to help remember how you felt when you first walked into Maine Road. I know I will.

I'm already missing Maine Road.

Gary James
September 2003

Below: Weeds grow on a pitch declared the best in the League only a few weeks earlier. This was the sorry sight at Maine Road in September 2003. The Kippax Stand in the background had the shortest life of all the permanent stands ever erected at the ground. The stand was only eight years old when City moved out in 2003.

Acknowledgments

AS always, I would like to take this opportunity to record my thanks to those who have helped with my research or have provided support for this publication. I have interviewed dozens of supporters, players, club personnel, media-types, and others along the way and have been astounded by their interest.

I have also received a considerable number of letters and emails – several hundred in fact – from supporters offering their views on the ground and their own memories. I was fascinated by their stories and have tried to incorporate a substantial number within the book. However, I must stress there were so many I have only been able to include a fraction, but would like to thank all those who took the time and trouble to write, and apologise if your own memory did not make the final edit.

It is worth mentioning also that in the final weeks of editing and proof-reading it became apparent a small number of memories had also been sent to fanzines and other publications. I removed some from this work to avoid duplication, however I decided to retain a few because of their quality or interest. The best example was Will Linsdell's memory of the 1985 promotion match with Charlton, which had also been sent to and included in *King of the Kippax*. I hope you agree it was right to leave that memory in.

One large group of people I must thank are the subscribers who backed this project without seeing a single page of print. I am delighted with the way fans have always supported my work, but was amazed by the response this time. More supporters have pre-ordered this publication than any other in the history of the club. In fact, it is unlikely any other book on a single club or football ground has matched the interest from ordinary fans. I hope it lives up to your expectations and I am truly grateful.

Naturally, I would like to express my thanks to Manchester City F.C. for making this the official history of the stadium. It's clear from my early discussions with

them, the Blues would not put their name to any historical work unless it was of the right quality and offered something different. I am therefore grateful to have been selected. It was Chris Bird who gave me this opportunity, and I am grateful to him and to David Bernstein for their support. I started researching and writing this while they still held posts at the club, and was delighted with the enthusiasm they both demonstrated. Thank you.

Of course, the present day staff of the club have been tremendously helpful. Bernard Halford has been most supportive, and I found his stories of key events in the stadium's history very entertaining. He shares the same passion for the ground as I and most fans do, but he's also worked there for over thirty years. It must have been a tremendous wrench to leave Maine Road.

Naturally, I'd like to thank Alistair Mackintosh, John Wardle, and all their staff, especially Janice Monk, Steve Sayer, Ian Howard, Vicky Kloss, Rosie Bass and Paul Kenyon.

Another major contributor was Eric Alexander. The Alexander family has been involved with Manchester City since the club was formed and to receive knowledgeable assistance from Eric was deeply satisfying. He helped provide background to key events but was also immensely interested in the story of the ground as it unfolded. Eric is a true footballing man and comes from a great dynasty of Blues. Thanks again.

Photographer Ed Garvey is another who has helped throughout my research and writing. Naturally, he has provided many illustrations of Maine Road during its final year or so, but has also offered support and opinion elsewhere and, like Eric, was keen on understanding the development of a place we all love.

There have been many others who have co-operated including, Malcolm Allison, Joanne Ashcroft, Ken Barnes, Mike Barnett, Noel Bayley, Ashley Birch, Graham Birch, Geoff Bramble, Harry Bramble, Colin Bottomley, Keith Casson, Ian Cheeseman, Roy Cheetham,

Right: Photographer Ed Garvey and author Gary James photographed after Maine Road's final League match in May 2003.

Left: The City players on a training session on the streets around Maine Road during the 1940s. One-time Beveridge Street resident and future Liverpool manager Joe Fagan is pictured fourth from left. George Smith (light suit, trilby hat, gloves and scarf - centre of photograph) remembers: "It was a bitterly cold day with snow on the ground. The pitch was frozen so Laurie Barnett took us on a training walk around the streets. We tried to make the best of it, but we'd have preferred to play."

Roy & Kath Clarke & family, Dave Clayton, Denise Daley, Mike Donaldson, Neil Dorsett, Rob Dunford, Paddy Fagan, Steve Fleet, Nick Harris, Johnny Hart, David Hilton, Pete Hollins, Simon Inglis, Paul James, Alan Johnson, Mike Kelly, Steve Knott, Paul Lake, Josh Langton, Eddie Large, Francis Lee, Bill Leivers, Roy Little, Colin MacBean, Malcolm McAlpine, Alistair Mann, Ian Mellor, Norah Mercer, Carl Morris, John Motson, Tommy Muir, Andy Noise, 'Turnstile' Ted Pearson, Heidi Pickup, Roger Reade, Stuart Renshaw, Steve Rigby, John Riley, Norman Rucker, George Smith, Ian Smith, Bert Trautmann, Dennis Tueart, Helen Turner, Jimmy Wagg, Dave Wallace, Andy Ward, Jessie Ward, Chris Williams, Johnny Williamson, Steve Worthington and Mark Wylie.

There are also a few people who have provided assistance but, due to a variety of reasons, I was unable to carry out a full-length interview as originally planned. They include Ian Niven junior and James H. Reeve.

The first person I consulted specifically for this book was Dennis Chapman. Dennis has helped enormously over the years with his statistical and historical knowledge, and I am grateful once again for all the help with this and my previous works.

Julian Baskcomb, Julia Byrne and their colleagues at Polar have once again performed magnificently. For over fifteen years I have been in contact with them and have always received enthusiastic encouragement. They have become renowned for producing quality publications, and I am delighted they have remained committed to producing quality books on City. Additionally, I am grateful for the tremendous design skills of Trevor Hartley. Once again, he has made this an attractive publication. Thanks.

Thanks to my family - Heidi, Michael, and Anna. You've provided me with terrific support yet again. Researching and writing a book of this type takes many, many months of hard work and long hours, and my family have sustained me through this period. Also, thanks to the other members of my family who have supported me throughout.

I am certain there are many others who have helped along the way and if I have overlooked your contribution please don't feel slighted. It's simply that the last few years have been exceptionally busy and it has not always been possible to record or remember every name. My apologies.

Naturally, I would like to pass on my thanks to those quoted within the following pages, and to all who have helped my research in other ways. You know who you are. Undoubtedly, there will also be a number of people who assist me in one form or another the moment this page is printed. Again, if you fall into this category thank you.

I hope you enjoy "Farewell To Maine Road", and that it gives you all you expect, although I believe this book will prove most interesting in a decade or so when all trace of the old ground has vanished for good. Then we'll sit back, pick up the book, and remember exactly what it felt like to stand on the Kippax, or sit in the Gene Kelly Stand!

I know it is inevitable some mistakes will have crept in, but I sincerely hope there are not too many. If you do find any then please write to me via the publishers. In addition, if you have information you feel may help develop the story of City's grounds, or unusual or rare photographs, then please write.

Thanks, GARY JAMES September 2003

PICTURE ACKNOWLEDGMENTS & ARCHIVE SOURCES

To ensure this publication covers Maine Road throughout its entire life has required the involvement of many photographers (both amateur and professional) and photo libraries. However, one supporter deserves a special mention - Emma Tamara Taylor. For over a decade Emma has deliberately set out to capture unique images of the stadium and the events staged there. Although at times her family and friends may have questioned her desire to capture all things City, it's clear she understood fully the importance of the old ground. Several of her photos are included in this book.

Many of the author's own photographs from the 1980s onwards also appear, while his collection of historical photographs and newspaper cuttings make up the majority of images used. Other articles and photographs have been supplied by the following:

Manchester City F.C., Action Images, Empics, The Hulton-Getty Collection, The Manchester Evening News & Guardian, The Manchester Chronicle, Daily Dispatch, Athletic News, Umpire News, The Weekly News, The Daily Mail, The Daily Express, The Daily Mirror, The Independent, The Sun, The Observer, The Times, The Telegraph, The British Film Institute, The North West Film Archive at Manchester Metropolitan University, The Illustrated London News, The British Library, the BBC, Granada TV and Sky TV.

Others who have supplied illustrations include: Frank Borson, David Djordjevic, Peter Feely, Phill Gatenby, Andrew Heydeman, Heidi James, Harry Potts (former Junior Blues photographer), Sefton Samuels, Graeme Thompson, Richard Tucker, Crosland Ward and Steve Worthington.

More than any other photographer connected with this book, Ed Garvey has been an inspirational presence throughout Maine Road's final season. He has spent many hours in the company of Gary James walking around the stadium and capturing images otherwise lost forever. His enthusiasm, interest and willingness to see his images used in this volume and in other ways by the club has been refreshing. He is clearly a talented sports photographer and the author, the publishers, and Manchester City FC would like to record here their thanks for his support for their work.

There are a number of other photographs included in this book, the source of which we have been unable to trace. The owners are cordially invited to contact the publishers in writing providing proof of copyright.

In the Subscribers' List (p 297) we asked some club officials to list their favourite match and favourite part of the ground. Shortly before publication Kevin Keegan told us his favourite match at Maine Road was, like many, the November 2002 Manchester derby (profiled on page 21), while his favourite part of Maine Road was Rose's Room. To understand the special nature of Rose's Room see page 191; Ashley Lewis' favourite Game was Huddersfield Town 7/11/87 (10-1 - profiled on page 220); Favourite part of ground: Middle of the Main Stand (always felt like home); Bryan Bodek's favourite Game was the Ballet on Ice (Spurs 1967 - profile on page 174). Favourite part of ground: Old Platt Lane Stand.

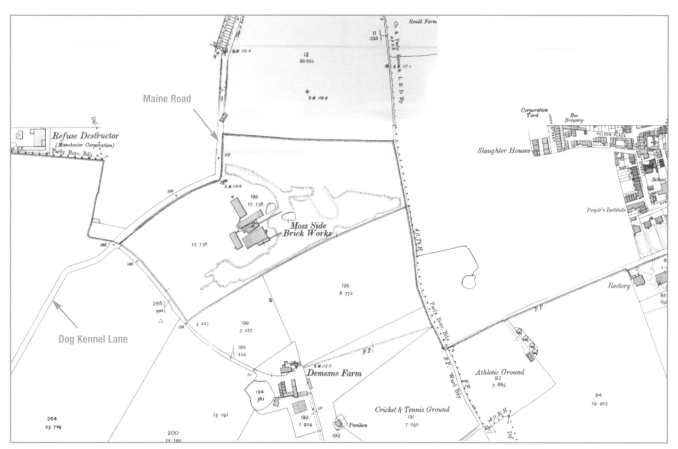

Above: An 1880s map of the area later to become the home of Manchester City. All of Maine Road was originally known as Dog Kennel Lane and as housing appeared (top of map) the road took on the more familiar name. The shape of the land later occupied by the ground and car parks is visible between Maine Road/Dog Kennel Lane, and the northern (later Claremont Road), southern (later Thornton Road) and eastern (later Yew Tree Road) boundaries of the Moss Side Brickworks. The Athletic Ground at the bottom right of the map is recognisable today as City's Platt Lane Training Complex.

Above: Maine Road seen from the air in 1971.

Left: This 1974 illustration of Maine Road shows the ground from the corner between Platt Lane and the Kippax, prior to the days of crowd segregation. Artist TONY WHITING says "It took me several days to correctly convey Maine Road. Stan Gibson was very interested in seeing the completed work. I now dedicate this drawing to the memory of my brother Neil, a true Blue".

Maine Road Terminology

1   MAIN STAND 1923 - 2003 Alternative name: Grand Stand

2   MAIN STAND 'J' BLOCK 1973 - 2003 (area between end of Main Stand and North Stand)

3   MAIN STAND 'G' BLOCK 1931 - 1993 (area between Main Stand and Platt Lane).
Alternative name: part of Platt Lane Corner; Family Stand; 'new' G Block (1993 - 2003).

4   PLATT LANE CORNER 1931- 1993 (corner of Platt Lane leading to Main Stand)
Alternative name: Apple Pie Corner; The Boys' Stand; The Boys' Corner; 'new' Family Stand (1993 - 2003); original unroofed terracing 1923 - 1931.

5   PLATT LANE STAND 1935 - 1993 Alternative name: 'new' Platt Lane Stand 1993 - 2003; UMBRO Stand (initial name after redevelopment); original unroofed terracing 1923 - 1935

6   PLATT LANE/KIPPAX CORNER 1923 - 1994 Alternative name: away section (away section also stretched into the Kippax); HH temporary stand (late 1990s onwards); Temporary stand also dubbed the Gene Kelly Two and by one fanzine the Alan Ball Stand (the fanzine cruelly reasoned: 'It's small and doesn't make much noise').

7   KIPPAX STREET STAND 1957 - 1994 Alternative name: Popular Side (1923 - 1957); 'new' Kippax Stand (1994 - 2003).

8   CHANTERS' CORNER (1960s - 1994) Alternative name: The Sways.

9   WINDY CORNER 1923 - 1994 (area in between Kippax and North Stand)
Alternative name: Temporary Stand UU (1997 - 2003); Gene Kelly Stand; original terracing 1923 to 1971 then rebuilt as part of North Stand development.

10   THE NORTH STAND 1971 - 2003 Alternative name: The Scoreboard End (1923 - 1971); The City End.

Chapter One

End of an Era

The result was almost incidental. One City fan said that he had paid £400 for a ticket. "I was working today so I didn't get there until half-time," he said. "But it's not about the game, it's the end of an era. I have to be there." I tried to empathise. It must be an emotional wrench leaving a ground after 80 years. "Yeah, true," he said, "but it's a bit of a dump to be honest."

Paul Connolly, writing in *The Times* following Maine Road's last League match, May 2003

SOME supporters had to be asked to leave Maine Road after its final League match on 11th May 2003. They found it hard to say goodbye. This was one of the most significant places in their lives. A place where they had experienced a range of emotions and gathered a wealth of memories. This wasn't just a football ground, this was their Utopia.

The final match was the culmination of a very important and emotional League campaign. Expectations were high. Kevin Keegan's side had entertained throughout the previous season and appropriately enough the Blues were competing in the highest division in English football, the Premier League. Promotion in 2002 had been achieved in style with City securing the League Championship. This meant the oldest national trophy in league football was housed on the premises during its final year. Keegan hoped to build on this with a finish in the top six and qualification for Europe. Understandably, this led to a mixture of anticipation and excitement, but was also coupled with sadness at the demise of Maine Road. There were times when this could have overwhelmed activity on the pitch, but fortunately neither the supporters nor club personnel allowed that to happen.

As with Hyde Road in 1922 the stadium was far too small to cope with demand and so the club pro-actively sought to increase the stadium's capacity. As during almost every pre-season since the erection of the Kippax in 1995, club officials walked around the ground considering how to squeeze in extra places. Already temporary seating was positioned in the corners on either side of the Kippax, in the 1993 tunnel area between the Main Stand and Platt Lane, and behind the stadium control box above J block of the Main Stand.

In the end City's options were limited, but additional seats were shoe-horned in with the most obvious change coming in the corner between the Kippax and Platt Lane where the uncovered block HH was enlarged.

The improvements helped to raise numbers slightly but it should be remembered that Maine Road's capacity had been severely restricted since the development of the Platt Lane Stand in 1993. Following the construction of the Kippax in 1995 Maine Road's capacity was the smallest for a City venue since 1905. The final capacity was a shade over 35,000 – some 50,000 less than the day the stadium opened in 1923.

The use of new turnstile technology, with admittance to the Family Stand controlled through the use of proximity cards, was trialed during the season. This new entry mechanism was able to verify the details of the person gaining entry, and, for example if a child ticket was being used by an adult this would be immediately highlighted.

With Maine Road given its usual summer brush-up, the first home match saw the Blues defeat Sir Bobby Robson's Newcastle 1-0. Darren Huckerby was the scorer at the Platt Lane end. When the next home match ended in a 3-1 victory over Everton, hopes were high that Maine Road might prove a fortress in its final season. New boy Nicolas Anelka scored twice that day - although it was initially believed he'd netted a hat-trick until the Premier League dubious goals panel took one from him - and went on to be City's top scorer with fourteen League goals.

Above: Old meets new as the Kippax Stand towers above the crumbling perimeter wall.

Below: Sitting in the temporary stands at either end of the Kippax was not a pleasant experience when the rain came down, even though supporters were given plastic macs. These fans sat in the green seated stand close to Platt Lane.

Above: The view as the North Stand corner was approached from Wansford Street.

Below: The skyline of Maine Road in its 80th year provides a contrast in architecture to the terraced houses viewed from the back entry of Wansford Street.

The best result of the opening months was without doubt the 3-1 victory over Manchester United. The crowd for the final derby may have been approximately half the attendance of the first at Maine Road (a 1-1 draw on 12th September 1925), but it's fair to say the passionate atmosphere was equal to any previous encountered.

Many fans remembered the 5-1 derby victory on 23rd September 1989 as the best at the ground. It was a match that rocked Manchester and amazingly, thirteen years to the day later, Maine Road felt a real tremor as an earthquake hit. The epicentre was at Dudley in the Midlands and the effect on the ground became a talking point, although greater tremors hit a month later.

A series of earthquakes – one measuring 3.9 on the Richter Scale – with an epicentre close to City's new stadium at Eastlands shook Manchester. A few buildings in the area were damaged, while the administration offices at Maine Road developed minor cracks in the walls. For a while Manchester was nervous, and then after a few days of activity each tremor was largely ignored.

By the end of September Maine Road had already held its highest crowd of the season when an official attendance of 35,131 witnessed a 3-0 defeat by Liverpool. The appearance of forged tickets brought considerable headaches to the club and the attendance was greater than the club would have desired by about 100 fans.

On Monday 7th October Dennis Tueart unveiled a tribute to former Groundsman Stan Gibson at his former house on Maine Road, while Chris Bird made a speech at the tunnel inside the ground. The club wanted to commemorate Stan's time at the club and erected a plaque on his former home, and a similar plaque at the spot in the tunnel where he used to stand during matches. It was a gesture much appreciated by Stan's family and friends. Another City staff member and devoted Blue, Gary Johnson, passed away in tragic circumstances on 12th November 2002. Naturally Gary's family and club personnel were devastated by the tragedy.

In December the club hosted a Christmas Carol concert. As with the Billy Graham event of the 1960s this demonstrated how Maine Road really was a multi-function venue. It also entered the record books as the largest event of its kind.

Left: One of the turnstiles bought by City in the 1890s and initially installed at Hyde Road in use for supporters using the 'Gene Kelly Stand'. A review of all turnstiles during May 2003 came to the conclusion that there were at least four turnstiles from around 1896 and a further eight or so from Hyde Road still in use at Maine Road for the final game.

Above: Temporary seat 48 overlooks turnstile 48 - possibly the oldest turnstile at Maine Road!

Above: Visiting teams were presented with a souvenir of their final visit to Maine Road. Here, West Ham's Joe Cole is handed an 'End of an Era' pennant by Ali Benarbia prior to the penultimate fixture.

On 11th January the Blues defeated Leeds 2-1 with Niclas Jensen scoring an exceptional vollied goal – many believed this the finest goal of the season. City were in eighth place at this point and Keegan's European ambitions looked achievable.

It wasn't long however before events suggested City might be about to self destruct. Issues in the Boardroom led to the resignations of Chairman David Bernstein and joint Managing Director Chris Bird. Both had been influential figures behind City's resurgence but immediately the remaining Board members – Bryan Bodek, Ashley Lewis, Alistair Mackintosh, Dennis Tueart, and John Wardle – stressed their commitment and desire to see the club continue to progress. John Wardle became acting Chairman (later he took on the role on a permanent basis) while Alistair Mackintosh continued as

Right: When fans arrived for the final home game the two semi-circular mosaics above the exit doors of the Main Stand had been painstakingly removed in fear of them being destroyed by souvenir hunters.

Managing Director. Unlike previous upheavals, the club continued successfully with its plans and aims.

By the end of April the realisation that Maine Road's final game was near seemed to create a mad rush for tickets. Everyone wanted to make their 'last' visit to the ground, while every game seemed to be the 'last' of a particular type to be staged. On 12th April Middlesbrough visited for the final Saturday match at the ground, while on January 29th the last night match ended in a 4-1 victory over Fulham. When Sunderland played in the last Easter Monday fixture (the whole concept of 'last' matches was getting rather silly by this stage) they became the first side all season to present the club with a commemorative souvenir of the day. City had been presenting each opponent with an 'End of an Era' pennant but Sunderland were the first to present something back. They gave City a rosebowl with an inscription marking their last visit to the stadium. Incidentally, the time span between Sunderland's first appearance at Maine Road and their last was greater than any other visiting club. The 3-0 victory over Sunderland was City's last win at Maine Road with Marc-Vivien Foe scoring the Blues' last goal at the stadium.

It was revealed at this stage that Maine Road was to be demolished at the end of the season and the media became more interested in the ground's demise. Television film crews appeared on a frequent basis. Photographers started to capture images they hoped would be unique, and on some days during the ground's final weeks several film crews and photographers roamed around the ground at the same time.

Internally, the club removed many important items of memorabilia and club material. Bar signs were removed; honours boards put into storage; and photographs discreetly withdrawn. Souvenir hunters had already made off with the away team bath plug, the press room sign, Kippax Store sign and the Frank Swift bar sign. The club had no choice but to remove key items.

With increasing concern for club property, steps were taken to secure and preserve the two semi-circular mosaics above the Main Stand exit doors. For many months Marketing Manager Ian Howard and club museum personnel discussed ways of preserving the mosaics and options for future use at the new stadium, but matters were brought to an head when rumours circulated that individuals had planned to smash the mosaics in order to salvage one or two sections for themselves. The club could not allow this to happen and with a determination to salvage these important features of the ground, City supporting Mosaic artist Mark Kennedy was brought in. He arrived at the ground on 6th May to perform the painstaking task of removing the mosaics tile by tile.

The job was far from easy and, largely due to the determination of the original mosaic experts that these would last forever, it became a nightmare operation. The tiles simply could not be removed in the manner anticipated without serious damage. After lenghty consultation with other experts different equipment was tried in an attempt to dismantle sections of the mosaics at a time. Although further tiles were damaged, the approach was far more successful and most of the material was removed.

It is anticipated that at least one of the mosaics will be reconstructed at the new stadium. Maine Road's last League match was the only professional game to take place at the stadium without the mosaics in place.

Behind the scenes the club was also taking steps to remove other items for preservation, and were working with the city council to plan for an auction of material and memorabilia from the stadium.

The final match of the season - played on the 35th anniversary of City's 1968 Championship win - was eagerly awaited by all fans but once over the realisation started to hit home that no further League match would be played there. City ended the season with an average attendance of 34,564 and a final League position of ninth. It was not as high as Keegan had hoped, but was still a highly respectable position and the club's highest finish since 1993 when Peter Reid was manager.

Keegan had hoped for European qualification and although City's League position fell short of a guaranteed place, the Blues still qualified via the Fair Play League. It may not have been the preferred route, but it did cap a perfect end to a great season and ensured the new stadium would host UEFA Cup matches in its opening year.

In the weeks that followed the close of the season, focus switched to the new stadium while Maine Road edged closer to destruction. The temporary stand in between the Platt Lane and the Kippax was taken down within a week of the last match.

Elsewhere there were obvious signs of demise. During the last match signs had been ripped off the walls; carpets had been cut; and a number of seats disappeared. Parts of Maine Road presented a sorry sight.

Many matches were still being played at the ground. Some former players took part in a game, sponsors hired the pitch, and charity matches were played, but the last ever match was the Supporters' Club Challenge between the Merseyside CSA and Prestwich & Whitefield CSA. Don Price's Prestwich side recorded a 17-0 victory but interestingly the Merseysiders missed a penalty in the final minute. The very first match at the stadium had also included a missed penalty.

The Merseyside branch had actually performed a sponsored walk from Liverpool to Maine Road in the days leading up to the final League match. The walk was completed in under fourteen hours. Norah Mercer, the widow of former manager Joe, is a pro-active member of the Merseyside branch and she attended the match with Prestwich on 12th June 2003. It was fitting Norah watched that final match as, it should be remembered, her husband was linked to many major events at Maine Road. He was manager during City's most successful period at the stadium and, as a player, had appeared in England's thrilling 8-0 victory over Scotland in October 1943, and for Arsenal in 1948 when the Football League attendance record was set.

Exactly a fortnight after that final match, millions of television viewers around the world witnessed the sight of Marc-Vivien Foe collapsing during Cameroon's Confederations Cup semi-final against Columbia. Sadly, Foe could not be revived and died at the age of 28. By lunchtime next day Maine Road's forecourt was covered with floral tributes, and the old ground's final days as City's home were extremely sad ones.

By the end of June the club had moved out of the office space and into the new stadium, while plans for the likely autumn demolition of Maine Road started to be revealed a little over 81 years after the initial announcement had been made to move there from Hyde Road. So how did City's occupation of Maine Road start? The Maine Road story begins in Chapter 2, once we've paid tribute to two of the most memorable days for City fans in that final season...

Above: Match days will never be the same again for this local resident in Chilworth Street behind the Kippax Stand.

Left: The teamsheet from the very last game played at the stadium.

Maine Match 02/03

CITY v MANCHESTER UNITED

DATE:	Saturday 9th November 2002	
TYPE OF FIXTURE:	Premier League	
ATTENDANCE:	34,649	
RESULT:	City 3 Manchester United 1	
TEAMS & SCORERS:	CITY	MANCHESTER UTD
	Schmeichel	Barthez
	Dunne	G. Neville
	Wiekens	(O'Shea)
	Mettomo	Blanc
	Jihai Sun	Ferdinand
	Berkovic	Silvestre
	(Wright-Phillips)	Solskjaer 1
	Foe	Veron
	Tiatto	(Forlan)
	(Horlock)	P. Neville
	Jensen	Giggs
	Anelka 1	Scholes
	Goater 2	van Nistelrooy
	Unused:	Unused:
	Benarbia	May
	Huckerby	Fortune
	Nash	Ricardo

The last League 'derby' to be played at Maine Road

For the first time ever, City started a game with eleven non-Englishmen, including Niclas Jensen, seen here with United scorer Ole Gunnar Solksjaer. It was fellow Dane Peter Schmeichel who led the team out against his former club (top).

In the run-up to this match City supporters had at first felt the Blues might be able to achieve a decent result, however defeat at Wigan in the Worthington Cup a few days earlier and injuries to defenders Sylvain Distin and Steve Howey seemed to turn the balance back United's way. The Reds were missing David Beckham and Roy Keane through suspension, but with so many internationals and world renowned players on their books they clearly should have held the upper hand but, City being City, this is often a situation the Blues thrive upon.

In the days leading up to the match this derby, more than any other during the period since 1990, was given the attention it deserved. It was as if the significance of the last League derby at Maine Road had focussed the media on the importance of the fixture. The attention was reminiscent of the 1970s with every newspaper covering the game in detail. One of the most quoted players before the match was United Captain Gary Neville. In The Times he talked about the importance of not making a mistake and then moved on to the hurt felt by the club in 1989: "Even though I was a 14-year-old playing for my local club at the time, it still feels part of my United history. It is a result that hangs over the club. They were embarrassing days. You carry them in the back of your mind on days like this to remind you of what is at stake and how bad you will feel if you don't give it your all and get the right result."

He added: "I know I will be getting my share of grief at Maine Road this afternoon but I wouldn't miss it for the world. Any game against City is massive, but this is a really huge match for us because we cannot afford to lose any more ground in the League."

While Neville publicly recognised the importance of the fixture, his manager tried to play down the game. City fans knew it was all psychological warfare aimed at belittling the Blues. At a press conference Sir Alex Ferguson told the world: "The atmosphere will not be a problem to us. My team has played on the biggest stages and is used to it now. There's more noise when we go to Anfield and Elland Road because they are bigger stadiums."

Ferguson seemed to forget that the size of a venue is unimportant as far as atmosphere is concerned. Maine Road had always generated a good atmosphere for the derby regardless of whether there were 78,000 present or 34,000, and this match in particular proved a point.

The pre-match atmosphere was incredible with City fans determined to show to a live television audience their side was THE Mancunian club, and by the end of the match no viewer could doubt who was the pride of Manchester. Incidentally, the away support for this game was only the ninth highest that season at Maine Road.

Immediately prior to the game City's public address system developed a fault which actually helped the atmosphere develop.

When the game commenced City were determined to attack the Reds and in the fifth minute the first City goal came. Peter Llewellyn wrote his impression of the goal for the email service MCIVTA: "City started confidently with a good passing game. On five minutes a superbly under-hit pass from Phil Neville gave his mate Rio some tricky defending to do. But he is a quick international defender and he did cost £30m, so no bother there then. Anelka apparently doesn't read reputations in English newspapers and so took the ball off Rio easily, slotting a lovely pass to Goater. Goater shot accurately but tamely at Barthez who parried when he should have caught it. Anelka finished the job and we were 1-0 up."

That goal brought a great deal of noise from City's support around the ground but a mere three minutes later Solskjaer gave United an equaliser.

The usual derby day nervous agony and the fear United might take the upperhand now engulfed the majority of supporters, but this was not going to be another of those desperate derby days despite considerable possession by the Reds for the ensuing twenty minutes or so. Svenn Hanssen wrote on MCIVTA his views of what followed: "After 25 minutes Foe latched a seemingly hopeless pass into the United area. Gary Neville trotted after the ball and looked certain to

just secure it over the line for a goal kick. When the ball kissed the line, it looked like the United Captain had a change of mind - or was it heart - and instead tried to pass the ball back to Barthez. But there was the everlasting Goater lurking; he snapped the ball from the English international superback, and curled it past Barthez for his first goal of the afternoon. Neville was subbed later in the game. Sad story, but that's one back for escaping the red card after flattening Rösler in '95."

Peter Llewellyn: "Gary Neville clapped his hand to his head as he realised that everyone would remember forever the instantly invented refrain: 'Gary Neville is a Blue, he feeds Goater'. After this, we gained confidence and looked more likely to win. Luck was on our side as last minute toes and feet foiled the hard working Van Nistelrooy and in the second half we pushed United more and more. Finally Goater's 100th goal for City. A first time dink from Berkovic of the kind we saw so often last season, bounced just right for Goater and he half shot, half lobbed the advancing Barthez for 3-1. We could have had more."

"The United fans occupied the usual North Stand position and the Gene Kelly. They were quite supportive and noisy but showed that they don't come here often. We haven't been in the same division as United for most of the years since 1989 so there have been precious few Derbies to win or lose. They pointed towards the Kippax when in jeering mode, which of course, is where the main city singing support used to be in the old days. It is of course now on their right in the North Stand not in the Kippax. To their credit they cheered their own side at the end after a sound derby thrashing."

As the teams left the field the chant of "Who let the Goat Out?" echoed around the stadium. Goater later admitted: "That was one occasion I wished I'd been out wide on the Kippax side of the ground when the referee blew for time. My walk would have been a lot longer and I could have enjoyed the moment more. I know one or two who might have walked right back out on to the pitch! Ultimately, it was just a League game that we'd won. It wasn't the end of the season or I might have come back out!"

Goater also admitted: "It was a very special day and

Right: Celebrations after Nicolas Anelka's opening goal (top), Shaun Wright-Phillips taking on Ryan Giggs (centre), and Shaun Goater scoring City's third goal of the game and his 100th for the club.

Maine Memories

■ Being born into a family of United supporters was never going to be easy. It would seem in recent years that they had chosen the sunnier side of the street, but every now and then something happens which causes the sun to shine so brightly on City supporters that the memories last forever. November 9th, 2002 was such a day.

Last time round we'd been undone by a Beckham free-kick at Maine Road but then held our own for the remaining 88 minutes. Disappointing but no shame. Keegan's arrival had transformed the team, and given us back the passion which had been missing.

Fasten your safety belts and hold on tight 'cos the City rollercoaster is about to start. Anelka swoops early 1-0. Everyone is on their feet, embracing those around them, sharing in the moment. Within minutes the mood all changes as United equalise. This however is a Keegan team, and they're up for the fight. Goater makes the most of a Neville 'assist' and we start to believe we can have them today.

Finally, the Goat's second hits the net, it's 3-1 and we've crossed over to the sunny side of the street again. I had waited all my adult life for this moment, and stood transfixed as the final whistle sent us all into dreamland. For me this wasn't about the three points, but about restoring family pride. The only sadness on this memorable day, was that my aunt with whom I'd had years of United/City banter was not alive to have shared this moment. Typical! We eventually win one, and there's no-one to share it with! God bless you, Norah.

Richard Barlow

a really significant occasion but it never struck me until we got back to the dressing room that I had reached the milestone and only then when the lads were saying 'That was your 100th'."

After the match, former Chairman Eric Alexander remained in the stand admiring the view: "This game I suppose in many ways is my favourite at Maine Road. Not because of the result or the performance, but because after the match I stood in the Main Stand and looked out across the pitch and around the stadium. I started to think of my father [former Chairman Albert Alexander junior] and of his father [founder member of the club Albert Alexander senior]. I wondered what they would make of Maine Road and of the team. I considered how they must have felt when the decision was taken to build Maine Road, and how they would feel now with the move to the new stadium.

"I simply stood there and looked around. I'm not a sentimental man, but I did consider the events that had occurred at the ground. I could picture my father at key moments in his life which, inevitably, all involved City and Maine Road.

"The November Manchester derby for me was a landmark moment. I don't believe I had ever stood and thought about the ground and my memories in that way before. Normally, you watch the match or work in the offices and that's it. You don't often stand and think about what you've seen over the years. The great players… the terrific matches… There's more to life than a building and a football team, but that doesn't mean they are trivial. For some supporters they are everything."

For every Blue that day, this was the greatest moment of Maine Road's final season.

In the Directors Box at the November 2002 derby are (left to right) Chris Bird, Dennis Tueart, Alistair Mackintosh, Bryan Bodek, Ashley Lewis and David Bernstein.

Maine Men David Bernstein & Chris Bird

All set for Maine Road's final game...

■ David Bernstein and Chris Bird will forever be linked as key figures behind the resurgence of Manchester City during the late 1990s and early years of the 21st Century. They gave the club direction, leadership and perhaps most importantly pride. As the club's history unfolds in future years historians may try to determine which figure was the more important and, perhaps, may claim one was more significant than the other. In truth, however, both men were major figures behind both the club and the development of the new stadium and, as with Mercer and Allison thirty years earlier, it is fair to say both contributed a great deal.

David Bernstein was the quiet, politely spoken, professional businessman with significant experience of major organisations, while Chris Bird was very much an entrepreneurial figure with a drive and a passion few could match.

Bernstein was the first of the two to become known to supporters when he joined the board under the Chairmanship of Francis Lee. His photograph and a mini-biography appeared in the 1996-7 City Handbook where it was revealed he attended his first match in 1955 and was Chairman of the French Connection Group. His pedigree was good – particularly his background in accountancy and with several major organisations - and, when the time came for Francis Lee to stand down, it was clear Bernstein was by far the best man to take on the most significant role at the club.

Relegation to Division Two in 1998 was a major blow but it was also the period when the strengths of Bernstein came to the fore. He immediately made a public apology to fans and pledged to do all he could to resurrect the club. His Board at this time included John Wardle, who with his business partner David Makin was a major financial backer of the club, while Chris Bird was involved as a PR expert.

From that point on Bernstein's time at City was dedicated to establishing sound business practice alongside success on the pitch. This won him many admirers. According to Times journalist Mark Hodkinson: "Bernstein was extremely popular with supporters. They liked his self-effacing personality and the fact he arrived at the club without any 'history'. He was often waylaid by City fans on train journeys to and from London. He regularly sat among them, sharing opinions, outlining his plans. He was approachable, friendly, a gentleman."

Bernstein's first full season in charge was not an easy one. Bernstein: "On 19th December 1998 we lost to York City and fell to 12th in the Second Division – the lowest point in our long history. I had been Chairman for eight months. We worked hard to stabilise and turn around the Club and I believed we were doing the right things. But results had gone from bad to worse. As Christmas 1998 grew close I was deeply worried. Wins at Wrexham and critically at home to Stoke started a recovery that culminated in what I believe

was the most important match our Club has ever played. The Wembley final against Gillingham."

That game led to promotion via the Play-offs in 1999. It also brought a stronger determination that City would return to the Premier League and the appointment of Chris Bird as Chief Operating Officer. From that point on every area of the club was reviewed. Bernstein concentrated on the overall direction, such as the move to the new stadium, while Bird initially focused on improving the day to day activities. With City out of the Premier League since 1996, there was much work to be done. Bird thrived on the challenge. Mark Hodkinson: "His capacity for hard work and long hours meant he soon became City's 'Everyman' – the club's interface between the media, the supporters and the directors. He was known to everyone within the club. The tea ladies joked with him, the ground-staff would stop and talk."

Early in the 1999-2000 season Bernstein signed the documentation guaranteeing City's move to the new stadium and, for the following three years he and Bird worked hard with the local council and various bodies to ensure the stadium matched City's ambitions. Of course they were not the only City men involved, all the directors and most of the staff played a part, but they were the two highest profile Blues. Both men performed exceptionally to bring about the move but they also ensured on the pitch activities improved as well.

Kevin Keegan's arrival as manager heralded the start of a new era, but less than two years after his appointment both Bird and Bernstein resigned. Bird tendered his resignation first, followed by Bernstein's on the day the Board were due to meet to discuss Bird's. Rumours circulated as to the main reasons, but Ged Isaacs writing in fanzine *King of the Kippax* summed it up nicely when he wryly suggested: "As for Bernstein, the most obvious problem was that he'd been sensible for about five years and that's just not acceptable for a City Chairman."

Immediately following both resignations the media suggested City were a club in crisis but the true legacy of Bernstein and Bird is they left the club in a good shape. It remained well organised and, as with most professional organisations, not reliant on any one individual. Clearly, the roles of the other directors, in particular future Chairman John Wardle and Managing Director Alistair Mackintosh, ensured the club continued to progress, but that would not have been possible had it not been for the firm direction set first by David Bernstein when he became Chairman, and secondly by Chris Bird when he became Managing Director.

In summary, Bird and Bernstein may have come from different backgrounds with varying styles and approaches but both proves key figures in the cliub's development. They were both true supporters of the club, were regular attendees before their time on the Board and continue to share that passion.

Maine Match 02/03

CITY v SOUTHAMPTON

DATE:	Sunday 11th May 2003	
TYPE OF FIXTURE:	Premier League	
ATTENDANCE:	34,957	
RESULT:	City 0 Southampton 1	
TEAMS & SCORERS:	**CITY**	**SOUTHAMPTON**
	Schmeichel	Jones
	Dunne	Bridge
	(Horlock)	Lundekvan
	Distin	M. Svensson **1**
	Sommeil	Telfer
	Jensen	Prutton
	Wright-Phillips	(Higginbotham)
	Benarbia	Oakley
	Barton	Baird
	(Belmadi)	A. Svensson
	Foe	(Tessem)
	Anelka	Beattie
	Goater	Ormerod
	(Fowler)	(Fernandes)
	Unused:	Unused:
	Nash	Williams
	Wiekens	Blayney

A game of this nature and result would normally only warrant a footnote, if that, in City's history, but as this was the last League match ever at the stadium it is of course a significant landmark.

The game had been eagerly anticipated all season with supporters desperate to attend. From the club perspective, the Blues had requested their final match be against opposition who would normally only bring limited support to Manchester. When Southampton was selected everyone felt segregation could be kept to a minimum and visiting supporters could be accommodated in a relatively small number of seats. This plan became impossible however as Southampton were enjoying one of their best seasons of all time. They had progressed to the FA Cup final and at one point looked likely to achieve automatic entry into European competition. This led to considerable debate between the footballing authorities,

Previous three pages: Fancy dress and painted faces were the order of the day as City fans arrived at Maine Road's final game with one object in mind - to make it a day to remember.

This page: Fans were treated to a parade of former Blues before kick-off and here's just a few (top to bottom, left to right)... Brian Horton, David White, Ian Brightwell, Paul Lake and son; Paul Dickov (being interviewed by Radio One DJ Marc Riley); Ray Ranson, John Bond and Nicky Reid; Georgi Kinkladze with Lorraine Firth; Tommy Booth, Alan Oakes and Francis Lee; Peter Barnes, Dennis Tueart and Mike Doyle; Gary Owen and Denis Law.

the police, government bodies, and the two clubs and Southampton were eventually allocated the 'Gene Kelly' uncovered stand between the North Stand and the Kippax. They were not happy, although City did receive letters and emails from Saints supporters apologising for their club's attempts to receive the maximum number of seats possible.

The day itself saw most City fans arrive at the ground mid morning. The weather was overcast but nothing could dampen the enthusiasm of the Blues. An exceptionally large group of fans stood on the main forecourt waiting to catch a glimpse of the club's leading figures. Every player received a cheer, but the biggest came for Shaun Goater who was scheduled to play his last match for the club. Fittingly, Goater had been awarded the captaincy – just as another cult figure of the past, Max Woosnam, had for the opening match almost eighty years earlier.

Inside the stadium, the festivities began with mascots selected from the crowd shortly after the turnstiles opened at 1pm, and then 45 minutes later a parade of legends saw stars from the 1940s through to the modern era brought out on to the pitch. Due to the nature of the day only a representative sample of leading players could be brought out, but supporters were thrilled

Tributes to Marc-Vivien Foe

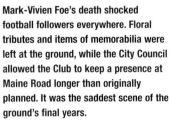

Mark-Vivien Foe's death shocked football followers everywhere. Floral tributes and items of memorabilia were left at the ground, while the City Council allowed the Club to keep a presence at Maine Road longer than originally planned. It was the saddest scene of the ground's final years.

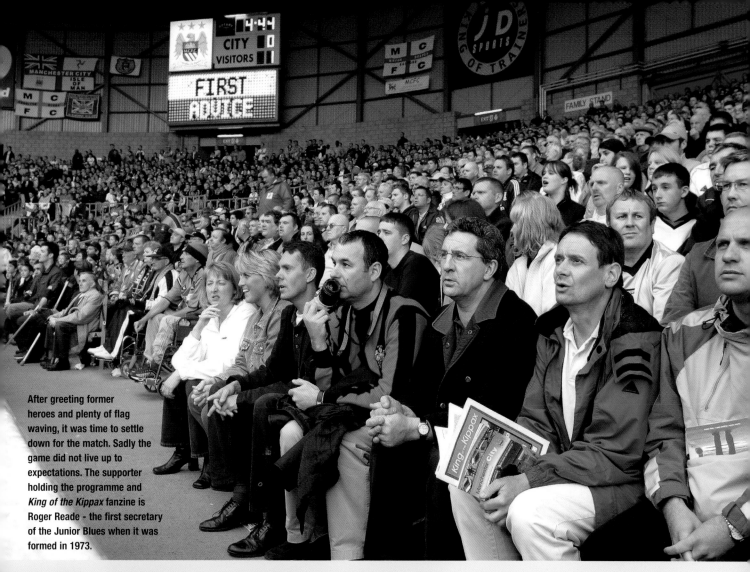

After greeting former heroes and plenty of flag waving, it was time to settle down for the match. Sadly the game did not live up to expectations. The supporter holding the programme and *King of the Kippax* fanzine is Roger Reade - the first secretary of the Junior Blues when it was formed in 1973.

to see many of the club's biggest stars. Roy Clarke delighted fans at the Platt Lane end of the ground when, after what appeared a gruelling walk around the pitch, he walked across the goalline as if it were a tightrope. The Platt Lane cheered. Other players, most notably Nicky Reid, Ian Brightwell and David White, stopped for a considerable time to sign autographs for large groups of young supporters. Perhaps the fact these had been local heroes meant they particularly understood the significance of the day.

At the North Stand end of the ground Georgi Kinkladze was given the biggest ovation although, sadly, those at the opposite end missed seeing the Georgian close up as rain cut short his journey around the pitch.

Prior to kick-off Colin Bell, Malcolm Allison, and Norah Mercer were introduced to the crowd. They were the club's chief guests and were introduced to the players. Significantly, Malcolm Allison made sure he took time out to also shake hands with each of the mascots and, on occasion, give them a gentle pat on the head or ruffle of their hair. Often dignitaries ignored the mascots, but Allison seemed to pay more attention to them than the players, extending his lifetime's rapport with the fans.

The match kick-off amid considerable noise generated from all sections of the stadium. Flags were passed around the stands – including the Main Stand – and the chant of "Feed The Goat" echoed around Maine Road. According to Paul Connolly writing in The Times: "The imminent departure of Goater has certainly proved the wellspring for almost as much emotion as the end of the Maine Road era. That became obvious when his name was greeted by the crowd before the game with a quite extraordinary tumultuous chorus of 'Feed The Goat'."

Left: The players huddle together in a show of determination to end this particular era with a win.

Shaun Goater in action for possibly the last time in a City shirt.

Likewise the much-missed Marc-Vivien Foe, who scored City's final goal at Maine Road on Easter Monday, shares a joke with Saints Claud Lundekvam, who appears to want to keep the goalpost as his souvenir!

Not likely, following the final full-time whistle (middle opposite), the goalposts are quickly removed by groundstaff before the post-match party begins.

Right: Shaun Wright-Phillips - "been there, got the t-shirt".

The Doves topped the after-match billing.

Blue and white confetti and fireworks, Moonchester and Moonbeam.

Some folks just didn't want to leave!

The game was not the great spectacle everyone had anticipated and in the 34th minute Michael Svensson of Southampton netted the last League goal ever at the stadium. The last City goal, incidentally, had been netted by Marc-Vivien Foe against Sunderland on Easter Monday.

At half-time three of the oldest surviving players were introduced to the crowd. Douglas Stewart was the eldest of the three and appeared in wartime matches for the club, while Billy Walsh, who played international football for both Northern Ireland and the Republic, and George Smith were both signed by the club pre-war, key players during the war, and then star men after the war. George was given a great reception when it was revealed he once scored four against United in a wartime match watched by over 60,000.

Due to the parlous state of the game, a number of supporters called for all three to be brought on as substitutes!

The second half followed the pattern of the first, although the substitution of Goater in the 63rd minute brought the first wave of emotion on a mass scale. By the final whistle chants of Blue Moon boomed around the ground and then, while the stage was being set up for the post-match concert, the present day squad came out for a lap of honour and then presentations were made to Goater and Schmeichel, who had ended his playing career with that match.

While these festivities were underway, groundsman Roy Rigby and his assistants Lee Jackson and Gary Conway, were removing the goalposts. For all three men, and all the other staff involved in the care and maintenance of the playing surface, this was a significant day. Maine Road had won the award for having the best playing surface in the Premier League and Roy was presented with the award earlier in the day. To many neutrals the Maine Road surface on its last League day was the best it had ever been on the final day of any season. It was significant that Roy and his team had achieved this with little publicity.

The post-match concert was hosted by Radio One's Marc Riley and featured a 'Blues Brothers' band, an Oasis tribute band, Badly Drawn Boy and the Doves, and ended with Badly Drawn Boy asking the North Stand to start off the final rendition of 'Blue Moon'. As the singing ended, fireworks were ignited and ticker-tape floated down from the Kippax. Moonchester and Moonbeam remained on the pitch partying, but in the stands many supporters remained seated contemplating what Maine Road meant to them.

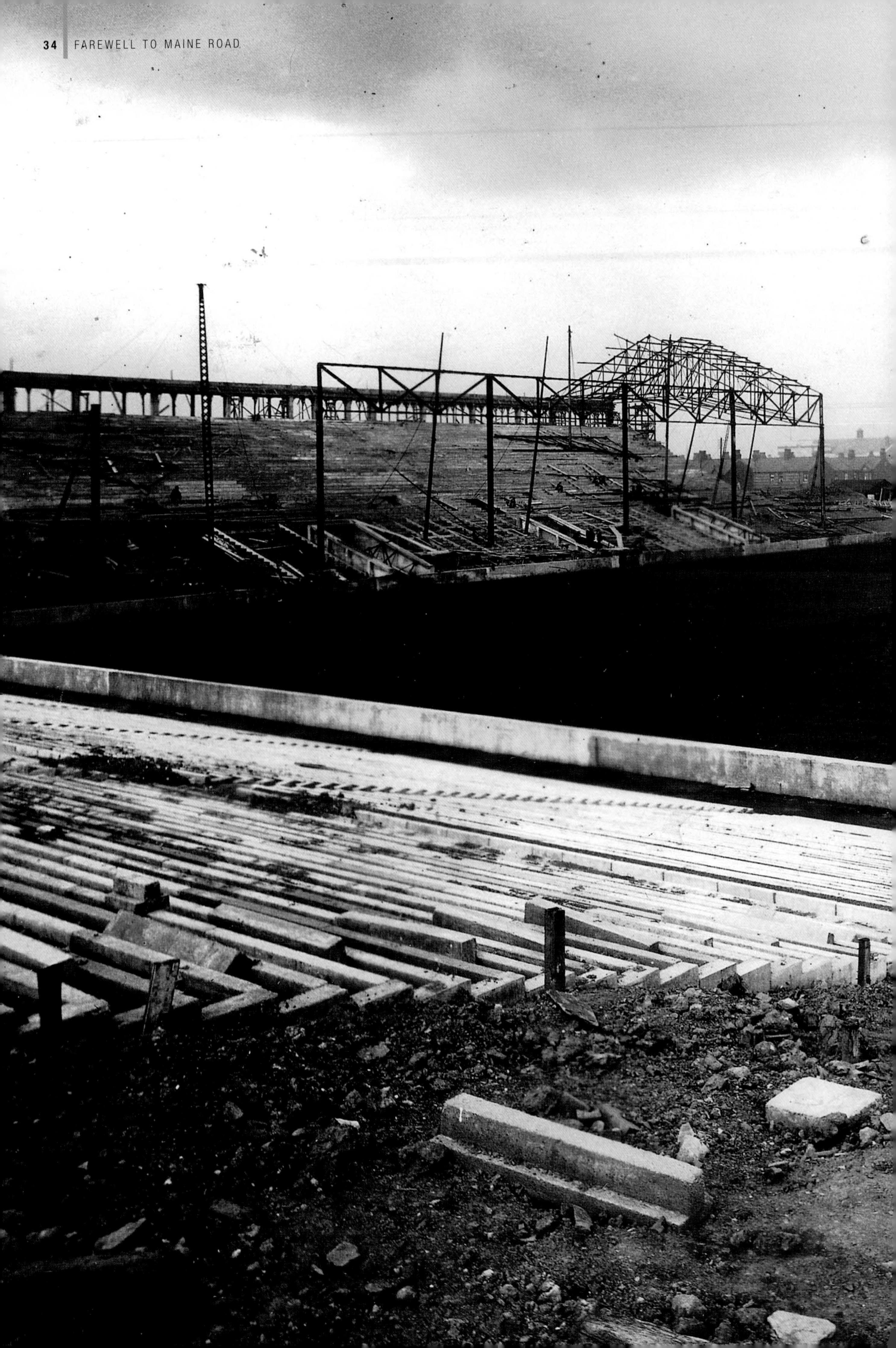

Chapter Two

Construction of Maine Road

This ground is the last word in the provision of comfort and security for – and against – the explosive force of the great crowds that follow the League teams. There is something almost barbaric in the impression which, when it is full it makes on the observer. As one comes on it suddenly from Claremont Road, a great rounded embankment towers up in front, and over it at one side looms the highly arched roof of a stand whose dim recesses cannot be discerned at all except from the ground level. Only the fresh green paint on the front of it picked out with gold, detracts from its broad impression of size and power, giving a rather incongruous air of neatness and modernity.

The Guardian, 27th August 1923

MAINE ROAD's final League game against Southampton in 2003 came almost 81 years to the day after the original announcement that City would be moving from their first League venue Hyde Road to a new stadium. Hyde Road was a well-loved footballing venue even if it was a little cramped, and so the announcement of the move away had to not only consider the feelings of supporters, it also had to offer something substantially better than Hyde Road.

City had always been based in the Gorton-Ardwick area of East Manchester and inevitably most supporters and the local newspapers considered the club would find a new home in that part of the city. For several years it had been common knowledge the Blues were keen to move, but it was assumed they would stay within a short distance of their birthplace at Clowes Street, West Gorton. The Belle Vue Pleasure Gardens seemed the obvious location, especially as this area was well known as the centre of Manchester leisure. There was already a sports ground there, and other sites were available including the land eventually developed as the Belle Vue Greyhound Stadium.

On August 30th 1920 the programme for the visit of Aston Villa actually stated City had agreed a lease with the owners, the Jennison family, for use of the Belle Vue Athletic Grounds, "More than that we cannot disclose at present." So it was clear City were determined to move, even before fire destroyed the Main Stand in November

1920. The reason it seems, was also revealed in the article: "It is doubtless well-known that we have decided to quit our present ground. We should have preferred to stay, if only for 'old times sake', had we been able to come to a satisfactory arrangement with the Corporation for more room for necessary improvements. For some years we have had in contemplation the re-modelling of the ground, which we think would have made it equal to any in the country, but the Corporation want the land and our tenancy expires in December 1924."

Some have suggested the comment 'the Corporation want the land' meant Manchester council required the entire ground to improve the tramway depot on Hyde Road, but that isn't entirely accurate. The Hyde Road tramway depot, later bus depot, was regularly being extended and improved and so any available land in the surrounding area was being consumed into the complex. City's plans to remodel Hyde Road had hoped to use some of the neighbouring land for new stands, approaches and facilities, but it was this very land which the council wanted. City had no chance of extending the ground's boundary and therefore little chance of increasing capacity and facilities. This meant a move to Belle Vue became the obvious choice.

The fire in November 1920, which destroyed the Main Stand and players' facilities, exacerbated the accommodation problems at Hyde Road, and made a move a near certainty.

Below: The Belle Vue Athletics Stadium was rejected by City in May 1922. For over two years the club had planned to move to sites within the Belle Vue Pleasure Grounds - a venue they'd used in 1889 for a floodlit friendly against Newton Heath. The ground eventually became the home of Belle Vue Aces Speedway team and these photographs were taken as it was being demolished in 1987.
The floodlight seen on the right could be viewed from the external steps of the old Kippax Stand.

Maine Memory

■ There was a quarry where the ground now stands. There was a deep pool and a man with a horse and cart slid into it and drowned. He has been seen many times over the years at certain points on the ground. The tea ladies called him Fred. There is something quite strange and inexplicable about the place. A door has been heard banging monotonously… yet the moment someone has gone to see what is causing it, the sound stops.

A figure has been seen in the foyer on countless occasions, but the moment the staff look at him he disappears into thin air!

There was something out on the pitch also that was quite inexplicable. During a match, even on a warm afternoon, I would be darting down the wing when suddenly I would find myself in a current of freezing cold air. It was quite extraordinary and there seemed no explanation for the severe change in temperature. It made you shiver.

Former Player Roy Clarke (1946-58)

MANCHESTER CITY'S NEW GROUND.

BELLE VUE ABANDONED FOR RUSHOLME.

The Manchester City Football Club have decided not to proceed with the scheme for a new ground at Belle Vue. They have instead obtained land in Rusholme upon which the work of building what will ultimately be one of the finest football grounds in the country will be started within a few weeks, and it is expected that the new headquarters will be ready for use by September, 1923.

The land has been bought outright, freehold. It is proposed to build a grandstand for 15,000 people and to find further accommodation for another 55,000, while in time the holding capacity may be extended to provide in all for a crowd of 120,000 under cover from bad weather. The model of the Hampden Park ground at Glasgow will be followed in some respects. The land has cost £5,500, and the estimated expenditure on building arrangements, &c., works out at some £7,000 more than for the Belle Vue project.

The site, which is on the Withington side of the Moss Side border-line, can be approached from Platt Lane by Yew Tree Road, and is bounded on three other sides by Thornton Road, Maine Road, and Carlton Avenue. The Greenheys terminus of the tramways is at the corner of Lloyd Street, 200 yards away from the plot. Wilmslow Road, whence Rusholme, Fallowfield, Palatine Road, and Chorlton circular route cars pass to and from the city, is near to the easterly side of the plot. The circular route trams from Cheetham Hill via Belle Vue, Dickenson Road, and Great Western Street pass the northerly side, along Great Western Street, 300 yards away. The Tramways Committee are at present contemplating opening up another route along Claremont Road, thereby getting a connection with Wilmslow Road on the eastern side, and Alexandra Park and Brooks's Bar on the westerly side.

The City management did actively consider the Belle Vue Athletic Ground for several years, and were also aware of other areas within the Belle Vue complex, but eventually the club rejected both these sites as too small. In addition, the Jennison family, who owned Belle Vue and more or less everything else in the area, would only give the Blues a fifty year lease.

Eventually the main Belle Vue ground became a major speedway venue - home to the Belle Vue Aces - but, although it lasted longer than the rest of the old pleasure gardens, it did not survive into the new century, being demolished in 1987. Its destruction was a sad moment for Manchester sport; remember it had staged a floodlit friendly in 1889 between Ardwick (City) and Newton Heath (United), and in 1929 Billy Meredith helped launch Manchester Central F.C. there. Manchester Central had high ambitions and capitalised on City's move from the area. They even launched a bid to join the Football League and were only rejected after a great deal of lobbying by City and United to keep them out.

Another Belle Vue development area eventually became a greyhound stadium, opening on 24th July 1926. This was the country's first greyhound racing track.

WHEELERS ASK FOR NEW TRACK.

Suggestion for City's New Ground.

WHAT OFFICIALS SAY.

Should there be a cement cycle track at Manchester City's new ground?

This is a question which is being freely discussed in athletic circles in Manchester, and efforts are being made to influence the Manchester City directors to this end.

The Manchester Wheelers have taken the initiative, and the President, Mr. F. T. Guilford, advances several reasons why, in his opinion, the proposal should be accepted.

Manchester, he points out, is very backward in this respect, compared with many other cities. The cinder track at the M.A.C. Ground at Fallowfield, he contends, is now quite out of date, and since it was built not only the sport of cycling but that of motor-racing has progressed.

"And here in Manchester there is no suitable place on which contests of this description can safely be held.

"In view of the fact that Manchester is now admittedly one of the greatest motor distributing centres in the country, this position of affairs does not redound to the credit of the city."

THE AMATEUR CYCLISTS.

From the point of view of amateur cycling alone, however, Mr. Guilford argues that there are many strong reasons why a track should be provided. Cyclists, he points out, are handicapped in their training owing to the absence of facilities obtainable in other cities, and the public interested in this form of sport cannot adequately be catered for owing to the scarcity of accommodation.

"I submit the provision of a cycling track at the new ground would not in the least detract from the enclosure for the purposes of football, but would be a paying proposition. For the purposes of athletics the ground would be used in the summer months, when otherwise it would not be earning any revenue at all."

FOOTBALL POINT OF VIEW.

So far, no overtures have been made to the City directors, and in an interview with an *Evening Chronicle* representative to-day, Mr. L. W. Furniss, the chairman of the club, said they had never considered the matter. Whilst he was unable to say what view the Board would take, his own opinion was that cycle tracks on football grounds were not to the advantage of spectators.

They meant that the people were so far away from the play, and as modern football grounds were constructed, they were almost impossible.

Most clubs had every sympathy with athletics, but they could not lose sight of the fact that it was football crowds they were catering for, and the distance objection had led to the removal of tracks on several of the leading grounds, including those of Bolton Wanderers and Aston Villa.

It was not a question of expense, but wholly and solely the convenience of the spectators.

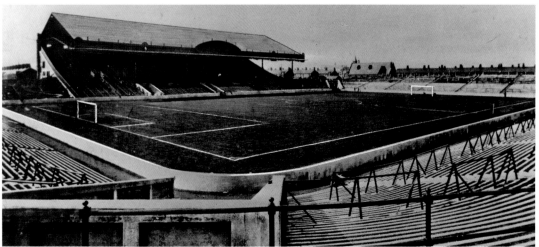

Top: The Main Stand roof takes shape while the stand's terracing is set in place. Note the three Main Stand tunnels were longer than in Maine Road's final season - they were reduced in length some 30 years after construction to squeeze in additional seating.

Middle: A completed Maine Road awaits its first match. The view is from the Platt Lane/Popular Side corner in August 1923.

Left: A similar view prior to Maine Road's final League match on 11th May 2003. The base of the Main Stand remains but the rest has changed.

Above: Most of the terracing is complete in this view from the Scoreboard End/Popular Side corner. Note the white perimeter wall initially had only one access point on to the pitch (players' tunnel). Also the opposite corner (Platt Lane/Main Stand) had the shortest life of all terracing at Maine Road. It was remodelled in 1931 and roofed as is described in Chapter Three.

Right: By May 2003 Maine Road looked considerably different as this image, taken from the temporary Gene Kelly Stand shows.

Top left: This photo was taken from the Main Stand seats and shows the general scale and size of the Stand and its roof. At the time of construction this roof had the largest span at any English football ground, including Wembley Stadium.

Left: Maine Road during construction as seen from the Platt Lane corner. These two photos and the one on pages 34/35 are extremely rare.

Above The Scoreboard End (North Stand) takes shape.

It is believed this was the land offered to City by the Jennison family when the Blues first chose to move away completely from the Ardwick/Gorton area. Clearly, the Jennisons were keen for City to move to Belle Vue and if the Athletic ground was deemed inappropriate then why not take on a totally free site, i.e. the future greyhound land? Once the Blues rejected Belle Vue completely the Jennisons worked with others to introduce the purpose-built greyhound track.

In 1987 the Greyhound Stadium became the new home of speedway following demolition of the Speedway/Athletics Stadium. This venue was still operating after the demise of Maine Road as City's home, and is the only surviving part of the original Belle Vue pleasure gardens still in active use.

In May 1922 Belle Vue was formally rejected with the Blues choosing a site on the border of Rusholme and Moss Side instead. The majority of Mancunians were deeply disappointed. Moss Side was not known for being a Blue area, nor was it easy for the majority of City fans to get to. City's homeland had always been East Manchester. In fact the initial development of terraced streets around the Gorton area had directly led to the formation of the club as St. Mark's, West Gorton in 1880.

The club were a little taken aback by the initial reaction, however they went to great lengths to explain to supporters living in City's heartland how it was utterly impractical to remain at Hyde Road and that all other possible venues were not suitable. They also deliberately outlined the bold plans held for the new stadium.

City boasted that the new sixteen and a quarter acre site on the edge of Moss Side was to be developed in two phases. The first phase, to be opened early in the 1923-4 season, would see completion of a grandstand

seating somewhere in the region of 15,000 with terracing for 55,000 looping around the other three sides. According to architect Charles Swain, the plan was based on Hampden Park which, in these pre-Wembley days, was regarded as the greatest venue in the world.

After a few years, the second phase would see City extend the terracing and erect a roof around the remaining three sides. The roof would link up in each corner with the grandstand and the eventual capacity would be 120,000. A phenomenal figure, but one the club were convinced would be filled on occasion. If nothing else the capacity would allow the new ground to stage events such as FA Cup semi-finals.

Other bold initiatives included the construction of a 500-space car park – a novel idea even for the 1920s – and in front of the grandstand a forecourt to allow at least 20,000 to gather. It would also be possible to allow ingress and egress on all four sides and Charles Swain had planned the venue so 120,000 people could evacuate within a 'very few minutes'.

The site cost £5,500 and had been considered around the time of the Hyde Road fire, but was initially discounted as part of it was covered by a tip and the rest was a clay pit, excavated for brick-making. The Blues called in soil experts and the builder Robert McAlpine to survey the site before making their announcement.

Despite the disappointment of moving away from Ardwick and Gorton, City fans became excited by the overall plans. Many doubted City could actually deliver a stadium of this quality and size and although the plans were amended a little over the following months, City came up with much more than originally outlined in their first plan.

The club had, by the end of 1922, decided that instead of one 'grandstand' seating around 15,000, City's

Main Stand would hold 10,000. The terracing issue however was debated for some time. One version of the plan shows the ground looking very similar to that delivered, however the terracing was still larger than that eventually erected. The areas behind each goal extended outwards with the terracing squared off. The eventual terracing gently curved around the ground as can be seen on the initial aerial view of the stadium (opposite), but one of Swain's plans from early 1923 was not to provide this gentle curve.

On the Popular Side Swain's plan was to have the terracing squared off in the manner that existed in 1957, after the roof was erected, although the close proximity of the houses on Thornton Road meant Swain angled the terracing to correspond with the direction of the houses at that end of the stand.

Eventually, the terracing was constructed to loop and curve around the pitch, and was designed to hold somewhere in the region of 75,000 spectators - some 20,000 more than the original plan. This meant the total capacity for the ground was between eighty and ninety thousand, although McAlpine's own archives claim the total capacity when constructed was 100,000, a point repeated in *McAlpine – The First Hundred Years*: "The grandstand at Maine Road measured 82m long by 43m wide and the total accommodation afforded at the ground was for 100,000 people". This was a phenomenal figure for a team used to playing in a cramped 40,000-capacity venue.

The questions supporters – and club officials - were now asking all focused around the scale of the development. Would the ground ever be filled?

When the Blues ended the following 1922-23 season - the last at Hyde Road - in eighth place, the final League game at Hyde Road attracted a crowd of only 20,000. The directors must surely have wondered whether their huge investment in the new stadium was just pie-in-the-sky.

Newcastle were the last visitors to Hyde Road on 28th April 1923. The game ended goalless and, as the match was played on the same date as Wembley Stadium hosted its first FA Cup final, very little space was afforded to the City game in the local newspapers. Instead they concentrated on Bolton's performance against West Ham and the exploits of Billy, the white horse, in clearing the Wembley pitch crowd overspill.

Ironically, the development of Maine Road – as City's new stadium was to be called - occurred at the same time as Wembley was being constructed, and as Sir Robert McAlpine & Sons were the builders of both venues there was a great deal of rivalry between their northern and southern divisions. The Empire Stadium, as it was known at the time, simply had to be finished for the 1923 Cup final, while Maine Road had an anticipated completion date of September 1923. Even then the September date was an optimistic four months earlier than the original forecast.

The land at Maine Road had previously been used as a brickworks – a very busy workplace during the latter years of the nineteenth and beginning of the twentieth century - and formed part of the Lloyd family estate. It was not a regular-shaped piece of land, being closer to a polygon. For hundreds of years the land had been distinctive on maps of the area and even the site of Maine Road itself was clear years before Princess Road or any of the other main thoroughfares surrounding the stadium were prominent, although the name, Maine Road, did not appear until the 1870s.

Prior to this, the road carried the image-provoking moniker of Dog Kennel Lane. It followed the present day route of Maine Road from its junction with Moss Lane East down to a point roughly in line with the start of the Platt Lane Stand, then turned south-westwards until it met Wilbraham Road. The final 500 yards or so later became part of Princess Road, just north of Hough End.

The top end of Dog Kennel Lane was the first to be renamed Maine Road. It appears that, as the development of terraced housing transformed the area from a rural landscape, a decision was taken to give the old lane a more modern name. Why 'Maine' was chosen isn't clear. Many streets in the Maine Road area are named after other places, for example Kippax is a town near Leeds and there are streets named after towns in southern England to the east of the Kippax and in the Victoria Park area, but Maine does not appear to fit into this pattern. For a start there appears to have been a conscious decision to rename a very old and traditional route, and also the name was chosen some time before Kippax Street and the others were named.

The most obvious link would be with the American state of Maine, or the French province of the same name, however investigations have proved inconclusive. There are two versions of a story which may have some relevance. In an early twentieth century newspaper article one journalist wrote of an event which had taken place around forty years earlier. He claimed that in the 1860s a prominent member of the land-owning Lloyd family paid for a group of local men to fight in the American Civil War.

If this is true then it is possible these men fought alongside forces from Maine, or were based in the area for a while. Maine forces were used in some of the most

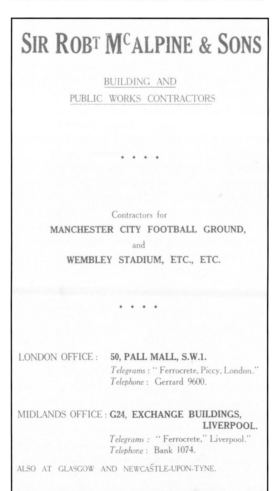

SIR ROBᵀ MᶜALPINE & SONS

BUILDING AND
PUBLIC WORKS CONTRACTORS

. . . .

Contractors for
MANCHESTER CITY FOOTBALL GROUND,
and
WEMBLEY STADIUM, ETC., ETC.

. . . .

LONDON OFFICE : **50, PALL MALL, S.W.1.**
Telegrams : " Ferrocrete, Piccy, London."
Telephone : Gerrard 9600.

MIDLANDS OFFICE : **G24, EXCHANGE BUILDINGS,
LIVERPOOL.**
Telegrams : " Ferrocrete," Liverpool."
Telephone : Bank 1074.

ALSO AT GLASGOW AND NEWCASTLE-UPON-TYNE.

Maine Memory

■ We lived on Princess Road when the ground opened. My father was a regular at Hyde Road and when Maine Road opened it was on his doorstep, and so for the first game my father brought my mother and I here. We sat in the best seats and it was a wonderful occasion. Since then I've sat and stood in every stand. I had a season ticket up until a couple of years ago but have had to give it up because of the cold and the stairs.

I was nine at the time of the first game so you can understand that this was the most marvellous experience a nine-year-old could have had. It was very exciting and according to my mother I sat next to her throughout the game shouting 'Come on Austin, come on Austin!' to Billy Austin who was playing outside right.

Seeing City on your own doorstep was a dream come true. What a wonderful day!

We had some interesting players then. Max Woosnam played that day and he had a rather strange characteristic. He would always carry a handkerchief in his hand to mop his brow. The goalkeeper was JF Mitchell and he was a teacher by profession. He wore glasses when he played and he brought off some fantastic saves over the years, but he also let in some really silly goals. I can laugh about it now.

Tommy Browell was another popular player when we came to Maine Road, but he was near the end of his playing days for us. He'd been at the club since before the First World War, and was very popular. When he stopped playing he became a tram driver in Blackpool. Up and down the front. It was said that some City fans would board every tram hoping to find him so they could say 'We've been on Tommy Browell's tram!'.

Harry Bramble

Maine Men Charles Swain

■ As the architect of Maine Road Charles Swain should be regarded as a major influence in the development of Manchester's architectural heritage, however it is typical of the perception of sport and more importantly sporting venues that little has been officially recorded about him. For example, The Royal Institute of British Architects have no information on him while, prior to research for this book, Manchester's own records paid little attention to his achievements at Maine Road.

What is known about Swain, however, is that he was born in 1881 in Newton Heath where his father, Hyde-born Matthew Swain, ran an iron foundry in Holt Street.

In 1901, at the age of 19, he was already known as an architect and was living in Buxton, and then in 1905 he set up his architectural practice. Four years later he designed his first cinema - The Kinemacolor Palace on Whitworth Street in Manchester. This now forms part of the Cornerhouse complex. From then on he became known for cinemas and theatres and designed several in the Manchester area. These included ones in Prestwich, Broughton, Stockport, Rawtenstall and even in Blackpool. He retired from practice in 1935 to concentrate on other business interests and died in December 1965.

Other Manchester buildings he designed (or was involved with in a major capacity) - Regent House, 30 Cannon Street (1927, since demolished); 44 Brazenose Street (1926); Old Colony House, South King Street (1925); 95-101 Market Street; and the "Empire Cap Works", Derby St, Cheetham - this was a well regarded building at the time of its opening. He also designed the Queen's Theatre, Great Bridgewater Street. Another Swain development was the Salford Poor Children's Holiday Camp in Prestatyn which he designed, free of charge, in 1928.

On 3rd July 1923 Swain became the proud owner of one share in the club, and the following May he purchased a further two hundred shares. He also became a director – often architects would be retained in some managerial capacity after the construction of significant developments – and by the time of the Platt Lane corner stand construction in 1931 Swain's official company address was: Lloyds Bank Buildings, King Street, Manchester. During the 1930s, possibly as a result of his retirement from practice in 1935, he sold his shareholding in the club.

famous Civil War battles and contained non-American volunteers (mainly Canadian).

Another version of this story appeared in the *Manchester Guardian* in 1904, except in this case the article clearly stated that the recruitment of men by the Lloyd family actually occurred during the American War of Independence. According to this version, landowner George Lloyd raised a corps of 150 volunteers from the area to fight against the American revolutionaries. The actual exploits of this corps are unclear, however it is true that considerable activity took place in the Maine area of America and that many Manchester men did fight in the war. Then in 1812 further battles took place with the British aiming to recapture Maine in a battle the Americans often refer to as the second War of Independence.

From a historical perspective it does appear clear Manchester men volunteered and fought in the War of Independence, and it seems likely many of these were based in Maine; however considerable research has not yet found conclusive proof that any of these actions may have led to the renaming of Maine Road. It may be nice to believe the name was changed to commemorate a historic incident, but may be rather foolhardy to do so.

Potentially, the returning volunteers or one of the Lloyd family members may have renamed Dog Kennel Lane to commemorate their stay in the US. Of course all this is pure conjecture, but it is known that Lloyd Street was named after the family, and it is clear the renaming of a road during this period was a very deliberate act and there must have been a reason. It would be entertaining to discover where the original 'Dog Kennel Lane' got its name as well.

At the top of Dog Kennel Lane, close to the corner with Moss Lane East, stood Moss Grove Farm which in November 1904 the *Manchester Guardian* admitted: "The only relic now remaining of old Moss Side is the farmstead at the corner of Maine Road." As far as can be seen, this is the first newspaper mention of 'Maine Road', while the farmstead was regarded as the last 'black & white' style building in the area. The rapid development all around caused that to be demolished soon after.

How the ground looked when it first opened.

The earliest mention of Moss Side came in 1533 when, ironically, it formed part of the Trafford family estate, while the first mention of football activity was in February 1904 when, under the headline 'A Moss Side Football Nuisance' the *Weekly Chronicle* newspaper stated: "Four youths named John Broughton, Stanley Parker, Daniel Brindle, and Harry Farrigan all living in the Moss Side District were charged with playing football in Great Western Street on January 28th. The defendants were each fined two shillings."

The first true mention of football in relation to Maine Road came in the same newspaper on 13th May 1905. This may sound like an old music hall joke but the article did appear under the heading "Moss Side – Localising the Kick". A case had been brought before the local magistrates' court of two young men who had been fighting over a football. One of the boys came from Maine Road. One boy explained to the court: "He told me he had got a new football and he kicked me!" Mr. Joshua Smith, the Chairman of the Magistrates, asked: "And was he kicking you for the football then?"

The boy said he was and the Chairman asked: "Where did he kick you?" The complainant replied: "In Moss Lane, Sir!" The court erupted in laughter and the case was dismissed.

The novelist Elizabeth Gaskell wrote of the area close to Maine Road, or Dog Kennel Lane as it was at the time, in her 1848 novel *Mary Barton: A Tale of Manchester Life*. She described the area as being full of greenery and quite picturesque, but a little closer to the city centre the scene was considerably different. She wrote: "women from their doors tossed household slops of every description into the gutter; they ran into the next pool, which over-flowed and stagnated. You went down one step from this foul area into the cellar in which a family of human beings lived. It was very dark inside. The window-panes many of them were broken and stuffed with rags, which was reason enough for the dusky light that pervaded the place at mid-day. After the account I have given of the state of the street, no one can be surprised that on going into the cellar inhabited by Davenport, the smell was so foetid as almost to knock the two men down. Quickly recovering themselves, as those inured to such things do, they began to penetrate the thick darkness of the place, and to see three or four little children rolling on the damp, nay wet brick floor, through which the stagnant, filthy moisture of the street oozed up; the fireplace was empty and black; the wife sat on the husband's lair, and cried in the dark loneliness."

Although it was a novel, Gaskell's account is typical of city centre Manchester during the mid to late 1800s. The streets around Maine Road were developed partly to rid the city of scenes like the one she describes. She was a great social reformer, as was Frederick Engels. Engels, a good friend of Karl Marx, was a wealthy businessman who deplored the poverty and conditions he witnessed in Manchester. He devoted much of his life to challenging the establishment of the day and sought to improve conditions for all. In the 1860s he lived at 252 Hyde Road, close to the location of City's first major ground, and at another time he lived at 374 Moss Lane East, close to the top of Dog Kennel Lane/Maine Road.

Other sites of interest in the Maine Road area included the four-acre Athletic Ground and seven-acre Cricket & Tennis Ground at the western edge of Platt Lane. The two grounds were separated by a narrow lane (present day Yew Tree Road) which led to the Moss Side

FOR local residents the prospect of City moving to their area was a major event. In 2002, 88-year-old Margaret Baker recalled how the news was greeted in her family: "We lived at the second shop along on Claremont Road and saw the stadium as a great opportunity. My parents felt the arrival of City would put the place on the map, and it certainly did that.

"When building work first started we were inundated with workmen – mainly from Scotland – coming to the shop asking if we knew of any good lodgings in the area. My family didn't really help a great deal at first but then a member of the McAlpine family – I think it was the owner's son or maybe it was his brother – asked if we could help because

they were having real problems. My father worked hard to help many of them find rooms, and he got quite pally with a few of them. He even created a football team for some of the men.

"Originally most of the land was just cinders and dirt. There was a great pool there and fairly early on a horse fell in. I remember how awful it was as the horse had to be left where it fell. Of course it didn't take that long before the stands started to be built. There was a lot of pride in the area. As far as we were concerned this was the best stadium in the world and it was being built on our doorstep. No-one was against City moving here – not the local residents any road."

A small group of people living in the area did oppose the

development but they were residents of a gypsy encampment, which had been set up, unofficially, on the land.

Bert Hindson, a City supporter living close to Maine Road in the 1920s, told journalist Alec Johnson what he remembered of this time in an interview in 1994: "They [the gypsies] were doing no harm whatsoever. I heard about the gypsies curse. They were upset at being told to clear off. They were doing no harm, just trading with the householders in the area. They were selling pegs and the like.

"Me and my little brother played on the croft in the centre of that area. There was a pond and I remember that a toy boat I was playing with suddenly sank like a stone. It must be just about under the penalty spot at the Platt Lane end of the ground."

According to legend the actual curse was placed on the ground – not, it should be stressed, on the club! – when over-zealous club officials ordered the gypsies to leave. The gypsies were planning to move on anyway, but the dispute with City caused one of the leaders of the group to confront the club. He said: "We have done no harm here. Therefore, hear this. No good will come to anyone who will dwell here."

Whether the gypsy curse affected the Blues over the eighty years that followed is anybody's guess and it is certainly true that in years when City have enjoyed success the curse has never received a mention, but during years when the Blues have failed the media have tried to create a story by suggesting the curse is the cause. Regardless of the true situation, with the original curse there is a final twist to the story which is

revealed here for the first time.

In December 1998 with the Blues struggling in Division Two a member of City's office staff was contacted by a third party interested in helping bring an end to the club's misery. He claimed to have contact with the descendants of the original gypsies who, according to his discussions, were now prepared to lift the curse – or at least counter it with a request for good luck. He said the gypsies had already taken four horseshoes, painted them a City Blue, and had performed all they could do to lift the curse. What the club now needed to do was house the horseshoes at Maine Road and good luck would counter the curse.

Clearly, the club official was sceptical. However, when the Blues faced Stoke on 28th December 1998 a member of the gypsy family arrived at the ground with a case containing the horseshoes and said City's luck would

change so long as the horseshoes remained at the ground. In the 31st minute third-placed Stoke scored. What followed was one of the most entertaining and enjoyable displays of the season. The most impressive part was City actually came from behind to take the points, something few City sides had managed in the previous couple of seasons. In fact it was the first time since Reading, nineteen months earlier. Usually, the Blues fell apart when in arrears, but not against Stoke. The crowd, recognising City's fire, burst into life and cheered, applauded, and chanted. All of this led to Paul Dickov netting a rather simple equaliser two minutes into the half. Dickov: "You could feel the confidence flowing through the side once I had scored."

From that point on nothing could stop the Blues, but they had to wait until the final five minutes for the next goal, when Gareth Taylor headed an 85th-minute winner. Had the horseshoes changed City's

luck and brought about a 2-1 victory? The City personnel didn't know what to make of the transformation, but decided keeping the horseshoes at the ground could do no harm and so they were stored in a secret location within the stadium for the next home match.

Division leaders Fulham were defeated 3-0 in the following Maine Road match and a decision was taken to keep the horseshoes for a while longer at least. Because of their positive impact the horseshoes were also taken to a couple of away games but to do this required the involvement of City's alien mascot Moonchester who managed to smuggle the items in with his football kit. Those games were won, however the realisation soon dawned that the curse was only supposed to be on Maine Road – not on City playing away – so the decision was taken not to push the luck too far and the horseshoes were then safely squirrelled away within the stadium.

As back-to-back promotions followed the horseshoes became

permanent fixtures hidden away at the ground, and were still present when the last Maine Road season ended in 2003. Of course the club has not been invincible since December 1998, but the gypsies did make it quite clear the horseshoes would bring more good luck than bad, and there was never any suggestion of invincibility.

Whether the original curse or the lucky horseshoes had any impact on City's life at Maine Road is clearly open for debate. Cynics will say success in the thirties, fifties, sixties and at other times proves the curse never existed, while those who believe suggest each success was followed by a major run of bad luck – relegation followed City's first championship; Bert Trautmann and Jimmy Meadows were both seriously injured during the mid-fifties finals; and the Mercer-Allison partnership was broken up when the club became the subject of a major take-over battle.

Fortunately, the move away from Maine Road ends the curse once and for all.

The story of a gypsy's curse

Brickworks. The Cricket Ground has since disappeared entirely, however the Athletic Ground is better known today as City's Platt Lane training complex with its facilities for the local community, such as the Dome.

Behind the Cricket Ground lay Demesne Farm. Over the years it has been suggested the name Maine Road developed as a corruption of the farm's name, however this seems unlikely as the name change from Dog Kennel Lane to Maine Road appears very deliberate, while the area closest to Demesne Farm never actually bore the name Maine Road. A Demesne Road was developed south of Alexandra Park (parallel with the farm), and another lane, Hart Road, south of modern day Platt Fields, was originally called Demesne Road as it led towards the farm.

Whatever the origin of the title 'Maine Road' this was to be City's home from 1923 through to 2003.

As the date drew nearer to Maine Road's opening match the local press began providing information for supporters. Very little to date had been forthcoming but on 13th August the *Manchester Evening News* provided "Some Impressive Facts & Figures – Details from McAlpines."

The article was aimed at informing readers of the size and significance of the new stadium. The newspaper revealed how the ground was unusual in that it was an 'island site'. What they actually meant was supporters would be free to walk around the external wall to reach turnstiles at any side of the ground, although free external access from the north end of the ground to the main stand was not possible, as the boundary wall joined to the club houses and the church wall, therefore supporters had to walk down a passageway leading from the scoreboard end boundary wall to Claremont Road, and then head westwards to the corner with Maine Road.

Many grounds, including the old Hyde Road ground, had restricted access. Supporters would have to walk down various streets to access each side of the ground, if indeed they were able to enter at any side of the ground. Although this seems like a pre-requisite in the modern era back in 1923 access on each side was perceived as an unusual selling point.

The article went on to describe the ground in statistical terms. The boundary wall – much of which was still visible in 2003 at the Kippax side of the ground – was an average of nine feet high. Its total length was 762 yards long and it stretched from the edge of the Main Stand towards the site of the club houses where it then angled behind the Scoreboard End (latter day North Stand) towards Kippax Street. It continued along the section still visible in 2003, passed behind the Platt Lane side of the ground, and eventually joined up to the south end of the Main Stand.

The design of the boundary wall had used the skills of Westminster-based civil engineering firm L.G. Mouchel & Partners. They had worked with Swain to design a strong wall. Original plans had shown the wall to have a large brick, concrete and iron base rising at an angle from a couple of feet under ground. Piers were to be erected every ten feet to create a strong footing. The original idea was to slope the wall inwards on both sides.

Built within the boundary wall were forty turnstiles and sixteen exit doors – each exit being nine feet wide - while the Main Stand, or Grand Stand as it was called at the time, possessed eight turnstiles and six exit doors.

Maine Men Ernest Mangnall

ROLE: Secretary-Manager

In terms of Maine Road's history, Ernest Mangnall is one of the leading figures behind the stadium's development. He is also the only man so far to have managed both Manchester clubs and it can also be recorded he was mainly responsible for United's move to Old Trafford.

Prior to joining the Blues he had been secretary with Burnley (1900 - 1903), and then United (September 1903 - August 1912). In 1907 while at United – managing the Reds at Bank Street (behind the present-day Asda Store) only a short distance away from the City of Manchester Stadium - he obtained the services of Billy Meredith, and many of the other banned City stars, for relatively small sums of money. With the City men he brought United two League Championships and the FA Cup. Without Mangnall's recruitment of these men it is highly unlikely United would have achieved any such success during this period.

In 1912 City stunned the football world when they snatched Mangnall from the Reds. Never in the history of the game had a manager left one major club for their biggest rivals after so much success. What made the story more of a sensation was the fact Mangnall actually remained in charge of United for the Manchester derby of 7th September 1912. Naturally City defeated the Reds 1-0 at the palatial Old Trafford on the Saturday, and the following Monday Mangnall moved into his office at the more homely, if cramped, Hyde Road.

At City, he developed a rather decent-looking side by the time of the First World War, with the Blues finishing fifth in Division One at the end of the 1914-5 season. During the hostilities he kept the club alive and even brought some trophy success in the first Wartime season.

Post-war he built a very useful team as games at Hyde Road regularly became sell-outs. In 1921 the Blues finished second and Mangnall worked hard to secure a new venue for the increasingly popular Blues. The 1920-1 season had seen many crowds of over 40,000 - the official limit - and Mangnall as secretary-manager received much criticism from the press who held him responsible for crowd control. It seems crazy now that the man responsible for team matters should also be in control of general ground and club matters, but right up until the 1940s, even later at many clubs, this was usually the case.

Mangnall, together with Chairman Lawrence Furniss, was instrumental in choosing Maine Road. Prior to 1922 City seemed destined to move to Belle Vue and the selection of Maine Road was a courageous one. It could so easily have all gone wrong.

In 1923 the Blues did move to Maine Road, and in Mangnall's final season (1923-4) he almost gave City an appearance in the FA Cup Final. With the 49-year-old Meredith in the side, Mangnall's men were beaten by Newcastle in the semi-final.

The following May the directors decided not to renew Mangnall's contract. Why is open to question, but it seems a grave pity that Maine Road's first manager was not allowed to continue his excellent work.

Mangnall died in 1932 after becoming a director of his home town team, Bolton. In addition to his roles at Burnley, United, City, and Bolton, he was also responsible for founding the Central League and the Football Managers' Association.

He remains one of the most influential football administrators of all time. Together with Lawrence Furniss he is probably the most influential figure in City's move from Hyde Road to Maine Road. Without Mangnall and Furniss it's possible the selection of Moss Side for the new stadium would never have been made. Without Mangnall it certainly would not have reached the size it did.

Maine Memory

The Grand Stand had originally been designed in a more elaborate manner. Architect Swain's plan wanted the windows to be marked out with terracotta, in a style reminiscent of many public buildings and Manchester warehouse construction (particularly around the Whitworth Street area) of the early twentieth century. This seems a little perverse for, at the time, Manchester's newest buildings were more or less all being constructed in Portland Stone, however the suggested use of terracotta and brick was perhaps more in keeping with the design of cinemas and theatres for which Swain was famous.

The plan had suggested the use of Accrington bricks for the pillars, with Common bricks used for the rest of the construction. A note on the original plan dated 10th July 1923 says "Elevation cancelled" and the design became more functional rather than decorative. The lintels and other more elaborate stonework did not appear on the final construction, although the two semi-circular mosaics over the main exit doors were surrounded by slightly more impressive white stonework than originally planned.

The mosaics were the work of two companies A. & O. Stefanutti & Co. – a terrazzo tile company from Johnson Street, Cheetham - and Conway & Co. - a tiling company from 67 Bridge Street. It seems Stefanutti designed the mosaics, while Conway installed them, although an advert for Stefanutti simply mentions the tiling erected at the main entrance.

As the name Stefanutti suggests many mosaic craftsmen came from Italy. Similar mosaics erected at Villa Park in 1923 were the work of Italians in business in Birmingham. It is believed these mosaics were first laid on a sheet of toughened glass before being mounted on the brickwork. City-supporting mosaic artist Mark Kennedy, who eventually removed the tiles in May 2003, believes this was how the Maine Road tiles were erected: "The

City mosaics are special because, other than the tiling in the Town Hall, these are probably the oldest quality mosaics in Manchester. They are of a thickness I have never seen before and clearly the craftsmen who created them were highly skilled. I believe they would have purposefully baked large square tiles – possibly about a foot square – and then smashed them to create the irregular shapes used. Then they would have painstakingly laid them out on either toughened glass or on a strong, smooth wooden surface, before mounting the entire mosaic on to the wall. This was not a simple tiling job, and clearly everyone involved in the construction wanted to make sure this was as perfect a job as possible. Great care was taken. This was an example of Mancunian pride."

The completed frontage was large but relatively plain in comparison with the original design. Nevertheless it was still an amazing construction at the time. Approximately 90 windows of varying size – the largest rectangular windows appearing in the second floor where the public tea rooms were – were positioned at four levels. Even the ground floor players' areas, including the dressing rooms, possessed windows, while the top ones provided light to the back of the seated stand.

According to McAlpine's the stand was 270 feet long, 140 feet wide and 56 feet high. It contained 54 rows of seats with the top seats being the equivalent of 44.5 feet above the pitch. It was stated that there were 186 yards from the back of the stand to the perimeter wall. The valuation of this stand alone amounted to £120,000 according to McAlpine's.

The roof, it was stated, had the largest span on any football ground, while the seats below included 1,700 best-quality tip up seats; an additional 8,000 spectators were accommodated on simple tip-up seats and some benches. The steelwork for the roof and crush barriers was fabricated by a company called C.J. Cooke & Co. at

Right: The Main Stand facade pictured during the 1960s. Apart from the floodlighting nothing had changed since 1923.

the Victoria Steelworks, Openshaw, while the seating was supplied by Goodalls, a furnishing store based on King Street in the city centre. According to their advert: "Goodalls make a speciality of tip-up seating and the whole of the seating on the Manchester City Football Ground was supplied by them." Some of Goodall's seating – most notably a section within the Directors' Box and the back row of the Main Stand - was still present at Maine Road for the final match in 2003.

In front of the stand lay a 12 feet wide cinder track, while inside the stand possessed three floors. Initially, the ground floor included the players' rooms, a gymnasium accessed via the home dressing room, the referees' and linesmen's room, a boiler room, a room for storing coal and coke, a laundry room and the initial entry points for spectators. Each of the rooms was positioned along a corridor stretching either side of the main entrance which, according to the original plan, was to lead directly into a ground floor lobby area. Housed there would be an ornate staircase, however it's clear a more modern entrance area was constructed instead.

Upstairs, the first floor contained - from the north end of the stand - the Directors' private room, the Boardroom, the secretary's office, the assistant secretary's office (with connecting door into the secretary's office), a large reception room, a lobby area containing first a gentlemen's toilet and on the other side of the main staircase a ladies' toilet with two cubicles. The corridor then continued towards the Platt Lane end with first the kitchen, then a room described as the "Rest or Games Room" which had a connecting door to the kitchen and another to a small toilet room. After the Games Room the architect had designed a Billiards Room and further along the Ground Committee Room.

By 2003 these two rooms formed the Executive Suite – or Joe Smith Suite as it was first known when opened in the mid-1980s - while the Rest or Games

Left: Mosaic artist and City supporter Mark Kennedy removes the first tile from the mosaic above the Main Stand exit at the Platt Lane end of the stand on Tuesday 6th May 2003.

Furnishers and Decorators
KING ST., MANCHESTER

Phone : 2200 City.   Telegrams : Allgood, Manchester

GOODALLS MAKE A SPECIALITY OF TIP-UP SEATING AND THE WHOLE OF THE SEATING ON THE MANCHESTER CITY FOOTBALL GROUND WAS SUPPLIED BY THEM

Below: Joe Mercer is pictured chatting to a TV reporter outside the main entrance in 1969. Note the central mosaic (which was hidden behind cladding in the ground's latter years). Apart from modifications to the door, the entrance had remained the same since 1923.

Room had become part of the kitchen, however for many years the Joe Smith Suite – named after the main force behind the early 1970s take-over - had been the Players' Lounge.

All the rooms on the north side of the lobby were redeveloped in the mid-1990s and were, for the final years of the ground's existence, part of the Boardroom Suite and connected kitchen. No rooms existed on the pitch side of the corridor at all in 1923, other than three passageways which led from the lobby into the Pressmen's Box, the Directors' Box, and the Ground Committee Box. These passageways were later developed into the Blue Room/International Lounge.

The top floor of the stand provided the main refreshment areas for spectators and housed two tea rooms plus numerous smaller catering bars.

Three large tunnels positioned at the front of the stand provided access at the lowest level of the stand. The middle of these was used as the players' tunnel throughout the life of the stadium.

The opposite side of the ground contained the main area of terracing. Here the Popular Side (retaining the name used for a similar area at Hyde Road), as it was initially known, reached a height of 38 feet above the pitch. The terracing contained 106 rows of steps at its highest point and from the back of the terrace to the front was a distance of 190 yards. Two giant tunnels were positioned within this stand for easy access.

As the pitch was built below normal ground level, the initial plans had actually shown these tunnels built lower than ground level. It was intended they would gradually slope up away from the pitch and then at the external end of the tunnel steps were to be built to bring the crowd back up to ground level. Fortunately, for safety reasons, the steps were never built. Instead the two Popular Side tunnels were built a little higher into the stand, and then a sensible gentle slope allowed supporters to comfortably walk back out at ground level.

The paintwork on the stand was mainly green (similar to Wimbledon's green), with details painted in gold for effect. This included the front of the Main Stand roof where, in the centre, a small semi-circular gable was positioned.

Behind the goals the terracing reached a height of 22.4 feet and contained 73 steps. The whole terracing was divided into two by a low wall and barrier positioned roughly midway from the front of the end terraces around the ground. The opening of the two Popular Side tunnels were positioned to line up with the wall. According to the *Manchester Guardian*: "With between twenty and thirty thousand people filling this great slope, there is to be seen a continuous sea of faces broken only by two great concrete pits in the centre and two tunnels at the end to which the many-headed monster is to disappear when the game is done. With the crowd actually there, with nothing to be seen but its heads and these pits and the containing wall, also of concrete, which bars it from the field of play, one cannot doubt that, it is indeed the monster Hydra for whom the architect has made sumptuous but fearful provision."

The two tunnels referred to were actually two of the four large white corner tunnels. McAlpine & Sons had worked with architect Charles Swain to create a stadium that could be evacuated quickly and efficiently. These tunnels and a series of exit steps at the rear of the terracing were considered at length during the planning phase - the aim being that all those spectators positioned below the midway dividing wall and barrier would leave by the six terrace tunnels, while those stood to the rear of the wall would leave by the twelve sets of steps positioned at the back of the banking. The plan seemed perfect, however, on matchdays supporters would leave by whichever exit point was nearest whether they were positioned behind the dividing wall or not, and so, on occasion, this wall made access a little difficult for those stood within a few feet of a tunnel but behind the wall. Those towards the back would primarily use the exit steps, however they would also risk running down the muddy embankment at the back. Photos from the early 1950s show a series of pathways where the earth had worn away following continual use as a means of escape.

According to the *Guardian* Swain had made his intentions clear: "Come in, he says, come in and take your ease, but here, inside these barriers you stay, and by these pits and tunnels, quietly and quickly you depart. This scheme, in its simplicity and great scale, suggests power and force in the way that a pyramid does, or a Babylonian tower, and there could scarcely be a better scheme to represent the passionate concentration of fifty or eighty thousand men and women on the fortunes of the field below. The grandiose effect is amusingly diminished by the small concrete enclosures, which are established at the base of either end of the great slopes. On a sunken seat in each sits two policemen and two first aid men. Their upper halves showing quaintly across the field, like marionettes or toy-soldiers guarding some prehistoric keep."

The comment regarding the policemen focused on corner dugouts built as a base for police on match days. These have long since disappeared, however, they were designed as part of the main wall structure and basically consisted of a four-seater stone slab with a small wall on either side. At least one of these corner dugouts survived until the 1950s. Supporter Fran Parker: "There was a dip in each corner and the ambulancemen and police would sit on a stone slab there. I can't remember ever seeing police anywhere else during the late twenties or early thirties, and there was one day when I didn't have a particularly good view. My dad suggested I go and tell the ambulancemen I had a headache, so I walked down to the corner and told them, and they let me sit with them on the slab for the rest of the game."

The material used for the development of the terracing was announced as the "Hennibique System" of Ferro-concrete construction. Hennibique was a pioneer of reinforced concrete, primarily for skyscraper construction, and also worked with another Maine Road contractor, Mouchel, on New Bridge Street Station in Newcastle.

In terms of overall size the club boasted that the total length of the terracing was the equivalent of 17 miles, and that the area within the 3ft high perimeter wall was 131 yards from end to end and was 92 yards wide. The goal and touch lines were positioned some eight yards in from the perimeter wall, and there was a 3.5ft track around the pitch. The total distance around the pitch was quoted as 440 yards.

The pitch itself brought immense pride to the club at the time of the opening. A steam navvy – a channelling device, or mechanical digger - had burrowed down eight feet and then cinders had been positioned on top. Only a few years earlier dozens of men, or 'navvies' – the nickname established during the construction of canals or 'navigations' - would have been used instead. Then 3,000 tons of soil from the Wilbraham Road area was deposited before a two-inch fibre pastureland turf from Poynton, said to be one hundred years old, was carefully

Below: One of the two Kippax/Popular Side tunnels photographed by City fan Emma T. Taylor in the early 1990s.
It's clear from its size Architect Charles Swain envisaged huge crowds. At the end of many matches supporters would be lifted off their feet by the sheer force of the crowd down these tunnels.

MANCHESTER CITY'S NEW FOOTBALL ENCLOSURE.

MANCHESTER City's new enclosure is one of the most palatial homes of football in Great Britain. The opening takes place to-day (August 25th), when Sheffield United visit the ground but it will be some time yet before the painters put on the last touch.

The structure has been erected in the residential district of Rusholme, and when the full scheme has fructified the ground will accomodate 120,000 people, mostly under cover.

The grand stand, which occupies nearly the whole of one side of the ground, will accommodate 10,000 spectators, of whom 1,750 will have lounge and numbered seats. Its span of 120 ft. without supporting pillars is claimed to be the largest of any in the country. The stand is 140 ft.

from back to front, 280ft. in length, and contains 54 tiers.

In several respects the enclosure has been modelled on the lines of the famous Hampden Park Stadium.

Facing the grand stand is a huge embankment with 109 tiers with a 14 inch tread, whilst behind the goals there is a terrace each with 53 tiers.

The lessons of Wembley have been taken to heart, and a feature of the ground will be six tunnels communicating with the terraces, giving easy access to all parts.

Built upon an island site of sixteen and a quarter acres, purchased for £5,550, there will be means of ingress and egress on all four sides. The main entrances will be in Maine Road, by which

name the ground will be known, for the time being at all events.

The playing pitch has been prepared by Anthony, the old Notts and Central Lancashire League cricketer, and is in excellent condition. In order to keep it so, all the usual training preparations and practice matches have taken place at Hyde Road.

A singular coincidence in connection with the building and opening of this new sport stadium, in the heart of one of the greatest sporting cities of the world is the fact that Mr. J. E. Mangnall, the secretary of the City club, was connected in a similar manner with Manchester United when their commodious enclosure was opened a few years ago.

Above: City's new ground was viewed as one of the most impressive sporting venues in the country when opened in 1923. This article mentions that the stadium has been modelled on Hampden Park and that the 'lessons of Wembley have been taken to heart' proving the point that Maine Road was seen more as a rival than a copy of Wembley.

laid to provide the playing surface. The pitch was designed to have a crown dropping by six inches from the centre to each goal line.

On 18th August, three months after the last League match of the 1922-23 season, the last-ever game, a practice match, was staged on the Hyde Road pitch. Afterwards the goal posts and several turnstiles were taken from the old ground and erected at Maine Road. At least 12 of these survived in the Kippax wall right up until the Blues moved from Maine Road in 2003.

One of the stands, believed to be the Galloway End, was taken down and sold to Halifax Town to be erected at the Shay, while others were dismantled and sold to various companies. In the late 1990s one section of roofing was discovered at a factory in Sale and when its girders and overall structure was compared with roofing at the Shay and photographs of Hyde Road, the metalwork appeared to match.

The Shay had opened approximately twelve months before Hyde Road's last League match and the stand, believed to be constructed at that time, does match the metalwork from the Sale factory. But why would City sell it before the rest of Hyde Road was dismantled?

The Shay stand was extended around the time of the demolition of City's ground, but the metalwork on the newer section is slightly different, and therefore unlikely to be from Hyde Road, although of course both sections could potentially be from that source. Basically, it appears the metalwork from one of City's multi-span roofs was dismantled and re-erected along the touchline at the Shay. It formed a traditional style roof, and still exists at the Shay today, although during the early 1990s it was re-clad.

Although much of the Hyde Road site was later used by the local tram and bus companies, for several years most of the site was still free from development. The outline of the pitch could still be seen on almost three sides, while the outline of the stands could be traced with a little imagination. Gortonian Paul James remembered seeing some banking in this area during the

early 1940s, although it's hard to imagine how it survived that long.

The only obvious landmark connected with City's tenure at Hyde Road was the Hyde Road Hotel. Ardwick was still a densely-populated area for another forty years following City's departure and for much of that time the Hyde Road Hotel was a popular drinking place for locals. Sadly, it was no longer quite the building it had been before, but still felt like home for many Blues.

Unfortunately, even the Hyde Road Hotel no longer stands – it was demolished shortly before the end of the 2001-02 season.

Three days after the last practice match at Hyde Road, the *Manchester Evening News* provided invaluable information on how to get to the new stadium. The article started: "The mammoth enclosure will accommodate at least 90,000 people and the first gate is sure to reach enormous proportions, even if that stupendous figure is not reached. Probably two-thirds of the crowd will wish to journey to their Mecca by tram car, and many of them are wondering how to do it."

The article went on to describe each of the main tram routes to the stadium and also stated how the local tramways department were already putting plans in place to lay new tram-tracks through Great Western Street, Monton Street and Platt Lane. Platt Lane was already a major route for trams, however improvements would be made to allow multiple trams to load and unload at the same time.

Clearly the switch from Hyde Road to Maine Road was perceived as a move of a considerable distance and as a result most of the local newspapers provided details on how to find the new ground. The opening game was treated in a similar manner to a major cup final with the local authority working with City and the tramways department to plan for transporting supporters from the city centre and, in particular, east Manchester, to the stadium.

According to one newspaper the authorities used the plans they had made for the Royal Show of 1916 -

which took place south of Alexandra Park, close to Maine Road - to plan for the opening match. The only issue was that attendees of the Royal Show arrived throughout the day, whereas City fans would all be arriving for a set time. More difficult for the authorities was the actual departure from the ground. They had no idea exactly how many fans would attend and had to plan for a figure of between 40,000 and 90,000 all leaving at the same time.

The opening of Old Trafford in February 1910 could hardly be used as a guide as a crowd of around 45,000 watched Liverpool beat United 4-3. That crowd was little more than the official capacity of Hyde Road.

Regardless of what public transport was available, it was clear this would be a major moment in the history of the city.

On the Friday before the season began, most newspapers carried stories of how the grand opening would overshadow all other football that day. The *Manchester Evening News*: "In the First Division there is only one game between two local rivals, and that is Birmingham where Aston Villa will visit the St. Andrew's ground, but big as the attendance is it is not likely to be as large as that seen on Manchester City's new ground at Moss Side, the opening of which is the chief event of the day."

The newspaper was correct as the Birmingham derby could only manage a crowd of 41,300. The article went on to stress the size of City's development: "That this vast stadium should have been practically completed between April 24 and August 24 of this year is the subject for wonder and admiration. It unquestionably creates a record in building construction, and it is a splendid testimonial to the organising powers of the contractors, Sir Robert McAlpine and Sons."

"Most people were freely sceptical as to whether the enclosure would be ready for tomorrow. A month ago it did not seem possible that it could be, but by the employment of hundreds of skilled workmen all but the internal work on the huge stand has been completed, and even this remaining task will not occupy more than a fortnight. As already stated the enclosure will accommodate well over 80,000 spectators."

"Sheer curiosity will attract many hundreds of people to this magnificent new ground in Maine Road, Moss Side, but the bulk of the club's supporters will be keen on participating in what is an historic event in local football activities because of the re-appearance of Max Woosnam, whose career as Captain of the team was so unluckily suspended for a whole season, owing to the fracture of his leg."

Woosnam's return as captain was a fitting tribute to the all-round sportsman. His injury came as a result of an unfortunate accident and not only deprived him of a year in football, it also prevented him from defending his Wimbledon Doubles title won with Lycett in 1921. He must have been immensely proud to lead the first City side into the new stadium.

The *Evening News* felt certain the Blues would win the match despite Sheffield United possessing some very capable players: "It is difficult to form an estimate of the home team's chances on what is virtually a strange ground, but with a player like Woosnam behind them, the three inside forwards should be effective enough to bring victory to City, and so give the Club a good send off on the new ground."

The City programme for the first match called the game "A memorable day in the history of the club" and added: "Today marks an epoch in our history. For the first time we have a ground worthy of the club, and we are hoping that it will bring us increased patronage commensurate with our enterprise, and which is necessary to maintain it. In that we do not think we shall be disappointed.

"Evidences have not been wanting that we shall command a big measure of support. The demand for season tickets has been very gratifying indeed."

The article provided further information on the ground and commented that the club had decided to call the venue 'Maine-road'.

The programme also asked supporters to be patient as not all of the building work had been finished.

The Daily Express saw the move to Maine Road as a new beginning for the club. Under the headline "Manchester's New Pitch: Fresh Lease of Life For The City Side" the *Express* stated: "Manchester City will begin a new lease of life when they remove from their old home in Hyde Road to the palatial headquarters at Maine Road. In the removal they may find the

Below: An invitation to Albert Alexander Senior, a founder member of the club, for the post-match celebration to mark the opening of the ground.

Below right: A proud day for the Blues. Lawrence Furniss, City Chairman and a player in the 1880s, and Max Woosnam introduce Councillor Cundiff, the Lord Mayor of Manchester, to the players prior to Maine Road's opening match.

Continued on page 56

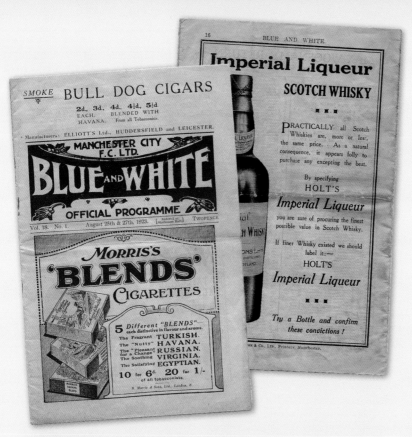

Maine Match 23/24

CITY v SHEFFIELD UNITED

DATE:	Saturday 25th August 1923	
TYPE OF FIXTURE:	Football League Division One	
ATTENDANCE:	58,159	
RESULT:	City 2 Sheffield United 1	
TEAMS &	**CITY**	**SHEFFIELD UNITED**
SCORERS:	Mitchell	Gough
	Cookson	Cook
REFEREE:	Fletcher	Milton
J. Rowcroft	Hamill	Pantling
(Bolton)	Woosnam	Waugh
	Pringle	Green
	Donaldson	Mercer
	Roberts	Sampy
	Johnson 1	Johnson 1
	Barnes 1	Gillespie
	Murphy	Tunstall

The match programme for the opening game contained approximately two pages on the new stadium; a half page on Max Woosnam; a couple of pages on the usual club detail – team line-ups etc.; and the rest was largely taken up with advertisements. There was even a half-page theatre review on page two!

The adverts made interesting reading. Fred Karno, the well known music hall comedian who ran his own troupe which, at one time, included Stan Laurel and Charlie Chaplin, was staging a show at the Palace Theatre. The Ardwick Empire claimed to be the brightest spot in Manchester and also boasted that 'Friday night is football night', while the Futurist Super-Cinema was showing for the first time in Manchester a film entitled 'The Romance of Mary Tudor' which claimed to be a magnificent coloured production. How is a mystery.

The Empire had competition from the Ardwick Picture Theatre which, on the same night, was to show the true life story of John Lee – "The Man They Could Not Hang". Lee had been found guilty of murder and was sentenced to the death penalty, however after having his head placed in a noose, the first attempt at releasing the trap failed and Lee did not hang. Two further attempts followed, after which it was decided to free him. Lee wrote his life story and also toured the country preaching that God had saved him because he was innocent.

Other adverts concentrated on cigarettes, cigars and pipe-smoking; beer and whisky and travel companies. There was also an advert for the Denmark Hotel - "The nearest high-class hotel to the ground" – which stood on the corner of Denmark Road and Lloyd Street.

The front and back covers of Maine Road's first programme are shown above and all the other pages (with the exception of pages 2 and 3) are reproduced overleaf.

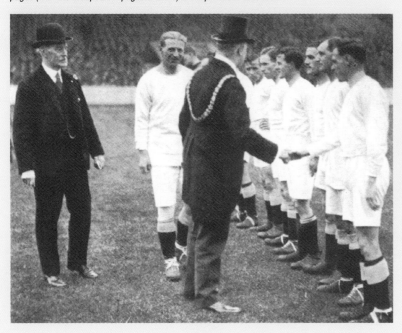

■ The family of City supporter Ron Meredith lived in the Maine Road area at the time the stadium was being built and his family took a keen interest in the ground and in the opening match: "My Grandmother, Edith Bowden, lived at 9 Ebberstone Street opposite the front entrance. She went to the first-ever match but what was remarkable was that, because of where she lived and her determination to attend, she was actually the third person to pay to get inside the ground for this opening game. After that she went to every home game, much to the amusement of my father because my grandfather wasn't interested in football and she went on her own.

"My father's name was Billy Meredith and we lived at 138 Maine Road, so we often received mail intended for the great player. My father would pop across to the ground and hand it in."

The build-up to Maine Road's opening game took a similar format to most other matches of the period. The Beswick Prize Band played a selection of music including the "Victor's Return" , "Casino Tanse", "La Traviata", "Ain't We Got Fun", "O, Star of Eve", and "Wana". Then local dignitaries were introduced to the players, before the action could begin.

Two players made their debuts in this match. For City - ex-Sheffield United man Alex Donaldson played his first game after signing from Sunderland, while the Sheffield team included George Green for his initial outing.

The match itself was amazing. Sheffield United's goalkeeper, Gough, was replaced by outfield player Pantling after thirty minutes, and the new 'keeper immediately faced a penalty taken by Frank Roberts. Pantling saved the shot – putting Roberts in the record books as the first man to miss a penalty at Maine Road.

According to the *Guardian*: "In the first half Sheffield were the better team, and the passing of their forwards and halves was delightful in its ease and accuracy. Gillespie and Tunstall on the left wing played admirably together. Tunstall combines speed and trickiness with a cool eye for the lie of the field, which is one of the principal secrets of success."

Despite Sheffield's control the game remained goalless at half time. During the interval the Beswick

Prize Band performed the American Belle March.

The Guardian: "In the second half Manchester City woke up and, after an even interval, were much the more aggressive. They got an excellent goal after a centre from the right wing, and another immediately afterwards when the left wing was allowed to dribble right in to the goal posts and put the ball across the mouth. But it is idle to pretend that the game mattered much on Saturday, except it was right that so great a crowd, so finely housed, should have taken so excellent a show to entertain them. May there be many such."

The Guardian also considered the age of the players and the celebrations that followed the City goals: "The game was good League football, played on the happiest green turf and fought as hardly and well as though the game had never stopped in April. There were few really young men on either side, but in athletics the day for youth and grace seems to have gone for the time. In cricket and football experience and stamina count for as much, and football runs to weight and 'build' and heavy shoulders. There can never have been so many half-bald heads as there are now, and the veterans hold their own. The only sign of the beginning of the season was that the players were not quite so melodramatic as they will be when the crowd's blood is up, though when a corner is to be taken there seems always to be six captains on one side and half a dozen on the other, and the extravagance with which a team throws itself on the colleague who has happened to score a goal would bring a blush to the cheek of the average schoolboy, that admirable standard of reserve."

The Blues actually won 2-1 with the historic first goal scored by Horace Barnes after about 68 minutes. Tommy Johnson netted the second, while Sheffield United's Harry Johnson pulled a goal back two minutes from time, thus providing the Blues with their first Maine Road victory.

It was fitting that Tommy Johnson was one of City's scorers that day. Johnson was a major City star and a very popular figure. He loved City and, living in the Gorton area, knew only too well the importance of the club. In May 2003 his son Alan Johnson provided his view of his father's time at the club and role in this opening match: "I wasn't born until after City had moved to Maine Road but my dad often talked about the first game. It seemed strange that two Johnsons scored that day – one for City and one for Sheffield. The opening game at any ground must be special, but for Dad to score one of the opening goals was an incredible moment, and it lived with him all his life.

"From the moment I was born I was brought to Maine Road and sometimes to other grounds – as a baby I was taken into the Directors' Box at Wembley for the 1926 final – and so this is a major part of my life also. Funnily enough one of my own personal favourite moments came in the 1950s when I managed a local amateur side to a final at Maine Road. Dad, or Tosh as he was known to most of his friends, sat in the Main Stand and watched. It must have been a strange feeling for him. It was certainly a proud moment for me."

Back in 1923 the opening match was watched by City's record crowd at the time. During the modern era a great deal of research has been performed on statistical information concerning City's history, and as a result most historians quote the attendance as 56,993, occasionally as 60,000. However, on 31st August 1923 most of the local press in Manchester carried an announcement by the club stating the total attendance.

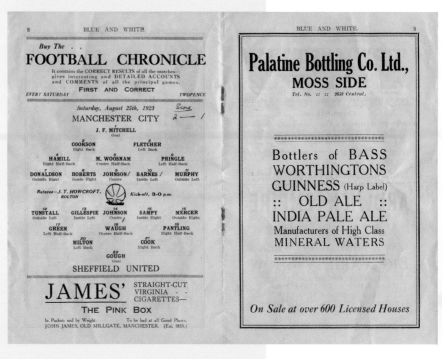

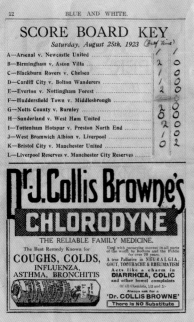

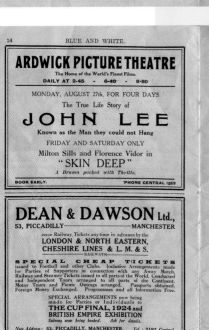

Under the headline "58,159" the *Evening News* reported: "The attendance at Maine Road last Saturday when Manchester City played their first League match on their new ground is officially returned as 58,159. This figure, in the words of a club official, includes everybody."

Many City attendances from this period are estimates and it is often difficult to prove conclusively what the attendance was. As the 1923 article occurred within a week of the game it's fair to assume this is the most accurate figure for this match. It's interesting to note however that the comment "this includes everybody" was made. It's possible the 56,993 was the total number of people who paid on the day, while the larger figure could include season ticket holders who, for many big games, were quoted separately. It's difficult to prove, however the larger figure should be used as the true attendance for this fixture.

One person certainly not included in the official attendance figure was eight-year-old Margaret Baker. Margaret had been extremely enthusiastic about the opening day and couldn't wait to see what the completed stadium would look like from the inside. She waited around the back of the Popular Side wall hoping she could get in. Early into the second half her chance came when the club decided to open the exit gates early. They were possibly concerned with the size of the crowd and wanted to ensure anyone wishing to leave early could do safely. What actually happened was that hundreds of local schoolchildren and several adults rushed into the ground to marvel at its newness.

Margaret: "We'd been waiting patiently for what seemed like an eternity when we heard the bolts being drawn back on the huge gates. When the gap was big enough we ran inside. Directly in front was the back of this enormous embankment, and midway along at the top was a flagpole with a beautiful flag flying proudly. It was a beautiful and, at the same time, powerful sight. None of us knew where to go, but being close to the corner we headed for the tunnel and as I walked through I could see the roof of the stand on the other side of the pitch.

It was amazing; there were so many people on the terracing that I froze. Prior to then I'd only seen crowds of a couple of hundred so the sight of 60,000 made me think the whole world had come to the bottom of my street!"

In September 2002 Margaret returned to Maine Road to see the stadium from the inside for, what she believed would be her last time. Looking out from the Millennium Suite at the top of the Kippax Stand she was amazed at what she saw: "I was impressed when I first saw inside the ground and now I'm impressed again. I didn't realise football grounds were this beautiful. There's even a lift. When I see this it brings back so many memories – Jim Mitchell with his bandanna; Meredith and his toothpick – I used to see the players walking around the streets. They were just normal folk.

"The ground is much better today than I thought it would be, apart from the Directors' Box. That looks so shabby. The Queen would never come here!"

On inspecting the dressing room area Margaret commented: "The away dressing room is very old. I bet it's not changed since 1923. But the home dressing room looks very smart. I could change here myself."

Continued from page 52

surroundings so strange that their play may be affected, but the larger ground should tend in time to improve play."

Although the media focused on the move, and supporters have given their views, little is known of how the players coped with the transition. They had little chance to practice at the new ground prior to the opening match, and with Maine Road being by far the best club stadium in the country, there couldn't have been a single player who knew what to expect. Presumably, they were delighted with the move and no doubt City's new surroundings helped to attract key players.

One player-related story from this period – still doing the rounds during the 1940s – concerned City's former captain Mick Hamill who was known as a bit of a prankster. It seems that shortly after the ground opened a young player noticed the initials "MH" chiselled into the white perimeter wall. He called for the manager, Ernest Mangnall, and his assistant, Wilf Wild, and told them of his find. The two City officials looked at the initials which were carved into the wall approximately a yard to the left of the players' tunnel, roughly where the away dug-out was positioned in 2003. The men were horrified to see their brand new stadium subjected to an act of vandalism at this early stage in its existence. To Mangnall and Wild there was only one explanation: "It's that bugger Mickey Hamill! Hamill... Hamill... Come here!"

According to one version of the story Hamill eventually arrived with a sheepish grin, while Chairman Lawrence Furniss also appeared on the scene when he heard the commotion.

It was only after a heated debate – which was exceptionally funny to the other players at the time – that the true reason for the MH carved into the stonework became apparent. It represented the fact that a 'Man Hole' was present on the cindertrack in front of that section of wall. Hamill was innocent.

The MH carving was visible at the ground for many years. In fact it is believed it only disappeared in the stadium's final fifteen years as the stonework and dug-out areas were modified.

The first match – in which incidentally Mick Hamill played his part - ended in a 2-1 victory to the Blues, but the general excitement of the initial game soon wore off as City found the League programme offered little in terms of enjoyment. The second Maine Road match ended in a 2-1 defeat by Aston Villa. Playing for Villa that day was Tommy Ball. A player with huge potential, 24 year old Ball was shot dead only a couple of months after this match in a tragic accident by his policeman neighbour. Tommy was the first footballer of many who played at Maine Road to die.

A crowd of 43,601 watched a 1-1 draw with Bolton in the third Maine Road match. Frank Roberts scored his first goal at the new stadium that day. According to one reporter: "There is no side in the country Bolton so dearly love to beat than the City." It seemed Bolton were still angry the Blues had defeated them in the 1904 Cup Final.

By New Year the Blues were not having the best of seasons. Many blamed the pitch which became muddy in parts following a rather wet autumn, although only the Villa game had ended in defeat up to Christmas. There had, however, been four drawn matches. Although that did not signify a disaster, it was not viewed as good enough by supporters. The stadium was an easy target and architect Charles Swain, by this time a member of City's Board, received much criticism.

Despite this, it wasn't long before the stadium proved its worth and the club flourished, although financially there were issues behind the scenes for many years.

Although McAlpine's are unable to confirm the exact details of the arrangement it is understood from other sources that the club owed £60,000 of the original cost (estimated at £100,000), and that McAlpine's were concerned the club were unable to pay off such a large amount. William Menzies Shaw – a McAlpine employee – became a City director in 1926 at the insistence of McAlpine's and his role was to monitor the club's finances and to protect McAlpine's interests. Even in the early 1930s articles in Manchester-based sporting newspapers would often include statements along the lines of: "City's heavy ground debt prevents them from making further acquisitions." It's possible these comments are related to further ground developments, nevertheless it does show how the period immediately following the development of the stadium was a difficult one financially.

From a spectator's point of view Maine Road was near-perfect. In October 2002, 95-year-old Randell Cockshoot gave his memories of this period: "When I was a youngster my school, Birley Street in Beswick, used to play cup and shield games at Hyde Road, and we used to have to walk from an area close to where the new City Of Manchester stadium is to Hyde Road. Although my father was a United man and went to Bank Street, Clayton, to see their cup-winning side [1909], my heart always lay with City because of playing school matches at Hyde Road.

"I always felt Hyde Road was homely. Although it was like a nice, popular holiday resort with men who always made sure the youngsters got to the front, we were always confined. Everyone looked after you, but there wasn't enough room. Maine Road, on the other hand, was massive and I enjoyed standing on the Popular Side for many years. In fact I was there until I retired at the age of 65. I thought Maine Road was a wonderful place and worthy of such a great team. I must stress that City were a truly great side when they first played at the ground.

MICHAEL HAMILL
MANCHESTER CITY

Above: This piece of lucky heather given to Albert Alexander Snr at the opening match has been preserved by the Alexander family since that date and is currently in the possession of former City chairman Eric Alexander.

Left: Mickey Hamill - not guilty of vandalising City's new ground!

Hamill was a very popular player and many humorous stories are connected with him. Hamill made his debut at Derby County on 9th October 1920, in a game which also saw Derby's Egyptian inside-right Tewfik Abdallah make his first appearance. According to Hamill, Abdallah entered the field asking 'where's me camel?' Of course he was actually asking 'where's Mick Hamill?' but the press enjoyed the thought that an Egyptian would be looking for a camel! Abdallah had the last laugh though, scoring his only League goal in a 3-0 Derby win.

"I worked on Saturdays from 1922, so my first memories of the ground all took place on Wednesday afternoons. It's difficult remembering much from these early years. I do remember the King coming to Hyde Road – that was my favourite moment – and I suppose another great moment at Maine Road was the Stoke cup match in 1934 when Eric Brook scored a wonderful goal in front of eighty-four thousand people.

"Maine Road has always been a grand ground. I remember going around the interior of the stand once and seeing the players at work. That was a real treat. My favourite players were always Max Woosnam and Billy Meredith. They were true gentlemen."

Maine Road's neighbours were also aware of how much the club was a part of their life. Local resident Marjorie Cooper lived on Beveridge Street throughout City's stay at Maine Road: "I was born in 1919 on Beverley Street – they changed its name to Beveridge Street some time later – and remember all the stories about the horse and cart falling into a pit and being buried where they fell. I also remember my parents using the name Dog Kennel Lane instead of Maine Road – the old name was still in circulation for a lot of the locals even then. We used to pay 9s 6d rent a week and a German man used to own most of the houses on our street. The Lloyd family owned much of the land and they chose most of the street names. I believe one of the family came from Yorkshire and named some of the streets after Yorkshire places – Beverley, Driffield, Pickering, Henbury, and Kippax – but I don't know the connection with 'Maine'.

"Matchdays were always something special. It wasn't so much the football, but the entertainment around the ground. Before and after the match there would be artists performing for any spare change you might have. I'll never forget the Meat-pie Man, the chap wearing a feather head-dress, just like an American Indian, and the Houdini character wearing a strait jacket! They were wonderful days."

Street entertainment around the ground made Maine Road a very special venue. Hyde Road was limited in its environment, but the new ground seemed to have so much space both in front of the Main Stand and behind the Popular Side terracing.

At the Claremont Road end of Maine Road lay a church, St. Matthias. Marjorie continued: "We used to go to the church and I remember the Whit Walks starting there during the 1920s. In front of the church was a small garden but at its side, between the church and Claremont Road, was a beautiful field. It was fenced off from the road and was home to many, many flowers. We used to go in there and pick the flowers. It was such a beautiful spot, and so close to the church and the ground."

Five years after the move to Maine Road the History of the Lancashire Football Association was published. One section focused on City and, with the stadium still in its infancy, the book considered City's move: "The Club was not lacking in enterprise at Hyde Road, but when you went to the ground you felt you were going along some subterranean passage to an enclosure that precluded enlargement and kept you under confinement willy nilly.

"How gentlemen like Messrs. John Chapman and Sam Anderson lived under such conditions was a mystery. That Ernest Mangnall could ever let his brains have full scope baffles me. What a blessing it was that the seeming misfortune of that disastrous fire led the Directors to look round Manchester, with the result that the Club now boasts a ground with the largest holding capacity outside Wembley, and with room for further extension and addition that could make the holding capacity of Wembley seem insignificant."

Below: Ten of the team who first represented City at Maine Road.

Back row (left to right): Pringle, Donaldson, Mitchell, Cookson and Fletcher.

Front: Sharp (the only man not to appear in Maine Road's opener - his place was taken by Woosnam), Roberts, Johnson, Hamill, Barnes, Murphy.

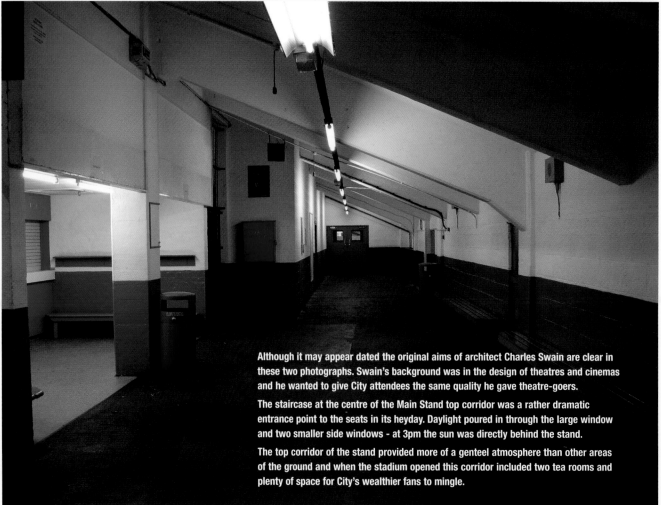

Although it may appear dated the original aims of architect Charles Swain are clear in these two photographs. Swain's background was in the design of theatres and cinemas and he wanted to give City attendees the same quality he gave theatre-goers.

The staircase at the centre of the Main Stand top corridor was a rather dramatic entrance point to the seats in its heyday. Daylight poured in through the large window and two smaller side windows - at 3pm the sun was directly behind the stand.

The top corridor of the stand provided more of a genteel atmosphere than other areas of the ground and when the stadium opened this corridor included two tea rooms and plenty of space for City's wealthier fans to mingle.

Left: When Maine Road entered its final weeks there were few recognisable original features, however in one or two areas of the Main Stand some of the original handrails, fencing and other woodwork remained. The rectangle and carved edges of these posts were typical of the style adopted throughout the ground. Most of the woodwork, and large scale stonework used similar patterning when first constructed.

Below: Originally there were two impressive stone posts at the pitch entrance from the tunnel (see page 75), sadly by 2003 each post had been remodelled to match the rest of the wall. However, this carved corner still shows an element of the styling used throughout the stadium at the time of its construction. Some say architect Charles Swain adopted an Art Deco style, but if he did his planning was at the cutting edge of design as Art Deco didn't become prominent until after 1926.

Above: Hidden away inside a paint storeroom behind the Kippax Stand is this old painted sign asking supporters to "Commit No Nuisance". Originally this wall would have been on public view but became hidden when the club built a series of storerooms and additional toilets in later years. Fortunately, this rare insight into the attitude towards supporter behaviour survived to the end.

Below: Many areas of the ground changed over the years, including the way the club numbered its turnstiles. The original number 3 can clearly be seen on the door of turnstile 18 in the Main Stand.

Below right: Underneath the Main Stand this room for programme sellers changed little in the stadium's lifetime.

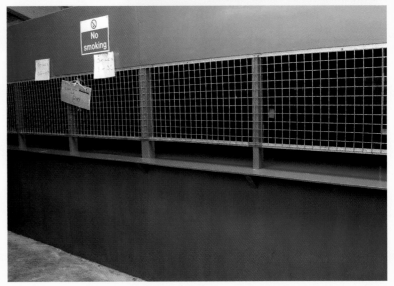

Left: Supporters approaching the Main Stand/North Stand corner of the ground in 2003. Cars can be seen parked on the field of Claremont Road Primary School.

Going to the Match

ALTHOUGH attending matches at Maine Road by the new millennium had become a common ritual for thousands of Blues, in 1923 the routine still had to be established. Supporters used to travelling to Hyde Road had to organise their own procedures and a whole manner of issues existed.

The bulk of City's support came from east Manchester – Gorton, Ardwick, Droylsden, and Denton were Blue strongholds – and many of these would walk to the Hyde Road ground, or travel by tram down fairly straight easy routes. With the close proximity of the Belle Vue Pleasure Gardens and the good public transport links that brought, travel to Hyde Road was simple.

Once Maine Road opened, City's support had to find new ways of getting to see their team. Some still walked to the ground, but the added distance meant more time was needed. For those working on a Saturday morning this presented further problems.

Some fans chose to get on their bicycles and cycle to the ground and this, for the majority, appeared the preferred route. Had aerial photographs been taken of the ground and surrounding streets during a match in the 1920s then the size and scale of City's cycling support would have been seen. Almost every backyard within half a mile of the ground would house bikes with each tenant charging supporters a few pence each to park their bikes.

Naturally, some supporters had travelled to Hyde Road on bikes pre-1923, however few ever commented on this as being a typical match day feature. The numbers increased enormously with the move to Maine Road.

At Hyde Road most walked to the ground and this was still a major way of getting to the new ground in 1923. Supporter Harry Bramble was nine when Maine Road opened and lived close to the stadium on Princess Road: "About an hour before kick-off I would look out of

the window and you would see crowds of people walking towards Maine Road. It wasn't one or two, it was large crowds. Of course I'd join the exodus when I felt it was ready and then you'd get to the ground and queue up. You had to get there earlier than today."

Other supporters travelled to the ground by tram with a large volume changing from city-bound trams at Gorton Town Hall to those bound for Longsight and Platt Fields close to the site of the present day greyhound stadium. Others would walk towards the university and board trams there. Clearly additional expense was incurred.

The greatest tram route – and later bus route – was the number 53. The 53 would travel through City's heartland encompassing the following main roads – Forge Lane (close to the new City of Manchester Stadium), Grey Mare Lane, Belle Vue Street, Kirkmanshulme Lane, Stanley Road, Dickenson Road (the majority of supporters would alight here, others would wait depending on pre-match activities), and Moss Lane East.

Below: A back page advert in the City programme of 1937, when cycling to the game was a popular choice.

16   BLUE AND WHITE

Ride to the Match on a thoroughbred British Bike

bought from Manchester's Leading Dealers—

SCOTT BRETTLE
Limited

All Leading Makes

Supplied on First Deposit of **2/6** Then from 1/6 weekly

2,000 to choose from—under one roof

MOTOR BIKES From **5/-** Weekly

TANDEMS ANY MAKE **10/-** Secures

SCOTT BRETTLE Ltd.
192, DEANSGATE, MANCHESTER

Branch Depot : 680/682, Ashton Old Road, OPENSHAW.

OPEN WEEKDAYS TILL 8 P.M. AND SATURDAYS TILL 6 P.M. 'PHONE: BLA. 8747

WITHY GROVE PRESS (ALLIED NEWSPAPERS LTD.), WITHY GROVE, MANCHESTER 4.

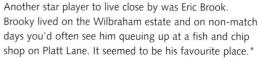

Above: Jimmy McMullan lived in one of the club houses on Maine Road during the 1920s, but was also believed to be the first City player to have a car. Jimmy was a major Scottish international star and was City captain when the Blues faced Bolton in the 1926 Cup final.

Below: By 1947 Frank and Doris Swift had not only purchased a car but also joined the AA (see badge on bottom of car) .

Fran Parker lived in Hulme during the late twenties: "Once I was out of my trolley we would get the tram from Hulme. It cost a ha'penny for me and a penny for my dad and it was always full of City fans. I remember once a woman saying to my dad: 'I don't know why you bring that young girl to football' and my dad said: 'I bet she knows more about City than you do' and so someone asked me if I could name the team. I named every single one of them and was given a penny by each of the fans!"

A small number of supporters would make their way to the ground by car. Those that did would find parking for 500 cars – a major innovation for football at the time – or plenty of space on any of the streets surrounding the ground. Few possessed cars in the 1920s, and those that did were usually the club's wealthiest supporters. Even players rarely owned cars. It wasn't until the 1930s that the club's biggest stars started to buy their own vehicles, but most of them had no need because the club would try to ensure its players lived close by.

The two club houses on the main forecourt were used by various players and staff over the years. According to Harry Bramble: "Jimmy McMullan was possibly the first player to live in one of those houses. He was City's captain and a major figure in Scottish football and yet he lived next door to the ground. We all knew he lived there and you'd often see him about the area, but in those days City had a policy that whenever a house came up for sale in Thornton Road, or the other streets, they would buy it and rent it out to the players. I think the players paid about a £1 a week and those with club houses thought they were well off. It was a real perk getting a house close to the ground at such a good rent.

Another star player to live close by was Eric Brook. Brooky lived on the Wilbraham estate and on non-match days you'd often see him queuing up at a fish and chip shop on Platt Lane. It seemed to be his favourite place."

Marjorie Cooper also remembers Jimmy McMullan living in the club house: "He was probably the first major star in that house, but we continued to have players living in the streets around the ground for many years. I remember that when Joe Fagan was at the club during the late thirties he lived on my street – Beveridge Street – opposite the ground. He used to come to our house and play cards with my parents. There was a woman who rented out a room to the club and she'd usually have three players in there. Joe was one of them – he married my friend Lil – and the other two I think were Albert Barr and Ray Freeman. It must have been pretty cramped with three players in one room, but that was fairly normal back then. Les McDowall lived in that same house for a while.

"Frank and Doris Swift lived in a council house on Lloyd Street South, while Albert Emptage lived in the next street to ours. Alec Herd – and his son David who went on to play for United – lived at 219 Maine Road. This is the house that became groundsman Stan Gibson's house. I remember Bobby Johnstone living at the Lord Lyon pub – not a good place to put a footballer!"

Once supporters arrived at the ground they would venture into public houses, such as the Parkside, or the Robin Hood further down Maine Road, or would visit the chip shops and cafés in the neighbourhood. Some supporters would bring their own sandwiches to the match.

Inside the ground there existed a couple of tea rooms in the Main Stand – supporters could sit down and enjoy a simple snack – and several bars around the ground, although supporter Fran Parker remembers these sold the usual football fayre of Bovril or Oxo: "I can't remember any beer being sold at Maine Road. In fact I think there was only one club – probably Bolton – in the League who sold beer. They did sell sweets like cough drops to keep you warm, but you would be on the terracing when they'd come around. Someone would throw a coin down and the man selling the sweets would throw the bag up to the right person. He never missed! His bag burst sometimes, but he usually got his man."

Once the match was over, supporters would rush away from the ground as quickly as they could to either retrieve their bikes or to force their way on to public transport. A scene reminiscent of the Tour de France must have existed as thousands of cyclists took to the streets of Moss Side.

Those in cars had a relatively simple drive home, with the only obstacles being those on foot, the bicycles, and of course the trams. Clearly travel by car in the 1920s offered the quickest means of travel, however few could enjoy that luxury.

Trams, by their very nature, were not the ideal form of transport post-match. Due to the limited number of routes initially and the fact trams had to travel at best in convoy, it was extremely difficult for supporters to guarantee they would make a certain tram or predict how long it would take them to get home.

To ease the situation additional tram-lines were laid over time, but the basic problem continued until transport by bus became the norm.

In 1984 former City player Billy Dale talked of how he got to games during the early thirties: "I lived in Harper Lane and had to catch two buses to every match,

or a tram. I'd lose all sense of the crowd when I concentrated on the match. I'd perhaps hear an individual voice when it was all quiet. I never took any notice unless it was someone I recognised. Once I heard a shout and it was an ex-playing friend of mine Jumbo Clements. He'd gone off to America some time before and I was astounded to see him. 'What you doing here?' I asked. 'I've come to see you'. I couldn't believe it."

For supporter Colin MacBean the prospect of travelling on the same bus as a player was very exciting: "The late Frank Swift was my hero and one day I managed to find out what bus he used to get to the ground. From then on I'd catch that bus. Several young supporters, myself included, would try to sit as near to him as we could. It was a mission I suppose. I think he must have realised this himself because the same boys would appear every game and surround him. He was a dream with the supporters. The very best and he treated us all exceptionally well."

As time progressed transport arrangements changed. Initially, getting to the match hardly changed at all, but by the time of the Second World War buses were a very popular form of transport. They were able to jostle for position and could move off whenever they chose. They could also line-up on any of the streets around the ground and this then allowed greater opportunities for movement after the match. Match specials would ferry supporters to the ground from Aytoun Street in the city centre and then back again after the match.

Supporters weren't the only ones to travel by bus. Forties player George Smith remembers his journey: "I had to get from Prestwich to Maine Road. We didn't have a car – no player did when I started. In fact I seem to remember that Wilf Wild banned us from having cars in case we got injured, although once Wild moved to purely secretarial activities that rule was relaxed I think. I do know for certain that we couldn't afford a car back then.

"At some point Billy Walsh managed to get a really old car and we were once travelling from the ground and had to stop at a policeman on points duty. When he waved us forward we were stuck! There were six of us squashed in his car and we couldn't get it going. I don't think we ever thought it was wrong to have so many squashed into it. Anyway, we eventually got her going. We also got a few funny looks from the policeman!

"But when there was no chance of getting a lift, I would get myself to Piccadilly and then get a bus – I seem to think it was a 95 but I could be wrong – straight to the ground. The supporters would be on there. That was all right before the match, but not always afterwards!"

Supporter Eddie Nevill was also a bus regular: "Following my demob from the RAF in August 1947 I lived near Andy Black, the City forward and Scottish international, in Sale. He helped me get my first season ticket and sometimes we would travel together on the bus to Maine Road for the match – imagine the players today travelling to the ground on an ordinary bus! Back then it was normal and no one thought anything was odd about it."

The volume of cars for both players and wealthier fans increased during the forties, but it wasn't until the fifties that the car started to become affordable for working class supporters. This increase in car-ownership led to parking issues. City's own car parks were no longer sufficient and the majority of car-owning supporters had to park on streets around the ground. Children now took

to the streets offering to mind cars, where once their parents had offered to store bikes in backyards. Some still travelled to the ground by bicycle and they still found a few locals interested in minding their bikes. Comedian Eddie Large was one such enterprising youngster: "I lived on Maine Road - second house along by the main car park - so it will be exceptionally sad for me when City move. As a kid I couldn't afford to go to the match so we had to wait until the gates opened at three-quarter time then we were in. I was not happy with this so I decided we would allow bicycles to park in the back yard at 7d a time. My sister used to help me but once I had enough money to go in I left her to it; she soon got fed up and so it was back to three-quarter time!"

By the sixties the car had replaced the bike to a large extent, while other supporters travelled in groups by bus. Chris Fogarty remembers his first journey to Maine Road: "I come from a family of City fans, who used to go every week, then one week I said I would like to go, so my Uncle Len decided to take me to see City play Blackburn Rovers in 1960 at Maine Road.

"I can still remember sitting on the bus from Ardwick; it was full of men that seemed about ten feet tall to me, all smoking and laughing, the bus was all smoky and I was beginning to cough, I had never been in so much cigarette smoke before.

Above: George Smith outside the Players' Entrance in the 1940s. He had to get the bus from Prestwich!

"When we got off the bus in what I now know as Lloyd Street, I could see what looked like millions of people all walking towards the ground, and I can still remember saying to my Uncle Len 'are they all going to the match?' He just looked at me and smiled and replied 'Yes, of course'. It's funny how some words still stay in your mind after all these years.

"When we got to the ground I couldn't believe how big it was, the front of the Main Stand was huge then I could feel myself getting excited.

"When we got inside it was like being in an ant's nest with everybody walking around talking and laughing. Then my big moment came, we walked up the steps and it just hit me - I was there stood at the top of the Main Stand looking down on the pitch. I was probably shouting 'Yes, I'm inside the ground!'.

"When we sat down I remember looking at the programme - just flicking through looking at the pictures. From then on I started to save the programmes, but sadly in the mid-sixties the house was broken in to and my programmes were stolen. To this day I have not been able to get hold of the City programme from my first match.

"After the match - which we won 4-0 - I couldn't stop talking about it to my Grandmother when I got home. I'm sure I must have given her a headache going on about the match over and over again, telling her about every kick, every goal and every tackle. From then on I was hooked on City, and have been ever since. I now have three grown up boys who all support City."

Roger Reade remembers that when he first came to the ground he would be brought by car: "We'd park up and then walk through the passageways. They all had numbers and as a child you'd always check which passageway was which. The Baseball Ground was similar, but after Maine Road's gone I don't think there'll be anywhere else like that. Once we'd made it to Maine Road we used to pop into the sweet shop that used to be right at the bottom end of the road. It's not there now, but it was our regular stop-off point and we used to get bags of Nuttall's Mintoes and Everton Mints. We'd sit through the game sucking and chewing them, but it was all part of the ritual."

The Parkinson family would also drive to the ground, but then follow a ritual many supporters still do to this day. According to Ian Parkinson: "We would park up on Clinton Avenue, opposite the house where my mother grew up, and walk up to the Parkside pub. We would often get fish and chips at the chippy opposite. At this particular time - early seventies - a blonde girl used to work there and always talked in a whisper. This habit became known to the locals and all the customers would in turn ask for their food 'in a whisper.' As adolescent kids, we just used to fall about with laughter every time. The poor girl (deadpan, never a smile) had no idea what all the hilarity was about.

"We then used to continue the 'lucky route' down the snicket opposite the pub to the far end of Maine Road. This procedure was a sacred ritual as in those days we very rarely lost a home game!

"The first thing we did on turning into Maine Road was to see if City were on the TV that weekend. Granada was always the preference as that was shown on a Sunday afternoon. We were always out on a Saturday night, and so never watched *Match of the Day*. Remember this was before video recorders were invented or television companies battled for the coverage rights.

"We would take our seat in the Platt Lane end or walk round to the Kippax. Midweek games, when my Dad used to take us, were always watched from the Platt Lane end - and we always won! The main recollection was the sheer joy and humour of the day. We had such a laugh. It was never serious, just fun. Maybe this was because we had such a wonderful team and never worried about relegation. The supporters had only one criteria, the team had to play attractive attacking football, win, draw or lose. I remember 'Helen the bell' at the scoreboard end and the many hilarious quips from the wittiest supporters in the land."

By the seventies the bus and car seemed to be the only methods of travel. Those wishing to travel by bike were unable to find many storage places, while the movement of Manchester's population limited walking. It's not often considered, but the general shift of Manchester's population during the slum clearance programmes of the fifties to seventies had a serious

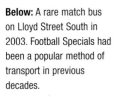

Below: A rare match bus on Lloyd Street South in 2003. Football Specials had been a popular method of transport in previous decades.

impact on attendance at Maine Road. Support didn't diminish – except for a brief period of failure in the early sixties – but the means of getting to Maine Road did.

City's heartland of east Manchester was ripped apart with the terraced streets of Gorton, Ardwick, Longsight, Beswick and Bradford flattened. The residents of this area moved mainly further east to the new overspill estates of Hattersley, Haughton Green, and Gamesley. Other supporters did move to Blackley, Wythenshawe and around the city, but those in the east were in some cases over ten miles further away from Maine Road than at any other point. They had to travel by car or bus, but even then bus travel necessitated a much longer journey and supporters had to change at Belle Vue on to the traditional number 53 route.

Some had to make sacrifices. The majority of residents living on the new estates still worked in the city, or in the Gorton/Ardwick areas and therefore travel to work costs increased. This limited their leisure money and with an increased need to use public transport – or an increase in fuel costs – attendance at Maine Road was something that had to be planned a little more. In the fifties a supporter living in Ardwick could have decided to go to the match as late as 2pm, possibly later, but by the time of the oil shortages in the early 1970s, a traditional Blue resident in Gamesley would have had to make that decision much earlier. Bus travel would take over ninety minutes, assuming connections were easily available, while travel by car could take a hour, depending on traffic, and parking could be an issue.

For players, travel to matches in the seventies was by car. Brian Kidd revealed his matchday schedule in the late 1970s: "My routine never varies. I have lunch at noon then sit around in my dressing gown watching the build-up to the day's sport on television. When we are at Maine Road, I generally leave home about 1pm ready to report at the ground for the pre-match briefing at 1.45pm. Living on the north side of Manchester, I have to come right through the city centre and there's always plenty of atmosphere to get you in the right frame of mind.

"City fans are parading through the streets in their scarves and, very occasionally there is the odd skirmish when they meet the rival supporters on the way from station to ground. But in the main, City fans are a good lot and we have little trouble home, or away.

"As you get nearer Maine Road, so the tempo of the build-up increases. Fans spot you in the car and if they are Blues it's cheers all the way. From the rival camp they'll just boo you till you are out of sight."

During the eighties car and bus travel was still dominant, however the 'Can I mind your car, mister?' approach of local schoolchildren had become a little menacing. Rumours circulated how refusal would result in tyres being slashed, mirrors damaged, and general minor problems. Some fans started to park further afield to avoid the issue altogether, while others parked further away simply to avoid the traffic post-match. It was felt walking a significant distance was preferable to sitting in traffic jams close to the ground.

The club worked with the local government and education authorities to improve car parking and by the late eighties a number of schools in the area started to open up their school yards for parking. This eased the situation on the streets – particularly as many of the streets closest to the ground were now only allowing parking for residents – and brought extra income to the schools. It also reassured those worried about car security.

Once de-regulation of the buses occurred the opportunity to travel by public transport to the ground reduced. Match buses still existed but in smaller numbers and post-match where there had once been traffic jams of buses heading towards the city centre and also eastwards towards Longsight, there now were jams of cars punctuated every so often by private hire vehicles and occasionally buses.

There were also, by 2003, once again large groups of supporters simply walking towards the city centre just as there had been eighty years earlier.

Below and right: Heading for home in 2003 usually meant a brisk walk to the car or a longer trek towards town.

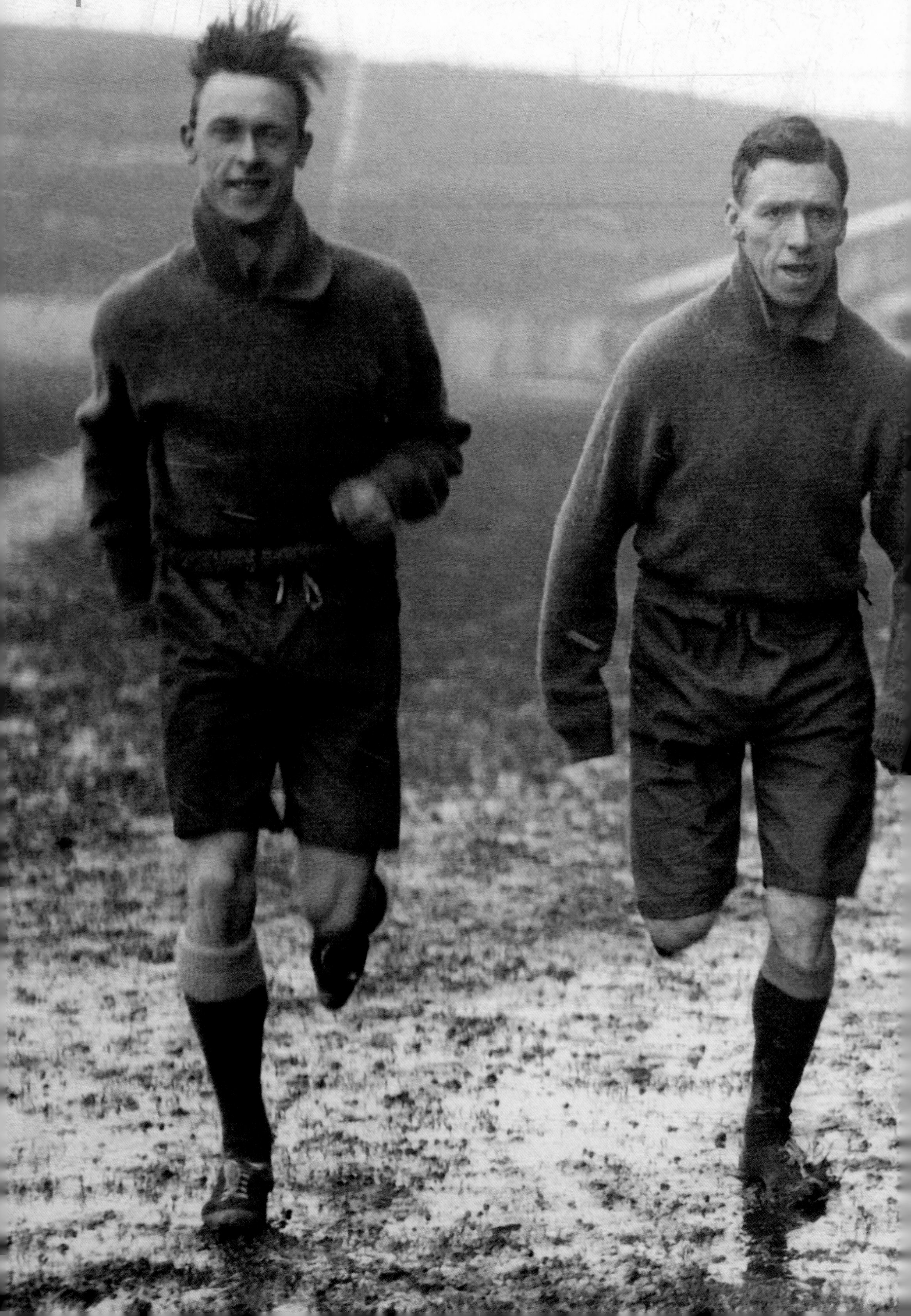

Chapter Three

The First Decade

Thus was formed the Board – Messrs, Furniss, Alexander, Ayrton, Dobson, Hughes, Moon, and Smith (Mr. Mangnall, secretary) – that made the decisions which transferred the club from its beloved but out-of-date home at Hyde Road to the palatial enclosure at Maine Road.

The greatest outdoor sport of the British people will continue to flourish; and under normal conditions advancement is sure. The present executive is judiciously blended and knows the needs of the Club as regards playing strength. Criticism of football management is often hasty and unfair. Success and failure are not such divergent possibilities after all. May the old Club continue to prosper, and the highest guerdon in football – the long-cherished League Championship flag – soon be flying at Maine Road.

Fred Johnson, author of "The History of the Manchester City Football Club", September 1930.

T HE 1923-4 season saw many complaints about the quality of the pitch, however these niggles were about to be pushed to one side as Billy Meredith, City's legendary player, returned to the team at the age of 49 to take part in a fabulous cup run.

Meredith's actual return had come in the third round FA Cup tie at Brighton on 23rd February, but his first match at Maine Road was on 1st March when the Blues met Middlesbrough in the League. City won 3-2 and Meredith's appearance made him the only man to have played home games at the four major Manchester venues – Hyde Road, Maine Road, Bank Street and Old Trafford.

Prior to that match, City had progressed through the early stages of the Cup by beating Nottingham Forest - in the first FA Cup tie to be played at Maine Road - and Halifax Town in a second replay (played at Old Trafford). The Forest match was watched by 33,849 (receipts of £2,050) – the highest home crowd at this point in time to witness a City first round tie – and was described as 'Max Woosnam's Return' match in the *Daily Express*. Woosnam had been missing from the side since the opening game of the season. According to the *Express*: "Max Woosnam assisted Manchester City to beat Nottingham Forest at Moss Side. It was distinctly unfortunate for Nottingham Forest that halfway through the first half Burton, who re-appeared after a long absence, was carried off the field, having displaced a cartilage.

"In the second half Manchester City the more often pressed, and eight minutes from the restart Barnes opened the scoring with a fine goal. Almost on time, after Hardy had saved from Morris, Roberts scored the second goal for City."

At Brighton in the third round Meredith & Co. helped the Blues to a 5-1 victory, and then City were drawn against First Division high-flyers Cardiff City at

Previous pages: City players training in front of the Main Stand during the 1920s. Left to right: Billy Austin, Frank Roberts, Tommy Johnson and George Hicks.

The Platt Lane corner in the background was the first to be demolished. It was rebuilt in 1931.

Maine Memory

■ We stood at the Platt Lane end for several years and this was before the roof went on. It cost us ninepence I think, and one day it was raining, so I said to my dad "Can we go over there Dad?" and I pointed at the Main Stand with its roof, and he said "Oh no, we can't afford it. It's half a crown!" and that was that. But he must have thought about it because before the next match he'd bought me a chubby umbrella for one and threepence, and so we had our own little shelter from then on.

He'd usually put me on the wall, and stand behind me to protect me, but then some jobsworth started to stop us from sitting on the wall.

At half time we used to get a cup of Oxo and a meat pie. I think it was tuppence for each one.

Fran Parker

Left: The crowd at the Platt Lane end of the ground in 1925, with the scoreboard in the background.

This was Maine Road's first scoreboard but it is believed to have been removed in 1935. In total three scoreboards have been positioned in this corner. None of these lasted more than a few years.

This still is actually from movie footage taken at Billy Meredith's Testimonial match (see page 72).

Maine Road in the quarter-final. A crowd of over 76,000 – the highest in Manchester for any footballing fixture (including two FA Cup finals) at that point – witnessed a goalless game.

According to City fan and local resident Margaret Baker the enormous crowds were good for the local economy: "The shopkeepers around Maine Road benefited enormously from the ground being built. Shops seemed to spring up on almost every corner around here. It was a real bonus for local trade, but some shopkeepers became a little too greedy and prices went up. Our shop stayed the same and we all benefited from the large crowds. Then of course there was the money to be made from storing bicycles in the back yards."

The replay ended 1-0 to City before a massive Welsh crowd of over 50,000 with Meredith setting up Tommy Browell for the only goal. The Blues were to face Newcastle United in the semi-final but prior to that Meredith made his final League appearance when he played in a 2-2 draw with Preston at Maine Road. He didn't play particularly well in that game. Similarly, against Newcastle Meredith was not convincing and the Blues suffered a 2-0 defeat ending the chance of their first Wembley appearance and, in the case of Meredith, a remarkable fairy-tale.

Back at Maine Road attendees at a reserve game eagerly awaited news from the semi-final. In those days supporters had to wait for a man carrying a sandwich board inscribed with the latest scores to walk around the pitch. Frank Brown was one such supporter who, speaking during the mid-70s, remembered the disappointment experienced each time the boardman appeared: "By the time he reached our part of the ground we knew the worst - City were a goal down. But plenty of time to go, all was by no means lost.

"Then again the figure started his death march down the tunnel, slower than ever this time. A groan, not a sigh, greeted him as, chalked on his board, appeared the never-to-be-forgotten figures of: Newcastle 2 City 0. That's how it had finished. Goodbye Wembley."

The chalking up of scores at Maine Road reserve games was a common occurrence and in those pre-transistor radio days was the only way of knowing for certain how the Blues were performing away from home.

After the Cardiff match the capacity of Maine Road wasn't really tested again until 30th January 1926 when a fourth round FA Cup tie with Huddersfield Town was watched by 74,789. The Blues won 4-0 but the biggest talking point concerned crowd safety. A crush barrier collapsed under the strain of the crowd causing many injuries. A number of spectators were carried away by stretcher.

City went on to play Bolton in their first Wembley appearance, but the game ended 1-0 to Wanderers. It was around this time that Fran Parker attended her first match: "I can't remember my first game but my father used to bring me in my trolley when I was three. It would have been 1925 or 1926. My dad used to sit me on the wall and if it was a very big match, like a cup tie, the staff used to put straw around the wall on the pitch side for us to sit on. So if you wanted to find a better place to sit you'd pick up your straw and move to another place. As I got older I used to make sure I got a good amount of straw but I also started to notice other things like Tip Top Tablets.

"Tip Top Tablets were like cough drops and cost a penny a bag. The man used to walk around the pitch with his box and you'd throw a penny down to him and

Maine Match 23/24

CITY v CARDIFF CITY

DATE:	8th March 1924	
TYPE OF FIXTURE:	FA Cup 4th round	
ATTENDANCE:	76,166	
RESULT:	City 0 Cardiff City 0	
TEAMS & SCORERS:	CITY	CARDIFF CITY
	Mitchell	Farquaharson
	Cookson	Nelson
	Fletcher	Blair
	Pringle	Evans H.
	Hamill	Jones
	Wilson	Hardy
	Meredith	Lawson
	Roberts	Gill
	Browell	Davies
	Barnes	Clennell
	Johnson	Evans J.

■ If television and media interest in 1924 was as prolific as today then this game would have been deemed 'Match of the Season' – possibly of the decade. There were many different angles - Cardiff were at their peak; Maine Road was hosting its first truly major match; and the legendary Billy Meredith was back in the side again at the age of 49 – and interest on the streets of Manchester was immense.

In addition possibly the largest travelling support, other than cup finals and semi-finals, journeyed to Maine Road from Cardiff. It's difficult to estimate exactly how many Welshmen made their way to Maine Road, but reports of the period stressed that six hundred tickets had been sent to Cardiff for advance bookings, while supporters arriving by train claimed in excess of one thousand fans would be making the trip. This may not seem a great number by modern day standards, but in 1924 with limited transport and little spare cash it was a significant number.

Queues outside Maine Road started a full five hours before kick-off. According to the *Athletic News*: "With all the ardour of first-nighters at the theatre football zealots – among whom were some sporting the Cardiff colours – began to assemble round the entrances to Maine Road as early as ten o'clock this morning. One lady, whose house adjoins the ground, and who stores cycles, said that she had four clients at that hour."

Margaret Baker remembers how local businesses prospered from City's early years at Maine Road: "Everyone who had a backyard would charge supporters to leave their bikes there while the game was on and after a while everybody seemed to have their own regular spot. You could make a tidy sum out of it, but it wasn't the only way we made money. All the shops In the area had a great flood of money coming in on match days and all those that had had shops before the ground was built couldn't believe their luck. Every type of shop seemed to benefit. Of course over time other people started to move in and I'm sure they expected to make a lot out of the supporters, but for those of us there before the

FIVE-HOUR QUEUES AT MAINE ROAD.

Manchester Sprinkled With Cup-Tie Colours.

WHOLE CITY AGOG.

Football Ousts Wireless and Golf.

ground it was a real bonus, and many shops made more on a Saturday than the rest of the week put together."

A large group of supporters decided to while away the time before the turnstiles opened by having a game of football. No doubt they used one of the exit gates positioned under the semi-circular "Manchester City" mosaics, as generations of supporters and locals have continued to do throughout the ground's history.

The Salvation Army, dressed in Japanese costume, mingled with crowds collecting money for the 'Self Denial Fund', while one report claimed the streets around the ground resembled an Eastern Bazaar: "There were date-sellers, coughdrop sellers and purveyors of button-hole cups and favours. All of whom anticipated a roaring business. The coughdrop seller had the most reasonable wares, because the wind across the ground was most biting, and even the policemen, who were much in evidence, found the need of some comforter of this kind."

According to the Athletic News: "By 12 o'clock there were literally hundreds awaiting admission, and contrary to the intention of opening the ground at one o'clock the gates were thrown open before half-past twelve, and the crowd began to pour in.

"One had expected to see a very much larger assembly by noon, but there is evidently considerable confidence in the holding capacity of the ground. It is not yet known how many exactly it will accommodate, but it was generally expected that it would be put to the supreme test by this afternoon's game."

Those final comments are very interesting in terms of the way the stadium, and indeed football, was viewed at this point. Major games – including the 1923 FA Cup final – could still be attended by anybody so long as they were able to pay their admission prior to the turnstiles being closed. All-ticket matches were unheard of. Naturally, some – though by no means all – seat tickets could be purchased in advance, but only a small proportion of fans actually bothered to do that. As far as football was concerned, the general rule was if the game was a major match, get there early to guarantee admission.

The other point worth pondering over concerns the capacity of Maine Road. The report makes it absolutely clear that nobody – not even club officials – knew exactly what the capacity of the ground was. Supporters were packed onto the terraces without any real consideration, or understanding, of how many could be accommodated safely. Why greater tragedies never occurred during this period is a mystery. At least Maine Road was a new stadium. What would the situation have been like if this game were to be played at Hyde Road?

About an hour before kick-off the stadium was relatively full, although reports still suggested the

capacity would not be reached: "Half an hour before the match was timed to begin the ground, at a casual glance, appeared to be well filled, but there were obvious gaps on the huge embankment, and it became a matter of doubt that the capacity of the enclosure would after all be really tested. Thanks to the exertions of the police, of whom there was a total of almost 150 on and about the scene, room was made for the foolish late-comers, and in a little while the congestion was so great that boys were extricated from the mass and rolled over the heads of the spectators in order that they might find sanctuary inside the concrete wall."

The official attendance was recorded as 76,166, with receipts of £4,909.

The pitch was in poor condition – architect Swain garnered severe criticism during this period – and understandably the game was littered with mistakes. The match ended goalless - despite City's superstitious wearing of their lucky away strip of scarlet. Billy Meredith had been unable to keep up with the speed of the game at times, but was still regarded as one of the better players on the pitch. According to the Manchester Guardian: "There was great interest in Meredith's play. He performs as artistically as ever that strange feat of magnetising the ball round his toes in a half-circle and then running down the field to the goal-line with a ferocious half-back somehow kept always on the offside of him. He was only beaten once or twice all Saturday afternoon."

Late in 2002, 89 year old supporter Harry Bramble remembered seeing Meredith in this match: "I'd been going to watch City ever since Maine Road opened in 1923 and, of course, my father remembered Meredith playing at Hyde Road. So we were excited by the news he was to play and I was not disappointed. My first sight of him in action was fantastic. He was the first player to outfox opponents really, and he was still doing it then when he was nearly fifty.

"Of course, because he played outside right he always had a chance to recuperate while play was going on elsewhere, but when he did have the ball he was outstanding. So much so that Cardiff and the other teams would put two men on him. I remember seeing two going for him… one either side, and at the moment when they were to go into him to attempt to get the ball off him, he'd put a spurt on and the two men collided while he moved forward with the ball."

The Daily Express was also impressed with the Welshman: "Meredith the veteran was always a great source of danger, controlling the ball with fine effect and centre-ing with his wonted accuracy. Indeed most of the opportunities which fell to the home inside men came from his wing, and the old international also tried on one exciting occasion to score himself."

The Express was not so impressed with the rest of the match: "It was a great disappointment to the record crowd at Manchester City's ground that no goals were scored in the great cup struggle between City and Cardiff City. It was a typical cup-tie battle, full of vigorous football, though the finer points of the game were only occasionally shown. Manchester City, who had to make several important changes, were rather the better side, but they were up against a magnificent defence."

Although this game was not a great spectacle, it is a very important match in the history of the stadium. The replay ended in a 1-0 City win, but the two stories – Meredith and Maine Road - which dominated 1923-4 were first brought together in this match.

Maine Memory

■ My first visit to Maine Road was at the age of four in 1933. This came about due to the fact that my father's brother was rather small and asked to borrow the stool from my desk to stand on. I must have lent it on condition I went along. I still remember the day. We were standing at the top of the Main Stand – this was allowed even though the stand itself was seated – and apart from being lifted up to see the pitch a couple of times, all I saw was a sea of legs. Nevertheless I was hooked and now, with my own children and grandchildren we have had five generations of Blue support.

Chas Betts

Right: This cartoon from the Daily Dispatch focuses on the size of the crowd at Maine Road's first derby.

Maine Men Max Woosnam

Role: Captain at opening game
Born: Liverpool, 6th September 1892
Died: London, 14th July 1965
City debut: v Bradford City (h) 1/1/1920

■ **Max Woosnam was an incredible sportsman and was one of City's most famous players during Maine Road's early history. During the First World War Woosnam had served with the Montgomeryshire Yeomanry in France, and after the hostilities were over he moved to Manchester. He almost joined United, but this would have clashed with his job, so he signed for the Blues in November 1919 instead. Pre-war he had been with Chelsea briefly.**

He became a major City star but his fame was not merely as a member of City's exciting early twenties side. He was a Wimbledon doubles champion, a member of the Davis Cup team, an Olympic Gold medallist, a Cambridge Blue at soccer, golf and lawn tennis, and 12th man for their cricket team.

He was also a committed and highly respected amateur player and felt the game of football was one to be enjoyed for sporting reasons and not financial. Several times during his career he joined the famous amateur side Corinthians. During his time with City he also captained England for a game, and appeared three times as an amateur international.

Woosnam was the archetypal English gentleman. On 6th May 1922 he received a broken leg in a collision during the match with Newcastle but, in typical style, refused to blame his opponent: "I went out to tackle Lowe, the Newcastle winger, pushed the ball into touch and got it just below the knee – as I deserved to do. Entirely my own fault."

Afterwards young supporter Joe Carley wrote about the events that followed: "After the game, I made my usual trip to the players' entrance for autographs, and stood amongst a silent crowd of sympathisers as Max, still smiling cheerfully, was carried to the ambulance on a stretcher. A small boy detached himself from the onlookers and calmly asked the injured player to sign his book. Before any of the amazed spectators could shoo the boy away, Max asked the stretcher-bearers to stop for a moment so he could sign the book."

Woosnam was brought back into the City team in August 1923 when he was appointed captain for the day at the opening of Maine Road. It was a fitting gesture and Woosnam enjoyed the accolade.

While with City he worked for Crossleys - a local motor manufacturer - and on one occasion he had told the Blues he wouldn't be able to play due to work commitments. When his manager found out, he insisted Woosnam play for City instead of performing his duties.

His last City season was 1924-25 and after that he played for Northwich Victoria, and worked for ICI. In later years he moved to the south-east as personnel officer for ICI. He died in 1965, and twelve years later a street close to Maine Road – "Max Woosnam Walk" - was named after him.

he'd throw a packet up to you. For some reason the club wouldn't allow the sellers on to the terraces. In fact the police never went on the terraces nor did the ambulancemen. If somebody wasn't well they'd be helped down, but if they'd fainted they'd be rolled down over your head. It happened often, and I used to wait for pennies to drop out of their pockets!"

Earlier that season a paying crowd of 62,994 witnessed the first Manchester derby at the new stadium. United were promoted in 1925 and the *Athletic News* enjoyed the return of the derby: "The first meeting of the Manchester rivals after a lapse of four years brought the City club the largest League gate they have ever enjoyed. It was not so great as that recorded at the Cup tie with Cardiff City in March 1924, when 76,166 spectators paid for admission, but over 62,000 people passed through the turnstiles and, with ticket holders, the attendance was officially returned at nearly 66,000."

That sentence clearly shows the problem with determining actual attendances from this period of City's history. The figures often simply quote those that had paid on the day and exclude season tickets, while at other times figures are rounded to include season ticket holders, causing the true attendance to be distorted. The only attendances that can be clearly understood are those for cup ties.

Regardless of the attendance the match was a major spectacle. The *Athletic News* described the play: "It was a magnificent spectacle and a game fought in a splendid spirit. That the City did not defeat their rivals was due primarily to the brilliant goalkeeping of Steward, a Manchester born player, to whose rich promise the Athletic News referred last Monday. It was fitting that on the only occasion he was beaten the success fell to Samuel Cowan, for these players were the outstanding figures in the contest.

"Cowan's headwork was a feature of the match. More, he tackled with grim determination and effectiveness, and distributed the ball with discrimination and accuracy. Cowan promises to be all that the City club expected when they bought him from Doncaster Rovers last season. He has all the physical requirements for a centre-half-back, and judging by his display in this match, he has the temperament for the big event. His equalising goal was a masterpiece in headwork and judgement."

The game ended 1-1 while the return, incidentally, ended 6-1 to the Blues before an Old Trafford crowd of 48,657.

A key feature of the Maine Road derby was the large presence of first-aid men who seemed to be forever removing supporters from the Popular Side. Little was said in the press concerning crowd safety, but it is clear a large number of spectators suffered minor injuries. This seemed to be a typical feature of every big match at every major stadium during the 1920s and 1930s, as few considered safety even at the country's newest venues. Despite these injuries Maine Road was still one of the safest venues in Europe.

Although Maine Road was considered a major stadium in every sense of the word there existed a feeling that the ground should have had more cover. Hyde Road had at one time boasted covered accommodation for over 35,000. This was a huge figure, nevertheless Maine Road's cover only sheltered around 10,000 fans, and even then these were all seated. The terracing had no protection at all.

The History of the Lancashire Football Association,

published in 1928, was critical: "Manchester is still primitive in its accommodation. At neither Old Trafford nor Maine Road can the ordinary one shilling spectator find covered accommodation. Our City friends launched out freely, but they and Manchester United must provide covered accommodation for the men who do not aspire to Grand Stands on which you sit, but are prepared to stand the game through, yet desire some protection from the weather."

The book did end its section on the Blues in a positive note however: "Maine Road is a great ground,

and great crowds assemble there, and the supporters of the Club look for results in keeping with the ground's surroundings and equipment."

Sadly the 1925-6 season ended with the Blues relegated.

The opening game of the new season saw City face Fulham in a match filmed for local cinema audiences. City were a popular club and as such movie companies were keen to film excerpts from key games and show them across the city and, often, nationwide. The earliest known Maine Road game to be filmed was the Cardiff

Maine Match 24/25

MEREDITH XI v RANGERS/CELTIC XI

DATE:	29th April 1925
TYPE OF FIXTURE:	Billy Meredith's Benefit Match

■ Billy Meredith remains one of the most famous early stars of football. Stories of the great man's abilities have been passed down through the generations and, even today, his name often appears in the footballing and Manchester press.

During the early years of the 21st Century a group of City supporters, led by Tommy Muir, contacted Meredith's daughter Winifred to ask her permission to erect a new headstone at his grave. In April 1958 Meredith had been buried in an unmarked grave. It had been his choice – he realised how popular football was and didn't want a fuss – but forty years after his death supporters felt he deserved something more fitting. Winifred, who had lovingly tended his grave throughout the intervening years, was delighted with the gesture. City, United, the PFA, and the Welsh FA each agreed to split the cost and a new headstone was commissioned.

The reason Meredith's name has remained so important is simply because he was the first true Blue hero. He joined City in 1894 and as captain lifted the FA Cup a mere ten years later. This was Manchester football's first major success and, with City also performing exceptionally well in the League, it was a sign Manchester was at long last proving its worth as a footballing city.

He played at Maine Road in the stadium's first season - the only man to have played home matches at each of Manchester's four major League grounds (Hyde Road, Bank Street, Old Trafford, and Maine Road). It should be remembered he was also instrumental in setting up the original Players' Union and in the mid-twenties helped create another Manchester team with League ambitions – Manchester Central. According to an interview with 1930s City star Billy Dale, Meredith was still coaching at Maine Road when he joined the club in 1931, although Dale wasn't particularly impressed with the Welshman: "He was too old. He tried to play with you but couldn't kick a ball above twenty yards, He was trying to show us how to play. He'd set up posts and try to dribble through them but he kept knocking over the posts. They had to sack him eventually – he was always swanking about."

A series of benefit matches and events were organised for Meredith following his retirement in 1924,

with this match being the most significant. Somehow Meredith convinced Rangers and Celtic to form one side to take on a team of Lancashire-based players selected by Meredith himself. The Meredith side, playing in red and white, contained City favourites Frank Roberts and Charlie Pringle, plus of course Meredith, and former City star Horace Barnes – a Preston player at the time.

The Glasgow side, playing in blue and white, contained five Celtic players – including Jimmy McGrory – and six Rangers men. Former City full-back Johnny McMahon was one of the linesmen, while the other was an ex-United star George Wall, who incredibly smoked a pipe throughout the match!

According to the *Manchester Evening Chronicle* report: "Many old friendships were renewed at Maine Road on Wednesday night, and we all laughed at Meredith trying the old backheel to the half-back business with very little success."

A few moments from the match, including the teams posing for photographs, were filmed making this quite probably the oldest surviving viewable footage of a match at Maine Road. The footage concentrates on Meredith pre-match, and also shows the Popular Side and Platt Lane end. The camera was placed in front of the Platt Lane end, close to the goal, for much of the action.

Appropriately, in 1977 Manchester City Council named a street close to Maine Road after Meredith, and in 1985 *Football Wizard*, a biography of his life, was published. In 1997 BBC2 Wales broadcast a television documentary about him.

In addition, it is a little-known fact that Billy Meredith was actually a City shareholder for many years. According to club records he became a shareholder on 5th November 1920 – the day before the Hyde Road fire – and remained so until March 1950. It's possible he had been a shareholder prior to November 1920 as the club shareholder records were destroyed in the fire, however as Meredith's date appears so precise in comparison with other shareholders from the period before the fire, it seems highly likely Meredith did purchase his shares on that date.

Billy Meredith's position in Manchester football is a major one. He was Manchester's first successful captain and helped to create both City and United's trophy-winning heritage, and deserves to be recognised forever more as one of Manchester's leading citizens. Without Meredith neither club would have established their name.

OFFICIAL
Souvenir Programme

W. MEREDITH
1894 — 1924

BENEFIT MATCH
On the Ground of the Manchester City A.F.C.
MAINE ROAD, Moss Side
WEDNESDAY, April 29th, 1925.
KICK-OFF — — — 6-30 p.m.

MEREDITH'S XI. v.
RANGERS & CELTIC XI.
PRICE 2d.

Below: Billy Meredith, the oldest player ever to turn out for City at Maine Road.

Above: Huddersfield goalkeeper Taylor scoops up a shot from City's Tommy Johnson during the 1926 FA Cup meeting.

Right: Two young girls, Marjorie Cooper and Annie Bruce, stand outside St. Matthias Church ready for the annual Whit Walk. The stadium can be seen in the background whilst on the left of the photograph a motor car is visible outside 219 and 221 Maine Road. This car is believed to have belonged to City star Jimmy McMullan. McMullan lived in one of the two houses and it is understood he possessed the only car in the district at the time this photograph was taken!

cup-tie in 1924 but unfortunately footage from that match is in a precarious state and cannot currently be viewed.

For many years the match with Fulham was believed to be the oldest known viewable footage of a Maine Road competitive match, however as recently as 2002 footage of City v Huddersfield (30/1/26) and City v Crystal Palace (20/2/26) has been discovered.

Cinema audiences were able to witness City's 4-2 demolition of Fulham on the opening day of the 1926-7 season as the Blues bid for promotion. It was a season of quality entertainment and high drama as City scored plenty of goals - 35 came in the opening 13 matches while the team averaged over three goals per game at

Maine Road during the first half of the campaign. The Blues were also well supported and continued to attract significantly larger crowds than First Division Manchester United.

As the season progressed City notched up several high scores. The best result at Maine Road had to be the 7-0 thrashing of strugglers Darlington on 18th April. A crowd of around 40,000 watched that game as the Blues nudged closer to promotion. Sadly, Portsmouth also kept up the chase and by the last Saturday of the season both sides were level on 52 points, while Middlesbrough were already certain of the title. Importantly, Portsmouth had the better goal average (82 for and 48 against, with an average of 1.708 as opposed to City's 100 for, 61 against at an average of 1.639).

The final match of the season saw City face bottom club Bradford City at Maine Road, while Preston were Portsmouth's visitors. Within six minutes of the start the Blues took the lead through Peter Bell. The *Athletic News*: "In less than six minutes the City were one up. From the kick off they were on their toes, and when Bell improved upon an inspiring piece of play by Roberts and swung a ball into the goalmouth which Boot caught but failed to hold, the huge assembly was delirious with delight. The cheering was deafening. Ten minutes later another peal of thunder announced a second success, and as fine a goal as anyone could wish to see. All the time in the sweltering heat the City had been playing football of the finest quality, and at an amazing pace. Their manoeuvring was bewildering, and their forwards were as nippy and as virile as they were clever.

"Boot had defied them courageously and dexterously when his backs were hopelessly beaten, and shots had missed by the proverbial inches, but when Hicks picked up a pass from Broadhurst and slipped it through to Johnson there was not the slightest chance for the Bradford guardian. Like a streak of lightning Johnson whipped round Russell with a deceptive swerve, and his left foot served him truly.

Maine Match 25/26

CITY v CRYSTAL PALACE

DATE:	20th February 1926		
TYPE OF FIXTURE:	FA Cup 5th round		
ATTENDANCE:	51,630		
RESULT:	City 11 Crystal Palace 4		
TEAMS & SCORERS:	CITY		CRYSTAL PALACE
	Goodchild		Callender
	Cookson		Little
	McCloy		Cross
	Coupland		McCracken 1
	Cowan		Coyle
	Pringle		Greener
	Austin 1		Harry
	Browell 3		Blakemore
	Roberts 5		Cherrett 2
	Johnson 1		Hawkins
	Hicks 1		Clarke 1

■ After defeating Huddersfield Town 4-0 in a Maine Road tie watched by 74,789 – many spectators were stretchered away after a crush barrier collapsed – a smaller crowd of under 52,000 (receipts of £3,358) witnessed one of City's most amazing displays since the opening of the stadium in 1923.

The Blues were clear favourites to win this match despite their poor League form as Crystal Palace were then a Division Three (South) side, relegated at the end of the previous season. The difference in class was clear, however the 1925-6 season was one of City's most unpredictable periods. They had already thrashed Manchester United 6-1 at Old Trafford in the League, yet had been defeated 5-1 by Huddersfield at Maine Road in the very next League fixture. Put simply, no one quite knew which City side would take the field for this Cup tie.

Palace were managed at this point by Alec Maley, the brother of City's first great manager Tom Maley. Although it's not entirely clear, it does appear that Tom,

who had been Southport manager briefly in 1925 but was by this point retired from management, attended this match.

The opening moments saw City attack while Palace seemed uncertain how to approach the match. Then in the fourth minute, as City's George Hicks posed a little danger, Palace's Bob McCracken fouled the City man to give the Blues a penalty. Palace were clearly disappointed at giving City the initiative so early and when Billy Austin netted the spot-kick Palace crumbled.

After thirty minutes City were leading 5-0 with a goal from Johnson and a hat-trick from Roberts. Tommy Browell netted twice shortly before the interval to give the Blues a 7-0 half-time lead. The result was a formality and the Blues entered the second half with an air of complacency only to be surprised by a spirited fightback from Palace.

In the 55th minute Percy Cherrett made it 7-1 but City replied three minutes later when Tommy Browell scored his third. Palace were surely finished but instead Cherrett netted his second, and then George Clarke scored following a penalty. City's popular 'keeper Jim Goodchild had at first parried the ball out before Clarke blasted it past 'naughty boy' Goodchild as he was known to the City fans.

Cherrett netted again to make the score 8-4 and for a spell Palace felt they could challenge, however managerless City got their act together again with Roberts scoring twice and George Hicks netting the eleventh shortly before the end.

At the whistle City fans raced on to the field, not to congratulate their players, but to hoist Palace's 'keeper Billy Callender shoulder-high. According to newspaper reports the Manchester men did this as recognition of a fine performance – apparently he'd saved far more than he'd conceded – however it seems highly unlikely he'd have been given such a reception had he managed to keep the score down to 4-4!

A few days later cinema audiences were able to re-live a few scenes from the match as Pathe News featured the game under the title: "Crystal Palace Overwhelmed" in cinemas nationwide. Incidentally, this was the first time Palace had featured in a match where one side reached double figures.

Below: Frank Roberts, scorer of five goals in City's 1926 FA Cup win over Crystal Palace.

This total was never again achieved by anyone at Maine Road in the competition, although Tommy Browell had also netted five times earlier in the same season against Burnley in the League, and George Smith did likewise in a 1947 League fixture with Newport County.

"Two goals to the good in sixteen minutes was a glorious start on such a momentous occasion. "

The Portsmouth-Preston game had kicked off fifteen minutes later and news was now starting to filter through of how that match was progressing. The *Athletic News* noted that tremendous cheering came from City's vast terracing. On investigation, their reporter discovered that Preston had taken the lead at Portsmouth. With thirty minutes gone Hicks 'coolly and deliberately' placed the ball into the net for the Blues' third. According to The Pilgrim, writing in the *Athletic News*, this was "not a raking shot that bulged the netting, but a coolly and deliberately placed ball from a 'take-me-and-get-one-pass' by Johnson".

Backed by a noisy 50,000 crowd the City players surged forward. In the 52nd minute Charlie Broadhurst netted the fourth via a fine long range shot. Six minutes later Frank Roberts made it five, then after about 66 minutes ace-goalscorer Tommy Johnson made it six. According to The Pilgrim City tore Bradford to shreds:

"All they could do was to kick at random, and except for two occasions their forwards never got a look in."

As always with crucial matches of this kind at Maine Road conflicting messages circulated around the ground. Some thought City were already promoted while others urged the side forward.

Nine minutes from time Johnson netted a penalty to complete his hat-trick, and then in the dying seconds Broadhurst made City's total eight. The whistle sounded and supporters surged onto the pitch to greet their City heroes. Wild celebrations followed.

The band came out and started playing 'Auld Lang Syne' as everyone was convinced the Blues were saying goodbye to Division Two and welcoming in the First. Then the atmosphere deadened a little as news filtered through Portsmouth were winning, although nobody seemed to know by how many. Club officials tried to discover the extent of Portsmouth's lead, but few supporters really cared because they thought 8-0 had to be sufficient.

Extreme right: A card from Gallaher's Cigarettes depicts action from City's 7-4 home win over Swansea Town in 1927-28. It shows the visitors' inside-right Deacon dribbling between City's Cookson and McCloy with Cowan behind him.

Above: Jimmy McMullan leads City out of the tunnel prior to the game with Fulham in 1926. When Maine Road was first built the Main Stand tunnels extended further than they did during modern times. A little over thirty years after this photo was taken the wall above the tunnel was removed and seating was brought forward several feet. Comparisons with later photographs will show that the Chairman and other figures moved forward into the new seated section. Note also the pillars adjacent to the perimeter wall. The back of these pillars still existed at Maine Road in 2003 but the front had been completely remodelled to allow improved dugout space for the manager and staff - a small bench as seen here would only accommodate a coach and a physio!

City's victory meant Portsmouth needed to win their game 5-1, and with those vital fifteen minutes' leeway they had the opportunity to control their own destiny, especially as they were already leading 4-1. The Portsmouth bench seemed to know exactly the state of play in Manchester and they bellowed at their players to score. The Fratton Park crowd started to sing the Pompey Chimes and also "To Be A Farmer's Boy" – a song sung to their popular ex-dairy farmer Willie Haines. Sure enough, Haines netted his fourth and Portsmouth's fifth goal. The celebrations in Moss Side quelled as Portsmouth now erupted. Haines, interviewed in 1969, explained what happened to him: "Yer know, I never had no pants on when I got in t' the dressin' room. They tore 'em off. It took me an hour to get off the pitch."

Haines became a cult figure on the south coast while back in Manchester the City directors learned their fate via ticker-tape. Portsmouth were promoted by the narrowest goal average margin in history. Their average equalled 1.7755, while City's was 1.7705. One more City goal would have given the Blues that vital second promotion spot.

It was a devastating blow. The *Athletic News* felt City had suffered more than most: "Wonderful and tragic. Those are the only words that can adequately describe the thrilling finale at Maine-road. It was a game that will never be forgotten. I have been watching football for many years, but I can recall nothing to equal it. The atmosphere was electric. There were over 50,000 spectators present, and the one concern was how many goals Manchester City would get. There was never any questioning their ability to win."

The report added: "By some infinitesimal fraction of a goal they have to go through it all again. Another goal would have done it, and that there was not another goal, and more than one, was due to Boot. He was fortunate on one occasion, but he played like one inspired, and though he was at fault when the first point was recorded, that is the only blemish on a display that, like the game will as I have said, never be forgotten."

Maine Road had never experienced such drama. Although City had been relegated the previous season this was the first moment of true disappointment experienced at the stadium. City had come so close. Somehow the Blues had to pick themselves up and look forward to the next season. It was difficult.

The first home match ended in a 7-4 victory over Swansea Town. Around 40,000 witnessed star man Tommy Johnson net a hat-trick. Further excitement followed as only one game – surprisingly a 5-3 rout at Swansea – in the first nine ended in defeat.

With a large, vocal crowd City charged up the table

and ended the 1927-28 season as Division Two champions for the fourth time. The average attendance had reached 38,000 - an incredible figure at this point in football's history - and one which gave the Blues the largest support in the League. In fact this was the highest average of any club since 41,100 had followed Newcastle in 1920-21, and was at this point the sixth highest average attendance of all time. For comparison the top eight were:

> 42,860 Chelsea (1919-20; 3rd Division One)
> 41,100 Newcastle (1920-21; 5th Division One)
> 38,140 Chelsea (1920-21; 18th Division One)
> 37,900 Chelsea (1913-14; 8th Division One)
> 37,850 Newcastle (1919-20; 8th Division One)
> 37,468 City (1927-28; Division Two Champions)
> 37,461 Everton (1927-28; Division One Champions)
> 37,160 Chelsea (1921-22; 9th Division One)

Two League games – Chelsea on 12th November and Preston on 25th February – were watched by crowds recorded as 60,000, while an FA Cup tie against Stoke on 18th February was watched by 73,668 – the third-largest Maine Road crowd at this stage.

On 2nd April 1928 Maine Road hosted its first FA Cup semi-final when Huddersfield defeated Sheffield United 1-0, and then the following season Maine Road celebrated its fifth anniversary. The opening home game was to be the 37th Manchester League Derby. It was not a great match, but a 2-2 draw proved City could more than match their neighbours. According to journalist Ivan Sharpe it was a good-natured game. This was important as only a day or so earlier a radio broadcast by Bishop Welldon had criticised the game of football for displaying selfish and unsporting behaviour. Ivan Sharpe took the opportunity of using his match report to stress the sporting nature of Manchester football: "The truer sermon was preached on Saturday where 60,000 odd frenzied folk urged the teams to extra effort, on a field as warm as a Turkish bath, and despite the ninety minutes of thrill and strain and continuous excitement, not one incident marred the match. That was a sermon worth noting. It was eloquent, silent preaching."

Maine Match 27/28

HUDDERSFIELD TOWN v SHEFFIELD UNITED

DATE:	2nd April 1928	
TYPE OF FIXTURE:	FA Cup semi final 2nd replay	
ATTENDANCE:	69,360	
RESULT:	Huddersfield Town 1 Sheffield United 0	
TEAMS &	HUDDERSFIELD	SHEFFIELD UNITED
SCORERS:	Mercer	Alderson
	Goodall	King
	Barkas	Birks
	Redfern	Sampy T.
	Wilson	Matthews
	Steele	Green
	Jackson 1	Partridge
	Kelly	Blair
	Dent	Johnson
	Stephenson	Gillespie
	Smith	Tunstall

■ On Monday 2nd April 1928 Maine Road hosted its first FA Cup semi-final when Huddersfield defeated Sheffield United 1-0. This was actually the second replay after both sides had drawn 2-2 at Old Trafford (attendance was 69,260) and played out a goalless match at Goodison Park (attendance 53,749). The Maine Road match was watched by 69,360 with the only goal coming nine minutes after half time from a disputed free kick. The Huddersfield scorer was Alec Jackson, but the significance of this match was clearly that it was Maine Road's first major neutral fixture and it passed with very few – if any – issues.

The match at Old Trafford had seen terrible crowd control problems – supporters took to the pitch on a couple of occasions to avoid crushing – but Maine Road had no such instances. According to *Adjutant* in the

Daily Dispatch: "The crowd was an amazing one, yet there was not a casualty save for an occasional case of semi-fainting, while I should like to add that Mr. Arthur Kingscott [former referee and senior FA official] went out of his way at the close of the game to tell me that the arrangements were perfect; that everything went off without a hitch. A well deserved tribute to the City officials."

Outside the stadium Manchester found the holding of a major cup game on a Monday afternoon caused several traffic issues. According to the *Daily Dispatch*:
"Manchester Tramways' timetable was considerably upset between the hours of five and seven o'clock last evening in the effort to deal with the crowd of seventy-thousand people who had attended the Huddersfield versus Sheffield United Cup semi-final at Maine Road.

"The difficulties of coping with so many people were made greater by the great number of motor-cars which blocked the main roads into the city, and by the outpouring of workers from office and factory just when the football crowd was streaming out of the ground.

"Pedestrians who had failed to board tramcars were soon congratulating themselves as they walked along Oxford Road and Upper Lloyd Street. For they were making far better progress than those in vehicles. For long distances motor-cars crawled along three abreast, and the whole roads were overhung by pale-blue clouds of oil fumes from the hundreds of chugging exhausts.

"At All Saints the crowds walking from the football ground met the little army walking homeward from the city. Stationary tramcars with every seat occupied, stretched back as far as the eye could see, past the university in one direction, and right into the city in the other. Crossing the road at points, other than those where policemen were stationed was a dangerous business."

The article went on to say that approximately three hours after the match ended the scene was back to normal. Clearly, the traffic chaos detailed in 1928 became a regular feature – with buses replacing trams – of Maine Road matchdays by the 1970s.

Maine Memory

■ I have supported City since attending my first game in 1930. The goalkeeper was Len Langford back then, but I was also at Maine Road when Frank Swift made his first home appearance. On Christmas Day 1933 Swift had played at Derby and we'd lost 4-1, so you could say that we supporters didn't know what to expect from him. On Boxing Day we beat Derby 2-0 and he played well and before long he'd helped us win the Cup and the League. He became one of my favourite players, alongside Doherty, Brook, Busby, and Cowan from that period.

F E Hillier

Maine Memory

■ I've witnessed many great moments at Maine Road and many painful ones too, including David Pleat's dance of delight in 1983 and City's time-wasting against Liverpool in 1996, but my worst moment at Maine Road has to be 7th May 1927. I've learnt to cope with disasters but when at the age of about ten you see your side win at Maine Road 8-0 and still miss out on promotion by 1/200th of a goal it's heartbreaking. I was desolate... blown away... impossible to describe the agony I felt that day. I can still feel it even now. Since then I have implored the team to 'pot all the goals you can'. I pray to be five goals ahead so that I can breath easily. I've seen too many of our 3-0 leads disintegrate.

I also remember that Maine Road was used for many local finals or Manchester Boys games. For the Manchester Boys games a second crossbar would be fitted across the goal, about a foot below the usual crossbar. I need hardly say there were occasions when the question arose 'Was the ball below or above the lower crossbar?' – the nets remained in their usual place! The biggest schoolboy moment came when Manchester Schoolboys drew 2-2 with Southampton Boys in the early thirties. It was the national final and each side held the trophy for six months. I remember there was a staggering crowd there, in excess of 30,000, and the Manchester Boys had never received such support. It was a great game.

Denis Houlston

Below: Tommy Johnson and Eric Brook training on the Maine Road pitch circa 1928. Johnson scored a club record 38 League goals for City during the 1928-29 season.

Tommy Johnson's goal in that match was the first of his record breaking 38 League goals. He scored a hat-trick in one Maine Road League game that season – against Bolton on 29th March – and netted two in six other home games, but his best performance came away from home when he netted five against Everton on 15th September.

Other than Johnson's achievements and a satisfactory season all round, little of note occurred to affect the Maine Road story. Johnson's record of 38 League goals that season remains the highest from any

City player in a single campaign, and during the early part of the following campaign, Johnson again shone.

As far as the stadium was concerned, the club valued it at approximately £125,000, which seemed a little low as McAlpine's had valued the Main Stand alone at £120,000 a few years earlier. The Blues claimed to have an outstanding mortgage of £75,000, but clearly the stadium was a major asset, especially as 1929-30 saw two attendances of over sixty thousand - 64,472 witnessed the fortieth League derby in February, while 61,574 were at a rare 2-1 defeat at home to Hull City in the fifth round of the FA Cup. In the previous round the Blues defeated Swindon Town 10-1 – a record for Maine Road only equalled in 1987 when Huddersfield Town were beaten by the same score.

The outstanding mortgage was, in the main, owed directly to McAlpine's. Malcolm McAlpine was a young boy during this period of the stadium's history and remembers how he first heard of football: "I became a Manchester City supporter as a child because it was the first football team I had ever heard of. I remember being at home early on Saturday evenings when the telephone would ring. My father would answer and I'd hear him say something along the lines of 'sixty-thousand excellent!' then other weeks it would be 'twenty-thousand! Why only twenty thousand?' You see, Manchester City still owed my father a great deal of money in relation to the building of the stadium and he had negotiated for a share of the gate receipts to be paid after each match. Naturally, I became a City supporter as a result, although I must say it had nothing to do with results. It was all about familiarity with the name and, I suppose, the need for the club to perform well."

Semi-Finals at Maine Road

■ The 1928 replay between Huddersfield Town and Sheffield United was the first FA Cup semi-final to be played at Maine Road, and proved City's ground was well equipped to stage major events. Unfortunately, due to various circumstances – most notably the fact City featured in three semi-finals themselves over the course of the following six years - Maine Road was not to stage another semi-final until 1946 when Derby and Birmingham met.

Staging FA Cup semi-finals and other neutral fixtures depends on a number of factors. These range from safety concerns to stadium capacity; from travelling distance to parking arrangements; the neutrality of the venue to involvement of the club. Until the late 1980s, Maine Road's capacity usually worked in the club's favour, however segregation was

weak for major matches with the Kippax often split down the middle by hastily-erected barriers and scaffolding. Wherever possible, the FA tried to ensure both competing sides would be given a similar allocation of standing and seat tickets. As Maine Road's segregation would usually split the Kippax roughly two-thirds of the way along this was not adequate, and as a result major fixtures during the late seventies until the demise of the Kippax in 1994 were difficult to segregate.

When Manchester United and Oldham met at Maine Road in the 1990 semi-final and replay, the decision was taken to give United a larger share of the capacity, and so segregation was similar to regular City matches, with United having the home section of the Kippax.

A major factor on whether a venue hosts a semi-final is the

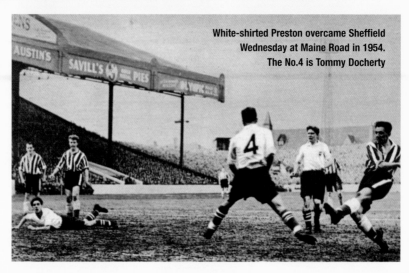

White-shirted Preston overcame Sheffield Wednesday at Maine Road in 1954. The No.4 is Tommy Docherty

location of the competing clubs. Maine Road becomes a serious choice when clubs from Merseyside, Lancashire, or Yorkshire meet. Only the 1946 semi-final (Birmingham and Derby) has been played between sides outside of these regions, although the 1951 match also involved Birmingham.

Looking at every season since Maine Road opened, it's clear City have faced stiff opposition from Old Trafford, the Merseyside grounds, and Hillsborough, yet considering the quality of these venues at various stages of their existence, Maine Road's record is impressive.

During the 1950s Maine Road became the first choice for a while with the ground staging five semi-finals during nine seasons. Even then the reasons Maine Road did not stage more was because other grounds were more appropriate due to travelling distances. The FA were always keen to ensure both sets of

supporters had a fair travelling distance and equidistant venues would be chosen wherever possible.

In 1952 the competing clubs were Newcastle v Blackburn (Hillsborough & replay at Elland Road) and Arsenal v Chelsea. City competed in the 1955 & 1956 semi-finals while the other games in those years were between Newcastle & York (played at Hillsborough, replay at Roker Park) and Birmingham v Sunderland (Hillsborough). The 1957 semi-finals were between Manchester United and Birmingham City (Hillsborough), and Aston Villa

Kevin Keegan played in the controversial all-Merseyside semi-final of 1977.

Maine Road's FA Cup Semi-Finals

Date	Match	Attendance
2/4/28	**Huddersfield T. 1-0 Sheffield Utd** (2nd Replay)	69,360
27/3/46	**Birmingham City 0-4 Derby County** (Replay)	*80,480
12/4/47	**Burnley 1-0 Liverpool**	72,000
25/3/50	**Liverpool 2-0 Everton**	72,000
10/3/51	**Birmingham City 0-0 Blackpool**	70,000
21/3/53	**Bolton Wanderers 4-3 Everton**	75,000
27/3/54	**Sheffield Wednesday 0-2 Preston NE**	75,213
22/3/58	**Blackburn Rovers 1-2 Bolton Wanderers**	74,800
26/3/60	**Sheffield Wednesday 1-2 Blackburn Rovers**	74,135
7/4/73	**Leeds United 1-0 Wolverhampton W**	52,505
9/4/75	**Birmingham City 0-1 Fulham** (Replay)	35,205
23/4/77	**Liverpool 2-2 Everton**	52,637
27/4/77	**Liverpool 3-0 Everton** (Replay)	52,579
31/3/79	**Manchester United 2-2 Liverpool**	53,069
17/4/85	**Manchester United 2-1 Liverpool**	45,775
8/4/90	**Manchester United 3-3 Oldham**	44,026
11/4/90	**Manchester United 2-1 Oldham** (Replay)	35,005

Record attendance for midweek game between two Football League clubs, outside of Wembley.

v West Bromwich Albion (St. Andrew's). The same pattern is true for other periods.

The first semi-finals the ground could have staged were in 1924, however City faced Newcastle in one match while the other was between Aston Villa and Burnley (Bramall Lane). This match could have been played in Manchester, however the FA believed holding the tie in Lancashire would give Burnley an advantage.

Of the matches played at Maine Road, it's clear the 1946 Birmingham v Derby tie and the meeting between Huddersfield and Sheffield United in 1928 are the most significant in terms of the ground's story, however when attendance figures are considered it is clear Maine Road has staged some of the most watched games outside of Wembley. Only one other League venue – Stamford Bridge – has held an attendance in excess of eighty thousand.

City fan Sean Riley remembers attending a 1970s Cup replay at Maine Road: "One memory, which I have from a game not involving City, was the FA Cup semi-final replay between Birmingham City and Fulham. As season ticket holders, we were able to apply for our seats in Block C of the Main Stand. I think there were about 35,000 people at the game, with 34,000 of them coming from Birmingham! We decided to support the underdogs, and I

remember well how the Fulham goalie, Peter Mellor, kept the Brummies at bay almost single-handedly. I saw Bobby Moore play that night as well. The Fulham goal came in extra time, and was greeted with almost total silence by the Kippax Stand, where the majority of the Birmingham fans were standing. It was undoubtedly the shock cup result of the season, and it happened at Maine Road."

BBC Commentator John Motson remembers the 1977 meeting between Liverpool and Everton: "This was the first FA Cup semi-final I had commentated on for the BBC and so it was always going to be special. With only a few minutes to go I remember that Everton's Bryan Hamilton managed to get the ball into the net for what would have put Everton into the lead but referee Clive Thomas disallowed it. It was a highly controversial incident and inevitably brought a great deal of attention. For any commentator great goals and terrific play are a delight, but controversial incidents also give you something to focus on. Liverpool won the replay and I went on to commentate on my first FA Cup final for BBC TV. I always enjoyed my visits to Maine Road and I am delighted that some of my key moments as a commentator occurred there."

The actual story of the Everton-Liverpool games of 1977 could make an entire

chapter of this book, however space doesn't allow that. Nevertheless, the incident Motson referred to does require further consideration. When the ball crossed the line most were convinced the goal was legitimate and as soon as the game was over referee Clive Thomas was bombarded with questions from Everton personnel and the media. When asked why the goal was disallowed he simply responded: "There was an infringement. Watch TV tonight… you'll see it then."

Later that night millions tuned in to Match of the Day to look for the answer. What they saw confused them even more. From one TV angle it looked as if Hamilton had been offside, but from another camera the goal looked perfectly legal. It became one of Maine Road's most controversial incidents.

Incidentally, it was estimated City made £60,000 for staging this semi-final – a quarter of the total profit generated by the tie – while over ten thousand fans had been locked out of the first match with a further three thousand waiting in the streets around the ground at the replay. Ticket touts made a considerable profit.

The 1979 meeting between Liverpool and Manchester United was, as far as chairman Peter Swales was concerned, a major landmark in the history of the stadium. At the time he claimed the game was: "Probably the most glamorous semi-final that has ever been played." Clearly this was hyperbole, however Swales was also rightly proud that Maine Road was to host the game. In his column in the semi-final programme he reminded supporters of both clubs that Maine Road had a fine reputation as a semi-final venue and outlined the key games that had taken place there during the 1970s. In fact this was Maine Road's fifth semi-final since 1973.

Another member of the McAlpine family, Alfred McAlpine, son of Sir Robert, was credited as being a City supporter.

Sir Robert McAlpine and Sons made three loans to the Blues early in the history of the stadium, and some stories suggest that on the Monday following each home game a City official would travel to McAlpine's nearest offices on Merseyside with a bag of money. The money would represent a share of the gate receipts and the City official would count out the cash to a member of McAlpine's staff. To ensure McAlpine's interests were looked after City had agreed to allow a McAlpine's representative on to the Board. William Menzies Shaw joined the City Board in 1926 and worked with the club on various ground improvement plans and on finance issues.

Eric Alexander, a former Chairman of the club and a director for many years, remembers that McAlpine's did provide support: "I seem to recall, although I would need to check the specific details, that we paid off the final instalment of the McAlpine loan during my time as Chairman. It must have been during the summer of 1973. The interesting point here though is that we did at least own the stadium. I suppose the McAlpine's loans were similar to a mortgage lasting fifty years, and when we paid that off in 1973 we were probably the only football club to have full ownership of its stadium."

Clearly, the financial position of the club in 1973 – the year Peter Swales succeeded Eric Alexander as Chairman - was very strong, but for those years prior to 1973 the McAlpine's loans may well have dictated how the club managed its expenditure.

In February 1930 Maine Road hosted its second neutral FA Cup game. The match was a fourth round second replay between Middlesbrough and Charlton Athletic and ended 1-0 to the north-eastern side, but the crowd was a miserly 16,676.

During May 1930 Cliff Stevenson, a City fan who was nine at the time and lived on Wansford Street opposite the ground, witnessed a remarkable sight when an airship, the R100 flew over the stadium. Cliff was a pupil at the school on the corner of Claremont Road and Maine Road and in May 2003 told City fan Dave Miller what he saw. Dave: "As Cliff was out in the playground he saw the nose of the R100 airship above his head. At the same time the tail was still above the halfway line at the ground. I've been amazed by Cliff's story and decided to find out more. This incredible flying machine was 709 feet (216m) from tip to tail and at its mid-section measured 130 feet (39m) in diameter. The interior contained fifteen gas-bags carrying over five million cubic feet of hydrogen, underneath was a carriage carrying the crew – about five people I believe and up to forty-five passengers. It could travel up to 83 miles per hour."

Dave's research has uncovered that the R100 travelled over Manchester on 22nd May 1930 at 11.30am, and that its sister ship the R101 had been expected to fly over the city the previous December. When the R100 traversed Manchester the city was mesmerised. Remember at this point in history few aeroplanes ever travelled across the city and the R100 was simply one of the most incredible sights around. According to the *Evening News*: "When the airship appeared, Manchester was taken by surprise. She was flying so low that the noise of her engines drew thousands of people to mill and office roofs and windows. The airship's number could be plainly seen. In the suburbs, housewives ran to their doors. The dirigible

Bolton's Gubbins scores the winner against Blackburn (in stripes) in 1958.

The Ground Committee

■ There is a band of men who, over the years, have contributed a great deal to the success of Maine Road without ever really receiving the credit they deserve. This band of unsung heroes forms the Manchester City Ground Committee – an organisation involved in the stewarding and development of Maine Road since the stadium opened in 1923. Prior to 1923 of course the Ground Committee were responsible for Hyde Road.

The Ground Committee lost a great deal of importance in recent years as the nature of policing and stewarding the stadium has altered since the late 1980s, however for most of City's history the Committee has been a very important organisation.

In 1975 club historian Bill Miles outlined the history and role of the Ground Committee: "It was formed in 1894 and all members of the committee are shareholders of the club and voluntary workers. In fact many past members of the committee have become directors of the club. The duties of the committee are the housing, comfort and control of spectators. We've always been proud of our tremendous record for crowd management. Some members are the third generation of their families to serve on the committee. People like Eric Kay, and David Homer who looks after the official car park.

"I was invited on to the Ground Committee by the late Alan Douglas [former Chairman] and I've really enjoyed it. Our social functions are the highlight of the year. We still have the traditional hotpot, but now it's graduated from a small room in a local pub to a plush affair for 150 people with guest speakers. We also have our bowling day every year, but we're considering cancelling the event next year if City secretary Bernard Halford enters again. He's won it for the past three years!"

In the days before the Hillsborough disaster the Ground Committee were also responsible for stewarding. Back in 1975 the organisation of stewards was becoming more of a police issue than a club issue, although the Committee were extremely well organised. Many Committeemen felt their approach was more appropriate than the perceived 'heavy-handedness' of the police. In 1975 the introduction of specific stewarding clothing surprised the Committee. Bill: "The stewards are easily recognisable these days with their fluorescent jackets which were issued on police instructions. I must admit they didn't go down well with some stewards at first. Professional men, of which we have a number, resented having to wear a jacket. In fact, some resigned. But I'm happy to say they relented and were back on duty recently. After all it's for their own good they wear the jackets. The police can easily spot them and help if any problems arise.

"There are around fifty stewards - 24 in the North Stand and 22 in Platt Lane. Members of the Ground Committee look after the directors' box, the main entrance and the official car park."

The Committee in 1975 consisted of fifteen members with three honorary members. Walter Nugent had been Committee chairman for ten years, while other figures included secretary Eric Kay – who was still serving at the ground during its final season, Fred Mars, and the treasurer was Alwyn Noden who was still a Maine Road regular in 2003. Other committeemen over the years have included both Albert Alexander junior and senior, and Lawrence Furniss, John Schofield and Eric Palmer.

Although modern safety concerns and security issues have reduced the perceived importance of the committee, a small group continued to assist with the match day organisation of the ground through to Maine Road's demise in 2003. Their importance to the stadium's history cannot be stressed enough.

Above: Bill Miles (left) and Eric Kay of the Ground Committee photographed in 1975. Eric Kay was still serving on the committee during Maine Road's final season and his family had been involved with the committee since the Hyde Road days.

came over Corporation Street and Cross Street and, watched by thousands of eyes, circled round the Town Hall with a wide and graceful sweep. It was a beautiful sight, the sun glinting brilliantly on the airship's hull."

The airship's future was not as brilliant as the day, unfortunately, and after its sister-ship exploded in France the following October Britain decided not to pursue airship developments.

By that time City were clearly Manchester's dominant force, while Maine Road always housed the greater crowds. The Maine Road derby of 4th October 1930 ended 4-1 to the Blues but the attendance was a disappointing 41,757 plus season ticket holders. This was still more than the return fixture at Old Trafford (won 3-1 by City), but was an indication the derby was no longer as even a contest as it had previously been and therefore crowds suffered. According to Ivan Sharpe, writing for the Athletic News: "Manchester United have become the football which the fates are kicking. It was like visiting day at the hospital, the visitors being nearly 45,000 strong."

With City a comfortable 4-0 up Sharpe commented: "The City obviously grew sympathetic and declined to rub it in, so that after Spence had headed a clever goal, the game became a drab runabout and everyone welcomed the end."

This Maine Road match saw the end of United as any kind of football force for almost two decades. The Blues capitalised on United being in Division Two, and Maine Road gained as a result.

Supporters were clearly enjoying life at Maine Road, although sometimes they would come under threat from an unlikely source. In 1984 Harry Godwin, City's chief scout in the Mercer-Allison era, told of the exploits of goalkeeper Lewis Barber: "Back in the thirties Barber was a bit of a character. He had his hair swept back and one

Right: The players get ready for a training run around the perimeter of the pitch. Two of City's greatest captains, Jimmy McMullan and Sam Cowan, are on the left of this photograph.

RECORD OF THE MANCHESTER CITY GROUND COMMITTEE

The Ground Committee was formed in the year 1894.
All members are Shareholders and voluntary workers.

Duties

The duties of the Ground Committee are entirely confined to the control and supervision of the spectators, and in no way do they interfere with the managerial side of the Club.

Record of Membership

There are still three members of the present Committee who joined at its inception 35 years ago. They are : Messrs. A. Windsor, H. Wood and C. Schwarz. Two other members, Messrs. Bennett and Denson, have 34 years' service. Other records of service are, one member 21 years, two members 20 years, four members 15 years, and three members 10 years.

Office Holders

Mr. S. Boswell, 21 consecutive years as Chairman. Mr. Windsor, 21 years Secretary, Chairman and present President. Mr. Hubball, 18 years Treasurer. Mr. Schwarz, 19 years Assistant Secretary and Secretary.

Directorate

Since its formation nine members of the Ground Committee have become Directors of the Club. The past Directors were Messrs. Healy, Forrest, Prowse, Royle, Chilton Boswell and Moon, and on the present Board, Messrs. Alexander and Smith.

Records

The City ground holds the record in England (outside Wembley) for attendances, the figures being 76,600, 73,000, 72,000 and 68,300. The management of the record crowd of 76,600 was mentioned in the House of Commons by the Rt. Hon. J. R. Clynes after the fiasco which occurred on the occasion of the Cup Final at Wembley.

The Ground Committee are also responsible for collections of £50 for the Meehan (the ex-Manchester United player who died in London) Fund, and of £117 for the widow of the late Sam Wynne (Oldham). Of this latter sum £98 was in copper.

Particulars of the organization of the Ground Committee have been sought by eight League Clubs, and also one Irish Club. Its policy has always been constructive, and non-interference with Executive affairs. Hence its continuous record of excellent work. Mr. H. Wood was appointed chairman, Mr. H. Irlam secretary and Mr. F. Barnes assistant secretary in 1930.

The Shareholders' Association has had almost an equally long career. It came into being when matters were not going well with the Club, and has undoubtedly been of service. The present Executive includes Mr. J. H. Westbrook (President), Mr. W. H. Whinnerah (Chairman), and Messrs. J. Stephens (the ever-green), C. Schwarz (who has three occupations in life, Fur, Football and Flowers), F. Jolly, W. Smith, and W. Leah (committee).

Another instance of long service is R. Roden, who became a gateman in 1888, and for 11 years was in charge of the Boys' Gate—their record being 3,200. After 42 years he is still serving, and also has a son on the staff.

105

Above: These comments from 1930 reveal that the handling of the 1924 Cardiff match - a record crowd at the time - was mentioned in Parliament.

particular day he wasn't having the best of games. A couple of fellas in the crowd shouted some abuse and Barber leapt over the wall and started to sort them out! Can you imagine a player jumping in to the crowd like that!"

A few exceptionally large attendances witnessed City's matches during the 1930s as can be seen by the cup run of 1931-2 when 56,190 watched a 6-1 demolition of Brentford in the fourth round, followed by a 3-0 defeat of Derby witnessed by 62,641. Fred Tilson scored a hat-trick against Brentford as City continued their reputation as one of England's best supported clubs.

The following November Maine Road hosted its first representative match as the Football League played the Scottish League. Although Scotland won the game 3-0, the match is significant as it proved Maine Road was viewed as a major venue. One of the reasons for this may have been the development of the corner between Platt Lane and the Main Stand. This area of the ground was quite popular, and during 1931 the club's first major development since the opening of the ground occurred. For some time complaints had been received about the limited amount of cover and so a decision was taken to redevelop the corner and build a roof.

Over the years the development of this corner has been largely forgotten, with supporters believing the corner section was erected at the same time as the rest of the Platt Lane Stand, but it was not so. Designs from March 1931 show elaborate plans for Maine Road's new corner stand. Architect Charles Swain submitted one plan which would have provided the club with considerable prestige. This included the erection of triangular gables on both the pitch side of the stand and the external view. The gables would have been positioned directly over the tunnel.

The plans also included the complete re-profiling of the terracing to enable it to match exactly the tread of the Main Stand. In addition the terracing would be extended further backwards, first with concrete and then an additional eleven steps would be made out of wood.

A new exit vomitory would also be erected between the tunnel and the Main Stand, positioned within the extended terracing. At the base of this would be two new ladies' toilets.

The section of terracing closest to the Main Stand – in its final years (late 1980s/early 1990s) this became the club's first Family Stand – was to be furnished with bench seats consistent with those positioned in various areas of the Main Stand.

According to the original plan, further seating would have been erected on the wooden steps across the entire back of this corner stand. These would be very basic bench seats with no backs, although this plan could not possibly have been seriously considered as those sitting on the eleven rows of benches would not have been able to see over the heads of those stood in front. It's likely this part of the plan may have simply been Swain's method of testing whether the club were interested in further increasing the seating capacity. Perhaps he held a view the stand should have been entirely seated. Certainly by increasing the terracing tread and by making such grand plans for the roof, Swain must have viewed this as a significant development.

The capacity of this new corner stand was to be 6,830 standing and 950 seated, however this may not have been the final figure as it is unclear whether this includes the proposed additional bench seating at the back. Considering the size of the terracing it is likely this figure does exclude the proposed rear seating.

The development created changes to the tunnel. Firstly it had to be extended a little so that its external end matched with the new exterior walling of the stand. Secondly, the re-profiling of the steps meant the tunnel walls were now too low. The parapet had to be raised.

Also, because the terracing was now higher than that behind the goal, a small staircase led from the back of the corner terracing down to the older Platt Lane terracing. Metal railings were erected the full length of the raised terracing to ensure supporters' safety.

The roof of the stand was held up by four new stanchions plus a connection to the nearest stanchion at the edge of the Main Stand.

The new corner stand when complete may have slightly increased the capacity of the ground, but more importantly what the corner stand actually did was to raise the status of Maine Road further. The stadium was only eight years old but it now contained covered seated accommodation for a little over 10,000 plus covered terracing for a figure quoted at almost 7,000. A further 60 to 70,000 could be accommodated on the uncovered terracing.

Swain's corner stand development may well have been consistent with his original development plan. The first published proposals had said City would build the stadium in two phases with the first phase creating a 15,000 seated grandstand with covered terracing holding 55,000 looping around the three other sides. In the end a smaller stand was built, but larger uncovered terracing was erected in the first phase.

The idea of a second phase still existed and it's possible Swain's corner stand was part of a more ambitious plan. Of the few Maine Road plans in existence, one does exist from March 1931 which shows a corner stand – of the style designed for the Platt Lane corner – positioned on the other side (the Scoreboard/Main Stand corner) of the Main Stand. In addition, a Swain produced design for a full Platt Lane Stand exists from this same period. Did Swain try to persuade the other City officials that the time had come to start phase two of his grand plan?

Only the Platt Lane corner was developed in 1931, and its clear the original plans for the ground – or at the very least a modified version of those plans – were still the template for the stadium's development. The corner stand was completed in August 1931, although the Manchester Evening News pointed out on the 24th August that the stand had not been completed in time for a practice match attended by 12,560 a couple of days earlier (City's senior team beat the Reserves 6-4 with David Halliday scoring five). It did state, however, that it anticipated completion before the first home League game on 29th August 1931 against Sunderland.

On 26th August details of the new stand pricing structure was announced: "The new extension to the stand will be ready and those who desire to use it will

Right: A 1932 press call sees Sam Cowan, Matt Barrass and Len Langford wrestling on the pitch (top) and boxing in the original Maine Road Gym. Seventy years after the opening of the stadium, the gym, positioned under the Main Stand, became the Joe Mercer Suite.

Below: This 1968 photo shows the external walling of the 1931 Platt Lane Corner roof, and the original turnstile entrances. Notice the sign for 'G' Block (closest to the Main Stand) - additional seating was installed in this section in 1931 while the rest of the corner remained terracing. The stand had also been extended a few feet towards Maine Road. The colour photograph, taken in 1981, shows the 1931 roof (the section with adverts for Covonia and DER), and the remodelled tunnel.

transfer when they have paid to get into the ground. They will pay a shilling extra for a seat and 6d for the standing accommodation under cover, but at Central League matches it is not the intention to make any further charge for the standing accommodation. This does not apply to the seats.

"Season tickets are going well, and all who still need them are urged to apply to the office before Saturday to avoid inconvenience."

Late in 2002 supporter Harry Bramble remembered standing in this corner for a League meeting with Huddersfield. The game was played on 31st October 1931 and resulted in a 3-0 City win: "We called it the Boys' Corner and there was a railing at the edge of the stand. The rail was to stop you from getting into the stand from the terracing. When play was at the opposite end of the ground the only way of seeing clearly what was happening was by pulling yourself up the railing. I pulled myself up and hung on to the railing for the entire match. I daren't lose my spot. Now, because it was such a wet day there was water everywhere, and when I went home my sleeve and all down that side of my body was wet. My mother wasn't too happy, but I told her I couldn't let go!

"Huddersfield had a centre-forward called Jennings in this match and he was a very dangerous player. He worried us."

The new corner, though it may appear relatively minor in relation to modern ground developments, was a major investment by the club. It was also proof, if any were needed, that City took the development of Maine Road seriously. This corner, together with other developments over the course of the following couple of years, would enhance the stadium's reputation enormously.

Maine Men The Alexander Family

■ The Alexander family have been linked with Manchester City since the formation of the club in 1894, and during that time three members of the family have held important positions within the City hierarchy - a memorable achievement.

ERIC ALEXANDER, the third generation to become a director at the club, is aware of how much City has always meant to his family: "Both my grandfathers were members of the club when it was originally formed, with Albert Alexander being a member of the ground committee. He became a director in 1912. He was a board member until 1953 when he died.

"Of course the family owned horse-trams and Hansom cabs in Manchester and so when City won the FA Cup in 1904 he drove the team around Manchester on his horse-drawn coach. Incredibly, when United won the Cup five years later, they asked him to do the same for them."

ALBERT ALEXANDER SENIOR was perhaps the first family member to become a familiar figure to most supporters. An article in January 1933 reminded supporters of some aspects to his City career: "One of the hardiest veterans in football is surely Mr. A. Alexander, a director of the Manchester City Club. He joined the club in an official capacity 39 years ago, was a member of the ground committee for eighteen years, and has been a director for the last twenty-one years.

"Mr. Alexander has never missed a match through illness – the only games he has missed have been on occasions when scouting for the City – and at 65 he is as active as many men at half that age."

Albert Alexander certainly did make his mark. For many years he was the club's vice-chairman, and took on considerable duties to help the club develop. On several occasions the opportunity to become Chairman had arisen, but each time Albert allowed others to take the role. He wanted the club to develop more than anything else and felt he would not be an appropriate Chairman. That is a major shame as it is clear from his other activities he would have been a most appropriate leader. Eric Alexander: "He always felt he didn't have the education to carry out the role. He had left school at thirteen I believe and, despite being a perfectly

respectable and well-mannered man and an excellent speaker, he simply felt he didn't have the right academic background to lead a club like City. It is a shame really because he would probably have done an excellent job. He was also an alderman and could have been Lord Mayor of Manchester but refused that honour for the same reason."

During 1925-6 Albert was thrust into the spotlight a little when he was placed in charge of the first team. City were managerless and, rather than make a permanent appointment, the club turned to Albert. Clearly this may seem a little odd in terms of modern day football, however it should be stressed Albert was a highly knowledgeable football man. In fact it's clear he possessed more knowledge of footballing matters than many secretary-managers of the period.

According to a 1930s profile written in an official club booklet: "He [Albert] was placed by his colleagues in charge of the League team. Had the good fortune of taking them to Wembley for the English Cup Final and the bad luck to see them lose 1-0 by 'a flick of the fingers'."

The article should have also highlighted that Albert's City side defeated United 6-1 at Old Trafford (the largest score in a Manchester derby), and also defeated the Reds in the 1926 FA Cup semi-final. Sadly, the Blues were also relegated that season.

Away from football Albert was a councillor for Ardwick and enjoyed playing golf. He was also a visiting justice and frequent visitor to Strangeways prison where he would talk with prisoners and generally show real concern for every area of society.

The Lancashire FA made him a vice-president in tribute to 21 years' membership, while City made him club president in 1951. He died in October 1953 and his death was reported in the Manchester Evening News edition of 14th October 1953 – the day City's floodlights were used for the first time.

The second member of the Alexander family to make his mark at Maine Road was ALBERT ALEXANDER JUNIOR. Like his father, Albert was a keen member of City's backroom staff for many years. He worked on the Ground Committee and managed City's 'A' team, and was generally eager to work through the ranks to help

Above: Albert Alexander Senior.

Right: An invitation to a 'Hot Pot Supper' in 1934 where Albert Alexander Senior's 21 years service were to be honoured.

Below: The Directors pictured in 1968. They are (left to right) Walter Griffiths (secretary), Chris Muir, Sidney Rose, Albert Alexander junior, Frank Johnson, John Humphrys, Eric Alexander, and Joe Mercer (manager).

The Directors of the
Manchester City Football Club
request the pleasure of the company of
Mr. A. V. Alexander

to a Hot Pot Supper at the
Stock Exchange Restaurant, Cross St., Manchester,
on Thursday evening, 15th November 1934,
at 6 p.m. for 6-15 p.m., on the occasion of
Presentations to A. Alexander, Esq. J.P.
(on completing 21 years as a Director of the Club,)
and to the Cup Winning Team.

MAINE ROAD.
MOSS SIDE.
R.S.V.P.   MANCHESTER. 14.

W. WILD.
SECRETARY-MANAGER.

City's success. Albert's son Eric remembers his father's love of football: "He was a very good footballer and cricketer but he was gassed in the Great War and had to give it up. It affected him throughout his life, although it's fair to say he recovered enough to fulfil a happy normal life apart from playing of course. He took up golf, but his love for football was such that he started the 'A' team at City. He started it in 1921 and ran it right through until 1963. He enjoyed working with the youngsters and developing them. He gained an awful lot of satisfaction from that, particularly when players like Matt Busby developed their skills and style as part of the 'A' team."

Above and right:
After Maine Road's last Manchester derby, former Chairman Eric Alexander took a few moments to consider what Maine Road meant to him.

Eventually, after many years of loyal service Albert Alexander junior became City's Chairman, and it's fair to say City's most successful spell was during his period at the top. Alexander guided City through the successful years of the Mercer-Allison period and was probably the first Chairman to be known – and more importantly liked - by the majority of supporters. Joe Mercer in particular was always complimentary about the support received from 'Little Albert'.

Albert understood every aspect of the club and at one point during his Chairmanship stressed that above all else: "I have always been a players' man." The comment was simple and to the point but behind it lay a lifetime's involvement with the club. He could never be accused of being involved in football purely for the prestige because he had carried out many, many behind-the-scenes tasks with the club over the years. Journalist Bill Fryer was a fan of Albert's and writing in 1970 he said: "He is highly revered in the game and by the public, and I have no doubt good deals have been done for City out of Albert's friendships because in reality the whole of football is a 'club'."

The third member of the family to make an impact was Albert's son Eric. As with his father and grandfather, Eric became involved with many aspects at the club: "I can remember my first visits to Maine Road as a young boy. I remember going into the kitchen with the steward Harry Clark. He gave me a bottle of pop and Sam Barkas, City's great captain, came in and ruffled my hair. They all knew me as Young Albert's son and it was thrilling to see the players behind the scenes. I was accepted in to the community from the start because of both my father and grandfather – Old Albert."

Like his father, Eric was keen on football from an early age and played for City's junior sides in preference to playing for his school side. After a spell in the airforce Eric had trained to be a commercial artist but continued to play football for various teams. Once his own playing days were over he became increasingly involved with the reserves and young players. Inevitably Eric joined the Board and continued his interest in the reserve sides, but also took on responsibility for other areas of the club, such as the pitch. "I worked with Stan Gibson to ensure we improved the pitch and I would push to find the appropriate funding. We became the first side to fit an automatic sprinkler system, and we also churned the entire pitch up. We dug up the top twelve inches or so in a bid to give the club a surface it could be proud of. Over the years the soil had compacted and was extremely poor from a drainage point of view, and so we took advice and brought in sand from the north-east and brought in soil. Then we re-sowed the pitch and by the time the new season started it was superb."

Eric was also involved with installation of the undersoil heating development, and many other forward-thinking initiatives during the 1960s and 1970s. He was also a key player in the redevelopment of the Scoreboard End into the North Stand, and had also pushed to see the Kippax redeveloped and City's training facilities improved. Not all of Eric's initiatives were followed up by the club, however it is clear that his ideas were all for the betterment of both Maine Road and the Blues.

During Maine Road's final season Eric, as an Honorary President, but more importantly as a fan, continued to attend matches and support his club. He is delighted his family have been so involved with the ground's development over the years, and is keen to see City surge forward at the new stadium.

In summary, the contribution the Alexanders have made to City's history is immense. It is highly unlikely any other family could have had such an involvement with a major English football club throughout its history.

Cult Heroes

■ There are some players who, immediately on arrival at Maine Road, achieved cult status at the club. Sometimes the reasons were obvious – a great performance, a promotion-winning goal, a rare talent – while at other times it was not so clear-cut. There have been many cult figures over the years, and here we highlight a small selection.

One of the earliest Maine Road men to achieve cult status was TOMMY JOHNSON. Johnson was an incredibly talented player who shares the record for most League goals (158) by a City man, but in March 1930 was transferred to Everton. Maine Road regulars demonstrated against the departure and the average attendance dropped by 8,000. Worse was to follow when in 1933 he helped Everton achieve a Cup final victory over the Blues.

In May 2003 Tommy's son Alan remembered his father's popularity: "It was two-way really. The

supporters enjoyed his style of play and his determination, but he also recognised their loyalty and commitment. The day he was told he was leaving he was absolutely stunned. He had no idea he was going to leave. We lived in Park Avenue, Gorton, at the time and he didn't want to go, but he had met Dixie Dean the great Everton star a few times and, because of Dixie, he felt that if he had to go somewhere it was better to go where he knew someone.

"At Everton he had a lot of success but City remained his club. Sometimes he'd bring Dixie Dean back to our house in Gorton and the two of them would go around pubs like The Plough and the others in the area. In fact Dixie became as well known in the pubs of Gorton as my Dad was.

"After he'd left City he kept coming back here and sometimes paid to stand on the Kippax side of the ground. If he was ever recognised he was always congratulated simply for being 'Tosh' Johnson!"

In the late 1960s he was a season ticket holder during City's rebirth under Mercer and Allison, and in the years in between a whole breed of heroes had come and gone.

In 1962 forward ALEX HARLEY arrived from Third Lanark in Scotland. He netted 23 goals in 40 League appearances during a period when the Blues desperately needed a hero, and is acknowledged as the first player ever to have his name chanted at the ground, although older supporters claim to have developed particular 'shouts' for players such as Eric Brook ('Brookie') and other stars of the twenties and thirties.

Harley only managed the one season with City which, in many ways, effectively guaranteed his status as a cult figure.

Another cult hero with a one-season career at Maine Road was MARK LILLIS. Lillis was not a great City player but he typified the spirit of the mid-80s. He was a Blue through and through and it was obvious to all he shared the same passion for the club as the supporters on the Kippax. In fact he had been a Kippax regular himself (critics suggested he should have remained on the terraces instead of on the pitch, but that's a little unfair).

Lillis gave his all and his first City match at Maine Road saw him score a goal and then perform a bizarre and difficult to describe celebration with his arm to the Kippax – it later became his trademark.

Around this time City fans' penchant for the local hero was much in evidence with PAUL MOULDEN the best example. 'Goalden Moulden' was the record-breaking youth player who burst into the first team in 1986. For City fans he could do no wrong and was a joy to watch, but he wasn't the only local hero. Other examples include TOMMY CATON, NICKY REID, PETER BARNES, GARY OWEN, MICHAEL HUGHES, and virtually every member of the 1986 Youth team.

One surprising cult figure from the 1980s was JOHN GIDMAN. It was very unusual for any former Manchester United player to be accepted at Maine Road, particularly during the 80s and 90s, but Gidman seemed to go out of his way to win over the fans. It helped that his first game was a 1-1 Maine Road draw with United which allowed him to 'get stuck in' and show he was no longer red, but

Above: Cult heroes Paul Dickov and Ian Bishop.

Below: Alex Harley, Nicky Reid and John Gidman.

Left: Maine Road's first hero Tommy Johnson.

Above and below:
Supporters pay homage to
Shaun Goater and Uwe
Rösler at Maine Road's
final game.

he also seemed to know what to say to the fans. He
stated publicly how City were the only side he would
leave Old Trafford for, and when he joined City added:
"There was nowhere else I wanted to go. As soon as I
met the lads I knew I was in the right place with the right
people. I am delighted to get this chance to play for
City."

IAN BISHOP was perhaps the biggest cult figure of
the 1980s. This was amazing as it was initially perceived
he'd replaced local hero Moulden and was under greater
pressure than most new recruits. Too many believe he

became a hero simply because of his role in City's 5-1
win over United, but that isn't entirely accurate as
supporters recognised Bishop's determination right from
the start of his Maine Road career. When he left, after
only 19 League games, his cult status was cemented.

In recent years UWE RÖSLER and GEORGI
KINKLADZE became major City figures. With both men it
was down to key performances on the pitch. These were
difficult days for City, and Rösler and Kinkladze helped
bring some much-needed joy to the Blues. Rösler's
displays, particularly alongside Paul Walsh during the
Brian Horton era, were extremely entertaining while
Kinkladze was, for many people, the only reason to
watch the Blues during the struggles of the Alan Ball and
Frank Clark days.

Another more recent hero was PAUL DICKOV. He
achieved cult status directly as a result of his never-say-
die attitude, and his goal at Wembley in 1999 typified his
City career, but wasn't the only time he'd saved the club.
His earlier equaliser in the first leg of the play-off semi-
final at Springfield Park, and his spirit and fighting
qualities, helped change a number of League games
between 1996 and 2002.

So who was the last cult figure at Maine Road?
Clearly, the real hero of Maine Road's final years has got
to be SHAUN GOATER. Goater achieved so much for the
club in the last few seasons that he will be remembered
for a very long time. He may not have been everybody's
idea of a perfect footballer, but he was a perfect hero.
His determination and endeavour for the Blues made him
a major star, while his goalscoring record alone made him
a worthy successor to Maine Road's first cult figure
Tommy Johnson.

Chapter Four

Record
Breaking
Years

Whew! 'Record' is too mild – this crowd was not only a record – several records in fact – it was a problem. 84,569. That is the figure. And they all came to see Manchester City and Stoke City battle out a cup-tie at Maine-road, Manchester, yesterday.

Oh yes, it was a record all right. A record for Maine-road and a record for any match (London and its teeming millions included) outside a cup final or international match in this country. The £5,426 receipts were also well ahead of Maine Road's best.

The *Sunday Graphic and Sunday News*, 4th March 1934.

B Y the end of 1932 Maine Road's reputation as a major stadium was substantial. The people of Manchester were proud of their ground yet once it started to be used for key neutral matches it was soon known nationally. The large City crowds brought the club considerable income and, apart from a figure of around £200 spent on general maintenance each year plus the regular mortgage payments, the club had little need to invest in ground developments, although it's clear some, most notably Charles Swain, harboured desires to continually improve the ground.

The seated capacity at a little over 10,000 was sufficient and still quite large in comparison to several First Division clubs, while the terracing was clearly still in very good condition. The major area of weakness concerned covered accommodation for standing spectators and, as non-Mancunians like to point out, Manchester does have a reputation for rain.

The only cover existed at the Platt Lane corner but, as this only housed around 6,800, it was still insufficient. Swain's plans to further develop the ground had been put on hold for the time being. However by the summer of 1933 the directors were seriously considering further improvements for standing fans. The obvious answer was

a roof, erected on one of the open ends – as Swain had suggested - or across the large Popular Side. The costs were calculated and the Popular Side discounted immediately. The terracing on that side curved too much towards the corners to be easily covered, and the cost of squaring off the terracing would probably have been too great at the time. Remember McAlpine's were still providing the club with much financial support.

This meant the club could either roof the other Main Stand corner, or cover one of the two ends as Swain suggested. Even then the curving nature of these stands meant alterations to the terracing which the club felt unable to undertake at this time. In addition it's possible plans put forward by Swain would involve increasing the rake of the terracing to be consistent with that in the corner.

Possibly the directors felt an increase in terracing – which the squaring-off of either stand would require – was not justified as the capacity of around 86,000 had not been met. In addition, apart from occasional comments in the media and by the Lancashire FA, little was said about this lack of cover. Mancunians were hardier than most it seemed!

After considering all the options Maine Road was

Right: Eric Brook demonstrates his culinary expertise in the Maine Road kitchen.

Below: Sam Cowan takes a shot in City's Billiard Room at Maine Road. The Billiard Room eventually became the Players' Lounge and then in the mid 1980s was redeveloped as the Executive Suite.

Maine Men Wilf Wild

ROLE: Secretary & Manager

■ Wilf Wild was a loyal and hardworking club servant. He joined the Blues as assistant secretary in 1920 and remained at the club until his death in 1950, but in between he achieved considerably more than any summary of his career can hope to relate.

The key story of Wild's time is undoubtedly the success he brought the club as manager during the 1930s, however the key role he had in the history of Maine Road is what this feature focuses on.

As assistant to Ernest Mangnall, Wild had a major part to play in the move from Hyde Road to Maine Road in 1923. Wild's first duties inevitably focused on the issues of crowd management and ground development.

After the Hyde Road fire of 1920 Wild helped Mangnall search for a new venue and, after rejecting Old Trafford and Belle Vue, the club decided to build Maine Road. As with the move to the City of Manchester Stadium in 2003, the move to Maine Road required substantial planning and much of that fell to Mangnall and Wild to perform. It was not easy.

Immediately after moving City's great pulling power ensured Maine Road was tested a great deal, again this impacted on both Mangnall and Wild who, with the support of Chairman Lawrence Furniss, basically ran the entire club.

The development of Platt Lane in 1931 and in 1935 would have been major activities undertaken by Wild at the time.

Wild was a great advocate of splitting the role of secretary and manager. It's difficult to fully articulate how the various footballing roles worked in the inter-war period, however it is fair to say that the man regarded as the manager was also responsible for every aspect of the day-to-day running of the club – paying wages, stadium developments, match day control…. you name it, the manager did it. In fact the only aspect the manager never quite got to grips with in those days was the actual coaching of the players. This was left to a 'trainer' who, invariably, was a former player who simply told the players to do the same things he'd been told to do twenty years earlier.

A good illustration of Wild's role came on a match day in the immediate post-war period. Player Johnny Hart – a man associated with City at various levels from office boy in 1944 through to manager in the 1970s – remembers the pressure Wild was under: "On a match day he was always, always busy. First there'd be the general office work. Then something connected with the ground. He was always on the go. As office boy I'd help of course, but he was the man in charge. It was his responsibility. I vividly remember him giving a team talk – obviously not the long drawn-out affair you'd get today. It was more along the lines of 'watch the first five minutes and the last five, and don't do anything silly', but it was appropriate for the time.

"Anyway, he'd then break away from the players, leave the dressing room, and head off down the tunnel. At the front of the tunnel he'd pick up the tannoy system microphone and would make an announcement: 'Could those of you on the Popular Side please move along into the centre. We're expecting sixty thousand here today so if you'd be so kind as to move along then everybody will get a good view'. Then he'd watch the crowd move and then head off back into the dressing room to check on the players."

Wild was clearly not the only football manager to have this multi-faceted role, but in terms of Maine Road's history it is vital his role is understood. Wild was probably the last City manager to take on this all-encompassing position. His successors varied in abilities, but none of them could ever have taken on that many responsibilites in the successful way Wild did.

In addition to his secretarial prowess, Wild was also City's most successful manager of the pre-Mercer period. He is also the longest serving manager, leading the side from 1932 until the end of the war. Despite the intense pressure, Wild performed exceptionally well in both roles. In 1933 and 1934 he guided the Blues to the FA Cup Final, and off the field found himself responsible for the organisation of the highest attended game at Maine Road - 84,569 v Stoke on 3rd March 1934. The stress on him during 1933-4 must have been immense, however he not only survived but seemed to thrive on it.

In 1936-7 he managed City to their first League Championship and then guided them through the difficulties of war. Eventually, the pressure of the war years and that first post-war season were too much and he stood down for his former captain, Sam Cowan. Wild remained as secretary until his death four years later. His wife Betty was a popular and familiar presence at the club through to retirement in the 1960s.

left to face the 1933-4 season without further change. Ironically, it was this very season which would really test the stadium. The 1933 season had ended with Blues losing to Everton in the FA Cup final and there were high hopes the new campaign would at least match that achievement. In the League, City achieved fifth place, while the Cup-run saw the Blues return to Wembley. This time they managed to lift the trophy with a convincing victory over Portsmouth.

The FA Cup run commenced with a home tie against Blackburn. It was a key moment in the career of 19-year-old goalkeeper Frank Swift, who had made his debut less than three weeks earlier.

A crowd of over 54,336 paid £3,415 to witness a great City performance, even if the tie itself was not as full-blooded an affair as supporters might have wanted. Nevertheless, the early stages proved fairly even with the majority of play in midfield.

Both Swift and his opposite number Cliff Binns were able to relax and watch the action for the first quarter, then City slipped up and Swift realised he was heading for trouble: "Harper, the Rovers' centre-forward broke through the light blue line in front of me. In my nervousness I anticipated too soon and dived before he kicked the ball. To my amazement and delight, the ball hit my right hand – and stuck. The roar of the crowd, as much as the save, helped give me confidence."

The save had been a lucky one, but it was enough to settle Swift. In the 20th minute Eric Brook put City a goal up with a half-volley, but shortly afterwards Bruton headed an equaliser. City remained the more positive side and it was clear that goal would only be a minor irritation. Ernie Toseland restored City's lead, then made it 3-1 midway through the second half. The *Daily Dispatch* reporter was particularly thrilled with the move: "This was a remarkable goal, for Toseland after running into the penalty area got so much power behind his shot that the ball travelled round the netting and came back into play.

"It was one of Toseland's brightest days. With Brook, he was the forward of the match. Though they were rarely extended the City defenders played very

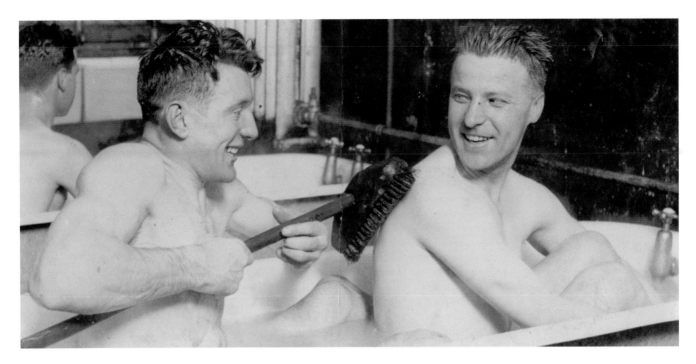

soundly throughout, and Swift made some excellent saves."

At this stage in his career Swift was trying to learn from his opposite number. He watched and tried to understand exactly what was happening at the other end of the field and, with more pressure being exerted at the Blackburn goal, he studied Binns. He witnessed a very good performance from a capable 'keeper. According to the *Dispatch*: "No one could have kept a better goal than Binns. He had not the slightest chance with any of the shots that beat him, and his judgement, courage, and safe handling averted disaster on other occasions when he could not have been blamed had he surrendered."

Overall the *Daily Dispatch* reporter was not impressed with the Blackburn performance: "Bruton headed a glorious goal, but that was all, and the undoubted craft of McLean was never in evidences. Like Harper, he had a very poor match, and apparently the occasion was too much for Duncan."

Thinking about the Blues the reporter added: "There was never any question which way the result would go. The City were the winners from the start. They jumped into their stride right away, and except for the brief period just about the time they scored their goal the Rovers never lived with them.

"Up to the interval there was no comparison between the teams, and if the Rovers did a little better after the change of ends, they were never the equals of their conquerors in skill, pace, and method.

"Though they were rarely extended the City defenders played very soundly throughout, and Swift made some excellent saves."

The victory brought City an awkward away trip to Hull City in the fourth round, but prior to that match they had to face reigning champions Arsenal in the League. Arsenal were already viewed as the team of the decade and were by far the biggest name in English football at the time. They were already topping the table and would go on to end the season as champions – their second of three consecutive successes. Arsenal were certainly the team to play well against, especially with a Maine Road crowd of 60,401 desperate to see a Blue victory.

City excelled, winning 2-1 with all the goals coming

in the second half. Alec Herd and Bobby Marshall scored for the Blues while Pat Beasley netted for the Gunners, but the scoreline was only an indication of how the match had gone. City had played exceptionally well causing Arsenal's goalkeeper Frank Moss a few anxious moments, but earlier the action had mainly been around City's goal. Young Frank Swift, under immense Arsenal pressure, produced a string of marvellous saves to thrill the crowd.

The match with Arsenal usually warrants no more than a footnote in City's history, but in terms of City's development and Maine Road's history it was a major landmark. Arsenal were the team of the 1930s, but the Blues were beginning to match them on occasion. The public recognised this and over the course of the following years this fixture became one of, if not the, biggest games in football. Huge attendances flocked to watch as City-Arsenal matches became a clash of the giants. No other League fixture – not even the rare Manchester derby – could match games with Arsenal during the 1930s.

Two days after the game City went to Southport for cup-tie training. At Hull, City surrendered a two-goal lead and the contest ended 2-2. The replay was watched by an incredibly high Maine Road crowd of 49,042. It says a great deal about the pulling power of City at this point in their history considering this was a midweek match, played in the days before floodlighting or evening kick-offs. How nearly 50,000 Mancunians could afford to take the afternoon off work in such a depressed period is a mystery, but as the season progressed, and City became more successful, the numbers increased still further.

Incidentally Main Stand seats for the replay cost four shillings each and were quickly sold out. Citywon 4-1 but the match was not as easy as the result implies: "Manchester City won their replayed cup-tie with Hull City at Maine Road yesterday, but by no means as comfortably as the score (4-1) seems to suggest. Swift, the Manchester goalkeeper had plenty of work."

Watching the match was Jack Hillman, the goalkeeper during City's 1904 Cup success and one of northern football's early century stars. After the game he sought out City's young 'keeper to congratulate him on a good performance. It's worth noting that articles from

Above: Sam Cowan and Bobby Marshall share a bath at Maine Road. Maine Road's dressing room initially contained a large team bath and two individual baths for a more private bathtime!

Maine Memory

Right: One key feature of Maine Road following its opening in 1923 through until the 1950s was the annual public practice match. These would often attract a great crowd. This match shows goalkeeper Len Langford in action during 1933 with the Popular Side terracing in the background.

around this period mentioned how Hillman owned a shop in Bolton and had on display in his window the ball from the 1904 Cup final. Where that ball is today is a mystery.

One memorable Maine Road match occurred between the Hull tie and the trip to Sheffield Wednesday in the fifth round of the Cup. This was a 5-2 City win against Middlesbrough played out in a dense fog. "Missed in the fog" read one headline which focused on the poor visibility experienced by supporters. "Spectators did not see how Manchester City won" read one report; "Amazing why so many paid to watch", said another.

The attendance was only 22,082, but two weeks later an enormous crowd witnessed the Blues face Sheffield Wednesday. The game was at Hillsborough, but deserves space in this publication because the events of that day do have a bearing on the state of football stadia at the time.

Most Mancunians eagerly awaited the fifth round tie and the hyperbole in Manchester was considerable. Many felt it was their year after the disappointment of the previous season when City fell apart against a Dixie Dean-inspired Everton at Wembley. Thousands were keen to travel to South Yorkshire to support their heroes.

Mancunian pride was at a high at this point and, on the day of the tie, hoardings were removed from Manchester's new all-white £425,000 Central Library to allow Mancunians to see what a prestigious new building their city was getting. This was a major moment in the industrial city's history and it's clear many City fans would have paused on their journey to London Road Railway Station – modern day Piccadilly - to admire the view of such a clean, pristine building in what was otherwise a dark, dismal and dirty city.

Enormous attendances followed City throughout the Thirties and this fifth round tie at Sheffield Wednesday saw a mass exodus from Manchester. They helped to create a Hillsborough record crowd of 72,841 with gate receipts of £5,566. Clearly, this was still less than Maine

Road's record of 76,166 set a decade earlier, but it was still a significant figure and remains Hillsborough's all-time highest attendance.

City fan Joe Carley was one of the many thousands of Mancunians who journeyed to South Yorkshire: "At the ground I joined the queue at one of the two shilling turnstiles (the popular side being almost completely filled), and rumours were rife that the gates were being closed. I pushed in with the crowd, paid my two bob, one other person was allowed in after me and then, no more!

"Things were not very comfortable in some parts of the ground and ambulancemen were kept busy. Just before the teams came out a stretcher party passed bearing the blanketed figure of a man killed in the crush."

Hundreds were injured as the stadium was ill-equipped to deal with such a large crowd, while in the tunnel City's 19 year old 'keeper, Frank Swift, also witnessed the general scenes of mayhem: "After we had changed, and were ready for the field, we found that the narrow tunnel from the dressing room to the pitch was blocked by ambulance men tending groaning casualties. After forcing my way through with the other players, I had to stand aside to let pass a stretcher bearing a man crushed to death against the railings on the Spion Kop."

These were comments Swift made in his 1940s autobiography. They appear rather cold when viewed today, however this says more about the style of football writing in the 1940s than it does about Swift's attitude and compassion. It's worth considering that Hillsborough, both in 1934 and at the time of the disaster in 1989, was viewed as one of England's premier venues with excellent facilities. If this was the best, what conditions were experienced by spectators in the worst?

On the day of the game Hillsborough's capacity was viewed as 75,000 but was this really possible given the crowd control issues? Despite these obstacles, the

players made their way on to the pitch. The match was frenetic but ended 2-2 with the replay the following Wednesday afternoon.

To all concerned the draw was a fair reflection of the game. GWC: "The Hillsborough game has been left behind and we are looking ahead to Wednesday's replay at Maine Road, but I look back and I see a packed ground with nearly 73,000 people overflowing the barriers. I recapture the excitement, the shocks, the hopes and fears for first one side and then the other, and that final satisfaction that all square was fair enough."

Looking back in 1948, Swift felt the game was one of the best he ever played in: "This I think was our toughest match of all on the path to Wembley. It was one of the most amazing games I ever played in. The 72,841 crowd, a record for the Wednesday ground, brought all the sights, scenes and sounds that are only provided by a cup-crazy mob."

The size of the crowd continued to be commented on after the match, although the mention of injured or deceased supporters was disappointingly ignored by the media. The focus was more on how the Wednesday manager Billy Walker 'packed them in'. The *Daily Dispatch* devoted its Gannon cartoon to the cup tie and the first few drawings depicted Walker throwing supporters into the ground and a solitary white horse keeping them in! Further proof, if any were needed, supporters were not treated in the same manner as if they were going to the Music Hall or cinema.

The replay, on Wednesday 21st February, would see City also pack in their fans for another interesting tie. With thousands taking the afternoon off work, the Blues attracted the incredible attendance of 68,614. City won the match 2-0 with two long-range efforts. Frank Swift described how he saw the Blues take the lead: "The two goals were both scored following long free kicks from our half. The first time Fred Tilson waited for the ball to bounce in front of Millership, nipped round the Wednesday centre-half, and went on to score. Bobby Marshall scored the winner in the second half, heading in a forty-yard free kick taken by Dale. Thus we passed on, after inflicting on Wednesday their first defeat in nineteen games."

The build up to the quarter-final with Stoke at Maine Road seemed to increase everyone's desire to attend and the match was watched by an astounding 84,569. Although official figures do not exist it seems likely the crowd was dispersed around the stadium in the following manner:

    Main Stand seats – 9,500
    Platt Lane Corner Stand seats – 2,000
    Platt Lane Corner covered terracing – 6,000
    Platt Lane uncovered – 17,000
    Popular Side uncovered – 28,000
    Scoreboard End uncovered – 22,000

It must have been seriously overcrowded in some areas. Potentially the safest place to be, from a standing perspective would have been the Platt Lane Covered Corner as admission to that area was by additional payment once inside the ground. This meant those watching from the corner would only be allowed in if space allowed. It seems likely this section would have been closed off some time before the main turnstiles were shut down, although it is known that even this area was crowded.

City's victory over Stoke took the Blues to Leeds

Road, Huddersfield – the same venue as the previous season's semi-final. This time their semi-final opponents would be Aston Villa on a wet and windy day. City won 6-1 – another record – while under the inaccurate headline "Huddersfield's Record Crowd" *The Guardian* focused on the scale of City's victory and how the Villa supporters felt in the minority. The report was also littered with references to City's Cambridge blue shirts. Clearly the reporter was a little pre-occupied with the University boat race which took place on the same day. For the record Cambridge – wearing City blue! – won by 4.25 lengths. Incidentally, the report of the boat race took substantially more column space than the two semi-finals. "It was indeed Manchester's day. What colour there was in the crowd seemed to be almost entirely the light blue that stands for the City as well as for Cambridge.

"An hour later they were listening to that almost

Maine Memory

■ In the first summer of the war the newspapers announced that Maine Road would be opened for the Army to provide training at night for young men in advance of being called up. There was the promise that after the drill we would have the chance to form sides and get to play on the pitch. We changed in the Main Stand and then were drilled by a typical army sergeant major for what seemed an interminable time. Eventually we complained that we had been promised a game and so we were eventually divided into sides. I don't recall how many sides there were but it seems in retrospect that we were at least twenty to a side, meaning that most of us just ran around without getting a kick. The City trainer, Laurie Barnett, was organiser and referee and I recall his caustic comment that after all our complaining at having to wait for the game, we were making a pretty awful show of it when we got the chance. If City were looking to make a discovery I guess they were disappointed!

Harold Entwistle

■ The build-up to the quarter-final with Stoke at Maine Road seemed to increase everyone's desire to attend and, indirectly, the game may have had a bearing on the general attitude of Manchester business folk that week. The Manchester Stock Exchange reported surprisingly brisk business on both the Friday and Saturday morning. In addition local traders reduced their prices for dairy products with eggs, bacon, and Lancashire and Cheshire Cheeses all down in price. It's highly unlikely the cost of such items had anything to do with the general excitement within the city, but it is clear from the general tone of the Manchester-produced newspapers the city was full of pride and vigour.

In addition to the mood of Mancunians, Stoke fans were excited by this tie. According to one newspaper "Thousands of Stoke City supporters invaded Manchester", and it is true many thousands did travel up from the Potteries. The scene in the city centre was outlined in the *Manchester Guardian's* "In Manchester" diary column: "The distinction of having helped, even by the addition of a single unit, to make a record crowd at a cup-tie, excluding the final, is one that involves a great deal of discomfort and commends itself rather in retrospect than at the time.

"A good judge of numbers might have prophesied the record any time after noon on Saturday, when a drab tide of humanity pressed relentlessly down Oxford Road and Wilmslow Road and loaded cars and cabs and trams crawled in the same southerly direction. The discomfort began early, for there was no eating-house but those full to the doors at lunch-time, and waitresses ran distractedly from table to table, never quite catching up with the orders of the hungry visitors from the Potteries.

"The thousands who stayed to eat in the city were proved foolish when the ground was reached, for two hours before the game was due to begin masses of people were standing outside the turnstiles waiting to enter and climb on banks that from all appearances were packed so tightly that no fish in a tin seemed an adequate comparison. So, indeed, it proved after having penetrated, triumphant, but bruised, those narrow entrances. The elation born of having achieved the apparently impossible, by getting in at all, was short lived, for it soon became all too clear that one would see little or nothing of the game."

Supporter Alwyn Noden had travelled to the match as early as possible: "I was fourteen at the time and as I walked down Platt Lane with my father it was obvious there was going to be a very large crowd, but at the time we never thought it would be a ground record. We stood in the Platt Lane corner next to the Main Stand. Before

Above left: Mr J Green presents the players with the most modern radio available at the time. This same wireless was used during the 1933-34 season to hear the FA Cup draw.

Left: This photograph is believed to have been taken during the March 1934 'record crowd' game with Stoke City (or during Stoke's visit in the following September). The photographer was stood in the 1931 Platt Lane Corner. Notice the shadow of the roof - this clearly demonstrates that the roof did not extend the full length of the Platt Lane Stand at that time.

Maine Match 33/34

CITY v STOKE CITY

DATE:	3rd March 1934	
TYPE OF FIXTURE:	FA Cup 6th round	
ATTENDANCE:	84,569	
RESULT:	City 1 Stoke City 0	
TEAMS & SCORERS:	CITY	STOKE CITY
	Swift	John
	Barnett	McGrory
	Dale	Spencer
	Busby	Tutin
	Cowan	Turner
	Bray	Sellars
	Toseland	Matthews
	Marshall	Liddle
	Tilson	Sale
	Herd	Davies
	Brook 1	Johnson

the match there were the usual scenes – the brass band were playing and youngsters were being passed over the crowd on the Popular Side to sit in front of the wall surrounding the pitch. I also remember that there were only a small number of policemen inside the ground. If memory serves me there were only four – two sat in dugouts at each corner of what became the Kippax Stand. There was also a man walking around the touchline carrying a large sign which read 'A tale of two Citys on the Maine Road to Wembley'. This was greeted with terrific applause from both sets of fans."

Alwyn was not the only one who had anticipated a good attendance as the match programme also focused on the crowd: "As there is sure to be a tremendous gate one may point out that the record attendance for our ground is 76,116 on the occasion of our cup-tie with Cardiff City on 8 March 1924, the receipts being £4,909. When we played Stoke City here in February 1928, 73,668 spectators paid for admission, the takings amounting to £4,352."

Interestingly, the programme also provided a profile on one of Stoke's young players, Stanley Matthews. Matthews was only 19 but as far as the City programme was concerned he was on the verge of an England cap and was "a player on the threshold of a great career." The author of the piece could not possibly have anticipated that Matthews would still be playing thirty years later after becoming one of the most famous footballers of all time.

In January 2003, City fan Fran Parker gave her memories of this day: "We knew it was going to be a large crowd because in those days the club would put out piles of straw in front of the white perimeter wall. Some people probably thought it was to help protect the pitch but we knew different. What it was really for was to help younger fans settle on the pitch side of the wall.

"We would climb over the wall, collect our pile of straw and then find a convenient place to sit to watch the match. Behind the wall would be my father and all the men, while the children sat in comfort on our straw. It was a great experience and ensured we had a good view and a comfy experience. I suppose it was safer as well, especially with such a large crowd."

Photographs for the period do show groups of supporters sat pitch-side of the wall and clearly Fran remembers with affection her early experience of these matches. Another supporter, BJ Walsh of Marple Bridge remembers being one of the last to enter the ground: "We were later than normal and arrived just as the turnstiles started closing. We rushed to try and get in and made it, but only just. The last turnstile closed after we got in. We then tried to get to our usual spot – the Platt Lane corner of the Popular Side terracing – and managed to squeeze in above the tunnel parapet. In those days spectators who had fainted were passed down over the heads on to the pitch. At this match a body was passed down and was disappearing over the tunnel, but was just retrieved before it fell down. It was set down next to me. I was upset thinking he was dead. He looked so cold and lifeless and didn't come round until half-time."

The official attendance that day was 84,569. For the players the site of almost 85,000 supporters packed in the eleven-year-old stadium must have been thrilling.

In the opening minutes the Blues were under considerable pressure as Stoke's Sale and Matthews attacked, causing Swift to gamble and come out to narrow the angle should one of them choose to shoot. It was a mistake, for the two players clearly had an opportunity to wrong-foot the 'keeper, but Matthews' inexperience and the sight of a giant 'keeper heading towards them was enough for both men to miss-kick. A short while later Matthews tried again. The *Manchester Guardian* described the scene: "Another chance fell to Matthews and after Swift had beaten away the ball it rolled the full width of the goal, not two feet from the line, with no one able to master this excitement sufficiently to be able to kick it one way or the other."

The newspaper went on to say "the famous Liddle-Matthews wing was thoroughly mastered by Bray and Dale" and "Swift had hardly anything to do."

Off the pitch the scene was not a pleasant one. In April 2003 Eddie Nevill remembered the difficulties the crowd faced: "I was nine years old and spent most of the game sitting on my father's shoulders or on a crush barrier in the old Platt Lane Stand. It was extremely difficult to see, but I will never forget the utterly fantastic atmosphere."

Supporters were sitting on the touchline – including Fran Parker - and Swift, in particular, was conscious of the large group of supporters sat around his goal. He tried to joke with them, however his thoughts must surely have drifted to the problems experienced at Hillsborough when he witnessed a dead supporter stretchered out. The *Manchester Guardian*: "For some time the late-comers lived in hope that the police would permit them to climb over the barriers at a certain point and range themselves behind the goalposts. Lively exchanges of badinage gave place to angry shouts from the back as the police proved adamant, but as those who were at the front could see there was no reason why they should risk any sort of collision with the law, which was represented in considerable force. At last those to whom the game was invisible accepted the inevitable and stopped pushing."

The *Sunday Graphic* reported, under the headline "Cup Fans Trapped in Amazing Crowd", of the problems faced: "Having got in, hundreds wandered about looking at a solid array of backs – spectators' not players' – and then tried to get out. But they were trapped, until a turnstile was opened to let them out. Some youths scaled a 12ft wall to get out. These unfortunate people did not

The "Sunday Dispatch" presents below and in the back page an astounding "new-view" of cup-tie fever. Our photographer moved behind the scenes at the Manchester match, where gathered 84,569 spectators—the biggest football crowd ever seen in England outside London

Sunday Dispatch

MARCH 4, 1934

THE ONLY WAY—CUP-TIE VERSION

ARTHUR THOMPSON, the "Sunday Dispatch" photographer, shows in this page of pictures the remarkable adaptability of the Cup-tie fan. These striking photographs were secured during his wanderings among—or behind—yesterday's record crowd of 84,569 at Maine-road, Manchester.

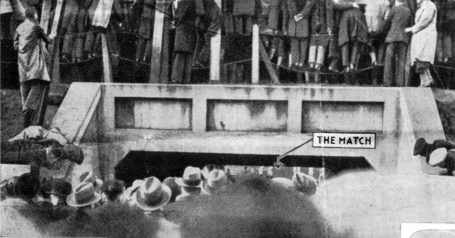

THE MATCH

"HIS WHITE SCARF made an excellent foot support."

"FROM A TUNNEL I saw minute headless players and spectators in many weird attitudes."

"A PRECARIOUS PERCH reminiscent of a pole-squatting record bid."

"NICELY BALANCED on a steel girder at the top of a 30ft. bank."

"HERE IS INGENUITY—It was only an old perambulator chassis, but it served."

"TWO MEN ON A BRICK, and a girl's tight-rope act."

"THIS FLEETING GLIMPSE of the ding-dong struggle I obtained by climbing on to a friend's shoulders."

Printed and Published by the ASSOCIATED NEWSPAPERS, LTD., at Northcliffe House and Carmelite House, Carmelite-street, E.C. 4, and Northcliffe House, Deansgate, Manchester 3, March 4, 1934.

even get a good look at the field, let alone the game. Besides this huge total London's crowd of 67,000 seems moderate.

"Ambulancemen were kept busy and treated about 100 people for crushing and abrasions. Three were taken to Manchester Royal infirmary."

With the terraces packed and supporters experiencing distress, in some areas watching the match became irrelevant in some ways, however there was still the need to know exactly what was happening on the pitch. One bright spark near the front decided to help. According to the *Guardian*: "An anonymous person at the front out of the goodness of his heart began to describe the game for them. At first they took it as a joke and there were derisive cries of 'Square Four' and 'Square Six' in the manner of the announcer at a wireless running commentary. However, this unofficial commentator stuck to his self-appointed task, and being something of an expert in the game, gradually won silence for his remarks. Thus it came about that several hundred people who might have got really bad-tempered and made trouble were satisfied with hearing about a game instead of seeing it. The only interruptions came when men who had fainted - and there were scores in this corner of the ground alone - were passed roughly but efficiently over the heads of the crowd to the grass, where the ambulance squads laid them about and splashed water in their faces."

The sight of so many supporters lying along the touchline must have been unnerving for the players.

Despite the initial Stoke pressure, it was City that took the lead. Eric Brook received a wide pass well out on the Kippax wing and raced for the Platt Lane corner flag. He was only feet away from the hundreds of supporters who had managed to climb over the white perimeter wall and sit on the touchline. He then made a speculative lob from the wing, which seemed to change direction in mid-flight. The Stoke 'keeper Roy John appeared to have it covered, jumped up and somehow missed it as it curled past the 'keeper and into the net.

"I don't think I have ever heard a bigger roar from the City crowd," admitted Alwyn Noden in May 2003. Alwyn went on to become a member of City's ground committee for forty years until the stadium move in 2003.

Fran Parker didn't see the goal: "I saw Brooky on the wing and he kicked the ball and it seemed to twist. I don't know how, but it did, and when it went in I closed my eyes tight. It was a great feeling and I was so excited at seeing such an amazing goal".

Harry Hughes, on the Kippax side of the ground, was unable to see the goal in detail. He was stuck behind several excited supporters and simply knew the ball had gone in. How was a mystery, but Joe Carley, standing at the Platt Lane end, had a better view: "Brook scored the only goal of the match – a goal which will be talked about by Manchester and Stoke supporters for many years to come. He received a wide pass well out on the wing and raced for the corner flag. That wily old veteran, Bob McGrory [Stoke], made no effort to overhaul the City winger, for he realised his speed was not what it was. Instead, he turned goalwards to intercept the winger's centre when it came across.

"Now I was on the terracing, midway between the corner flag and the post, and had a full view of Brook's high lobbing shot or centre, taken from a position only a yard or two from the flag. With the exception of Roy John [Stoke goalkeeper], no other player was in the penalty area as the ball travelled and dipped near the far post. Stoke's goalkeeper watched it carefully, appeared to have it covered, and – as I thought – jumped to make sure the ball would go over the bar and land on the roof of the net. I heard a comparatively faint shout of 'goal' from the crowd at the rear of the posts, and then to my amazement saw a blushing, annoyed goalkeeper stoop to pick the ball out of the net!"

Fran Parker felt it was an intentional shot from Brook: "He was a great player. He played for England, and was one of our biggest stars. He knew what he was doing. From where I sat on the edge of the pitch it was

Maine Memory

■ Two of the finest players ever to play for City were Tilson and Brook. They were marvellous players and in the thirties we had a great time watching these men, especially Brook. He always seemed to have the ball, and if the opposition had it he'd rush and take it off them. It was unknown at the time for a forward to take the ball off opponents. Most forwards waited for it to be passed to them.

Brook was such a major star that they used to say he would put ten or even twenty thousand on the gate at away matches. Of course he was a very famous international player but I missed seeing his wonder goal against Stoke when the record crowd was set. We had a business by then and only one of us could go to the match, so my father went to Maine Road and I looked after the business.

Harry Bramble

THE WAY TO WEMBLEY
BROOK'S AMAZING SHOT BEAT STOKE

Above: Eric Brook.

Left: Eric Brook's wonder goal against Stoke was captured by the *Daily Dispatch* photographer. Brook is the City player closest to the Popular Side terracing.

Right: The homecoming of the 1934 Cup-winning team on a bus through Moss Side, close to Maine Road. Players are Eric Brook, Matt Busby and Sam Cowan (holding up trophy). Local residents decorated the streets around the ground with blue and white buntings and flags to celebrate City's success.

as clear as day that he had shot at goal. He may have been on the touchline himself, but goalscorers like that look for openings all the time. Most players probably wouldn't have been able to score it, but Brooky was different."

As time progressed the City players enjoyed the game further as the pressure was all on Stoke. Then in the last minute Stoke somehow found an opportunity. Frank Swift: "Stoke forced a corner and everybody, bar the goalkeeper crowded into our penalty area in an effort to force the equaliser. Over came the ball, and up went the heads of what seemed every other player on the field. Big Arthur Turner, the Stoke centre-half, got his head to the ball, and with me standing helpless – and with 84,000 hearts in a similar number of mouths – the ball curled slowly over the bar. Then the whistle... "

Joe Carley, leaving the ground, thought of what he had witnessed. He had been impressed with the City men but wasn't so keen on their opponents: "It was my first view of a much-talked-of star of the future, young Stanley Matthews, but I was very disappointed in him. The occasion and the record crowd seemed too much for him."

Fran Parker was unable to remember Matthews at all in that game, while Harry Hughes was a little more blunt: "None of the Stoke players could play! Not even Matthews. City were too good for them."

Denis Houlston was 17 at the time but clearly remembers the day: "The highlight of my time watching City has to be this cup tie. It was a lovely warm day and Eric Brook's winning goal came from the area I stood. I was always a third of the way along the terracing from the Platt Lane corner, and about twenty yards back from the wall. I think Brook played in every position for the club – he certainly went in nets once – and was a very good player. When the goal went in it was marvellous. Nirvana. On the final whistle I didn't need to use my feet to leave I was wedged in a solid wall of human flesh and swept through the exit gate like a surfboarder."

For BJ Walsh the sight of the unconscious supporter had unnerved him for most of the first half but when the fan came round he began to see the funny side: "The unconscious supporter came round at half time and once he'd gathered his thoughts he started talking to us all. It transpired he was a Stoke City supporter. At full time we commiserated with him, as you did in those days, but he amazed us all by saying that Stoke had been the better side in the first half!"

City entered the semi-final for the third consecutive season while Maine Road entered the record books. The official attendance that day was 84,569 - the largest ever crowd in the provinces and to this day the record for any club fixture.

savage chant by which the City supporters both reminded their team how many goals had been scored and revealed their appetite for more – 'one-two-three-four-five-six!'"

Later the report outlined what happened in the final five minutes: "A 6-0 lead breeds magnanimity! Five minutes from the end the City cheered as hard as the Villa when Astley got a consolation goal – 'Come on Villa, there's just time!' came a shout from the crowd."

One report suggested the City defenders were too bored to tackle Astley! A view shared by Blue Joe Carley. Carley called the match "City's finest exhibition in living memory."

The attendance was surprisingly only 45,473, some twenty thousand below Huddersfield's record at the time.

In the final City defeated Portsmouth 2-1. It was a major success and back in Moss Side, the locals prepared for City's return. Marjorie Cooper lived opposite the ground on Beveridge Street: "We had a real party when City won the cup. The entire neighbourhood was decorated with blue and white flags, banners and the like. It was a wonderful sight. We were all very proud of what City had achieved and because we lived next to the ground we treated it like a major occasion. Everyone was happy and in party spirits and the bus came down Maine Road with the cup. They must have been pleased with the reception they got from the local residents and the fans who had come to the ground."

June Brown remembers the day well. She lived in 221 Maine Road, one of the two club cottages next door to the ground, and was the daughter of club steward and stewardess Harry and Gladys Clark. Harry had become the club steward in 1928 – the same year as June was born – and was responsible for the day to day running of the club's facilities such as kitchens, bars etc.
June: "When the cup was brought back to Manchester the club didn't know what to do with it and the

Team	Attendance	Capacity	Match
Arsenal	69,064	72,000	Derby County, 30/3/34
Aston Villa	74,600	80,000	Walsall, 25/1/30
Birmingham City	66,544	79,000	Portsmouth v Leicester 17/3/34
Blackburn Rovers	62,522	65,000	Bolton Wanderers 2/3/29
Chelsea	77,959	95,000	Swindon Town, 11/3/11
Derby County	37,727	38,000	Wolves, 27/1/34
Everton	66,737	70,000	Liverpool, 15/10/27
Grimsby Town	23,644	28,000	Chelsea, 29/3/29
Huddersfield Town	**67,037**	**68,000**	Arsenal, 27/2/32
Leeds United	56,988	58,000	Arsenal, 12/12/32
Leicester City	**47,298**	**50,000**	Tottenham, 18/2/28
Liverpool	61,036	62,000	Tranmere, 27/1/34
Manchester City	**84,569**	**86,000**	Stoke, 3/3/34
Middlesbrough	43,707	45,000	Manchester City, 27/12/27
Portsmouth	39,080	42,000	West Ham, 2/3/29
Preston North End	40,180	42,000	Northampton, 17/2/34
Sheffield Wednesday	**72,841**	**75,000**	Manchester City, 17/2/34
Stoke City	43,689	46,000	Aston Villa, 18/2/22
Sunderland	75,118	76,000	Derby, 8/3/33
Tottenham Hotspur	57,246	58,000	Arsenal, 16/9/33
West Bromwich Albion	64,612	70,000	Aston Villa, 21/2/25
Wolverhampton W.	52,110	54,000	Aston Villa, 27/12/32

Notable attendance details outside of Division One are detailed below. The division the side was playing in is detailed in brackets after the name.

Team	Attendance	Capacity	Match
Bolton Wanderers (2)	**69,920**	**70,000**	Manchester City, 18/2/33
Burnley (2)	**54,775**	**65,000**	Huddersfield, 24/2/24
Manchester United (2)	73,000	80,000	Bolton v Sheff Utd, 24/3/23
Newcastle United (2)	**68,386**	**70,000**	Chelsea, 3/9/30
Oldham Athletic (2)	**47,671**	**52,000**	Sheffield Wed., 25/1/30
Cardiff City (3S)	54,000	60,000	Tottenham, 24/2/23
Reading (3S)	**33,042**	**35,000**	Brentford, 19/2/27

Above left: The FA Cup is carried around Maine Road on a wooden stretcher prior to the League game with Wolves. Children climbed over the perimeter wall to get a better view.

Chairman, Bob Smith, came up to my father with the cup and said 'Harry look after this tonight and take it to the bank tomorrow for safe keeping'. My parents didn't know what to do with it. We were all so worried, and they ended up putting it under their bed while they went to sleep, thinking that had to be the safest place for it. So the FA Cup spent its first night in Moss Side under my parents' bed! The next morning my father took it straight to the bank as soon as it opened. I'm not certain which bank it was, but I think it was probably the one on the corner of Claremont Road and Lloyd Street. Apart from special events, the cup remained there until City had to give it back."

On 5th May the FA Cup was brought out of the bank vault for supporters to see prior to the League meeting with Wolves. The famous trophy was carried on a wooden stretcher around the pitch by club officials. It was the first time the Cup had been seen at Maine Road and some climbed over the perimeter wall to get a good view of the trophy. Two policemen walked alongside to ensure the trophy remained safe.

Success in the cup caused City's directors to consider ground improvements again. The Stoke attendance had tested the limits considerably, although the club still boasted Maine Road could have held more. The official capacity was, for the first time, quoted as 86,000. How this figure was arrived at is a mystery.

The directors viewed the options again, and may well have seriously considered the erection of another corner stand at the northern end of the Main Stand. Swain's plans still existed of course, as did his 1931 drawing of a roofed Platt Lane End, and so it's likely only these two options were seriously contemplated. The Popular Side was again not likely to have been considered for financial reasons. After a little debate the conclusion was to put a cover over the terracing at the Platt Lane end of the stadium. Over the course of the following year plans were made and the stand was developed in time for the 1935-6 season.

Prior to this improvement though it's worth pausing to consider how Maine Road compared to other leading venues. According to the *Topical Times* City's stadium possessed the second highest capacity after Chelsea's Stamford Bridge which claimed to be able to hold 95,000. The highest attendance for a Chelsea match was recorded at the time as 77,959 for a game with Swindon in 1911, but this was beaten in October 1935 when 82,905 attended a League match with Arsenal, thus surpassing the record League crowd set when City faced Arsenal in February 1935.

In terms of record crowds the following details are taken from the *Topical Times* of 1934. These show the highest attendance and capacity of each Division One club's ground at the start of the 1934-5 season. Those in bold are still records today.

Following the success of 1933-4, the following season was always going to be difficult. Expectations were high, especially as the Blues had proved good cup-fighters for three seasons running, but the Cup was a disappointment as an away third round tie at Tottenham ended in a 1-0 defeat.

As usual Maine Road housed a few enormous crowds. Sheffield Wednesday, Leeds, and Stoke each attracted over 50,000, while the game with first-placed Arsenal on 23rd February attracted 79,491 (including season ticket holders). This was a new record for a League match.

Another momentous occasion during the season was the visit of the Duke of York (future King George VI) to Maine Road for the League match with Derby County on 20th October 1934. The visit brought back memories of when the Duke's father had visited Hyde Road fourteen years earlier but, unlike that occasion, the visit seemed to have got the better of the City players as the Blues lost 1-0 before 44,393.

In February 1935 the Blues scored six in successive games at Maine Road. On 2nd they defeated Leicester 6-3, then the following Saturday Middlesbrough lost 6-2. Those games put City third, but poor results in April caused the Blues to end the season fourth, one position higher than the previous season.

In May 1935 plans were finally submitted to the city council for the redevelopment of the Platt Lane end. The plans for a 'New Grand Stand' were compiled by Redpath, Brown & Co., a company from Trafford Park, and looked very similar to those initially drawn by Charles

Above: The Platt Lane Stand roof was constructed in 1935 and can be seen in this aerial photograph taken in the summer of 1953 (before the floodlights were added in the October). Note that there are very few, if any, cars in the picture.

Swain in 1931. Significant delays affected the planning and construction of this stand according to the City Council planning department.

Why Swain was not involved is not clear, however it is known he retired from practice in 1935.

To install the roof City had needed to square off the terracing to some extent. The directors and architects had considered how best to achieve this and, rather than reduce City's capacity, the decision was taken to extend the stand, as they had done with the corner, although this extension was to be significantly larger. This was a bold and potentially costly move. However City decided to keep costs as low as possible by using wood for the main terracing instead of concrete. Swain's corner construction of 1931 was eventually completed solely with concrete – his wooden plans had been abandoned – but the 1935 plans felt wood was a cost-effective way of achieving the increase.

Basically, the club extended the main section of terracing between the two edges of the pitch by 24 terracing steps. This brought the top of the stand in line with the end of the original muddy banking behind it. A structure of wood, metal and brick was erected from the ground to hold the new wooden terracing and the back of the roof. Two large flights of stairs were built out of

the back to allow access from the rear, while the original staircases were also left in position.

The outer walling was constructed using a similar shade of red brick as the Main Stand, with the bare concrete of the main supporting structure showing in places. Light was also allowed into the stand via windows of glass blocks. There were sixteen such windows within the main section of the stand.

At the pitch side five large stanchions held the main part of the roof in place, and this joined well with the 1931 corner section. Unfortunately, this meant viewing matches from this stand would always offer a restricted view.

Iron railings were erected at the other end of the stand to divide it off from the uncovered corner between Platt Lane and the Popular Side. A similar divide was erected behind the stand in the public areas.

With these developments the capacity of Maine Road must have increased. If 86,000 was the official capacity in 1934 then the addition of 80 yards of 24 wooden steps must have added in excess of 5,000 to the capacity, although some would argue that the capacity should never have been quoted as 86,000 in the first place.

Maine Road now provided cover for around 35,000,

Maine Match 34/35

CITY v ARSENAL

DATE:	23rd February 1935		
TYPE OF FIXTURE:	Football League Division One		
ATTENDANCE:	79,491		
RESULT:	City 1 Arsenal 1		
TEAMS &	CITY		ARSENAL
SCORERS:	Swift		Moss
	Dale		Male
REFEREE:	Barkas		John
Mr. E. Wood	Busby		Crayston
	Cowan		Roberts
	Bray		Copping
	Toseland		Bowden	1
	Marshall		Davidson
	Tilson		Drake
	Herd		Dougall
	Brook	1	Bastin

■ The largest League crowd at the time came to see the League champions take on a City side determined for league success themselves. The *Daily Express* reporter Henry Rose felt it was not a classic encounter: "Crowd of 80,000 – the biggest ever for a League match in England – a crowd out for the Arsenal's body, as it were, roaring at every kick and miskick, gave the game at Maine-road between Manchester City and Arsenal an atmosphere as grim as the grimmest cup tie. The game contained all those incidents that make the heart beat faster, though there was little class football."

"My pad was nearly 'all Arsenal' in this first half, yet it was the City who almost took the lead from a free kick just outside the penalty area. Eric Brook, instead of his usual 'whizz-bang', lobbed the ball gently over the Arsenal players' heads, and Tilson ran forward past a hoodwinked defence, but sent the ball over the bar. A move worth a goal this."

Arsenal managed to score through the determined efforts of Bastin. The Arsenal man latched on to a ball that seemed destined to go out of play – it would have given the Gunners a corner and it's possible City were caught unawares – and then banged it back into the goal area. Bowden, in acres of space, slotted it into a seemingly empty net.

City fought back, but Arsenal defended well – according to Rose Arsenal proceeded to "pack their own goal in the usual Arsenal fashion" – and as the game entered its final fifteen minutes the Blues looked beaten. Fortunately, with only eight minutes remaining, Busby set Tilson up for a shot. The strike was blocked but the Arsenal 'keeper could only push it a few yards forward. Goal-poacher Eric Brook saw his chance and, according to Rose, Brook "sent it crashing into the top of the net and jumped almost as high in his ecstasy."

The match ended 1-1 and City finished the season fourth, while Arsenal were champions for the third successive season. A poor run of four defeats during April had caused the Blues to miss out on their first title. Immediately after the game with Arsenal *Daily Express* Sports Editor Arthur Simmons revealed that most neutrals wanted City to win because they were utterly fed up of Arsenal: "Heart-cry of the 80,000 at Maine Road was 'City must win'. Arsenal stick it! But we must not praise them for that. What I mean is, as a correspondent writes: 'I know directors and managers who are sick of Arsenal!'"

This game remains the record crowd for a League game involving City at Maine Road and it should be remembered that at the time it was set City, and Maine Road, held the record for the highest club fixture (84,569) and the highest League fixture.

including the 10,000-seater Main Stand. This figure was comparable with the largest covered accommodation provided at Hyde Road and, considering the club still allowed its vast Popular Side terracing and Scoreboard End to be uncovered, proved Maine Road still offered great potential.

Whether redeveloping the Platt Lane in such a way meant the club had abandoned its original plan of creating a 120,000 stadium is unclear. That plan must surely have allowed for all the terracing to reach the same height as the Main Stand.

The views of Charles Swain would need to be understood before reaching conclusion on this point. Swain's plans for the Platt Lane End may not have been developed in their entirety, however it's clear his masterplan had been consulted at length. It seems possible – and probable – that the next stage of Swain's plan would have been to erect another corner section at the northern end of the Main Stand, followed by a replica Platt Lane Stand at the Scoreboard End.

Swain's plans for the Popular Side are completely unknown. It's possible he would have wanted to erect a roof similar to the Main Stand side, or maybe he would have wanted to continue the Platt Lane roof around that side of the ground. In truth he would have needed to construct stands similar to that erected in 1931 at each of the corners, and then would have been free to roof the Popular Side in any style he preferred.

Looking objectively at the Platt Lane Stand of 1935 and the corner of 1931, it's clear City did attempt a balance between architectural consistency and the obvious needs of the supporters and management. The Platt Lane roof was not by any stretch of the imagination a copy of the Main Stand roof, however there were

Below: City and Luton players pay their respects following the death of King George V in January 1936.

Maine Memory

■ It was May 1934 when I first fell in love with the Blues. I can still remember vividly being taken by my Mother to the corner of Kippax Street and Claremont Road to watch City bring the cup home. Finglands coach was decked in blue and white and Freddy Tilson held the cup aloft.

I went to Heald Place School and when City were playing an afternoon game we kids, instead of concentrating on lessons, would listen out for the cheers, hoping each one signalled a City goal. Some games, especially cup replays, were played on Wednesday afternoons pre-floodlights.

When I was old enough my mate and I would stand outside Maine Road waiting for three-quarter time, when the gates would be opened. I can still see the small knot of OAP's who always seemed to know which gate would open first. Then we'd rush up the stairs at the rear of the Kippax, under the flag, and hope to have a glimpse of Peter Doherty or Alex Herd and big "Swifty".

Supporting City for 60 years means many memories, but I'll always remember the semi-final played at Villa Park in 1955. Mud, rain, more mud and rain, and that glorious headed goal by Roy Clarke made it all seem like a beautiful summers day, but to no avail. Newcastle beat us 3-1 and Jimmy Meadows was badly injured in the final.

On to the new stadium. I wonder if it will be as inspiring as the 84,000 v Stoke City in '34 or as miserable as the 8,000 v Swindon? Dear old City, thanks for the memories. I don't suppose you'll ever change. Perhaps I secretly hope you won't!

Brian Wood,
Heald Green

enough similarities to provide a consistency to the ground. A similar construction at the opposite end would certainly have given Maine Road uniformity to a degree.

The new stand was used for the first time on 24th August 1935 for a public practice match between the Blues and Maroons. The attendance was approximately 12,000 and, according to the local press, many of those had come to admire the new stand. In fact it seems much of the ground was empty with the majority housed under the new roof.

The following week West Bromwich Albion visited Maine Road for the first proper match in front of the Platt Lane Stand; 39,826 witnessed a good City performance as Alec Herd netted the only goal. The *Daily Dispatch* described the match as "Manchester City's Thriller" and claimed: "There was a spirit of gay enterprise about the play of both teams at Maine Road on Saturday, and only the acrobatic performances of two great goalkeepers prevented the rival sets of forwards from taking several goals. But what a contrast in methods!"

The *Dispatch* went on to claim that Albion's 'keeper Pearson was 'cold and calculated' while: "Swift, who plays his football like some jolly schoolboy, makes his job a swashbuckling adventure. He takes risks; he indulges in prodigious leaps and strange attitudes; he reveals a technique that follows no example. Rather has he developed it himself from his own athletic prowess outsize in hands and supreme courage."

With Swift entertaining City's crowd in the new Platt Lane Stand – the 'keeper would often chat to fans behind the goal during matches - the next home fixture saw Liverpool annihilated 6-0 as the Blues enjoyed a glorious time.

During the course of the 1935-6 season Maine Road staged further entertaining fixtures. In December Aston Villa were defeated 5-0, and in March Middlesbrough suffered a 6-0 drubbing. At the time the Boro fans had expected their side to put in a better performance than the previous year. The pity, from a Blue perspective, was that only 20,094 attended, but even that was more than 7,000 higher than City's match with Blackburn on 19th February. The Blackburn game was City's first home League game since the death of King George V but it's unlikely that held any bearing on the attendance, especially as the cup match with Luton had taken place a few weeks earlier and had been watched by 65,978. A minute's silence was held for the King before the Luton game. Incidentally, City defeated Third Division Luton 2-1 – The Hatters' first defeat since 28th September.

On 11th March Arsenal were beaten 1-0 before a Maine Road crowd of 32,750. Again, in comparison with previous fixtures between the sides, this seemed a poor figure, however the match was played on a Wednesday afternoon and should therefore be viewed in a more positive light. Ten days later a 7-0 annihilation of Bolton Wanderers was watched by 40,779. Eric Brook scored a hat-trick, while new signing Peter Doherty netted twice.

The first home match of the 1936-7 season saw Leeds defeated 4-0 followed by a 6-2 victory over West Bromwich Albion three days later, but a run of poor results ensued. When supporters slow-hand clapped the goalless match with Chelsea at Maine Road on 26th September no one could anticipate how the season would end.

On Halloween, Sunderland defeated City 4-2. The Blues were totally outclassed, although everyone recognised the defeat could have been much greater.

Maine Match 36/37

CITY v ARSENAL

DATE:	10th April 1937	
TYPE OF FIXTURE:	Football League Division One	
ATTENDANCE:	76,000	
RESULT:	City 2 Arsenal 0	
TEAMS & SCORERS:	CITY	ARSENAL
	Swift	Boulton
	Dale	Male
REFEREE :	Barkas	Hapgood
Mr. G.C. Denton	Percival	Crayston
(Northampton)	Marshall	Joy
	Bray	Copping
	Toseland 1	Kirchen
	Herd	Bastin
	Tilson	Bowden
	Doherty 1	Davidson
	Brook	Nelson

■ With both sides occupying the top two places in the League this was a must-see match. The attendance was quoted in the press immediately after the match as 76,000 including season ticket holders. If the ticket holders are excluded a figure of 74,918 actually paid on the day.

Trevor Wignall, writing in the *Daily Express*, saw this as the match of the day: "The semi-finals in the Cup will naturally claim most attention today, but there is another game that is equally interesting and important. It will be played at Maine Road, Manchester, between the City and the Arsenal, and the result will, in all probability, determine the Championship of the First Division. Manchester City were my selection as winners of the Cup. They gave me a good run for my Cup tip, and as a consequence I fancy them for this afternoon's game."

After thirty-five minutes the Blues took the lead through Peter Doherty. This is how journalist Arthur Simmons saw it: "Tilson should have ranged about more. One of his few dashes to a wing made the City's first goal. He caught a badly placed ball from Joy inches inside the touchline; centred cleverly; Doherty got on. Boulton was drawn out. Doherty had to make his close-in shot from awkward position. He judged it perfectly. That's where ball control comes in. Doherty could spare some, and still be an artist. A nice goal."

According to Doherty: "With Eddie Hapgood in close attendance I hooked the ball into the roof of the net from a very narrow angle. Boulton looked amazed, as well he might, for I was very nearly on the goal line when I shot."

Toseland scored a second for the Blues 24 minutes into the second half to give City victory

In 2003, 76-year-old supporter Harry Holland remembered the goal: "Into the second half, with City gradually getting on top and with not long to go, City scored a second goal. The amazing thing though, was that it was a headed goal scored by Ernie Toseland – a player who had never headed a goal before for City. In fact he was legendary for rarely heading the ball at all! He played at outside right and his theory was that he centred the ball – which he did to perfection – and the job of others was to head the goals! This time however, the ball was played into the Arsenal goalmouth, bouncing just right for 'Twinkletoes' Toseland. With no other City players around he headed home. The crowd were cheering and laughing at the same time!"

Shortly before this goal City had felt a little aggrieved when a penalty appeal was turned down. Simmons: "Arsenal had a curious escape. Herd drove pretty hard, though it was not one of his 'bullets'. Boulton was the other side of the goal. Hapgood stood under the bar in a direct line with the shot. He jumped and threw up his hands in a feverish attempt to save. The ball hit the bar. The City wanted a penalty. The referee shook his head. It all happened in a jiffy. Only Hapgood knows whether his hands touched the ball. In any event not my idea of back play."

Lucky Arsenal!

There was further controversy when, with fifteen minutes to go, Arsenal's trainer (later manager) Tom Whittaker was reprimanded for touchline coaching. He had whispered something to Hapgood from the edge of the pitch and according to Simmons: "The referee came over to investigate. Whittaker had returned to his seat. The referee beckoned to him, put a hand on his shoulder, spoke earnestly. The incident was rather dramatic. A section of the vast crowd at Maine-road booed vigorously before the referee acted. Obviously, they considered Whittaker had given an instruction from the touchline. And that, of course, is not allowed."

After the incident the game was played out with little controversy. In February 2003 Mr. G Renshaw remembered this as his first City match: "I've tried to remember every moment of this first match but all I can remember was being passed over the heads of the spectators down to the front of the Platt Lane Stand. This was common practice in those days for youngsters – I was nearly twelve years old and so only just qualified for this special treatment. How I found my dad after the game and in such a large crowd I will never know. It was this game and this result which made me a City fan for life."

Simmons ended his match report with an interesting comment on City's position: "Well, Manchester City have played eighteen League matches without a defeat. In these days of fierce competition an extra-ordinary run. Can they stay though?"

The answer was yes and, after extending their run to 22 undefeated matches the Blues were champions.

Simmons congratulated City in the *Daily Express*: "Congratulations are being showered on Manchester City as League Champions. The honour is new to them. They have achieved it by splendid team work, artistry, and consistency. They have defied all comers to lower their colours in a League match in 1937. From Christmas to now without defeat is grand work. Well done Manchester City!"

According to Peter Doherty: "The Wearsiders gave a sparkling exhibition of scientific soccer, and Raich Carter had one of his best days – which means, of course, that he was magnificent. We were outclassed and outplayed that day, and only a wonderful display of goalkeeping by Frank Swift kept the score down to 4-2."

A few good victories followed in November and December, including a 4-1 Maine Road hammering of Everton and a similar defeat of Preston, but the real turnaround came at Christmas with a 2-1 victory over Middlesbrough at Maine Road on Boxing Day. 56,227 witnessed that, but only 16,146 bothered to attend two days later when a meeting with Grimsby ended 1-1. Clearly many supporters preferred to spend the immediate post-Christmas period at home.

Fred Tilson scored one of the easiest goals of his career in the Grimsby draw. All the player had to do was tap the ball over the line and afterwards he bemoaned the modern game to the other players telling them: "The game's not what it was. When Brooky and me were at Barnsley they wouldn't have counted goals like that!"

The first Maine Road derby since 1930 attracted 64,862, but the game was a rather dull affair. As anticipated City defeated the Reds thanks to a solitary goal from Alec Herd. The United side included future England Manager Walter Winterbottom, who played his one and only Manchester derby. The derby victory became part of a glorious unbeaten run which allowed the Blues to progress up the table.

A 2-1 home victory over Brentford on 7th April put City second behind Arsenal, who were due at Maine Road on Saturday 10th April. A magnificent 2-0 win brought a great deal of satisfaction to all at Maine Road, and was a crucial moment in City's season. Victories at Sunderland and Preston followed leaving the Blues needing only two points from their final two matches to win the title.

A 4-1 victory over Sheffield Wednesday at Maine Road on 24th April brought City their first championship. It was a stylish performance and proved to all football fans the strength of the Blues. According to journalist

Left: Centre-forward Fred Tilson was undoubtedly one of the driving forces behind a successful 1930s decade at Maine Road.

8 BLUE AND WHITE

THE NEW MANCHESTER

HIPPODROME

TWICE NIGHTLY 6-35 8-50 ARDWICK GREEN 'Phone: ARD 4101 Box Office 10—10

WEEK COMMENCING MONDAY, APRIL 26th, 1937

SANDY POWELL

The Ever-popular Comedian in His

1937 ROAD SHOW

WITH

ROY JEFFERIES CINGALEE GREAT GARCIAS
Versatile Entertainer The Silent Man of Mystery " Seeing is Believing "
10 MOONBEAMS KENNETH COOPER JIMMIE FLETCHER
" Fireworks " 14-year-old Syncopated Pianist Boy Soprano with the Silvery Voice

SATURDAY, APRIL 24th, 1937.

MANCHESTER CITY

1
SWIFT
Goal

2   3
CLARK   BARKAS
Right Back   Left Back

4   5   6
PERCIVAL   MARSHALL   BRAY
Right Half-Back Centre Half-Back Left Half-Back

7   8   9   10   11
TOSELAND HERD TILSON DOHERTY BROOK
Outside Right Inside Right Centre Inside Left Outside Left

Referee :   Linesmen :
R. W. BLAKE, Middlesbrough   A. BILLINGTON, Blue Flag
KICK-OFF 3 p.m.   G. SALMON, Red Flag

ORDER HYDES PALE ALE

12 13 14 15 16
RIMMER DRURY DEWAR ROBINSON LUKE
Outside Left Inside Left Centre Inside Right Outside Right

17   18   19
RHODES   HANFORD GROSVENOR
Left Half-Back Centre Half-Back Right Half-Back

20   21
CATLIN   ASHLEY
Left Back   Right Back

22
SMITH
Goal

SHEFFIELD WEDNESDAY

SLACK & COX, LTD.

For Bass, Worthington, Guinness (Harp Label) & Mineral Waters
Specialities : VITONICA, VI-MALTO and PERIANDER
"FRUENTA" Super Fruit Crushes.

HYDE ROAD :: MANCHESTER 12

MANCHESTER CITY F.C.

Hon. President : L. W. FURNISS.
Directors : R. SMITH (Chairman), A. ALEXANDER, J. P. (Vice-Chairman).
Dr. J. B. HOLMES, F. R. JOLLY, W. M. SHAW and H. WOOD.
Secretary Manager : W. WILD. Registered Office : MAINE ROAD GROUND

CLUB GOSSIP

WILL TO-DAY BRING US THE CHAMPIONSHIP ?

TO-DAY we bring our season to an end so far as our home League engagements are concerned, and we are hoping it will be the happiest wind-up we have ever had in the sense that it will consummate our first Championship year.

Two points from the match with Sheffield Wednesday this afternoon and the prize for which we have striven so long and which would complete for us the full round of honours in the game, will be ours.

We have had the F.A. Cup and the Championship of the Second Division of the League, but never the trophy which is now within our grasp.

WE are not counting our chickens before they are hatched. We recognise that we are up against a desperate opposition. The match is of the utmost importance to the Wednesday, to whom defeat might mean the loss of their position, and they are sure to make a tremendous fight.

When we were at Hillsborough in December they inflicted upon us the heaviest defeat we have sustained throughout the season. They had what we should say was their very best day.

They beat us by 5—1, after we had run through six successive matches without a reverse and, except in the following game with Grimsby Town, six

Manchester City 4, Sheffield Wednesday 1.

MANCHESTER staged a miniature Wembley all on its own on Saturday. Excited "fans" swarmed over the field— policemen lost their helmets.

Manchester City had won the championship for the first time in their history. Great stuff.

And how they won it!

This was no scrambling victory but a triumph gained by some superlative football and three goals that memory will treasure for a long time. Oh, boy, what goals! Three in twelve minutes. Each is worth framing. Cold print cannot do them justice.

Henry Rose: "This was no scrambling victory, but a triumph gained by some superlative football and three goals that memory will treasure for a long time. Oh boy! What goals! Three in twelve minutes. Each is worth framing. Cold print cannot do them justice."

Clearly Rose enjoyed the victory, as did all City fans, and he went on to describe the goals: "The first. Percival to Doherty then a master touch by the Irishman to Brook, and that left of the wingman's seven-league boots almost broke the net.

"The second. A 'dummy' by Doherty to the Sheffield defence. A pass to Tilson, who scored with an effort that reminded me of the two he scored when the City won the Cup against Portsmouth. Then the third – the gem of the lot. I never want to see a better. Forgive me but truth must bring in Doherty's name again. He started it at the halfway line. A dribble for twenty yards, a cross pass to Tilson. Another dribble. A cross pass to Doherty. Back again, and again, and a crashing shot home by Doherty.

"I intended to criticise Brook for some inaccurate centres and wild shooting, but how dare any one criticise a player who can come across with two such goals as he scored? His second – the last of the game – was from the centre forward position from a pass by – you've guessed it – Doherty. Just before, the Wednesday, who never gave up trying, had made it 3-1 when Rimmer scored after Swift had made a brilliant save from Luke's shot."

Rose clearly enjoyed watching City's first championship victory and, although extremely busy at the whistle trying to compile his match report he must have wished he could have joined the thousands celebrating on the pitch. He managed to make a brief comment on the scenes in his report: "Manchester staged a miniature Wembley all on its own on Saturday. Excited 'fans' swarmed over the field – policemen lost their helmets. Manchester City had won the championship for the first time in their history. Great stuff."

At the whistle, supporters charged across the pitch in celebration. They sang, shouted, and cheered, until captain Sam Barkas, manager Wilf Wild and Chairman Bob Smith appeared. The Chairman paid tribute to the team: "It has been a fine achievement, especially as they have not been beaten since last Christmas. On behalf of myself and my fellow directors, I take this opportunity of thanking the players. We are tremendously proud of them."

Sam Barkas stressed City's teamwork, "We have all pulled together. We have been a happy family, and that is one of the secrets of our success."

Maine Road had witnessed its first League championship and had proved a worthy venue for such a successful season. As a result, the following November the stadium staged its first Charity Shield match. The Blues had played in the Charity Shield once before – away at Arsenal in 1934, but this was the first time they had hosted the game.

The annual fixture between the League champions and FA Cup winners was usually played at the home of the champions during this period of football history and so a crowd of about 20,000 witnessed the Blues defeat FA Cup winners Sunderland 2-0.

Sadly, the rest of the season was a stark contrast to the previous campaign, or indeed that one match with Sunderland. In fact it proved a major shock as the Blues could not find any consistency. They struggled despite

---

Below and right: Pages from the City programme for the championship-clinching game with Sheffield Wednesday in April 1937.

Bottom: Henry Rose's opening words in his report of the game in the *Daily Express*.

possessing some excellent international players, and were relegated. It was completely baffling.

Despite the struggles there were still a few high points as far as Maine Road games were concerned. Supporters saw a 6-1 defeat of Derby on 18th September, while the best Maine Road result was a 7-1 thrashing of West Bromwich Albion on 16th April. Eric Brook netted four in this match, but City were still a shade fortunate in these pre-substitute days as the visitors' goalkeeper, Little, badly bruised his shoulder in the 22nd minute and was forced to leave the field for a while. When he returned he was unable to move his right arm. Another player, Finch, Albion's full back, also suffered a gashed head following a collision with Eric Brook. When he returned he joined the wounded Little out on the wing.

Prior to Little's injury the Blues were already two goals up - a Brook penalty in the second minute and a Doherty header twenty minutes later - but once he'd left the field City could not be stopped.

Two weeks later Leeds arrived at Maine Road. For Dennis Chapman, a supporter from the Stockport area, this was his first sight of City in the flesh. Dennis went on to become a major researcher of City's history as a result of attending Maine Road during this period. Dennis remembers the Leeds game well: "I was eleven when I went to my first game in April 1938. I sat at the top of the Main Stand with a friend of mine, and I remember seeing Eric Brook chasing down the left wing and putting crosses in for Jimmy Heale – who played a brilliant match – but the real outfield star was Peter Doherty. With Doherty's delicate dribbling he managed to score a fine hat-trick. It was a great 6-2 victory and of course Frank Swift played superbly, although he was rarely put under too much pressure.

"The half-time score was 3-1 so it shows that City were on top throughout the match. There was no particular reason why I chose this match for my first. It was the Easter holidays from school and my friend and his father – who were both good City supporters – decided to take me along. We went on the bus and I enjoyed every minute of it. The crowd was only about 27,000 which wasn't particularly large, probably because of their erratic form, but it was a very exciting game. I couldn't wait for my next sight of Brook, Doherty, Swift and all the other players – they were all great players, although at the time we didn't realise quite how great some of them were."

Despite the 6-2 victory the Blues remained in danger. The final match was away to Huddersfield, who were also struggling. Huddersfield netted a scrappy goal twelve minutes from time and the Blues ended the season in 21st place despite incredibly scoring more goals than any other team in the division.

In the cup, City reached the sixth round – losing at Aston Villa 3-2 before a then Villa Park record crowd of 75,540 – with Maine Road hosting two matches. The first was a 3-1 victory over Millwall in a third round replay, while the other was the fourth round victory over Bury. City won this game 3-1, but the crowd was a huge 71,937 – by far the highest at Maine Road all season and the last great Manchester crowd before the war.

City finished the 1938-9 season fifth in Division Two and, as far as Maine Road was concerned, there were no developments of note within the stadium. An international was played in Manchester during November 1938 but Old Trafford staged the game.

The 1939 close season still saw a significant Maine Road moment when professional tennis was played on the pitch. The tournament proved very popular as it allowed fans to see leading American stars - something even Wimbledon could not do.

Unfortunately, the international situation was worsening as the 1939-40 season opened, with City defeated 4-3 at Leicester.

Prior to the match manager Wilf Wild told reporters: "We shall start with promotion our aim. Manchester City and the First Division are synonymous terms, and we hope to succeed this coming season."

Behind the scenes there had been a number of changes to support the club's bid for promotion. The Blues had appointed a masseur – the first in the League – and put former player Laurie Barnett in charge of the reserves. In addition a fourth team was created to play in the newly-formed Lancashire League. This fourth team were expected to play all their matches at Altrincham's ground, while the third team would play at Droylsden. Wild made it clear he wanted City's reserve and youth set-up to be the best. He told reporters: "If any youngster in the district desires a trial we shall be ready to accommodate him if he gets in touch with us."

On 30th August City entertained Bury in a 1-1 draw. Understandably, the crowd was a rather subdued 20,000, and then on Saturday 2nd September the Blues welcomed Chesterfield with Jack Milsom scoring twice to give City a 2-0 victory before 15,000.

Then on Saturday 2nd September the Blues welcomed Chesterfield while Wilf Wild made one alteration to his line-up, replacing Jimmy Heale with Jack Milsom. The former Bolton forward netted twice to give City a 2-0 victory before 15,000.

Milsom received all the headlines but both goalkeepers were also praised. Middleton, in the Chesterfield goal, was cheered at the end by the City fans for an outstanding performance while Frank Swift was also credited with putting in another 'brilliant show'.

Later that day news came through that 21 people had died following a German air-raid on Warsaw. At noon the next day Prime Minister Neville Chamberlain announced: "This country is now at war with Germany. We are ready."

An announcement was made that the League programme would be cancelled and all players contracts suspended. City's chance of promotion had ended. The future of all City's players lay in doubt. Even Maine Road's future was uncertain. With no football how could the stadium survive?

Fortunately by the end of September, there had been a change of heart and permission was given for the organisation of mini-leagues or competitions consisting of teams within straightforward travelling distance. Attendance would be restricted to ensure safety, and spectators would have to carry gas masks and the like.

MANCHESTER CITY
F.C. LTD.

BLUE AND WHITE

OFFICIAL PROGRAMME

NOVEMBER 3rd, 1937.   ONE PENNY

F.A. CHARITY SHIELD
•
MANCHESTER CITY
v.
SUNDERLAND

AT MAINE ROAD
WEDNESDAY
NOVEMBER 3rd

MR. W. PICKFORD
F.A. President

Left: The programme from the first of three FA Charity Shield games staged at Maine Road.

For the staff though this period was extremely difficult as the cancellation of the League programme inevitably brought a reduction. Gladys Clark, the club's stewardess, was released, as were most of the club's non-essential personnel. According to June, Gladys' daughter, few remained at Maine Road: "My mother was told she couldn't stay on due to the war, but my father was viewed differently. He was kept on and we were allowed to stay in the club house at 221 Maine Road, but in total I think two-thirds of the staff were given notice. In fact, I think the only staff remaining were my father, the groundsman Ernie Smith, an odd job lad called Mark Royle, and then in the offices there was Wilf Wild but that was about it.

"Ernie Smith and my father were told to keep the place in best shape possible and they also became involved with the local air wardens and defence organisations. Ernie, I think was a special constable, and both he and my father became 'spotters', looking for enemy aircraft. They would patrol the Main Stand roof at night time looking for 'planes. I remember my father telling me how they had to be positioned on the roof. They had an extremely good view of Manchester and all directions from there. It was a key spot and at the same time it must have been a very scary place to be, particularly when bombs would be landing across the city."

Although Maine Road itself was not hit by enemy bombs the area around the ground was. Marjorie Cooper remembers: "Houses on Kippax Street were hit. In fact there was a gap for many years where a couple of houses had disappeared. Carlton Avenue was badly

damaged and so were some of the other roads south of the ground. One of my friends was killed in the houses close to City's Platt Lane training ground, and it was a major tragedy because her family originally lived in the terraced houses close to us and moved to the houses with gardens across Platt Lane because they were spaced further apart – they thought it would be safer."

June Brown remembers vividly a number of wartime stories which modern supporters may be surprised to read: "Maine Road was a key centre during the war, and many local figures took on dual roles. Walter Crickmer, United's secretary, was in charge of the distribution of butter and other products and turned up at Maine Road one day and asked if the ground could be used to store items. I think they wanted to have essential items spread across the city in locations not normally associated with the product in case the usual places were hit by bombs. So, for a while butter, lard and similar products were stored in the tunnels and ground floor rooms of the Main Stand.

"Also, across at the Popular Side of the ground the two large tunnels built into the terracing were used to store newsprint for the newspaper industry. Manchester was still a major area for printing in those days and it was essential the paper was stored in a safe location to keep information circulating. So the tunnels housed these large wheels of paper. They were enormous. I remember one air raid. It may have been the first we'd encountered. My father was on the Main Stand roof looking out for 'planes and my mother and I needed somewhere safe to shelter. We didn't have a shelter nearby and so we went into the ground and hid in the Popular Side tunnels

Below: Professional tennis was played on the Maine Road pitch in July 1939. The four competing Americans were all major stars of the day.

Three years later American soldiers were seen around the ground.

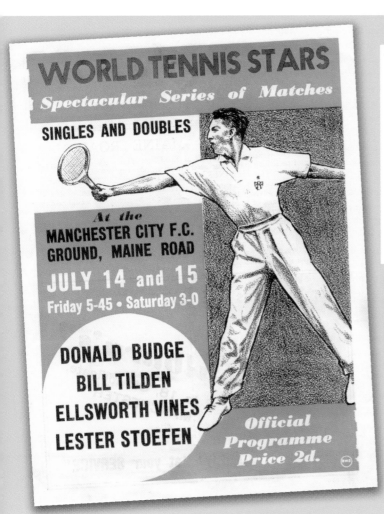

between the rolls of paper. It was a frightening experience. It was dark, naturally, but we could also hear the buzz of the airplanes, the sound of gun fire, and the noise the bombs made as they came down.

"When it was safe to leave, we returned home and the next day my mother insisted a shelter was made in our back garden. My father and Ernie Smith dug out a shelter, but when we came to leave it the next night we could hardly get out! They'd made it well enough to get into and it was excellent protection, but it was too difficult to get out. So they kept working at it."

Another incident concerned Manchester's air defences: "One morning my mother woke up, opened her bedroom curtains and saw nothing. Everything had vanished. I rushed in and we tried to work out what was happening, and then we realised something was against the window blocking the view. When we went outside we saw that it was a barrage balloon used to block out enemy planes. The balloon was normally positioned at the south end of the ground in the directors' car park but it must have broke free and somehow came to rest against our house.

"In the directors' car park there was also an Ack-Ack gun manned by a couple of British soldiers. The car park was fenced off and we weren't allowed to go inside, but after a short while the British were replaced by a small group of American soldiers. I can't remember the date but it would have been about 1942. Now they were so different to the British. Every morning they would parade up and down the forecourt chanting their chants as they marched. Most of the children would follow behind imitating them. Because we weren't allowed near the car park, I don't know what they did at night time, but I believe they had either tents or small huts erected in the car park. I also remember that one day they had gone. I think they'd gone off to prepare for D-day, but all we knew at the time was that one day they were here, the next they had vanished."

June recalls a dramatic incident from around the time of the Manchester blitz: "We all woke up with the rather exciting news that a German 'plane had been shot down in the area. I'm not certain exactly where it came down but there was shrapnel everywhere and all of us children were running around searching for anything we could find. It was terribly exciting and then even more thrilling news reached us – the German pilot had baled out of his 'plane before it came down. The adults now started searching. Although we'd seen the 'planes, and the bomb damage, this was the first time the enemy had felt close.

"While the search was progressing the news came through that he'd been caught. Later that day I was told by my father that Uncle Ernie (Ernie Smith, the groundsman) had caught him inside the Maine Road ground! Apparently, he'd parachuted to the nearest open space he could find and, presumably, Maine Road was the perfect spot. I can't ever recall the story appearing in the 'papers, but I do know that it was kept relatively quiet because the authorities didn't want to cause too much alarm. In fact it may be that only those working at the club knew the full story."

The capture of a German pilot within the Maine Road ground is a remarkable moment in the history of the stadium. Extensive research has failed to produce a specific date, however June's memory of the day and her proximity to the situation suggest the story is accurate. Naturally, it would have been better if the captured pilot had turned out to be Bert Trautmann!

On 28th October 1939 Maine Road staged its first wartime match as 4,000 watched Wrexham defeated 6-1.

Due to the difficulties in wartime, Maine Road customers were never certain who would turn out. Dennis Chapman remembers the general excitement of the time: "We never knew who would be playing. Of course we always hoped Swift or Doherty or some of our other favourites would be able to get back to Manchester in time to play but we never knew for sure. Even the Saturday morning press wouldn't know for certain. It would often say things like 'Doherty may be with us today', or it would say that 'Swift will definitely not be available today'. It was terribly exciting, although often we'd be disappointed. You just had to accept whoever came along.

"The City match programme was a penny sheet, although it was extremely good in comparison with certain other clubs. Alf Clarke, the famous local reporter, seemed to know exactly where each player was in the country, or even overseas. Naturally, he couldn't always tell us, but his articles in the City programme usually gave enough information to keep us up to date.

"I remember a board coming around Maine Road with the team changes from the programme. As it made its way around the pitch supporters would either groan or cheer depending on which 'name' would be playing. It was vital you jotted down any guest players because you wouldn't always recognise them of course.

"Until you saw the board with your own eyes you would hope and hope that your favourite would be there. I remember hoping Peter Doherty would be there, and also of course hoping Frank Swift would be there. Sometimes I'd be disappointed because a reserve goalkeeper would be put in. One time I remember someone saying that Frank Swift had just arrived at the ground half an hour before kick off, and so the board came round with his name on and everyone cheered.

"One match Swift managed to get back for was

Above: Beveridge Street pictured during the 1940s. Marjorie Cooper's children Pat and Ian can be seen in the foreground with St. Matthias Church in the background. By the time this photograph was taken the Church was no longer a place of worship and was used to store antique furniture. When the building was demolished City groundsman Stan Gibson rescued the font and placed it in his garden next door. It remained there until June 2003 and now resides at his daughter's house in Hyde. During the Seventies the font was used as part of a ceremony to 'christen' new Junior Blues. The Social Club was built on this site in the mid-sixties while the bollards - clearly visible above - were still in place when the Blues left Maine Road in 2003.

Maine Memory

■ My story of Maine Road is one of longevity rather than of an individual magical moment. I saw my first match at Maine Road in 1940, the opposition I do not remember, the programme cost 2d (less than 1 pence in new money!) with a player called A.N.Other playing in several positions. This was due to manager Wilf Wild not knowing which professional players would be in the area and available at the right time. We had a centre forward called Williamson from Rangers and a collection of other strays making up the team.

During the war we saw many good players come and go but my personal favourite was the great Frank Swift. Swifty could often be seen before games walking to the game down Maine Road carrying his boots with him. Imagine that today!

Jim Burrows, Didsbury

against Blackpool in April 1943. He'd played in the previous couple of games – a 4-0 win at home to Blackburn and a 3-1 defeat at Blackpool – but we didn't know whether he'd be at Maine Road that day or not. In the end he was, but it was one of only six appearances for City that season. So you can appreciate how lucky we felt to see him that day.

"The match itself was an excellent 1-1 draw. It was a Wartime League Cup tie and this was the third round. Blackpool were riddled with star players. Many were guests. They had Stanley Matthews, Ephraim Dodds... Burbanks of Sunderland, and City also included King of Wolverhampton, Bellis of Port Vale, and Williamson of Glasgow Rangers. There was a huge crowd, considering the circumstances, of 53,204.

"I had been up to the Lake District on holiday and decided to call in at Maine Road on my way home. I had a rucksack with me, which or course I had to take off. I stood on the Popular Side – it became known as the Kippax of course - and put the bag on the floor and at the end of the game I discovered the rucksack was soaking wet! I thought 'This is strange, it hasn't been raining', then I realised what had happened. No one wanted to lose their place during the match and so a visit to the toilet was out of the question. That was the last time I ever put a bag on the floor of the Kippax!"

Throughout the war the situation described by Dennis existed with Maine Road hosting many interesting games with several entertaining players as football provided a release from the day-to-day pressures of war.

As well as regional league football the FA also allowed several international matches to take place. The FA insisted these games be regarded as 'unofficial' internationals and refused to award caps. There was no doubt at the time however these games were true full-blooded international affairs and the same degree of commitment was shown as in any pre-war internationals. In fact, many players displayed greater commitment because of the circumstances. The stubborn refusal by the FA to issue caps was an insult to all those players, particularly so as these games were tremendous morale-boosters.

Dennis Chapman travelled to watch several

Maine Match 43/44
ENGLAND v SCOTLAND

DATE:	16th October 1943	
TYPE OF FIXTURE:	Wartime International	
ATTENDANCE:	60,000	
RESULT:	England 8 Scotland 0	
TEAMS & SCORERS:	ENGLAND	SCOTLAND
	Swift	Crozier
	Scott	Carabine
	Hardwick	Miller
	Britton	Little
	Cullis	Young
	Mercer	Campbell
	Matthews 1	Waddell
	Carter 1	Gillick
	Lawton 4	Linwood
	Hagan 2	Walker
	Compton	Deakin

■ Maine Road has hosted many international matches over the years, but none could have been more satisfying to Mancunians than this meeting between England and old rivals Scotland.

Future Liverpool manager and wily Scottish international Bill Shankly was delighted to miss out on this game: "When I heard the team I said two prayers. One of thanks to the Scots for leaving me out, and one on behalf of Adam Little who had taken my place. I knew then we'd do well to get away with less than five goals against."

Shankly saw this as the greatest side England had ever selected, and he had good cause to worry. England were in devastating form and had defeated Wales three weeks earlier, and even then the nation's most gifted player, Stanley Matthews, had hardly been given the ball. The press claimed jealous team mates had frozen him out. The truth, according to England captain Joe Mercer, was more understandable. Mercer claimed the Welsh left-back Billy Hughes had boasted how Wales could easily handle Matthews, so the English decided to focus their attacks elsewhere, leaving Wales to concentrate on an isolated Matthews. It worked a treat.

The game with Scotland at Maine Road was approached differently. Matthews was to be an integral part of the side and, as if to prove England's dominance further, Tommy Lawton was recalled for his first international in a year.

EIGHT goals were fired into the Scottish net in the International with England at Manchester City's ground yesterday. Here is the fourth — by Lawton (Everton) on the ground. Scots' consolation is that this top score of all these tests does not count in the records—it was only a war-time game and therefore "unofficial."

The two gifted players helped punish Scotland with an awesome wartime display, but it was Matthews who received most of the plaudits. According to the *Daily Express's* Frank Butler: "Matthews, at the top of his form, provided the best entertainment with his uncanny footwork and body-swerve, which gave Scotland's defence ninety minutes of nervous strain."

By half-time the score stood at an incredible 5-0. Scotland felt relieved when Raich Carter missed a penalty, however England continued to dominate and the match ended a record-breaking 8-0. The eighth was appropriately enough netted by Man of the Match Matthews, who received a tremendous ovation. According to City man Frank Swift: "I think this will go into history as Stanley's match. At times he seemed to bamboozle the whole of the Scottish rearguard on his own. When he got the eighth, entirely on his own, the whole crowd rose as one man and cheered for minutes on end. Even some of the Scots clapped their hands as Stanley made his triumphant way back to the middle."

In later years it was claimed the Scotland side was particularly weak however that claim was always disputed by Bill Shankly: "You cannot even argue about this. This was a great England team. They had wonderful players in the side, and just as many waiting to get a game. If I had been picking a team from the best players in the country at the time they beat us 8-0, I would have picked that same side. It was hard for all of us [in wartime] but it was no harder for the Scots. I can't think of any players that were not available for Scotland because of the war."

The only Scottish player who could have complained was Shankly's replacement Adam Little. The previous day he sat his degree and travelled to Manchester through the night, although the media singled him out as being the best Scottish player on the day.

Wartime internationals helped boost morale and this Maine Road match, in particular, came at what was clearly a turning point in the war. Only a few days earlier Italy had 'changed sides' by declaring war on their former ally Germany, and general optimism was spreading throughout the country.

Thousands of spectators travelled from all corners to attend Maine Road, although many found accommodation difficult to find. As a result the local authorities opened up one of the large air-raid shelters in Piccadilly Gardens to afford travelling fans a place to sleep, while the black market also flourished with forged tickets helping to make ticket touts a few pounds.

England's defeat of Scotland had a positive effect on English morale, and for Mancunians in particular the sight

of so many world class players – including their own goalkeeper - was encouraging.

Frank Swift naturally wanted to impress at Maine Road. He made a couple of fine saves, but otherwise claimed he had little to do: "It was sheer delight to be the goalkeeper on this great side. For long periods I was able to watch the machine swing into action, to note the brilliant half-back play of the three musketeers, Britton, Cullis, Mercer; the terrific shooting of Lawton; the methodical destruction of the Scottish defensive plan by Carter and Hagan; and the sheer wizardry of Stanley Matthews."

City fan Sefton Woolf was 13 years old at the time: "It seemed the most exciting day of my life. A first-ever opportunity to see the greatest players in the world sent me to the ground a month before the match to queue for a half-price standing ticket. Price one shilling.

"My friend and I had left our homes in north Manchester in the early morning, each clutching a parcel of food to last the day, and arrived at the ground at 11am. We took up our positions at the Scoreboard End, sitting on the wall behind the goal. Only a few dozen people had arrived and we had four hours to read and re-read the programme, and to listen to two kilted men explain how Willie Waddell was going to destroy our defensive left flank and lay on a multitude of goals for the Scottish forwards."

Dennis Chapman also attended this match to see the brilliant England side on his favourite ground: "We all wanted to see this one. There was 60,000 there and the atmosphere was fantastic. Both sides contained household names all the way through. I was stood in the corner between the Platt Lane and the Main Stand, near the tunnel, and I still vividly remember Stanley Matthews running towards me for the eighth goal. He came running down the right touchline, almost to the corner flag just in front of me. He cut inside and put in a beautiful centre-cum-shot into the goal.

"Of course, Swift had played his part a little. I know he had very little to save, but he set up Lawton for his fourth goal. He made one of his famous long throw-outs which Lawton got hold of and without anyone else touching the ball he scored the seventh."

Maine Memory

■ I remember the wartime match with Blackpool on 10th April 1943. It was the Football League Cup North and City drew 1-1. I was fifteen years old and went with my two brothers Roger, age 13, and Peter age 11. We travelled from Heald Green to Mauldeth Road station and were met by our school sports master Mr. Frank Moseley who lived in Burnage. He had played for City's junior teams in the 1920s and sadly died at Maine Road in 1974. We all walked to Maine Road from Mauldeth Road station. Mr. Moseley only had one stand ticket which he gave to Peter, being the youngest. The rest of us went round to the Kippax side of the ground and found an exit door ajar. We went through the gap and saw the game. I remember that Blackpool fielded a great forward line which included a few guest players. Their side included Dix from Tottenham, Burbanks (Sunderland), Dodds and Finan, and Stanley Matthews, who was a Stoke player at that time. The Blackpool side was one of the best sides you could possibly see at this period of time.

Dennis Chapman

—And this is Matthews (No. 7) scoring goal No. 8

Maine Memory

■ I first went to Maine Road when I was ten in 1943/4. My father was in the RAF and took me to the ground whenever he was on leave. We stood on the Scoreboard End, about the same spot as he and my mother had stood at Maine Road's opening match in 1923. The problem was that I was a small boy and had a problem seeing. So I was sat, uncomfortably, on one of the safety barriers! However, on his next leave he solved the problem by bringing home a small ammunition box for me to stand on. So after that, whenever he came home on leave, I would carry the box to the match with me. Nowadays my son and I have season tickets in the North Stand – more or less that same spot my parents had stood at in 1923!

My father lived in Stretford during the 1920s and although that is known as a United area, he chose to support City. When he was out of work he walked from Stretford to Hyde Road to get in at three-quarter time when they opened the gates, and then he walked all the way home again. That's what you call a supporter!

Keith Murfett

"Swift was by far the pick of the bunch when it came to northern 'keepers at this time, and was a major star. With the match being played in Manchester a lot of people went to watch him. Although, it would be unfair to say everyone came to see Swift. A good many did of course, but we had a lot of chances to see him play. The real stars most 'neutrals' came to see were Lawton, Carter, and Matthews. I've got to mention, of course, another man playing that day was Joe Mercer. He made the sixth goal with a terrific run from defence.

"The Scottish players I wanted to see were Tommy Walker – a wonderful player – and Willie Waddell of Rangers. Having said that the rest were all household names."

In the years that followed Swift, Mercer, Cullis, Lawton, and Matthews each claimed this to be the greatest performance they had participated in. Respected journalist Ivan Sharpe rated it highly and claimed wartime conditions actually helped foster team spirit and co-operation between the players. Overall the general feeling was that England possessed some excellent players who, due to wartime camaraderie, worked exceptionally well as a team.

Even Tommy Lawton, a man regularly pilloried over the years for his blunt, often negative opinions, recognised the brilliance of his team mates. In particular the four-goal hero claimed the match belonged to Matthews: "We all had moments when we've been exasperated with Stan because he'd taken the ball off down the wing as if he was playing on his own. That day at Maine Road he played as well as he had ever done. People talk about the Cup Final in 1953, but I think he was even better in that game against Scotland. It was ninety minutes of sheer wizardry." He also had praise for City's Swift: "We all played well that day and well did we deserve the applause and nice remarks at the end. Even Big Swifty, who for most of the game was a spectator, had his moment in the second half while making a smashing swallow-dive save from Campbell!"

In October 2001 *The Times* newspaper profiled the match as one of the most memorable of all time, and the following month the same newspaper claimed Matthews' performance that day was the third greatest performance by a footballer of all time. Back in 1943 journalist Frank Butler felt Matthews' performance was incredible, but he also rated the contribution of the entire team: "I doubt if an English crowd will enjoy a football exhibition as much again." It remains the largest margin of victory in the England-Scotland fixture and clearly deserves a special place in English history.

For Maine Road to have hosted such an important game says a great deal about the stadium's position in international football. This match will always be mentioned when it comes to great England performances and those Mancunians who attended feel the atmosphere and interest generated by the sixty thousand crowd helped the players succeed.

The game brought in receipts of £10,600 with some supporters – those seated in the Main Stand – paying a guinea to watch the spectacle. Swift was the only player from either of the Manchester sides to appear in this match showing the Manchester public were not simply interested in seeing their heroes, they also wanted to support their country.

'unofficial' matches during the war and there's no doubt in his mind the players showed full commitment: "These players were professionals. They enjoyed playing and wanted to put on a good show for the thousands who had paid to watch. The quality of the sides during wartime was superb."

He also believed the morale-boosting efforts could not be ignored: "When Swift and Brook and Matthews and the like were playing nobody cared whether they should have been on the front line or not. Occasionally, people would comment on them playing football rather than fighting, but nobody complained about George Formby or Will Hay entertaining the troops or making films. To my mind their performances for England and for the other clubs during wartime is equivalent to the role played by leading entertainers of the period. In fact, they were considerably more entertaining than Formby for the vast majority of the public!"

On 16th October 1943 Maine Road hosted one such international match between England and old rivals Scotland. It was a classic spirit-raising match and brought a great 8-0 victory to England. There appeared an even greater interest in international matches during this period than at other times. Perhaps this owed much to the waves of patriotism felt across the country, but it's fair to say many Mancunians were interested in hearing national football news. The City programme always tried to help.

When City met Crewe in October 1944, the City programme contained over a page (out of only four) of detail on the national side, although it's fair to say most of this focused on the role of Frank Swift and the possible selection of George Smith. Swift was a very busy player during this period. As well as playing for the national side he was also a key member of the British Services' team. On 23rd September 1944 he helped City

beat Stockport 6-2, then a week later played for the Services side in Paris. Two days after that he played another Services game in Brussels, and on 7th October kept goal for City in a 1-1 draw with Crewe. In between the Stockport match and the game in Paris he was very nearly involved in a plane crash when an Allied aircraft narrowly missed the Services' plane. According to the City programme: "Newspaper reports speak of only twenty feet separating the two 'planes from collision, and I am told that the 'near miss' caused one famous international player in the party to be violently sick."

Other than the October 1943 international, only one other first class City match attracted a crowd of over 60,000 and that was the North Regional (second period) League game with Blackpool on 22nd April 1944.

As far as the development of Maine Road was concerned, once the Second World War ended, all prospect of improving the stadium had to be put on hold until the city itself returned to normal; within a mile of Manchester Town Hall 165 warehouses, 150 offices, and 200 other business premises had been destroyed or badly damaged by bombing raids.

Significant damage occurred in the Shambles area off Cateaton Street (close to the Cathedral), in Piccadilly and close to the Irwell. According to the *Guide to Manchester and Salford* published in 1948: "Mainly in two 'blitz' raids at Christmas 1940 hundreds of factories and thousands of houses were damaged and destroyed. The Free Trade Hall, classic home of music and oratory, was destroyed; the Royal Exchange, largest of its kind in the country, was partly gutted; the massive Assize Courts were demolished; the Cathedral was hit; frightful gaps

were torn in Portland Street and Mosley Street, the finest commercial thoroughfares in Britain; the quaint historic survival known as the Shambles was burned out."

Curoiusly many of these badly damaged areas – particularly the Royal Exchange and the Shambles – were the same areas targeted by a terrorist bomb in 1996.

It seems likely the development of Platt Lane in 1931 and 1935 would have been followed in the late 1930s/early forties by the covering of the Scoreboard End and Main Stand corner had war not intervened. Development after the war would have to wait. Maine Road was not in its best state – even general repairs and upkeep of the venue had taken a back seat during the war – but it was still a major venue, and with many other issues in the wider sporting world, the stadium was about to prove its worth to several major clubs.

Above: George Smith and Eric Westwood in training. Smith, a guest at Maine Road's final game in 2003, always kept his injured right arm and hand covered by his sleeve.

Maine Memory

■ I had five uncles all born within half a mile of Old Trafford and, not surprisingly they were United fans. All except my Uncle Jim that is. For some unknown reason he was a die-hard City fan and was determined his nephews would follow in his footsteps and not his brothers'. On Christmas Day 1943 all the uncles were in the Army and the only one who managed to get leave was Uncle Jim. I suppose it was luck really, but he decided to take me to Maine Road for a match with Everton. I was not much more than a toddler then and I remember being fascinated by the colours and the noise. City lost the match 5-3 but that didn't matter. I'd tasted my first Maine Road match and I was a Blue for ever more. Despite the ups and downs over the years, I have always been grateful that it was my Uncle Jim who got leave and not one of the others. After all if my first match had been at Old Trafford I might have been a... No! Perish the thought!

Frank Thompson

Chants and Songs

THE history of supporter-singing and noise-generation could fill an entire book in its own right, however it's worth pausing in this story of Maine Road to consider the sounds generated by City fans at home games over the years.

During the club's 36-year stay at Hyde Road supporters would often sing along to the band prior to the match and then, once the game commenced, would give encouragement to the players. One report from the 1890s described the Hyde Road atmosphere as being electric – this is significant. Electricity was still in its infancy as far as domestic use was concerned and it's fair to say it was viewed as being something fantastic and even futuristic. In many ways the use of the word 'electric' meant this was considerably better than the norm. Over the years the term 'electric atmosphere' has been overplayed, but in 1890s Manchester this was a major recognition that the Hyde Road support was something powerful and unique. It should be remembered also that supporters were known for wearing fancy dress costumes and bringing musical instruments into the ground on occasion during this period.

By the time the club moved to Maine Road the fancy dress and musical instruments had long since been forgotten, but the atmosphere remained. City fans were great believers in fair play and would support any player if he played in a positive manner, but they would also react strongly to those who were seen as ungentlemenly. During the 1925-6 season Manchester United's captain and hardman Frank Barson laid out City's Sam Cowan. According to reports he 'totally flattened' him and then feigned injury himself. The City faithful made sure he knew how they felt and, according to the *Manchester Football News*, they "hooted more vigorously than had ever been heard" and then every time Barson obtained the ball they "booed and hissed with grim determination". Barson, incidentally, had been given a pub by United as a bonus for achieving promotion within three seasons!

Throughout the pre-World War Two period supporters continued to sing along to the band either before the game or during half-time. They also would encourage the players by shouting phrases such as 'Give it to Tommy [Johnson]' or 'Play Up City!'

Sometimes songs would be published in the local papers about players such as Billy Meredith or Sam Cowan, but whether these were ever sung at the ground is unknown, although it does seem unlikely. Newspaper cartoons would often suggest that songs or even primitive chants had been heard at the ground. Tommy Johnson's son, Alan, remembers his father's view of the crowd: "He loved the supporters and enjoyed playing here. It meant a lot to him and he particularly enjoyed it when the crowd started to shout his name. I can't remember exactly what they shouted but it always included the name 'Tommy' or 'Tosh'. I think he was the fans' favourite at the time."

Fran Parker, who first attended Maine Road around 1926, remembers how the crowd was very noisy at that time: "It used to be a thrill to hear the crowd in those days. They'd be making lots of noise. 'Up the Blues!' and 'Come on you Blues' were two of the most popular shouts of the time."

Another fan, Denis Houlston, also first attended Maine Road in 1926: "In those days no-one ever wore club strips or replica shirts. We all wore caps and drab clothing, but we were well behaved with no malicious banter. However, when cup-ties came along we paraded with our scarves, rattles, bugles and rosettes – these were usually home-made from paper with a silver cardboard FA Cup. They'd be brought out for each tie and then safely put away until the following tie."

In 1984 Harry Godwin, City's Chief scout during the Mercer-Allison era, told of one popular saying of the late 1920s: "The ball would be pushed forward for Toseland to chase after and every time the ball was sent in front of him the crowd would call out, 'Get after them pigeons, Tosie!' It happened every game and everybody shouted it. I don't know why we called 'em pigeons."

On occasion supporters would burst into popular ditties of the period, or would sing songs of celebration. "Auld Lang Syne" was sung in the 1920s while "For he's a Jolly Good Fellow" was sung frequently to players who had married in the morning prior to a match, and was heard extensively when City won the Championship in 1937. Even in the early 1950s "She's a Lassie From Lancashire" could be heard emanating from the ground during key cup matches.

Over time the popular songs of the period gave way to ones naming City's players or key events. One of the earliest and most well-known songs of the fifties was a City version of 'Bless Em All':

Bless 'em all, Bless 'em all;
Bert Trautmann, Dave Ewing and Paul;
Bless Roy Little who blocks out the wing;
Bless Jack Dyson the penalty king;
And with Leivers and Spurdle so tall;
And Johnstone, the Prince of them all;
Come on the light Blues;
It's always the right blue;
So cheer up me lads;
Bless 'em all.

From the fifties onwards chants started to develop but there was still the old-style one-liner that would prove popular. Fran Parker: "Because Dave Ewing was a good header of the ball we used to shout 'There's only one head bigger than Dave's and that's Birkenhead!' It always brought a laugh."

Another Fifties song was 'City is the Team':
City's the team;
They're the best team in the land;
Playing the game;
Always in command;
We may lose a point or two;
But never do despair;
Cos you can't beat the boys in the old light blue;
When they come from Manchester.

According to numerous sources Alex Harley (1962-3) was the first player to have a chant specifically created for him, although supporters from the twenties and thirties were the first to focus their shouting at a particular player.

Many of City's most recognisable chants came from the sixties with the most important, from an historical context, being the anthem celebrating City's triumphs under Mercer and Allison (sung to the tune of Auld Lang Syne):

In '62 the boys in Blue fell into Division Two;
The Stretford End cried out aloud;
It's the end for you Sky Blues;

Joe Mercer came;
We played the game;
We went to Rotherham;
We won one-nil and we went back into Division One;

Since then we've won the League;
We've won the Cup;
We've been to Europe too (And Won!);
And When we win the League again;
We'll sing this song to you;

City, City, City....

Other memorable chants from this period included 'Singing The Blues'; 'The Mighty Glyn [Pardoe]' (also became Mighty Wyn after Davies and Mighty Quinn after Niall); 'Hi ho, hi ho, we're off to Mexico, with Bell and Lee and Summerbee, hi ho, hi ho..', and various other traditional Blue hits.

The late sixties and early seventies saw the first abusive chants as well. Most of these were directed at Manchester United, but other teams, such as Liverpool were also featured. These do not make pleasant reading, but are important in terms of the history of chanting at Maine Road. One of the earliest examples uses the song 'From the Halls of Montezuma to the Shores of Tripoli':

From the banks of the River Irwell to the shores of Sicily;
We'll fight, fight, fight for City to win the Football League;
To Hell with Man United, To Hell with Liverpool;
We'll fight, fight, fight for City to win the Football League;

We will stop on the banks of the Mersey on our way up to the top;
The right will take the Stretford End and the left will take the Kop;
We will hang Fitzpatrick by his balls and we'll paint Old Trafford blue;
Then as we march down Wembley Way we will sing this song to you.

The name Fitzpatrick refers to United's John Fitzpatrick who, in the August 1968 Maine Road derby, performed a number of crunching tackles on Colin Bell. Though not a legendary player as far as United are concerned, his inclusion in this song makes it clear what City fans thought of his determination in derby matches.

Another song from this period, 'Kippax Boys', focuses on City fans' loathing of United and warns Reds not to enter the Parkside pub or walk down Kippax Street before ending with:

We are the boys from the Kippax;
We're loyal and we're true;
And when we play United we are ready for a do;
We don't carry razors;
We don't carry lead;
We only carry hatchets to bury in your head.

Clearly these songs were hardly likely to give a good impression of football banter, but they do help to outline how supporters' attitudes had changed. All major clubs had songs like these coming from their more vocal supporters during the early seventies, and little was done to change views. Sadly, songs referring to the Munich Air Disaster have also been heard at Maine Road at various points since the seventies, although the most familiar – if that's an appropriate word - of these chants was first sung by Bolton supporters.

Of course, only a minority created and sang these songs and throughout the seventies other tunes were heard on a regular basis. Often television adverts, such as British Airways' 'We'll take more care of you', or popular tunes of the period such as Rod Stewart's 'Sailing' (We are City, we are City, super City from Maine Road) were adapted. Occasionally traditional songs such as 'Jingle Bells', 'White Christmas', 'You are my Sunshine', and 'London Bridge is Falling Down' would be converted into Blue chants.

In the 1980s, once away fans were housed in the old Platt Lane Stand and it became obvious how many opposition supporters were in attendance, the Kippax would often sing 'We've got more in the Junior Blues, doo dah, doo, dah'. On occasion chants would seem a little surreal. Shortly after Channel Four commenced broadcasting in the eighties, City fans on the Kippax pointed at fans of Everton and sang 'We all agree, 'Corra' is better than Brookside'.

'Blue Moon' became popular during the 1989-90 season after first being sung at Anfield on the opening day of the season. By the time of the Manchester derby in September it was already one of the club's most powerful anthems. Another hit followed when fans created the 'Niall Quinn's Disco Pants' song. When he moved to Sunderland the song travelled with him and he's even been seen on television singing the song himself.

The last decade of the ground witnessed more humour from the fans with self-mocking songs sung frequently. 'We never win at home and we never win away' had been popular in the eighties, but was resurrected during the Alan Ball reign. At derby matches United fans were astounded when City took hold of their supposedly humiliating remembrance of how many years it had been since City had last won a major trophy - 'City is Our Name' - and firstly sang it in its original form, then adapted it to say '17 years and we're still here, City is our name'. The number of years has altered a little since its first airing of course, but the message it continues to get across is the loyalty of City fans.

Many heartfelt chants became popular during the nineties. The strongest is 'City 'Till I Die' – a song which came to epitomise the loyalty of supporters during the struggles of the late nineties. Other songs such as the 'Pride of Manchester', or 'The Only Football Team To Come From Manchester' stress Mancunian attitude, while 'We're Not Really Here' has been used by supporters frequently in the final years. Its origins have been disputed frequently over the years. Some claim it refers back to a League game at Luton in the 1980s when Luton Town banned visiting supporters and a small group of Mancunians created the song, while others point to a friendly in Ireland when a disturbance took place in a bar. Whatever the truth, the song came to symbolise the disbelief of playing in Division Two and, more recently, the demise of Maine Road.

One of the most entertaining features of games during Maine Road's final seasons concerns the territorial chants between the stands. The North Stand has reclaimed its rightful place as City's most vocal stand and would on occasion goad the Kippax with chants of 'You're Not Famous Any More' and then follow up with 'We Are The North Stand'. The Kippax would retaliate and the general atmosphere would improve. Occasionally, the Platt Lane and Main Stand would be brought into the battle of the stands.

It was this territorial style of chanting which brought great laughter to inhabitants of the Platt Lane and southern end of the Main Stand when, at a fairly quiet moment of Maine Road's final game the children and adults of the Family Stand started their own version of the chant. 'We are the Family Stand' started by a small group but within seconds the entire corner stand erupted. It is highly unlikely the North Stand heard the noise, and when the Family Stand began singing 'North Stand, North Stand, Give Us A Song' City's more vocal fans remained silent prompting the children to make mocking noises.

Although Maine Road has ceased to be a venue, it's clear those present in the Family Stand on that final day will ensure they play their part in making City's new home a passionate venue.

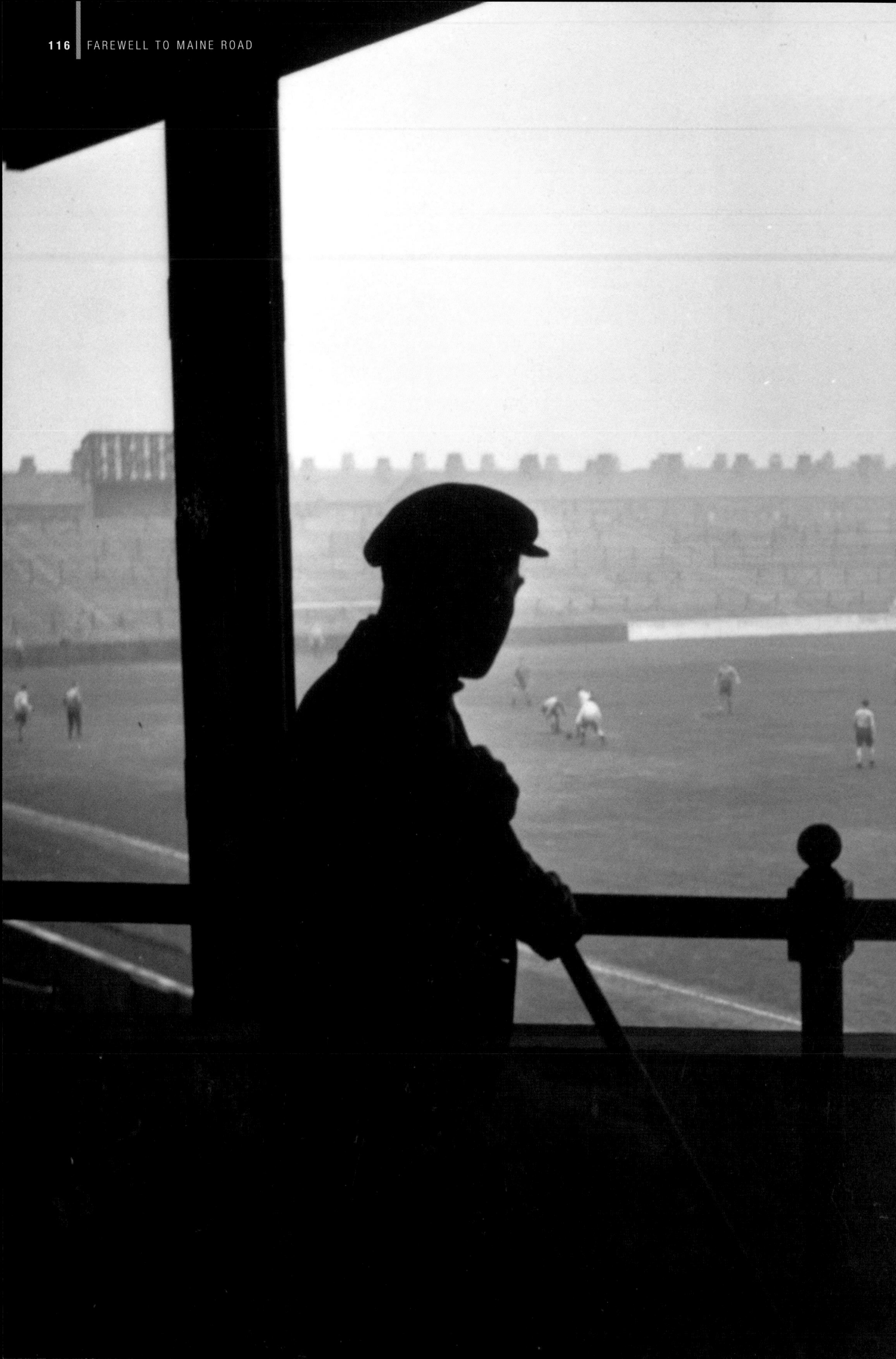

Chapter Five

You're Supposed to be at Home!

Everyone wanted to see Yeovil, the greatest giant-killers since the war, and when they were drawn against cup holders Manchester United at Maine Road there was sure to be a crush for tickets. Yet nobody anticipated little non-League Yeovil would attract 81,565 spectators. With twenty minutes to kick off all Maine Road's gates had been firmly shut with thousands more locked outside. It was one of the biggest gates ever outside London.

Stephen Kelly, Back Page United 1990

THE biggest Maine Road story of the immediate post-war period had to be the continued use of the ground by arch-rivals Manchester United. United's home, Old Trafford, had suffered bomb damage on the night of 11th March 1941 with the main stand almost destroyed and an area of terracing damaged. The pitch had also been badly scorched. The Reds were unable to stage first class football there and so the Blues offered the use of Maine Road.

Once the Old Trafford pitch was improved both the City and United reserve sides used United's home, while the first teams both resided at Maine Road.

This had not been the first time both sides had considered sharing their grounds. Shortly after the First World War, City had mooted moving away from cramped Hyde Road to join the Reds at Old Trafford but the City management eventually ruled against it. Then in

1920, after the Hyde Road main stand had been destroyed by fire, City asked United if they could temporarily share Old Trafford. The Reds agreed to this but according to the *Athletic News* from November 1920 there were significant conditions: "The basis which the United suggested last week was the City should take the equivalent of last season's 'gate' in the corresponding match and the remainder should belong to the United. As gates have increased by 30 per cent, at the very least, the Manchester City directors declined to entertain the proposal and no wonder.

"Manchester United did not in our opinion manifest the much vaunted League spirit. They missed a great opportunity to make the club popular by a fine sporting act. The followers of Manchester City have a greater affection for the old club than ever. And they have formed a just appreciation of their neighbours."

Below: This photograph of the original Main Stand was probably taken during the City-United derby matches of April 1946. The interesting point is that the roof of the Main Stand is still blacked out following the war. Originally the gable carried the club's name but this was painted out during the war. Sadly, it was never painted back and within a few years the gable and front of the roof was covered with advertising.

Above: This cartoon appeared in the United programme prior to a Maine Road derby.

In 1920 City had regularly played in front of 40,000 capacity crowds at Hyde Road – at Old Trafford these could have increased to 60,000 plus – and to see the receipts for an additional 20,000 make their way straight into the pockets of United was too much to ask.

Understandably, United's use of City's ground during the post war years has occasionally been reported as making City a great deal of money, but the truth is rather different. City did benefit but the major winner from United's time at Maine Road was United themselves. They were able to attract significant crowds – larger than any held at Old Trafford – and as a result made substantial profits.

When City offered Maine Road to United the Blues were not concerned with how much they could make from of their lodgers, but simply offering their neighbours a chance to continue. United could have turned City down and chosen another venue – clearly any of the other League grounds in the greater Manchester area would have welcomed them. Also other sports venues, such as the Belle Vue ground where City almost moved in 1923, could have accommodated United for a while.

The sharing of Maine Road was simply to allow United to survive. Nothing more, nothing less. Sadly, from a Blue perspective the dual use did have a detrimental effect on City's long-term direction.

The immediate post-war period was a boom time for football and many clubs recorded huge gates. In

Manchester however supporters' loyalties were tested. Few fans ever travelled to away games but Mancunians were desperate to watch good football. United's use of Maine Road brought a solution for many former soldiers. In the 1980s one such squaddie, Fred Burden, described his experience of football during this period: "As a boy I'd been a City supporter. Whenever I could I'd go to Maine Road and watch Big Swifty, Busby, Brooky and Doherty. There was only one team for me. Then after the war it seemed natural to keep going to Maine Road. It was like home. It had a familiar feel. Of course with United playing there I then started to watch City one week and United the next. It was a natural thing to do.

"United had been the poor relations throughout my boyhood and when they came to Maine Road they were managed by a City player - Matt Busby. It seemed right to support him and to see United reborn. My first United games were really just out of interest or perhaps even sympathy. We'd all suffered in the war and there wasn't really any rivalry between the clubs.

"But when it came to proper League and Cup football after the war that's when it all started to change for me. Busby's United were a better side than City and, with a young family, money became tight. I had to make a choice. By the time the Reds moved back to Old Trafford, I moved back with them. I didn't have enough money to watch them both and, in my mind at the time, I was still supporting Manchester. Busby was a Blue and I'd grown up watching him. When United won the Cup in 1948 all of Manchester was happy."

Former City Chief Scout Harry Godwin also told of this time during the 1980s: "United played at Maine Road just after the war, and because they were a better team than City they took over a lot of the support of the men whose loyalty had strayed while they were away in the services, and of their youngsters who were just getting interested. United were looking like a team, and they won the Cup in 1948."

In 2002, City supporter James Dowd gave his view of this period: "There were about equal numbers of Blues and Reds at school. The banter and leg-pulling was friendly and there was none of the nastiness which has sadly infected many rival supporters in a city like Manchester. We would often go together to Maine Road every week to see City and United alternately. United shared City's ground because Old Trafford was a bombed wreck.

"We Blues grudgingly admired Red players like Johnny Carey, Stan Pearson, Bert Whalley and, above all, Jack Rowley with his thunderous shot. But we staunchly insisted we liked the great Frank Swift better than all the United players put together! I am certain it was Frank who single-handedly retained the loyalties of many younger fans.

"When United moved back to Old Trafford several of my former school Blues moved with them. They preferred to watch the more successful team. Illogically I felt they were traitors. Go to Old Trafford? Never! It was a football lesson that a successful team will attract hangers-on. United have certainly gained a lot of hangers-on over the years from all over the country. In contrast nobody can accuse City of having fair weather fans for we have had to endure a lot of bad weather!"

It's clear from those present at the time the great rivalry between the clubs that exists today, and indeed had existed at times pre-war, was not a major factor during this period, although there was still some needle as City forward George Smith remembers: "We always

Evening Chronicle

FOOTBALL EDITION

FLAG SAUCE —of course!

No. 15,186   Threehalfpence   SATURDAY, APRIL 6, 1946   A KEMSLEY NEWSPAPER

SMITH'S FOUR AGAINST UNITED

City's magnificent win in a game of thrills

MANCHESTER UNITED 1   MANCHESTER CITY 4

By ALF CLARKE

MANCHESTER'S "Derby" match at Maine-road this afternoon was a game of thrills and sensations, and if the result was surprising it was no more than the City deserved. Hero of the match was Smith, three of whose four goals were scored in seven minutes.

Aston got the only goal for United after 53 minutes, and so atoned, to some extent, for his previous failures.

For the greater part of the game the United attack was a disappointment. The forwards played much too closely. On the other hand, the City opened out the play. They were strong alike in attack and defence.

For once in a way the United left wing had no punch.

Both teams were as announced.

UNITED. — Tapken; Whalley, Walton; Carey, Chilton, Cockburn; Delaney, Aston, Hanlon, Pearson, Rowley.

CITY.—Swift; Williams, Barkas; Walsh, Cardwell, McDowall; Dunkley, Herd, Constantine, Smith, Emptage.

Whalley won the toss for United and they had the sun at their backs in attacking the city end goal.

Rowley made progress down the left, but he was forced to put behind when tackled by Williams.

In the next minute the City became very menacing. Herd pushed the ball down the middle to Constantine, who bore down on the United goal, only to see Chilton make a magnificent tackle and charge down his shot.

THE CITY POINT OF VIEW

EVERYBODY thought this was going to be a walk-over for United. On the contrary, the City were much the better side in the first 20 minutes, and had their inside forwards finished better City might have been further in the lead.

City, forwards did everything except score. Smith and Constantine failing close in, but I can remember Swift making two great saves from Hanlon.

A game of thrills, and when Smith headed a goal from Constantine's centre after 35 minutes it was no more than City deserved. There

the ball off his head. The goalkeeper next made a smashing save from Hanlon when all seemed lost. He was injured in the effort and had to receive attention.

SMITH TAKES A CHANCE

After 35 minutes City took the lead. The goal followed a throw-in. Constantine broke through, veered to the right and centred, and SMITH, running in, got his head to the ball to deflect it out of Tapken's reach.

It was a lead which, on the play, City had scarcely deserved, though their fast, open play had always looked menacing.

The surprising thing about United had been the lack of thrust on their left wing. Indeed, there had been little effective shooting by any of their forwards.

Just before the interval City nearly got a second goal when Chilton only just succeeded in blocking a shot from Constantine. Then Herd shot wide.

Half-time: Manchester United 0, Manchester City 1.

SECOND HALF

After an early attack by United had been beaten back, City made progress, but Chilton turned the ball back to Tapken to clear. United's weakness in attack was young Aston, who just lacked the experience neces-

NEARLY A GOAL. Constantine of City, m?s a great effort but fails (above). Tapken, U. d's goalkeeper, goes down to make a great save (left).

Bury outclassed at Middlesbrough

MIDDLESBROUGH 3   BURY 0

BURY were well beaten at Middlesbrough, where the home team playing fast, clever football soon established the mastery.

Taylor, in the Bury goal made several brilliant saves, but little was seen of the Bury attack. Middlesbrough's forwards, with Murphy and Mannion outstanding, kept the Bury defence on the run.

Bury improved for a time after the interval, but Nash in the Middlesbrough goal dealt confidently with several shots. Mannion who returned from service in the Middle East after four years' service in the Army, captained Middlesbrough. The crowd numbered more than 20,000 at the start.

Bury made two late changes

Aston; Howarth, Hart, Halton; Roberts, N. Berry, Livingstone, Quigley, Kilshaw.

Middlesbrough, with the slight breeze, were first to attack, but Dews' final pass was short. Mannion was prominent, but Aston cleared.

Spuhler after a tussle with Aston, worked an opening for Dews, but Taylor easily saved the inside left's shot. Middlesbrough were doing most of the attacking.

IN THE AIR

Mannion often troubled the Bury defence. Walker worked his way through, but his shot was

HAGAN STAR FOR ARMY XI

F.A. XI 3, A.P.T.C. XI 5

HAGAN, of Sheffield United, was the star of the International Trial match at Wembley to-day. Partnering Compton again, he gave the F.A

---

wanted to beat them! I watched United at Maine Road if we didn't have a game, but I don't think I ever wanted them to play well. When we played against them we always wanted to win well. We didn't want to take it easy, ever."

Smith often performed well against the Reds with one game in particular bringing out his determination to beat City's tenants: "It was April 1946 when I scored four goals and we beat them 4-1. They were never really part of the game. We didn't let them get into it, but I suppose it all started in the dressing rooms. You see with United being at home for this match I suppose they should have used the home dressing room, but we wouldn't let them. It was our ground and so it was our dressing room. They had to use the away dressing room which, throughout my time at Maine Road, was also the second team's room. I suppose this meant they would be uneasy from the start."

A crowd of 62,144 watched a thrilling City performance with Smith's first goal coming after 35 minutes. According to the *Manchester Evening Chronicle*: "The goal followed a throw-in. Constantine broke through, veered to the right and centred, and Smith, running in, got his head to the ball to deflect it out of Tapken's reach."

City remained in front until the 53rd minute when Aston headed an equaliser, but that's when the game really came to life with Smith in outstanding form: "A foul by Whalley on McDowall led to City scoring their second goal after 65 minutes. McDowall took the kick, dropped it at the far side of the post, where Smith and Tapken went for it. Smith got there first and put it at the

Left: The front page of the Evening Chronicle makes very good reading for George Smith and all City fans following the Maine Road derby of April 1946 - United's home game.

Below right: Former Maine Road idol Peter Doherty returned with Derby County and scored twice in the 1946 FA Cup semi-final replay.

Below: City's forwards line up for the camera in 1946. Left to right: Maurice Dunkley, Andy Black, Jim Constantine, George Smith and Tommy Capel.

back of the net. But worse was to follow for United. Two minutes later, when Tapken was adjudged to have handled the ball outside the penalty area, the free kick on the line, taken by Herd led to a short centre, and Smith, on the line, again headed it home.

"This hat-trick by Smith – a grand individual feat – was no more than his brilliant play deserved."

Smith's fourth goal was a little unusual: "Smith had veered over to the right wing and, from an oblique angle, he put in a shot which went between Tapken and the upright, and then struck the far upright and went into the net. This was after 72 minutes."

Scoring four goals - three in seven minutes – made Smith the undisputed star of the game. Smith: "I wasn't much of a drinker... I never went wild or anything... but beating United in that manner and by scoring four goals was a wonderful moment. I enjoyed the day and enjoyed most of the games against them during this period. It was nice for the landlords to put one over the tenants."

Four years prior to the game Smith had suffered greatly when he was on the receiving end of what would in the 21st century be described as 'friendly fire'. He was on active service in Africa when he and a few army colleagues were shot at from an allied aircraft. A bullet entered his right arm above the elbow and emerged a good six or seven inches further down his arm. He was lucky the bullet had only entered his arm, but desperately unlucky to have been fired at by servicemen fighting on the same side.

Smith spent some time recovering in Africa before being able to return to Manchester. When he did come home the situation was not particularly good. Not only was the use of his right arm seriously limited, but City was uncertain whether he could continue to play. Inevitably, life for most Mancunians was difficult during the war years, and with his future in doubt Smith needed reassurance from the club. However, the club were undoubtedly keen to ensure they kept the wage bill down as much as possible and needed every player to demonstrate his fitness. After a series of trials and much heartache Smith returned to the club and on 26th August 1944 celebrated his restoration to the first team with a hat-trick against Tranmere in the opening match of the new season. This was his first appearance at senior level since 25th April 1942.

Although Smith and the City players had little time for United, the Blues did appear to accommodate United as best they could at a managerial and public level. Indeed, the Blues always advertised United's fixtures in their match programme, and always tried to help when it came to fixture allocation. City could have been awkward and insisted their fixtures always took priority but they didn't. The Blues would often negotiate with the Reds when fixtures clashed and often – though not always – City would let United have Maine Road first – a point best demonstrated at the start of the 1946-7 season.

United's first post-war Football League match at Maine Road was a 2-1 victory over Grimsby Town in Division One on Saturday 31st August 1946. The game was watched by 41,025, while City's first home game of the period was played in the late afternoon on Wednesday 4th September. Because of this the Blues could only attract 28,000 for the visit of Bury in Division Two. The following Saturday however City drew 47,319 for a goalless game with Chesterfield.

United's spell at Maine Road lasted until August 1949, but there were many other non-City related stories connected with Maine Road during this period. One of

Maine Match 45/46

BIRMINGHAM CITY v DERBY COUNTY

DATE:	27th March 1946	
TYPE OF FIXTURE:	FA Cup Semi-final replay	
ATTENDANCE:	80,480	
RESULT:	Birmingham City 0 Derby County 4	
TEAMS & SCORERS:	BIRMINGHAM	DERBY
	Merrick	Woodley
	Duckhouse	Nicholas
	Jennings	Parr
	Harris	Bullions
	Turner	Howe
	Mitchell	Musson
	Mulraney	Harrison
	Dougall	Carter
	Jones	Stamps 2
	Bodie	Doherty 2
	Edwards	Duncan

■ One of the biggest matches ever to be played at Maine Road was the 1946 FA Cup semi-final replay between Birmingham City and Derby County. An incredible 80,480 – a record for a midweek game played between two Football League clubs - witnessed it. Peter Doherty, the former City great, played for Derby in this match and wrote about it in his autobiography *Spotlight on Football*: "Neither side had scored when the game had run its normal span, so we turned round for extra-time – and then things happened! Five minutes only had gone when Duncan slipped a neat pass inside to me, and I tore in to hit the ball past Merrick into the net, colliding with Duckhouse, the Birmingham right-back, as I did so. Duckhouse's ankle was broken, unfortunately, and he had to be carried off the field on a stretcher. It was purely an accident, as I couldn't possibly avoid the collision, so great was the speed at which I was travelling. The ball had been played however, and was, as a matter of fact, curling up the back of the net before Duckhouse hit the turf.

"With an inside forward at full back, Birmingham fell away, and Stamps and I added further goals to give us a comfortable victory."

The game ended 4-0 to eventual cup-winners Derby and gate receipts totalled a record £28,205. City fan James Dowd had wanted to see the game: "It's the match I most regret not seeing. Derby included great players such as Raich Carter, Dally Duncan and, of course the former Blue Peter Doherty. Doherty was Dad's favourite player and, according to him, was the best player ever to wear a City shirt. One of the few times I saw Dad angry was a few weeks after his demob when Doherty was transferred to Derby County. 'What the hell are those directors playing at?' he said to me, as if I could give him an answer. 'You watch. He'll win something for Derby and we'll win nothing'. Derby did win the FA Cup after this game with Birmingham and Dad merely shrugged. There was nothing he could say.

"I arrived at the ground for the semi-final at my usual time to find the gates closed and disappointed fans leaving the ground in droves. It wasn't all-ticket for standing room and the fact admission had been doubled to 2s 6d – twelve and a half pence in today's money – did not deter anybody. Yet I heard descriptions of some of the play and goals that were relayed to a few of us by a sailor who had scrambled up inside the steeple of a derelict church that stood where the City superstore was later built."

Derek Bennett received permission to attend: "I was allowed by my father to wag a day off school to watch this match. We were so crushed at the northern end of the ground that I was passed over the crowd by hand down to and over the wall finishing up watching the game sat on my handkerchief leaning against the wall. It was a game I shall always remember for the crowd and atmosphere. In the game Peter Doherty clashed with the Birmingham right full back who suffered a broken leg very close to where I was sitting."

Bob Knowles was at the opposite end of the stadium and remembers the match more for events off the pitch: "Even though I am a City supporter I had to be at this match. It was one of the first major matches of the immediate post-war period and for it to be held at Maine Road was a major honour for the club. We normally stood on the Kippax side of the ground but we had decided to go behind the goal at the Platt Lane end to avoid the crush. We knew the Popular Side would be packed on a day like this. I remember seeing a couple of supporters climbing up on to the Platt Lane roof. I think they shinned up a drainpipe at the back of the stand.

"I was about sixteen and stood on the terraces with my uncle. We were close to one of the staircases that used to come up at the back of the concrete terracing but before the wooden terracing. As we waited we heard a crash and a supporter had fallen through a skylight on the roof and landed about ten yards away from where we stood. St. John Ambulance men soon arrived. A few people had been injured by the incident but I don't think anybody died."

Several supporters recalled this incident with some claiming there were fatalities, although no evidence has been found to support that. Clearly, though, this was a match everybody wanted to see.

the biggest was the 1946 FA Cup semi-final replay between Birmingham City and Derby County, watched by 80,480.

Two other major games were played in 1946. One was the victory international with Wales in November, but the first was the England-Scotland match played in aid of the Bolton Disaster Fund. These internationals were followed in November 1949 by a tremendous match between England and Ireland. The English won 9-2 but the match was also newsworthy because it was actually the first World Cup qualifying match ever played in England.

On a domestic level Maine Road became a familiar venue for FA Cup matches. In December 1946, Lincoln played Wrexham in an FA Cup replay, while the following April Burnley and Liverpool met in the semi-final. A crowd of 72,000 witnessed a well-deserved Burnley triumph.

Stockport and Shrewsbury met for a Cup replay in January 1948 and then Crewe and Oldham met at City's ground in another replay in December 1949.

Above: In August 1946 Frank Swift, seen here taking the ball off Willie Thornton's head, captained England in a 2-2 draw with Scotland at Maine Road. The game was played to raise funds following the Burnden Park disaster. Thirty-three people were killed and over 500 injured when crush barriers collapsed in a huge crowd at Bolton's FA Cup tie with Stoke the previous March.

He did not know he had won 352 minutes cup-tie

BILLY McCULLOCH, the Stockport County left half-back, will never be able to describe how he scored from a free kick to win the cup-tie against Shrewsbury at Manchester City's ground on Monday afternoon. He was suffering from concussion, took the kick "from memory," staggered off the field at the final whistle with other limping and tired players, and was taken to Stockport Infirmary, where he was operated on for a blood clot.
Stockport won 3—2 by this goal of his, netted in the seventh minute of extra time, and after a 352 minutes' struggle against a non-league club, Stockport are now at home to Torquay United in the third round on January 10.

Maine Road hosted four semi-finals in five seasons at the start of the 1950s. Firstly, Liverpool beat Everton (1950), then Birmingham and Blackpool played out a goalless match. This was followed in 1953 by a victory for Bolton against Everton. Interestingly, Everton have never won a semi-final at Maine Road.

In 1954 Sheffield Wednesday and Preston met at Maine Road, but during the same year the ground also staged an inter-League match when the Football League faced the League of Ireland.

A point worth noting about the semi-finals is that with City's involvement in both the 1955 and 1956 finals, Maine Road's chance of staging a semi-final was severely reduced.

Other neutral matches such as local finals were regularly staged at Maine Road. James Dowd remembers attending Maine Road regularly for non-City matches:

Right: Sam Cowan photographed in the manager's office at Maine Road during his brief spell in charge of the team.

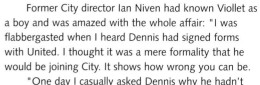

Maine Memory

■ When my two sons were boys I used to take them into the Platt Lane. There was a railing that used to go around the terracing and I'd put them on there and then stand in front of them. I think this was the most enjoyable time watching City because I was there with my young sons and we'd all be sharing the fun of it all.

Harry Bramble

"One of my most vivid memories is going to see Manchester Schoolboys, in their rugby style shirts, play in 1946 or 1947. One quick-moving and clever forward stood out. He was called Dennis Viollet. Later, of course, he achieved fame with United. As he had showed his skills and promise on their ground why didn't the City management snap him up?"

The game James refers to may have been the Lancashire Schools Cup game between Manchester Boys and Salford Boys in April 1949. The match was covered extensively in the *Daily Dispatch* with respected journalist Archie Ledbrooke also commenting on Viollet's skills. As James pointed out Viollet should have been a Blue. His family were all City fans and he even played with Alex Herd's son David. City goalkeeper Frank Swift had noticed Viollet's skills and had mentioned him to the City management but for some unknown reason City ignored Viollet's obvious talents. Swift became angry with the club and insisted they meet with the Viollet family.

A meeting was organised with the Viollets waiting in reception for over an hour. Dennis' father demanded to know what was happening and was told the Scout had decided to go out instead. The Viollets, understandably, swept out of Maine Road and the following day, when a cheery Frank Swift popped around to see how the meeting had gone, they told the City 'keeper what had happened. He was furious and marched to the ground to confront the scouting team. After an unproductive debate Swift decided to speak with his old friend Matt Busby and the following day the United manager personally visited the Viollet family. Inevitably Viollet signed for the Reds.

Former City director Ian Niven had known Viollet as a boy and was amazed with the whole affair: "I was flabbergasted when I heard Dennis had signed forms with United. I thought it was a mere formality that he would be joining City. It shows how wrong you can be.

"One day I casually asked Dennis why he hadn't signed for City because I distinctly remember that all his family were 'dyed in the wool' Blues. He told me that he was waiting for someone from Maine Road to call and speak to him and his parents but nobody came."

Although this story doesn't directly concern the Maine Road stadium it does indicate how it was around this time that the Blues started to lose out locally to the Reds and suggests that for the first time in their history the club did not really have a cohesive plan either on the pitch or off it.

Another Maine Road development during this period, though, was its role as a Rugby League venue. The first Rugby League Championship Play-off Final to be held at Maine Road occurred pre-war on 13th May 1939 when Salford beat Castleford 8-6, despite being 5-6 down at half-time. The match was watched by 69,504 with receipts of £4,301.

For a while Maine Road became the home of the final with the first ten post-war finals held there. The highest attendance at one of these games was 75,194 for the Huddersfield-Warrington match in 1949. This was the largest provincial crowd for a game of Rugby League at the time, although an amazing 102,569 attended Odsal five years later for the Challenge Cup replay.

These matches at Maine Road brought a lot of media interest. Some were broadcast on BBC Radio's North Home Service. Among the commentators for the 1954 match was Eddie Waring, who later became famous along with City fan Stuart Hall for TV's *It's A Knockout*.

There was also sadness at the 1954 Warrington-Halifax match when a 65-year-old supporter – John Lynskey of Bewsey - collapsed and died. Perversely this was the third spectator death to occur at a match involving Halifax during the tail end of the 1953-4 season.

Throughout this period City matches at Maine Road also hit the headlines on several occasions, and for some supporters the immediate post-war period gave them their first taste of Blue life. James Dowd remembers how he became hooked on the club: "My status for being a Blue rose at school during the first weeks of 1946 when City won five out of six matches and drew the other. Then came my first big City letdown. That year FA Cup ties were played over two games. City had smashed Barrow 6-2 at Maine Road in the third round and in the first match of the fourth round they easily won 3-1 at Bradford Park Avenue.

"I was so sure of another City win that I skipped school the following Wednesday afternoon to see the formality of the second game. On a sodden pitch City lost 8-2! I couldn't believe it. I was so upset I threw away my match programme in the street – how I wish I'd kept it! We Blues were only saved from the sniggerings of our Red pals because United lost at Preston 3-1. For me it was the sweetest revenge and definitely one of my Maine Road highlights when in the 1946-7 promotion campaign City thumped Park Avenue 7-2. In those days Park Avenue had the then unknown players Len Shackleton, Downie and Ron Greenwood."

CONTINUED ON PAGE 127 >

United at Maine Road

THE use of Maine Road by Manchester United came in two distinct phases. The first was following the bombing of Old Trafford during the war, the second came when United needed to play European Cup matches under floodlights.

Old Trafford was hit by bombs dropped by the German Luftwaffe on Tuesday 11th March 1941. The highly industrialised Trafford Park had been the target and by daybreak news of damage to Old Trafford was circulating around Manchester, although the *Manchester Guardian* did not mention the ground by name. Due to the wartime situation the newspaper did not want to give away too much information and reported: "Slight damage was done to dwelling-houses in one or two working class districts and slight outbreaks of fire were reported from a football ground and a training institute."

The 'slight damage' saw a bomb hit United's Main Stand. The stand was almost completely wrecked, while the pitch was scorched by the blast. City contacted United and offered the use of Maine Road and the first home United match to be staged at City's ground was the 5th April meeting with Blackpool in the North Regional League. The Seasiders' won 3-2 before a crowd of 2,000.

Further wartime matches followed over the course of the next four years with United paying the Blues an annual rent of £5,000 plus a share of the gate receipts. City were to use United's training ground, The Cliff, for reserve fixtures.

In 1945-6 the FA Cup returned and then the Football League returned for 1946-7. The first crowd of over 60,000 to watch United at home at Maine Road was 65,112 for a game with Middlesbrough on 14th September 1946.

During 1947-8 the first United home League derby at Maine Road took place on 7th April 1948 and was watched by 71,690 – around 6,000 less than the City home fixture. City player George Smith missed that game but did play in other away derbies at Maine Road. He claims that despite City being the away side, the Blues always insisted on using the home dressing room. Supporters did not have the same opportunity to retain home advantage. Those sat in the Main Stand would have to choose other seats if United had sold those tickets to their own supporters. The game ended 1-1, but for United the visit of Arsenal proved to be their greatest League attendance. A crowd of 83,260 watched the Championship duel between United and Arsenal on 17th January 1948. Joe Mercer captained the Gunners to a 1-1 draw and his side went on to win the Championship.

The crowd for this game has occasionally been recorded as 81,962 or 82,950, but the figure of 83,260 is the total submitted to the League in 1948 and remains the record crowd for any League fixture. Significantly, the total was almost 13,000

higher than United's previous record (70,504 v Aston Villa 27/12/20), but was still not a record for Maine Road.

The following season 82,771 watched United draw 1-1 with Bradford, while 81,565 witnessed their 8-0 victory over Yeovil. Both matches took place in the FA Cup with the Yeovil match gaining national coverage. Yeovil had developed a fantastic reputation as giant killers after knocking out Second Division Bury and First Division Sunderland, and everybody wanted to see them play. Over seven thousand travelled from Yeovil, while many neutrals – including several thousand City supporters – also joined the queues for the tie. Main Stand seats which had a face value of five shillings

Above: Johnny Carey (left) and George Smith in action during City's 'away' derby at Maine Road in 1949. All four League derbies played at City's ground during United's time there ended in draws. A packed Platt Lane Stand can be seen in the background of this picture.

UNITED'S "GOLDEN ERA" AT MAINE ROAD

It may be a £75,000 profit for 3 seasons

BY TOM JACKSON

POST-WAR football has brought a financial boom to Manchester United. Final returns from their "golden era" at Maine Road, when they hired City's ground for senior matches, will probably reveal an aggregate profit of £75,000 on the last three seasons.

United's balance-sheet for 1948-49—their closing spell at Maine Road—will soon be issued to shareholders. It is believed to show all-time records in attendances, gate receipts, and profit on the season's working.

The second period when United used Maine Road for home games came in 1956-7 when the Reds became the first English side to enter the European Cup. Wolverhampton Wanderers had been invited to join the competition the previous season, however the English footballing authorities put pressure on the Molyneux club not to take part. When United won the title in 1956 they accepted an invitation to play in the competition and so the first competitive European match on English soil took place on 26th September 1956 with United at home to Anderlecht in the 2nd leg of the Preliminary round. The only problem was that Old Trafford did not possess floodlights. United had not seen the need to erect floodlights of any description and so once again City offered them the use of Maine Road.

In total three matches were played at Maine Road, with the match against Athletic Bilbao regarded as the best victory. United had lost the first leg 5-3 and managed an amazing fightback thanks to a noisy Mancunian crowd.

United's European Games at Maine Road (1956/7)

Attendance	Date	Result	Round
40,000	26/9/56	United 10-0 RSC Anderlecht	Preliminary
75,598	17/10/56	United 3-2 Borussia Dortmund	One
70,000	6/2/57	United 3-0 Athletic Bilbao	Qtr-final

The Reds progressed to the semi-final to face Real Madrid. They lost the first leg 3-1 but chose to play the second leg at Old Trafford. Surprisingly the attendance was 65,000 and the Reds could only manage a 2-2 draw. Had the game been played at Maine Road there would undoubtedly have been a significantly higher attendance and potentially the atmosphere might have helped United reach the final.

Above: The official programme for United's European Cup quarter-final with Athletic Bilbao in 1956-57 and a 'pirate' issue also on sale around Maine Road that night. The unofficial version labels the game as a World Cup quarter-final!

and seven shillings and six pence were exchanging hands for figures between three and six pounds.

Twenty minutes before kick-off the ground committee chose to close the gates. According to reports there were still hundreds locked outside. The attendance was not a record – even United's game with Bradford had attracted more – but because of the involvement of Yeovil the match has become one of Maine Road's landmark moments.

The following August United returned to Old Trafford and their first 'home' fixture – a Lancashire derby with Bolton Wanderers on 24th August 1949 – attracted 41,748. Interestingly, their last match at Maine Road had been watched by 49,808.

United's Best Attendances at Maine Road (1941 to 1949)

Attendance	Date	Opponents	Type of Fixture
83,260	17/1/48	Arsenal	FL (Arsenal Champions)
82,771	29/1/49	Bradford	FA Cup 4th round
81,565	12/2/49	Yeovil Town	FA Cup 5th round
74,213	28/2/48	Preston NE	FA Cup 6th round
71,690	7/4/48	Manchester City	FL
71,623	26/3/48	Bolton W	FL
70,787	4/12/48	Newcastle United	FL
70,434	7/2/49	Bradford	FA Cup 4th round replay
66,967	7/4/47	Wolves	FL
66,485	22/1/49	Manchester City	FL

United's Average League Attendances at Maine Road
(1946 to 1949)

Season	Average (Att Position)	Lowest Attendance	Highest Attendance
1946-7	43,945 (4th)	8,456 (Stoke)	66,967 (Wolves)
1947-8	54,890 (3rd)	35,509 (Everton)	81,962 (Arsenal)
1948-9	48,808 (3rd)	20,158 (M'brough)	70,787 (N'castle)

Right: Action from non-league Yeovil Town's visit to Maine Road in 1949. The FA Cup giant-killers played United in front of over 80,000 fans!

NOTE: United's average attendance for the first season back at Old Trafford was 43,282, and reduced to 39,008 in 1950-1. By 1954 it was down to 35,458, and didn't surpass the 1946-7 figure (United's lowest at Maine Road) until 1956-7 (45,481 – the best in the League).

City did achieve promotion in 1947 with the most significant match, in terms of attendance and importance, being the 10th May meeting with Burnley. A crowd of 67,672 – the highest League attendance in the greater Manchester area since the City-Arsenal game in April 1937 – watched the Blues win 1-0 against one of their biggest challengers to guarantee promotion. Writing under the headline "City Go Up – Herd Makes It Certain" Tom Markland reported on the match: "City have won promotion. They needed one point to be sure, but Herd gave them a couple when he scored the only goal against Burnley at Maine Road. For 85 minutes the battle swung to and fro, the tackling was determined and all the attacks failed. Then, five minutes from the end, Burnley were caught napping, and Herd banged the ball in from a few yards out."

In another report Gilbert Hoare recorded: "This was the game Manchester was anxiously waiting since their descent into the Second Division in 1938. The Hampden Roar wasn't in it when in the 82nd minute Alec Herd, Manchester City's long-serving Scot, hit the goal which assured the club of promotion to the First Division. Among the 67,672 watching the quick-thinking Scot were representatives of the Bury Club who, earlier in the season were all set to sign him, but fortunately for City did not do so.

"It was one of those games for the soccer historian. Hard, action-packed and thrilling, with a certain amount of vigour, so that referee J.M. Brown of Ormskirk had to use pencil and notebook to record the names of two players."

As with many other games during Maine Road's history, one newspaper report suggested the crowd of 67,672 still did not include every person present: "The official attendance was 67,672. If members' tickets are added the gate must have reached 70,000."

Manchester City go into Division 1

MANCHESTER CITY 1   BURNLEY 0

MANCHESTER CITY will be playing in First Division football next season. Their victory over Burnley was well earned. The result was in doubt until five minutes from the end, when Smith, who had moved over to the right wing, sent across a centre which probably for the first time in the game put the Burnley defence in two minds. Woodruff only partially got hold

Top left: City players take to the stand for the annual press call, this one on the eve of the 1946-47 season, the first season of Football League action since the war.

Bottom left: A 1950 picture of Roy Paul and trainer Laurie Barnett examining a new dressing room clock while the other players look on!

The thorny subject of whether members' tickets, season tickets and the like should be included in attendances always seemed to crop up when big games were played at the stadium. From the modern perspective, it's clear the figures should be included, however for many years the official attendance or gate recorded in the media only considered those who paid on the day. As these are often the most accurate figures these tend to be regarded as the official attendance, but they do not accurately reflect the true attendance.

City's promotion meant the Blues were more positive about the future and a loudspeaker system was installed for the benefit of some – by no means all – supporters. James Dowd: "In 1947 I remember we fans suddenly had the luxury of team changes being relayed over a new loudspeaker system. Or at least those in the Main Stand did. The changes would percolate back to we mere mortals on the standing terraces.

"All football fans on the terraces wore flat caps

Maine Match 46/47

CITY v NEWPORT COUNTY

DATE:	14th June 1947		
TYPE OF FIXTURE:	Football League Division Two		
ATTENDANCE:	25,431		
RESULT:	City 5-1 Newport County		
TEAMS & SCORERS:	CITY		NEWPORT	
	Swift		A. Smith	
	Sproston		Emanuel	
	Barkas		Oldham	
	Fagan		Rawcliffe	
	McDowall		W. Smith	
	Walsh		Batty	
	Dunkley		Williams	
	Herd		Haddon	
	Black		Roffi	1
	Smith	5	Carr	
	Clarke		Harper	

■ The Blues were already promoted and were certain of the Second Division title by the time they faced Newport in June. This was the latest finish to a season ever experienced by the Blues – brought on by the cancellation of games due to arctic weather conditions – and the occasion became newsworthy for this and for a couple of other reasons. Firstly, the match saw the debut of Roy Clarke – a Sam Cowan signing shortly before the season ended – and then the game itself brought an incredible goalscoring feat from George Smith.

Smith netted all five goals to help City to a convincing 5-1 win. In 2003, Smith was modest about his achievement that day: "It didn't matter so much that I scored five. It was good that we won. I ended the season as top scorer but promotion was the main aim."

Musing on the general atmosphere around the club, Smith believes this was a great period for City: "The players really trained hard and we had a thoroughly enjoyable time. Sam Cowan was the manager. He was City through and through because he'd spent so long at the club before the war as captain. He was the first to talk tactics with us I suppose, although our training pattern had to take account of his circumstances."

Cowan was living on the south coast while managing City and had to commute from the Brighton area to Manchester for the preparation prior to games. It appears he travelled home after each match and returned to Manchester midweek – probably Tuesday – to train his players and take part in other managerial activities. Smith: "Tuesday night and Thursday night tactical sessions were organised, although I don't think these were compulsory. Most of the first team would attend though - or at least those interested enough would! In these sessions a board would be brought out and we'd talk about the style of play we'd adopt. We'd also comment on the opponents, assuming we knew something about them that is.

"Other training would occur each day during the day. We'd run around the perimeter of the pitch, and up and down the steps of the terraces. Sometimes we'd go for a brisk walk. That was about it really. After training we'd go upstairs to the players' lounge and play snooker or table tennis. There was a bar in there so we'd also get a drink if we fancied it. I didn't really drink, but if you wanted it you could. Food was also available across the other side of the corridor towards the Boardroom."

Smith clearly enjoyed this time at Maine Road and seemed to regard Cowan's time as manager with affection. Despite this, and the success Cowan had brought to the club, the manager was asked to leave after this match with Newport. The commuting was thought to be too much of an issue.

For debutant Roy Clarke this was inevitably a significant moment: "I was from Newport so that was an interesting aspect to it, but I had also played in Division Three South in my previous match – for division champions Cardiff City – and then in Division Two for City and then my next match was in Division One. Three divisions in three consecutive games!

"Moving to Manchester was a terrific ordeal in many ways. I didn't know what to expect and I don't mind admitting that I was a little frightened. It was a colossal stadium and many of the pre-war greats were still around. I don't remember much about the game, but I do remember some of the other aspects to the day. We lived in Fallowfield and I borrowed Kath's [his wife] bicycle to get to the ground – a woman's bike for a footballer! When I got to the ground I thought they would all pull my leg, as footballers do, but I think they were a little envious. They'd all walked or caught the bus with the fans. No traffic problems for me!

"After the match I had to follow the routine all City players adopted. In the dressing room there were two single baths – the sort you'd get in any bathroom – and a large team bath plus one shower. All players had to dip into the single bath, usually with another player, to wash off all the mud – not that there was much mud in June – and then once you were free of mud you'd move into the team bath. You couldn't get into the big bath until you were clean enough to do so!"

then. I heard on a television programme that the traditions of football being a working class sport was demonstrated by the fact football fans used to wear flat caps whereas racing fans, for example, would wear trilbies. What tripe!

"Football fans wore flat caps for two reasons only, nothing to do with their social status. One - as most terracings were uncovered a hat was necessary as protection from rain. Two – any fan who was foolish enough to wear a wide-brimmed trilby risked abuse and having it snatched off his head for obscuring somebody's view! 'Get that bloody hat off' was not an infrequent shout."

Following City's promotion, several large crowds came Maine Road's way; 67,782 watched the opening 4-3 victory over Wolves, and 67,494 witnessed the cup game with Preston, but the two biggest crowds of the season were for the Manchester derby games with United. The first – City's home game – took place on 20th September 1947 and was watched by 78,000.

By the time of the return match in April it was clear to most Blues that United's use of Maine Road was having an effect on City's support. Over the 19 League games United had played at home at Maine Road they had averaged approximately 54,000, while the Blues were watched by an average of around 43,400 over a similar number of matches. Pre-war the disparity between the figures always worked in City's favour but the increased interest in sport following the war, and the fact the two sides were playing at City's venue created this major shift.

As with the first post-war derby the second ended in a draw. This time the result was 1-1 before 71,690 fans (the second highest League derby), but the significance of this game is it was the first League game at Maine Road in which City were the visitors. United's season ticket holders sat in their regular seats while City fans had to find alternative accommodation; the match programme was United's not City's; and even the flag had to be United's not City's. It was all very strange.

James Dowd remembers these two derby matches because of the size of the crowds rather than the football on offer: "When City returned to the First Division the

Below: An early 1950s photograph of players in the home dresssing room bath. Left to right: Roy Clarke, Jack Oakes, Joe Fagan, Dennis Westcott and George Smith.

Right: Joe Fagan (far left) appears on another bathtime picture. The home dressing rooms used to contain a large team bath, two single baths and one shower.

Maine Memory

■ I was three years old. My dad had always been a fan and so one Saturday I got my coat ready for when Dad was going to the match. When he saw me he said: 'little girls don't go to football matches', but I wasn't to be put off. So he took me and in those days there was no cover over the Kippax and Dad sat me on the wall of one of the corner tunnels so that I could see. In my excitement I over-balanced and nearly fell off but Dad managed to grab my arm and pulled me back up. In doing so he pulled my arm out of its socket. At that time they used to have St. John Ambulance men and one came along and just pushed my arm back in its socket. Never once did I cry although I wanted to scream, but I was frightened Dad wouldn't take me again, so I kept quiet and didn't even tell my mother. She would have gone mad!

Mrs. M E Atkinson

■ The first post-war League derby with United – City's home game – took place on 20th September 1947 and was watched by 78,000 fans. It remains the largest derby crowd ever, although it still falls short of Maine Road's record by around 6,000. Despite the inevitable excitement of only the third League derby since 1931, the match itself was not a classic. According to the *Daily Dispatch*: "A crowd of 78,000 left Maine Road yesterday with no man able to boast to his neighbour about the result of the Manchester 'Derby' game. Nor could anyone boast about the display of his favourite team. Manchester City did not live up to their promise and the United never displayed their true capabilities. Both sides finished poorly, but the City were the more dangerous side before half-time, and one of the highlights of the game was Crompton's daring save at the feet of Wharton as the ball flashed across the United goalmouth."

The *Dispatch* added: "Another highlight was the full-back display of City's Sproston. His interceptions in the first half particularly were brilliant."

Overall the game was a disappointment but in terms of significance this was a crucial derby match.

Maine Match 47/48

CITY v MANCHESTER UNITED

DATE:	20th September 1947	
TYPE OF FIXTURE:	Football League Division One	
ATTENDANCE:	78,000	
RESULT:	City 0 United 0	
TEAMS & SCORERS:	CITY	UNITED
	Thurlow	Crompton
	Sproston	Carey
	Westwood	Aston
	Walsh	Warner
	Fagan	Chilton
	Emptage	McGlen
	Wharton	Delaney
	Smith	Morris
	McMorran	Rowley
	Capel	Pearson
	Clarke	Mitten

two matches which are most vivid in my mind are the two draws against United. Over 70,000 packed into Maine Road for both games. On the Kippax we standing fans would be bodily carried down three or four steps by the surge of the crowd and then carried back again. We were literally packed in like sardines in a can. Yet nobody was nervous. It makes me nervous now to think about it! I wasn't nervous even when some old terrace veteran advised me 'Don't stand against a crush barrier. The crowd can push you against the bar'. Yet those crush barriers were supposed to be for crowd safety!

"I now look back on my early days of watching games at Maine Road with some retrospective astonishment. Why on earth were we never bothered about our safety? In the seasons after the war nobody was bothered much about crowd safety. Neither were we fans bothered.

"On a few occasions I saw some man, unable to get out of the crush, urinate where he stood. There were dark tales of some unsuspecting person's overcoat pocket being used by somebody standing behind him! Things are decidedly more civilised today."

Throughout the forties City seemed destined to play

second fiddle to United. This was a major shame especially as the Blues had generously come to the rescue of the Reds in a move that ultimately caused City much harm. However, City were keen to regain the upper hand. On the pitch the appointment of former player Les McDowall as manager was helping to re-establish the club, while off it Maine Road was about to prove its worth once again as the club invested heavily on a relatively new innovation – floodlights.

As time progressed floodlights became a vital part of football, however in 1953 Maine Road was one of the first venues to install permanent lights. This confirmed that no matter how the Blues were performing on the pitch the Maine Road stadium would continue to be at the forefront of innovation. It was also a wonderful place to start your playing career. Roy Little joined the Blues in 1949 and made his debut in 1953. He vividly remembers his first impressions of the place: "I signed a contract under Jock Thomson for £10 signing-on fee and wages of £10 a week on a yearly contract, and I felt as if I'd made it to some extent. I was part of Manchester City and my first experience of training at Maine Road was awesome! Simply looking around the stadium and imagining the sound of the 1934 record crowd was terrific. It was a great place to be, but there was also a real hierarchy within the club.

"The home dressing room was reserved for the first team squad while the possibles and also-rans had to use the away dressing room. You wanted to graduate to the home dressing room but it took some doing. Any player that made it through the Juniors, 'A' Team, Reserves and into the First Team was welcomed by the others. I think everyone appreciated the lengths you'd gone to progress and so you were immediately welcomed. I remember that when I reached the dizzy heights of the first team, I was accepted into a great bunch of lads. They made me feel a real part of MCFC. We had Roy Paul as skipper who played in front of me. His guiding words before the game were simple 'win the ball son, give it to me, and I'll do the rest'."

The mid-fifties were to be a wonderful period for players and supporters alike.

Maine Men Roy & Kath Clarke

ROLE: Social Club manager & manageress

■ Roy Clarke's on the pitch role has been documented many times over the years, however what isn't so well-known is the non-footballing role of Roy and his wife Kath.

Kath and Roy arrived in Manchester in 1947 when Roy joined the Blues as a player. Initially they lived in Fallowfield. Kath: "It was funny when we first arrived. We'd been married about a month and moving to Manchester was a move into the unknown for us. In fact Roy was so worried it would be much colder than South Wales that he bought a heavy, thick coat. It seems silly now but back then you really did not have any concept of what Manchester would be like – it was cold in the north we were told!"

Naturally, Roy's playing career brought a great deal of success and satisfaction to the family, but it was his later work with the club which is significant from a Maine Road point of view. Firstly, Roy was one of the key players behind the Development Association and spent considerable effort trying to increase income for the club. One of his ideas was Scoreboard Scoop – a regular feature which gave supporters the chance to win money if scores displayed on the scoreboard matched the panel printed on the back of the programme. Scoreboard Scoop increased programme sales and proved a very popular game. In fact fans complained when it was dropped in the early seventies.

The Development Association went on to raise a great deal of income for the club while Roy Clarke's reputation as a player, and his general rapport with the regular man in the street, led to him taking on the role of Social Club manager when it was opened in 1966. For the next 22 years or so Roy and Kath made the Social Club a major venue. Leading stars appeared on a regular basis while Roy and Kath went out of their way to give the club a real family feel, but it took a great deal of work. Roy: "It was too popular at the start. I had to stand on the roof once when the queue stretched down Maine Road – we couldn't let them all in!"

Kath remembers the change it brought to their lives: "We were still living in our own house and one of our daughters was only 12 months old. Also, we were never drinkers and hardly knew what went on inside a pub, so taking on a social club was a bit of a challenge. Closing time was 10.30pm in those days, so by the time we'd cleaned up and locked the doors it was nearly midnight before we could go home. We'd have to get back to the club early morning for deliveries and cleaning, so we could never rest. After the first couple of days I remember telling Roy that we couldn't continue."

Fortunately, the couple came up with a cunning plan. The roof of the Social Club had deliberately been flat – the view being that over time the building might be extended upwards – and the Clarkes felt a flat could be constructed over part of it. Roy discussed the possibility with Walter Griffiths, the club secretary, and within six months an apartment was built. The Clarkes moved in. Kath: "It was ideal being above the club because it meant we could plan our time more."

Being that close to work meant they had little free time. They were supposed to have one day a week off, but usually worked, they enjoyed their time there and indirectly contributed enormously to the development of the football club itself. According to Arthur Hopcraft's *The Football Man* – a highly respected football book written in 1968 – the Social Club was a major reason for City's popularity at the time. In one chapter Hopcraft wrote: "Talking to members of City's Social Club I was told with much delight that they had never before felt so involved with the footballers they had watched over the seasons. Players, club directors and the management went to the social club frequently, not only to give talks and to comment on football films but just to be in contact with the fans and available for conversation."

By the late 1980s the Social Club was no longer as popular as it had been a decade earlier, nevertheless, it was still accepted by its regulars. Sadly, the world had moved on since 1966 and one day Roy was mugged outside the bank on Claremont Road. Roy: "I didn't know what had hit me. I'd been pushed to the ground and they'd snatched the bag with all the change in, but I'd hidden the notes. I went inside the bank and handed all the notes – I don't know how much but it was the full weekend's takings! – to another customer. Then I ran outside to see if I could find my attackers but they'd all gone. I went back inside the bank and, fortunately, the customer had handed the money over to the clerk."

Retirement followed a year or so later, but both Roy and Kath continued to be regulars at Maine Road. Roy was, by this time, already hosting a number of tours of the ground on match days. City's former historian Bill Miles had asked him to get involved during the early eighties and by the time of Bill's death in 1984 Roy was a popular guide. He brought to life the stories of the ground and the club.

In retirement both Kath and Roy continued to attend Maine Road until its final match. Roy was escorted on to the pitch at the final game, alongside heroes from every era, and he enjoyed performing a lap of honour, waving to the fans. The ovation he received came from every generation of support.

Swift's Last Home Match

■ Frank Swift announced that the match with Arsenal on 27th April 1949 would be his last at Maine Road. He was keen to retire at the top and wanted the 1948-9 season to be his last. For supporter Eddie Humphrys the Arsenal match was a memorable occasion: "I was a boy and Swift was naturally City's great hero - a man we all admired and wanted to see. The news of his retirement was seen as a bit of a blow. How would we ever survive without him? I had to be there for his final match to send him off in the right way."

Another young supporter was 10-year-old Paul James: "I lived in Gorton and would cycle across to Maine Road whenever I could. Sometimes I would wait outside until three-quarter time because I had no money, but then I got a job as a paper boy delivering the sports edition of the *Chronicle* and that gave me the money to pay to watch from the start. The only problem was that I had to get home early enough to collect the *Chron* and start delivering it. In those days the *Chron* was eagerly awaited in Gorton as it was the 'City' 'paper while the *Evening News* was the 'Red' paper.

"When City played Arsenal I managed to cycle to the ground for kick-off. I didn't know it was supposed to be Swift's last home game and so I was confused when, despite the fact we were losing, he was getting all the applause. It puzzled me why a goalie could get so much support when he'd let the goals in! Anyway, with City losing and 'papers to be collected I left about fifteen minutes before the end – the time I used to get in! I cycled home and it was only when I picked up the *Chron* I realised it was Swift's last match and that he'd been chaired off the field. I'd missed all the celebrations!"

Eddie Humphrys managed to become part of the celebrations: "I don't remember quite how it happened, but I ended up on the edge of the pitch in front of the tunnel as Swift was chaired off. As he neared the tunnel I shook hands with him and the moment was captured by a photographer. Arsenal's Joe Mercer and Les Compton were nearby, as were Roy Clarke, George Smith and a few others. It was a great feeling and as we shook hands the fans and officials stood close by started cheering. Swift was a huge hero."

Frank Swift celebrated his final match the following week away at Huddersfield but, due to a number of goalkeeping issues, he was persuaded to play a few games the following season while the club searched for a new man. So Swift's 'final match' wasn't quite as final as he'd hoped.

Main picture: Frank Swift launches a goal kick into the air during Grimsby Town's visit to Maine Road in 1948.

Right: Supporter Eddie Humphrys shakes the hand of Frank Swift after the goalkeeper's last home match for City, against Arsenal in April 1949. Arsenal skipper Joe Mercer watches (under signature) and other players in the picture include Billy Walsh, Eric Westwood, Joe Fagan and Johnny Hart.

Maine Match 53/54

CITY v HEART OF MIDLOTHIAN

DATE:	14th October 1953
TYPE OF FIXTURE:	Floodlit Friendly
RESULT:	City 6 Hearts 3

■ In the 1880s City's predecessors Ardwick had played charity and friendly matches under lights. One match was against Preston, the other a charity match against Newton Heath (United) at Belle Vue, however the use of floodlights for first class football didn't occur until the early 1950s. In 1951 Arsenal installed lights for a friendly with a side from Tel Aviv and another against Rangers, while Southampton spent £600 installing lights of high enough quality to allow Football Combination games to be played. A highly successful first match caused the Southampton manager – and former City Cup finalist – Syd Cann to comment: "Floodlit soccer has come to stay."

Over the course of the following two years most forward thinking clubs looked at ways of installing lights. Wolves switched on their lights in September 1953, but at the time neither Football League nor FA Cup matches could be staged under lights. This meant any club investing in floodlighting was taking a major gamble.

As well as Wolves, City were keen to experiment. During the summer of 1953 they erected four 90ft high floodlight pylons to house their new lights which were first switched on for a friendly with Hearts on 14th October 1953. Interestingly, City narrowly missed out on being the first side in the North-West to switch on their lights when Bury turned on theirs for a friendly a mere eight days before City!

To celebrate this great event the club invested in shirts with a shiny finish. According to one player: "They weighed about three tons. We sank to our knees when we put them on."

Johnny Hart remembers: "They wanted the shirts to stand out under the lights and they did dazzle to some extent but they were so cold compared to regular shirts.

None of us enjoyed wearing them, but I suppose it was more about the spectacle of the event than comfort."

The shirts did help the entertainment value of the evening, but the real stars were the lights themselves. City was incredibly proud of their development. According to the City programme for the Hearts match: "Maine Road officials were so determined City should have nothing but the best they spared no expense getting the finest possible equipment and leading experts to install it, so their claim to have the finest floodlighting system in the country is well founded."

The programme went on to describe the floodlighting system: "The pitch is illuminated by one hundred 1,000 watt projector lamps operated in three batteries of 24 and one of 18 on the top of the towers at each corner of the ground. There are ten more as ancillary lighting on the stand.

"Apart from the floodlighting, many smaller lamps have been installed for the benefit of those leaving and entering the ground, and in case you are wondering what will happen if there's a 'fuse', an automatic emergency system will cover every contingency. Individual or complete control thus can be made at any point and at any time.

"For the technically minded, the system is controlled by a 200 amp main breaker, and each of the four batteries of lights has its own switch control in a cubicle at the base of the tower. Total load for the floodlighting and amenity lighting is 150 kilowatts, and approximate cost of current consumed in say two hours before, during and after the game is £3."

The companies involved with the project included Philips who, thirty years later, became shirt sponsors for a while.

For the record this first floodlit match ended 6-3 to City. The following week Fenerbahce – a name forever linked with City for the first ever European Cup game played by the Blues – were defeated 5-1 under lights and on 28th Celtic and City played out a 1-1 draw in a third floodlit celebration.

Maine Memory

■ I came down from Scotland on holiday at Christmas 1951 and went with a friend of mine to Maine Road to see City v Chelsea on Boxing Day. City won 3-1 and there were almost 50,000 there. That was it. I have been a Manchester City fan ever since.

John Gibson

MANCHESTER CITY IN FORM

Manchester City played excellent football in defeating Heart of Midlothian 6-3 at Moss Side last night in their first flood-lit match.

City's young centre forward, Sowden, who was playing in his first game of the season, scored three goals. Forward altogether Manchester had the better of their opponents, who, though clever in their midfield work, lacked finish. Hearts, indeed, missed several chances in the first half and though their forwards always fought hard, they never were so precise and controlled as were City's. Hart (2), and Broadis scored City's other goals, to which Hearts replied through a penalty goal by Parker, a somewhat scrappy goal by Wardhaugh, and a lucky one by Cumming.

Left: Johnny Hart jumps for the ball in the shiny shirt worn by City players to reflect better under the floodlights.

Rugby League at Maine Road

Halifax and Warrington met in the Championship Final at Maine Road in May 1954.

Above: The Scoreboard End can be seen in the background as Halifax's Tommy Lynch runs with the ball.

Below: The only try of the game, scored by Halifax's John Thorley.

■ Maine Road was the home of the Rugby League Championship play-off final between 1939 and 1956 with eleven finals taking place at the ground. City player of the 1940s and 50s, Johnny Hart remembers: "The ground would take on a different feel and I remember watching them take down the football goalposts and erect the rugby posts instead. At that time the club had a dog which would chase anyone it could see if it heard a raspberry noise. While the men were putting the finishing touches to the post I sneaked around to the Platt Lane Stand and blew a loud raspberry and then hid. The dog looked over and saw the two men working on the posts and immediately ran towards them. They panicked and climbed up to the bar and ended up sitting there for about an hour while the dog sat below staring at them, waiting. They daren't get down because they knew what would happen!"

The details of the play off finals held at Maine Road are:

DATE	TEAMS & SCORE	ATTENDANCE	RECEIPTS
13/5/39	Salford 8 Castlefield 6	69,504	£4,301
18/5/46	Wigan 13 Huddersfield 4	67,136	£8,386
21/6/47	Wigan 13 Dewsbury 4	40,599	£5,894
8/5/48	Warrington 15 Bradford Northern 5	69,143	£9,791
14/5/49	Huddersfield 13 Warrington 12	75,194	£11,073
13/5/50	Wigan 20 Huddersfield 2	65,065	£11,500
12/5/51	Workington 26 Warrington 11	61,618	£10,993
9/5/53	St. Helens 24 Halifax 14	51,083	£11,500
8/5/54	Warrington 8 Halifax 7	36,519	£9,076
14/5/55	Warrington 7 Oldham 3	49,434	£11,516
12/5/56	Hull 10 Halifax 9	36,675	£9,179

In addition to Championship play-off matches there have been individual League matches played at the ground when other venues have struggled due to poor weather. In 1987 Maine Road staged Oldham v Featherstone and Warrington v Barrow. Neither match was particularly successful as far as attendance figures are concerned. Oldham's 20-16 victory was watched by 2,719, while Warrington's 24-20 win was attended by 2,215. The games took place on 18th and 19th January.

Another interesting Rugby match to be staged at Maine Road was the Bath v Wigan challenge of the codes game. The match was a showpiece event aimed at proving that the strongest club from each code could outplay their opponents at their own sport and possibly match them at the other sport. The game was split into two halves – one for each code – and inevitably both sides easily won their own half. In 2003 the concept was revived and there were even suggestions that Maine Road would stage another challenge with Sale Sharks hosting a game at the ground, however once Sale announced they would not be moving to Maine Road the possibility of such a game at City's ground ended.

Internationals at Maine Road

MAINE ROAD's role in international football is rarely considered, yet the ground has staged some incredible fixtures over the years. The 8-0 defeat of Scotland was clearly a great morale-booster during the war, then in 1946 another match with Scotland brought home the importance of stadium safety. The City board offered the use of Maine Road for a fundraising international to raise money for the victims of the Burnden Park disaster.

Although these first two internationals were significant events, they were not regarded as full official internationals. The following November, however, Maine Road did host a full international. The game was the England-Wales Home International. Naturally hosting any international is a major honour, but the FA were quick to point out that the honour of staging this match in particular was greater than normal as this was the first full international to be played in England since 16th November 1938 – ironically that had been staged at Old Trafford.

Of local interest was City's Frank Swift – described as 'a former fisherman, he is now a Manchester innkeeper' – and Bolton-born Tommy Lawton, the only man remaining in the side from the November 1938 match.

Writing about the match a couple of years later, City reporter Eric Todd gave his view of the match: "England beat Wales by 3-0 and it should have been a good deal more. England took the lead after nine minutes when Carter sliced his drive and Mannion, at hand to accept this pass, flicked the ball away from Sidlow. Thereafter England dominated the proceedings, but the forwards played too close together and Sidlow was not troubled unduly.

"Wales hit back and Swift saved brilliantly from Ivor Powell, but five minutes from the interval Tommy Lawton made it two following grand work by Carter and Mannion. Wales fought well after half-time and Swift made the save of the day from Edwards, flinging himself full length to divert a well-placed header. As the game advanced, however England rallied and while Wales were appealing for offside, Mannion went through to score England's third."

Todd finished his article by stressing: "England, however, missed many chances and Wales were defeated more soundly than the score suggests."

In 1949 possibly the most important international to be staged at Maine Road saw England defeat

Above: Frank Swift makes a flying save for England against Wales at his home ground in 1946.

Full England Internationals played at Maine Road:

Date	Opponents	Score	England Goalscorers / Team	Attendance	Type of Fixture
16/10/1943	**Scotland**	W 8-0	Lawton 4, Hagan 2, Carter, Matthews	60,000	Wartime International
			Swift, Scott, Hardwick, Britton, Cullis, Mercer, Matthews, Carter, Lawton, Hagan, Compton		
24/4/1946	**Scotland**	D 2-2	Welsh 2	70,000	Burnden Park Disaster Match
			Swift, Walton, Hardwick, Wright, Leuty, Mitchell, Matthews, Welsh, Lewis, Fielding, Mannion		
13/11/1946	**Wales**	W 3-0	Mannion 2, Lawton	59,121	Home International Tournament
			Swift, Scott, Hardwick, Wright, Franklin, Cockburn, Finney, Carter, Lawton, Mannion, Langton		
16/11/1949	**Ireland**	W 9-2	Rowley 4, Pearson 2, Mortensen 2, Froggatt	69,762	Home International & World Cup Qualifier
			Streten, Mozley, Aston, Watson, Franklin, Wright, Finney, Mortensen, Rowley, Pearson, Froggatt		

The Road To Rio

By IVAN SHARPE

TO-DAY it's a double-barrelled match—England v. Ireland in the International Championship and also in the World Cup.

The International Championship, our own yearly tournament, needs no explanation. The World Cup is a new experience for the British countries, so let us see how it works.

Thirty-three countries entered—

Argentina	Ecuador	Italy	Scotland
Austria	Eire	Yugoslavia	Spain
Belgium	England	Luxembourg	Sweden
Bolivia	Finland	Mexico	Switzerland
Brazil	France	Paraguay	Syria
Burma	India	Peru	Turkey
Chile	Ireland	Philippines	Uruguay
Cuba	Israel	Portugal	U.S.A.
			Wales

Three (Belgium, Burma and the Philippines) fell out. So 30 remain.

First these countries were divided into 10 geographical groups. In Europe and the Near Orient, six of these qualifying competitions are now being decided, plus similar tests in Central and North America, South America (two), and Asia.

In four of these 10 zones two countries will qualify, making 14 teams bound for Brazil to play-off the competition proper next June and July at Rio de Janeiro and three other cities.

Add the exempted World Cup holders, Italy, and the country organizing the competition proper, Brazil, and the required number of 16 finalists is reached.

THE WORLD CUP

Our own International Championship is down to supply two finalists—(1) the winners and (2) England, as Scotland, Wales and Ireland have announced that they will only go to Rio if they are top of the British table. So, if England are the British winners, the World Cup competition will be one short, a gap that will soon be filled.

How do the last 16 play-off in Brazil? On the League-Cup system. They will be divided into four separate sections of four countries apiece. Call the teams in the first section A, B, C, D. A plays B and C and D; that is, each team plays the other *once*. Thus each plays three matches.

Two points for a win and one for a draw, and goal average doesn't count. Teams finishing level on points play-off. This applies also in the *Deciding group*: The winners of these four

sections enter the deciding group and, again, each plays the other. Thus the competitors reaching the last lap will play three more matches apiece, and the country at the top of this final table wins the World Cup.

Already Rio is all agog. Over a thousand workmen are building a mammoth stadium to hold 150,000 people, of whom 120,000 will have seats. Reckon this ground as about twice the size of Maine-road and you won't be far wrong, as the Manchester City record is 84,000 spectators consisting chiefly of people standing up.

TAKE THIS FIRST STEP TOWARD A REAL HOLIDAY for **1950**

LAST Summer we successfully pioneered Air Cruising holidays. For 1950 we have an even bigger and better programme planned, at prices which compare very favourably with coach tours. Write now for details.

Send us your name and address

CHARTER AIRCRAFT ALWAYS AVAILABLE AT EXCEPTIONALLY LOW RATES

FINGLAND'S AIRWAYS LTD.

213 WILMSLOW RD. 14 MANCHESTER

'PHONE: RUS 2894 (5 LINES)

3

Left: The programmes from England games with Wales at Maine Road in 1946, and the World Cup qualifier with Ireland three years later.

Above: Page three of the Ireland programme explains how the World Cup qualifying competition works. It's also interesting to note that while the home countries were hoping to qualify for a tournament in South America, Manchester travel company Finglands advertise that "Last summer we successfully pioneered Air Cruising holidays". All of a sudden the world was becoming a smaller place.

Other International and Representative Matches played at Maine Road:

Date	Match	Type of Fixture
9/11/1932	Football League 0-3 Scottish League	Inter-League Match
10/2/1954	Football League 9-1 League of Ireland	Inter-League Match
19/10/1955	England 'B' 5-1 Yugoslavia 'B'	'B' International
21/9/1960	England U-23 v Denmark XI	U-23 International
12/10/1973	England v Northern Ireland	Amateur International
20/3/1974	Football League v Scottish League	Inter-League Match
8/3/1978	England U-21 2-1 Italy U-21	UEFA U-21 Championship q/f 1st leg
2/5/1978	England U-21 1-1 Yugoslavia U-21	UEFA U-21 Championship s/f 2nd leg
28/4/1982	England U-21 1-1 Scotland U-21	UEFA U-21 Championship s/f 2nd leg
18/4/1984	England U-21 3-1 Italy U-21	UEFA U-21 Championship
26/3/1986	England U-21 1-1 Denmark U-21	UEFA U-21 Championship

Note: *City also hosted two Inter-League matches between the Football League and the Irish League at Hyde Road on 6/11/1897 (8-1) and 14/10/1905 (4-0)*

Ireland 9-2. This is important as it was not only a Home International match, but it was also the very first World Cup qualifying game ever to be played in England. The importance of the fixture has largely been forgotten over the last fifty or so years, however this game must surely be a landmark both in Maine Road's history and in English international football.

The World Cup had been in existence since 1930 but England had chosen not to take part. Once the Second World War was over England's attitude had changed and as a result the Home International Championship was to be used as qualification for the finals.

As the World Cup was relatively unknown to English fans at this point, City took the opportunity of explaining what it was all about in the match programme. Respected journalist Ivan Sharpe told supporters: "The International Championship, our own yearly tournament, needs no explanation. The World Cup is a new experience for the British countries, so let see how it works. Thirty-three countries entered."

Sharpe listed all the entrants then went into specific details of how these groups were divided into zones to reach the required number of sixteen who would travel to Brazil for the finals. He then outlined how the competition would progress in Brazil.

The most interesting element of the qualification was that the opportunity for two sides to qualify out of the Home International tournament existed as FIFA believed that two of the four British nations should reach Brazil. Interestingly, England were guaranteed to qualify as, according to Sharpe, Scotland, Wales and Ireland had stated they would only go to Brazil if they were top of the British table.

In the end England topped the British table and were the only side to make it to Brazil.

In addition to international matches at a senior level, Maine Road has hosted a number of Amateur, 'B' and Under-21 internationals and inter-League matches.

The inter-League match with Ireland in 1954 was viewed as an incredible occasion. Eric Thornton of the *Manchester Evening News* remembered the match in 1960: "That Irish visit was fantastic. The English boys were two up through Don Revie and Jackie Sewell within three minutes. Then they eased up, led by only 2-1 at the interval, but, drawing their second breath, took seven terrific goals in a second-half power display. Guess those who were in the team? Such personalities as Billy Wright, captaining the team from right-half, with Albion's Jimmy Dugdale and Ray Barlow on his left.

"Nat Lofthouse had the number nine spot. Johnny Berry formed the right-wing, Sewell and Vic Metcalfe the left. Great names for anyone to conjure with, especially in these times when there's a dearth of real talent."

Another match he remembered was the 1955 'B' international with Yugoslavia: "They [Yugoslavia] made so many team changes that a special slip of the line-up had to be inserted in the programme. Even then no one knew whether they were going or coming after the team had been announced over the tannoy!"

The Under-21 UEFA Championship matches played at Maine Road during the late 1970s proved quite popular with City fans, especially as Blues Joe Corrigan, Peter Barnes, Gary Owen, Paul Futcher, Ray Ranson, Nicky Reid and Kevin Reeves made appearances for England. Other England youngsters included future Blues Clive Allen, Justin Fashanu, Adrian Heath and Steve Mackenzie.

Don Revie in action during City's 2-2 draw with Aston Villa at Maine Road in August 1955.

Chapter Six

Birth of the Kippax

Now everything is ready for the 'go-ahead', and it is expected the foundations will be laid before the end of the season, probably as soon as the home League programme has been completed. Work will proceed apace during the close season and by the time the 1957-8 kick off is due, most of the Popular Side facing the Main Stand will be under cover.

The Manchester City F.C. Match Programme 1956-7

BY the mid 1950s Maine Road was certainly on the map as far as its status as a neutral venue. It had attracted a significant number of semi-finals which, considering the close proximity of other semi-final venues Old Trafford, Hillsborough, and Goodison Park, and also the likes of Bramall Lane, Burnden Park and Anfield, was a major achievement. In addition City themselves were once again becoming a major force for the first time since the war.

The club consistently attracted average attendances of over 30,000, and individual matches could still generate crowds of sixty and seventy thousand depending on the status of the fixture and opponents.

In terms of accommodation the Main Stand still housed around 9,000 plus the directors and press, while the Platt Lane provided covered accommodation for about 20,000 standing spectators and seats for around 2,000 next to the Main Stand. The Popular Side and Scoreboard End were still uncovered but this was fairly typical for most football grounds during this period. Even the national stadium at Wembley, built the same year as Maine Road, still only had two sides of the ground covered.

None of this was of particular concern at the time. More than anything else supporters wanted a successful team and in the mid-fifties they got their wish. The early matches in the FA Cup run of 1955 gave rise to optimism. First Derby County were swept aside 3-1 then City defeated Manchester United 2-0. Supporter M.E. Cummings remembers that match and his own involvement in Maine Road's history: "Every one of the players on both sides was a household name; internationals in abundance. United had the Busby Babes but we had Bert Trautmann, the finest goalkeeper, and Don Revie at his best. United lost their Captain Allenby

Chilton when he was sent off and nearly all the City players begged the referee not to send him off! Joe Hayes and Don Revie scored and I feel privileged to have been there to witness such an important derby.

"Years earlier, when I was a 13-year-old schoolboy I used to carry the large blackboard around notifying supporters of team changes. At first – in 1942 – I would parade in front of the Main Stand and the Platt Lane as these were the only stands City were allowed to open, and then in February 1943 they announced the rest of the stands would be open, so I then had the entire pitch to walk around. The board was quite large and was split into two for City and visitors, but I also had the job for United's home matches at Maine Road as well. I had no end of problems with United's changes. They always seemed to have players with long names such as Wrigglesworth and so I had to start abbreviating them. That was not an easy task! Then there were the days when it rained and my changes kept disappearing. I'd stop every few yards to chalk up the names again.

"Later I had the job of putting up the half-time scores in the scoreboard situated at the back of the terracing where the North Stand was later built."

The United cup match was City's only tie at home during the 1955 Cup run, but Maine Road still had its part to play when it came to ticket distribution. City fan Peter Leckenby: "As a child I lived in Eileen Grove off Platt Lane and naturally became one of those boys who would wait until three-quarter time before getting in, but my first specific memory of the ground was in the weeks leading up to the 1955 Final. In those days tickets were sold at the ground on open sale and the queues snaked around the streets of Moss Side and into Rusholme where I lived. People slept overnight on the pavements, leaving many things behind. Us kids in the area had a

Below: Maine Road 1954. Where once the club name was proudly displayed on the gable of the Main Stand, City had now resorted to filling every available roof space with advertising. The gable advertised 'Pauldens' - a department store which eventually became Debenhams - while the perimeter wall around the pitch was still free of any advertising.

Right: Jack Dyson in action during the goalless Liverpool cup-tie at a snowy Maine Road in February 1956. 70,640 braved the conditions to witness this game. City won the replay 2-1 en route to Wembley.

Maine Memory

■ I have been a City Supporter for over 50 years and went to my first game at age eight in 1950. I then started to go to every home game with my brother, now sadly passed on to the big ground in the sky. We always went on the Kippax in those days and always on the corners so we stood adjacent to whichever goal City were kicking into. We always moved to the opposite end at half-time. You had freedom of movement in those days and it was a freedom we enjoyed.

I remember the cries of "Give it to Joe" at every game Joe Hayes played in. I also remember the great goalscorer Billy McAdams, and I have to say that Billy Mac was a lesson in how to be a traditional centre-forward. Another man I remember with affection was Big Dave Ewing. The crowd used to shout "Pull up at Daves'" and Ewing was a man who would have died for City.

Andy Handford

field day combing through all the debris to see if there was anything useful, and at my age, almost anything was!"

Ken Barber was one fan who had queued through the night: "I arrived home about 12.30pm on the Sunday after an 18-hour wait for my 3s 6d ticket and then discovered my brother was already at home with his ticket! He had arrived at the ground about 10.15 on the Sunday morning and bought his ticket from one of several young lads who had jumped the queue! He paid a few shillings more than me but was I envious! Fortunately City introduced the voucher system in the programme after that which made it a lot easier."

City were defeated by Newcastle in the final but Peter Leckenby's first City match as a paying customer came during the next season's cup run: "It was the third round match against Blackpool. I hardly saw a thing – thick fog had descended and the match was abandoned with the score 1-1! It didn't put me off, I had caught the bug. I quickly became a regular.

"My dad was a policeman and was on duty inside the ground for many matches. As a kid I used to see if I could find him – he was usually behind one of the goals. I was the 'bee's knees' to my mates, because that was my dad on duty!"

Ken Barber was also at this match: "Blackpool had scored in the first couple of minutes and then the fog came down. We were stood on Kippax Street and couldn't see a thing. We knew we were pressing for the equaliser when it was passed round that we had been awarded a penalty and that Jackie Dyson was taking it. Then a terrific cheer meaning we had scored was followed by utter silence. We were wondering what was happening and then after about ten minutes it was announced that the match had been abandoned!"

City progressed to Wembley for the second year in succession and defeated Birmingham in a highly memorable final. The 1955 and 1956 finals – and well-attended Cup matches at Maine Road - brought City considerable income and it was highly appropriate when the decision was taken to erect a roof over the Popular Side terracing. The decision to improve Maine Road was actually taken following the 1955 final and prior to the cup run of 1956, with the intention that the new development would be ready by summer 1957.

The decision to roof the Popular Side was potentially the first ground development – other than the use of floodlights which could not have been predicted in 1923 – to break away from Charles Swain's vision of how the stadium should be progressed.

Clearly any improvement at Maine Road had been on hold during the war years. Before the war, further

development of the stadium had occurred despite the depressed financial state of the country, and the Manchester area in particular. The Platt Lane Corner (1931) and Platt Lane Stand (1935) showed the Blues were keen to enhance the ground and it seems likely the Scoreboard End and Main Stand corner would have followed to a consistent plan during the period 1939–1945 had the situation allowed.

By the mid-1950s however so much had changed in the twenty years since the Platt Lane had been roofed that the original Charles Swain plans must have been either lost, forgotten about, or simply dismissed as being out of date.

Structural engineers from Bolton – John Booth & Sons – were brought in to look at what could be done with the Popular Side. In February 1956 the company submitted its initial plans, but it wasn't until the following season that real progress was made. City's planning application was formally granted on 13th November 1956. Announcements appeared in the City programme during the 1956-7 season stating the club's intentions.

The roof was raised during the summer of 1957 but brought a great deal of controversy City's way. For example the terracing had to be squared off - as Swain had initially planned then discounted way back in 1923. This meant the ends closest to each corner were extended; not a problem at the Scoreboard (north) end of the stand but at the Platt Lane end this meant those living in houses on Thornton Road would lose a little light. The residents were far from happy and a petition was set up.

Fortunately for the Blues, the local council supported the club and by August 1957 the stand was midway to completion. On 14th August City announced the £40,000 roof had been hit by a number of problems, most notably strikes by contractors. This left the job only half complete and meant this terracing area would be closed for the club's annual trial match.

Thornton Road resident Alan Liptrot wrote for *The Kippax – A Celebration* his boyhood memories of the stand being constructed: "As I set off to Heald Place Primary School each day, I watched the stand growing. The enormous upright girders went in first, then the thin lattice of roof girders spread along the construction. Sometimes the workmen – 'spidermen' – could be seen climbing across the exposed spaces and rumour had it that two or three actually fell to their deaths although I never knew if this was true or not.

"It was while the stand was being built, before the roof went on, that something really odd happened. My mum was a very calm and unexcitable woman. If she drank at all, it was the odd sherry at Christmas. She was not given to imagining things either, but she was

Maine Memory

■ One of my best memories is the day Ray Haddington scored a goal from the half way line in the good old days when City played a match at Maine Road in the fog. They wouldn't play a game like that today!

My wife Hilda and I have been going to watch City for 68 years now at Maine Road. We were both 12-year-olds when our respective dads took us. One other memory comes to mind; just after the war I was in the crowd behind the goal in the Platt Lane stand, the crowd that day was over 80,000. My poor old Dad was so crushed he could not even get his hand in his pocket to get a fag out... Good old days!

George Court

Haddington signed in November 1950 and appeared in six League matches. He scored in the first four of these, with two taking place at Maine Road (West Ham & Southampton).

Maine Match 55/56

CITY v EVERTON

DATE:	3rd March 1956
TYPE OF FIXTURE:	FA Cup Sixth Round
ATTENDANCE:	76,129
RESULT:	City 2 Everton 1

TEAMS & SCORERS:	CITY		EVERTON	
	Trautmann		O'Neill	
	Leivers		Moore	
	Little		Tansey	
	Barnes		Farrell	
	Ewing		Jones	
	Paul		Lello	
	Spurdle		B. Harris	
	Hayes	1	Wainwright	
	Johnstone	1	J. Harris	1
	Dyson		Fielding	
	Clarke		Eglington	

Above: Joe Hayes heads City's equaliser against Everton.

Roy Clarke was a major doubt for the game after injury had kept him out of the previous couple of League matches. He strove hard to make it but was a little surprised by the medical given him by trainer and former player Laurie Barnett: "I had a fitness test before the game with Laurie. He said 'Right... laps... sprints... now get your boots on'. I thought 'Great, I'll be kicking the ball now, I can really test my knee'. He takes me to the touchline puts my hands on the wall and says, 'right... kick the hell out of the wall with the toes of your boots, then we'll know if you're fit!'."

Clarke did make this sixth round tie with Everton, and supporter Bernard McAlinden remembers how he felt about the player: "'Tricky' Roy Clarke was always likely to score an important goal so it was great news that he could play in what was a terrific tie for City. They'd already knocked out Liverpool and were desperate to progress to the semi-final. The side was incredible – Trautmann, Paul and Johnstone were outstanding players. Players that would have been great in any era, but Everton also had a good side. When the game kicked off Everton dominated as they attacked the scoreboard end."

The Toffeemen spent the first 45 minutes pressing forward in style. Bert Trautmann, who had been another injury worry prior to the match, was kept on his toes, finally succumbing to an angled drive from Jimmy Harris. One goal was never going to be enough though, and in the second half Everton started to struggle. McAlinden: "Right from the kick-off City tore into Everton and played like a team possessed. They chased the equaliser and it came mid-way through the half from an accurately-taken free kick by Paul. The penalty box was packed as he stepped up to take the kick, about 25 yards out and around 25 yards in from the touchline on the left. As the ball was swung in, Joe Hayes made a vital yard of space on his marker and nodded in a beauty from point-blank range. Maine Road erupted with one of the loudest roars I have ever heard."

Around eight minutes later Bobby Johnstone scored the City winner when he threw himself at a Roy Clarke

centre. According to McAlinden: "Nobby took one touch and swung in a gem of a cross with the ball met by Johnstone running onto it and his quite brilliant header found the bottom corner of the net. Magic!"

It was a very good victory.

Another fan, Dave Harries, remembers this game because it was also his first Maine Road match: "I was nine years old and went to the game with my friend Billy who was only eight at the time. We both lived near Preston Street in Hulme from where we walked to the match, probably a distance of two miles. Neither of our dads were particularly interested in football but they gave us the entrance fee, probably to get rid of us for a couple of hours. Imagine it, my very first match and the gates ware locked an hour before kick off with 76,000 fans inside the stadium!

"Billy and I were put astride one of the entrance tunnels by a helpful supporter, very close to where I held a season ticket with two of my sons, near the corner flag in block L of the North Stand, next to the Main Stand. In those days it was the Scoreboard End, and I remember how both sets of fans were mixed together with not an ounce of trouble.

The City fans would sing a song followed by one from the Toffees, and it was fascinating to watch how the fans swayed with the sheer pressure of so many people being in the ground. The attendance was greatly increased 20 minutes from the end of time, when the gates were opened and many thousands more entered the ground in the hope of getting a glimpse of the game.

"My outstanding memories were of Bobby Johnstone who scored that day, the skill of Ken Barnes and the driving force of our captain Roy Paul. The 2-1 win was the icing on the cake for Billy and me as we made our way back home. Although the song had not been penned at that time, it was inevitable that I was 'City till I Die' because of that match.

"I was in Albert Square when the team returned without the cup in the previous season, and my abiding memory was Roy Paul announcing from the Town Hall steps that 'City would return with the cup next year'. And sure enough I watched the team come home with the cup from a vantage point somewhere on Market Street after they defeated Birmingham 3-1 in 1956. This was the game in which Bert Trautmann, my favourite player as a schoolboy, played on with a broken neck."

Maine Memory

■ During the early fifties and for the following decade or so, I had made a 'pen-friend' of Betty Wild who worked in the City offices. She was the widow of former City manager Wilf Wild and had been sending me City home programmes. She invited me to the ground on the day before City's match with Sheffield United in August 1954. Jimmy McClelland, the trainer/coach took me around. I met Bert Trautmann in the boot room; he had a badly bruised and swollen right hand and so shook my hand with his left one. I remember thinking that he stood little chance of playing for a week or so, but 24 hours later Bert was in goal for the visit of Sheffield United. City won 5-2 and he played well, but I have always wondered how he got through the game as I could see no signs of holding back in his handling of the ball.

Dennis Chapman

convinced she had seen a UFO, hovering over the part-finished stand. She had gone into the backyard on her way to our outside toilet when, over the stand, she saw it! She described it as having a body a bit like an aeroplane but it was flying very low and much too slowly. It had a faint glow to it, and she said it had windows in the side through which she could see figures moving about. She watched for a while and then hurried back in to tell my dad, but by the time they had both gone out again the thing had gone.

"Of course we never knew what she had seen that night, but many years later I read in a book about UFOs that sightings do tend to increase whenever large metal structures are being built, but you never know how much of it you can believe.... so what was it?"

Maybe the answer is that the UFO carried the ancestors of Moonchester – City's mascot – and from that day on the aliens from the Blue Moon became City fans!

Living so close to the ground gave Alan a different feel for Maine Road than most. Attending on match days was fantastic for most, but being in close proximity at other times meant Maine Road was a part of everyday life: "I lived at 62 Thornton Road from 1948 to 1971. Thornton Road is the one that backs on to the car park behind the Kippax. City's ground was not just somewhere I visited for matches… it was there all the time. I played football on the car park – the 'croft' as we called it – using the exit gates for goals. I used to climb the wall into the ground to get the ball back whenever it went over. The slopes at the front of the ground were the only places in the neighbourhood where you could get a half decent ride on your 'bogie', and the old wooden fence around the car park – down the 'Pink Entry' - was great for climbing.

"From my bedroom window I could look down into the ground. The banked terraces prevented me from seeing the actual pitch, but I did have an uninterrupted view right along the back of the Kippax to where the

Maine Memory

■ When I was a kid I lived in Hulme and I remember my dad took me and some friends to watch Manchester City. We used to play football behind the scoreboard end (now the North Stand) and every time there was a goal we used to run up the embankment only to find out that most of the time it was not in our favour.

We also used to jump the walls eventually getting round to the main stand where we would slither under the railing into the main stand. We thought it was great sitting in the main stand, such luxury for a few working class boys from Hulme.
Alan Forrest

wall of the ground angled left towards the open Scoreboard End.

"I have one clear memory from the days when the Kippax was open terracing. Watching the man putting up the flag on mornings prior to home games was as much a part of the Saturday morning ritual as *Children's Favourites* with Uncle Mac. The flag flew from early morning until shortly after the game was over. It seems surprising now that no one ever tried to steal it, but these were different days."

Remembering the time when City announced they would redevelop the Kippax Side, Alan added: "When we heard that City were going to cover the Kippax, I was eight or nine years old. I remember the excitement and curiosity in the houses along Thornton Road although the mood soon changed when the first large support girder was erected. People had naively imagined the new stand would follow the curve of the old terracing but of course it didn't, it ran straight along and was extended by quite a distance towards our houses. The upright girder on the back corner of the stand was much closer to the houses than anything else in the ground and it rose to a tremendous height."

As expected the stand was not complete in time for the annual practice match, causing the programme to apologise but announce that the new stand would be called The Kippax Stand: "Owing to circumstances beyond the club's control, the new covered stand – to be known officially as the Kippax Stand – could not be completed in time for today's practice game, but the contractors have given an assurance that it will be ready for the League match with Sheffield Wednesday next Saturday."

City's shareholders were already aware of this fact however. During the AGM on 14th August Chairman Alan Douglas told supporters "The seating enclosure will in future be known as the Main Stand; the covered enclosure as the Platt Lane Stand and the newly covered terraces as the Kippax Street Stand. The other terraces will be known as the Scoreboard End."

These names were already in use to some extent, but it seems this was the first formal statement outlining the club's preferred name for each stand. Ground plans and the like often named the Main Stand as the Grand Stand, while the Kippax had always been known as the Popular Side. Both the Grand Stand and Popular Side were in common use at Hyde Road and seem to have been naturally carried forward to Maine Road. Douglas also outlined how admission charges would range from 2s to 7s 6d.

Despite the expectation of an official Kippax opening against Sheffield Wednesday on 24th August, the game did not take place. Some have suggested this was because the stand wasn't complete, but the truth is there was an epidemic of Asian 'Flu and Sheffield Wednesday were seriously affected. The League agreed to Wednesday's request to cancel the fixture – a decision made public only two days before the match was due to be played. City were hugely disappointed and immediately asked the League and the FA if they could bring a continental side to Maine Road to officially open the stand on the same date.

Despite considerable negotiations, the Blues could not find appropriate opposition and another trial match was played instead. So, the first home game in front of the Kippax Stand was City's 5-2 victory over Chelsea on 4th September. Both the first and last League matches (April 1994) played in front of the Kippax roof were against Chelsea.

Below: The roofed Kippax Stand photographed in the 1970s.

Left: When the Kippax roof was built in 1957 the stand was extended (see left of top photo) over the original banking. This photo was taken in 1993 by which time the extended area had become the away section of the stand. The original 1923 tunnel and steps can be seen on the 'home' side of the segregation fence.

Local residents objected to the extension and in the 1994 photo (centre) the Kippax roof can be seen through a passage in Thornton Road.

Above right: The view from the Kippax car park during the early 1960s. Note the original Main Stand roof was still in place at this point while the floodlight towers were those erected in 1953. The floodlights on the roofs of Kippax and Main Stand were erected in 1957.

King of the Kippax editor Dave Wallace remembers his first sight of the completed stand: "City's raucous type supporters sported bob hats and scarves, waved rattles and congregated on the Scoreboard End terrace. Only when the rain hammered down was the threepence paid to transfer to the Kippax, but without the Scoreboard End's vociferous backing the atmosphere inside Maine Road was sadly lacking! My first observation of the Kippax then was on a Wednesday night in 1957 [the opening home match] when we clinched the double over Chelsea. We won that game 5-2 after Bobby Johnstone was sent off for swearing at the ref – only to be followed later by a Chelsea player. A placatory refereeing decision no doubt! Boy wonder Jimmy Greaves didn't play in this particular game after being injured on the previous Saturday at Birmingham in a collision with Gil Merrick, the Birmingham goalie."

After the match Bobby Johnstone told reporters: "If I am penalised I shall seriously consider giving up football." Johnstone was penalised but fortunately decided to continue playing.

The next home match was another eventful day as Dave Wallace remembers: "Then came my first time on the Kippax, a rainy September evening when City manager Les McDowall unveiled his latest plan against Preston. Keith Marsden was picked to play at number ten, dropping back to play twin centre-half with Dave Ewing. City won 2-0."

The booklet, *The Kippax – A Celebration*, produced by Noel Bayley to mark the end of the stand in 1994 contained many views of the roofed terracing, but one contribution – from Pete Hollins – also commented on the original floodlights and the enormous wall behind the stand. Pete: "I recall my first impressions of the stand as being overwhelming. I observed a high brick wall edged with barbed wire to deter the more adventurous fans who – frequently in those days – endeavoured to scale it. In the wall there appeared to be hundreds of turnstiles, one of which we'd pass through having been relieved of our money by a faceless figure standing in the darkness beyond the mesh.

"Once inside, I remember looking at the bases of the floodlight pylons which seemed to reach up beyond the sky although at that time, I suppose, my perceptions of size and scale must have been somewhat exaggerated as in later years, those same floodlights were dismantled and sold to a non-League side before being replaced by others that were twice the size. Elsewhere, the perimeter wall was also rebuilt to its present height and now it could only be scaled with the aid of a ladder!

"On the inside of the wall, I well remember some rather unsanitary toilets of which only rats and cockroaches would have been proud and, although I cannot remember the existence of any bars, I can recall the smell of the pies – on sale in small kiosks – which was more appetising than the smell we get these days."

Interestingly, the development of the Kippax roof also contained plans by John Booth & Sons to erect

floodlights on three towers on the new roof. A similar arrangement was planned for the original Main Stand roof as well. It is believed this would have provided enough light to enable the original corner lighting pylons to be removed.

Roof-style floodlighting has become the norm since the 1980s, however in the mid-fifties this would have been a significant departure. City's original lights were not the best in the football world, but 1957 was still a time when many football clubs had no lights of any description.

John Booth & Sons plans were refined in October 1957 and one solitary floodlight tower was put on the Kippax and one behind the gable on the Main Stand roof. The original corner lights were left in place for a few more years.

Prior to the Kippax Roof being built a number of very important games were staged at Maine Road. These were mainly FA Cup matches, such as City's thrilling

encounters with Liverpool and Everton in 1956 and the match with Newcastle in 1957. Other important games during the mid-fifties included Manchester United's first foray in Europe. The Reds had gone against FA advice and decided to take part in the European Cup, however they had overlooked the fact Old Trafford did not possess floodlights and so the Blues offered to help. This led to Maine Road becoming the first English ground to stage European football. In total three European matches were played at Maine Road during 1956-7 before the Reds returned home.

With United out of Maine Road, City were able to concentrate on their own club. Maine Road staged another semi-final in March 1958 – Blackburn v Bolton – watched by 74,800 illustrating the ground's importance once more, and gradually the Kippax started to develop a reputation as THE place to stand.

One Maine Road attendee during this period was future City player Ian Mellor: "My dad used to take me

Maine Match 56/57

CITY v NEWCASTLE UNITED

DATE:	9th January 1957			
TYPE OF FIXTURE:	FA Cup third round replay			
ATTENDANCE:	46,988			
RESULT:	City 4 Newcastle 5			
TEAMS & SCORERS:	CITY		NEWCASTLE	
	Trautmann		Simpson	
	Leivers		Keith	
	Little		Batty	
	Barnes		Scoular	
	Ewing		Stokoe	og
	Paul		Casey	1
	Fagan	1	White	2
	McAdams		Davies	
	Johnstone	2	Tait	1
	Clarke		Curry	1
	Fagan		Mitchell	

■ The Blues were comfortably winning this third round cup replay 3-0, but a penalty early in the second half prompted a spirited fightback by Newcastle. After 86 minutes the scores were level at 3-3. City made it 4-3 in extra time but the Magpies won 5-4 despite being a player down after having lost Dick Keith in the second half of normal time. A crowd of 46,988 witnessed this stupendous match.

Supporter John Barber remembers the last goal of the tie: "This became a really catastrophic memory. My father had a friend who left when it was City 3 Newcastle 0 because he thought it was all over. How wrong could you be? The final result of an absolute humdinger was City 4 Newcastle 5, with the second goal for Newcastle scored by a young unknown called Tait. He took the ball behind the halfway line and beat about six City men on his way to what was the goal of a lifetime. Aren't City supporters gluttons for punishment? What a club!"

According to City fan David Buxton this ranks as the best cup tie he ever saw, but above all else he remembers

the role played by Newcastle's Jimmy Scoular: "Strange that I should choose a game we lost as the greatest! Looking back, it was a terrific game to watch, although at the time I didn't appreciate City throwing away a three goal lead! What still stays vividly in my mind is the leadership shown by Jimmy Scoular, a player we loved to hate. Without him, the Tynesiders would never have turned the game round - he threatened and cajoled and got the best out of his team in terrible conditions. Steam was rising from his massive thighs and balding head. Rather like our own Roy Paul, I regard Scoular as an inspirational captain. I can't imagine either of them jumping in the air to avoid a tackle or wearing a sarong!"

This game is also significant for comedian and one-time Maine Road resident Eddie Large: "I remember taking the afternoon off school to go to watch City v Newcastle. City were leading 3-1 then it went to 3-3, and extra time with City winning 4-3. Yes, you have guessed it we got beat 5-4. I made sure I got home about the same time as I would from school, five minutes later my Dad walks in and says 'I have just seen one of the best games of all time. I wouldn't have blamed you for having the afternoon off school to watch that'. I never told him!"

For player Roy Little this is not a game worth dwelling on: "This was a game to forget! Especially for myself. At half time we were 3-0 up and thought we could get our own back for the cup final defeat of 1955. Come the second half and a series of mistakes let them draw level 3-3. We got in front via a Bobby Johnstone goal and were playing well. But then a long clearance went over my head and I played the ball back to Bert, but this ruddy zebra – Len White – poked a foot out and sent the ball past Bert! My mistake was termed 'the diabolical back pass'. White then scored the winner but my back pass virtually cost us the game.

"After this Newcastle disaster a few supporters on the Kippax corner used to have a bit of banter with me. 'Watch out, White's about' they used to shout."

Right: Maine Road as it looked at the end of the 1950s. The gable on the Main Stand once proudly displayed the club's name but advertising for rain macs gave the stand a less prestigious feel.

Below: Looking down Wansford Street towards the Scoreboard End in the early 1960s. The view down the same street in 2003 appears on page 17.

and I've always been a Blue. My first memory of Maine Road is of a 1958 England versus Germany Under-15 match. I was about eight years old and can't really remember too much about the day other than there was a ginger-headed player – that seemed to stand out for some reason – and that we sat in the Main Stand. My Granddad had been a season ticket holder in the Main Stand, and by the end of the fifties me and my father had moved to the Kippax. We usually stood towards the Platt Lane end near the edge of the penalty area. I remember us playing against Spurs and to me, as a young boy, there seemed to be this player using his wrong foot to kick the ball. I couldn't understand what he was doing and I asked my dad 'why's that player using his 'wrong' foot'. Dad told me it was Jimmy

Greaves and that he was left-footed – it wasn't his wrong foot! This may seem a little odd, but that was the day I realised I was left-footed. I always kicked with my left leg but no one had ever said anything to me about being left or right footed, so when I saw Greaves I just thought it was wrong. After that I understood and looked out for left-footed players and, of course, that day helped me understand my own style of play."

By 1960 Maine Road looked fresh and bright but on the pitch the club began to struggle. On 2nd May a crowd of almost 66,000 came to the final match of the season with Burnley, but the large crowd had not turned out to celebrate City's success, they had arrived to see how the mid-table Blues would cope against Championship-chasing Burnley.

Royal Blues

Over the years Manchester City has proved a very popular club for visits by significant members of the British Royal family and of other nations' royalty. Whether this has anything to do with the club's success, the stadium's importance, or the role of Manchester in terms of industry and commercial activity is unclear.

There have been two major royal visits to Maine Road and there has been one significant visit to the club's former ground at Hyde Road. In addition, the Queen and the Duke of Edinburgh have already visited the City of Manchester Stadium twice for the Commonwealth Games. Prince Philip created history by becoming the first senior member of the Royal family to visit two of City's venues.

The first Royal visit to Maine Road was on 20th October 1934 when the Duke of York (future King George VI, Queen Elizabeth II's father) watched City's 1-0 defeat by Derby County. Prior to the match the Duke was introduced to both sides and then took his seat at the front of the Directors' Box. The previous year he had witnessed City's FA Cup final defeat to Everton.

The next major Royal visit came on Thursday 7th May 1964 when Prince Philip witnessed a City-United derby match. The game had been organised by the Variety Club of Great Britain as a charity fundraiser for underprivileged children, and it had been hoped a capacity crowd of over 60,000 would be present, however appalling weather limited the attendance to approximately 36,000. Philip, as with the Duke of York thirty years earlier, sat in the Directors' Box, although this time, according to newspaper reports, the box had been decked out with flowers and was christened the Royal Box for the evening.

The game ended with Philip presenting the Duke of Edinburgh Cup to United's captain Denis Law on the pitch in the pouring rain. Thousands of children, according to local reports, swarmed onto the pitch as the Duke became drenched. Interestingly, Philip's visit to the Commonwealth Games in 2002 also saw him suffer with the rain. Maybe he recalled his 1964 visit as he waited for the 2002 Games to end.

Since 1964, Maine Road has seen several visits by middle-eastern princes, but the most significant Royal visit of all to a City venue has to be the 1920 appearance of King George V at Hyde Road. This was the first visit to a provincial ground by a reigning monarch and as such is of immense importance.

There is also a suggestion that another royal visit occurred at Hyde Road, however this appears to be a myth. According to some sources it has been suggested Queen Victoria's son, the Prince of Wales (future King Edward VII), attended Hyde Road in 1900. Some sources have even produced a photograph purporting to be the future Edward VII at Hyde Road. Extensive research however has led to the conclusion this visit did not occur, and that a simple explanation for the confusion exists. Back in 1930 the club's first true history, Manchester City Football Club Souvenir History by Fred Johnson, stated "The Hyde Road Ground was honoured with the presence of His Majesty the King on March 27th 1900 when Liverpool were opposed." This is clearly a

typographical error as the incident it refers to is the visit of King George on 27th March 1920 (when Liverpool were the visitors).

Clearly this explains the confusion but what about the photographic evidence? This photograph (below) is clearly from Hyde Road – the stand in the background is undoubtedly the Stone Yard Stand – and according to some sources the two gentlemen wearing top hats are members of the Royal Family, however when this photograph is compared to photos taken during the visit of future Prime Minister Arthur Balfour in September 1900 it's clear this photograph was taken on the same day. Balfour was the only prominent guest that afternoon and can even be seen on this photograph (his head appears in the background between the ladies and the top-hatted gentlemen).

In addition, further investigation shows the top-hatted gentleman in the rear

Left and above:
King George V is introduced to Eli Fletcher (left) and the rest of the City players (above) during a visit to Hyde Road in 1920.

is City director Mr. W. Richmond (a director between 1896 and 1902), while the gentleman in front looks suspiciously like Joshua Parlby (the club's former manager and a key member of City's Board in 1900). One of the ladies is described as the daughter of Arthur Balfour in another photograph from this day.

As it is though, the fact the King attended Hyde Road in 1920 is a major landmark, and that his son (future King George VI) attended Maine Road, and his grand-daughter (Queen Elizabeth II) has already attended the City of Manchester Stadium gives City a unique place in history. How long will it be before Prince Charles or Prince William attends a City venue?

Maine Memory

I have been a City supporter for over fifty years and some 48 years ago my parents asked me what I wanted for my 7th birthday. The only thing I wanted was to meet my hero Bert Trautmann. My Dad managed to arrange this through Eric Todd who was the City reporter for the Football Pink in those days.

Match day arrived (City v Sunderland, which City won 1-0) and my father, my brother and I were invited to meet Bert before kick-off. A photograph was taken of this meeting; alongside myself and Bert were Roy Little and Paddy Fagan. This picture made the Football Pink evening edition and also features on page 96 of Bert Trautmann's autobiography *Steppes to Wembley*. The club also kindly invited us to sit on the bench and watch the match but unfortunately my father worked for himself and had to get back to his hardware shop. There was some consolation for me however as the club gave me a football signed by the team for my birthday.

More recently we have managed to reproduce the same photo, albeit we are 48 years older. This was kindly arranged by our now family friend Roy Little.

Chris Brunt

Above: Maine Road seen from the air in 1961.

Burnley won the title with a 2-1 victory. Dave Wallace: "A crowd of 65,981 rolled up for this Monday evening tussle and the roads to Maine Road were choc-a-block, causing me to abandon the 76X and leg it for the last couple of miles. The ground was packed and there was no chance of getting on either the Scoreboard End or the Kippax. I ran the length of the back of the stand although the Venturi effect of the roar through the tunnels – an incredible punch of sound – nearly floored me! Amazingly, I found a spot with room to spare in the corner between the Kippax and the Platt Lane, and that was where I always headed for if I was late, or if we had a big crowd, because there was always room."

According to Dave it was over the next couple of years when the atmosphere within the ground really altered: "During the 1961/2 season the situation gradually changed. The Scoreboard Enders drifted away; fans started to get wise to protection from the elements and a whole new breed gathered on the Kippax. By the 1962/3 season that support was well established and preparing for relegation in that cold, cold winter, a new hero emerged, having his name chanted throughout – "H... A... R... L... E... Y!" The Scot from Third Lanark – who scored 32 goals in a relegation season – specialised in scoring against United even when he was transferred to Brum at the end of the season."

Eric Thomas, a City fan living in Australia, also remembers the Harley chant: "From my early days as a young supporter in the 1950's, I have witnessed many memorable events at Maine Road. I can remember those days when the ground was full to capacity, and they would allow us kids to sit over the barrier wall around the pitch. I'm talking 64,000 for a derby game when Roy Paul was City's captain, and Allenby Chilton was United's. I can remember when I heard the first noise and chanting erupting from the terraces "Harley!, Harley!" for that great goalscoring machine Alex Harley. But probably my most interesting memory has more to do with the culture outside, rather than inside, the stadium. Back in the days when cars were a luxury, and players wages were twenty pounds a week. A lot of fans used to cycle to Maine Road, and the enterprising

neighbours living around the back of the ground used to open their back yards and charge you sixpence for minding your bike."

Back in 1960-61 the derby match with United became newsworthy for the simple fact it was to be the only Maine Road derby ever to be abandoned. The match, played on 27th August 1960, was attended by 51,927 – the largest crowd for an abandoned match at Maine Road. John Barber was present that day and remembers the role played by referee – and future "It's A Knockout" referee – Arthur Ellis from Halifax: "The weather was appalling and the pitch became waterlogged to some extent. The referee was that fussy Arthur Ellis and I think the match went City 0 United 1; City 1 United 1; City 1 United 2; City 2 United 2 and then the match was called off in pouring rain to the rage of the fifty odd thousand supporters massed inside the ground. Finally Arthur Ellis came over the intercom system and in a broad Yorkshire accent said helplessly 'Aam as disapawnted as wot you aare'. Denis Law scored that day as did another prolific scorer of vital goals, Joe Hayes."

Another fan, Ted Knott remembers the pre-match entertainment and also the importance of the club's scoreboard at the end opposite the Platt Lane: "During the fifties and early sixties the pre-match and half time entertainment was provided by The Beswick Prize Band conducted by Albert Risby, and occasionally backed up by female vocalist Miss Silvia Farmer. Sometimes the band would march around the pitch and the baton would be tossed into the air. It was quite a sight, particularly when the baton wasn't caught! This brought great amusement to the crowd. It wasn't until the mid-sixties when the entertainment changed to chart music, but I must say the public address system was never much good at Maine Road.

"Of course, we had to rely on the old green scoreboard for news of how teams were faring. I can recall one particular reserve match at Maine Road against Wolves. The first team were playing at Molineux on the opening day of the 1962-3 season. In those days the scores of the first team were relayed to the green scoreboard every 15 minutes. The scores must have been telephoned through because I clearly remember that as soon as we all heard the telephone ring our attention was immediately switched to how our first eleven were getting on. The moment arrived and we all awaited with baited breath, especially as Wolves were THE team of the period and we had just had a good pre-season. To say we were hopeful is an understatement. Then up came the latest score Wolves 0 City 2. We all cheered. We'd hoped it'd go our way but we couldn't believe we'd be winning 2-0 so early in the match. Then we realised... the scoreboard attendant had put the plates up the wrong way round, and we were in fact losing 2-0. Oh the groans! I can still hear them now. I'm sure he did it to wind us up. We ended up losing 8-1 that day and the reserves also got a 5-0 drubbing! Whenever anyone talks of the old green scoreboard I always remember that particular day!"

City were relegated at the end of that season but it's fair to say Maine Road had continued to develop. Benches had been installed on the Platt Lane terracing increasing City's seated capacity to approximately 18,500. This meant the stadium now housed more seats than any other League ground. The transformation of terracing to seats was relatively uncommon at the time, but the City view was clearly to increase seating to a level in keeping with a major stadium. Sadly, by simply bolting benches on to the original terracing the view from this stand – particularly for children – was exceptionally poor.

Nevertheless, in the early sixties few questioned City's decision although in truth the seating of Platt Lane in this manner was looked on in future years as a poor move. According to stadium expert Simon Inglis, writing in the 1980s: "The stand has bench seats bolted onto the old terracing, and has been built up at the back on wooden terracing. The rake is therefore unchanged, and with a line of uprights along the front, viewing is not always ideal. Compared with the North Stand opposite, the arrangement is positively archaic."

Despite the stand's inadequacies in later life, it's fair to say the Platt Lane became a great home for many City fans. It was a good introduction to Maine Road for young supporters and the atmosphere within the stand was relatively good. Over time a large contingent of season ticket holders took up residence on the Platt Lane benches, and the stand developed its own identity.

Supporters now had real choice within the stadium. The most expensive seats were clearly within the Main Stand, while those craving a good atmosphere while wishing to be seated could pick Platt Lane. For standing spectators, the Kippax would protect you from the elements, while those more traditional diehards could still stand on the uncovered Scoreboard End. Every type of Sixties supporter could be accommodated.

It is worth stating as well how there were minor changes within the structure of the Main Stand during the late fifties and early sixties. The three familiar tunnels, regarded by many as the most recognisable feature of the ground throughout its existence, were altered slightly. Viewing the tunnels in the club's first thirty years of existence it is clear they were longer than at the time of the ground's demise in 2003. The Players' tunnel retained the full length of white walling on either side, however the seating was brought forward to allow a small enclosure for the senior directors in between the two white walls. The other two tunnels were reduced by a similar distance with the two white walls demolished for the final six feet or so.

These tunnel changes had no effect on their use as exit points, but it did mean additional seating could be installed where the tunnels used to extend. A review of this area in 2003 showed how concrete from the original end wall of the tunnel was still positioned under a few of the seats.

Roger Reade, a key figure behind the PFA's community programmes and an ardent City supporter, remembers attending Maine Road during this period: "My first actual game was City against Swansea Town – they didn't become a city for a few years – on 2nd

Maine Memory

■ The first match I ever saw was on 3rd March 1962. I was six years old, so don't remember much about the game, although when I look back I actually saw my first City hat-trick by Peter Dobing. Spurs were Champions, City were mid-table and sliding towards relegation the following year. What else could happen but City win 6-2. I do remember the Spurs goalkeeper was called Hollowbread, which seemed a great name to me at the time. That first match was watched from the Platt Lane end, but as my dad started taking me regularly we moved more towards the Main Stand, near the corner flag. We always had to get there early to avoid the view of the goals being obstructed by the pillars.

Over the years since then I have stood or sat in almost every place in the ground, including the dug-out, and the best spot to watch from was the old Kippax Stand. No matter what time you got there, you could always reach your usual spot by a bit of shoving and pushing, and the atmosphere was always lively. And although it looked packed from other parts of the ground, there was always room to move around. Streaming down the big steps or through the low tunnel after a match, everybody singing and banging - it doesn't get any better than that!

Graham Elliott

Left: Geoff Hurst scores to seal City's relegation in 1963. West Ham beat the Blues 6-1 in both League games that season and, although this match took place at Upton Park, the photograph is included to show the traditional City colours as described by Roger Reade on page 149.

Below: Bert Trautmann's Testimonial Match in 1964 attracted an official crowd of 48,000. Thousands were locked out while those that did make it into the ground believe there were in excess of 60,000 there. The ground at this stage was easily capable of holding over 60,000 and these scenes of chaos demonstrate how high the attendance was. Somewhere amongst this crowd of supporters and police are a couple of the players!

November 1963. Unusually we watched the match from the corner, in between the Kippax and the old Scoreboard End. The Platt Lane became our regular spot at the time, not the Kippax. I remember the vivid colours worn by both sides. City were in their brilliant sky blue – and that looked incredible when seen in the flesh for the first time – while Swansea wore an away kit of orange. It was very vivid and to a young boy it really stood out. Alan Oakes scored and we won 1-0 but that day was everything to me. I couldn't wait for the next match. We then became regulars in the Platt Lane, and I loved being at the ground. I think that ground means everything to me. I've been going there for forty years – half its life – and I can't imagine how my life would be if I hadn't gone to matches and been a City fan. Saturday afternoons would have been dull, but not only that, the club and the ground have given me and many, many fans focus. Imagine a life without City – what would we

Maine Memory

■ My father was a football supporter for as long as I can remember and specifically a City supporter. It was great when City won the cup in 1956, and my Mum took my cousin and myself to Piccadilly in Manchester to watch the team bring the cup back to Manchester. I can remember seeing Bert Trautmann sitting on the top of the bus and I think he was holding a big teddy bear or something. It could have been the cup, but I couldn't tell.

Of course it wasn't until after the team returned that it was found that he had broken his neck.

I can't remember how long he was actually out of the game, but when it was announced he was going to play in the reserves my father bought tickets as a surprise for myself and my cousin - who I might add was a United supporter.

This has become my favourite Maine Road memory. We travelled there by bus and were very excited. My first impression of the stadium was that it was huge. I hadn't seen anything like it before so it was pretty amazing at the time. We had seats in the stands which were about half way down on the right hand side from the director's box.

The atmosphere was fantastic and one of the many things that stick in my mind is how much the crowd reacted to Trautmann. Every time he touched the ball the crowd cheered. Bearing in mind he came to this country as a German POW the Maine Road crowd really took him to their hearts.

This experience definitely made me a blue for life, but I think at the time it was more the man than the game! Not long after this game my father and me started to go to Maine Road home games on a regular basis, eventually buying season tickets. There was however one thing we disagreed on and that was that my father thought Frank Swift was the best goalkeeper City ever had, but for me Bert Trautmann was the best. We never agreed on that!

Jean Preston

A quieter moment for Bert Trautmann as he watches the action at the Scoreboard End of the ground during a League game in 1964.

be doing now? Remember in 1963 going to Maine Road, even when City were poor, was a major day out. It was by far the most exciting part of the week and it was the closest we could get to a proper trip. Obviously, if you were lucky you'd go to Blackpool once in a while, but other than that, Maine Road was it. No Alton Towers, no weekend breaks at Disneyland… in fact even trips to garden centres and DIY places were unheard of, so Maine Road had no competition for me, my parents, or my peers.

"Once we made it into the ground the excitement of entering the Platt Lane Stand was immense. I just could not wait. We'd walk down the Platt Lane tunnel and the whole Maine Road scene would open up. It was like entering the stadium via the Player's tunnel. It was a terrific feeling and I can't ever remember entering the stand by the steps at the back, or any of the other means. It was always the tunnel, and it was always passionate. Even on cold dismal days with relatively low crowds. That tunnel signified Maine Road's passion. It was a major piece of the ground."

In 1964 the floodlights changed. This time club officials boasted how City's new lights, erected on 180ft towers, were the tallest in League football. They were also considerably more powerful than the earlier ones. The floodlights cost £36,000 and the Blues expected to open them with a prestigious friendly against either Manchester United or Rangers in December. Sadly, the Reds rejected City's offer immediately claiming they were too busy with European football – perhaps forgetting it was City's investment in floodlighting which had enabled United to compete in Europe in the first place.

Rangers also rejected City's offer. The Blues then decided not to bother with a specific opening match, and the lights were eventually switched on for the League fixture with Bury on Boxing Day 1964. According to Peter Gardner at the *Manchester Evening News*, the old lights were eventually sold to Lockhead, Leamington in the Midland League, although it had initially been hoped they would be sold to Cheshire League side Runcorn. Sadly, a Runcorn official wrote to City's secretary Walter Griffiths to say: "We have run into financial trouble and find that the cost of transporting and installing the lights is beyond our means."

The Boxing Day meeting with Bury ended goalless, but the lights proved considerably better than the previous set. Inevitably, the switch-on was used by many headline writers to criticise the team. "City Blunders All Too Clear" read one, while another said "City Lights Dimmed." The supporting reports all followed the same theme: "There was nothing festive about this Boxing Day scramble. The brightest part of the proceedings was the switching on of City's new lights, but they only revealed to a greater extent the weaknesses of both sides."

Maine Memory

■ My first game at Maine Road was over 40 years ago on September 8, 1962. I went to see City against West Ham. One year earlier our primary school teacher sent the boys home with the task of finding out who City's goalkeeper was and why he was famous. We all came back enthralled by the Bert Trautmann legend. Unfortunately, the rest of the class were brainwashed shortly afterwards. Living in Flixton they became Reds. We were only six or seven at the time and she set the question when she realised we knew little about football, but what a spark she lit! I was well into war stories in the Hotspur and other comics, so I was so taken with the whole Bert Trautmann legend. After that I had to play in goal, despite my tiny stature.

Finally I persuaded my dad to take me to see Bert, David Wagstaffe, Peter Dobing and my other heroes. I was overwhelmed by the occasion - the noise, the crowds, the colours, the shirts, the pitch! I felt crushed in the Kippax/ scoreboard corner.

The result? …err, City were beaten 6-1 and Bert Trautmann got sent off defending the Platt Lane end after one of the goals. I remember him picking the ball out of the net and kicking it in the back of the ref! He stripped to the waist and walked off; a show of temper I didn't really associate with Bert. We lost track of the goals, thinking it was 7-1 but there was a disallowed goal. I didn't hold it against Bert as his wartime record and '56 heroics put him on a pedestal. I was probably more disappointed with the younger heroes, especially David Wagstaffe who I regarded as City's best player. I was really upset when he was sold to Wolves.

Why did I stick with them? Well the following week I went to Old Trafford for the first time to see us beat United 3-2, and former Blue hero Denis Law fresh from Turin got booked. I remember walking away from the ground with the Man U fans really upset. That compensated hugely for the previous week. Of course that was the peak of the season. The bad tempered 1-1 draw with United at the end of the season put City down, instead of United and they won the Cup. Ever since I get really nervous when City get a landmark result. The rollercoaster had started back in 1962-3!
Ged Parker

Another report said: "The lights served only to illuminate City's faults."

Further construction work was being performed around the ground. Prior to the lights' illumination Peter Gardner wrote how City were a modern progressive club, always looking at ways to improve facilities. He was correct but, as both Peter Swales and Francis Lee were to discover in the eighties and nineties, any ground

Maine Memory

■ My very first visit to Maine Road was in August 1960. My dad took me to see City play Arsenal. Walking to the ground through the streets and back alleys surrounding the ground, my memories are of countless numbers of bicycles being parked up in the back yards of the houses. Threepence per bike I think it was, and queues of buses dropping people off. The bikes have long since disappeared and the buses are greatly reduced in number but the pilgrimage continues - by other means of transport. We sat in the Main Stand in Block H. The images were of the pitch way down below us, the views across Moss Side beyond the open Scoreboard End, the noise of the crowd, the smell of Bovril which seemed to be the only refreshment available as far as a small eight-year-old could make out. The players seemed so far away but I was held by the magic of it all and have now been a regular for over 42 years! Over the years I have stood in the Scoreboard End and the Kippax Street, sat in the Main Stand and the Platt Lane, I have enjoyed and endured all the emotions that go with supporting a football team, and when that team are the mercurial Manchester City everything is magnified. They are family.

Phil Taylor

development had to be carefully considered alongside the overall direction of the team on the pitch. All supporters wanted improved facilities, but they also wanted success. City needed to get the balance right, particularly in the mid-sixties.

Another major development taking place was the building of the £60,000 Social Club. According to Gardner: "Next stage in development will be the exciting new Social Club planned for the spare land at the corner of Maine Road and Claremont Road. Plans for this are going well and the club could be in operation by early 1966. Some critics of the club will be quick to question the wisdom of attempting such an expensive venture when the money might have been better used to strengthen key positions in the team fighting to make a return to the First Division. But where to find such players in these days of highly-inflated prices is a different matter. The club did make positive steps towards promotion last season when nearly £70,000 was spent on three players – Derek Kevan, Jimmy Murray, and Alan Ogley."

He added: "City appear to be relying on the strength at their disposal to pull them through this season, and the money they are now ready to pay out is for the benefit of their supporters."

The investment in players was nowhere near enough, while the building of the Social Club seemed a distraction. True it would help in the long run but by December 1964 City were going nowhere. The Bury match typified the club – great investment in facilities (floodlights) but little motivation on the pitch.

Another improvement announced was the expansion of the Development Association offices. Former player Roy Clarke was managing the association out of an office at the Platt Lane end of the ground but it was nowhere near good enough. The club announced a modern office would be erected on the main forecourt although this became consumed within the Social Club building work.

While the stadium had moved on during the late fifties and early sixties sadly the team had not. Occasional flashes of brilliance couldn't disguise the fact City were struggling. A silly defeat at Shrewsbury in a third round FA Cup replay brought more misery. Some supporters asked 'What's the point of having a major stadium if the team is so poor?'.

The frustrations came to a head with Swindon's visit on 16th January. The attendance was a miserly 8,015 – the lowest City League crowd at Maine Road – and when the season ended on 28th April only 8,409 bothered to watch the Blues beat Charlton 2-1. The season ended with City in eleventh place in Division Two. The average attendance was 14,753 – the lowest ever at Maine Road and the lowest since 1899.

There were even worrying stories of a potential merger with United. George Poyser was dismissed weeks before the end of the season and former cup hero Fred Tilson asked to act as caretaker manager. Tilson had strong support from the Board, in particular Albert Alexander – a very knowledgeable football man – and the Blues were undefeated in their final four games, but clearly City were in a mess.

Supporters demonstrated against the Board; bricks were thrown and windows smashed. The Blues appeared to be dying while Maine Road was, for the first time in its history, the scene of considerable unrest. The forecourt became a meeting point for disheartened fans. Something had to change.

Maine Match 64/65

CITY v SWINDON TOWN

DATE:	16th January 1965	
TYPE OF FIXTURE:	Football League Division Two	
ATTENDANCE:	8,015	
RESULT:	City 1 Swindon 2	
TEAMS & SCORERS:	CITY	SWINDON
	Dowd	Hicks
	Bacuzzi	Dawson
REFEREE:	Sear	Trollope
J.E. Carr	Kennedy	Morgan
(Sheffield)	Gratrix	McPherson
	Oakes 1	Atherton
	Pardoe	Shergold
	Murray	Hunt
	Ogden	Summerbee 1
	Kevan	Brown 1
	Connor	Rogers

■ This match has gone down in history as City's lowest League crowd – only 615 more than watched Fourth Division Stockport that weekend. It is also viewed by many as the lowest point in the club's history. Clearly, relegation to the third tier of league football in 1998 was the lowest in terms of performance on the pitch, but when other factors are considered – mainly support – January 1965 saw the club blundering forward with little idea of how to turn the situation around. Supporters felt alienated with demonstrations taking place, while one director had even suggested the best way forward might be to merge with Manchester United! Clearly life couldn't get any worse for the Blues.

A Cup defeat at Shrewsbury ensured this League affair with Swindon would only be attended by absolute die-hard City fans. This game has been commented on a great deal, but the full story of the match has rarely been published. To put the situation into perspective the following text has been compiled based on the events recorded at the time.

The general feeling in Manchester was this would not be a well-attended game. Swindon were not an attractive side and the embarrassing cup defeat was a convenient excuse for some to miss the match. In addition, there was general unease around the city as stories of potential bus strikes were developing, while the weather was poor. Snow had been forecast, although it didn't arrive until the following week.

Prior to the match Chairman Albert Alexander, working with former cup-hero Fred Tilson, gave the City players a team talk. He urged them to give all they could to help ease the situation while manager George Poyser was away desperately searching for new players.

Alexander's pleas certainly had some effect and City played with real determination. No one could fault their attitude as they made most of the play. But Swindon were solid in defence and the visitors had luck on their side. Jimmy Murray missed a couple of sitters for the Blues, while other shots – including one from Alan Oakes – hit the crossbar.

Two surprise attacks by Swindon saw Brown and

Summerbee score, while Alan Oakes managed a 67th minute consolation goal when he netted a 30-yard rocket. According to reporter Wilf Dowding: "Forget Manchester City's troubles and here was a game to enjoy – cheeky Swindon's planned retreat against City's enthusiastic approach. In the 67th minute left-half Alan Oakes tried a glorious 35-yard shot. By then Swindon were playing confidently with a two goal lead – the reward for simple effective moves completed by Denis Brown (20 minutes) and Mike Summerbee (64). Both goals were against the run of play but went to the side in control - even though Swindon were mostly retreating. Indeed the more City attacked the more Swindon seemed likely to score."

The game ended in defeat and according to *Sun* journalist Arthur Walmsley that was a fair result: "They tried, oh, how they tried, but at the end they confirmed what was known before – that this City team is just not good enough. It might be claimed that luck didn't go City's way, but good teams mostly make their own luck and City are not a good team just now. With Murray and Kevan having nightmare games, it was not surprising that teenage forwards Ogden, Pardoe and Connor hardly looked the immediate answer to City's problems."

City did need players, but one man the supporters were keen to see had been dropped – Matt Gray. On the Kippax a banner was fastened up proclaiming "We want Matt", although this statement was misconstrued in one newspaper with reporter David Jack believing it could have meant the City faithful wanted Matt Busby as manager!

Left: Derek Kevan jumps with Swindon right-back Owen Dawson. Swindon had taken the revolutionary step of wearing numbers on their shorts continental style.

Above: A deserted Scoreboard End as Maine Road records its lowest ever League crowd for a City game, just over 8,000 for the visit of Swindon Town in 1965.

Left: The Platt Lane Stand / Kippax corner is just as sparsely populated!

After the match youngsters demonstrated against the Board. This was probably the first time in history City fans had publicly criticised the directors. There were even letters in the local papers. D Lett of Salford wrote: "Many thousands of City supporters must be wondering how much longer we are to be subject to the way our club is slowly sinking. The supporters have given everything but their blood in believing City are not finished. But even to a City fan time has a limit and this is surely burning to a rapid close. We who work in various jobs five days a week, but whose opinions are never heeded, could tell you the present board should go. Let's face it – over the past 15 years we have had players and managers. The only thing that hasn't changed is the board."

Journalist Don Evans felt the club's failure had developed over time: "After the sale of David Wagstaffe to Wolves; the report of an alleged merger approach to Manchester United; the Cup exit at Shrewsbury, and the transfer request of Matt Gray, the Maine Road fans have been frustrated and fed-up. And surely the ultimate in misery was reached yesterday when just 8,015 saw the defeat against Swindon… a sorry contrast to the golden days.

Maine Memory

■ I remember when Dave Ewing got married. He was married in the morning and then played in the afternoon. The players carried him around the pitch and the band played 'For he's a jolly good fellow'. I think quite a few players were married on the day of a game.

When I was pregnant with my eldest daughter I went to the hospital on a Wednesday morning and the midwife said "You'd better come in this afternoon. You're almost ready." I told her I couldn't because there was a midweek match on but I managed to persuade the midwife I could wait and went home. Anyway, time came to go to the match and I couldn't get through the turnstile! So they opened up a gate and let me in, but I had to promise that I would stay at the end of the match and wait for the crowd to go before I tried to leave. My daughter was born the following Saturday.

Another time I was with my daughter and Cliff Sear was playing. She was mad on him. Anyway, he stopped on the pitch in front of us to sort his socks out and he threw a piece of tape on to the pitch. She had her eye on it for ages, but a lad went and picked it up and she said to him "I had my eye on that. I wanted it," and a policeman asked her what she wanted. She explained and the policeman took the tape off the lad and gave it to her.
Fran Parker

Maine Memory

■ I was one of 14,698 to attend Maine Road on Saturday 8th February 1964 and witness the League debut of Colin Bell. As a 17-year-old, no-one was to know the influence he would have at City. He was playing for Bury and scored for them in the 25th minute.

Harry Dowd playing in goal for City injured his shoulder just after the interval. These were the days before substitutes were allowed, and Matt Gray pulled on the goalie's sweater with Dowd moving outfield to take up the centre forward position. Eight minutes from the end and playing better than all the other forwards, Dowd netted the rebound from a Derek Kevan shot which had hit the bar to earn City a 1-1 draw. In honesty, whilst these two incidents were in their own way history making, the game was memorable for little else.
Peter Hall

"There was a minor demonstration yesterday, incidentally, by schoolboys behind the stand. But it was good natured enough."

In another article Frank Steele felt the demonstrations were a little more serious: "It was yet another dismal day for Manchester City, the club which is existing from crisis to crisis. After the game a minor demonstration by young fans outside the main entrance was dispersed by police who are accustomed to such things at Maine Road."

In the *Sunday Express* James Mossop claimed: "After yesterday's match about fifty fans stood at the main entrance shouting 'Sack the lot'.

Chairman Albert Alexander – a Blue through and through – did not hide from fans. Instead he spoke truthfully about the situation: "It is distressing, but we shall continue to do everything in our power to bring about an improvement. I can reveal that in the past few weeks we have asked several clubs about players we would have liked, but it has not been possible to obtain them.

"We have been losing money for quite a while and the urgency of the position is such that the day may be near when we may have to pay more than we ever intended."

City's playing problems were endemic throughout the club. According to reporter James Holland: "One of the most disturbing features of the situation, however, is that the reserves are next to the bottom in the Central League, for the strength of any club is governed by the quality of its reserves."

Eric Cooper, the 'Sports Voice of the North', considered City's situation and decided: "It isn't soccer experts or players Manchester City need right now so much as a psychologist. A man who might analyse the transitions from optimism to pessimism. A man who by his enthusiasm and drive might fill the gaps between the potential City have shown so often and the failures that have labelled them the most unpredictable team in soccer. Here is a club that between the wars were Manchester's favourites, reaching the Cup final three times besides winning the League Championship in 1937, while neighbours United were regarded as a music hall joke."

Cooper went on to consider where City's failure began: "Old timers will tell you that the decline at Maine Road set in when they were relegated a year after winning the League title and a cynical fan lowered the flag to half-mast. Since that time City have twice won promotion from the Second Division and twice more returned. They have also won the Cup, but somehow they have never recaptured the old glory.

"Supporters – and they could probably command more potential fans for a winning team than their successful United rivals – have been buffeted between hope and frustration until they are tired. The image of Manchester City has changed from the glamorous cavalier football of the 1930s to one of abject apathy."

Away from the misery of City's position, the game was noteworthy for an innovation Swindon were trying out – numbers on their shorts. According to a Swindon official: "We first noticed that some of the continental teams adopted this system, and, as it seemed such a good idea, we thought we would copy it."

One newspaper thought this was taking things a little too far. Who knows what they would have thought had Swindon put names on the back of their shirts instead!

Maine Men Stan Gibson

ROLE: Groundsman

■ Stan Gibson was one of the unsung heroes of Manchester football. He was City's groundsman for forty years and together with a team of hard working staff created a playing surface worthy of the club's stature, particularly during the sixties and seventies. Roy Clarke, who managed the Social Club for over twenty years, remembers Stan with affection: "He was a great neighbour and terrific friend. He was a regular in the Social Club – table number one was his table – and he always said he was there to help if we needed him. His work at City was incredible and he truly loved the club."

Born on 10th September 1925, Stan worked as a stoker in the Navy during the war. Always a keen sportsman - he was a Naval boxing champion and had football trials with Burnley – but by his 30s was becoming well known as a groundsman. He arrived at Maine Road from Chorlton Cricket Club in 1959 after a recommendation by City 'keeper Steve Fleet, and in the years that followed worked hard to create a perfect pitch.

By the time of City's promotion in 1966 Stan had made the surface one the club could be proud of. Both Joe Mercer and Malcolm Allison were keen to use Stan's expertise to develop the pitch further, and thereby increase City's chance of success. Working with Allison and director Eric Alexander, Stan made the pitch the biggest - and many would say the best - in the League. Alexander: "Stan and I spent many hours discussing what we could do to improve the pitch. We worked hard to make sure the pitch was in good condition. Stan understood the need for a quality surface and I would try and secure the funding through the Board – it wasn't easy. Stan spent many hours trying to get everything perfect."

Both Mercer and Allison recognised Stan's contribution to City's success. It's a little known fact that Stan was entrusted with the job of looking after the FA Cup following City's homecoming in 1969. He chose to put the prized possession in the safest place he could think of, and the trophy spent its first night in Manchester locked in his toilet!

Stan loved City – he was even on the club's books for a while

Merger Talk

TO most supporters the idea of a merger with another football team will sound ridiculous and, perhaps, a pure flight of fancy. However, throughout the 1964-5 season City appeared to be seriously considering the possibility. What made the suggestion even more unpalatable was the shock that a City official had actually approached Manchester United.

According to reports from the period the City man at the centre of the storm was Vice-Chairman Frank Johnson who, five years later, found himself thrust into the spotlight again when his decision to sell shares led to the acrimonious 1970 takeover battle.

It seems Johnson had already angered supporters – and Chairman Albert Alexander - by suggesting the entire Football League should be split into North and South sections, and followed this up with a formal approach to United directors to merge. How far the merger would go was unclear, but at the very least, it was suggested, City and United would share one ground

– Old Trafford. Hence the reason the story is included here as, had the merger gone ahead, Maine Road would have ceased to exist in the 1960s.

The approach by Johnson came towards the end of the 1963-4 season and was confirmed as genuine by an Old Trafford director, but the discussions – which seemed to occur several times during 1964 – were not made public until January 1965. By that time a group of 'rebel' shareholders led by Peter Donoghue were pushing for changes at Board level. They had already asked for an Extraordinary General Meeting where they were to demand the resignation of the Board. Donoghue was dismayed with the merger discussions and told Peter Gardner of the *Manchester Evening News*: "If what we have heard is true this is the last straw. We are determined not to let City die as a club. A merger would only go through over our dead bodies."

Around the same time Donoghue's group issued their ten-point plan to save City. This included the appointment of a marketing manager who would be expected to generate his own salary after six months, £30,000 per annum after three years and over £100,000 per annum after five years; special ticket prices for married couples; open up the ground seven days a week

Left: Stan Gibson at work in the late 1960s. Notice the old scoreboard in the background.

Below and right: In October 2002 two plaques were unveiled in memory of Stan at a ceremony attended by family, friends, former players, club officials and local media. One was unveiled by club director Dennis Tueart at 219 Maine Road, where Stan lived, and the other on the tunnel wall at the spot where Stan used to stand during games.

In Memory of
STAN GIBSON
Head Groundsman
Manchester City Football Club
Who passed away on
24th Dec 2001
He will be missed by us all.

in his youth – and felt the pitch was his own. He could never relax during a match though: "I watch the pitch rather than the game! I shouldn't really, because I get very upset if I see a divot, especially if it is the opposing side who have churned it up."

Inevitably, the pop concerts in the eighties and nineties brought him a few headaches, but when the first was held during the early seventies the singer, David Cassidy, was welcomed into the Gibson home. Cassidy seemed to enjoy the experience, although he was on the receiving end of some advice by the Gibsons. Janice Monk, Stan's daughter, remembers: "We had the biggest popstar in the world in our house on Maine Road and my mother embarrassed us all by telling him he was 'too spotty'! She went on to give him advice on how to get rid of his acne. I must say he did have bad acne though at the time."

Stan did welcome other innovations, such as the undersoil heating implemented in 1979.

Stan was always an important influence and others often sought his views. At one stage Rod Stewart tried to lure him away to tend his own turf, while Ken Bates was desperate for him to join Chelsea. Stan would have none of it: "I know I'm biased, but to me there's nowhere better than Maine Road, and there's nothing nicer than someone coming up to me on a Saturday and saying how great the pitch looks. Makes all the toil worthwhile."

His love for the club and Maine Road was never in doubt, and was perfectly summed up in 1994: "City is my life. That pitch out there is my baby. I can't keep away from it, and I couldn't imagine my life without it."

Stan died on Christmas Eve 2001, but late in 2002 the club unveiled plaques to Stan at the house on Maine Road where he used to live and at the spot in the tunnel where he used to stand during matches. Since City moved out of Maine Road the plaques have been removed and given to Stan's daughter Janice. It is anticipated one will be placed in the club's museum at the new stadium.

by erecting bars and restaurants; telling the manager to 'buy the best'; work closely with schools and youth football; introduce season-tickets for the Kippax and create a special enclosure for fan's described as the 'faithful'; and to open up the space under the Main Stand to allow community use.

Clearly there was some merit in Donoghue's plan, especially the idea of community use, links with schools etc. Naturally, the club argued that by building the Social Club (due to open by 1966) they were already moving in that direction.

Eventually, the City board and Donoghue's group announced they would work together to make City successful, although it was interesting to note how Albert Alexander's statement

stressed the emphasis would be on finding the right players, not on the other aspects of Donoghue's plan. This made sense, as City desperately needed a lift. As Peter Gardner put it: "Team performances and playing problems must be placed ahead of any plans to make Maine Road a neon-lit nightclub or the employment of expensive psychological experts to probe the minds of absent City fans to find out what they want to make them return to the fold. All the advertising and market research in the world will not fill the vast Maine Road terraces if the club is struggling to pick itself up off the Second Division floor."

Donoghue's group included Michael Horwich and Chris Muir – both of whom later became directors – and although their involvement helped to kill off the merger debate, it's clear the togetherness didn't last. By the end of the 1964-5 season friction returned, and ultimately both Horwich and Muir formed part of the group that battled for control of the club in 1970.

As far as the merger with United was concerned, furious letters appeared from both City and United fans. In the end the merger debate appeared nothing more than an ill-conceived idea to reduce City's financial burden by moving the club to Old Trafford.

CITY SOCCER ROW LOOMS OVER TEAMS "MERGER"

BY PETER GARDNER

CUP day found Manchester City fans on the receiving end of a huge shock—off the field. For a big boardroom row seems to be brewing at Maine Road over a sensational plan to link up with Manchester United.

This is the second bombshell this week, and vice chairman Frank Johnson is at the centre of both.

And on the Seventh Day...

SUPPORTERS have always worshipped their heroes at Maine Road, however the ground has also been the scene for several religious meetings and festivals over the years. During the 1980s and 1990s Maine Road was a regular venue for Jehovah's Witness meetings and festivals, and in 2002 the largest Christmas Carol Service in the world was staged at the ground, but back in 1961 Maine Road hosted a religious festival lasting several days. This was a very popular event as it was fronted by the energetic American evangelist Billy Graham.

Present at the Jehovah's Witness meetings was Peter Leckenby: "In 1990 I attended Maine Road for the Convention of Jehovah's Witnesses out of curiosity. It felt strange. I was amazed at the peaceable atmosphere and love among the delegates, who cleaned up the stadium afterwards – and before the convention I was told. So much so, I decided to study bible truths with them and returned to Maine Road in both 1992 and 1993 for the full three days duration of the Conventions before I got baptised in 1994. The conventions moved to Goodison Park in 1994."

Another City supporter, Bob Smith, was among the congregation for one of the main days of the Billy Graham festival: "In 1961 when studying for a Degree in Mechanical Engineering at Loughborough, where I had joined the Christian Union, I was one of a group who visited Maine Road for a rally led by the American Evangelist, Billy Graham. It seemed strange to be at Maine Road for a non-football event but it has had similar long-term consequences. Four of us arrived at Maine Road from Loughborough in the early evening. It was a very pleasant warm day although it did get a little chilly later.

"We sat in the Kippax stand opposite the centre-circle area. A platform had been built out from the goal area at the Platt Lane end. Behind that was a massed choir composed of choristers from many churches in the north of England. I have since been told that there were over one thousand in the choir. There was a typically American "warm-up" before the famous Gospel singer George Beverley Shea sang 'How great Thou art'. This was followed by a very moving address by Billy Graham, after which people who had been "called" were invited to go forward to meet counsellors. It was very atmospheric and many people from around us did go forward. As I was already a committed Christian I did not move but I may well have done so had my circumstances been different. My guess is that there were over 30,000 present but it is difficult to be more precise than this."

Bob's recollections of the day ties in with photographs and news stories from the period. This event is believed to be the first occasion when seating appeared at both the Platt Lane end and on the Kippax terracing. The organisers had worked with City officials to

Below: American Evangelist Billy Graham preaches from a stage erected in the Platt Lane End goalmouth.

Note the semi-circular gable on the Main Stand roof had disappeared completely by 1961.

create temporary seating in the two stands and many thousands did attend over several days. One attendee was future Chairman Albert Alexander junior. His son Eric remembers the event as a landmark moment in the stadium's history: "Maine Road was always a major venue as far as sport was concerned – rugby, football, even tennis, had all been played there – but this festival proved the ground could stage many other events. It was a major honour to stage such a tour and it did bring national coverage to Maine Road. I didn't attend the festival, but my father did. He didn't go for any religious reasons. I suppose he was more interested in the stadium, but I do know he enjoyed it. The choir... the crowd... and the speeches were all very impressive."

Inevitably the event was a great success, and was often referred to over the years that followed. In January 1965 shortly after City's lowest League crowd, one angry City supporter (R.C. from Shaw, Lancashire) wrote to the *Manchester Evening News* to complain about the direction of the Blues and ended by saying: "As it has been said often before, it will take Billy Graham to fill Maine Road again."

Clearly R.C. was wrong, but it helps highlight how popular the Billy Graham festival was.

May 1971: The North Stand is under construction and Stan Gibson works on re-laying the Maine Road pitch.

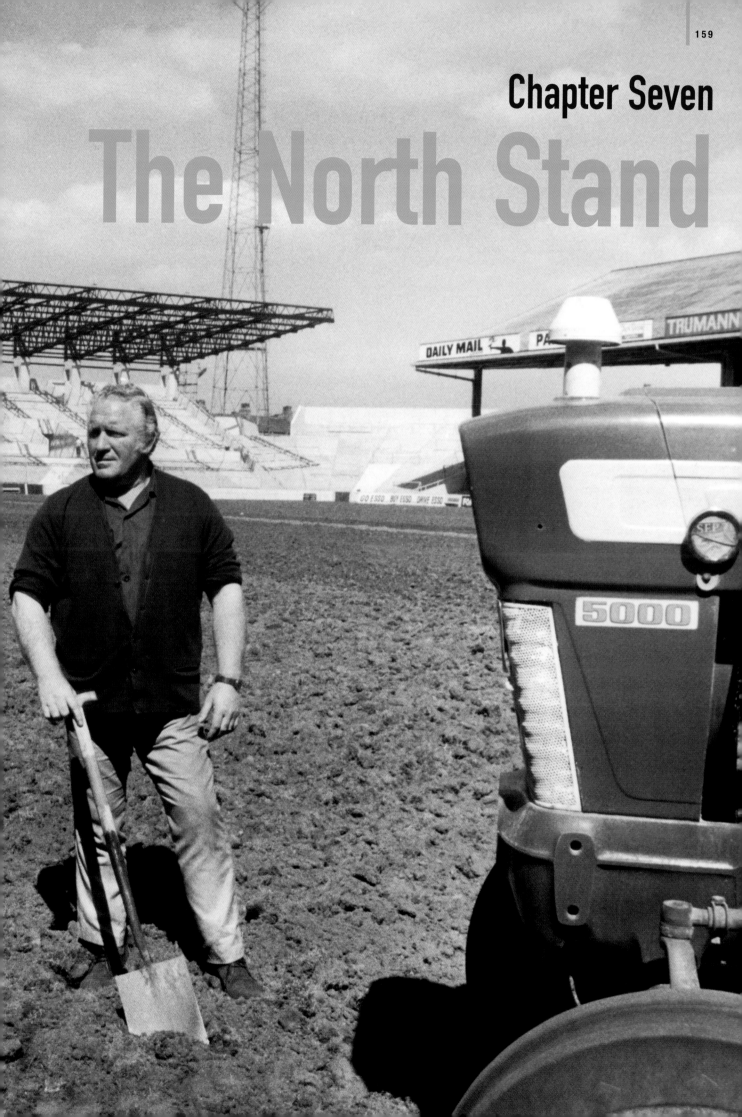

Chapter Seven

The North Stand

During the Summer of 1969 the Directors of Manchester City Football Club decided to reward the fortitude of the hard-core fan who has loyally turned out to support the team in all weathers – wearing a programme on his head like a pitched roof, as protection from wet, snow and gale – jostling at half-time to buy a cup of tepid tea and a warmed-up pie, consumed standing at a mobile counter, water teeming down the back of his neck. Cheshire Design Group of Stockport was commissioned to prepare a report on the feasibility of producing a new 'Scoreboard End' stand.

Jim Andrew, Cheshire Design Group publicity, 1970

THE supporters demanded change during the early Sixties. City were in decline and struggling to find a way out of the downward spiral engulfing the club. In addition Maine Road was starting to lose its status as one of the North's leading venues. With England selected to stage the World Cup in 1966 Maine Road should have been one of the key venues, however with games spread across England a decision was taken to select only one venue in the Manchester area, and Old Trafford was chosen.

In 1965 the City Board decided to act. They needed to substantially improve matters on the pitch, while at the same time find ways to enhance the ground. Joe Mercer was appointed manager and was joined a few days later by charismatic young coach Malcolm Allison. They arrived with the brief of restoring pride to the club. Within five years they had taken City through their most successful period ever.

This success and increased attendances helped the club fund ground improvements and as a result Maine Road underwent a great deal of change over the next decade or so. Despite this, ground developments at Old Trafford allowed United's venue to overshadow Maine Road for the first time in the stadium's history.

Bernard Halford, who became City's secretary in the early 1970s, felt the World Cup was a major turning point in the history of Manchester's venues: "Maine Road had become England's first choice for many years and, although it didn't always stage semi-finals and cup final replays, it was regularly shortlisted ahead of Old Trafford. So when the decision was taken to stage World Cup matches at United instead of City it gave United the chance to improve their ground with funding from the FA and others, while City had to pay for all their developments during this time."

This viewpoint does make sense. Many important games had been staged at Maine Road over the years, while others were scheduled to take place there if circumstances allowed, for example the 1965 FA Cup

final replay would have been played at City's ground had the initial fixture ended in a draw. The World Cup decision was made in 1962 – just when City were entering their downward spiral. At that time Old Trafford consisted of one completely open end; the main stand (completely roofed by 1951 following bomb damage); an 80 yard basic terraced cover opposite the main stand (erected between the wars); and the covered Stretford End (covered in 1959). The Stretford End covering was intended to be extended around the open end and the United Road side, however a grant of £40,000 afforded the Reds more extravagance.

By 1966 United had pulled down their old United Road cover and erected a two-tier cantilever stand costing approximately £350,000, and including the first executive boxes at a League ground. Hillsborough, another northern ground, developed along similar lines for the World Cup, leaving Maine Road a little outdated. Had the World Cup decision gone City's way, it's possible Maine Road would have continued to be viewed as the major stadium in the Manchester area, but sadly this high point in English footballing history left Maine Road in second place as far as the outside world was concerned. Ironically, the World Cup matches at Old Trafford only attracted crowds in the range of twenty to thirty thousand.

City could have felt sorry for themselves at this point, but chose instead to improve the stadium using their own funds. The Blues could not afford wholesale changes at first and instead chose to redevelop parts of the ground when and where appropriate. The middle section of the original Main Stand roof was remodelled. Viewing from this stand had been restricted via six stanchions. These had been necessary in 1923 to hold the largest spanned roof in the country, but by the mid-sixties such a restricted view for the best seats in a major stadium was inconceivable and so the Board demanded change.

In retrospect, the club should have built an entirely

Below: Until the completion of the North Stand, four years after this photo was taken, it was not possible to walk all the way around the perimeter of the stadium. The Scoreboard End turnstiles and external wall stretched to the club houses on Maine Road. Apart from the painted signs and the graffiti (reading 'No Wage Freeze') this wall looked the same in 1968 as it had in 1923.

Right: This photo from 1968 shows the club houses on Maine Road - Stan Gibson was living at 219 on the left of this photo at the time. The building marked 'Ticket Sales' was the Development Office (later Souvenir Shop and in 2003 the Junior Blues office), and the hut was City's first Souvenir Shop at the ground. Another opened behind the Kippax a year later. Over the years the houses have been the homes of various players - including Jimmy McMullan in the 1920s and Bill Leivers in the '50s, as well as other club personnel.

Below: The new Souvenir Shop advertised in the matchday programme.

CITY SOUVENIR SHOP

NOW OPEN

THE POSITION OF THE SHOP IS BETWEEN THE NEW SOCIAL CLUB AND THE OFFICIAL MAIN ENTRANCE

Items Available will include

Colour Photographs, Club Badges, Scarves, Bob Hats, Rosettes, Pennants, Programmes, Calendars, Car Stickers, Blazer Badges, Programme Holders, Teddy Bears in Club Colours, Shoulder Bags, Duffel Bags, Airline Bags and Holdalls, plus many other items.

THE SHOP WILL BE OPEN EVERY MATCH DAY

All Orders and Applications for Lists should be sent to :

**CITY SOUVENIR SHOP
MAINE RD., MANCHESTER 14**

Enquiries: MOS 3392

Right: City supporters celebrate with Mike Doyle after the FA Charity Shield in 1968, which saw champions City overcome FA Cup winners West Bromwich Albion at Maine Road in some style.

new roof, possibly even a cantilever, however the depth of the stand and general scale of the roof was still enormous for the period. Building a cantilever over such a huge stand at this point in construction history would have proved highly expensive and, potentially, nigh on impossible. So when the Board settled for something which allowed a clear view for those in the middle of the stand – mainly the Directors' Box – cynics in other seated areas questioned the decision. They were right to challenge the new construction as it didn't actually improve the stadium by much.

By removing two of the roof's stanchions the view did improve for most in the Main Stand, but this still left four placed in positions which restricted the view of the goalmouth for many others. In addition, the roof looked ridiculous. Where there had once been a proud gable proclaiming the name Manchester City F.C. (although this had been hidden by advertising hoardings for many years) there now appeared to be a disjointed roof.

Although this can rarely be described as an architectural improvement, it did improve the view to some degree for up to 9,000 spectators. Outside, on Maine Road itself, there was no visible change to the stand. The large brutal brick exterior still gave an impression of a northern factory. The only relief came from the three mosaics which picked out the name of Manchester City Football Club in blue and white tiles. Those same mosaic tiles also appeared on the internal walls of the main entrance for a short distance.

Most major developments during this period occurred outside the stadium. A wooden hut was erected in front of the Scoreboard End turnstiles to sell City souvenirs on match days - primitive by today's standards but this was the birth of the souvenir era.

Another stall was opened at the Kippax side of the ground on 1st February 1969 and the two official shops advertised Boys Blue & White Football Shirts at 14 shillings and 11 pence; a Framed Team Photo at 6s 6d; a

Francis Lee Coloured Photo at 3s 6d; a Paper Knife (with City emblem) at 16s; and a Can Opener (with City emblem) at 5s.

Two books were also on sale *Meredith to Mercer* and *The FA Cup* by Eric Thornton, priced at 25s and Peter Gardner's *Manchester City Football Book* at 16s.

The biggest change of all during the mid-sixties was the development of the City Social Club and small ticket office. This really was a major advancement; the Social Club was built on the site of a former church, and meant the ground was no longer hidden down a side street as the Social Club faced Claremont Road and therefore increased City's presence.

Of course the major story for City throughout the late sixties and early seventies was the success of the Mercer-Allison team and the joy it brought all Blues. Promotion in 1966; the League title in 1968; FA Cup in 1969; and the double of the League Cup and ECWC meant Maine Road was a great place to be. Fan Bob Storie remembers the Charity Shield match against West Bromwich Albion as being one of the key days of celebration: "When you're only fifteen and living in Scotland, visits to see your adopted English team are obviously rare and infrequent. For me, the Charity Shield match captured a team still climbing to further summits, having established themselves as the new force in English soccer.

"That day will remain with me forever. Like Gods walking in my dreams of Sky Blue persuasion, City put on an awesome display of pace, stamina and finishing on that warm August day. Albion were a useful side themselves, but no one could have lived with City that day. After years of mediocrity, the club were at their height as League Champions, and that game was a

Maine Match 65/66

CITY v EVERTON

DATE:	26th March 1966	
TYPE OF FIXTURE:	FA Cup Round 6	
ATTENDANCE:	63,034	
RESULT:	City 0 Everton 0	
TEAMS & SCORERS:	CITY	EVERTON
	Dowd	West
	Kennedy	Wright
REFEREE:	Horne	Brown
TW Dawes (Norwich)	Pardoe	Labone
	Heslop	Wilson
	Oakes	Harris
	Summerbee	Harvey
	Crossan	Scott
	Young	Young
	Doyle	Temple
	Connor	Morrisey

■ This cup tie is significant as it shows how far the Blues had come under Joe Mercer and Malcolm Allison. Almost exactly one year earlier City had lost 4-1 away at Ipswich during a period when demonstrations, protest groups, and talk of merger with United filled the air. By March 1966 the Blues were surging forward towards promotion and enjoying a fine cup run.

This tie was the first sell-out crowd for a decade, but as the capacity of Maine Road was now approximately 64,000, this would be the first capacity crowd of under 70,000. The Platt Lane Stand had been seated three years earlier and that had reduced numbers by around 10,000. Nevertheless, the volume was proof City were a major force once more. According to Peter Gardner in the *Manchester Evening News*: "This is more conclusive proof of the re-birth of the Blues, particularly when just over 12 months ago there was an all-time low attendance of 8,015. With the 64,000 crowd due on Saturday it will rocket the average attendance for four home FA Cup ties to over the 52,000 mark. These totals represent cash takings of more than £40,000, of which City's cut is one-third."

The attendance was higher than any domestic crowd at Old Trafford that season.

The tie was anticipated to be immensely entertaining and both the BBC and ITV had wanted to cover the match but City and Everton agreed not to let either station film the game. Why is a mystery, although it does signify how back in the late sixties television once had to fit in with football's demands.

The match itself was not the great fixture everyone had hoped. Peter Gardner reminded fans of the television issue: "Manchester City and Everton directors must be commended for their excellent foresight in slamming the doors on television cameras. For this boring, frustrating sixth round tie was hardly fit for the eyes of 64,000 disappointed Maine Road fans, never mind those of the fireside millions."

Journalist Frank Clough blamed Everton for the negativity: "This was the big flop! Ninety minutes of muscle and mayhem, thud and blood, and so little exciting constructive football. It was also dour, dull and unenterprising. And the major portion of the blame must go to Everton. They were cautious to the point of being chronic. Pulling eight or nine men back, all sights set firmly on a home replay."

Joe Mercer was delighted with the result and still felt City stood an excellent chance in the replay. He dismissed Everton's claims that City had deliberately gone out to injure their players, and laughed at suggestions that Everton's sick list would be a factor in the return: "I always had a bump after a Cup tie. If you haven't had a knock you haven't been in the game. Of course it was hard. Cup ties are always hard."

City 'keeper Harry Dowd was acclaimed as the hero, particularly as Everton threw themselves forward in the final minutes. According to reporter Norman Wynne: "He pulled off two saves in a minute that would have done credit to a Cup final itself. And the cheers from the anguished City fans will not be bettered if England win the World Cup."

All focus during 1966 was on the forthcoming World Cup finals being played in England for the first time, and one of the Maine Road attendees for this tie was England Manager Alf Ramsey who, according to the press, had come to watch Mike Summerbee. As Ramsey had already adopted his 'wingless wonders' style of play, Summerbee's chance of appearing seemed poor, but that didn't stop supporter D. Carr of Wythenshawe writing in to *The Pink* with his views on Ramsey's approach: "When Alf Ramsey decided to start playing 'silly beggars' by not selecting any orthodox wingers England's chances of winning the World Cup fell from slender to nil!"

The City-Everton replay ended in another goalless game causing a second replay to take place at Molineux. It had initially been decided to hold the replay at Blackburn but unfortunately, on the Monday night, poor weather meant Ewood Park was unable to stage the game and so it was moved to Wolverhampton by the FA without consultation with City and Everton. As a result the game only attracted 27,948 and the poor atmosphere affected City more than Everton. The match ended in a 2-0 defeat, but the three matches did prove the Blues were on their way back.

Below: Despite losing out eventually to Everton in the FA Cup quarter final City did go on to pick up some silverware in 1966, as Second Division champions. Manager Joe Mercer pours champagne into the trophy being held by skipper Johnny Crossan, whilst groundsman Stan Gibson is left to look after the lid!

Above: Bobby Kennedy
and Francis Lee bathe in
the home dressing room in
1968 whilst young Gary
Lee, Francis' son, drinks a
bottle of pop.

clinical demonstration of the Mercer-Allison dynasty at its
very best. There were of course further triumphs at home
and abroad, but Maine Road will never invoke happier
memories for me than that day in 1968 – the high
summer of a wonderful era, and for me a golden
memory of the club on its own field of dreams."

Inside the Main Stand, despite the glory, the players'
amenities had changed little since the 1920s. Ian Mellor
remembers signing for the club on 18th December 1969:
"Down near the tunnel in the players' area was a small
room for the coaches and I was taken in there to sign for
the club. Like all young footballers you think your arrival
is a major piece of club history and you expect it to be
glamorous and exciting but the reality was somewhat
different. The coaches' room was small, dark, miserable
and damp. Johnny Hart had all the forms and asked me
to sign and I looked around and thought 'Where's
Granada? Where's the BBC?' I expected all the media
there and for the signing to be in the best room in the
stadium, instead we were hidden away in a dark,
depressing room. I do remember that Johnny said to me
'I wish you all that you wish yourself' when I signed
which probably sums it up nicely. At that moment
though I wished Granada were there!"

Mellor made his debut on 20th March 1971: "We
were playing Coventry and Malcolm Allison told me I'd
be playing on the Wednesday prior to the match. I knew
I'd be facing Wilf Smith who Coventry had bought off
Sheffield Wednesday for about £200,000. He was the
most expensive full-back at the time, and in the days
leading up to the match I was a nervous wreck. I couldn't
sleep. All my confidence went.

"The game kicked off and we were attacking the
North Stand end of the ground but my energy had totally
gone. I was awful. Just before half-time Malcolm Allison
had a real go at me from the touchline. He bellowed at
me. He was right but I couldn't do anything. When the

second half started I just had a go. I didn't worry about
anything. In fact I didn't think about anything, I just did
my own thing and as a result I settled and ended the
game well. We drew 1-1 and I must have done enough
because I kept my place for the ECWC match with
Gornik four days later."

Mellor scored his first senior goal for the club in the
Gornik game and on the last day of the season netted his
first League goal in the Maine Road derby with United:
"This was a strange day really. Being a Manchester lad
and a City supporter the derby meant a great deal to me.
Still does. But this match also started differently to most
matches. Just before we left the dressing room we were
told we would be lining up on the pitch because Eamon
Andrews' was here to present Matt Busby with a *This Is
Your Life* book for the TV show. So we all lined up on
the pitch and Eamon Andrews came out, said something
like 'Today, Sir Matt Busby This Is Your Life', presented
him with the book, everyone cheered, and then we got
back to normal and played the match."

For the ground itself the most significant progress of
the 1970s was the North Stand. In fact, looking back at
all of City's developments since the stadium opened in
1923 until its closure as City's home in 2003, the North
Stand was perhaps the most satisfying ever undertaken
at the ground.

The stand evolved in stages with the first phase
completed in time for the 1971 season. Architectural firm
the Cheshire Design Group was commissioned to design
and develop the new Scoreboard End. According to the
City programme: "The new stand puts a completely new
face on Maine Road, and will mean that some 20,000
spectators will be able to watch the games in
considerably more comfort. It's been a long business but
considering what was involved, it's been one of rapid
development. The action started in the summer of 1969
and while the basic football watching side of the contract

is complete, phase two of the construction – the bars, refreshment and souvenir shops is still to be added. One outstanding feature of the stand is the division of the terraces into pens with a capacity of some two thousand spectators each. This greatly improves the safety factor, comfort and speed of dispersal. The terracing is stepped higher than the old scoreboard end... which means a better view for those at the back."

The North Stand was a major development and, although the stand looked rather dated by 2003, a stylish construction. The club was immensely proud of the result. Earlier, in February 1970 the Blues had first publicly announced their plans for the stand. At the time they said the construction would cost around £325,000 and would see a 22,000 capacity terraced stand covered by a cantilever roof. They also said they would extend the Main Stand roof and seating to ensure the stand would reach the corner flag rather than end mysteriously some yards away from the end. This would have meant an additional section of around 1,000 seats, but the construction costs were excessive considering the payback those seats would bring.

Inevitably, City abandoned the Main Stand plan and the awkward portion in between the new North Stand and the Main Stand was left roofless until 1982, but the rest of the North Stand construction did match the original plans.

While it was being built Maine Road's capacity was restricted significantly. The entire end terracing was put out of action, at times causing lower attendances than usual for several fixtures. However, once the stand opened it proved very popular, offering as it did a completely unhindered view of the pitch, which, apart from a few thousand seats in the middle of the Main Stand, was a rarity at the time.

Surprisingly, unlike most other major clubs at this period, City's initial plan did not include the installation of seats. The club seemed perfectly happy to provide for standing spectators. Perhaps most clubs would have developed a seated stand, but with so many seats on offer in the Main Stand and Platt Lane, the Blues concentrated their efforts towards standing spectators. There was a long term plan to install seats, but this was not public knowledge at the time.

The view from the North Stand was unlike anything else at Maine Road. Because of the cantilever roof, and the increased rake of the terracing – on a par with the best areas of the Main Stand and certainly better than the Kippax or the Platt Lane Stands - standing spectators had a perfect outlook.

The exterior view of the new stand was impressively sleek and modern. The club's use of black, grey and blue provided a modern contrast to the red-bricked terraced houses of Manchester and, from an architectural viewpoint, it was certainly more stylish than any of the modern buildings being erected elsewhere in the suburbs, or even in the city. Don't forget the yellow-tiled Arndale Centre was Manchester's big architectural contribution of the 1970s!

Across the roof of the stand at the pitch side the club erected a series of small upright flagpoles, and on match days approximately twenty different flags fluttered from the roof. It was a tremendous sight, but over time the flagpoles became damaged and by the early 1980s the club had removed most of them, leaving three in the centre of the stand. These were not always used but, when they were, the North Stand regained some of its original prestige. In the late seventies and early eighties the flag poles usually held a Manchester City flag, Junior Blues flag, and occasionally a Union flag.

At the back of the stand the club erected a new 90ft long electronic scoreboard. It cost £11,000 and was proclaimed as one of the most modern in Europe. According to Gerry Harrison, writing in the programme: "About the only thing it can't do is predict the half-time scores. Messages can be typed up letter by letter as a complete line; the brilliance can be varied; the script flashed on and off. The electronic memory circuit can hold a message in reserve so the scoreboard need never be blank; facts and figures can be prepared on tape and fed into the system... and incidentally, for the record, the individual letter blocks, 54 of them, are made up of massed lamps, seven high and five wide. Hird-Brown, the Bolton firm who supplied the scoreboard were also responsible for the electronic scoreboards at Wembley Stadium, at Edinburgh's Meadowbank Stadium where the Commonwealth Games were held, at Sheffield Wednesday's ground... and they will also be supplying Everton and the Munich Olympic Games swimming pool with scoreboards."

This scoreboard was in use until the mid 1980s by which time it had started to incorrectly display messages. Frequently teams' names and scores were jumbled up with messages such as "Eve5t81 21 0P5 0" appearing

CONTINUED ON PAGE 168 >

Maine Memory

■ Years ago Eric Todd wrote a story in the *Manchester Evening News* about the referee getting injured at the start of a City v Stoke game in the '60s. A substitute linesman who had been sitting near to Joe Mercer in the Main Stand came on when the senior linesman went in the middle. Todd described the linesman as appearing from the stand looking like a painter dressed in a City track suit. At half time the linesman had time to change into his official kit which he had with him in the boot of his car. All went well for City won, though the substitute linesman didn't half get his leg pulled by his mates. I know this to be true because I was that linesman.

Brian Warwick

Maine Memory

■ Simple things seem to take on almost magical proportions when you're a child. As a schoolboy in 1971, we, the football team from High Lane CP school, visited Maine Road for a tour of the ground and the facilities, to watch the players train and collect as many autographs as was possible. Looking up, quite literally, at your heroes and favourite players, Lee, Summerbee, Bell, etc, signing your book, was, simply, a never-to-be-forgotten great feeling.

Over thirty years ago in March 1970, I remember sitting on a bench in the old Platt Lane stand with my dad, and can recall the roasting and ear-bashing Joe Corrigan received from captain, Tony Book, and maybe even Colin Bell. Joe was walking back to his goal after having taken a goal-kick, when the ball was returned, unbeknown to Joe, courtesy of Billy Bonds of West Ham, from what seemed, at the time, to be the half-way line, over his head, and into the net. It was Jimmy Greaves' first game for West Ham. He scored twice and we lost 5-1!

Lawrence Ivory

Below: The old Scoreboard End becomes a building site as Malcolm Allison takes the players on a Maine Road training session.

Left: Capacity was reduced whilst construction work went on at the stadium. Here City defend the building site end as Francis Lee attacks the other. The West Bromwich Albion goalkeeper is Jim Cumbes, then also a Worcestershire cricketer, and in 2003 Chief Executive of Lancashire CCC.

North Stand Design

■ The Cheshire Design Group (CDG) were commissioned by the club to compile a report on the possibility of a new stand at the Scoreboard End of the ground. The club was keen to improve the stadium and re-establish Maine Road as Manchester's leading venue, and the report focused on the view that regular supporters should be rewarded by this development.

The brief given to CDG by City made clear City's aims, even if it did sound more like a mathematical examination question: "Fit six and a half miles of people into approximately one three-hundredth of a square mile of space, so that they all have a clear unobstructed view of the match, protected from the weather and with adequate refreshment as far from the old 'pie and pea' stall image as modern first-class football is from the ancient village kick-about. Incorporate into this toilet facilities, souvenir shops, first-aid room and an efficient turnstile system. All designed with the maximum comfort, safety and control of spectators in mind – all to be fitted in one three-hundredth of a square mile."

The CDG documentation makes interesting reading, and their approach was very unusual as they were keen to fully understand what makes a football club and a football spectator tick. They appointed professional architects and designers as you would expect, but also used the skills of knowledgeable football people, including author Jim Andrews who had spent considerable time and effort understanding the behaviour of football supporters. The report went on: "The design team began by conducting an extensive programme of research into the behaviour of the football supporter.

"The popular image of a football fan is a brightly coloured muffler

streaming like a challenge to battle from the window of a speeding car; a rhythmic handclap culminating in a window-shaking roar in the middle of the night; an empty beer bottle bursting like a hand grenade; a greasy half-eaten packet of fish and chips flung from a coach; a standard item on British Rail's profit and loss accounts expressed in broken light bulbs and toilet fittings. But it was soon concluded that this unfortunate image was the result of a small – although expensive – minority.

"Basically the football supporter is an average hard-working man who on Saturdays, freed from the restrictions and monotony of factory or office, is for one afternoon a wild rover following his team at home or away come hell or high water – for he is more than a mere spectator. When he's on the terraces he can feel the turf pounded by his own feet and it's him kicking the ball – and if one of his team gets clobbered he'll double up in agony and in that foul tackle – by God it's as if it was his own leg chopped off six inches below the knee. As moods change from ecstatic joy to bitter despair, according to the fortunes of the opposing teams, a highly-charged emotional climate is created in which the small hooligan element thrives. Because of the problems and dangers caused by this minority it was concluded that the safety and control of spectators must be considered of paramount importance. Also it was felt that by improving the spectator facilities and their environment generally, a reduction in the amount of vandalism would be achieved."

The first major debate between CDG and the club centred around the turnstile area, the outcome being the old turnstiles and boundary wall would be removed and replaced by modern turnstiles built into the stand. This would allow the club to control access to individual areas of the stand, and also provide much-needed space behind for match day fan movement. Remember, prior to the North Stand

Right: The new North Stand was for standing fans when it was first built. This picture was taken on 28th August 1971 when City beat Spurs 4-0.

Below: The Cheshire Design Group's drawings show plans for the ground level of the North Stand and an artist's impression of the how the stand would look from the outside the ground.

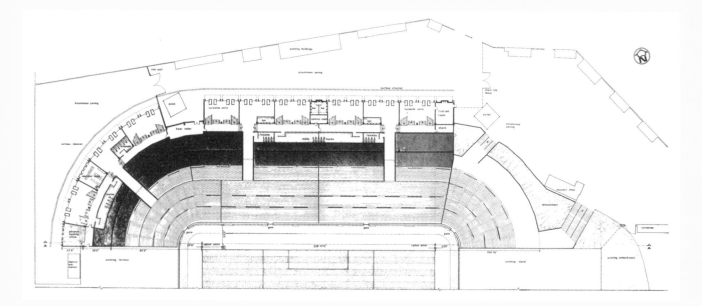

development, supporters wishing to go from the Main Stand forecourt to the Kippax turnstiles would either have to walk through the Pink Passage – the dark alleyway between the exterior wall of the Platt Lane and the main car park – or down Maine Road, up Claremont Road and down Kippax Street. Basically, there was no way of cutting through from Maine Road to the Kippax at the Scoreboard End of the ground.

Removing this section of the boundary wall was in itself a significant decision as the space behind the stand contained a number of bars and toilets. This meant the club really did intend creating a completely new image for this end of the ground. When the Kippax was rebuilt in the 1990s, the external wall was retained mainly for security purposes, however it is clear the club saved a great deal as the existing turnstiles would be retained and the existing toilet facilities preserved, but during the 1969 discussions the club were keen to build something totally new and fresh. They wanted a modern stand with good access and that could only be achieved if the boundary was changed.

Unfortunately, the club were unable to go as far as they would have liked with the stand's development. The report stated: "The scope for additional amenities in the way of entertainment, health and sports facilities outside the present short ground usage was considered but regrettably these could not be considered for economic reasons at this stage of the club's development."

Although the club were unable to develop other health and sports facilities, it does show that the Board of 1969 were forward-thinking enough to consider including these items. At this stage in the history of football few clubs ever thought beyond match day.

The author of CDG's report into the development tried to explain to the club how much time and effort they had put in to the initial proposal. Clearly, this did not follow the usual professional approach of a design group, but it was refreshing to read and, again, helps give the impression that the designers and the club wanted to achieve more than simply create a football stand: "Heads were scratched and splinters extracted from fingernails. Midnight oil was burnt. Marriages almost broken up, but somehow put together again. Bright ideas over glasses of beer became pure strokes of genius over more glasses of beer, but were discarded over congealing breakfast bacon and eggs to be resurrected with the eleven o'clock cup of coffee and finally consigned to perdition after lunch. But, at last, somehow put together out of holes worn in carpets by rhythmic pacing; snarls at early beloved wives and offspring; obscenities shrieked at other drivers in the rush-hour; acres of paper plastered on shaving cuts; sudden kicks at hitherto pampered pets; was assembled a list of conclusions:

1. A cantilever roof with no obtrusive columns
2. Increased angle terracing
3. Integral turnstiles
4. Extensive toilet facilities
5. Licensed bars and snack bars
6. Simple lines and aesthetic acceptability both internally and externally
7. Replacement of Scoreboard
8. Most of all the comfort, safety and control of spectators"
CDG were determined to design something unique.

ONE HELL OF A PROBLEM TURNED INTO A HELL OF A LOT OF PROBLEMS!

"By hysterically repeating to themselves the old maxim, that to know the problem is half way to solving it, the design team worked on ... and on. By the Autumn of 1969 a satisfactory design had been formulated and was presented to the club's Board of Directors."

The key elements of the proposal were:

1. The Terracing
Ten pens with a capacity of approximately 2,000 in each, were to be erected. Each pen would be divided by concrete walls.

2. The White Perimeter Wall
The retaining wall at the front of the terracing would be rebuilt to allow a more modern design. The terracing would commence a little way below pitch level with the retaining wall angled inwards towards the spectators. This would offer a smooth footholdless barrier to discourage 'pitch invaders' (or so it was hoped!).

3. The Cantilever Roof
The roof would extend 101 feet over the terracing on cantilever supports of black plastic-coated steel-clad trusses ten feet deep, at 17' 6" intervals. The actual roof to be slung underslung beneath the structure so as to form a clean uncluttered surface without the need for additional false ceilings (a novel and unique form of construction at the time). The concrete supports to be built on piled foundations extending some forty feet into the ground to bore three feet into the actual bed-rock.

4. Turnstiles
One turnstile to be constructed to every thousand spectators. Each turnstile to be connected by electrical impulses to the central control point, thus ensuring accurate calculation of the attendance. Access to each pen would be controlled to ensure safety and capacity control.

5. Amenities
In addition to extensive bar areas and toilet facilities, the stand would incorporate an Advance Ticket Office, First Aid Room and a Souvenir Shop.

6. Aesthetic Appearance
The external and internal appearances were considered to be of equal importance. The mezzanine level was to be emphasised in the formation of protruding white concrete boxes. The turnstile line was to be set in the form of a dark recessed plinth. The roof cladding would extend down to the mezzanine roof in the form of a textured light blue wall, the clad trusses projecting above the roof at regular intervals forming black fins silhouetted against the skyline. Throughout natural textured materials were to be used to give the structure an overall clean and functional appearance of simplicity.

7. Statistics
The stand would contain over 6.5 miles of terracing; 210 tons of steel roof; two acres of roof sheeting; 500 high tensile steel bolts (22' long, 2" diameter) holding the roof on.

The club were delighted with the proposals by CDG and immediately sent an invitation to tender to seven major construction companies. In June 1970 John Laing Construction were selected and they commenced on site the following month.

The development brought Maine Road into the 1970s, but even thirty years later the stand, though a little dated in some areas, was still regarded as a magnificent construction. It's external image was clearly modern when first constructed and, although the quality of subsequent developments elsewhere made the North Stand appear old hat, it is clear this was the most appropriate development constructed at Maine Road post World War Two. The 1993 Platt Lane Stand was ridiculed; the 1995 Kippax seemed out of place, but the 1971 North Stand feels as if it was designed to fit Maine Road. The designers themselves felt immensely proud of their development, while they also recognised that stand development wasn't simply a case of identikit building: "Cheshire Design Group feel this solution was the right one for Maine Road, but realise it might be completely wrong for another ground. Each must be considered on its own merits using a logical design process."

The club claimed the stand cost around £325,000 while CDG were always keen to point out: "It is important to note that the cost of this stand is no more than that of other stands recently erected on traditional lines."

instead of "Everton 2 QPR 0". Fans joked they needed a code-breaking machine to understand the scores! However, back in 1971 this was another forward-thinking installation and one which opened up many possibilities for the club. Simple advertisements could now be displayed on the board, alongside important ticket information.

By the late eighties the board was completely switched off, and then in the late 1990s it started to be hidden behind adverts for kit manufacturers. Firstly Kappa's name was emblazoned across it, then Le Coq Sportif.

Away from the stand development, the summer of 1971 also saw significant pitch enhancement. At the request of Malcolm Allison it had been increased in size to 117 x 79 yards – two yards wider than the previous season. According to groundsman Stan Gibson this made his pitch the largest in the League: "It's certainly bigger than Wembley… and last year there were only two First Division pitches bigger than ours. If you look closely you'll also see the pitch has been crowned to help drainage. It's been almost ideal grass growing conditions in July… so I reckon it will be in great condition."

In May 1971 a special machine was used to make vertical slits in the soil and then fill them with sand to form vertical drainage channels to take surface water quickly to the drains. These were spaced at 12 inch intervals across the pitch, making a total of over 15 miles of slits in the pitch. In addition, a large quantity of sand was mixed with the soil and then the whole area was sown with special grass seed after proper fertilisation.

When the 1971-2 season commenced Chairman Albert Alexander announced that phase two of the North Stand development would commence in October. This would include the completion of the turnstiles – attendees had to use those in the perimeter wall when the stand first opened – and the development of toilets, bars, and shops. He stressed the stand would be completely finished by the end of the season.

He also announced the famous Scoreboard Scoop competition had been dropped from the programme. This competition – which at one point in the sixties was won by BBC GMR's Jimmy Wagg – used the old scoreboard and a series of football pools style predictions pre-printed on a label attached to the programme to give each programme buyer a chance to win up to £200.

The idea had to be abandoned in 1971 as the new scoreboard would not have been suitable for this type of competition.

Elsewhere in the stadium other initiatives were being pushed. Season tickets for the Platt Lane Stand were on sale at £9. Supporters would be allowed to attend Maine Road on a weekday, pay their money and then walk around the stand to select the seat they wanted. Club officials would then paint the words 'Season Ticket' onto the benched seat and from that point it would be reserved. It was a simple approach but very popular.

With Maine Road now roofed on all four sides the ground was to many people complete. Vocal support was now divided between the Kippax – which for most of the sixties had become the home to City's noisiest support – and the terraced North Stand. Captain Tony Book particularly liked the atmosphere emanating from the new stand: "Against Liverpool I won the toss and because the new North End terraces have got so popular with our vocal supporters I decided to play into that goal. The crowd were really tremendous and the lads and myself were spurred on by their support."

Above: Chairman Albert Alexander visits Joe Mercer's office.
Below: Notification of new £9 season tickets for the Platt Lane Stand. This is when the benches were first painted maroon, yellow and green.

RENEWAL OF SEASON TICKETS

There will be **NO INCREASE** in the price of your 1970-71 season ticket. The present prices of £14 for Blocks B and C, £12 for Blocks A, D, E ,F, G and H and £9 for the Platt Lane Stand will continue to apply.

All members are requested to retain the renewal form in the back of the season ticket book **PENDING RECEIPT OF RENEWAL INSTRUCTIONS** which will be despatched very shortly. Incidentally, if you have changed your address during the current season and NOT informed the Secretary please drop him a postcard immediately or else your renewal circular is likely to go astray.

NEW MEMBERS WELCOMED : Next Season City will once more be competing in a European tournament and demand for big match tickets is certain to be great. Why don't those of you who are not season ticket holders save yourself unnecessary outlay by purchasing a Platt Lane Season ticket. Remember your own seat is made available for all City matches at Maine Road.

PROPOSED NEW SCHEME FOR THE PLATT LANE STAND : In future all seats in the Platt Lane Stand for capacity matches will be sold on a **RESERVED BASIS.** The scheme will operate on the same lines as the Maine Road Stand which will benefit not only spectators but also the stewards controlling the crowds. Present season ticket holders will be informed by a comprehensive letter that they will be allocated a particular seat in the centre section. Briefly the new system will work on the following lines :

(1) All seats will be numbered and a ticket will be sold for each particular seat when it is an all ticket match.
(2) The centre sections will be reserved solely for season ticket holders who will occupy specifically reserved seats for all matches.
(3) The stand will be divided into sections. The seats in each portion will be painted in a respective colour.
(4) For all ticket matches tickets will be sold in each section i.e. Holder of Yellow ticket, Row A Seat No. I, shall occupy the seat in the yellow portion of the stand, and so on. Also spectators will have to enter through the same coloured turnstile as their ticket.

There is an increasing demand in football today for more and more reserved seats and this is what Manchester City aims to provide. What other First Division club can offer a season ticket for a reserved seat at the bargain price of £9. Write to the Secretary now and ask to be put on the waiting list and so make life easier for yourself on Saturdays.

The Social Club

■ The Social Club became the heart and soul of the club for many years and was managed by former star player Roy Clarke and his wife Kath. The Club was officially opened on 1st April 1966 by the Mayor of Manchester, Bernard Langton and soon became a key entertainment venue in its own right with many big acts performing there.

As early as November 1967 the club was advertising a cabaret show starring Kenny Lynch. Lynch became more famous in later life as one of Jimmy Tarbuck's close group of showbiz pals, but in the late sixties and seventies Lynch was a major star in his own right. Other shows included comedian Colin Crompton, who later found fame with Bernard Manning as hosts of the 'Wheel-tappers and Shunters Social Club' on Granada TV, and an act called Roy & Jackie Toadruff described as the 'greatest comedy duo'.

The Grumbleweeds were another popular act at the club during the late sixties and early seventies, while on 20th November 1971 Bob Monkhouse was booked to appear, although his presence was not popular with all fans. Fran Parker: "We were members of the Social Club when it didn't even have a carpet! But we decided to stop going and to cancel our membership when

Bob Monkhouse was coming. Not because we didn't like Mr Monkhouse, but because they were after £4 a ticket. He was going to be the big star guest and I thought we should have got in as normal, so we wouldn't pay."

Few others complained however and the show was a huge success. Kath Clarke: "Bob Monkhouse went down a storm and he was a really nice man. When it was Roy's testimonial a few years later he helped a little and seemed to enjoy his connection with the club. Other stars included Ken Dodd, the Nolans when they were just starting out... Lisa Stansfield when she was very young, and we also had Frankie Vaughan. In fact we made a special effort with him and allowed him to use our bedroom as his changing room – it had more space and was much nicer – so afterwards I kept telling people that Frankie Vaughan had been in my bedroom!"

Roy Clarke: "The Social Club was a very popular venue for both entertainers and for supporters, and we tried all sorts to ensure it worked. In the early days we even had a casino room – roulette wheel and all the works – and we also had amateur boxing nights, film shows, you name it, we tried it. We also had very popular events at Christmas and New Year. The whole family had to help then, as well as all the usual staff, because we had

to cater for 600 diners. They were tough days.

"Of course, other City events such as Junior Blues meetings and Luncheon Clubs started at the club, and we also gave opportunities to several up and coming entertainers, or entertainers who were in need of a pick-me-up."

One of the latter was Bill Tarmey, Coronation Street's Jack Duckworth. In the days before he became a Coronation Street regular Tarmey had been ill and found it difficult getting bookings once he returned to full fitness. The Social Club was in need of a new compere and so Roy offered to give Tarmey a chance. The

opportunity helped relaunch Tarmey's career and many years later he publicly recorded his thanks to Roy and Kath Clarke.

The club attracted many famous names while the compere for most of the club's best years was Frank Ford – a very popular figure.

Although the Social Club was a seven day a week venue, match days were its original focus, and for many people the day always started with a trip to the club. In addition to the bars and cabaret room, the Social Club offered the 'Blue Grill' restaurant. This was situated on the first floor overlooking the main club room – the area later became home to

the City Forty Club and then offices for the City Superstore. The Blue Grill advertised itself as: "The happy restaurant for the North's leading chompers. The best steaks, the best wine, the best company – only at the Blue Grill."

During the 1980s the club began losing its non-match day popularity; society was changing. When the Moss Side riots occurred in 1981 Roy and Kath were away in Tenerife and were shocked to hear of the problems. They were naturally concerned for many of their regulars and for the Social Club itself. Many buildings close to Maine Road had been badly damaged, particularly on Princess Road, and the Social Club could have been a target. Fortunately, a combination of City's and the Club's position as part of the local community and the fact the police were to use it as a base meant the building was safe.

Roy and Kath left the Social Club a few years later and, despite considerable effort following their departure, it was never the same again. It closed in 1997 and re-opened as the City Superstore in October of that year.

The Social Club and Maine Road pictured in the mid-1960's.

On 28th August 1971 City beat Tottenham 4-0, but the exciting news as far as the Maine Road story was concerned was detailed on page three of the match programme. Director Eric Alexander – a man keen on the development of the ground and City's facilities – outlined how investigations into the redevelopment of the Kippax Stand were taking place. Alexander became City's Chairman the following November, and it's clear he cared passionately about ensuring Maine Road was a leading venue. He took the opportunity of revealing the latest ideas to all supporters: "At Maine Road itself, the new North Stand is now nearing completion and naturally we are eagerly looking forward to the next stage in the ground's development. As an industrial designer, I have spent many absorbing hours 'pipe dreaming' about the future Maine Road. One particularly interesting and possibly controversial idea concerns the Kippax Stand. Think about it! If we could rebuild part of the stand, incorporating a second tier containing about 8,000 seats, and build into the back of the stand a multi-storey car park spectators could then drive their cars straight into the car park and reach their seats without ever going outside. And private boxes would be incorporated in the back of the stand. Wouldn't that really be catering for the modern spectator?"

Alexander explained how the next stage would see the club carry out a feasibility study before ending: "City are one of the very few clubs who can consider such a project, as we own a considerable amount of ground around the stadium proper. This is the result of either good fortune or amazing foresight on the part of our 'forefathers', but which ever way it gives us the opportunity for endeavouring to make Maine Road a truly 'Superstadium' with access, amenities and comfort to compete with the finest."

The land Alexander referred to was indeed considerable in comparison with most other grounds of the period and was directly a result of good planning by the likes of Lawrence Furniss, Ernest Mangnall, Charles Swain and Eric's grandfather Albert Alexander senior. The original intention had been to extend the ground over a number of years and, although the Second World War ended City's redevelopment plan, the land was still free to allow forward-thinking City directors to search for ways of improving the stadium.

The redevelopment of the Kippax would have seen the capacity of Maine Road increase to some extent – possibly by around 4,000 when the impact on the terracing was fully assessed – but the biggest advantage would have been the installation of executive boxes. Clearly these would not have appealed to the majority of fans, but they would have been important income generators, especially when the unique car-parking arrangement was considered. Parking in the early seventies was becoming an issue around Maine Road as the volume of vehicles increased. The idea of driving into the stand to then take a seat in your own private box would have appealed to many of City's wealthier patrons.

The Kippax development was debated for some time but the club was still suffering from the takeover battle and, by the time Peter Swales became Chairman in 1973, ground improvements had begun to take a back seat. Executive boxes were not installed at the ground until 1993 – incredibly late for a leading club – while the Kippax was not redeveloped until 1994 – the season after Peter Swales had left the club.

Another major plan outlined by Eric Alexander in 1971 was the expansion of City's training centre at Cheadle. According to Alexander: "Cheadle will have two full size pitches, both floodlit and possibly heated so that

Above: This aerial photo taken shortly after the North Stand seats were installed shows the extent of the club property. The car parks behind the Kippax Stand (left) and the Platt Lane (top) could have been utilised, while the Main Stand forecourt area also offered potential. In addition to the ground, the club also made the Platt Lane Training complex (top left) their own during the Seventies, and in 2003 this remained City's most visible presence in the Moss Side/Rusholme area. At the bottom of this photograph are two areas (marked yellow) on either side of Lloyd Street South later redeveloped with Walks and Closes named after former City players. It's also worth noting that the area marked (pink) between these player streets and Claremont Road became the playing fields for Claremont Road School which, on match days, became parking for supporters.

Above: Police patrol on horseback at the Platt Lane end of the ground prior to the September 1967 derby.

Below: Francis Lee and Tony Book enjoy a sauna at Maine Road, watched by Harry Godwin and Malcolm Allison. However Eric Alexander's dream of having the "best available amenities" at the Cheadle training centre never came to fruition.

training can continue under most conditions. A running track and ancillary facilities will also be provided. A gymnasium and medical equipment will be available and a first class remedial centre will be incorporated including sauna, aerotone and hydra-therapy baths. It is the intention to provide our staff and players with the best available amenities.

"The buildings will be ultra modern, low-line style with great attention being given to landscaping the whole centre to match the rural atmosphere of the area. All the team management and training staff will have their offices at Cheadle and will normally only go to Maine Road on match days."

It appears that due to the pressures within the

boardroom Alexander was not able to progress the Cheadle development. At the time he was replaced by Peter Swales in 1973 he admitted: "I was a little bit deflated that we were not in a position to pursue our ideas to establish a training headquarters at Cheadle with super facilities. This was a grand project aimed at making our facilities the best in the land."

Not until the development of the Dome at Platt Lane in the late 1990s and then the complex at Carrington at the turn of the millennium, did City possess facilities of the level desired by Alexander in 1971.

At football grounds across England, violence and crowd disorder had started to become an issue, however Maine Road was usually a calm place during the late sixties and early seventies. Unfortunately, incidents did still occur. In the main these centred around missiles being thrown from either City supporters or from the opposition fans. Often Peter Blakey the club physio would be called on to help injured fans. Against Sheffield United on 23rd October 1971, Blakey stitched the scalp of a ten-year-old Sheffield boy, and a Manchester nine-year-old. Both boys had gone to the game with their fathers and both had been on the receiving end of missiles – one a bottle, the other a brick. The club tried to discourage aggressive behaviour by placing notices in the programme detailing the consequences on both the club and the individual. This was still a period, however, when the club and the police were uncertain how to control those determined to cause trouble.

There was an increased police presence when City faced United in the November 1971 derby. In addition, the club had taken steps to ensure the stadium was in perfect condition in the days leading up to the game. Vandals had regularly tried to get into Maine Road on the day prior to derby matches and so Stan Gibson went on a 24-hour patrol of the ground with his seven-year-old alsation: "Sheebah loves a roam round. I can't say I like the hours much but it has to be done. All sorts of strange things happen at a derby game. At a recent one here, two hours after the final whistle we were working on the pitch and I saw a figure come staggering across from the far side. He had obviously had a few. 'How long before the game starts?' he said. It appeared he had been asleep in the toilets since half past two!"

For the derby Colin Bell had been made team captain: "I like the idea of being captain. I seem to thrive on the extra responsibility – and that is the idea behind it. I was captain at Bury, a few years back, and so far the greater involvement on the field suits me."

A very memorable match ended 3-3, but the most significant news from a Maine Road perspective is that the attendance was 63,326. This was the last 60,000 plus crowd housed at the ground as the City management now realised that the North Stand offered great potential as a seated area.

There were a number of reasons why the decision was taken to install seating. The club claimed it was taken as a result of the Ibrox disaster of January 1971. Sixty-six people died in a crush at the end of the Rangers-Celtic match. According to one witness the crowd just "caved in like a pack of cards. It was as if all of them were falling into a huge hole."

The disaster would ultimately lead to increased legislation connected with stadia design, control and safety, however City's decision to seat the North Stand could not simply have been as a result of the disaster because the terracing at that end was actually the most modern in the country. It's design was good, especially

Maine Memory

■ My love for City goes back to the early Sixties, despite being born in Newton Heath. If you listen to my good mate, Noel Bayley, the editor of Bert Trautmann's Helmet, he'd have you believe I am some Johnny-come-lately who has only supported City for six years. That tongue in cheek comment cannot be true, because who in their right mind would have jumped on a bandwagon heading downhill?

The truth is I was hooked on the Blues long before Noel's umbilical cord was cut. That was when my Dad took me to my spiritual home for the first time, on May 6th 1967. I'll never forget walking up the stairs at the back of the Main Stand, setting foot inside the amphitheatre, and seeing that lush green turf. I was hooked. Thanks Dad!

The game was against Sheffield United in the penultimate home Division One match of the season, and ended 1-1 with City skipper Johnny Crossan scoring for us. Despite that team including Colin Bell, Crossan was my first hero, even though he left City two games later! However, it didn't take long for Colin the King to become my all time City legend. I also remember declining the offer of a trip to the Cup Final in 1969 with Dad, preferring to watch the match on the Beeb. Why? Sounds more like the action of a fan of Stretford Rangers.

I also vividly remember spending the night of 29th April 1970 scouring the European airwaves (without success), using a super-duper Zenith multiband UFM \ MW \ LW radio that my Uncle Bernard had brought back from Chicago. There was no such thing as Teletext or Sky Sports News in those days, but the biggest barrier was the fact Chelsea and Leeds had to replay their drawn FA Cup Final at Cold Trafford that night, and all the world's media seemed to focus on this game, rather than a European "showpiece" in rain-sodden Vienna. I remember the late BBC News almost mentioned in passing that we had beaten Gornik Zabrze 2-1. How times change.

But back to Maine Road. I rarely missed a home game in the early '70's, taking up various vantage points on the North Stand and Kippax terraces, and remember going to quite a few local away games with Bob and Phil Aitken, and their grandad, Alf Owen. I was quite privileged really because Alf was a member of the "40 Club" in the Supporters' Club and we had our own little pre and post-match table on the balcony. I probably used to look down on some of you lesser mortals! Alf was on City's books, though he never played for the first team, and was so well-connected within the club that, before the 4-1 home win against Leicester City on November 23rd 1974, I was privileged enough to be sat in the Manager's office, chatting with Tony Book and his assistant, Ian MacFarlane. After the match, I remember wandering around the Players' Lounge and nearby corridors, seeing Barney Daniels being interviewed by the Press following his "brace" that day. Great days!

I was at Wembley in '74 and '76, but thinking back, City's barren period, between 1976 and 1997, seemed to coincide with my career in retailing. Having to work every Saturday meant very few live City games, but I was always there in spirit, including the "5-1", when I was roped into a "lads 'n dads" weekend away with my son Ashley, at Beaver Camp in Ashworth Valley, Bury. Fortunately the Scout Master was a Blue, so he sneaked off home and returned with his portable TV, so we could enjoy Match Of The Day, whilst consuming our home made chilli con carne and Tom Caxton's lager. Not quite the same as being there, but good nonetheless. I did manage to make the Full Members' Cup Final in 1986, and memorable nights such as David White's four at Villa in 1991.

My current "obsession" with City began in May 1997 when, following a change of career, which finally gave me weekends off, my wife Karen bought me a season ticket in the upper Kippax for the next season. Kinky had just signed for two more years and City, after one season in the First Division following relegation in '96, were nailed-on favourites to get out of the First Division. After all we always went back up at the second attempt, didn't we? As we all know, we did get out of the Division that season, but it was the wrong end!

The Kippax Street Stand has a unique feature that we all take for granted, but will surely miss in years to come. After all, how many other modern stands have an enclosed open area inside the ground, where fans can chat and drink with their mates? I can't think of any!

Steve Kay

---

the notion of using pens – a concept encouraged throughout the seventies and eighties and which became most familiar at Old Trafford. In addition, if the club were truly concerned with terracing then the enormous near-30,000 capacity Kippax needed first attention.

In truth, the reason City decided to install seats on the North Stand was probably financial. The standing terraces had brought in greater funds than anticipated and this allowed the long-term seating plan to be brought forward. Eric Alexander: "We'd always planned to do it, but our increased income allowed us to do it earlier. This was deeply satisfying for all concerned."

It has to be said that by installing modern plastic tip-up seats on the new terracing the club could charge a higher admission fee. City brought in 7,800 grey plastic seats in time for the 1972-3 season, and by September 1972 the stand was reported as holding 8,120 fans. It is assumed this included the uncovered block between the North and Main Stands. The admission price was 70p per game, while those standing on the Kippax would be charged 40p.

The other areas of the ground were priced: Main Stand Blocks B & C - £1; Main Stand A, D, E, F, G & H – 80p; and Platt Lane 60p.

Naturally, the reduced capacity did impact attendances. The first Manchester derby following the installation of seating was attended by 52,050 – some eleven thousand lower than the previous home derby. This was bettered by the FA Cup tie with Sunderland, which attracted 54,478 on 24th February 1973. Many felt this exceeded the capacity of the ground and it's true the attendance was never bettered over the following thirty years.

With the development, Maine Road once again housed more seats than any other ground. The total number stood at around 26,000 – almost half the capacity – and this figure was only surpassed during the early 1990s with the demolition of the old Kippax Stand and the move towards all-seater stadia.

In 1981 Coventry City's Highfield Road ground was transformed into the first all-seater ground in England, but even then the Maine Road seated capacity was still significantly larger than Coventry's figure of 20,616.

In November 1972 groundsman Stan Gibson was delighted with another innovation – Maine Road's new sprinkler system: "This system is the most modern in the country, and we are the only football club to have it. It's

been used by golf clubs, but a football pitch is much more complicated. If you wanted to you could flood the pitch in a matter of minutes. You can have individual sprinklers on. You can set a time limit of anything between a minute and ten minutes on each one. Say for instance I wanted to water just one goalmouth for a couple of minutes I would do it just by turning a knob down below.

"Beneath the stand is the nerve-centre of the system... the pump which pushes out the tremendous

Left: Throughout the 70s and 80s wooden seats in the Main Stand were replaced in stages by blue plastic tip-up seats as finances allowed. Unfortunately, not all the seats were the same shade of blue! These were some of the first to be installed.

Below: Francis Lee poses with his new car outside Maine Road.

pressure, the knobs and dials which put it all into action... as well as the little matter of a 12,000 gallon water-tank.

"It's really sophisticated. It's even got a time clock. For instance, if I went away for a few days I could set the sprinklers to pop up say next Thursday at 2.30pm to water the pitch for three minutes. You can't beat that. You've got to be a technician as well as a groundsman these days!"

The pitch actually housed 24 pop-up sprinklers - 16 around the touchlines and eight in the middle of the pitch. When Stan pressed a button hidden under the Main Stand the sprinklers would pop up from their base two feet below the playing surface and spray water across an area of 50ft.

Later in the 1972-3 season lightning hit one of the four giant floodlight pylons. Stan described what happened: "Three of us had been on the pitch working. We were just coming off when there was a tremendous crack. The flashes of lightning seemed to be all round us and then blue smoke started to rise. It was a frightening experience and we dived for cover I can tell you. We could even feel the heat of it. You should have seen us fly up that tunnel!

"We can laugh about it now, but reckon that Wilf O'Neil, Albert 'Ted' Heath and I are lucky to be alive. I was in the Navy, but I never heard a noise like that from the big guns. They heard the crack in Cheadle I'm told. Anyhow, it was blue smoke, not red, I'm glad to say."

The lightning had created a large hole in the tarmac and concrete at the base of the pylon. Despite the damage it's fair to say Maine Road was in a very good shape as the Mercer-Allison partnership broke up and the Chairmanship of Peter Swales commenced. Maine Road was also about to enter one of its most exciting and electric periods with entertaining football and large crowds.

Maine Memory

■ My first and most memorable moment was Saturday 1st February 1969. I was seven years old and my United-supporting father agreed to take me to see City for the first time against Newcastle. Why is it so memorable? It was one each and after 41 minutes the game was abandoned for fog. Even though my first visit was cut short I have stuck by them through thick and thin and now my 8-year-old son attends whenever he can. I remember asking my dad when the game was abandoned 'Is this the normal length of a game?' Being my first visit I suppose I didn't know what to expect. He explained there should have been a second half.

I do remember that we didn't get our money back, and by the time the game was abandoned we couldn't see the pitch at all. I also remember we were in the Main Stand which is where I became a season ticket holder. As my parents are both United fans it's worth mentioning why my dad agreed to take me to see City. I was a big fan of Francis Lee and I think Dad just wanted me to see my hero. Seeing Lee made it for me.

Neil Branham

Maine Match 67/68

CITY v TOTTENHAM HOTSPUR

DATE:	9th December 1967			
TYPE OF FIXTURE:	Football League Division One			
ATTENDANCE:	35,792			
RESULT:	City 4 Tottenham 1			
TEAMS &	CITY		TOTTENHAM	
SCORERS:	Mulhearn		Jennings	
	Book		Kinnear	
REFEREE:	Pardoe		Knowles	
D Smith	Doyle		Mullery	
(Stonehouse)	Heslop		Hoy	
	Oakes		Mackay	
	Lee		Saul	
	Bell	1	Greaves	1
	Summerbee	1	Gilzean	
	Young	1	Venables	
	Coleman	1	Jones	

■ Back in 1967 City were delighted to publish a letter in the match programme from Bobby Greenroyd, a United supporter. He watched this game with Tottenham on *Match of the Day* and wrote to Maine Road afterwards: "I am a regular Manchester United fan, but after Saturday's game your next home gate will be increased by one."

City fan David Edge: "We supporters at the time knew we had a team capable of playing some great football with a 'never say die' attitude, believing that if we did go a goal down we were more than capable of coming back at the opposition. This is what happened on that memorable day against Spurs. To go a goal down in normal conditions is one thing, and so early on, but to come back by playing some fantastic football, given the conditions, it was poetry. Breathtaking!"

The Spurs match entered City folklore and is regarded as one of the deciding factors behind City's 1968 championship success. Heavy snow had put the game in doubt, however coach Malcolm Allison was adamant the game would go ahead. The presence of the television cameras may have had something to do with Allison's determination. He wanted the nation to accept City were now a major force, and viewed this match as the perfect opportunity. However when Jimmy Greaves netted in the seventh minute Allison's plans appeared in some disarray.

Earlier he had encouraged the players to treat the game as any other. He had even made them participate in a 45-minute training session on the frozen pitch. As City went a goal behind he was frustrated. He had expected so much more and bellowed: "Don't think about the ground. The ground is only there to be run over!"

Allison knew how to motivate his players and his words, together with one or two more vociferous comments, encouraged a different approach and the game turned. From then on the Blues tore into Tottenham with attack after attack. They produced a performance of tremendous quality and determination. In fact they attacked so much their own defence could have left the pitch, they had so little to do!

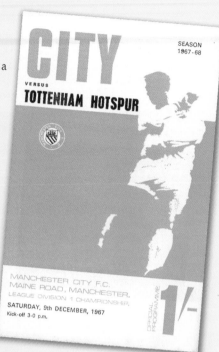

Colin Bell, in sparkling form, scored the equaliser. Neil Young, too often the forgotten man of City's glory years, also mastered the conditions superbly. Manager Joe Mercer rated Young as "the player with more talent than anybody else at the club." Young ended the season as City's top scorer and, against Spurs, he helped Tony Coleman and Mike Summerbee to score, and then added the fourth goal himself.

A very talented Spurs side were defeated 4-1 in a match later described as the "Ballet on Ice".

Supporter Geoff Eckersley: "'Ballet on Ice' is the perfect description as the conditions required the highest skill levels from each side and the snow-covered pitch made for a theatrical feel to the occasion. It's a simple

Left: Jimmy Greaves puts Spurs into an early lead at the Platt Lane end of the ground.

Colour action photos from this period are rare and these are believed to be the only surviving examples of colour action from this match. Note the use of the orange ball - a regular occurence on days when visibility would be hampered by the conditions during the sixties and seventies.

point but one worth making that when the conditions are at their most difficult you will then see who can play and who cannot. Every City man played that night. Spurs weren't allowed to."

This victory was only the beginning for City. As Allison anticipated, their appearance on *Match of the Day* brought attention from all over the country. Letters flooded in to both City and the BBC. Even Tottenham fans wrote to say how much they enjoyed the performance.

Former players and rival managers contacted Allison and manager Joe Mercer to congratulate them on creating such a fine side. Dixie Dean, a man Joe idolised as a youth at Goodison, wrote: "I was looking at your match on Saturday and I think you have the best workmanlike team I've seen since the old days – nothing fancy, just a set of lads making it easy for themselves as it should be."

Didsbury-based City fan Ged Jepson remembers what this match meant to him: "It was memorable for several reasons. The match was played on a pitch earlier covered in snow, and even when cleared the game was still in doubt because of the frozen conditions. However once started we were warmed by the magnificent football played by the Blues and forgot about the cold!

"Having gone a goal down early doors to a Jimmy Greaves goal - a fortuitous deflection from a free kick - City set about their task with relish. A deserved equaliser from King Colin soon followed but it was not until the second half that we took the lead our efforts deserved. A Summerbee header past Jennings made it 2-1 and Tony Coleman lashed a shot in after Frannie Lee had hit the post. Neil Young hit the post before crowning the display with a goal after Colin Bell's shot had cannoned off Jennings.

"What a great match! The quality of attacking football was the fruition of Joe Mercer's and Malcolm Allison's bold and brave philosophy. A group of us had travelled from Liverpool where we were training to be teachers and we returned to college in time to savour the match, before an appreciative if begrudging audience (Liverpudlians, Evertonians, Geordies and possibly the odd red!), which crowned a magnificent day. We knew we were good but our intent to move to the top was signalled to a much wider audience that day. One of many memorable matches in the season of our lives."

Another fan, Alan Whitney, remembers how impressed he was with the game: "City played so well that this was the night we realised what a great team we had. My Dad and myself arrived late - just as Jimmy Greaves scored at the Platt Lane End from a free-kick. We always stood on the corner of the Kippax near the Platt Lane Stand. City were outstanding as Bell, Lee, Summerbee, Young, and Coleman tore Spurs apart. The

Above: City on the defence as No.4 Mike Doyle heads clear. Other Blues in the picture are (left to right) Neil Young, Glyn Pardoe (3), Alan Oakes (6), George Heslop (5), Francis Lee, Tony Book and Colin Bell.

Below: Tony Coleman celebrates putting City 3-1 in front.

4-1 scoreline could have been eight or nine. That game was eventually voted *Match of the Season*."

In Stockport one family were concerned for the well-being of one of their eldest relatives. City fan Paul: "I was 10, and my grandfather lived with us in Stockport. A more ardent fan would be hard to find. I remember the day was freezing cold and snowing, and my grandfather chirps up that he was going to City. At the age of about 68, the family didn't think it would be a wise move. Undeterred and armoured with his trusty flat cap and overcoat off he went. Well 6pm, his usual time of arrival back home, came and went. In fact *Match of the Day* was about to start and still no sign. We were worried! Where was he?

"After the game the weather closed in and grandad decided to walk up to the A6 for the 92 bus only to find that no buses were to continue past Lloyd Road in Levenshulme. He decided he would walk – a distance not far off 10 miles in polar conditions! When finally arriving home, *Match of the Day* over, his words were: 'Bit celd out, a grand match... buses just like Spurs... couldn't get past half way!' He was home. We were amazed!

A week later City faced Liverpool and Bill Shankly turned to Allison and warned him: "You're not going to tear our team apart like you have torn the others apart, you know!" Shankly was right as far as the result was concerned - the Anfield match ended 1-1 - but according to the *Liverpool Echo* the Blues were still the more impressive side.

The Blues set out to thrill in every match from then on. After a 7-0 victory at Reading in the cup, the Elm Park announcer proclaimed: "Ladies and Gentlemen, you have just seen one of the greatest teams England has produced in a long time." Few disagreed.

With thrilling performances City challenged for the title. In March they defeated Manchester United 3-1 in a gripping game at Old Trafford, afterwards the *Mail's* Ronald Crowther described how the balance of power had swung from the Reds to the Blues and, after another action-packed game on the last day of the season – City defeated Newcastle 4-3 at St. James' Park – the Blues snatched the title in style from Matt Busby's United.

United, who were defeated by lowly Sunderland at Old Trafford, were reigning champions. Before their match the League Championship trophy was on display, however at some point during the afternoon it mysteriously disappeared. Joe Mercer quipped he would walk all the way back from Newcastle to search for it if necessary, but fortunately the Reds rediscovered it in time for City to be officially presented with it at a friendly against Bury a few days later.

For the next few years tremendous success followed the Blues with Joe Mercer, a man written off by Aston Villa in 1964, and Malcolm Allison forming one of the most successful partnerships of all time. Mercer was the calming influence; Allison the showman. Together they were unstoppable.

At the friendly against Bury both men appeared on the pitch to receive the championship trophy, but afterwards they each followed their natural instincts and sought out the roles they most craved. Allison donned a City shirt, came on as substitute, and with chants of "Allison for England" ringing in his ears had a goal controversially disallowed! Mercer, on the other hand, soaked in the atmosphere then, as the game neared its end, he was seen leaving Maine Road. A local reporter searched for him. He discovered him on his own eating a bag of chips he'd sneaked out to buy.

Now that's the Mancunian way to celebrate winning the championship!

Right: Joe Mercer lifts the championship trophy at the friendly with Bury on 14th May 1968 watched by Bobby Kennedy, Malcolm Allison, Colin Bell, Ken Mulhearn, Mike Doyle, Glyn Pardoe, Tony Book (hidden), Francis Lee, Tony Coleman and mascot Paul Todd. Allison made an appearance for City in the game, but Mercer celebrated with a bag of chips!

Maine Memory

■ In 1968 the Blues had to play Newcastle away on 11th May and win to take the First Division Championship. Four days before the game I had the most memorable evening when we visited Maine Road on Wednesday 8th May 1968 to play for the Shell Wythenshawe team in the Manchester Industrial League Cup Final against Grasmere Rovers.

Can you imagine the feelings of a lifelong City fan, knowing for weeks that we were to play at Maine Road? Absolutely fantastic! The continuous rain had made the pitch doubtful and the groundsman wanted to call off the game when we arrived. It was only the intervention of great stalwart big Dave Ewing that allowed us to go ahead, since he saw the stand held quite a few supporters from both teams looking forward to the game.

We were then lucky to be given City's changing room. The match was great and we went on to beat Grasmere Rovers 2-0 to lift the cup. A great week was completed when we travelled up to Newcastle on the Saturday with the other thousands of Blues supporters to see our team lift the Championship ahead of United, who lost to Sunderland at Old Trafford. The memories are still as strong today and it was one of the major highlights of my life to have been in the Champions-elect changing room only days before the Blues became Champions. Fantastic!

Geoff Nolan

Maine Memory

■ My first memories of the Kippax are of watching the swarming masses as a youngster from the relative comfort of Block G in the Main Stand or from Platt Lane. I used to love watching the Kippax at night matches, transfixed by the continual little flashes of light which would permeate the dark crowds under the roof of the stands as people lit up cigarettes.

I remember wishing I could walk along the steel walkway which ran along the top of the Kippax Stand roof to the small floodlight in the middle of the stand, with its yellow sign proclaiming "Steelwork by Booths of Bolton". I remember the distinctive white entrance and exit tunnels which I used to walk through always in excited anticipation at the start of a game once I made it on to the Kippax. And the sky blue pillars which always seemed to obstruct your view, wherever you stood! It's amazing how often those prominent features of the stand can be spotted in the background of photographs taken during City matches.

The Platt Lane Stand also has good memories for me. Reached through the turnstiles on Maine Road, I used to love the climb up the steep steps at the back of the stand, from where you could gaze out over the rooftops of the rows and rows of terraced houses in the side streets surrounding the ground. The coloured benches were unique -with a numbering system which confused all but regular City fans - odd numbers only in some sections and only even numbers in others. There was also the creaking wooden boards hanging from the roof informing you of your Block Number - mine was Y (for Yellow!) 2. I used to love my place in the stand so much - row 26, seat 26. I used to worry what I would do if my seat was moved. I could never imagine life without Platt Lane... nor Maine Road.

One vivid memory of Platt Lane is waiting inside the turnstiles as a season ticket holder at a City-Liverpool match in 1975, and being absolutely devastated, thinking my Dad and sister had been unable to gain admission when the turnstiles were closed, with thousands still queuing outside. They had entered without me spotting them and much to my delight, I found them when I took up my seat a few minutes after kick off.

Andrew Heydeman

Maine Memory

■ My choice of favourite game at Maine Road may not have been that eventful for some – Manchester United 18/11/72 - but it was my first derby. I just remember the atmosphere, Colin Bell's goals and a moment that has stayed in my memory that typifies Manchester derbies. Just before the game, Malcolm Allison came over to the Kippax arms raised above his head applauding the City supporters, a City fan ran onto the pitch shook hands with Allison, went over to the United supporters and made a two-fingered salute. I'll never know who that supporter was, but I was one impressed 11-year-old.

Noel Halliday

Maine Memory

■ Of my 37 years as a City fan, for 35 of them I have been living away from Manchester. Consequently I have only seen two reserve games at Maine Road, separated by 19 years.

The first of these was against West Brom reserves at the end of the 1965-6 season. It was played on a Saturday afternoon, as most reserve games were then, and kicked off at three o'clock. The first team were away at Leyton Orient, the score at this game being letter 'A' on the old mechanical scoreboard at one end of the ground, and this was as much a focus of attention as the events on the pitch. I don't know how large the attendance was, but it would certainly have been well into four figures. Dad and I took our places on the Platt Lane End. I didn't know any of the players in City's reserve side, but can see now that they were mostly experienced players no longer able to command a first team place. Assuming, however, that my notes on the teamsheet are correct (I was only 9 at the time), a young and then unknown Stan Bowles was City's no.11. Roy Cheetham gave City an early lead from the penalty spot at our end, but they couldn't build on it. At half time Dad and I changed ends with the teams, through a gate in the corner of the stand and along the front of the Kippax to the Scoreboard End. This, of course, was uncovered, but it was a nice sunny day so no problem. The idea was that we'd see City's second half goals. Instead, West Brom equalised and I can only remember the play going on in the distance, up at the other end. Dad wasn't for going back to the Platt Lane End - I'm not sure whether we could anyway - and I got thoroughly bored. Perhaps that's why this was the last reserve game I saw for 19 years.

In March 1985, I ended up in Manchester on a business trip on the Tuesday night of a reserve game against Bradford City reserves. By now, reserve matches were generally midweek, and I think they usually kicked off early too. This one was 6.45pm. Only the Main Stand was open and only a few hundred people attended. The atmosphere was relaxed although all who went were certainly interested in what they were watching. This time the team was made up of players whose best years were still ahead of them, including Earl Barrett at centre-back. City won 3-2. Darren Beckford headed the first from Paul Simpson's corner. Steve Redmond, playing in midfield, hit the second from just inside the box. Paul Moulden claimed the winner with a delightful strike. Back to goal with his marker tight to his back, Moulden flicked the ball over both their heads and wheeled round to volley it into the net when it dropped behind them.

One interesting aside from this game was that, with the ticket office being open before the match, it was a good opportunity to renew my season ticket for the following season. Relative to the price of other things, football was much cheaper entertainment then than is the case now, to the extent that my new season ticket cost £27 and I paid for it in cash – three ten pound notes, receiving £3 change. Unthinkable now, paying cash for a season ticket at a club of City's stature!

Simon Clarke

City in Europe

THE first European match involving City and staged at Maine Road was the European cup tie with Fenerbahce on 18th September 1968. Sadly, City underestimated the quality of the Turkish side – neutrals had told the Blues Fenerbahce were equivalent to a mid-table Division Two side – and in the first leg City missed chance after chance. The result was a shock 0-0 draw with Mike Summerbee on the receiving end of some abuse by the crowd. The second leg saw the Blues defeated 2-1 in front of an exceptionally hostile and volatile crowd.

In 1969-70 City returned to European competition with the European Cup Winners' Cup. The first tie in Manchester was the second leg of the first round game against Atletico Bilbao. This was supporter Tony Breslin's first game: "Apart from my parental family, City and Maine Road are the longest features of my life – over 35 years – and as a result I have so many memories. So many ups - and downs! I first went to see City in 1969 against Atletico Bilbao in the ECWC. We won 3-0. This is perhaps my quirkiest memory.

"Being young and living what seemed at the time a great distance away - Oldham! - I and my friend Michael were required to have a parental escort. Why was a mystery to us but we finally persuaded my friend's dad to do the honours. Given that it was a nice sunny evening, a top First Division side, and an exotic European tie it is still hard to believe that as my friend and I stood in the old Scoreboard End watching our heroes in awe, my friend's father sat on the terrace and read a book! He was not interested at all. He was just doing his fatherly duty! "

Home victories over SK Lierse (5-0) and Academica Coimbra (1-0) helped the Blues reach the semi-final against German side Schalke 04. The first leg had ended in a 1-0 defeat. Supporter David Smith: "Even though we were one goal down from the first leg I was still confident we would go through. In fact I was so confident I'd already booked two travel tickets with the City Club to Vienna!"

Smith's confidence was justified and the second leg saw a glorious 5-1 victory. According to supporter Graham Elliott: "The 5-1 Cup-Winners Cup Semi-Final v Schalke was the best European game I saw at Maine Road. There was always a special atmosphere under the smoky floodlights and that night was just magic."

Elliott was right. The atmosphere at midweek European matches was exceptional. There was always something magical about the lighting, the noise, and the general hustle and bustle of the crowd. During the sixties and seventies few supporters ever saw top-quality European players as television coverage was limited, and so a visit by any European side was felt to be something truly special.

Dave Bracegirdle remembers the Schalke match with affection: "Being in my fifties there are so many matches to choose from as the most memorable but if I had to pick just one I would say it was probably the second leg of the European Cup-winners' Cup semi-final when City were trailing 1-0 from the first leg with Schalke. City were brilliant that night and won 5-1 to take us to the final in Vienna. The emotion of that night was unforgettable, especially as I had been to all of City's away legs in Europe that season."

The Schalke match set City up for the 1970 ECWC final victory over Gornik Zabrze in Vienna, and the following season the Blues reached the semi-finals. Home victories over Linfield (1-0), Honved (2-0), and old foes Gornik (2-0) carried City to an intriguing meeting with Dave Sexton's Chelsea.

A 1-0 away defeat meant the Blues had to attack, but a series of injuries to key players meant they would always be struggling in the return, and Chelsea managed another 1-0 victory. City still received much positive coverage – "It's another super show from those Mercer minors" – but it was a major blow to the club at the time.

City had to wait until September 1972 for their next European match. This time Valencia were the visitors to Maine Road. Goals from Ian Mellor and Rodney Marsh helped City to a 2-2 draw, but a 2-1 defeat in the second leg ended City's progress.

The next European night at Maine Road saw the Blues defeat Juventus 1-0 thanks to a goal from Brian Kidd. Andrew Heydeman remembers the atmosphere on this occasion: "The noise and unrivalled tenacity and wit of the Maine Road crowd was at its best. I recall the Kippax chanting 'We hate spaghetti' to the Juventus fans and then singing with delight 'Fish and Chips'. The crowd was great on nights like this, but my all-time favourite chant came at a League Cup tie against Luton Town in the late 1970's. Roger Kirkpatrick, the short and plumpish referee, had to go off injured during the early stages of the game. When his replacement gave a dodgy decision against City, the Kippax started singing 'We want that fat ******* back!'."

A difficult return game in Turin ended in a 2-0 defeat. Then the following September Polish side Widzew Lodz arrived at Maine Road in the UEFA Cup. Manager Tony Book anticipated a 3-0 win, but the game ended 2-2. City had been leading 2-0 with goals from Channon and Barnes. An injured Dennis Tueart watched the match: "We were 2-0 up with ten minutes to go and then Boniek scored from a penalty and a free kick. At 2-0 with ten or fifteen minutes to go we were cruising… justifiably 2-0 up. Then he scored direct from a free kick, followed by a penalty when one of their guys dived. Suddenly it's 2-2."

The game caused City a few problems. A fan had run on to the pitch to confront Boniek causing UEFA to fine the club.

The final season of European football at Maine Road was 1978-9 and it proved the best since 1970-1 For David Djordjevic this season was special: "Some of my favourite Maine Road memories are the European nights of the seventies. The first positive was that it meant a day off school as I lived so far from the ground. The second was the chance to go to Manchester during the week and see a floodlit match as I feel this always seemed to add to the atmosphere. We would normally have to change trains in Sheffield to get to Manchester and would then have tea at a Greek cafe on Oxford Road, in front of the student 'toblerone' buildings - in one of which I later lived for two years while studying.

"Once I was old enough to go to Maine Road on my own, and then when I was old enough to drink, the rituals changed somewhat - usually leaving home at some unearthly hour so that we could meet lads from Derby, Leicester, Nottingham etc. on the train and then be in some pub like the Brunswick, the Old Garratt, or the Salisbury by 11am. Many of the games from this point on were watched from the Kippax in a sort of haze and I rarely saw a kick-off. But before all of that I suppose my favourite game of all time was City 3-0 AC Milan in December 1978.

"We had got an unexpected 2-2 draw in the San Siro and absolutely stuffed them in the return. The atmosphere was great and we were three up at half time. Tommy Booth, Asa Hartford and Brian Kidd scored the goals and we played the best football I've seen at Maine Road against one of Europe's top sides. The game was made even sweeter by the memory of seeing us beat Juventus 1-0 a couple of years before when they kicked us off the park only for us to lose 2-0 in the return. The whole European campaign at Maine Road in '78-79 was special. I saw us score three goals in the last five minutes to beat Liege 4-0 and us take a 1-0 lead against the eventual winners Borussia Mönchengladbach only for a little Dane called Alan Simonsen to score a cracking equaliser."

The game with Borussia Mönchengladbach on 7th March 1979 was the last European tie staged at Maine Road. Malcolm Allison was back by this point and had started to choose youth over experience; eighteen- year-old Nicky Reid made his debut, and the Blues drew the game 1-1. Mike Channon netted the first goal (City's last at Maine Road in Europe) but it wasn't enough. The away leg ended 3-1 with experienced Pole Kaziu Deyna scoring the consolation.

With a lack of major success in the years that followed City failed to qualify for Europe. In 1991 and 1992 the Blues finished fifth in the League – in many years that would have been enough to qualify – however entry to Europe was limited at this time as English clubs were still feeling the repercussions of the Heysel ban. In fact City didn't return to European competition until 2003. The new City of Manchester Stadium was given the honour of staging a home UEFA Cup match against Welsh side TNS on 14th August 2003 as its first competitive fixture.

City's return to Europe was via the UEFA Fair Play League. England topped the League - set up to reward countries with good disciplinary records - with City finishing fifth in the Premier League's version of the competition. As the four clubs above the Blues had all qualified for European competition, City gained entry into the preliminary round of the UEFA Cup.

This was a major boost to supporters, and gave the new stadium the opportunity to be seen across the continent.

Highest Home Attendance: 49,664 Atletico Bilbao 1/10/69
Lowest Home Attendance: 21,698 Valencia 13/9/72
Highest Home Win: 5-0 SK Lierse 26/11/69
Only Home Defeat: 0-1 Chelsea 28/4/71

Fanzines

■ The first 'unofficial' publication compiled on a regular basis was a magazine by the name of *Out of The Blues*. It first appeared in August 1968 and received the full backing of the City players. In fact copies were available from the Players' Committee shop at No. 37 Beveridge Street, directly opposite the City Store and offices.

The editor was Paul Doherty, son of former City legend Peter, and a sportswriter with *The People* newspaper. It's clear from looking at the early editions that it was more a magazine than a fanzine. Nevertheless, it did try to campaign at times. In the first edition, produced only a few months after City had secured the Championship, Steve Gage accused the *Manchester Evening News* of being biased: "Quite a few City fans will never forgive the Manchester Evening News in their end-of-season souvenir for putting United – yet to win the European Cup – on their front page with City – already Champions – relegated to the back page!"

Stories with a similar angle still appear in City's fanzines today with the *Manchester Evening News* known in most City fanzines as the *MUEN* ('U' standing for United!).

Peter Crabtree was one of the *Out of the Blues* salesmen: "My most abiding memories of many visits to Maine Road are those of the late sixties during the early days of the fanzine. Several friends and myself, all in our early teens, used to turn up at a small office just across the road from the ground to collect batches of these magazines to sell as the fans arrived for the match. For the first few weeks all went very well as most fans thought they were buying a programme rather than a magazine. This did not endear us to the programme sellers although we did very well in commissions!

"After a few weeks, sales dropped dramatically as more fans realised the difference between the two publications and obviously elected to buy match programmes. After a few months I stopped going although whether it was the lack of sales and income or simply because of the weather turning colder, I no longer remember. I often wonder what happened to the magazine but always recollect with pleasure those first few weeks where I not only got in to see the games for free but also made quite a bit of pocket money into the bargain."

Ultimately, *Out of the Blues* ceased but it did have a major impact on City's publications. Paul Doherty became City's programme editor and the match programme improved considerably as a result. Doherty also went on to become head of sport at Granada TV.

Right: An article from *Out of the Blues* in March 1969.
Below: Fanzine sellers prior to Maine Road's final game include Noel Bayley (right), Sue Wallace (centre).

OUT of the BLUES

The magazine for Manchester City fans
Editor: PAUL DOHERTY

THE word OFFICIAL is getting a lot of usage round Maine Road these days. For instance, a very impressive sign hangs over a wooden hut on the Maine Road forecourt, proclaiming it is the OFFICIAL souvenir shop of Manchester City F.C.—meaning, I presume, that it has nothing at all to do with the souvenir shop across the road which the City players joined in opening and support.

The OFFICIAL sign didn't appear until round about the time the City players started attending The Players Pitch, which are the premises they have an interest in. I suppose The Players Pitch then became the only OFFICIAL souvenir shop of the Manchester City F.C. players. Curious?

★   ★   ★

This magazine is not allowed, by Board ruling, to affix the word OFFICIAL to any page. We've asked for this permission, we've even asked the club to produce it. But we have been told to remove any suggestion that we are OFFICIAL, so we are content to tell the public who supports us. Ironic?

So long as we provide the public with the information they require, give fair value in the publication, and have the co-operation of the City people whom spectators are really interested in at Maine Road, we feel we are being reasonable and can be acceptable to the fans without being OFFICIAL.

★   ★   ★

My last letter from City secretary Walter Griffiths, in reply to a request for an answer to a fan complaint, informed me that he would be giving the answer in the OFFICIAL programme. And if I cared to send him the letter of complaint, he would answer it OFFICIALLY. Naturally?

OFFICIALLY, I can let you into a secret . . . we haven't been making much headway with our intentions of providing a closer contact between City and the supporters through a magazine.

What puzzles us is that the players decided to support a souvenir shop, making personal contact with the public, BEFORE the club wanted to start an OFFICIAL one of their own. Odd? The players and management want this magazine . . . that's OFFICIAL.

We believe that our appearance has brought about an improvement in the match-day OFFICIAL club programme, which we felt was badly needed anyway. So we haven't done much harm if this is all we have achieved. Agreed?

Not all OFFICIALDOM should be resented. It is essential to have authority, and we don't want to be among the generation that knocks OFFICIAL people.

We view the players and managers as OFFICIALS of Manchester City, and we support them solidly. They support us.

But strictly off the record . . . could somebody put us totally in the picture about what's going on at Maine Road.

2

The following is not meant to be a comprehensive list of all City fanzines/supporter magazines, more an indication of the size of fanzine production at Maine Road since the late 1980s:

Are you Blue or Blind?
Bert Trautmann's Helmet
Blue Murder
Chips and Gravy
City 'Til I Die
City 'Til I Cry!
Electric Blue
King of the Kippax
Main Stand View
Purple Reign
Singing The Blues
The Blue
The City Set
The Cityzen
The Fightback
This Charming Fan
True Blue
Wig Out

As far as the fanzine story is concerned, City fans had to wait until the 1980s before another supporter-focused magazine appeared. *Blue Print* first appeared during the 1987-8 season and was originally edited by Mike Kelly, then in September 1988 Dave Wallace brought out *King of the Kippax*. This has gone on to be the most prolific and popular of the City fanzines, and by the start of the 2003-04 season was the only one of the original 1980s fanzines still in production.

During the 1988-9 season Noel Bayley brought out City's third fanzine, *Electric Blue*. This continued until the end of 2002-03 as Noel felt the move to the new stadium was an appropriate time to say farewell. Noel's view of the history of his publication makes interesting reading: "In the beginning was the word ... Well, there were two actually: 'Electric' and 'Blue'. City were blue alright, in every sense of the word, but electric? Hardly. So the title mixed a combination of truth and lies. Nowadays, cuter writers call anything that's wide of the mark irony, cross their fingers and hope to get away with it! It was 1989 and City were languishing in the old Second Division. Having jacked in my job at Whitehall in the summer of '88 - on the day before City lost 1-0 at Hull in the first game of the season - I had no job prospects whatsoever and plenty of time on my hands. A little earlier a fanzine called *Blue Print* appeared. Now, there were many things *Blue Print* became before long, but to begin with it was an inspiration to me just as the *Manchester Evening News* was, but for all the wrong reasons! Its chronic bias towards that other team grated... It still does.

"I wasn't political enough to be into causes, boycotts, demos or anything else, but the *MEN's* overt favouritism to the team in red spurred me on to attempt to redress the balance in some way, however small. I considered writing for *Blue Print*... briefly, until I had a brainwave. I'll do my own fanzine, I thought. At the time football was in the doldrums and there was plenty to say. However, the PC revolution was some way off and internet and email was confined to a handful of geeks in Silicon Valley. The printing press was still king and, allied to the typewriter and Letraset, I set of on a voyage of discovery."

Electric Blue's first edition was printed on dark blue paper. Noel: "If only I knew then half of what I know now! As Oscar Wilde said 'youth is wasted on the young'. With the benefit of hindsight, black ink on dark blue paper didn't make for the best contrast, but I persevered. It was a Red, funnily enough, who suggested I print blue ink on white paper; it seemed quite revolutionary at the time and in my own small way, I've pushed the boundaries out ever since. EB - as it's still fondly known to many people - led the way in terms of technological advancement amongst City fanzines. From duo-colour to full colour, desk top publishing and now, under a new title and masthead, it's a fully digital operation.

"To use the parlance of the dreaded human resources department, my 'personal development plan' has come a long way. I've had to teach myself first, typing, and then computers; I started with an Atari ST which had 1 megabyte of RAM and a single floppy disk drive, before upgrading via a PowerMac to an iMac so beautiful it seems a shame to use it! Ditto, the software. The technology around today is so 'out there' it is truly humbling.

"As for my own development plan it has lasted longer than any university course, any apprenticeship and, in all likelihood, most marriages. Needless to say, I'm not married myself, I haven't had the time, but my bride-to-be Leanne has suffered every anguished moment with me as my blood pressure has reached boiling point and, like the volume controls on Spinal Tap's amps, my stress levels have often gone up to 11 when 10 should have been the limit. And that's before I've even got onto the street with a bag full of fanzines, only to be asked, 'What's that?' and 'Is that the programme?'

"In the meantime, I've shunned the limelight... turned down TV offers, and hung up on the *Manchester Evening News* whenever they've called. However, I've obliged *Teletext* and various websites, and contributed to *The Observer* and *The Times* whenever they've come knocking, all for the princely sum of zero pence. Big time baby... No really, the established media like to 'borrow' ideas from fanzines and keep us at arm's length, but are happy to refer to us as 'scurrilous rags' as the *MEN* once did.

"Eight years ago I had to change the name from *Electric Blue* to *Bert Trautmann's Helmet* when Northern & Shell - one of Britain's biggest publishers and owners of the *Daily Express* - threatened to sue for copyright infringement. In the end they settled for my changing the name. It cost sales, but it could have cost a lot more had they flexed their corporate muscles even slightly.

"Over the years, I've met many, many City fans, I've welcomed more writers than your average college of journalism - many of whom have cut their teeth on other titles – and managed to lose one or two, but not many. The fanzine has reached a peak and come down again and, like yesterday's papers, fanzines in general have all but been sidelined by the internet, radio phone-ins, text messaging, *Teletext* and a dozen other instant gratification devices.

"Still, I've received a few bouquets, many more brickbats and I've interviewed my biggest City hero, Dennis Tueart. It took me ten years but, like the Mounties, I always get my man. There were others too. Peter Barnes was the most gentlemanly, closely followed by David Bernstein, while Francis Lee was the most crafty - he wouldn't let me run the tape! But Dennis was the best. My fanzine has changed beyond all recognition from what I started off with at Ewood Park in April 1989. We've gone from Bald XIs, City's Worst XI and similar to what I like to describe as a compendium of essays and photos which wouldn't look out of place in a newspaper or magazine. Come to think of it, *Bert Trautmann's Helmet* is a magazine without adverts. Unless, of course, anyone can explain the difference. So why am I jacking it in then? It's a question I get asked most days. There are many questions and almost as many answers, but football's changed, the world's changed and I've changed, but if you ask me whether I'd do it all again then yes, I probably would! But now, it's time to do something else..."

In recent years the supporter-driven email service MCIVTA has provided another means for those with internet access to get their views across, and as a result some fanzines have found it difficult to keep the momentum. Nevertheless, City fans now have a rich history of fanzine production and over the years there have been many different publications. Some lasted for several issues, others were only seen by a handful of supporters. In fact, the very nature of fanzines means there will undoubtedly be publications produced by small bands of supporters for their own interest which never become known by the wider public.

During the final days of Maine Road *City 'Til I Cry!* seemed to be one of City's most inventive fanzines, and also one with staying power. Tom Ritchie, one of the forces behind the fanzine, remembers why it started: "*City 'til I Cry!* first saw the light of day in July 1998 as the result of a couple of devoted City fans' response to the incredible situation facing their beloved club... Third Division football! While both of us - Steve Hudson being the other - had written for other fanzines, we both felt it was time to do our own thing. The money was better! The first time it was sold at Maine Road was against Blackpool. We won 3-0, and the fanzine has been sold at every first team game since that day, as well as at hundreds of reserve and youth games.

"At the time, it felt like an act of defiance, a show of faith that come what may we would not be bowed... even though the team and the club were deep in crisis. And that atmosphere and attitude pervaded our time down amongst the dead men, as City fans turned out in their thousands and gave a backing to the club that may never be equalled again.

"Five years and forty issues later, we're still here, if only the same could be said about our home. We will depart our wonderful Maine Road stadium and step into the unknown of the new place. I say "wonderful Maine Road stadium", but, as you obviously realise, the place is anything but. Four non-matching stands, cramped conditions, not enough capacity, dodgy car-parking... the list of negatives could go on a lot, lot longer, I can assure you! But that would diminish what Maine Road actually MEANS to those who have followed the sky-blues for any length of time. I've been coming to the place since about 1965 when it was almost falling down... crumbling terraces, leaking roofs, bench seating, barbed-wire everywhere! But Maine Road was not, and never will be, about something as transient and ornamental as "facilities"; it was always about the performers. And by that I mean not only the players on the pitch, but the support that congregated there.

"The stadium has seen the largest ever crowd for an English league ground, and the huge bank of the Kippax will forever be remembered by those who stood there. And while the present ground was less than half the size of the original place, the atmosphere on occasion was no less dramatic and intimidating. For me, Maine Road will always have a piece of my heart, and no new stadium will usurp that. If truth be told, I don't really want to go. I've seen the new stadium. I've been told how wonderful it is when you are inside, but new stadiums didn't do footballing traditionalists such as Derby County and Sunderland that much good, did they?

"If I could I'd start up a petition right now and get a campaign going to keep us at Maine Road. I'm sure thousands of Blues would forego the new corporate world in front of us for a re-run of the

memories when we faced Wigan Athletic, Birmingham City and the tumultuous times of the 60's and 70's.

"So many great memories. Routinely stuffing the Reds in the Mercer/Allison days, 10-1 against Huddersfield Town, Boro' in the League Cup semi, the 5-1 against Charlton Athletic, THE 5-1, Kinkladze, Marsh, Tueart... never-to-be-forgotten times. And the people I've met - the happy, the optimistic, the miserable, the moaners - the whole world in microcosm was there at Maine Road!"

Steve Kay has contributed to both *Bert Trautmann's Helmet* and *City Til I Cry!*: "After the first few games of the 1996-97 season, I placed an invitation in the unofficial internet newsletter MCIVTA, for passengers to travel in my car to Ipswich, and Noel Bayley responded, asking if he and his girlfriend Leanne could cadge a lift. Soon, *BTH* scribe Mike Billinge completed the "Gang of Four" that travelled the length and breadth of the country on the record breaking Man City Millennium Ground Tour, which took in sixty-odd different grounds in three consecutive seasons. Today, I am still an unpaid chauffeur in Bayley World, but hey, that's show business! Leanne and Mike are as appreciative as ever, but Noel sometimes says I should feel privileged to have such an icon in my car. I have news for Noel - I have bigger icons on my PC desktop!

"My current "fanzine boss" Tom Ritchie, (*City 'Til I Cry!*) also travelled with us to many games. In fact some times I have had 50% of the Manchester City fanzine editors in my car; *King of the Kippax* and *Chips 'n Gravy* being the only exceptions. What an honour... not! Instead of in-depth, meaningful discussions about the current rumours and gossip surrounding the comings and goings at Manchester City F.C., the pair constantly bitched about such trivial matters as the content, grammar, photographs, layout and font size of each other's production, rarely agreeing on anything. What both fail to see is that *City 'Til I Cry!* and *Bert Trautmann's Helmet* are as different as chalk and cheese, and do appeal to different people, though many people buy each fanzine. It's like trying to compare *The Sun* with *The Daily Telegraph*, and I will let you decide which fanzine equates to which newspaper!

"Currently I sell *City 'Til I Cry!*, but have been known to contribute articles to both. Sadly Noel has hung up his mouse, and *BTH* is no more, but the unique style he brought to fanzine world will be missed by those who read his fanzine. The great thing about selling fanzines is the opportunity it gives me to meet other supporters who stop and chat, whether buying a fanzine or not. There is some perception that the "ace space" to sell around Maine Road was on Fanzine Corner at the end of the North Stand, but the truth is that anybody wanting to buy a fanzine will usually find a seller.

"Surprisingly, fanzine sales remain remarkably constant, whatever City's fortunes on and off the pitch. Some fans just collect fanzines in much the same way they collect programmes, without reading them, but most are read for the unofficial, uncensored, alternative views of those that really matter... the fans! Fans can relate more easily to another fan's point of view, rather than that of some overpaid journalist with no affinity to Manchester City. The popularity of fanzines appears to be dwindling as more people gain access to the internet, but *City 'Til I Cry!* and other fanzines will still be around as we move to the new stadium, and will present the fanzine sellers with a new challenge... staking a claim at Fanzine Corner, if indeed one will exist."

As Steve suggests, the future for fanzines is unclear, but there will surely always be a place for quality City fanzines such as *King of the Kippax* and the others. No matter how widespread club publications become, or how up to date internet and email news services are, nothing can compare with the freedom of the fanzine.

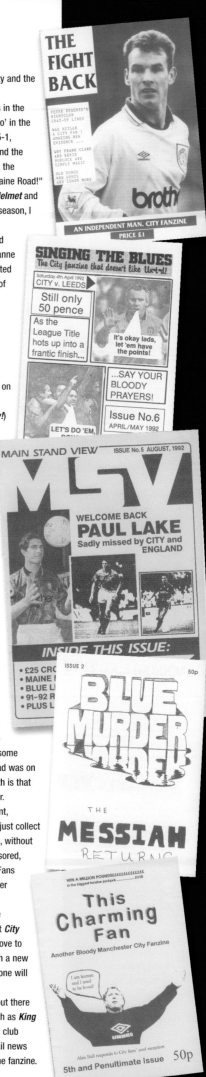

Maine Road on Film

Maine Memory

■ My first impressions of Maine Road are very vague but I do remember the smell of Bovril and pies. At the time I lived in Droylsden and when my mother finally let me go with my brother to first team matches, we used to travel to Manchester city centre and get the match bus from Chorlton Street to the ground. Or if we didn't catch that, we'd just walk down Oxford Road to the ground.

I remember there used to be a bloke who would walk round the ground wearing a sandwich board with the slogan "Jesus Saves" on it in big black letters. Anyway, he must have got taken short and left the board propped up against a wall outside the Kippax while he went for a pee and whilst it was left there someone had written underneath the slogan "and Tueart puts in the rebound" which creased me up!

I also remember when I went to the League Cup semi-final that no one wanted to go to the toilet in case they lost their place. So one entrepreneur brought with him a football without the bladder inside and decided to use that as a portable toilet and then poured it out onto the steps when it got full.

Jed Hutton

CITY fans are always delighted when they see Maine Road used as a backdrop in a film or TV series. Over the years City's ground has been seen on many occasions and in many different scenarios. Two of the highest profile uses of the stadium in recent years are for the film *There's Only One Jimmy Grimble* and the television drama *Second Coming*.

Possibly the first use of the ground, although it must be stressed that actual proof of whether Maine Road was utilised cannot be found, was for the filming of scenes for *The Ball Of Fortune* starring ex-player Billy Meredith. Only a few seconds of footage survive of the film showing Billy Meredith running down the wing, but it is believed this scene was actually filmed on the Maine Road pitch in 1926.

A review of the film mentions scenes were filmed at 'the great grounds of the North and the Midlands' and, because of Meredith's City links (he was a trainer with the club around the time of the film), it does seem likely Maine Road would have been used. After all it was the newest most exciting League ground in the country at the time.

In the 1930s Maine Road was featured in a couple of Pathe News documentaries screened at cinemas across the country. In one the star players of the day are seen on the pitch practising, while manager Wilf Wild is seen waving a number of pound notes around. The commentary says something along the lines of 'Manchester City are one of the country's wealthiest clubs and here's Wilf Wild counting the takings'. It's a delightful piece of film.

Maine Road matches between 1930 and 1960 were regularly filmed for cinema audiences and, with the advent of television, it became obvious that local company Granada TV would show an interest. In 1956 Granada's first outside broadcast showed City's cup homecoming live to those who had decided not to venture on to the streets, and then in the sixties Maine Road was used by the company in a series of programmes.

The most famous use of the ground during the sixties was in Jack Rosenthal's situation comedy *The Dustbinmen*. One of the binmen was Winston Platt, a City-obsessive played by Graham Haberfield. His cap had been adapted to pay homage to the Blues, while the dustbin van, Thunderbird 3, also contained a City slogan in some episodes. In one programme Winston stood on the dustbin van, which was parked up at the northern end of the main forecourt. From there he shouted instructions to the players (out of sight to the TV audience) as a City training session was in progress on the pitch. Another time he forced the rest of the dustbinmen to sit and chant City songs at Maine Road, after winning a bet with them.

In another episode he returned to the depot in a joyful state after emptying Colin Bell's dustbin, while another scene once depicted him being baited by a United-supporting boy who asked him if he supported City because he worked with rubbish? Winston lifted the boy up and threw him into the back of the dustbin van. This scene has been regularly shown in Granadaland, and even featured in the Granada Studios Tour for a while.

Away from Maine Road the Winston character was also filmed on the pitch at Wembley celebrating with the players.

Interestingly, the actor Graham Haberfield was also filmed at Maine Road for another television programme – possibly the most famous British serial of all – *Coronation Street*. In *The Street* Graham played Jerry Booth, a colleague of builder Len Fairclough.

The Street has regularly featured characters with a soft spot for City – Curly and Alma are two recent examples – but in the late sixties an entire story line lasting for three episodes focused on the Blues.

The basic gist was that Rovers' Return landlady Annie Walker was debating the behaviour of football supporters with Stan Ogden and Len Fairclough. As a result she was challenged to go to a football match at Maine Road. Being the type of lady she was she accepted and decided to go with young female supporter Lucille Hewitt. Lucille, it seems, was a regular Maine Road attendee who went to see all the star 'pin-up' players of the period.

Annie's husband Jack worries about Annie's safety and asks Stan Ogden, Jerry Booth and Len Fairclough (all wearing City scarves) to accompany Annie to the match. When Annie emerges from the Rovers' back room wearing a City scarf the three men refuse to accompany her, but after the offer of free beer they reluctantly agree. As the three men, Annie and Lucille leave the pub Annie asks Stan Ogden for the toilet roll she knows he is carrying. She then places it in her pocket and the general impression is that Annie wants to act like an average City fan, i.e. throwing toilet rolls on to the pitch, shouting at the players etc.

The five characters are seen travelling to the ground on a match bus – Annie gets into a debate with an uncouth away supporter! – then they alight on Lloyd Street. The men discuss which part of the ground to take Annie into. They want to take her into the Platt Lane but Annie asks them where they normally go. The say 'The City End', meaning the Scoreboard End, but stress that it's quite rough and so Annie insists they go there.

All of this is clearly filmed on a match day at the ground and later scenes show the five characters stood on the Scoreboard End during a match. The general impression is the match was against Liverpool, however supporter Rob Dunford believes the match was against Leicester in November 1967. This ties in with the details of the game seen on film.

As the programme progresses Annie Walker gets involved with the game and asks Lucille Hewitt about various players, especially the number nine. Lucille replies: "That's Mike Summerbee... isn't he dreamy?" Annie simply replies: "He is rather."

After the game the men and Lucille insist on going to the local chippy, although Annie sees no logic in this as they can get a perfectly good meal back at the Rovers. The men explain to her this is a football tradition and then they go to the chip shop. Meanwhile Lucille and Annie discuss the match with Lucille reminding Annie, who by this time is getting a little irritated about having to wait, that she was using foul language when her 'darling Michael' was fouled!

Annie is then left on her own outside while Lucille joins the men. Inevitably, a couple of away supporters (one of whom was John Challis, later known as Boycie in *Only Fools and Horses*) arrive outside the chip shop and start winding Annie up about being a City fan: "A lady of your age should know better!"

Annie retaliates with a series of intelligent remarks which makes the situation worse and then snatches the rattle of one of the supporters and in a rage throws it. It smashes a window just as a policewoman arrives. Annie is questioned about the incident and when her pockets are searched the toilet roll she took off Stan Ogden is found. She is immediately arrested as a football hooligan.

The next episode shows Annie being questioned at a police station and, eventually, Len Fairclough and Annie's husband Jack manage to get her released with just a caution.

The whole storyline, though a little farfetched at times, was an excellent piece of television history and the use of Maine Road during an actual match added enormously to the story. At one stage in the programme Annie's husband Jack is seen at Coronation Street talking to battleaxe Ena Sharples. Jack explains where Annie is and Ena responds with a comment along the lines of: "Annie Walker at a City match! By eck, I've heard it all now!"

According to City supporter Andy Noise another Granada programme from this period featured Maine Road: "I've only seen the one reference, but in *The Lovers*, Geoffrey (played by the late Richard Beckinsale) turned out to be a Blue. For those who don't remember it, and I only saw a re-run in the 90's, it starred

Beckinsale and Paula Wilcox, as young lovers and their mixed views on consummating their relationship. Anyway, it emerged that Geoffrey's needs were otherwise satisfied at the Academy. In one 'classic' episode, and proving the series was indeed fiction, Geoffrey went to watch City play Spartak in a European tie. Not content with just mentioning his favourite team, Geoffrey was actually filmed at Maine Road, waiting to meet his mate outside the northern end of the Main Stand. Viewers could see the edge of the scoreboard end terracing in the background and hear the pre-game chanting of the Blue fans."

Above: This unique photograph shows Billy Meredith (striped shirt) in action during the 1926 feature film *The Ball of Fortune* - believed to have been filmed at Maine Road.

Below: A prop used in the film *There's Only One Jimmy Grimble*.

Maine Memory

■ I have been going to City since about 1967 and have missed only a handful of games. I have many memories, including Tony Towers scoring in the Cup-Winners Cup; Buzzer missing a sitter against Fenerbahce, and so on. Many years ago I lived in Moss Side and any spare time I got I would hang around the main entrance, waiting for the players. One of my greatest memories is when I got a job as a newspaper boy and on my round was a certain Maine Road. One day I took a paper to the old social club, and outside was a true gent in every sense of the word - Harry Godwin. I asked if I could have his autograph, but at the time he was holding a box. I took the box off him, and followed him - to my surprise - straight up the steps, and into the main entrance. I was in wonderland! He took me into his office, gave me some sweets and led me out of the Main Stand so I could watch my heroes training on the pitch. It was an incredible experience.
Edwin Sparrow

Harry Godwin was a very popular member of City's staff for many years. He was chief scout under Joe Mercer, but later became 'Uncle Harry' to thousands of Junior Blues. Two seats were donated in memory of him at Maine Road to the Junior Blues.

Interestingly, these 1960s programmes all featured a typical fan's view of Maine Road, and gave television viewers the impression that City was very much a club for its supporters. Across at United, Old Trafford's use in film showed an entirely different approach. The film *Charlie Bubbles* (1968), starring Albert Finney, depicts a great deal of sixties Manchester, but also shows the main character taking a boy to Old Trafford for a game. They watch the match from an executive box and the entire scene tries to demonstrate how much the main character was out of touch with the boy. The boy wanted to be on the terraces watching the game and is clearly disappointed about being behind glass. Perhaps Albert Finney should have taken the boy in the Platt Lane Stand!

There have been many other references to City on television – 'Little & Large' shows, 'Two Pints of Lager & A Packet of Crisps', Steve Coogan's 'Paul Calf', 'Playing the Field', 'Clocking Off', 'Linda Green', 'Cutting It', 'The Big Impression', Craig Cash's 'Early Doors' etc. – while back in May 1971 Maine Road was used for the opening of one edition of *This is Your Life*. On that day Eamon Andrews presented Matt Busby with the famous red book before a Manchester derby. Many City-related players and personalities have been featured on the show over the years.

During the seventies the TV news show *Nationwide* had a series of weekly features on the club, and then during the 1980-81 season Granada made the seminal documentary *City!* This featured the end of Malcolm Allison's reign and the beginning of John Bond's.

In 1989 a drama was made at the ground featuring a player from a team called 'City' who was kidnapped. The actual match filmed for this was in December 1989 and the stadium Control Room was used to give the impression of an executive box.

The 1990s saw several scenes in *Cracker* filmed close to Maine Road. In one scene a man is murdered in a back entry and the following day Cracker and the other characters are seen discussing how the death occurred. At the start of the scene a general shot of the area shows part of the Main Stand in the distance and it's clear the scene must have been filmed somewhere in the Lloyd Street area. In the very first episode Cracker's son wears a *Blueprint* 'Better than Best' Colin Bell Tee-shirt.

In recent years the *Second Coming*, starring red Christopher Eccleston, showed a miracle taking place at Maine Road – where was he between 1996 and 1999 when City were in dire need of a miracle? – while *There's Only One Jimmy Grimble* showed plenty of Maine Road. Even Robert Carlisle's character, a former player who had scored a hat-trick in a Manchester derby, lived on Maine Road opposite the stadium.

Of course various other documentaries and news stories have featured film of Maine Road, while the early morning children's television show of the late eighties/early nineties the *Wide Awake Club* featured the City Ladies team at the Platt Lane training ground.

The end of Maine Road attracted the interests of a number of media companies and both Granada and BBC produced programmes about the stadium's history.

Interestingly, the day after Maine Road's final League game in May 2003, *Coronation Street* had a scene which talked of the great stadium at its best. Was this *The Street's* own tribute? In the scene, bad boy Joe Carter is revealing to Karen MacDonald his feelings as a young unwanted boy. He told of finally arriving with foster parents who were so interested in him that the

father took him to City for a midweek match. Joe described the scene and painted a terrific picture of Maine Road under floodlights, and then revealed how the father gave him his own season ticket. Joe was delighted until he discovered the ticket was actually the father's real son's ticket and he was to hand it back the moment the other lad returned.

In the story Joe described the pain he felt at having that ticket snatched away from him, and how his entire life had followed a similar course. Surely, as any Blue will know, Joe's character would have felt more anguish had he been forced to watch City week in week out instead!! It also makes you wonder what Club secretary Bernard Halford would have done had he found out the season ticket was being transferred!

Since then City have been referred to extensively in two other shows. *The Big Impression* has seen Alistair MacGowan impersonate Kevin Keegan, Noel Gallagher and various other Manchester-based personalities during his sketch *Sex and the Man City*. According to supporter Phil Lines writing on the MCIVTA email service: "I have seen three instalments now of *Sex & the Man City* and have to confess (a) Its very funny; b) The take-off of KK is spot on; c) It really puts us on the map - you have to remember this is a time slot with an audience that for the most part would not know about teams other than Man Utd & Arsenal. In PR terms it is good exposure and is taking a chance a bit with references to Anelka & Tiatto. His impression of Kevin is well observed and is much understated and all the better for it and is the first time I have seen anyone take KK off without resorting to the rather pathetic Frank Spencer "Oooh Betty" type rendition of him saying "luv it luv it etc".

Cutting It is another programme with regular City coverage. There is a City-loving character who, at the end of May 2003, attempted to propose to his girlfriend after making his room a romantic setting. City memorabilia could be seen everywhere while the playing of 'Blue Moon' aimed to give a romantic feel.

Clearly, City's place in television comedy and drama will continue for some time, but as the new stadium develops its own place in television history we should not forget the great history Maine Road has as a set for television and film.

The following provides details of key Maine Road matches on film.

■ **EARLIEST KNOWN MAINE ROAD GAME FILMED:** City v Cardiff City, 4th round FA Cup, 8/3/24. Maine Road's first season was captured on film, however this footage is not currently viewable and is awaiting preservation. The attendance was 76,166.

■ **EARLIEST SURVIVING VIEWABLE MAINE ROAD GAME:** Billy Meredith's testimonial match was filmed on 29th April 1925, and is stored at the North West Film Archive at Manchester Metropolitan University, although it is incorrectly recorded as 'Meredith 1926'.

■ **EARLIEST KNOWN VIEWABLE MAINE ROAD GAME FEATURING CITY:** City v Huddersfield Town, 4th round FA Cup, 30/1/26. City beat League Champions Huddersfield 4-0 before a crowd of 74,789.

■ **MAINE ROAD'S FIRST TELEVISED MATCH:** City v Wolves, Division One, 15/12/56. This was Bert Trautmann's first game back after breaking his neck in the 1956 final.

■ **MAINE ROAD'S FIRST APPEARANCE ON MATCH OF THE DAY:** City v Tottenham Hotspur, Division One, 9/12/67.

Classic Maine Road. To many supporters the ground reached its peak during the mid-70s. The facilities were still basic in many areas (note the original curled armrest benches in the Main Stand), but the atmosphere was passionate.

Chapter Eight

Undersoil and Off the Pitch

"City probably have less trouble than most clubs when it comes to hooliganism. But I am not pretending we are trouble free. We endeavour to educate our supporters through our excellent Supporters' Club and Junior Blues organisations. These meetings are always attended by directors and players and their very presence is a big help in spreading the gospel. We also have a wonderful understanding with the police – they are exceptionally co-operative. Overall, I would say hooliganism is a Government problem. It's about time they got their fingers out and did something more positive."

Secretary Bernard Halford, November 1979.

AFTER the development of the North Stand, the 1970s became a decade of gradual change at Maine Road. Improvements to the Kippax car park seemed forever to be occurring, while inside the stadium the decision had been taken to replace the wooden benches in the Main Stand with blue plastic seating whenever possible. Unfortunately, the seating changes occurred over a decade and happened only when the club had a spare dollop of cash. This meant that blocks of seating were replaced at different times and often with different shades of blue. There seemed no coherent plan and by the 1990s, when the replacement process had ended, almost every shade of blue from a very pale sky shade through to a very deep royal existed in what was the club's most prestigious stand.

No doubt those responsible would say the important issue was replacing benches and wooden tip-up seats with modern plastic ones, however from an aesthetic point of view the stand started to look a little ragged during the seventies; the roof still had the raised section in the middle, and a gap between the Main and North Stands.

Outside the ground City's merchandise operation was beginning to improve. The wooden hut erected in the sixties had disappeared and in August 1973 the club opened their new City Sports & Souvenir Centre. This was housed in the building next to the Social Club and, although heavily criticised by the mid-1980s, was a major step forward in 1973. Under Manageress Yvette Price the shop boasted it stocked over 120 items of genuine City souvenirs. According to a press release at the time: "It is a magnificent centre and is well worth a visit. All your City souvenirs from a suit – ladies or gents – to a tie clip are available. The suits are made in Crimplene to an exclusive City design. Hats, scarves, ties and cardigans are available in the same material. A selected range of goods to commemorate the Golden Jubilee at Maine Road are also available. If you have a birthday present to buy, why not call at the centre after the game, where we are sure there will be something to fit the bill!"

Player of the Year Mike Summerbee officially opened the store. Items for sale included satin scarves at 65p; Maine Road jubilee pennants at 37p; and City bikinis at £2.65.

One of the key stories nationally during the early 1970s were the regular mining disputes. During the 1973-4 League Cup campaign City's progress through the competition was dependent upon midweek afternoon kick-offs and the use of electricity generators to ensure power. City fan Roger Reade: "I sneaked out of school to watch the Coventry match on 16th January. It was an

afternoon kick-off and the club had been forced to find a generator to ensure the ground had power. At the time the strikes had caused power to go off at set times each day and so big events like football matches were in jeopardy, but this game went ahead and as a result we progressed to the semi-final against Plymouth and then the final against Wolves."

Another supporter, Barry Evans, was also present that day: "This game was played on a cold wet January afternoon and was the most entertaining match I have watched. The power strike caused the game to start in the afternoon. The pitch was in the worst state I have ever seen before or since. It was mud from goalmouth to goalmouth. How the teams played football in those conditions was a credit to both sets of players. Twenty minutes had gone when Mike Summerbee crossed the ball from the wing to Colin Bell to head for the top corner of the net, when the Coventry 'keeper pulled off the save of his career!

"That save was only a small part of a great game played by two very good sides. The next morning the 'papers hailed City the Muddy Marvels after their 4-2 win."

Power cuts forced some matches to be rearranged and Andrew Heydeman remembers this allowed him to attend Maine Road by his own means: "One of my most vivid Maine Road memories was the first time I ever went without Mum and Dad. It was a league match against West Brom in City's championship-chasing 1971-72 season. The country was severely affected by power

Right: Rodney Marsh scored both goals in a 2-1 win against Tottenham at Maine Road in September 1972. This was before the days of fencing and segregation on the Kippax.

Below: Mike Summerbee officially opens the City Sports & Souvenir Centre (Souvenir Shop). Notice Bernard Halford (back, far left). In 2003 Bernard's office was a room above the old shop. During the late 90s the club converted the shop into office space.

Maine Memory

■ I've got a few memories of Maine Road, all of course from my younger days when me and my Dad were Kippax season ticket holders, which was from about 1975 through to the second relegation in the eighties. And yes, we always stood in the same place with the same folk around us who we only ever saw every other Saturday, and who always came out with the same lines such as "yours are in blue" or the "don't kick it so high Joe, you'll get snow on it". At the end of one season a six inch piece of concrete broke off the corner where we stood, so my Dad decided to take it home as he felt that he'd paid for it over the years of buying a season ticket. He painted Kippax St on it and stuck it on the rockery back home.

My first memory of watching City was when we beat Burnley 7-0 - around 1969 - yet the first game I ever saw was at Old Trafford for a birthday treat. Probably in 1967 or 1968, when the Reds won something like 5-2, but despite that I chose City. It seemed the natural choice. It has certainly been the right choice.

Andy Poole

The 7-0 victory over Burnley was played on 7th December 1968.

cuts at the time, meaning the West Brom game was rescheduled for a Wednesday afternoon in March.

"My parents were both therefore unable to attend and although only just ten years old, I was given permission to go to the match with my eight-year-old sister. We caught the train from Bury to Victoria and were given detailed directions to get to Maine Road by bus from City Centre Manchester because I was used to travelling to Maine Road from Bury by car. Extensive rebuilding work on St Mary's Gate - where special matchday buses used to run from in those days - meant the street signs were obscured (at least that's still my excuse!) and we wandered from Victoria station all the way down Deansgate unable to locate the bus stop.

"At the end of Deansgate, I fortunately recognised the Mancunian Way and we struggled anxiously down the middle of the pedestrian-free dual carriageway towards Moss Side. We passed the brewery and through those distinctive streets of red-bricked terraced houses and were delighted when we finally arrived at Maine Road. By this time, it was about five minutes after kick off and just as we approached our G Block Main Stand season ticket turnstiles, a massive roar went up and I was paradoxically devastated that City had scored and I'd missed the goal. Colin Bell had scored City's opener and went on to add another in a 2-1 victory for the Blues in front of 25,677. Whilst disappointed to have missed the goal - it remains one of very few goals I have ever missed during matches I attended at Maine Road - I was proud we'd eventually found our way there and arrived home in Bury safely afterwards. I'd also managed to buy the cheaper reduced-page programme specially produced for the match because of the power cuts. Many brilliant Maine Road memories were experienced in subsequent years but that very first visit there 'under my own steam' will always be a vivid and special memory."

Roger Reade remembers other national situations affecting life for City fans during this time: "I remember one game, and I think it must have been around the time of one of the IRA's bombing campaigns in the early seventies, when there was a proper bomb alert. A

message came over the tannoy that we all had to check under our seats to see if there was a suspicious package there. I remember looking under the Platt Lane bench I sat on and didn't see anything – other than our flask! I don't know what we'd have done if we'd found a bomb, but I do remember the referee – I think it was Roger Kirkpatrick – stopped play, picked up the ball, put his ear to it and shook it to see if there was a bomb inside! It's hilarious thinking back, but I do remember that on the day it was all so dramatic. I don't know if we seriously expected a bomb or not, but it was typical of the time."

Despite these worries, the early Seventies continued to be an exciting time for City fans with the great entertainer Rodney Marsh thrilling many with his acrobatics. Roger Reade: "I remember seeing City's old scout Harry Godwin throw a sweet towards Rodney who then proceeded to juggle with it before knocking it into his mouth. It was all controlled well, but Marsh was the great entertainer and loved to be different. I remember he had a car but unlike most cars he'd had it carpeted throughout – and I don't just mean the floors! Every bit of wall or ceiling space was carpeted, as were the pedals. He had this reputation for never wearing socks and I think once he got into his car he would take off his shoes to drive. Eccentric but a great player!"

Apart from the North Stand, most other developments inside the stadium during the seventies centred around crowd safety and control. An increase in crowd disorder throughout football led to the Blues being forced to erect fencing and formal segregation for potential problematic fixtures. Old Trafford was the first English ground ordered to install fencing but sadly the disease was widespread and 1975-6 was the first season in which the Kippax terracing was split by an iron fence from the back of the terracing to the bottom. The fence was positioned in such a way as to separate a third of the stand from the rest. The visitors stood on the Platt Lane side of the divide, while City fans were housed in the rest of the stand.

During 1975-6 formal segregation was used selectively. The 27th September 1975 derby match was the first fixture in which it was impossible to walk from one end of the stand to the other. Pre-segregation supporters enjoyed moving to follow the way City were attacking. If the Blues faced the North Stand, fans would move to the North Stand end of the Kippax, and then change at half-time. Once this opportunity was removed some became a little disgruntled.

After the derby match, segregation wasn't enforced again until the visit of Leeds on Boxing Day; followed by Aston Villa (7th February), and Everton (21st February). Interestingly, fixtures which a decade later would be viewed as high risk matches – Newcastle, Burnley, Tottenham, Birmingham and West Ham – were not deemed enough of a risk to insist on formal segregation. Of course throughout the sixties and seventies supporters did initiate their own unofficial form of segregation.

That same season Ian Niven, the director in charge of ground improvements, reported that £100,000 was to be spent on various initiatives around the ground and the Moss Side area. One of the most significant was the purchase of a four acre site at Platt Lane which had been used as a police sports ground. The aim was to house City's first team training headquarters close to the ground. Over the years this training ground developed further and by the close of Maine Road in 2003 the Platt Lane complex was a key City presence in the local community.

Other developments included the £24,000 rebuilding of the Kippax external wall. Ian Niven: "The wall is falling down and is beyond redemption. It was never pointed in past years and now it is too late to save it. The new wall will be 12ft high which is three feet higher than the existing one. The intention is to rebuild the whole wall, starting at the North Stand end."

£1,700 was spent on installing 'trainers' boxes' to replace the concrete dug-outs the club had used for many years, while £8,000 was spent on the installation of 860 plastic tip up seats in 'D' Block of the Main Stand replacing the more traditional bench seats. Ian Niven revealed how these were similar to the seats erected in Blocks 'B' and 'C' in previous seasons. A further £3,500 was spent on strengthening the back of the Platt Lane Stand. Niven: "It was in a dangerous state of repair two years ago and we have gradually moved around each area doing the necessary work. The wall is stripped right down to the steel, which is scaled and cleaned, then re-bricked and pointed. There is one more phase of this project to do after the coming summer."

A couple of extra rooms were created in the main corridor of the offices around this time. It was anticipated these would be a committee room and a store room, although Ian Niven added: "It might be used for Junior Blues offices because this section of the club has become an exciting development with membership of young fans increasing weekly by large numbers." According to 1976 figures these rooms cost around £900 to construct while other office improvements cost £3,000. The rooms created were modified in the mid-nineties and subsequently became the Chairman's Lounge and Boardroom.

Roger Reade, who was working for the club at this time, remembers another development then: "Money was spent on general improvements to the offices, but it was about this time we started to consider sponsorship and we came to the decision we needed a room. Bernard Halford asked me to get involved and we concocted a plan whereby a space between the main corridor and the terracing of the Main Stand would be filled with a new

Maine Memory

■ The corner of the old Platt Lane enclosure where it adjoined the Main Stand was an excellent vantage point, but due to its popularity it used to fill up by about 1.45pm on match days so you had to be quick. My father used to take me and my younger brother there when we started to attend regularly during the late '60's, still too young and small to stand in the Kippax.

On a cold January day in 1967 we arrived a little late to watch the match from my favourite corner so we took up our place behind the goal. I have to admit I have since seen some technically better games and witnessed some more exciting moments, however, that particular match sticks in my mind more than any other for a variety of reasons. City had just won the Second Division championship and had reached the top level for the first time since I had started watching them and England had just won the World Cup. So, to a 12-year-old football was the most important thing in the world. The first time I saw an England World Cup medal winner in the flesh was when Gordon Banks ran out for Leicester City to face the Blues in that FA Cup 3rd round. This was the first time I had watched a cup tie but I knew all about the magic of what is still the finest knockout competition in the world courtesy of some well-recounted stories from my father. City were on the wrong side of a 1-0 scoreline at half time and yet again it was a first for me when I saw a side come back from behind to win. A goal each from Mike Doyle and Glyn Pardoe put my team into the hat for the 4th round draw.

David Rothband

room. This eventually became the Sponsors' Suite and one of the key features was that the sponsors would be taken straight out of the room and through into 'D' Block of the stand."

The club had realised by the mid-Seventies that the Main Stand offices could be improved simply by building on the pitch side of the main office corridor. Architect Charles Swain had left this space as a void, and so with careful planning the club were able to fill in the corridor in stages to create extra offices or function rooms. This also meant staircases would have to be altered at times. The Sponsors' Suite was built over a staircase and so for Maine Road's final 25 years new supporters would wonder why a staircase existed that mysteriously rose to the ceiling with no exit point.

Above: Staircase to nowhere! The Sponsors Suite was built over this staircase in the late 1980s.

Below: Maine Road celebrated its 50th anniversary in the 1973-74 season, commemorated on the cover of programmes for that season.

Maine Memory

■ My granddad Leslie Appleton used to attend Maine Road in the days of 80,000 crowds when, on one occasion, he could barely move due to the amount of people packed in closely together. This particular day sounds like a typical Mancunian day as it was pouring down and my grandad said he came home with a pocketful of water. Children were passed down over the heads of the crowd and total strangers would help you along. As for going to the toilet the spectators just did it there and then in the space they found themselves - very primitive!

Tracy my wife remembers her name being called out during the all-standing days at the Kippax. She contacted her nearest steward only to be relieved to hear it was a Police Officer, also with the name Tracy Edwards, who had dropped her warrant card.

When I first went to Maine Road I was in awe of the size of the ground. It just looked so massive. I first attended the ground to buy tickets for a first team game when the reserves played there on a Saturday afternoon at 2pm. My grandad shouted out "Come on City, Simon wants to see a goal." They promptly scored four against Blackburn if memory serves me right!

My grandad lived on Brompton Road approximately three blocks from Maine Road and spectators used to pay to leave their bikes in his back yard. As he lived so close he obviously walked to games and when he was much younger and couldn't afford to go regularly he used to turn up at three-quarter time. City would open up the gates to all and sundry free of charge.

Simon Edwards

Rose's Room

■ **Tucked underneath the Main Stand, hidden at the bottom of the tunnel closest to the Platt Lane Stand was the photographers' tea room. To many people a tea-room is a tea-room but this one at Maine Road was different. Rose Woolrich looked after the club's photographers for thirty years and only missed a few games. Once, when she had broken a leg she even turned up for work in a wheelchair!**

Rose: "Stan Gibson was the man who asked me if I'd do this in the early Seventies. Back then the club was like most others and didn't really look after the photographers. There was originally a room in the Players' Tunnel but one day a photographer went a little too far and took photos of an incident that occurred as the players went down the tunnel. It was then decided the photographers should not be encouraged to go down there, so a room was created in the next tunnel.

"There was nothing special about this room – it was just a space made under the stairs and next to the toilets! – but over the years I've managed to improve it."

When Rose says she managed to improve it, there's not a hint of exaggeration, as most of the effort to paint and furnish the room has came from Rose and her son: "We brought carpets in… managed to get odd pieces of equipment… a bit of paint here and there… and of course some of my photographers gave me photos to help

Above: Photographers received a warm welcome in Rose's Room in 2003 (top picture) just as they had in this 1978 photograph, as Rose Woolrich does the honours with the urn.

decorate the place. The club provided some help over the years, but initially it wasn't felt important. In my eyes you've got to look after the photographers because they'll then look after you."

Club photographer Ed Garvey agrees: "I've not been to many other grounds, but it's clear from what the long-standing photographers say Rose's room was by far and away the best in the League. She treats us all like her own extended family and that makes you feel special. Sometimes she makes you feel so welcome it's a drag to go out for the start of the match!"

Rose enjoys her part in City's history: "Rooms like this are important but I just get on and do what I need to do. I make four dozen scones per match, and have the usual collection of grapes, cheese, crackers, nuts and so on. I've got to

know what each photographer likes or if they have a particular allergy or whatever. I also provide scones for Bernard Halford and for other members of staff. During the last year or so Kevin Keegan started popping in. I don't know how it started but he seemed to enjoy it. He was the first manager to set foot in my room and he's a really nice man. I think he liked the fact it's just a normal tea room. Nothing fancy. Of course, once Kevin came in others started to follow. We even had John Wardle in here."

Rose's unique room is the sort of area which will be missed enormously at the new stadium. Sure a new one can be created, but it's unlikely to have the same atmosphere as that left behind at Maine Road, although Rose will no doubt do her utmost best to make sure it's a home from home for all.

At the start of the 1976-7 season an announcement appeared in the match programme stating segregation would now become a permanent feature and Kippax turnstiles 52 to 56B would be made exclusively available to visiting supporters. Secretary Bernard Halford said it was an unfortunate but necessary step and added: "The object is to control any hooligan element which may arise at matches."

Fencing at the front of the Kippax was also permanent. Ian Niven said at the time: "This is to comply with the new crowd safety regulations and a dry moat will be built into the area between the grass verge and the perimeter wall. A 4ft 6ins high rail will be erected as protective cover to the moat. It will not interfere with the view of the spectators standing at the front of the Kippax. We have tested the plan and the rails, which will run from ground height, and they will not obstruct any part of the play."

Fencing behind each goal did not seem a concern for some time. The perception was that the more volatile supporters would only ever watch games from the Kippax terracing, however an incident in the UEFA cup tie with Widzew Lodz on 14th September 1977 shattered that illusion. Basically, a fan from the North Stand attacked Widzew's goalscorer Boniek. The incident had major repercussions for the club.

Firstly UEFA fined the Blues £400 then a 19-year-old supporter was found guilty of using threatening, abusive and insulting behaviour. He was fined £100 and banned from Maine Road, but City were also instructed to erect fencing behind both goals. Initially, the club, in consultation with the police and local authority, erected the fencing for only high-profile fixtures, but as time went by the fences became a permanent barrier between players and fans.

City were keen to publicise the prosecution, hoping it would act as a deterrent. The supporter's name appeared in the programme as the club chose to make an example of him. Bernard Halford said at the time: "We trust that our supporters will take notice of this case, what it has resulted in for the individual and the club, and realise that at all times it has got to be important to uphold the very good name which Manchester City have got.

"Believe me, we are totally aware of the great effort made by the fans to support City and we are delighted with the numbers who turn up on the Kippax and follow the team away from home. But we have to make every effort to reduce trouble, provocation and make the ground a place where any person is proud to come. I have been asked to implore the City fans to cut out the abusive language. It is doing no good for the club and is often at the root of troubles by its very provocative nature. We can do without it and if the fans responsible feel anything for the club they claim so strongly to support, then they will listen to this appeal."

Across football, grounds were beginning to resemble fortresses. Fortunately, Maine Road was still relatively safe compared to other major venues, but the Blues could not be complacent, and serious attempts were made to control fans while the club was determined to retain its family image.

The fencing at the Kippax side was positioned between the perimeter wall and the pitch – a move which allowed the view not to be too seriously restricted, while the fencing behind the goals, when erected, was placed on top of the white perimeter wall. The Kippax contained a typical iron bar style fence, while the other

Maine Men Bernard Halford

ROLE: Secretary

■ Bernard Halford was a popular figure at Maine Road throughout the final thirty years of the stadium's life. As Club Secretary, he was involved with all the major deals the club has negotiated over the years and at various times has played a dominant part in transfers, crowd control, security, office management, ground redevelopment... you name it he's done it (apart from play of course!). Bernard: "I have been fortunate enough to enjoy this rollercoaster ride and spent 50% of my life at Maine Road in my capacity as Club Secretary, also helping stage cup semi-finals, numerous pop concerts, and other events. One man I'll never forget was our long-serving groundsman Stan Gibson."

Previously, before moving to Maine Road in 1973 Bernard had been the Oldham secretary: "I'd always been a Blue. At school I'd get into fights over City. It meant so much to me and I used to love coming here as a youngster and watching all the stars. I first came here in 1949 and from that day I was captivated by the ground. It was a marvellous place to be then, and it remained a marvellous place throughout the years. No matter what anyone says about their own ground, that one of ours is the most special. The range of emotions we've gone through there is incredible."

The first game Bernard had full organisational responsibility for was City's cup tie with Sunderland in 1973. An official crowd of 54,478 attended that match, the highest number since the North Stand became seated the previous summer. Some felt the attendance exceeded capacity. Bernard: "I wanted everybody to see this because being new to the job I didn't want to let any of the fans down. Being a fan I knew how disappointed I'd feel if I couldn't get in to a game so I suppose I was keen to fill the ground. Nevertheless, we didn't break the safety certificate and everything passed off okay. The worst part of the day was that we only got a draw!"

Over the years Bernard has been one of the most consistent features of the club. The Board has changed, managers have come and gone, but Bernard has remained. From time to time immense pressure was placed on him, but he always continued to perform to the best of his abilities to keep the club moving forward. There cannot be a more experienced and knowledgeable secretary anywhere in the Premier League.

Leaving Maine Road probably means more to Bernard than most. A fan first, Club Secretary second, Bernard is inevitably emotional about the place: "I've had some wonderful times at Maine Road and I've found that even when I'm not due at the ground I'll sometimes make an excuse to drive past just to look. When we've moved out and the ground's long since gone I know I'll be drawn back on occasion just to look and remember what's happened there."

Above: Maine Road in the late 1970s seen from the floodlight tower behind the 1931 Platt Lane corner roof, looking towards the North Stand. Note the three flagpoles on the North Stand roof and the 'Welcome to Maine Road' sign beneath the floodlight on the Kippax roof. If it was possible to take a photograph from this position in 2003 the City of Manchester Stadium would be seen in the distance behind the North Stand.

fences were more of a lattice affair thereby reducing the visible impact. Nevertheless, fencing was not welcome.

While some were attending games in the hope that violence, or at least banter, with opponents would be available, Barry Rutter's attendance at the 1977 derby saw his life take a turn for the better: "I was 17 and living at home with my parents in Clinton Avenue, Fallowfield, while attending college. I used to go to most of the home games with my dad, Bill. However money was tight, and I was desperate to see the 1977 Manchester derby at Maine Road but the game was a sell-out.

"My friend Buddy - Stephen Budsworth - worked for Stadia Catering as a tray boy and said if I didn't mind going into the ground a couple of hours before the game he could "blag" me in as a new tray-boy. So, lending me his spare tray-boy jacket, we entered the ground through the small door on the front of the Main Stand, passed the security guard and into the ground. The idea was for me to hide in a toilet until the ground filled up and then take my place in the Kippax.

"However as there was the potential threat of trouble at the game, most of the regular tray-boys cried off and the Stadia supervisor was going mad! Buddy introduced me to her and she gave me a tray. I actually got to see most of the game and earned a few quid as well! I ended up keeping the job all season.

"A few games later City were playing Coventry and while working as a tray-boy before the game kicked-off, I borrowed 5p off a pretty young girl so I could give another woman her full change. I got chatting to the girl

- whose name was Karen - and after cashing in, just after half time, I joined her in the Kippax Stand. One thing led to another and in June 2002 we celebrated our 20th Wedding Anniversary. We ended up being season ticket holders and went on to sit roughly where we met in the Kippax stand all those years ago."

During the 1970s the area around Maine Road was in the process of redevelopment. Modern housing was replacing traditional terraces and the City Council decided it was time to honour some of Manchester's best footballers by naming streets after them. Peter Leckenby worked for the council at the time: "I was employed as an engineer by the Council at Pollard Street Highways Depot. It was my job to name the streets on redevelopment areas. One such scheme was the Upper Lloyd Street Housing Site.

"At the suggestion of Councillor Morris, the streets were to be named after famous City players of the past. I had to contact the club to discuss proposals and had many a long chat to the late Bill Miles, the club historian at the time. One of the problems we faced was which players' names to use. It was Council policy that streets could only be named after people if they were deceased. The names were eventually agreed – with the most recent player being Frank Swift from the 1940s – and Bill Miles eventually rang to invite me behind the scenes at Maine Road. I was taken around the ground, which included the Boardroom with all the trophies, where I spoke to director Ian Niven for a while. I also saw the dressing rooms and the players' bar. It was a marvellous day."

Maine Match 77/78

CITY v NEWCASTLE UNITED

DATE:	26th December 1977	
TYPE OF FIXTURE:	Football League Division One	
ATTENDANCE:	45,811	
RESULT:	City 4 Newcastle 0	
TEAMS & SCORERS:	CITY	NEWCASTLE
	Corrigan	Carr
	Clements	Nattrass
	Donachie	Barker
	Booth	Cassidy
	Watson	Bird
	Power	Blackley
	(sub: Bell)	(sub: Gorry)
	Barnes	Martin
	Owen	Burns
	Kidd 1	Cannell
	Hartford	Craig
	Tueart 3	Robinson

Left: Seeing Colin Bell back in action gave every City fan and player a massive lift....

Below: ... none more so than Dennis Tueart who rattled in a hat-trick as Newcastle were swept aside in an unforgettable second half.

■ One of Maine Road's saddest stories was that of Colin Bell's injury and fightback to fitness. Bell had been badly injured after a tackle by Manchester United's Martin Buchan in the 1975 League Cup tie between the sides. That game ended 4-0 to City, but the talking point was the injury, not the goals. Sean Riley remembers Bell's injury and his own unusual way of entering the ground: "It was the first time I had been inside Maine Road with over 50,000 people inside, and what an atmosphere it was. We actually gained access to the ground that night via motor-car! My late friends' uncle had a pass with his three-wheel invalid car, and he smuggled at least six of us in, so we were able to watch the game from the corner of the Platt Lane and Main Stand. Of course we never really understood at the time how serious things were when Colin Bell was stretchered off the field, yet I feel privileged to have seen the King play at all."

Colin Bell was named as substitute for City's game with Newcastle on Boxing Day 1977. It was a remarkable day. Manager Tony Book: "My plan had been to give him a twenty minute run at the end of the match, but an injury to Paul Power forced my hand. It wasn't planned the way it happened."

For Julian Cooke, Colin Bell's return became his favourite Maine Road match: "Of course all the talk for days in advance and on the bus too was whether Colin Bell would be named as sub and finally make his return. I'd only ever seen him play on TV, but knew he was a genius and that every City fan loved him. I'd followed his progress via the *Manchester Evening News* and the match programmes and was dying to see him play.

"The ground was packed and we managed to get our usual spot, high up in the Kippax. The first half was pretty disappointing, both teams looked as if they'd eaten too much Christmas pudding the day before. As the second half was about to start we could see the players begin to emerge from the tunnel opposite, and amongst them there he was!

"The roar from the Kippax was deafening, as they realised he was coming on as sub - Maine Road went

berserk. As everyone there witnessed, City were inspired by Bell's appearance and played brilliantly. Three goals from Tueart and one from Kidd swept Newcastle away. I remember Colin Bell's long-range effort that just went over the bar - if that had gone in it would have been the perfect return for him. After the game we walked up Maine Road to get the No.53 back to Belle Vue. The bus was packed and extremely hot. I was stood on the lower deck at the foot of the stairs - about half way through the journey I suddenly puked up, decorating a good part of the stairs. I seem to remember this amused or annoyed fellow Blues depending on how close they were to me - still at least I got a seat as some kind woman took pity on me. My schoolfriend just pretended he wasn't with me. We met my dad at Belle Vue and despite his concern about my sickness I was more interested in talking about Colin Bell. I suspect it was all the excitement of the day, the heat and too much indulgence the day before.

"The reason this game is still my favourite is because it was the first time I really experienced one of those extra special Maine Road days - something magical happened on the pitch, the fans were as one, all sides of the ground singing and making lots of noise, the team driven on by the passion of it all and the opposition powerless to resist the onslaught. That's when I realised how great it was to be a City fan and how special the atmosphere at Maine Road when everything goes our way."

The match is many supporters' favourite memory. Terry Morley: "My eyes were moist, as I'm sure were many thousands of others at the sight of Colin Bell coming on as a sub in that match. We could have lost 10-0, it didn't matter, the most important thing on that day was to see Colin finally make it back. Sadly though he was never really the same all-action player we always admired but even so he was still a class act and still better than most. We all loved Colin the King."

Paul Demby: "Whoever says a player cannot change the course of a match was not at Maine Road that day. I don't recall who went off, it's irrelevant anyway, it's who came on that's important. After over two years out of the game Colin Bell returned. I saw grown men weeping - at a football match in front of their mates. His influence was incredible, not because he had a great game but because of the lift he gave to the team. Four second-half goals later without reply and King Colin left to another standing ovation. There have been many other memorable moments at Maine Road but without doubt this left an indelible stamp on me."

Rachel Zoe McDonald: "Although I was only 10 at the time of this match, it is the one that really stands out and can still raise the hairs on the back of my neck. I have been lucky enough to witness many famous City moments, yet over and above this match is the one that stands out. Although I was only young I knew that what I was witnessing at the time was something very, very special, and that something was Colin Bell. The ovation for Colin Bell was unlike anything that I have ever heard since for any player, and I feel very lucky that I was there to witness his magic in bringing about that 4-0 demolition. When I close my eyes I can still hear and feel that atmosphere on the famous old Kippax that day."

For the players too this was a remarkable day. Joe Corrigan revealed to the Junior Blues in 1978 how he felt at the time: "That was a tremendous time. I've known Colin ever since I've been at the club – in fact, he was in the side when I started. I respect and admire him for his courage and determination not to quit. He's some character, and deserves to be back. Just to see him come out for the second half of the game with Newcastle was a boost to all the team."

The City Chairman at the time was Peter Swales and, in the mid 1990s, he recalled how great the atmosphere was that day: "It was certainly the best ovation I've ever seen given to any player in any game. I've seen most of the England games over the last twenty years and all of City's. I've certainly seen plenty of tremendous occasions – players getting hat-tricks… United getting beat 5-1 – but the Bell reception was far and away the best I've ever heard a player get. Bell was the best, no question."

Pitch problems will 'meltaway'

MANCHESTER City may well be on the way to creating a precedent in this country if they go ahead with the installation of a revolutionary undersoil heating system at Maine Road.

For it will be the first time the Swedish "Meltaway" system has been used in this country.

The plan is the brainchild

by Steve Bott

of Eric Alexander, director in charge of the ground at Maine Road, who sees the system having many advantages, apart from keeping the ground frost and snow free.

Firstly it will not involve digging up the pitch to install. A piece of equipment called a mole pulls the one-inch diameter man-made pipes eight inches into the soil, but above the drainage. Afterwards the pitch is rolled and three or four days later you wouldn't know it had been done, said Mr Alexander.

He added: "It allows the moisture to go through into the drains whereas other systems melt the snow or ice on the surface leaving it there where it can turn to mud or freeze over again. Because of its depth it also means the ground can still be spiked."

GROWTH

The revolutionary part of the system is that it prevents frost setting in in the first place and stimulates the rate of growth of the grass and generally keeps the ground in condition.

The system is switched on at the end of October and kept on until the weather improves. It is thermostatically controlled and automatically follows changes in temperature. Grass starts to grow a little earlier after the dormant winter period because the soil is warm.

"The pipes are virtually an overgrown central heating system. It operates on hot water from either gas, electric or solid fuel — we will be using a gas boiler.

"The system also has its financial advantages. Costing between £45,000 and £60,000 it compares favourably to one electrical system

currently in use in this country which I heard cost £100,000 to install," said Mr Alexander.

The job would be done by the Sandbach firm, who deal with City's pitch maintenance as well as being installation agents for the heating manufacturers.

The firm dug up the Maine Road pitch in 1970 and put new drains in after it got very heavy.

"The soil was too rich and the water wasn't getting away. The drains were adequate, but the water just wasn't draining. Now it gets away without any difficulty. They also put automatic sprinklers in, one of the first in the country, which are capable of pouring 12,000 gallons of water on to the pitch in a relatively short space of time," said Mr Alexander.

REDUCE

"The system can't stop snow falling, ubt it would melt it. I've seen it reduce an eight-inch layer of snow to two inches in six hours.

"And it has had a very good grounding. It keeps streets, car parks and sports pitches clear throughout Scandinavia.

"Over the last three or four years I've looked at all sorts of undersoil heating systems.

This one interested me earlier, but it was a little too near the close season to do anything about it."

Mr Alexander added: "This bad winter we have had with all its postponements has lent a lot of strength to my argument.

"There is only one thing that might lead to criticism of the system. The last two bad winters have been 16 years apart. Therefore many people would say it was a bad investment to spend £60,000 on something that was only going to repay such an outlay once every 16 years.

"But it's not just a case of keeping the pitch frost free, it's also keeping the pitch in good condition at the same time."

Maine Memory

■ I have been attending Maine Road for over 30 years and used to stand on the Kippax from 12 years old – I'm now in my mid-forties - and get there at 1pm when the gates opened so we could try and get a good view. The Kippax was always my favourite because of the atmosphere. The 1976 League Cup semi-final against Middlesbrough was a special night. We overcame a one-nil loss from the first leg, playing superb football on a brilliant night for the City and then we went on to win the cup itself!

The other key memory from this period was Dave Watson's headed goal in the 2-1 victory against Ipswich on 2/4/77. I was behind him when he ran in at speed for a corner and nearly broke the net with his header that won the game... the best goal I have ever seen at Maine Road.

Mark Chung

Maine Memory

■ I suppose my best memory has to be the goal I scored against Ipswich in April 1977. City and Ipswich were second and third in the League, and were both putting considerable pressure on Liverpool. We couldn't afford to lose, and Peter Barnes sent a great ball in. I met it about eight feet in the air and headed it in from about twelve yards out. Mick Mills said that I'd rose up and headed it in before he'd even had chance to move. We won the match 2-1 and ended up runners-up that year to Liverpool, missing the title by a point.

Dave Watson (1975-79)

Colin Bell hangs up his boots
in the home dressing room
after announcing his
retirement in August 1979.

Maine Memory

■ I remember going to a First Division match in the late '70s. After a liquid lunch I was stood right at the back of the Kippax with a great view and a bursting bladder. The ref was still blowing for half-time and I was off - first out of the stand, first down the steps, first into the toilets. Pick your spot! Bliss! Heaven! Ladysmith and Mafeking had got nothing on me! I was aware of the bog filling up around and behind me; but nothing would make me abandon my place until the last drop of lunch had been shaken into the atmosphere.

At last I was ready - and I looked down.... Pee was flying past me on both sides – several streams, at different heights - as well as between my legs. The punters must have been quick on the draw and taking aim the instant they saw even a square centimetre of wall in front of them, standing four, five, six feet away. I have to say in fairness - not a drop wet my jeans: they were better shots than the City forwards that day. But I didn't dare move until the last one had finished. I might have been the first man in, but I was also the last to leave!

Phil Williams

Ten Streets were named after players and those streets will remain long after Maine Road has been demolished. The players selected were: Horace Barnes, Eric Brook, Tommy Browell, Sam Cookson, Sam Cowan, Tommy Johnson, Jimmy McMullan, Billy Meredith, Frank Swift, Fred Tilson and Max Woosnam. Councillor Harold Collins, a United fan, was the man City claimed was responsible for the idea.

In 1979 City made one of their most innovative moves when they paid £45,000 for a Swedish undersoil heating system called 'Meltaway'. At that time football clubs were experimenting with many different systems, but none had considered the benefits of talking to companies based in countries well used to snow and ice problems. City Director Eric Alexander met representatives who were able to demonstrate how the system operated in Scandinavia: "Over there they used to heat the car parks of hospitals and the like, and this company had developed a system whereby they took waste material and generated the heated water for the pipes. It was very economical and, I suppose in today's terminology, very eco-friendly. We saw great potential but due to various reasons we were unable to benefit from the use of waste energy and so had to use boilers and the like to heat the water.

"Nevertheless, it was still a great innovation and one which led to our views being sought by many, many clubs."

Bernard Halford feels the system helped the club enormously: "We could immediately guarantee the game would be played no matter how bad the weather. So the cost of programmes, catering and all those other expenses that come about from abandoned games didn't affect us again. It was great. The only down side in my eyes was that the piping was installed in such a way that the entire pitch would have to be heated. That probably sounds sensible, but once in a while only the Platt Lane end would be frozen, or another area would need attention. Had we been able to section it off across the pitch we would have been able to apply heat in one or two places when needed, instead of everywhere. We'd have saved some further money that way. But no matter what we say about the system, it has to be stressed that this really was a major boost to the club and it was the envy of football."

At the time City boasted there were about 16 miles of pipes, nine inches below the surface, and the life expectancy of the system was fifty years – circumstances meant it only needed 25!

By the summer of 1981 Maine Road claimed to have a capacity of 52,600 with 26,500 seats. It had each

Maine Memory

■ Mud! That's my overriding memory of the classic 6th round replay at Maine Road between City and Everton, during our 1981 cup run. In my first regular year at Maine Road I thought I'd got used to the fortnightly trudge from Halls of Residence in Salford - dodging the little United oiks on Littleton Road, refuelling at a chippy near Piccadilly, then the remaining trudge to the Shrine, with an ale or two en route. And back again. Reckon it was 10 miles all told for the round trip - all to avoid the bus fare. How my friends used to laugh.

But the night of 11th March 1981 changed all that. We'd somehow sneaked a draw at Goodison and, prized ticket in hand, this was my big chance to see us have a pop at glory. Manchester had served up its finest specially for me - dark, scowling clouds and wet, wet, wet! By the time I'd made my way as far as Whitworth Park, it felt like I was carrying 30lbs excess in clinging, wet clothes - and the park had become Manchester's first aquatic theme park into the bargain. My Everton supporting friends were unimpressed.

Rarely has the Kippax seemed so welcoming. A huddle of steaming humanity, generating its own Special K warmth. A buzz to match the Liverpool League Cup semi a few weeks earlier and, outside this warm haven, a real sod of a pitch. Mud in the middle, mud at each end, rain sheeting in, water table tipping over at the touchlines. It was made for us. And so it proved. A combination of the ball stuck in the goalmouth, flicked-on near-post headers from corners, water splashing all over the shop, and Bobby McDonald in his best game ever for City, condemned the Toffees to a sticky end. With the League Cup run ending in valiant defeat, and the FA Cup semi now looming these seemed the best of times.

The walk back was just as wet. But it didn't matter. My Everton friends never forgave me and forced me to buy a bus ticket for some of the journey back - a legacy that lasted for the remainder of my time in Salford. I've still got that mud-spattered, tatty old 6th round ticket and, looking at it again today, I know that something magical will be lost for ever when we leave Maine Road.

Simon Taylor

Maine Memory

■ My first memory was of City beating Burnley 2-0 in October 1976. I was 12 and went with my two uncles, eldest sister and brother. It all seemed so big I could hardly see over anybody in the Kippax. The noise was fantastic and the atmosphere electric. I can remember the smell of Bovril at the side of the pitch. The honesty of people passing money down through the crowd, getting their drink and change back has strangely remained with me. I guess that the honesty of being a blue and not doing to others that you don't want done to yourself epitomises what it is like to be CTID. At the end of the game a Burnley fan threw his scarf into our side of the stand. I kept it for a while as a trophy. I live in Norwich now, but my son is a Junior Blue and his middle name is Peter after Peter Barnes. Maybe one day I will get to meet my hero and son's namesake! Carrow Road just doesn't hit the spot, if you know what I mean.

Phil Hume

side of the ground covered and was regarded as one of England's premier venues. The Kippax had a reputation as a passionate, noisy stand, while the rather out-dated Platt Lane stand now housed younger supporters – Junior Blues and the like, their families and pensioners. It was also beginning to house an element who saw the opportunities it presented for aiming abuse towards away fans. The impressive North Stand housed families who could afford the additional expense, while the Main Stand remained the preserve of the club's wealthiest support.

The club were proud of the venue, but significant developments were also occurring during this period at other grounds – Wolves had spent £2m on their 9,500 capacity John Ireland Stand; Aston Villa had developed their North Stand; and Nottingham Forest had created a £2.5m East Stand. Each of these stands contained executive boxes and afforded better corporate facilities than Maine Road could offer. With a cup final appearance in 1981 and an expectation that Maine Road and Manchester City would always rank amongst the best in the country, it was clear the club had to consider giving the ground a major facelift. The summer of 1981 was spent considering the options.

Crowd Control

■ Crowd safety was a very serious issue for Maine Road throughout its existence. It should have been the number one concern, but there were various times when spectator safety took a backseat. Sometimes this was simply because it was not perceived as an issue, for example during the 1930s when supporters were packed in. At other times the emphasis was very much on controlling fans' behaviour rather than ensuring their safety.

City were no different to the majority of clubs in these situations but, as Maine Road was for much of its existence one of – if not the – biggest League stadium, the issue was significant.

Images appearing in publications today show supporters during the 1920s as happy, flat-cap wearing people. They rarely show photos of disgruntled fans, or print stories of fans causing problems. Even the scenes at Wembley's first cup final in 1923 focus on the role of one white police horse controlling in excess of 120,000 people. The impression given is that fans were easily controlled, but this is not entirely accurate. The Wembley crowd, for instance, was shepherded by many mounted policemen –

black and white footage doesn't easily pick out the darker horses – while fans at all grounds would on occasion break down gates to gain access to watch their team. City's old Hyde Road stadium suffered at the hands of determined fans on several occasions. Gates were smashed open, while other supporters climbed into the ground via ropes and other means.

Maine Road however was less easy to access, and for the first few years of its existence crowd disorder was not evident. Instead the problems were all about capacity management.

During the stadium's first fifteen years the key aim appeared to be to pack as many supporters as possible onto the terraces. The record crowd of 1934 became famous in some quarters because fans said they 'got in but couldn't get out', suggesting the stadium was too overcrowded. No one really worried about the size of crowds and issues of safety – or at least, nationally, little was said. Then on 9th March 1946 the Burnden Park disaster saw 33 spectators die in a crush. According to the *Manchester Evening News* this was the result of around 200 to 300

people, many of whom were servicemen, charging through a gate to gain admittance. The newspaper simply stated: "Possibly the war has left some people with less respect for law than they used to have." It's hard to explain the reason behind this comment, and it may be the people of Bolton and Stoke (the two competing sides when the disaster occurred) were as angry at those comments as the population of Merseyside were when they read *The Sun's* wild accusations following the Hillsborough Disaster.

Naturally, an enquiry followed and clubs were now forced to consider safety. At Maine Road little changed because the stadium was still relatively new and it was felt the freedom to move around the three large terraced areas – note Platt Lane was still terraced at this stage despite being roofed – gave everyone the scope to avoid the more crowded areas.

It wasn't until the sixties that the emphasis started to move more towards controlling behaviour. Platt Lane attendee Lawrence Ivory remembers his

first sight of poor behaviour at the ground: "Football hooliganism had not quite reared its ugly head in the late 1960s. When watching City take on the Leeds team of Bremner et al in 1970, some Leeds supporters were messing about in the Platt Lane. They were burning something, probably a programme, and were waving it around. A City devotee - a middle-aged woman - decided enough was enough and sorted them out by giving them a good hiding with her umbrella, much to the amusement of the home fans!"

Supporters were still allowed to mix freely with opposition followers and, in general, the atmosphere between rival fans was good-natured, but that began to change at many clubs around this time. A hooligan element had started to follow most teams, and their main aim during the late sixties and early seventies was to occupy the area where City's more vocal support would stand, so the Scoreboard End first, and later the Kippax, became the two places most likely to see some form of confrontation.

Games with Everton became a little tense during the mid to late sixties. Simon

Clarke remembers a meeting from November 1966: "1966/7 was my first full season as a City fan, having 'made my debut' the previous April at the home match against Bolton Wanderers. My dad and I weren't going to all City's matches, so this was to be the fourth top-flight game I'd seen, but it was clear long before we got anywhere near the stadium that this one was going to be different. Everton fans were everywhere. I had a City rosette pinned to my coat, which the bus conductor commented on. 'You're outnumbered today' he said. 'The top deck's all Everton. There's three of them got a banner up there'. Sure enough, Maine Road was fuller than I'd ever seen it as we took our seats behind the goal at the Platt Lane end.

"In those days, home and away fans were still not segregated, though usually relations between the two sets of fans seemed cordial enough. At the FA Cup tie against Leicester later that season, the Leicester fans arrived late, and I remember great efforts being made on the Kippax to part the crowd enough for their young lads to squeeze through and take up places along the wall at the

A WARNING TO ALL SPECTATORS

IN AN attempt to stamp out the continuing nuisance of young fans running onto the Maine Road pitch, especially after the final whistle, City have decided to investigate the matter legally, with a view to taking out a civil action against any offenders who are caught.

"We have taken steps in this direction and it is certain to be the strict line we will pursue in the near future. This is why we wish to warn all fans, particularly the younger ones, that the club will prosecute acts of trespass on the Maine Road pitch" said club secretary Bernard Halford.

He added: "Fortunately we have not suffered from the same amounts of vandalism which have been afflicting many other clubs, but the invasion of the pitch by youngsters is becoming a major problem and unless it is curbed it could have serious consequences.

"Incidents of this nature could lead to steps being taken by the Football Association against the club because they

are determined to stamp on the practice.

"The last thing we want here is any form of fencing around the ground — yet measures like this could be forced upon us if we do not find a cure for this problem.

"We have the full co-operation of the police in this matter and they wish us to stress that they will apprehend any offenders they catch.

"This is why City are asking all our young fans to refrain from running onto the playing area, particularly at the end of matches. We would like the assistance of parents and adults to stop them, if at all possible.

"This nuisance is now getting out of hand, and it does have dangerous possibilities for the players and officials."

We can only emphasise what the club secretary says:

BE WARNED . . . or you could, as an offender, find yourself involved in a serious civil action.

November 1966: A sign of the times as police line up to prevent the toilet roll throwing Everton supporters from continuing their disorder.

front alongside their City counterparts. Later still, at the West Brom game, Dad spent most of the second half chatting to a couple of Albion fans, all three of them being only half interested in what was happening on the pitch. This Everton game was different, though. We were four or five rows back from the front of the stand. The rows in front of us were all occupied by Evertonians, mostly young men probably still in their teens. They were not so well disposed to the massed ranks of the City fans behind them, and a tense atmosphere built up. This was added to over the course of the afternoon by events on the pitch.

"I can't remember much detail from the match. Everton seemed to have more of the ball. City were determined not to let them do anything useful with it. Goal chances were few. Alan Ball became increasingly irate, to the extent that at one point, protesting after yet another heavy challenge, I was convinced he

was going to take a swing at the referee. He didn't, of course, he just looked as though he would.

"With this being November, it got dark long before the end of the game, which only served to heighten the atmosphere still further. Then the tension exploded, as Colin Bell timed his arrival in the Everton box perfectly to collect a low centre angled in from the right and sweep it low first time past the right hand of the diving West, right in front of us into the Platt Lane end goal. The City fans erupted, the Evertonians in the front few rows turned and there were some angry exchanges between the two sets of fans. I can well believe there were fights in other parts of the ground, although it didn't quite get physical where we were. Things settled again, briefly, as Everton's strenuous efforts to force an equaliser took the attention of the watching crowd. Everton won a corner on the right. The kick was played in to the near post,

from where Jimmy Gabriel despatched it to the back of Harry Dowd's net. Up went the Scousers, only to be left gawping in disbelief as the referee made them take the corner again instead of pointing to the middle for City to re-start. No-one knew why. Dad's best guess was that the ball hadn't been correctly placed when Everton took the corner, but, since it was down the other end of the ground, none of us could tell. Not that I cared that much. City were still leading, and that was what counted. The re-taken corner was also played in to the near post, but this time City were ready for it and Everton couldn't score.

"Dad and I left before the end, Dad saying we could leave early because City were going to win. It was only much later that I began to understand that he was worried about trouble at the final whistle and didn't want to get caught up in it. At the time I just thought he understood football so well he could tell

Everton wouldn't equalise. We got straight onto a bus and away from the ground quicker than usual, so it was worth it. And Everton didn't score."

Often away support would try to be first into the ground en masse and would choose the location where they felt the younger, vocal home support would normally gather. This would then lead to City fans charging the away support out of 'their patch'. Supporter Tony O'Grady remembers one such encounter: "Before segregation there was often conflict between home and away fans before the match. I used to hang around the gates waiting for them to open at first and one day just after we got in about 300 Birmingham City fans came on to the Kippax. There was only a relatively small number of City fans on the terracing and Birmingham seemed to see this as their chance to take the Kippax. They chased the early fans from one end of the Kippax to the other. The City lads then chased them back across the stand before Birmingham tried again. It continued like this for ages until the number of City fans increased to a number Birmingham couldn't cope with."

Many fans talk of this early form of tribalism occurring in the pre-segregation days, but interestingly little is said about the role of the police. It appears they allowed this behaviour to continue to some extent, although there were occasions when they did act. Certainly throughout football, hooliganism was becoming a hot topic by the end of the sixties and clubs were expected to improve the situation.

At Maine Road it was decided high-profile games would have a form of segregation. Tony O'Grady: "When we played United it was decided to separate the fans by putting a rope from the back of the Kippax to the front wall. Police manned the rope to separate the fans, but it was hardly the best segregation. I suppose it worked to some extent. But there were a lot of odd scenes, particularly at

derby matches. I remember when we were two goals down in a derby, a City fan couldn't take it any more and just jumped over the segregation line and into the United area. A couple of minutes later he was stretchered out. At another derby the United fans were throwing acid bottles into the Kippax. It was a real battlefield at times."

Due to City's success other teams' supporters would come to Maine Road looking for trouble and at times the atmosphere could be grim. Inevitably the club took the decision to divide the Kippax with a permanent barrier and on 27th September 1975 the Manchester derby became the first game to use the new segregation. The initial barrier was an iron railing which stretched from the back of the Kippax to the front roughly a third of the way along the stand. It still meant home and away supporters could position themselves within a yard of each other but at least it was a start. Remarkably, though this permanent barrier was still not used for every match.

The feeling of the club was that to segregate fans was a distressing action. The initial design of Maine Road had allowed freedom to roam around the terraces and so the new barrier meant fans could no longer move from one end of the pitch to the other. It was generally accepted a large number of Maine Road attendees enjoyed moving from one end of the Kippax to the other to watch their side attack. The barrier restricted movement and limited freedom. The club despised that approach and would have preferred not to have used it.

As well as the game with United, matches with Leeds, Aston Villa and Everton were the first to see the gates between the two sections closed.

For FA Cup semi-finals segregation varied depending on the competing teams. When Liverpool faced Everton in 1977 journalist Brian James wrote: "Segregation of the fans is part of the semi-final tradition, but never has the

Perimeter fencing at the front of the Kippax meant an obscured view of the game for many fans.

A MAJOR CONCERN

It is a sad state of affairs that we have to devote the front cover of the Manchester City match magazine to project another serious warning to all spectators who attend matches at Maine Road. The concern within the club about spectators trespassing on the pitch has to be brought home in this manner because of the further repercussions which have followed last month's "invasion" of the playing area by City followers.

That unthinking act, which may well have been an expression of jubilation after the Full Members' Cup success over Sunderland, has caused more swift action to be taken by the authorities and the full impact of all these measures will be in evidence as a permanent eye-sore by the end of this year.

We have had to spend £50,000 on the erection of a fencing around the perimeter of the ground. It is a drain on City's resources which need never have happened but for the thoughtless, reckless behaviour of some supporters who felt justified invading the pitch at the end of the game. IF THIS TYPE OF ANTIC DOES NOT STOP THEN THE SITUATION FOR EVERYONE WHO WATCHES FOOTBALL AT CITY WILL GET FAR WORSE.

Unless this behaviour is stamped out we are going to have a ground looking like Alcatraz prison, which a great shame for the club, for such a fine stadium and for the thousands of followers who do conduct themselves properly at home games.

The strengthened fencing had already been installed in front of the Kippax terraces and in front of the Platt Lane end of the ground. Today it should be completed and operational at the North Stand end of the local stadium. By the end of the year we will have, by order of the local authority, completed the entire fencing of Maine Road. The Main Stand will then be fenced in.

Fencing has been re-inforced and been built to a height of 2.4 metres. If this is not effective then we may well have to increase the fencing height to 4.4 metres (around 14 feet). And if there are still "fans" who consider this a challenge to be scaled then the height will be increased yet again.

We have also been warned that any breach of the fencing perimeter will result in additional modifications being needed and the top of the fencing will have to be raked back to provide an even greater obstacle to would-be invaders. But who wants to be caged-in to watch a football match.

We have consistently requested YOUR co-operation. 'Keep off the Pitch' has been a constant plea—but some "fans" have chosen to ignore us and in the process have needlessly cost the club a lot of money and a great deal of inconvenience and spoiled things for the genuine supporters.

We estimate almost 200 "fans" ran onto the pitch after the Sunderland game just over one month ago. It has caused untold problems and made life even more difficult with the authorities who are following strict Government instruction about the safety and condition of sports stadia throughout the land.

There was no justification for that "invasion". Indeed, there is none for any such act of trespass. If the guilty wish to justify their stupid behaviour by claiming the deed was an expression of their joy at the result let us say straight away that their foolishness should be a cause of concern to themselves as well as to City. Just one untoward act from a spectator on the pitch could lead to the closure of this stadium. Be aware of that. And if you genuinely support City you will help us to improve standards of conduct at our games.

The manpower costs have risen astronomically in recent times because of the needs to ensure acceptable behaviour. We will be paying £100,000 over this present season to the police for providing resources to make the ground a safe place. These overtime costs could be avoided and the money could be spent on proper football matters—if EVERYBODY supported City and our aims.

More problems mean more police and more stewards. It will mean more fencing. We need the help of our public. We need YOUR help. If it is not forthcoming then Heaven help what will be the view we can offer our fans for watching football in the future.

MANCHESTER CITY v COVENTRY CITY

'split' seemed so clear as today. Looking across the pitch to the opposite terrace [the Kippax] you see a six-foot wide no-man's land running from top to bottom... only patrolling policemen move there. Everything to the left of that mark is red... banners, flags, rosettes, scarves. And everything to the right is blue. If there are neutrals in the ground they can only be behind you, in the stand."

By the end of the seventies, segregation was permanent while a fence was also erected at the front of the stand (between the white perimeter wall and the pitch) to prevent fans from invading the pitch. Also a wire mesh had been erected at the end of the Platt Lane Stand to prevent those in the seated stand throwing material towards the terracing.

The away section during the eighties contained a series of fences and gates and, depending on the opposition, it was possible for the club to hand over the entire Kippax/Platt Lane Corner and the first third of the Kippax if away support was large enough. Likewise the club could restrict away support to the top corner of the Kippax Stand, and leave home fans in the bottom section of the segregated area and the open corner.

Access to the away section was via turnstiles at the Thornton Road end of the Kippax, and then within the public area between the turnstiles and the stand, supporters were divided by a tall narrow fence, although initially temporary barriers had been used.

The whole dynamics of watching football on the terraces at Maine Road changed as a result of this enforced segregation. In many ways separating the fans increased the territorial chanting and the view that the Kippax was a battleground. Supporters on either side of the segregation fence would throw items at their opponents – these could be anything, stones, darts, socks filled with material or coins – and folk on both sides of the divide would be injured. Some would be innocent victims, while others would class it as a battle wound.

While this was going on, the police would man the line looking for potential troublemakers and try to keep the peace. Often they would move into the stand and remove supporters they felt were guilty in some way.

The section of the Kippax behind the tunnel closest to the away fans became known as Chanters' Corner, and this is where an extremely large volume of fans would congregate. In the main this group would consist of City's more vociferous fans supplemented by many younger fans keen to graduate. Watching any match from this corner provided a tremendous feeling of belonging, and the atmosphere was certainly very, very powerful, but it could also be a dangerous place. The volume of support was too great for the area and so injuries were more commonplace. It was also the place opposition supporters would target and with the police (or 'Dibble' as they were nicknamed after the character in Top Cat) pro-actively looking for offenders, people were more likely to be arrested here than elsewhere in the stadium.

There was also a certain attraction for younger fans in Chanters' Corner. Julian Cooke remembers being there as a boy during the mid-1970s: "I was 12 when I started attending the Kippax and my older mates would take me near the back of the stand, towards where the away fans used to be, in the corner nearest the Platt Lane. They'd sit me on the crush barrier at about 1.45pm and I'd still be there three hours later, despite the swaying crowd behind me. Like lots of lads of my age I seemed to perfect a technique of leaning on the shoulders of those stood in front, in order to stay on the barrier and see the match, that and clinging on for dear life. I usually fell off when we scored - which was quite often in those days and would be lifted back on to the barrier by my friends. From this vantage point not only could I see the game but the away fans too and would happily join in with the taunts of the visitors, safe in the knowledge I was far enough away from them not to be in any danger. "

Another fan, Jeffrey Cheetham, remembers this area being known as 'The Sways' due to the pushing and shoving of the crowd. He was there in 1977 to witness Colin Bell's return.

By the mid-eighties, pitch invasions after a number of high-profile games were common, most notably Luton in 1983, Charlton in 1985 and Sunderland (Full Members' Cup) also in 1985, and the club increased fencing around the entire stadium. The whole of the white perimeter wall was now topped with a perimeter fence and viewing was severely restricted. At times in the early eighties fencing had been erected in front of the Platt Lane and North Stand for high-profile matches. Again the club was reluctant to make it permanent but was forced to over time. Then in December 1985 the club devoted the entire front page of the City v Coventry programme to the prospect of enlarging the size of fencing. Under the heading "A Major Concern" the club stated: "Fencing has been re-inforced and built to a height of 2.4 metres. If this is not effective, then we may well have to increase the fencing height to 4.4 metres (around 14 feet). And if there are still 'fans' who consider this a challenge to be scaled then the height will be increased yet again.

"We have also been warned that any breach of the fencing perimeter will result in additional modifications being needed and the top of the fencing will have to be raked back to provide an even greater obstacle to would-be invaders. But who wants to be caged-in to watch a football match?"

In 1985 the situation throughout football was grave; the Heysel disaster, rioting at Luton and at Birmingham, and many, many other stories of football violence made the Government determined to act. Even the Bradford fire was inadvisably often lumped into debates about crowd control. Margaret Thatcher's Government insisted clubs take action and membership schemes and increased fencing became the norm, but still more was demanded. Ken Bates at Chelsea suggested,

The Blues second goal in the 3-3 derby of 1990. Note the ridiculously large 'no man's land' between rival fans.

and then installed, an electric fence. Fortunately he didn't turn it on, but it was clear the view across Britain was that English League clubs had to increase segregation, fencing and security. All fans were labelled trouble-makers.

Supporters responded to the negativity by publishing their views and the fanzine industry was created, but on the terraces fans were viewed as animals at all grounds. During the early eighties away supporters wishing to sit would be placed in various areas of the Main Stand and for a while 'J' Block (the section between the Main and North Stands) was home to seated away fans. Then in 1985 the Platt Lane Stand was given over in its entirety to away support.

Prior to this the make-up of the Platt Lane had started to change. Due to its proximity to away support in the Kippax, home fans interested in baiting the opposition began sitting here. Often, before the final whistle, a large group of youthful Platt Lane-enders would leave the stand – a very visible act at times – with the sole intention of ambushing away supporters. The passageway behind the Platt Lane Stand became a key battleground.

After 1985 increased policing and segregation seemed to occur with every game and for many it was not a pleasant experience. Attendances reduced as a result. For those in Chanters' Corner there existed a strange philosophy. Basically, they felt they were protecting the honour of the club and were

up against the away team's supporters and the police.

The police presence became increasingly visible. During games a large contingent would march into the ground. As they paraded around the edge of the stands, Chanters' Corner would erupt into song with the majority whistling and humming the tune made famous by Laurel and Hardy. Others would laugh at the sombre-faced police officers, mocking them with a tune familiar to all as representing ineptness.

While the atmosphere at other football grounds worsened, Blues fans came together. By Christmas 1988 the famous banana craze had become a major event with Maine Road a focal point for fun. With every home game the number of inflatable objects increased. The largest display came at Stoke on Boxing Day 1988, but Maine Road was the epicentre of the fad and promotion in 1989 will always be linked with fun on the terraces. By the time of the Manchester derby in September 1989 the craze had subsided somewhat but it

helped show not all fans were hooligans - something the Government found hard to accept - until tragedy struck in Sheffield.

Football faced one of its blackest days in April 1989 when the Hillsborough disaster occurred. The whole subject of fencing, membership schemes and other initiatives was reviewed. Unfortunately, it took a disaster of this magnitude to force the authorities to act, and ultimately the decision was taken that fencing had to come down. Naturally, this impacted every ground.

In April 1992 City announced fencing would be removed from in front of the Main Stand at the season's end, but also stressed the club would only be allowed to remove the fences in front of the other stands if behaviour was good.

The following March the new Platt Lane – or Umbro Stand as it was initially titled – was opened with a Cup match against Tottenham. It wasn't fenced and, with City fans feeling desperate, supporters rushed on to the field from the new stand to interrupt play.

The media claimed this was a cynical ploy by City supporters to have the match abandoned, but the truth was much more complex. Put simply, Maine Road customers were far from happy with the direction of the club and this was a signal they wanted change.

Despite the pitch invasion, the fences were removed from the North Stand and when the new Kippax was erected they were not included in the design. Attending football matches became a more pleasant experience, although there were still occasional problems. When City were relegated in 2001 supporters charged onto the field from the North Stand as the game entered its final minutes. The match never lasted the full ninety minutes but the referee, perhaps fearing further problems, quickly blew his whistle to end it - the ugliest finish seen at the ground for several years.

More recently, matchday control involved significant use of CCTV cameras to monitor the crowd. Club Stadium and Safety Officer Peter Fletcher was totally responsible for crowd control within the stadium complex and worked closely with police, opposing clubs and other local authorities to ensure each match was policed and stewarded in a manner appropriate for that game. At Maine Road, from the Stadium Control room behind 'J' block in between the Main and North Stands, Fletcher and his team were aware of all potential hotspots and utilised all available resources - staff, the police, and technology - to

ensure these areas were well managed. A sophisticated set-up allowed every area of the ground to be monitored.

As any Maine Road regular will appreciate, the most obvious areas to police were those closest to the away fans in the North Stand, however the games with the highest risk meant other areas of the ground might require greater control. For example, during the final Maine Road derby, additional police and stewarding were present in the Main and North Stands because it was understood United supporters had managed to obtain tickets within the home sections. The club's policy was to find those supporters and evict them as they represented far more of a concern than those sitting in the away section. The entire operation went well and, as far as the stadium and club property was concerned, the derby proved one of the safest since the late sixties.

From a safety point of view, although crowd violence and hooliganism is still present in football, the actions of the club since the late 1990s have focused on preventing situations occurring rather than having to react. Maine Road in its final season was arguably the safest it had been since the pre-hooliganism days.

Even the final League match passed with very few incidents or problems. In fact most supporters had given up all hope of invading the pitch or ripping up seats by the time the entertainment had ended!

This pitch invasion by home fans brought an early end to City's final game of the 2000-01 relegation season.

Junior Blues

THE Junior Blues club became a model for young supporter involvement throughout football, and no one connected with the original idea could have predicted how important it would become. Who initiated the concept is open to debate. Like many great ideas there are usually a number of people responsible for their crystalisation. Over thirty years on from the initial concept it would be unfair to state categorically who was responsible for first suggesting it but according to a 1984 interview with Harry Godwin, City's chief scout who became known as 'Uncle Harry' to a generation of Junior Blues, the origins of the Junior Blues club lay in a letter he received: "It was formed following an idea by a man in the north-east – Albert Howell. Ian Niven had just started at the club and got involved. I was also involved from the start. Albert suggested 'The Young Citizens' club'. I took the letter into the general office and we had a little meeting. Johnny Hart was involved as well. It started in a very simple way."

From within the club, as well as Johnny Hart and Harry Godwin, directors Bill Adams, Tony Miles and Peter Swales were supportive, but the key City director from the beginning was Ian Niven. He was the prime figure and continued to play his part in the running of the organisation right up to the move to the new stadium.

The club was created during 1973 with Francis Lee as the first president. The 5th December 1973 programme for the League Cup tie with York City carried the following message: "The response to the Junior Blues Club has been fantastic. At the time of writing we have received nearly 300 membership applications. You can still join. Just send your full name, address and date of birth to the Junior Blues Club, Manchester City F.C. Also enclose a 20p Postal Order as the membership fee and you will receive a membership card and a club badge within a few days."

"It promises to be a thriving club with Saturday morning film shows; Christmas Party; 'Top of the Form' quiz; Regular Competitions; Chances to meet the players; A mascot of the day for every home match. And there are plenty of other activities planned. So join now and don't miss the fun!"

According to Roger Reade, Junior Blues Club secretary and later Chairman: "The initial club didn't offer a great deal in terms of what it provided – a membership card was more or less it – but it did prove the interest. I was interested and because of that I managed to get involved. In 1974 I became the secretary while another man involved was Richard Sutton who was Chairman of the Junior Blues club. It quickly became a model for every club.

"In 1976 we organised the first rally. We booked the Free Trade Hall, and you've got to understand that at that point we had no idea who would turn up, or whether there would be any interest at all. We spent ages planning it. It was a very nerve-wracking time. Then on the day itself we were at the Free Trade Hall and nipped out to see if anyone was waiting and was astonished – the queue stretched as far as we could see. Thousands turned up!"

The Free Trade Hall rally was a very popular event

Right: Richard Sutton and Roger Reade plan the 1976 Junior Blues extravaganza at the Free Trade Hall. The 'Manchester en bleu' magazine pinned to the notice board was an article on City which appeared in French publication *l'equippe*.

Below right: Mike Summerbee (PC Wee Long), Tony Book (Emperor Tyfoo), Francis Lee (PC Wee Non) and Joe Corrigan (the Genie of the Lamp) pictured in rehearsals for the 1972 pantomime production of Aladdin. There were six performances beginning the week of January 24th, but the two policemen, the Emperor and Genie were given the Friday night off so they could concentrate on the following day's game with Wolves!

Below: Nigel Rothband was a regular helper at Junior Blues meetings during the 1970s.

typically City, so we decided to get the players down there and lots of special guests and make this a great event.

"In the end we had John Stapleton, who was already known as a BBC presenter by this point, compering the jamboree, and almost everyone connected with the club you can imagine. Roy Clarke put in a phenomenal amount of work, but I suppose everybody did."

Little and Large, who were major stars by this point, provided a special message on a giant screen, while the real stars as far as the children were concerned were Tony Book and his playing squad. Joe Corrigan, the Junior Blues President, was very popular, while music was provided by a band called Harmony Blend. According to the City programme in August 1978: "The Harmony Blend pop group flew in specially from their show in Jersey with the 'world premiere' of a brand new City theme song. They look like having a major hit on their hands when their new record 'Blue City' reaches the record racks. To the catchy tune of 'Uno Paloma Blanca' – a gigantic chart success of recent years – they have injected words which went down a treat. And by the end of the show they had everybody singing along."

Another highlight of the event was the banners and signs created by young supporters. One read 'Corrigan Stops Concorde', while others said 'Knickers To The Rest, City Are The Best', and 'The Futcher Looks Bright At Maine Road'. A seven year old girl, Heidi Ward, was present that day. In June 2003 she remembered: "My dad and I had made a banner out of polystyrene with players' names and pictures on. We used the letters from the words 'Junior Blues' and put a typical City eleven next to them. There were so many banners there we stood little chance of winning, but we were surprised to see in the next match programme a photo of us and our banner at the event. The funny thing was neither my Dad nor I knew the photo was being taken and so you can only see the sides of our heads."

and two years later Roger, who had become Chairman of the Junior Blues at this point, and the rest of the committee organised their next big event: "Meetings by this point were very popular but after the success of the Free Trade Hall rally we decided we had to do something perhaps a little bigger. That's when we decided to do something at Belle Vue. The Belle Vue King's Hall gave us the potential to do something

The Junior Blues continued to grow and develop with regional clubs being set up. Roger Reade: "I think most supporters' branches set up their own Junior Blues, and the rally became a focal point for each group. It was an incredible sight when you stood back and saw banners with names of different places - not just British places either."

By this time Jessie Ward was one of the club's most recognisable figures. Jessie was an influential – some would say the most influential - person behind the Junior Blues for most of its first thirty years. She brought great direction to the organisation and was clearly one of the main reasons it developed and became such an important area of the club. Others to have played a key part include Nigel Rothband, Harry Godwin, Roy Clarke, Gary Lewis and Liz Douglas, plus of course Ian Niven and the original committee.

Many players have been involved over the years, the more popular being Francis Lee, Joe Corrigan, David White and, in recent times, Shaun Wright-Phillips who took part in the 2003 pantomime, just as Lee and Corrigan had thirty years earlier in the days before the Junior Blues had been officially formed.

As Maine Road entered its final weeks, the Junior Blues remained an important arm of the club.

Rock the Stadium!

■ Maine Road became familiar as a major footballing venue, but it has also staged some of the biggest concerts in the country with performances by leading artists of the period. Many supporters are familiar with the concerts of the 1980s, but City's role as a music venue commenced in May 1974 with a performance by the leading pop idol of the period, DAVID CASSIDY.

Roy Clarke, City's former player and Social Club manager, was involved from the start: "We wanted to try something different. The Social Club had already proved very popular for a variety of acts but staging a pop concert on the pitch offered so much more."

Roy's wife Kath remembers how it all came about: "Roy put the David Cassidy idea to the club suggesting it would be very popular and would bring in quite a bit of income and possibly even a few new fans. Showaddywaddy were the support act."

Cassidy had already appeared at London's White City stadium but widespread hysteria at the venue led to poor crowd control and a serious injury to 14-year-old fan Bernadette Whelan. Sadly, Bernadette died shortly after the Maine Road concert, but prior to Cassidy's performance in Manchester the media focused on crowd issues, and the plight of Bernadette Whelan was clearly at the forefront of thinking. City worked alongside the police and Cassidy's management team to determine what could be done to control the crowd and limit potential problems.

The anticipated attendance was 18,000 but the recent traumatic events in London deterred some from attending. Eventually it was revealed 10,500 had paid to see the event, while the club had brought in 400 stewards and 100 police. Considering the size of the crowd and the fact the audience was mostly comprised of teenage girls this was an astounding number. It certainly made the Manchester derby look like a teddy-bear's picnic in comparison.

According to journalist Ian Fowler: "Officials at Maine Road – where 10,500 screaming, banner-waving girls, some with anxious parents as escorts, packed the Main Stand – had mounted a massive security guard to ensure no repetition of London's White City show where there were 850 casualties. At the start of the show DJ Ed Stewart pleaded for good behaviour from the crowd – and he got it!

"The girls – aged between 11 and 16 – were outwitted as Cassidy raced to the stage disguised as an ambulanceman."

City secretary Bernard Halford remembers the concert well: "The stage was on the centre of the pitch and after the trouble in London we had to think long and hard about how we got Cassidy out on to the stage. The concert would have been off if we couldn't sort something out. Eventually we came up with the idea of dressing him up as a steward and he walked towards the stage through the crowd with other stewards. I think one or two photographers noticed but the girls didn't. We managed to get him on the stage, then he ripped off his steward's coat and the girls went crazy. It was nothing like a football crowd! They kept whooping and screaming. Mass hysteria I suppose you'd call it."

Cassidy had almost cancelled the concert for other reasons it was later revealed. After the London show Cassidy had been horse-riding and had fallen, injuring his back. With his back giving some pain the club and Cassidy's management considered the options and eventually club physio Freddie Griffiths was brought into action.

Griffiths: "I was called in about an hour before the concert was due to start because he was in pain and I found he had a damaged joint. I worked on him for about an hour and got him right. He seemed genuinely pleased afterwards and said, 'Gee, Freddie, I feel great'. His entourage said they had never seen him as mobile and relaxed as he was."

With Griffiths' soothing hands Cassidy was able to "gyrate around the stage for seventy minutes of non-stop action" according to the Manchester Evening News. His final song was 'It's all Over Now, Baby Blue'. Bernard Halford: "When the concert ended he jumped off the 8ft high stage and ran to the Kippax. He waved good bye and ran down one of the tunnels to a waiting car and that was it as far as the fans were concerned; he had gone."

City fan and former staff member Roger Reade remembers the concert: "This was a big event in everyone's eyes. Sure it wasn't a football match, but it was Maine Road and grabbed our attention because of that. It wasn't really known for grounds to stage events like this then … certainly not outside of London. I remember buying the newspaper the next morning and seeing a photo of David Cassidy singing on stage wearing a City shirt. That was a major boost to us at the time because Cassidy was the biggest pop star in the world. No ifs and maybes - he was it as far as pop was concerned and for him to be wearing our shirt meant a great deal whether you liked his music or not."

As concert-goers left the ground there were a few stories of crowd disorder - nothing of the magnitude of football violence, but there were still a few newsworthy scenes. A girl was attacked close to the ground as she waited for a bus. She was wearing Cassidy merchandise and according to newspaper reports a gang of youths terrorised her because she refused to hand over her pictures of Cassidy to them. It all seems a little surreal today, but it must be stressed at that time Cassidy-mania was immense.

Janice Monk, daughter of groundsman Stan Gibson, was present at the concert: "I remember the concert well because David Cassidy was the biggest pop star around at the time and, like all young women, I wanted to see him. The show was very, very good and afterwards I got to meet him but I must say my instincts changed when I met him. He seemed so young and nervous I suppose. He was like a little boy and he was no longer the major pop star we'd all gone to see. I think I wanted to mother him. I certainly felt sorry for him. He seemed to want to disappear into the scenery but being the big star he had to be the centre of attention. Eventually he went with my parents to our house next door to the ground. I suppose he

Oasis

Queen

David Bowie

Rolling Stones

Status Quo

Dire Straits

Rod Stewart

Jean Michel Jarre

David Cassidy

Guns N Roses

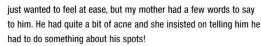

Above: Freddie Mercury of Queen, Status Quo and David Bowie.

Right: The pitch is engulfed with fans as Bowie plays in front of the Platt Lane Stand.

Below: The stage for the Guns N Roses concert was in the demolished Platt Lane end.

Bottom: It's every City fan's dream to play at Maine Road!

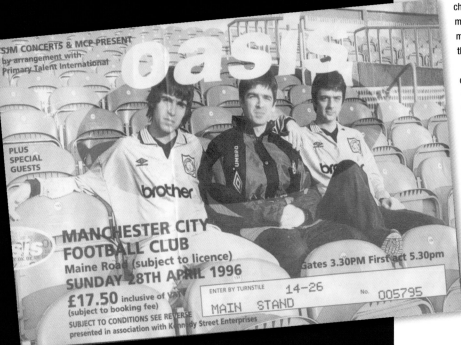

just wanted to feel at ease, but my mother had a few words to say to him. He had quite a bit of acne and she insisted on telling him he had to do something about his spots!

"I often wonder if he ever comes to Manchester and thinks about the time he spent talking with my parents. They treated him like a normal regular young man, whereas he was so used to being seen as a millionaire pop star. He seemed to like being normal for once."

After the concert Cassidy gave up touring. In fact he didn't tour again for approximately twenty-five years by which time his audience had grown up, and the type of venues he played were more traditional. At another gig in Manchester almost thirty years later he donned a City shirt again and reminded his audience of his 1974 performance; perhaps he really did remember the Gibsons.

The Maine Road concert should be seen as the largest Cassidy event in Britain.

In the ensuing years, rumours that other concerts would be staged at Maine Road often circulated but nothing ever came of them until 1985 when it was announced **QUEEN** and **STATUS QUO** would play there in July. From that point on the stadium became a recognised venue for leading stadium tours with **DAVID BOWIE**, **DIRE STRAITS**, **JEAN MICHEL JARRE**, **THE ROLLING STONES**, **ROD STEWART** and **GUNS N ROSES** all playing there.

Then, in April 1996, the concert City fans had been demanding came to Maine Road when **OASIS** performed two sell-out concerts. It was a dream come true for Noel and Liam Gallagher, but it was also a major moment for City fans and for the stadium. Noel Gallagher: "It was our place, wasn't it? So it was bound to be a bit special."

For most of these concerts the stage was erected in front of the stand at the Platt Lane end of the ground, but when Guns N Roses played there in June 1992 the stage was erected on the site of the old stand. This concert, more than any other, led to complaints from concert attendees and from local residents. Axl Rose and other band members went on stage approximately two hours late, while the litter left on the streets surrounding the stadium was considerable. Local residents complained to the council who responded: "We have cleaned up after a lot of concerts – but this is the worst we have had. The mess left by the concert goers was so big it is taking longer than it usually does to clean the place up."

According to Carl Johnston's review in the *Manchester Evening News* the concert was not Maine Road's best: "Two hours late and without the slightest hint of an apology, Axl Rose stormed on stage at Maine Road like a jet at take-off, and guitarist Slash roared in with a tidal wave of chords. The chanting crowd, their anger fuelled by the wait and an alcohol ban, surged forward.

"Axl, in trademark white underpants, spent more time changing than treading the boards. After an hour and 55 minutes it was all over. It wasn't value for money and mostly not that spectacular. Axl and Co can be better than this."

Another man who wasn't entirely happy with the concert was groundsman Stan Gibson. Janice Monk: "It's not that my dad was against the concerts themselves, it was more the effect on the pitch. No matter how they tried to protect it, it was always damaged. The weight of so many people on the pitch would press the turf, while items such as nails and screws from the stage rigging would be left on the pitch. Dad and the others had to clear it all up.

"He usually went to the concerts - I suppose part of him wanted to make sure they didn't do too much damage – and I remember him talking and drinking with Freddie Mercury and others. The after-show parties were always good and dad loved them, but the concerts were not something he particularly wanted to happen on the pitch. He had objected to the players training on there, so what chance did the singers have!"

The morning after... Stan Gibson was not a fan of these concerts!

Bernard Halford felt the concerts were important for a number of reasons: "By staging them at Maine Road we were able to raise vital income. It's no coincidence that the Queen concert came at a time when we were desperate to raise additional funds. Thankfully that concert went exceptionally well and I think it gave everyone a lift to some extent. I remember Freddie Mercury saying it was one of the best concerts they had ever done and it was clear he enjoyed it. David Bowie was the same.

"Attracting these stars also meant the names of Maine Road and Manchester City would be in the headlines. Concert adverts, reviews, tickets, posters, tee-shirts – they'd all carry the venue as either Maine Road or Manchester City F.C. It was all free publicity.

"Of course, the concerts sometimes had their down sides. The pitch took a bit of a hammering at times, but we also had problems occasionally when guests turned up unexpectedly. Now, I only found out about this afterwards but when we had the Queen concert Freddie Mercury's sister turned up shortly before he came on. We didn't have a seat for her in the Directors' Box because the first half of the concert had already been and gone and all seats had been allocated. Now the guy who was sorting it out was under a lot of pressure and had been told that Freddie wouldn't go on if he knew there was a problem so he had to find a seat for Freddie's sister.

"He looked around the box and spotted an empty seat, so he just put her in there without thinking. It turned out the seat belonged to a senior official at another football club who had nipped inside for a drink or something. When he came back out he wasn't happy somebody had taken his seat so he turfed her out. The City staff member who had put her there then panicked. Queen were about to start and he had no idea where to put her, so he ended up getting her to stand in the entrance tunnel throughout the show. She couldn't have been happy, although she never complained.

"I don't know if Freddie Mercury ever found out his sister had not been treated properly but I don't think he did. If he had I'm sure he wouldn't have been as complimentary about our organisation as he was."

For City fan and Radio One DJ Marc Riley the Oasis concert was memorable: "It was a fantastic breakthrough gig for the lads. My most fond memory of the shows? Standing in the Centenary Suite with the great Noddy Holder as he watched Liam rattle through 'Cum On Feel The Noize' for the first time!"

Maine Memories

Semi spectacular

■ What a great night the Maine Road 1975-6 League Cup semi-final was. We had thrashed United in an earlier round on the ill-fated night of Colin Bell's injury. It was a fitting tribute to this great player that we won this competition. We had lost the first leg 1-0 at Ayresome Park so the stage was set for a pulsating encounter. I remember standing with my mates under the half-burnt red & white scarf hanging from the rafters of the old Kippax stand, our usual spot. The City team that night was a terrific blend of experience (Tueart, Watson etc.) and youth (Barnes, Keegan etc.). Well we all know which City side turned up that night, they simply tore into Boro' from the off and ran out 4-0 winners (4-1 on aggregate). We were on our way to Wembley! The emotion and sheer feelings of ecstasy at the end have remained etched into my memory. The more recent play-off semi-final win over Wigan felt similar, but not quite as good as the thought of a Cup Final visit pending. Of course that was another fantastic day out, five in a Mark 1 Ford Escort that seemed to take all day, the best cup-winning goal ever, the celebrations the next day in Manchester! I still have the 'I was there' badge! Lets hope the current team can give us moments like these.

All in all this game stands out as a fabulous Maine Road memory for me, even more poignant as it represented the last stepping stone to our last Cup final success (which I still find hard to believe).

John Wild

Unplanned tour

■ The semi-final of the League Cup in January 1981 was a particularly significant occasion for me, as it was responsible for me buying my first ever season ticket at Maine Road. In early December I'd seen City come from behind to win a tense and atmospheric quarter final against West Brom, a bogey team of City's at the time, and was now convinced we were going to win that cup. A couple of weeks later, the match programme versus Leeds announced the sale of some cut-price season tickets for the Platt Lane end. Purchasers would have the same rights to a Wembley ticket as existing season ticket holders. This was too good an opportunity to miss, so on the Monday I duly made my way across from Liverpool, where I was a student, to Manchester, and arrived at the ticket office late morning. Only one window was open, but there was hardly anyone about so I quickly got served. The cashier gave me a scrap of paper with the numbers of some vacant seats on it and told me to "go through that gate there, go up into the stand and choose your seat". Then I was to come back to the ticket office to complete the transaction.

This was where things started getting complicated. I went through the gate I thought he meant, and ended up in a maze of corridors under the main stand. I wandered around for a bit, trying to find the way through with no success. There was nobody about, so I wasn't challenged, nor could I ask where to go. As a result, I got a very unofficial, totally unguided tour of that part of the stadium. I ended up in what I think was the laundry room, with one pile of sky blue shirts neatly folded up on a table while others, including Tommy Hutch's number 10, were hanging up to air. I was too awe-struck to touch one. The next corridor I tried turned out to be the players' tunnel, leading straight out onto the pitch. This was my moment to imagine that I was really playing for City, coming out onto the famous turf opposite a packed Kippax. Dreams over, I found someone at work on the Platt Lane stand, showed him my scrap of paper and chose a seat that didn't have a pillar in the way of some vital part of the pitch.

By the time I got back to the ticket office it was lunchtime but there was still only one window open. While I was sorting out the paperwork for the season ticket a big queue was building up behind me, as working City fans used their lunch breaks to come and buy their Liverpool tickets. Unknown to me, the queue got bigger while I used the forms in the ticket book to order tickets for the Liverpool semi-final, and the FA Cup tie with Crystal Palace. More time went when I filled in one of the papers wrongly and had to do it again. Finally, as I turned away from the ticket office window, a big cheer went up from the long line of Blues stood behind me. Only then did I realise how many were in the queue, and crept sheepishly away.

Simon Clarke

All in stitches!

■ I suppose the funniest moment I ever witnessed at Maine Road was when Rodney Marsh was the victim of a slightly high tackle - in his stomach! The ref missed it, but the ball went out for a corner at the Platt lane/Kippax end. Summerbee saw the rip in Marsh's shirt and pretended to thread a needle with cotton, and then proceeded to stitch the shirt. Everybody else was in the box waiting for the corner. The ref eventually noticed what was going on and ran over blasting his whistle and insisting that Summerbee take the corner.

Steve Kelsall

Ring leader
■ My earliest memory of trips to Maine Road in the early seventies would have to be the sound of the crowd yelling "Helen, Helen, ring your bell!" and she did! It was a typically City moment I suppose. I am excited about the prospect of the new stadium being in the Clayton area, as this is where my dad was born and grew up.
Sally Myatt

Kippax and sardines!
■ My favourite game at Maine Road was the FA Cup replay with Everton in 1981. This game for me had it all. I'd gone to the first game on the Saturday and we'd got out of jail with a really late equaliser. It was on the way home after this game that I believed we would go all the way to Wembley. The replay at Maine Road was a cracking game played in an incredible atmosphere and ending with a 3-1 win for the Blues. Other than derby matches at Maine Road this was the best atmosphere I'd ever encountered there and that's my main reason for picking this game. It was one of the last occasions when we were packed in like sardines on the Old Kippax. That was what football was all about - great games played in a superb atmosphere and not being able to move unless the people around you moved also. That was all part of the fun of standing on the Kippax and that's why it will always remain my favourite part of the ground. I missed it more than I thought I would when I started taking my son in the Family Stand.
Graham Dyson

European champions humbled
■ I was 16 years old at the time of the match with Liverpool in 1977, and my friend and I had only just been given permission to go to matches alone. It was an 110-mile return journey from Mansfield by bus, so this journey in to the relatively unknown added to the excitement of the day.

We had only seen an odd few games prior to this at City, and our expectations of the great mid-70's City side were high. We adored watching Dennis Tueart burn down the left wing, and Peter Barnes doing likewise on the right. From low down on the Kippax steps you got a real appreciation of their skill and you could feel the anticipation and excitement of the tens of thousands of City voices behind you whenever these winged wizards came in possession.

The Liverpool game came at a time when Tony Book's team was going though a rough patch. City were amongst the favourites to lift the title having taken Liverpool to just one point of the Championship the previous season. The signing of Mick Channon was meant to be the final piece in the jigsaw. Alas it wasn't to be and the Blues came in fourth at the season's end. But on that autumn afternoon when Liverpool, the reigning European Champions, came to Maine Road with their new hot property Kenny Dalglish more than compensating for departed Kevin Keegan, few could have predicted the hammering that the Blues were about to hand out.

Close to 50,000 packed the ground, the noise was deafening - it was the Kippax at its very best. Trailing at half-time to a David Fairclough goal, the blues came out for the second half and stormed it. Thrilling strikes from Kiddo, Channon and Joe Royle sealed it. Barnes ran Alan Hansen in to the ground and big Dave Watson was commanding at the back.

Anything seemed possible after that game, but it was to be the last hurrah for Booky. The next season it all began to fall apart, Big Malcolm Allison came back to recreate the glory days but it was never on. Liverpool came to Maine Road in the following years and handed out humiliating defeat after defeat (0-4, 1-4, 0-3, 0-5 all spring to mind). However, some 25 years later and in spite of other great glory days (the 5-1, the 10-1 to name but a few) my mind always drifts back to that day in 1977. I remember the day, I remember Gerald Sindstadt's commentary the following Sunday afternoon and I remember buying a badge a week or two later from a market stall just outside the North Stand ticket office - it read 'Liverpool RIP 28-9-77: City 3-1' - I wore it with pride.

".......it's Barnes storming down the middle, Hansen is all over the place and now brings him down, but the ball runs kindly for Royle - bang - its 3-1........"
Andy Wragg

■ *I was 10 years old, nearly 11, when City beat Liverpool 3-1 in 1977, and this remains one of the best City performances I can remember. Liverpool had just won their first European Cup and pipped us to the title by a point the previous season. We were running a coach from Shirebrook, Warsop and Clowne to the City games at the time and a massive crowd saw a great spectacle. The first half was a predictable game against Liverpool with us having a lot of the ball and them taking a one-nil lead. I can't remember who scored for them but think it may have been a deflection off Kenny Dalglish's bum - he did that a lot against us! As well as the game itself another reason it was memorable was that the City youth team were watching from behind where I was sitting - Main Stand H Centre, right at the back, and one of those offering his opinions on the 'square ball charlies' from Anfield was Michael Barnes (younger brother of Peter).*

Anyway, the real football took place in the second half when Brian Kidd turned in a corner to equalise. After that it was all City. Mike Channon, managed to stay off his backside for ten minutes to score a cracking second from the left hand side of the box and then Barnesy produced a wonder run which culminated in Hansen bringing him down, but luckily the ref played advantage and Joe Royle hit a cracking third. Mike Doyle missed an excellent chance to make it four but it still ranks as one of my top ten City games!
David Djordjevic

Escorting Germans
■ In the late 1970's, I worked for a local authority and a volunteer was sought to take a group of German visitors from one of the twin-towns of the borough to a football match. I volunteered so long as the match was at Maine Road. I later discovered the Council's Chief Executive would also be with the group, and that tickets had been obtained for the match against Arsenal. It was, however, up to me to make sure that everything went right for the visitors as the borough were their hosts.

I arranged transport to pick up the visitors at their hotel. The Chief Executive would meet us there. When I arrived, I could see he was already inside, so in I went to do my best. To my surprise, he was speaking German, and was, in fact, quite fluent. This made things a lot better. We got to Maine Road and before the match had a meal in the Social Club restaurant. Before the food was served, two people sat down at the next table, one of whom I instantly recognised - a former player, but not any former player. A fellow countryman of our visitors and legend of post-war football, the great Bert Trautmann. Our German visitors were soon shaking hands with the City great. What a coincidence! Things had turned out well. The result was 1-1, and the Germans were impressed with the size of Maine Road and the crowd.
Paul Templeton

Gaining an early advantage
■ As many a schoolboy discovered you couldn't see in the old Kippax. So early arrival was required for three or four key areas in the stand where the fortunate few could elevate themselves above the general mass. These were:

1. The front wall - fine when the weather was good, but as soon as the rain came you got soaked and the people behind you disappeared into the dry areas, leaving you isolated, cold and wet. You had to master sitting facing the crowd with your head revolving 360 degrees to see the action. Of course when the fencing went up this viewing point was completely ruined.

2. The tunnel entrances astride the huge concrete walls. You had to sleep there the night before to get on the back of these with the people running in below you, but the sides could usually fit an extra one on, especially the smaller ones amongst us who favoured this area.

3. You could perch on the barriers, but just as the action became exciting somebody would nudge you and you would end up on the floor, so the better one was the almost unbroken barrier that ran the width of the stand about half way down which had a lower rail that was just right for resting your feet on, giving increased stability. Again, this was a prized position and necessitated instant arrival and a running attack when the gates opened at 1.30pm. Side effects were, in the old days pre-segregation, you had a close-up view of the attempts by the away fans to take the Kippax, before the vast army arrived and prevented too much running about.
John Geary

20th April 1981 - Paul Power takes a corner during City's 3-1 defeat of Everton in their penultimate home match before the FA Cup Final. City's goalscorers were Dave Bennett (City player closest to goal), Kevin Reeves and Steve Mackenzie. Other City men visible are Bobby Macdonald (far left), Tommy Booth and Tony Henry. Note the uncovered J Block between the Main Stand and North Stand, and the space behind the stadium control box - 20 years later temporary seating was erected on scaffolding in this space.

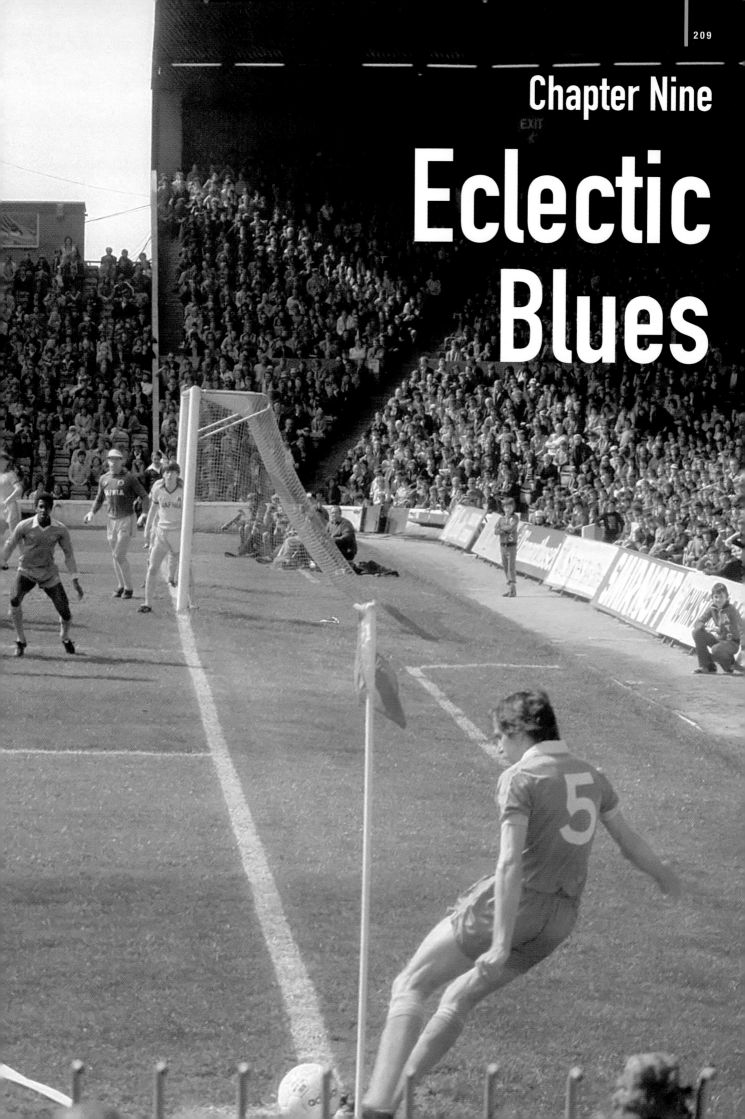

Chapter Nine
Eclectic Blues

"These are exciting times for City. Not only have we a successful team in the top four of the First Division, but we are also planning a super stadium for our supporters. We have undertaken extensive research at all major English and Scottish grounds and the best elements of these have been incorporated into the design. Other features will include restaurant, shops, and a special area with the disabled in mind."

Chairman Peter Swales commenting on the Platt Lane Stand plans, April 1991

T HE period between 1981 and 1993 saw City suffer two relegations and enjoy an equal number of promotions while from a ground perspective a similar roller-coaster ride ended with Maine Road having an eclectic appearance. Four stands from four different periods of development ensured the stadium lacked a cohesive style.

Maine Road's problems actually began during the summer of 1981. This was a great time to be Blue and the club's management team decided the time was ripe to improve the stadium. This promised so much but delivered little.

A tour around Maine Road during July 1981 would have made interesting viewing. The Main Stand, with its raised middle section, now housed a selection of original wooden tip-up and bench seats, plastic tip-up seats and padded ones in the directors' areas. Various shades of blue existed.

At the Platt Lane end of the ground, bench seats – mostly maroon and yellow – bolted on to the original terracing of 1923 (behind the goal) and re-profiled terracing of 1931 (corner) still existed. The large number of pillars made viewing from that area difficult.

The Platt Lane/Kippax corner remained terraced. In fact, apart from improved barriers, this was exactly as it had been when first constructed. The same was true for much of the Kippax, although the 1957 developments afforded a roof on the stand and squared off the terracing.

The North Stand appeared slick in comparison to the rest, but its grey seats looked dull. In later years they seemed out of place but as the Platt Lane housed red, yellow and green seats, and the Main Stand possessed various shades of blue, the North Stand was still the most perfect looking stand in the ground. It was by far the most modern area for regular spectators, even if the grey seating was a little unusual.

The weakest area of the North Stand was J Block. This was the uncovered section between the North and Main Stand.

In the concourses and other public areas little of note had changed since the 1920s. Bars had been redeveloped over time; the perimeter wall strengthened and raised; toilets improved and so on, but in essence anyone accessing Maine Road via the Platt Lane turnstiles, for example, in 1981 for the first time since 1935 would have noticed little difference.

In August 1981 City held a press conference to

Top Right: The Main Stand, with raised middle section and a selection of seat types and shades. City's first segregation fence (in front of Kippax) was a relatively simple affair and, surprisingly, did not continue in front of the corner terracing.
The Platt Lane end's multi-coloured benches were bolted onto 1923 terracing and pillars interrupted the views of spectators.

Bottom Right: The Platt Lane/Kippax corner was pretty much as first constructed back in 1923.

Below: The grey seats of the North Stand viewed from the dark at the back of the Main Stand.

£6m plan starts next May

publicise the plans. Models of a re-developed Maine Road looked very impressive and it was clear to all present that City aimed at creating one of the most modern and impressive venues in the United Kingdom.

The plan – costing a figure in excess of £6m – was to commence on 10th May 1982 and was expected to be complete by August 1987. By that time, the club boasted, every spectator would be under cover and there would not be an obstructed view in the entire stadium. It was a bold prediction, but there was little reason for doubt. It was also reassuring that, after the abandonment of Swain's grand plan around the time of World War Two, the club was now embarking on a serious redevelopment programme.

The planning details were impressive; three sides of the ground – Main Stand, Platt Lane and Kippax – would be re-roofed while the capacity would be increased slightly to around 54,000 within two years. The final 1987 figures were not released, but it's probable the final capacity of the ground would have reduced as the plan clearly showed an increase in the number of seats but a reduction in terracing.

The first phase would see the Main Stand roof replaced by a new all-white construction costing in excess of £1m, although the first doubts appeared as it became clear this new roof would not be a cantilevered stand as predicted. The original drawings of this roof clearly show stanchions at each end meaning that at best the roof would be a propped cantilever. The drawing also showed an intention to extend the Main Stand to the North Stand and to the Platt Lane Corner for the first time. This would be achieved by constructing a total of

23 barrel-styled roofing sections. The final three, at each end of the stand, would be extended out beyond the façade towards Maine Road itself. Within these sections would be lifts for the wealthier fans.

The plans also proposed a new restaurant within the Main Stand, together with 36 private boxes. These boxes were to be suspended from the ceiling along a gigantic lattice work of metal girders.

Above: In August 1981 the City programme v West Bromwich Albion pictured a model of the planned stadium re-development with a headline promising that work would begin at the end of that season.

Above: In 1982 the old roof came off the Main Stand and a new one went on.

Below and left: Initial artist's drawings of the new cover showed executive boxes 'hanging' from the roof. These never materialised, despite the fact they'd all been sold! The finished structure also featured less barrels.

They also showed that the old Platt Lane boundary wall would remain.

The new Platt Lane would however sweep around the corner at the Kippax side in a similar manner to the North Stand at the Main Stand corner. It was suggested this would provide further seating. Likewise, the North Stand would be extended at the Kippax corner.

Chairman Peter Swales told the media: "We are committing ourselves to a lot of money, but I'm sure it is the right way to spend it. There's no question of putting the ground before the team. The money for this comes from the club's Development Association and cannot be used for transfers. The supporters are building this stadium – and I am certain they will be extremely proud of it."

Supporters were immensely proud of the plan and, with the FA Cup final appearance in 1981 and a League Cup semi-final, the future looked bright. In addition, the introduction of executive boxes seemed to capture the imagination of wealthier fans and corporate supporters. In September 1981 the club released details of the amenities these boxes would provide. The number had now reduced to 32 – the reason became apparent the following May – but the facilities were impressive for the period.

The boxes, it was claimed, would be built during the 1983 close season, opening in time for August 1983. Each would hold eight people and would offer: "lift-access, first class dining facilities, air-conditioning, refrigeration, armchair seating, television and a GPO line [telephone] connection. They will be built on a two-tier basis. The club will accept bookings on a first come first served basis once the price details, exact dimensions and furnishings can be packaged to interested parties."

Within a month the club announced the scheme had already proved a complete sell-out: "All the options on the specially-designed boxes were taken up in a meeting called recently by club officials to have a question and answer session with the interested parties. A deadline date has been set for all the box reservations to be paid for. Meanwhile, City are compiling a waiting list in the event of any box vacancies occurring."

Entry to the boxes would be achieved by walkways constructed into the roof, leading to the extended sections of the stand.

A new television gantry would be installed under the roof, while the floodlighting system would be replaced by fitting lighting underneath each of the barrels.

According to the plan the later phases would see a similarly constructed roof on the Kippax, while the Platt Lane Stand would be remodelled to look similar to the North Stand. Whether this would see the stand completely rebuilt is questionable. Certainly the club implied it would, but then models of the new stadium showed the Platt Lane/Main Stand tunnel still in place.

The popularity of these boxes should have sent a strong message to the club that many wealthier fans desired facilities of the sort described. Clearly, regular supporters felt the emphasis on improving the ground should always have been on areas attended by the majority, however City needed to attract income from corporate clients. A total sell-out of the boxes a good 20

months before completion suggested the club could make a sizeable sum from corporate support. The beauty of City's plan was that by hanging the boxes from the roof of the Main Stand, regular support would not be affected. Other clubs had reduced sections of terracing to accommodate boxes – Aston Villa installed theirs under the balcony of their Trinity Road Stand, Everton on the terracing of their Main Stand – but City appeared to have the wisdom to create a totally new location for the corporate spectator.

By the time the first phase commenced in May 1982 the roof design had changed a little. Instead of 23 barrels, a roof stretching the full length of the pitch would be erected, using 18 larger ones. Even then the decision was taken to only erect 16 barrels (hence the reduction in the number of Executive Boxes to 32) initially. These 16 would cover the existing Main Stand and J Block, but would leave the entire Platt Lane corner roof of 1931 intact, thereby giving a lop-sided feel to the roof.

Maine Match 82/83

CITY v LUTON TOWN

DATE:	14th May 1983	
TYPE OF FIXTURE:	Football League Division One	
ATTENDANCE:	42,843	
RESULT:	City 0 Luton 1	
TEAMS & SCORERS:	CITY	LUTON
	Williams	Godden
	Ranson	Stephens
	McDonald	Goodyear
	Reid	Horton
	Bond	Elliott
	Caton	Donaghy
	Tueart	Hill
	Reeves	Aylott
	Baker	Walsh
	(Kinsey)	Turner
	Hartford	(Antic) 1
	Power	Stein

■ All City needed to do was draw this match to avoid relegation. A draw at home against a very poor Luton side seemed so easy but sadly the game did not go City's way. Supporter Kevin Bould remembers this as one of City's blackest days: "I have watched several relegation matches at Maine Road but none of them sitting with the away fans, alongside my future wife's Luton-supporting family. I will re-live the torture of this day forever more. I married a non-believer… a mad hatter… a committed Luton Town fan I met at college! I compounded the mistake by stupidly persuading my father to lend out our season tickets and accepted the offer of a lift to the game to sit with my wife's entire family. I was confident of victory – I was young and had not yet become tarnished by the many years of underachievement and cock ups – and failed to foresee the misery ahead. I was even planning how to conceal my delight on the coach journey back so as not to upset my newly-acquired relatives.

"Near the end of the game I was consoling my wife with the usual meaningless platitudes of 'You'll be back next year' and 'It's only a game' when I missed that goal by Raddy Antic and David Pleat's beiged-suited jig. My father's mouth just dropped open and we sat there speechless as the tango men and women of Luton sucked the breath from out of me. I could not move or understand what had happened. I remember leaving the Main Stand guiding my new family out of the ground away from the abuse directed at the Luton fans for the

short walk to the coaches where the nightmare continued - a four-hour coach journey back to Luton.

"My wife was very sympathetic on the day, and during the next few weeks – she really tried to talk about anything but football although I was bad-tempered and harboured a very rational hatred of the mad hatters of Luton etc. She tried to avoid football as a conversational topic but a combination of the local and national news ensured I watched countless reruns of David Pleat's stupid jig.

"Living in the South since my late teens, my principal contact with my father was at Maine Road and so many of my memories of him relate to football, but this game will remain without doubt the lowest point. We always referred to it as "that game" and we promised each other never to sit with the away fans or in that part of the Main Stand again. Even now it remains the most painful jointly-shared experience with him. I live 100m away from my family of mad hatters and gracefully they have restricted themselves to only mentioning "that game" once or twice a month but it still hurts. When we leave Maine Road it is a memory which, no matter how hard I try, is bound to resurface. My father died the day after the end of the 1996/7 season and every time I return to Maine Road I can see his face at the end of this game. Many periods of my life and my relationship with him are framed by football matches thankfully not all of them as painful as this one."

For the BBC's highly respected commentator John Motson this is one of three significant Maine Road matches he has commentated on: "My first memory was the 1977 FA Cup semi-final at Maine Road, and my last was the great game between City and Tottenham in October 1994 – a thrilling 5-2 City win. But the most significant for many reasons was the relegation match with Luton. As a commentator you sometimes need a piece of drama to give the game a focus and this match certainly had its drama.

"A draw was all City needed and Luton were not really expected to achieve anything at Maine Road, but my good friend Bernard Halford regularly tells me that City have always been unpredictable. This was one of those days.

"When Luton scored it was truly amazing. Nobody had expected it and for neutrals it was great drama, and then of course the match ended and David Pleat performed his jig of delight. A great visual moment for the BBC but not for City supporters. City seem to have a few moments like that – the 1981 Ricky Villa FA Cup Final goal is a good example. I had mixed feelings after the match. I had commentated on a great footballing story but I also felt a great deal of sympathy for all those City supporters and club officials I had got to know. Maine Road was such a welcoming ground."

Maine Memory

■ My first visit to Maine Road was when I was six as a treat for my brother's birthday, along with my parents. It was January, and City were playing Birmingham City. I remember feeling very overawed getting to the ground for the first time. We were sat towards the back of the Main Stand and City won 4-2. However, all the goals were scored in the first half and I think the crowd must have been quite subdued in the second half as I managed to fall asleep! My brother and my mum now have season tickets and I go and watch City as often as being a nurse in London allows - which isn't as often as I would like! I must stress that I've never fallen asleep watching them since.
Emma Faraday

City defeated Birmingham City 4-2 on 30th January 1982 with Kevin Reeves and Trevor Francis scoring two goals apiece.

Far right: Liverpool skipper and match-winner Graeme Souness lifts the Milk Cup at Maine Road.

Maine Memory

■ As a Blue living in London, I had few opportunities to get to Maine Road when younger. My first visit to the Academy was not to watch a match, but occurred at the age of 10 in the summer of 1982 when my family were visiting relatives in the North. My parents arranged for a tour of the ground, which unknown to them was the same day as City signed their sponsorship deal with Saab. I remember being shown around by the late Harry Godwin, taken into the trophy room and meeting some of the players; Kevin Bond and David Cross in particular. I know my parents were impressed that Peter Swales took time out to have a word with me and check I was having a good time. And my first-ever glimpse of the hallowed turf wasn't of 11 blue-shirted heroes running out to the roar of the crowd, instead there were a number of Saab vehicles in the centre circle alongside, bizarrely, Eddie Large with a few young ladies!

Six years later I saw my first match at Maine Road. Again I was visiting relatives so it was August and the first home match of the '88-89 season; City 1 Oldham 4. Roger Palmer scored a hat trick for them and Lakey got our consolation, but as we had seats in the Main Stand, my abiding memory of that day is someone chucking an egg at Swales at the end of the game! Having lost to Hull the previous Saturday, two defeats was clearly too much for someone to bear! An interesting introduction to Maine Road life.

Andrew Cleaver

At J Block the new roof, once constructed, appeared to float some way above the stand.

Throughout the summer of 1982 supporters flocked to Maine Road to watch the new roof take shape. The feeling of pride was enormous and, although the roof would be mocked by some over time for its barrel design, there was satisfaction it was not simply a copy of a stand elsewhere. Throughout football history the appearance of a magnificent new stand at one ground has led to similar ones at others as football officials seemed happy to settle for imitation, but the new Main Stand roof was different. It appeared modern and, to a large number of supporters, quite refreshing.

Its white colouring, and the use of maroon-coloured ventilation panels at the back actually meant the Main Stand was now a much lighter place to sit than previously. The old roof gave a rather drab feel to the stand – particular for those sitting at the back.

The first game in front of the new roof was on 1st September 1982 when Stoke were defeated 1-0 before 27,847. Despite the new construction, supporters were a little dissatisfied to say the least. Trevor Francis had been sold after less than a year with the club and many jumped to the conclusion he'd been transferred to pay for the building work. The atmosphere was very different to that a year earlier when Francis had arrived. Bernard Halford: "The day Francis arrived was incredible. The news had leaked out we were going to sign him so on the day thousands of fans stood on the main forecourt waiting for him to arrive. It was incredible. When he got here he had to push his way through the crowd and then into the stand. Of course, the sight of so many fans made him realise just how big a club we are and how important his signing was, and in return we got a major buzz out of his arrival."

Francis was an expensive purchase and only managed a total of 29 games for the club. Some thought he was an expensive luxury, but most wanted to see him remain and progress. Manager John Bond saw him as a key piece of his jigsaw. He expected to build a team around Francis but when the player was sold Bond felt the jigsaw didn't even have the corner pieces in place.

Clearly the roof looked magnificent, but the benefit of such a covering seemed small when the team suffered. The 1982-3 season was an exceptionally poor one and ended with relegation.

This was the third Main Stand roof and apart from an improved view for about 8,000 spectators and a new television gantry the roof provided little change for the majority of fans. The perception now existed on the Kippax, and in the rather dated Platt Lane Stand that those in the Directors' Box had once again looked after their own interests first. Whether this is true or not is debatable, however the events of the following May would have serious repercussions for the ground. In effect the events of May 1983 would herald the beginning of the end for Maine Road as a major stadium.

Relegation for the first time since 1963 caused an immediate postponement of the redevelopment plan. The boxes - already fully booked if the club's press announcements were to be believed - would not be developed during the 1983 close season. The Blues were struggling financially after spending record sums on fairly average, some would say mediocre, players during the late seventies and early eighties, and the investment needed in both team and stadium could not be found. Peter Swales' comment that the development plan was to be funded solely by the Development Association

Maine Match 83/84

LIVERPOOL v EVERTON

DATE:	28th March 1984	
TYPE OF FIXTURE:	Milk (League) Cup Final Replay	
ATTENDANCE:	52,089	
RESULT:	Liverpool 1 Everton 0	
TEAMS & SCORERS:	LIVERPOOL	EVERTON
	Grobbelaar	Southall
	Neal	Stevens
	Kennedy	Bailey
	Lawrenson	Ratcliffe
	Whelan	Mountfield
	Hansen	Reid
	Dalglish	Irvine
	Lee	Heath
	Rush	Sharp
	Johnston	Richardson
	Souness 1	Harper

■ This game is essential to the history of Maine Road as it is the most important national final ever staged at the ground. The first encounter between these sides at Wembley had ended goalless, although Liverpool were a shade fortunate when Hansen prevented a goal by the use of his thigh and hand. The Evertonians unsuccessfully appealed for a penalty, and so the two sides met the following Wednesday at Maine Road.

Although the Blues were a Second Division side at this point, the replay had been awarded to City because of its proximity to Liverpool and because the stadium was still regarded as a leading English venue. The development of the Main Stand roof in 1982 was still very much talked about, and television footage of this match seemed to delight in showing the unusual roof at every opportunity.

The game was played at a ferocious pace with Everton displaying a great deal of passion in the early stages, although they struggled to be effective. Future Blue Alan Harper shot wildly, while another future City man Peter Reid saw a great effort saved by Grobbelaar.

Despite the Everton pressure it was Liverpool who took the lead when, in the 22nd minute, Souness received the ball on the edge of the area and sent a left foot shot past a diving Southall.

The rest of the match was played at the same blistering pace as the opening minutes but Liverpool remained in control and at the end of the game they became the first English side to win the same major competition four years in succession.

seemed ludicrous because, if that had been the case, relegation would not have altered anything.

By not installing executive boxes during the summer of 1983 the club limited its income streams, however it's fair to say regular supporters would not have been happy to see money invested in corporate facilities at a time when the first team clearly needed strengthening. New manager Billy McNeill was forced to buy bargain basement players and this situation would certainly have worsened if expenditure had gone on building work.

Officially City's redevelopment plan was only on hold, but no further work was ever carried out on this plan. This meant City's £1m roof seemed rather extravagant. A much simpler construction could have sufficed, without any provision for private boxes. As a comparison it's worth noting Norwich City spent £1.7m in 1985 on a replacement Main Stand containing executive boxes, while Manchester United spent £1.5m on a cantilever roof, executive boxes and a new office block for the club's administration at their Main Stand in 1984. Had City's boxes been built then, the money would have proved a good investment.

Maine Road now gave the impression of a half-hearted stadium. Gone was the uniformity of the early years; gone was any hope of sensible redevelopment; and as the eighties progressed Maine Road's capacity and its position as a major venue was hit by a number of factors - crowd control, safety and general facilities.

Before this became apparent, the stadium played host to the 1984 Milk Cup final replay between Everton and Liverpool. The Milk Cup was the sponsored name of the League Cup and this replayed final attracted a crowd of 52,089. Liverpool beat Howard Kendall's Everton 1-0 and in April 1985, 45,775 witnessed an FA Cup semi-final between Liverpool and Manchester United.

On 11th May 1985 promotion from Division Two was achieved with a thrilling 5-1 victory over Charlton Athletic. An official crowd of 47,285 - in truth there must

have been more inside the packed stadium that day - celebrated a superb victory but across the Pennines similar scenes of celebration (Bradford were promoted from Division Three) turned to tragedy as the Valley Parade fire cost 56 lives.

A riot involving Leeds fans at Birmingham caused the death of one young fan. A further 200 injuries made this one of the blackest days in football history. Then on 29th May, Liverpool fans rioted at Heysel prior to the European Cup final. English football was at its lowest ebb.

Justice Popplewell was appointed to investigate the state of football grounds and make recommendations for the future. The upshot, for City and dozens of clubs in similar situations, meant major expense. Stands such as the 1935 Platt Lane Stand were a serious worry and with such a large amount of timber - the stand contained wooden benches and was built at the back with wooden steps - the club were concerned it would be forced to close.

Above: The Development Association was created in the Sixties to raise funds for ground developments. With the building of the North Stand these new offices were erected. In Maine Road's final seasons the front section of this room became a City souvenir shop open only on match days, with the Development Offices hidden behind.

Maine Memory

■ I remember getting stuck in Middleton with a mate one freezing November day in 1982, and we walked the rest of the way to Maine Road, paid at the turnstiles at the end of the Kippax near the North Stand, and stood on those seemingly massive terraces to watch the most awful game ever witnessed, City were playing Birmingham City and the match finished nil-nil I recall.

The only reason I remember the game was because a dog ran onto the pitch at the start of the game, and it took about 100 people what seemed about 30 minutes to catch it before the game could start. The dog definitely had more ball skills than the players that day!

Chris Whittaker

Left: By mid to late Seventies saw several changes to the Main Stand facade and, by the time this photograph was taken in 1981, a cage had been erected around the entrance to improve security. Other changes included the dark blue paint at ground level and the billboard above the entrance. The 1923 mosaic proudly displaying the name Manchester City Football Club was no longer visible, hidden behind advertising boards.

Right: David Phillips scores City's first goal in the 5-1 defeat of Charlton.

■ This was a vitally important match. The financially struggling Blues were desperate to gain promotion to Division One under Billy McNeill and put simply, City had to win. Richard Billinge remembers this because of the way the importance of the day grew: "I remember the Charlton game because of what happened before it. I travelled with three of my mates to the Notts County game. If we won at Meadow Lane we were promoted. It was that simple.

"I went to Nottingham for the first time and decided to follow a car full of City fans - it was only when they pulled over and started to talk to a policeman that I became concerned about their knowledge of the area! We got to the ground just in time to see Notts County score their second goal. So we were 2-0 down within fifteen minutes and the City fans were restless. Billy McNeill came on the pitch to calm us down at half time but we eventually lost that game 2-3. This meant we had to beat Charlton. I knew we'd do it, but this is City after all!

"There was a packed crowd – in truth it must have been over 50,000 as the Kippax was full to bursting. You had to get there early to get a good spot and so I set off travelling down on the bus from Cheadle early. Once the match started I remember the euphoria of being back in the top flight and watching a game I knew City had won from the start, which is unusual. The pressure of those crash barriers was immense but this was the way footy used to be. I remember dreaming of the glory years to come - I was young... naive... or just plain daft, but I wouldn't change that feeling for anything."

Supporter Will Linsdell remembers this as one of his favourite City matches: "The day before the game I awoke at home in Honiton, Devon, with £5 in my wallet and a sudden burning desire to get to Manchester for the big game. Those were the days when it was not necessary to be an official member of the club or give one month's notice to have even the slightest chance to get a ticket for a vitally important match – you could just turn up and pay on the gate. It wasn't only fifties fans who had that privilege.

"A few weeks previous I had experienced my greatest ever away day – a 2-1 victory over Alan Ball's Pompey, our only serious rivals for the third promotion

Maine Match 84/85

CITY v CHARLTON ATHLETIC

DATE:	11th May 1985	
TYPE OF FIXTURE:	Football League Division Two	
ATTENDANCE:	47,285	
RESULT:	City 5 Charlton 1	
TEAMS & SCORERS:	**CITY**	**CHARLTON**
	Williams	Harnsworth
	Lomax	Friar
	Power	A. Kimble
	May 1	Gritt
	Clements	Dowman
	Phillips 2	Aizlewood
	Simpson 1	Harris
	McNab	Curbishley
	Melrose 1	Lee 1
	Tolmie	G. Kimble
	Kinsey	Flanagan

spot behind Oxford and Birmingham. A young Paul Simpson had lobbed the winner over Alan Knight late in the second half to send the away contingent wild and surely book City's place back in the big league. However, City being City, we had stuttered a little since that vital win and the third promotion spot was to go down to the wire. With one game left, City and Pompey were level on points with City having the all-important advantage of a superior goal difference. I seem to think it was two goals advantage.

"Portsmouth however had the advantage of a settled side, whereas City were unable to put the same side out two games running due to injuries to the likes of Graham Baker, Jim Tolmie, Gordon Smith, Jim Melrose and Derek Parlane. Pompey were away at Huddersfield while we were due to entertain Charlton. The papers the previous week had been full of stories about the time Portsmouth had pipped City to promotion in the Twenties by the narrowest goal average margin ever.

"Being flat broke, I had already decided I would have to listen to the game on the radio and wait for *Match Of The Day* highlights on Saturday night. But I

realised the game could be something extra special and I had to be there. Sometimes you just know you have to be on the Kippax. As I travelled by train to Exeter for work, I hatched a plan. I would forge the date on my expired Young Person's Railcard so that I could get a cheap day return to Manchester - cost £15.

"That evening I would cash a cheque in my local pub, not to spend on drinks, as the landlord would have hoped, but to pay for my big trip. I did not have enough money in my bank account to meet the value of the cheque, but I could worry about that later. So I arrived at work with my thoughts only on forgery – not the recommended actions of a 20-year-old bank employee!

"My railcard had expired on 5th May. By the skilful application of the number two in black ink on the end of an eraser, I was able to imprint the 2 before the 5th on the card to magically transform the expiry date to 25th May. Only a very eagle-eyed British Rail employee would spot the card had been tampered with – mission one accomplished. I saw out the rest of the day thinking only about mission two – I would need at least thirty quid from the pub and the maximum encashment usually allowed was fifteen. I was a little nervous that evening as I entered the White Lion at 7pm – it seemed the immediate footballing future of City relied upon my ability to extract £30 from behind the bar.

"The landlord had a deserved reputation of being tight and I had figured that if I arrived early enough, his wife would be behind the bar – a far easier option. I was to be unlucky. She had gone away for the weekend and I was only allowed £20 on the understanding that I also cleared my £5 slate. That meant that I was left with a grand total of £20 with my existing fiver – not enough for the train fare, match entrance and some beers. My only option was to play cards and hope to win off my mates. By 8.30pm I had won a few hands of three-card brag and had £35 to my name. Rather than risk my good fortune, I really annoyed my mates by going home.

"The following day I woke at 6am full of nervous energy. I hadn't really slept to be honest and couldn't stomach more than a quick cuppa. My train was due at 7.15am with a couple of changes each way. It was a fragmented journey lasting a total of ten and a half hours. At the station I saw another Devonian Blue standing outside the ticket hall. Mike was to be my surprise companion for the day of reckoning. He was more nervous than I was and had arrived at 6am to ensure he did not miss the train. Tickets purchased – my railcard easily passed inspection – and the train was on time, so far so good.

"I had pinched a four-pack of Carling from Dad and Mike had some cans of cider. As it was such a special occasion, we started early. By Taunton we were well into the second. Two more Blues alighted at Taunton and the party had begun. It was now 8am and Mike, Harvey, Nick and I were already toasting Billy McNeill, Jimmy Frizzell and Andy May. By Brum, we were all light-headed but managed to find our connection. We were now

joined by a mad Charlton fan called Sparky. He informed us Charlton had a 17-year-old in goal making his debut and some teenage twins at full-back. Lambs to the slaughter!

"A strange thing happened at Stoke. Sparky was arrested for criminal damage to the train toilet. He would have got away with it if he hadn't worn the toilet seat around his neck! Our alcohol was now finished and it was time to start getting nervous again as the effects slowly wore off. The singing of 'There's only one David Phillips' was replaced by quiet contemplation. We arrived in Manchester at 1.30pm and made straight for the Aytoun Street matchday specials. You could tell that today was special. There was singing on the bus and plenty of nervy chatter.

"Time for a couple in the Parkside where the atmosphere was fantastic 2.30pm – I think it was about £5 to stand on the Kippax and I took up my favourite position to the left of halfway, about mid way up the terrace. Well that was were I had stood on the previous half dozen occasions I had visited the Hallowed Place. We were all buoyed by the pre-match warm up. Jim Melrose had passed a fitness test and Charlton had a small boy in goal – surely we could not fail this time?

"By 2.45pm the ground was heaving. Well over the 48,000 they announced had crammed in and the whole ground buzzed with excitement. We were bound to win and Pompey had a tricky away match – today was going to be a celebration. The Kippax throbbed and even the Main Stand seemed lively. I was surrounded by teenagers, who took great delight in pushing forward to make the crowd surge. I loved those pre-Hillsborough and Heysel days when everybody

Below : City fans swarm onto the Maine Road pitch to celebrate promotion after crushing Charlton. Jubilant fans Dave Powell and Colin Quilter parade their flag in the North Stand goalmouth whilst a policeman watches a young boy swinging from the crossbar.

squashed together and you plummeted twenty rows, carried on a tide of ecstasy and beered-up bodies, each time your heroes scored. Nobody had a thought in those days about the dangers of crushing and the odd rib injury was part and parcel of terrace residence.

"On a gorgeous summer's day in May, the beered-up and sweaty bodies were already in evidence en masse and we just awaited the moments of ecstasy. Our heroes were announced to the crowd – one by one the boys were greeted with loud cheers and their personal songs – "Simmo" for Paul Simpson. Charlton were greeted with cries of "Who?" Kimble and Kimble, sounded more like a building firm than a pair of teenage, identical twin full-backs. You could see the young goalie was wearing brown underpants!

"The roar that greeted the kick-off was deafening and City were soon playing good attacking football, no doubt fired-up by a big crowd and the knowledge that a rookie Charlton side did not really have a lot of danger in their ranks. As the sun shone brightly, so did Simmo who was roasting one of the Kimbles at will down the left-flank. When the first goal arrived the crowd did indeed surge forward and I was carried some distance just as a complete stranger was about to hug me. I did not see Mike again until the train home and as Harvey and Nick were in the Platt Lane End, I watched the rest of the match on my own so to speak. I did not feel lonely.

"I managed to fight my way back up to near my original position but then we scored again and the whole episode was repeated. The only difference this time was that I was vaulted forward while in a bear-hug with a large denim-clad gentleman who for some reason kissed the side of my ear. City can invoke strangeness in people!

"Two-nil up and Pompey would have to win by five now to stop us. No chance! We scored another before half-time and all the talk during the interval was about how we would be a force again next year in Division One. Even Peter Swales was a good guy at that moment and we were sure we would be able to spend some real money, instead of relying on the odd thirty grand signing and free transfer. The second half was a stroll in the sunshine. 4-0 then 5-0 and the crowd, now devoid of tension, were even a little subdued. Ironic cheers and polite applause when The Addicks pulled one back. Nobody cared. City were back!

"The crescendo of noise returned at the final whistle to salute the Blues back into the top flight. We all laughed at Pompey and Ball who had won at Huddersfield but had just missed out on promotion again. The Boys came out for a lap of honour and my journey had been worth it. I could not have missed that day."

Despite the importance of the day for City fans it was also a tragic day for football. Gary Knight put it all into perspective: "Charlton in 1985 - 5-1, sunny weather, big crowd, big result and promotion... a perfect day until we heard the news filtering through on the radio about the tragedy at Bradford. How could that happen at a football ground?"

The Bradford fire resulted in the deaths of 56 fans on the same day as City's game with Charlton.

Above: City sides appeared in two memorable cup finals in 1986.

Blues youngsters lifted the FA Youth Cup in front of 18,164 fans at Maine Road after defeating Manchester United 3-1 on aggregate. It was a great triumph for captain Steve Redmond and the backroom staff of Tony Book and Glyn Pardoe.

Two months beforehand the first team won through to the final of the first ever Football League Full Members Cup, where they lost a thrilling game 5-4 to Chelsea. The official squad picture for the Wembley final was taken in the Maine Road boardroom.

Fortunately, the Platt Lane survived but there was to be a major change with the local authorities insisting the stand be designated for away fans. They felt it would be easier to control visiting supporters there (seated away fans would be housed in the Main Stand or in 'J' Block causing two areas of segregation prior to this decision). City fans were disgusted, especially those season ticket holders who had been regulars for decades. The club offered them seats in the North and Main Stand, but many were far from happy with this enforced move.

The disgruntlement increased during the 1985-6 season as some clubs brought only a handful of fans seated in a stand that could hold around 9,000. This limited City's income from big matches, angered supporters and also caused the ground to appear half empty whenever a match was televised.

Once the stand became designated for away fans it was clear the ground was no longer the premier location it needed to be, and by 1987 there was a feeling something had to be done to bring Maine Road up to scratch. The club were still investing in minor improvements – lighting, fencing, the car parks, and the never-ending investigations into the public address system - but these were not cheap and serious improvements seemed to rely on the involvement of other parties.

Rumours of the Kippax car park and part of the stand being sold to a supermarket chain were rife during the period. In 2002 both secretary Bernard Halford and former director Eric Alexander admitted serious discussions had been held with Tesco and Sainsbury's, but fortunately these never really amounted to much.

Maine Match 87/88

CITY v HUDDERSFIELD TOWN

DATE:	7th November 1987		
TYPE OF FIXTURE:	Football League Division Two		
ATTENDANCE:	19,583		
RESULT:	City 10 Huddersfield 1		
TEAMS &	**CITY**		**HUDDERSFIELD**
SCORERS:	Nixon		Cox
	Gidman		Brown
REFEREE:	Hinchcliffe		Bray
K. Breen	Clements		Banks
(Maghull)	Lake		Webster
	Redmond		Walford
	White	3	Barham
	Stewart	3	May 1
	Adcock	3	Shearer
	McNab	1	Winter
	Simpson		Cork

■ On paper this game was hardly likely to be a thriller, and with attendances falling and little prospect of promotion, City were in desperate need of a boost. Few crowds had exceeded 20,000, with matches against the likes of Leicester only attracting a shade over 16,000, and the general feeling around Maine Road was not good. The club had dropped to the twelfth best-supported League side – their worst position since 1964-5 – with an average of 19,471. City had featured in the top four average attendances nine years out of the previous twelve.

Only die-hard fans seemed to attend games in 1987, but those that did knew City possessed some excellent young players.

The banana craze had started during this season and season ticket holder Steve Cummings remembers how this helped to lift the general atmosphere over the following year or so: "When City were at there worst... when the football was at its poorest... City fans were still having fun! Along came the bananas and all the other inflatables, the great Man City humour was making us the talking point of the football world. There was one game in particular when an absolutely huge inflatable ball appeared in the Kippax. It was passed from stand to stand, missing out the Platt Lane as they were the visiting fans. We didn't win that day, but people still went home laughing."

Steve was one fan who was desperate to attend, but was under orders not to go: "I was a season ticket holder in the old Kippax stand, and I had never missed a home match for many years but if it wasn't for my teenager attitude to defy my parents I would never have seen this perfect game. I was suffering with 'flu, the real horrible version that makes your body like ice one second then a sauna the next. But I just wouldn't listen to my parents orders to stay in bed, I dragged myself to the match and what a match it was!"

Another fan who remembers this as one of his favourite games is Mike Vickerstaff: "My most unforgettable match has to be the 10-1 against Huddersfield in '87. I have been coming to Maine Road since the opening day of the 1955/56 season - a 2-2 draw with Aston Villa. During that time I have obviously seen some memorable victories, many of

Below: It was the kind of scoreline you just had to stare at in print before you could quite believe it!

In the 1980s sponsorship and promotional activity became regular occurences at Maine Road - note the sign above the Main Entrance on page 216.

Above: The brewery Greenalls sponsored a new scoreboard.

Left: Fans look bemused as Winners Matches promote their goods at the ground. It is also interesting to note in this 1983 picture taken in front of the Main Stand, that there is no fencing (the North Stand was fenced) and supporters can be seen with pints of beer.

Supporters during the eighties had heard the plan had been to demolish the Kippax and build a smaller but more modern stand in its place.

No matter how much the fans wanted the Kippax roof, and view, to be improved, it's fair to say sacrificing capacity for these was not something supporters would have desired.

Other developments in this period included a new scoreboard. During the first months of the 1986-7 season fans became aware of a new structure being erected at the Platt Lane/Kippax corner, in front of the floodlight pylon, and then on 13th December 1986 the club officially announced this was an 'information board', donated by Greenalls Brewery. According to Peter Swales: "The new Information Board will help us to keep our supporters in touch with everything happening at Maine Road. It is a tremendous gesture by our friends at Greenall Whitley and we are most grateful for their generous donation."

The scoreboard had been installed by HB Control and Information Systems Limited, a Bolton company,

with similar ones at Ibrox and Wigan RLFC's Central Park. Rather than use illuminated bulbs, the scoreboard relied on a series of electro-mechanical moving spots. This, according to the club, gave greater flexibility in the style of notices displayed and, for a while, it impressed with its messages urging the team to 'Attack' while displaying a picture of a tank. The most interesting aspect for many was the fact the board could quickly reveal the scores of City's main rivals during a match. Those on the Kippax had to crane their necks to see the board and many a match during this period was affected by a sudden burst of excitement on the terracing as the message 'Latest Score' appeared in yellow. A pause would follow before the score was revealed. Often a huge cheer would greet a scoreline, and the entire atmosphere could change simply as a result of the latest news.

Unfortunately, the life of this board was even more limited than the old North Stand board. Messages began to get stuck, but for a brief spell it added a new dimension to watching the Blues. Interestingly, the old scoreboard was used briefly for private messages. By paying a small sum - sometimes as modest as £5 - supporters had the chance of having a few words, such as a Valentine's Day message, displayed. This concept didn't last long due to a lack of interest and the high cost of keeping the old board operating, but it was a fascinating diversion.

The late 1980s and early 1990s saw little stand

Above: The 10-1 mauling of Huddersfield featured hat-tricks from a trio of City players - Paul Stewart, Tony Adcock and David White.

which feature the team from Stretford, but how many supporters of any professional football team can lay claim to seeing their team score TEN goals against a team from the same division? I certainly never expect to see it again. One memory from that game has stayed with me; I watched the match from a seat in B Block near the Directors' Box. When the score was about 8 or 9 nil, I looked over to the area where the visiting directors and their entourage sat. My eye was caught by a very attractive, smartly-dressed lady who was trying, unsuccessfully, to hold back the tears. Someone told me she was Malcolm Macdonald's wife - he was the

Huddersfield manager at the time. I wouldn't go so far as to say the sight ruined my day, but I did feel a pang of sorrow for her."

The actual game had seen Huddersfield in control for much of the opening period. They could have taken the lead on a couple of occasions but thanks to the tenacity of players like Neil McNab and John Gidman the Blues survived the opening ten minutes. Then in the 12th a clinical strike from McNab gave the Blues the lead. McNab went on to dominate midfield and Huddersfield collapsed in quite an extraordinary manner.

Seventeen minutes later Paul Stewart scored City's second and then the Blues pushed forward with attack after attack. Tony Adcock scored five minutes later and three minutes before the interval David White made it 4-0. The game had turned completely and supporters on the Kippax began to make bold predictions about the final score. For many it seemed possible the Blues could double their half-time lead, while others felt Huddersfield would return to the pitch in a more composed manner.

The game restarted with Huddersfield offering little. Mel Machin's half-time team talk had encouraged the Blues to surge forward with more determination than in the first and City started to score at will. Once City had made it to seven, the Kippax started to chant "We want eight!" Every subsequent goal was immediately greeted by a corresponding increase to the chant. When it was 9-0, former Blue Andy May scored a penalty for Huddersfield prompting a conga in the Platt Lane by the travelling fans and a cheer from City.

In the 89th minute David White made it ten. "We want eleven!" roared the Kippax, but the whistle went, and the match entered the record books as City's highest victory at Maine Road. Three players had scored hat-tricks and within days of the match Granada TV were selling 60 minutes of footage on video for £15.

development - though plenty was needed - other than the usual mix of segregation and fence changes; exit gates, stairways, lighting improvements; and the replacement of wooden bench seats with plastic ones in the Main Stand.

Of course Maine Road's greatest story during the late Eighties was the role of supporters in creating a carnival atmosphere. The banana craze, started by fan Frank Newton at Boundary Park, had by late 1988 become a major news story. Thousands of bananas were brought to matches and a real carnival atmosphere existed. The away game at Stoke on Boxing Day 1988 came at the height of Bananarama with over 12,000 fans travelling in fancy dress, but Maine Road also had its moments. The FA Cup tie with Leicester in January 1989 saw the players take to the field carrying inflatable bananas, which they threw into the crowd. Then on 25th February, City's 2-0 victory over Plymouth was attended by journalist Richard Littlejohn who came specifically to find out about the craze.

Littlejohn loved every minute of the day and wrote: "From the packed Kippax terrace to the posh seats by the Directors' Box, a forest of bright yellow inflatable bananas was raised above heads, interspersed with blow up aeroplanes, turtles, snakes and cigarettes. Coupled with the celebratory singing and dancing, the atmosphere was like the Notting Hill Carnival without the muggings.

"By the corner flag, one fan played a giant saxophone. Behind him, a six foot long tube of smokers' toothpaste waved in the breeze. Elsewhere another City supporter wielded an enormous tennis racket. In the cheap seats, those who couldn't run to a six quid Big Banana brought lilos and rubber rings left over from last year's summer holidays in Blackpool or Benidorm."

The attendance figure when announced also brought a bit of laughter. The Greenalls scoreboard revealed: "Today's attendance 22,451 and 7,000 bananas!" Interestingly, although the attendance appears rather small it was the third largest crowd in England that day. In the days before the creation of the Premier League attendances were considerably smaller than they were a decade later for most clubs.

The banana craze livened up many dull games, but it also saw the resurrection of the club in 1989. Whether the craze had a direct impact on the team's performance is debatable, but surely it did help to lift spirits for most people connected with the club even if it was a little embarrassing for older supporters. John Marsland: "I do have happy memories of the time when inflatables appeared, but it is slightly embarrassing to recall that as a 25-year-old I used to take an inflatable coiled snake to matches. We called him 'Hissing Sid'!"

Promotion came in 1989, followed by a most memorable Manchester derby, and as football moved into the 1990s City felt they were on the verge of establishing themselves as a true power again. Ground improvements followed. Again most of these were relatively small scale, or developments few would notice.

In 1991 around £500,000 was spent on improvements such as these, but the biggest visible change saw the grey seats in the lower half of the North Stand replaced and some of the walls erected in the early

Right: Pictures taken outside the stadium around 1987 showing (top to bottom) the expanse of the new roof on the Main Stand, the City Social Club, the Souvenir Shop, the back of the Kippax and the away section at the Thornton Road end of the Kippax.

Below: A photograph taken through the Main Stand fencing shows the players running out for the Leicester Cup tie armed with bananas - the Kippax is already a mass of the yellow inflatables!
It was a strange site to see supporters walking to the ground carrying plastic fruit!

Maine Match 89/90

CITY v MANCHESTER UNITED

DATE:	23rd September 1989	
TYPE OF FIXTURE:	Football League Division One	
ATTENDANCE:	43,246	
RESULT:	City 5 United 1	

TEAMS &	CITY		UNITED	
SCORERS:	Cooper		Leighton	
	Fleming		Anderson	
REFEREE:	Hinchcliffe	1	Donaghy	
N. Midgeley	Bishop	1	Duxbury	
(Bolton)	Gayle		Phelan	
	Redmond		Pallister	
	White		Beardsmore	
	Morley	1	(Sharpe)	
	Oldfield	2	Ince	
	Brightwell		McClair	
	Lake		Hughes	1
	(Beckford)		Wallace	

■ Victories over Manchester United are always sweet, but this became a landmark result for many reasons. City had been promoted the previous May and optimism was widespread, particularly as two new players - Ian Bishop and Clive Allen - had arrived. Bishop had impressed while playing for Bournemouth at Maine Road towards the end of the 1988-89 season, while Allen had a proven pedigree. He was also the club's first £1m signing since Trevor Francis during the crazy days of the early 1980s.

The season hadn't progressed particularly well – one victory and one draw out of six League games – and also a series of injuries meant Mel Machin would not be able to pick his preferred line-up. Two of the most influential players - Clive Allen and Neil McNab – were to miss the match. Another casualty was City's first choice 'keeper Andy Dibble.

For the Reds, Alex Ferguson had spent a considerable amount of money, for the period, on several major signings. They included Gary Pallister (£2.3m), Paul Ince (£1.7m), Danny Wallace (£1.2m) and Neil Webb (£1.5m). Webb missed this match, as did Bryan Robson, but to say United possessed a weak side is clearly incorrect, especially as they had defeated League leaders Millwall 5-1 a few days

before, while City had lost 1-2 at Brentford in the League Cup.

City fans were nervous pre-match and for Steve McCarthy this was a very important day in his family's support for the Blues: "This was my son Carl's first ever derby game.

I'd spent ages before the match explaining about the unique atmosphere of a derby and of how normal people would 'change' and come out with words and phrases he'd never heard before. I even said he might see and hear a different Dad to the one I'd tried to be."

When the game started Carl McCarthy was prepared for a hot-tempered match. After only ten minutes, a large contingent of United fans in the North Stand started to wreak havoc. The players were taken off the field while the trouble-makers were moved to the empty corner of the Platt Lane Stand, close to City's Family Stand. City fans were livid. Surely they should have been removed altogether, but the authorities felt evicting them would have caused more trouble outside the stadium. Interestingly, a book, purporting to be a biography of Alex Ferguson's first six years, produced a few years later, wrongly claimed the game had been stopped due to disturbances in the Kippax.

When play resumed City totally controlled the action, and those Reds removed from the North Stand must have wished they had been evicted. David White turned Mike Duxbury inside out. Gary Pallister was made to look an expensive failure, while Jim Leighton seemed particularly ill at ease in goal.

David Oldfield scored the first goal after only 11 minutes, then Trevor Morley netted a second less than a minute later. After 36 minutes Bishop headed City's third past a nervous Leighton.

At half-time some United fans left. Around the rest of the stadium City fans felt relatively comfortable although they also knew City being City anything was possible in the second half.

Shortly after the break Mark Hughes shot a spectacular but ultimately unimportant goal past Paul Cooper at the North Stand end. City fans worried this might cause their relatively inexperienced side to panic, but they didn't and the Blues continued to dominate. Oldfield scored his second in the 58th minute at the Platt Lane end. More United fans left, while City supporters around the ground chanted 'Easy, easy!"

By this point Steve McCarthy was delighted he had brought his son to the match: "When City's fourth goal went in the atmosphere was incredible. Everybody was singing and dancing and Carl turned to me and said 'Do you know what Dad? I really like derby games'. After fearing the worst this made me feel deliriously happy."

Four minutes after this moment Andy Hinchcliffe headed home City's fifth. He held up his hand with five raised fingers. Paul Lake loved the moment: "When Andy did that he was saying what we all felt. He was showing the United fans what this game meant to us and as a team we'd been groomed for that day. All our lives we'd waited and hoped for that moment, and then it came. There couldn't have been a better result."

Chants of "Fergie out!" emanated from the old Platt Lane, although the numbers sitting in the away section were reducing at an alarming rate.

The rest of the game was played out with City in control and United offering little. Reports after the match focused on the determination of the Blues and also on

Below: David Oldfield's shot has Jim Leighton well beaten (top two pictures) for City's opening goal. In the bottom picture Trevor Morley runs towards the Kippax to celebrate after making it 2-0.

Above: Either side of David Oldfield's second goal came headers from Ian Bishop (top) for number three and Andy Hinchcliffe for a magical fifth.

the cost of the two sides. One newspaper revealed the entire City side had cost less than £1.9m - £400,000 less than Gary Pallister.

Stood in the away section of the Kippax that day was City fan Graham Dalal: "This game took place on my birthday. I have never been a season ticket holder at City – in those days I couldn't afford it and now I live away from Manchester. Tickets for derby games are notoriously hard to come by, so when my best mate – a United fan – said his uncle had a couple of tickets going, I jumped at the chance. The only drawback was the tickets were in the away end of the Kippax [away fans would be given the Platt Lane seats and away terracing on the Kippax].

"The game was unbelievable – 3-0 to City at half-time and 5-1 at full time. Everything City did went right – all passes found the man, every shot seemed to threaten. Not surprisingly, the mood in the away end was black to say the least, and any thoughts I had about celebrations had to wait. I'm surprised my bottom lip wasn't bleeding by the time the game ended! This was the only occasion I have been to Maine Road and watched City win and been glad to get out!

"After the fifth goal had gone in I vividly recall all the United fans around me throwing their match programmes on to the pitch and chanting 'Fergie Out'. If only! Even though I think the old Kippax is possibly the worst football stand ever designed – especially the away section – it still has to be my own favourite stand simply because this is where I watched City completely and utterly take United apart."

Another City fan Steve Cummings believes this to be his most enjoyable Maine Road match: "I have many memories from all the years I have been watching City at Maine Road, but beating United 5-1 was such a fantastic day. The form book was completely against us, and I just wasn't looking forward to the trip home as I was sharing a car with four Reds. Never in my wildest dreams could I have predicted that scoreline, needless to say it was the four Reds who hated every minute of the journey home."

seventies demolished. The new seats were mainly blue in colour although the letters MCFC were spelt out in white and black lettering.

Other changes included the removal of the old floodlight pylons - lighting had been put on top of the Main Stand and Kippax roof. Interestingly, roof lighting had been planned back in 1957 but the club chose to erect the four floodlight pylons.

While these developments were being carried out, the club started to confirm interest in moving to Manchester's proposed Olympic Stadium. Back in the late 1980s Peter Swales had gone on record saying the club would be interested in moving to the proposed stadium close to the Ship Canal in West Manchester, but privately he believed the city would never get the Olympics and so it was never really clear whether City's interest was genuine or not. Manchester first bid for the 1992 Games and failed, but by the time they bid for the 1996 Games plans had changed drastically and the new stadium was to be in East Manchester. This seemed a much more realistic proposal, and City continued to claim interest in moving, although the chance of a new stadium being built still appeared slim.

Of course, the most important footballing story of late eighties and early nineties concerned the events at Hillsborough in April 1989 when the FA Cup semi-final between Nottingham Forest and Liverpool resulted in terrible tragedy. The biggest disaster in British footballing history brought radical changes to the sport, and Maine Road had to be reviewed as a result.

The recommendations of Lord Justice Taylor's Report into the Disaster had to be considered with the most radical being all First Division clubs had to have all-seater stadia by 1994. Clearly, the Kippax's days were numbered, but in the Boardroom at Maine Road the directors realised the club had other necessary changes to make.

The Platt Lane Stand was struggling to obtain its safety certificate and each year following the Bradford

Maine Memory

■ Maine Road is all independence... going to games on my own... braving the Kippax... feeling a part of something real... something interesting... cultured in a way... something completely unlike the experience you'd ever have at Old Trafford. It's winter midweek evenings watching talented blue-shirted kids called Lake, Brightwell, Hinchcliffe, White, Moulden... all playing so well, promising so much and doing all the running around while Neil McNab and Kenny Clements, resplendent in 'tache and perms do the orchestration and late tackles. It's the Kippax shouting at Kenny incessantly to give us a wave... he's past his best, perhaps not that good, but he's doing a job for the team and wearing a City shirt. It's about fun, good football, comradeship with a bunch of strangers that is the crowd around you. It's the complete other-worldliness of starting the inflatable craze, it's bananas and Blue Moon. It's about seeing, years later, the City fan and art critic Paul Morley on some late-night show describing that his favourite memory of Maine Road was the first time he heard for himself the Kippax sing 'Blue Moon'. In my memory it was raining, it was cold and we were probably under-performing but as Paul said it brought a tear to the eye. It was beautiful, it's City and they are always there and I'll never forget.
Richard Clarke

fire the club found it increasingly difficult to persuade the authorities the stand was safe; its construction, particularly with the use of wooden steps at its rear, was viewed as a major risk and it was claimed they had to sort out this issue before moving on to the Kippax.

Supporters heard the news Platt Lane was to be rebuilt and immediately assumed the new stand would be based on the proposals of 1981, i.e. a replica of the North Stand. The club said time had moved on and those plans were no longer valid, instead the new stand would contain executive boxes. There was also a story circulating the stand would be a two-tier development similar to the North Stand at Villa Park. At the AGM Peter Swales revealed the stand would contain some form of shopping mall, although when questioned the details appeared a little sketchy.

On 30th April 1991 a drawing of the proposed new stand appeared in the *Manchester Evening News*. Supporters were mortified despite the hyperbole. The stand would cost around £5m according to the article, but what really surprised everyone was the fact it appeared to be dominated by a significant number of Executive Boxes. Peter Swales tried to sell the redevelopment with positive comments about the direction of the club and then added: "Eventually, the Kippax Street terraces will have to be seated at a cost of almost £1m and then we will have a 40,000 all-seater stadium which is certain to be one of the best in the country."

It was this paragraph that seemed most worrying. If the new Platt Lane was going to cost in excess of £5m then surely redeveloping the Kippax would be substantially more? It seems City hoped simply to bolt plastic tip-up seating on to the original 1923 terracing,

Maine Match 92/93

CITY v QUEENS PARK RANGERS

DATE:	17th August 1992	
TYPE OF FIXTURE:	FA Premier League	
ATTENDANCE:	24,471	
RESULT:	City 1 QPR 1	
TEAMS &	CITY	QPR
SCORERS:	Coton	Stejskal
	Hill	Bardsley
	Brightwell	Wilson
	Simpson	Wilkins
	Curle	Peacock
	Vonk	McDonald
	White 1	Impey
	Lake	Holloway
	(Sheron)	Ferdinand
	Quinn	Bailey
	Holden	(Thompson),
	McMahon	Sinton 1

■ Despite its result this match is an important moment in the history of football as well as in the story of Maine Road. Although the game was not a classic it was the first League match to be shown live on Sky Television on a weekday evening (Nottingham Forest had defeated Liverpool the previous day on Sky), and was also the first Premier League match played by City.

The whole of Monday evening was geared around entertainment for the television viewers. Dancing girls were brought on to lift the atmosphere – they actually killed it – while supporters were urged to look skyward as a parachute team were to land on the pitch. Everybody looked and waited and then they saw the parachutists head for the pitch. At first fans appeared delighted but then they noticed the words 'Red Devils' on the parachutists' uniforms and began to 'boo'. This may seem a minor point or an irrelevance to many but there's nothing supporters dislike more than the media or the club misjudging the mood, or the feelings of supporters. The idea of parachutists was entertaining, but surely the authorities could have been a little more sensitive to the fans and perhaps transformed the 'Red Devils' into the

'Blues Brothers' for the night. Some supporters already began to wonder what was happening to the game.

Other activities on the night included a band singing 'Baker Street'. Oh, and there was also a game of football. The match was noteworthy as it saw the return of Paul Lake after almost two years out of the game. Understandably he received tremendous support and applause but, sadly, this was to be his last playing appearance at Maine Road as injury at Middlesbrough two days later ended his comeback and ultimately his playing career.

After the match fireworks exploded from the space where the Platt Lane Stand had been. The old stand had been demolished and the area utilised for the erection of a stage for concerts held during the summer. This meant when the season opened there were no signs of the new stand. This seemed a little surprising as the new stand would increase capacity and therefore it was felt it should be progressed quickly. Though once construction did start the building work rapidly developed.

The firework display at the end of the match gave a strange feel to the ground as regulars left the Kippax, and the following day secretary Bernard Halford was amazed to discover it had also brought other problems. Bernard: "I got a call the morning after to say there was a man at reception who demanded to see me. I went down the corridor and saw this guy carrying a bird cage. Now this is going to sound a lot like a Monty Python sketch but I swear it's true.

"The man looked at me and said 'You've killed my parrot!' My mind was racing. What had I done? I couldn't understand. Then he explained he lived close to the ground and was settling his bird down for the night when the first blast of fireworks came from the Platt Lane end of Maine Road. The noise was so great his parrot had a heart attack or something and fell off its perch! I didn't know what to say. Clearly he was very upset – that's understandable – but the whole situation was so strange. I was waiting for Jeremy Beadle or someone to pop out to tell me it was some kind of wind-up, but it wasn't.

"He actually told me we should have warned him because he said if he'd known the fireworks were going to go off he could have warned his parrot! I don't know what he would have said to him to prepare him, but I suppose he must have had some idea how to get his bird ready for the shock."

Maine Memory

■ Back in 1992 my six-year-old son Adam was coming with me to his first-ever game. It was 1st February 1992 and City were at home to Spurs. At the time we were living in Sheffield and had travelled the previous night and stayed with my mother in law in Whitefield. During the night the house was burgled and amongst other things my wallet which contained our tickets for the match was stolen out my jacket pocket.

Can you imagine the panic that set in that Saturday morning when we discovered what had happened? Adam was distraught, and come to think of it so was I. Quick action was needed, I raced down to the ticket office and explained what had happened and they were brilliant about it and fixed me up with duplicate tickets. So I dashed back to Whitefield to pick Adam up and then back to Maine Road just making it in time for the kick-off. Adam was overjoyed at the way things had turned out and really enjoyed his first-ever match at Maine Road. Of course it helped that City won 1-0 with a goal from David White. It was an occasion, given all the surrounding circumstances, he will never forget.

Dave Bracegirdle

erected the Olympic Gallery in a similar location at the national stadium. Perhaps the real reason was cost.

Regardless of the views of the majority of supporters, it's clear the new stand would bring extra income into the club and, as far as the boxes were concerned, the development was a considerable improvement on boxes at certain other venues. Each of the 48 boxes would contain an external viewing area which allowed boxholders the choice of whether to sit inside or outside during matches.

It was also clear the old Platt Lane capacity of around 9,000 was rarely tested – Manchester United couldn't fill it for any of the derby matches during the late 1980s and early 1990s. The last great crowd to be housed in the stand was Sunderland, on the final day of the 1990-91 season, when they filled the main section of the stand (approximately 6,000 seats) as they watched their side fail in their bid to remain in the top division.

The final game played in front of the stand was against Notts County on 25th April 1992. On that day Alex Williams, working on City's Community activities, brought a few thousand youngsters into the stand as part of an initiative to attract young local support.

The demolition of the stand was swift and relatively uncomplicated although in November 1990, eighteen months before its scheduled demise, Leeds United followers had done all they could to destroy it. Several rows of benches had been wrecked as Leeds fans celebrated – although that hardly seems an appropriate word – a 3-2 victory. The club had to replace those benches, even though the capacity of the stand wouldn't be tested, to ensure compliance with safety certificates, and so for the final year or so of its existence the stand contained several rows of blue plastic seating in one section.

The scheduled demolition saw an end to the final two tunnels positioned in the corners. The original 1923 Kippax/Platt Lane corner tunnel and the Platt Lane/Main Stand tunnel modified in 1931 disappeared without an outcry. Had architect Charles Swain still been around it's likely he would have raised an objection, but as far as the redevelopment was concerned the tunnels had to go.

Above: The morning after. Despite their 3-2 win over City in November 1990 Leeds fans started the demolition of the Platt Lane Stand 18 months early by wrecking several rows of bench seating.

and it has since been revealed by a source close to the Chairman during this period that the club had at times during the eighties even considered installing benches on the terracing. Had that been the case then Maine Road would not have been viewed as a 'super stadium' by any stretch of the imagination. Instead the ground would have brought considerable embarrassment City's way.

Manchester Evening News journalist Peter Gardner claimed the £5m Platt Lane and £1m Kippax developments would make the ground a leading contender to stage World Cup matches if the FA's bid for the 1998 finals proved successful.

Fortunately, the Kippax redevelopment did not occur until 1994 by which time the club had moved forward, but regrettably the Platt Lane development did go ahead. Clearly, the main aim of the new stand was to cash in on the need for corporate facilities. Maine Road did lag behind many other grounds and the original plan to have boxes built as part of the Main Stand roof had been abandoned. The club claimed the Bradford Fire had brought worries over safety, however Wembley somehow managed to overcome similar concerns when they

Right: An aerial view of the stadium shortly after the MCFC seats were put in the North Stand in 1991. Notice the rear view of the Platt Lane Stand. The left hand corner was constructed in 1931 with the rest of the stand extended and roofed in 1935. Architect Charles Swain had planned for a mirror image of this stand to be erected at the opposite end of the ground but war prevented the club from furthering those plans. In addition, it is believed Swain wanted to extend the Kippax side in a similar way.

Clearly, the plans for the new stand had shown a new corner linking up to the Main Stand, but the Kippax corner plans seemed vague.

This corner had always posed a problem for redevelopment due to its proximity to Thornton Road, however the original corner could have survived for a little longer. Perversely, when the new Platt Lane Stand was finished, the Kippax corner was empty. Surely the club could have left the old terracing in place – and thereby kept the capacity at a figure in excess of 40,000. The capacity, as recorded following the opening of the new stand was 39,800. The Kippax corner would have added at least 2,000 standing to that figure.

The club, no doubt, would have argued this corner would have to come down in 1994 to comply with the Taylor report, however a little foresight may have actually allowed some form of uncovered seating to be developed here to help the transition to an all-seater ground. This corner, it should be noted, saw an increasing number of temporary seats erected during the new millennium.

The new Platt Lane opened - with the disappointingly sponsored name of The Umbro Stand - for an FA Cup quarter final against Tottenham in March 1993, but the day became one of major disappointment as supporters invaded the pitch; a move borne out of frustration at the club's direction rather than any motivation to cause trouble. A simple glance around the stadium showed the lack of foresight at the club. An eclectic mix of stands, styles and colours gave a clear indication the club no longer housed enough visionaries like Furniss, Swain, Alexander and others responsible for the stadium in the 1920s and 30s.

In the months that followed the Spurs fiasco, Peter Swales took steps to change the management structure of the club, while the fans grew increasingly dissatisfied with the overall direction of the team they loved. From a Maine Road perspective, however, most were now wondering how the ground would be made all-seater in time for the 1994-5 deadline. City had just 18 months to replace the Kippax Stand. The clock was ticking.

Above: The 1935 Platt Lane roof starts to come down in April 1992. The terracing was an original feature of the ground built in 1923, while the 1935 extension saw the terracing extended at the back with wooden steps.

Below: The Platt Lane Stand during construction. For a large part of the 1992/93 season the blue boarding behind the goal provided an unusual backdrop for teams attacking that end of the ground.

■ This game should have been one of the high points of Chairman Peter Swales' reign, but it became one of the lowest, possibly this is the match above all others which prompted City fans to bring to an end his chairmanship. Swales later admitted: "I should have gone then! That game was a real low point for me. New stand... Big crowd... Everything right, except the result and the fans on the pitch. I was going to resign but a few friends and other directors persuaded me to stay. They convinced me. I don't know if it was self-preservation or what, but they all convinced me to stay. Now I realise I should definitely have gone... No question! From that point on, it wasn't me. I made a few mistakes and I stopped learning. Stopped listening."

The day started brightly. The new Platt Lane Stand was to open for the first time and with live television coverage on the BBC there was an air of optimism around Maine Road. In fact the only negative point pre-match was the announcement the new stand would be given the moniker of the Umbro Stand. Although the stand was far too small for City's needs it did offer supporters the best sightlines of all the seated sections of the stadium at this time. There was substantially more leg room than in the North or Main Stands.

The game kicked off with supporters in full voice, and when Mike Sheron gave the Blues the lead the atmosphere developed further. This was to be City's year for the cup! Sadly, the Blues frustratingly inconsistent streak reappeared and Spurs became the only side with a chance of glory. First Nayim, totally unmarked, scored from about twenty yards out, then Sedgley ran unopposed on to a through ball to give Tottenham the lead.

Early in the second half Nayim made it 3-1 and City were dead. Five minutes from time another unopposed

Below: One of the first tickets issued for the new Platt Lane Stand.

Below: City chairman Peter Swales with Peter Lee of the Football Trust and Peter Kenyon of Umbro at the opening of the new Platt Lane Stand two days before the FA Cup quarter final with Spurs. The TV box in the corner near the Kippax is already in place for Sunday's BBC presenters.

Maine Match 92/93

CITY v TOTTENHAM HOTSPUR

DATE:	7th March 1993			
TYPE OF FIXTURE:	FA Cup Quarter Final			
ATTENDANCE:	34,050			
RESULT:	City 2 Tottenham 4			
TEAMS & SCORERS:	**CITY**		**TOTTENHAM**	
	Coton		Thorstvedt	
	Hill		Austin	
	Phelan	1	Edinburgh	
	Simpson		Samways	
	Curle		Mabbutt	
	Vonk		Ruddock	
	White		Sedgley	1
	Sheron	1	Nayim	3
	Quinn		Anderton (Turner)	
	Flitcroft		Sheringham	
	Holden		Allen	

effort gave Nayim his hat-trick and the City fans were totally and utterly dejected. Spurs had another disallowed, and then City's Terry Phelan set off on a thrilling run. He scored a superb goal in front of the Umbro Stand and within seconds fans streamed on to the pitch.

The stewards failed to stop them and it wasn't long before the number of invaders increased. Over time supporters started to invade from the Kippax as well, and the BBC claimed there were around 200 City 'hooligans' on the turf. The majority of those were not hooligans but simply frustrated supporters. In fact some were uncertain why they'd gone onto the pitch in the first place.

The police seemed slow to act but when they did they certainly over-reacted and sent about ten officers on horseback onto the pitch to charge at the supporters. This sight made the situation look considerably worse than it actually was.

The game resumed and Sheringham missed a penalty for Spurs – some fans felt he'd deliberately missed to avoid further invasions – and then Niall Quinn missed an absolute sitter. The game ended 4-2 and the media turned the invasion into a major news story.

The main reason for the invasion was undoubtedly frustration at seventeen years without success, but indirectly, the opening of the Umbro had also affected morale. It was clear to almost everyone in the stadium that the building of this stand had actually killed off all hope that Maine Road would ever be the greatest stadium in England again. Even the name 'Umbro' smacked of the club not listening – supporters were far from content with the kit suppliers at this point. The stand was a rather tasteless construction with too few seats and too many executive boxes. In simple terms it was very much 'small time' as opposed to the stands being constructed elsewhere.

The media missed the real story entirely, but the fans understood and, when the following season saw the poorly-timed sacking of manager Peter Reid, the frustrations reappeared with dramatic consequences for the club.

Maine Memories

Exit doors as goalposts

■ I grew up on Thornton Road, next to the ground, and so it wasn't just a football ground to me it was my playground. We played football on the forecourt, using the exit doors under the mosaics as our goalposts, and sometimes the players would join in as they left the ground. Could you imagine the joy of playing football with Joe Corrigan – England's goalie - in nets!

We also knew what time the players would set off for their jog to the Platt Lane Training ground so we'd all be waiting on the forecourt for them. When they came out we'd join them and jog along as if we were part of the team. The players didn't seem to mind, in fact I think it was probably quite entertaining for some of them, but for us this was special. Everybody looked as we ran, and I suppose in our young minds we probably thought that we looked the part.

Years later I started working at City, joining the Football in the Community scheme in 1988. City were one of the first clubs to set up a community scheme and they eventually became a model for clubs across the country. For me it was a dream job.

I'd been a season ticket holder since I was six and my main job was to travel around Manchester coaching football to school children. Most of the kids thought we were players and it was difficult explaining that you weren't, but as a job it was as good as you can imagine. Every day was a pleasure.

As part of my duties sometimes I'd be left to lock up the ground. In every room there were tiny electric wall heaters, even in the Boardroom. The place was always freezing and I had to remember to go around the ground and put on these heaters prior to the ground tours I gave. Than afterwards I had to go around and switch them all off. If I forgot I was in serious trouble – wasting even a penny of the club's money was a serious offence!

Every May there would be a staff game on the pitch against Tom Garner Motors. Quite often some of the first team would play as well as regular staff. I remember Howard Kendall giving me a nip of whisky before one match to 'help me relax'. I was spluttering for the first five minutes. My main memory from these games though came halfway through when the ball went out of play. I chased it to the hoardings in front of the Kippax terrace to take a throw in. Then it dawned on me. That's where I used to stand with my Dad. This is Maine Road. I'm playing on Maine Road!

Neil Mather

In your face
■ The Platt Lane is being rebuilt and a big temporary fence protects the pitch from the building site. David White is down on the by-line on his right side of the Maine Road pitch. In frustration at the ball running out of play, Whitey lashes the ball at the temporary wall and it rebounds straight into his face!

J. Tomkinson

There could only ever be one winner!

■ Although I have been to Maine Road many times over the years, the game with Leeds on 4th April 1992 sticks out in my mind more than most, for the simple fact that I travelled to Maine Road that day unsure about whether I wanted a City win or not. This was due to Leeds and United contesting the championship, and knowing that a City win would only help United's chances. Being only twelve years old at the time, all that I could envisage over the coming months would be constant gloating from United fans at school if the unthinkable was to come true. I thought that maybe just this once, a City defeat might not be the end of the world.

Once the game kicked off though I changed my mind. I may hate United, but I love City more - a feeling I think most Blues share. The atmosphere on the Kippax that afternoon was brilliant and City played just as well. It didn't seem long before Andy Hill had put us one up, and then Steve McMahon played a great through ball to Sheron who lifted it over Lukic to make it two. I remember Leeds having their moments, but they couldn't get past our excellent defence, well-marshalled by Keith Curle. Steve McMahon and especially Fitzroy Simpson had good games. Simpson was always snapping at somebody's heels, normally Strachan's, and I thought he was going to turn into a tremendous signing for City over the years to come.

The goal of the game was undoubtedly Niall Quinn's. To chip John Lukic, who was standing on his goal line, from the corner of the area took some doing, but that was exactly what he did. We were in cruise control from then on and Mark Brennan smashing in number four was the icing on the cake. The great thing about the game though was that the result didn't harm Leeds' chances of the title, because as we all know they went onto win the League at United's expense. For the next couple of months, it was me doing all the gloating at school instead of the United fans.

Andrew Jackson

It's not like it used to be!

■ *My best memories of watching City are when I was about six or seven and my dad was a steward. The terraces were still up and he would take me to watch the game. I got to sit in front of the terrace opposite the dug-out and had the best seat in the stadium. My idol was David White - players were different then, nowadays they seem to be untouchable superstars. David was down to earth. I am 22 now and have a season ticket and sit in the Platt Lane Stand. It's a good seat but the atmosphere is nothing like it used to be.*

Andrew Jackson

Moody Blues

■ The summer of 1983 was too much for an 11-year-old boy to bear. The events of the previous May cast a long shadow over the summer. For me, I was to experience the first (and unfortunately, not the last) occasion of City being relegated whilst 'you know whom' won a trophy. I don't know how the former happened. Admittedly, City had always struggled a bit, ever since I started going to Maine Road in 1978. Although these days I can smell a relegation in the offing, this one caught me unawares. The innocence of youth maybe, but we'd been top of the League in August and weren't in the bottom three until Raddy Antic popped up and invited David Pleat to do a sponsored lap of Maine Road.

I'd spent the summer sulking, taunted by new-found United kids who'd never set foot inside Old Trafford, basking in the glory of a fluky win over Brighton. All of a sudden, Oldham Athletic kids popped up from nowhere and were having a dig. In hindsight, I suppose young City fans of the 1990's can relate to all this but it was unprecedented back then. I'd left Maine Road in a flood of tears after the Luton game. Throughout the summer, I was determined to give it up. However, Manchester City is to this day, a habit that cannot be kicked. So after missing the first two games of the 1983-84 season as a result of my parent's insistence that I regularly spend the first two weeks of September, marooned in a caravan in Wales, I was back in my Block N seat for the Blackburn home game.

Times had changed. Big Joe had gone, King Dennis and Kevin Reeves sold and Bobby Mac sacked. Billy Mc & Jimmy Frizz came and brought with them strikers Parlane & Tolmie. Manchester City had turned Scottish! Who cared when you won six-nil? I can't remember the game vividly – I was only 11 after all, but I do remember losing count of the goals. You couldn't see the old scoreboard from where we sat in the back of the North Stand. We'd scored six. I'd never seen City score so many.

I can remember that Parlane scored a hat trick while my new hero Tolmie had a massive perm. He was the same height as I was back then. City were back – well we were winning more games anyway. Most of the wins came against teams I didn't know even existed.

I held my head high in school on the Monday morning. We'd scored six and we had a cool two-tone blue striped shirt that looked magic in PE. Along with Chelsea, Newcastle and Sheffield Wednesday - but not Leeds incidentally - we were part of the big four of Division Two. A pity then that we finished fourth but hey, don't let facts ruin a good story. Promotion wasn't actually achieved until the following season but the Blackburn result was enough for me to save up my pocket money and become a 'life member' of the Junior Blues. The silk scarf has already been handed down to my one-year-old son Jamie.

David Sigsworth

Demonstrations

ONE of Maine Road's most important aspects has always been the way supporters of the club have felt free to express their opinions. Sometimes demonstrations have been performed in a peaceful manner, but on occasion there have been ugly scenes outside the main entrance.

Prior to the 1960s all criticism of the management was carried out within the stadium or through the local newspapers. Supporters complained about the transfer of players - in 1930 they threatened to boycott the club following the removal of hero Tommy Johnson to Everton - but there was never any serious complaint about the control of the club. Fans seemed to accept the Board had the best interests of the club at heart and the manager was a figure to be respected. Sure they talked about his selections and transfers but they did not demonstrate.

By 1963 however the club was in decline and supporters began to vocalise. It's no coincidence that the empowerment of supporters also came at a time when demonstrations were occurring for civil rights and against war. Two years later a small group of young City fans demonstrated outside the main entrance. In later years the media claimed these fans had thrown bricks at the windows, but at the time little was said about that. The focus was simply on the fact a number of fans were now protesting against those in charge of the club they loved.

Around the same time a group going by the name of "Forward City" were accused of stirring up trouble in the *Manchester Evening News*. In May 1964 "Forward City" had been accused of forever comparing City to United. The *Evening News* claimed this was a silly thing to do, but in truth it was the newspaper that was out of touch. If nothing else "Forward City" were creating a situation whereby supporters could debate the direction of the club. The group's aim was to alter the course of the club and, although they did not directly bring change, they had sown seeds.

In 1965 Joe Mercer and Malcolm Allison arrived and City's fortunes were reversed. Members of the "Forward City" group later formed part of the 1970 takeover which, ironically, eventually led to the installation of Peter Swales as Chairman.

Relative peace followed until the beginning of the 1980s. Supporters first complained about Malcolm Allison's spell in charge, then in 1982 they began to openly criticise Peter Swales. The departure of £1m man Trevor Francis was seen as a major body-blow and even caused a small group of fans to later create the "Bring Back Trevor Francis Campaign". The campaign was doomed, as were City, and when relegation struck in 1983 the first chantings of "Swales Out" were heard.

The demonstrations against the Chairman came and went with alarming regularity. If City were relegated or performed exceptionally poorly, the stadium erupted and demonstrations would follow on the main forecourt. If City were promoted and even if they performed well during a poor season, the demonstrations would cease. Some tried to ensure the demonstrations occurred regardless, but the majority did not. When City were heading for relegation in 1987 the final home match of the season was expected to host the largest "Swales Out" demonstration of all time, however City beat

Nottingham Forest 1-0 thanks to an Imre Varadi goal and most supporters went home. A few committed fans did demonstrate but it wasn't enough to bring any change.

Further demonstrations followed at times throughout the eighties and early nineties - the sacking of Mel Machin briefly brought criticism Swales' way - and then in 1993 the largest demonstrations ever witnessed at Maine Road made national headlines. The trigger was City's abject failure in a cup quarter final with Tottenham in March, but the dismissal of Peter Reid only a few games into the 1993/4 season saw a sustained attack on the management of the club by the fans. Some thought Reid's dismissal totally wrong while others deemed it should have happened a few months earlier during the close season. Whichever viewpoint was held, it was clear the move was ill-conceived.

Demonstrations followed every home game and when former player Francis Lee announced he wanted to take over the club, the supporters felt they could rally to somebody who was able to seriously challenge the Board. A long bitter campaign followed with protests during games - former players stood on the Kippax; candles were lit to make a visible demonstration; and supporters stayed behind in the stands to show their determination - and on the forecourt. Maine Road became a battleground and at times the atmosphere was too intense. Francis Lee would be cheered as he took to his seat, and then moments later Peter Swales would be booed and verbally abused as he made his way to his chair.

Eventually, after a stormy AGM and numerous meetings, Peter Swales stood down and Francis Lee took over, but it wasn't the end of demonstrations at Maine Road.

The arrival of Alan Ball as manager set City off on another downward spiral and supporters became vocal again. Supporter Dante Friend set up a protest group called "Free the 30,000" which aimed to challenge the direction of the club once more. Supporters had clearly grown used to demonstrating during Peter Swales' reign and Francis Lee's honeymoon period was over. Lee stood down as the Blues headed towards relegation to the third tier of football but it wasn't the fans that had brought the change, it was pressure from the shareholders. Although, to be fair to Lee he had always stated he would stand down if the fans demanded it, unlike his predecessor.

During the final years of City's stay at Maine Road there was little to demonstrate against. The resignations of first Chris Bird and then David Bernstein in March 2003 caused some to question the Board set-up. A petition was organised urging Bernstein to return and some suggested demonstrating at the Birmingham match, however this came to nothing. Fans have generally been happy with the direction of the club since 1999.

It's worth remembering that supporters remain the most important part of Manchester City and it is abundantly clear that whenever they feel disgruntled with the direction of the club they will make their feelings known.

Maine Memories

We could have blown it!

■ Manchester City v Bournemouth, League Division Two, Saturday 6th May 1989 - This was supposed to be the day when City clinched promotion, assuming they won. If so, and Crystal Palace failed to win at Leicester, City were up. Given this state of affairs, and the fact it was a gloriously sunny day, I was expecting a huge crowd to turn up to acclaim the Blues. It seemed strange then, parking up at Wilbraham School, how quiet the area round Maine Road seemed, even allowing for it being still quite early. In the end only 30-odd thousand turned up, compared with 47,000 four years earlier in very similar circumstances. But since then we'd had Heysel, and English clubs were still banned from Europe. Football fans were very much under the threat of having to carry identity cards and the game generally was in the doldrums.

Whatever the reasons, it took a little while for the anticipated party to get going. Moulden put City one-up after only three minutes, seizing on a loose ball in the Bournemouth box, but afterwards City's play went rather off the boil. The fans on the Kippax were beginning to warm to the occasion, though, with news coming through that Leicester were also 1-0 up. On the pitch, City's meandering play was refreshed by a beautiful goal from Trevor Morley on 38 minutes. Turning his marker on the left side of the box, he then bent a glorious curling shot around the goalkeeper into the far corner of the net. City's renewed sense of purpose was quickly rewarded (41mins) when Hinchcliffe's long shot came back off goalkeeper and crossbar for Moulden to net the third from close range. Even the half time score from Filbert Street (Palace had equalised) couldn't dampen the sense of optimism, and once the second half got going, so did the promotion party. This was the age of the inflatable, and there were some large specimens around this afternoon. First a huge beach ball, then a rubber dinghy, were passed round three sides of the ground over people's heads while the promotion songs (particularly the Karma Chameleon one – the KC & The Sunshine Band 'City's Going Up' seemed to have been forgotten by some fans) were sung with gusto. On 63mins Shearer, the Bournemouth centre-back, headed in a corner and was applauded by most of the City fans, such was the confidence that the Blues were home and hosed. City had lost the initiative, though, and the goal gave the visitors a sense of hope. Apart from a glancing header, off target, from Moulden, the pressure was all on the City end, and the party atmosphere was swiftly replaced by a feeling of anxiety. When, after 79mins, Matthew Holmes threaded a carefully-placed shot through a crowded penalty area and inside the right post, anxiety gave way to near-panic.

There had been a number of stoppages during the game, and the referee was quite right to add on, by my watch, six minutes of what then was still called 'injury time'. The fear on the Kippax reached fever pitch as minute after minute ticked by and still the final whistle didn't blow. Finally, four minutes in, Blissett got goal-side of Hinchcliffe chasing a long ball into City's box. It was one of those horrible situations where you could see what was going to happen before it actually did. Sure enough Blissett, under pressure, managed to stay on his feet for long enough to get into the box, then down he went. The referee knew the script too and pointed to the spot. While Blissett received treatment, Kippax fans looked around for anyone with a radio on. One lad had. "Palace are leading." he solemnly announced. Blissett recovered and sent Cooper the wrong way from the spot. There was time for a bit more play, but not much, and when the final whistle finally went it was greeted by angry chants of "Machin out!", and worse. True, City could still go up by winning their last game at Bradford City, but I don't think anybody seriously had any confidence that the necessary victory could be achieved.

Thoroughly depressed, I deflated my banana as I traipsed up the Kippax terrace towards the exit at the back, and stuffed it into my coat. Wanting to be absolutely sure of the situation City were in, I fetched my little transistor radio out of my pocket, switched it on and pressed it to one ear. 'Sport On Two' - no Five Live in 1989! - was going round the various First Division grounds for final scores as I descended the steps behind the stand. Then they broke into the sequence for news of an important goal at Leicester. Incredibly, it was an equaliser for the home side after eight minutes of injury time! "YEEEESSSS!!!" I yelled, and a dozen or so faces looked up at me from the crowd down below in the forecourt, wondering what was going on. I was so shocked I couldn't get any words out. Fortunately, a bloke to one side of me had a walkman on and more presence of mind than I could muster. He raised both arms aloft, each hand with two fingers raised, victory style. "It's two-two Leicester," he announced, triggering a celebration down below as enthusiastic as any for any of City's goals that day.

Simon Clarke

Gordon Banks eat your heart out!

■ I have been going to Maine Road since about 1988 and one of my favourite memories was a game against Derby County (April 1991). Niall Quinn, a man who is only good in the air and can only score goals with his head, took a cross from the left on his chest, controlled it with his knee then volleyed into the top corner. World Class. But the best was a minute later Tony Coton got sent off and a penalty was awarded. Step up big Niall, somehow he got right down to the bottom left hand corner of the goal and tipped the ball over the cross bar. Gordon Banks eat your heart out.

Gary Waters

Just visiting

■ As a Norwich City supporter Maine Road was a ground I always wanted to go to, but my first visit didn't come until 16th September 1987, and then I was a neutral fan. At the time I worked for a good old Manchester firm called Refuge Assurance and I was on a course for a week. A few colleagues and I decided a worthwhile evening's entertainment would be to watch City play at home to Millwall. City were in the old Second Division at the time and managed by an old Canaries favourite Mel Machin.

I remember Machin's programme notes included a berating of his team for an inept performance in the previous home game – a 2-1 defeat to Blackburn Rovers. His public criticism obviously worked well as City swept aside Millwall with ease. The visitors included a young Teddy Sheringham, sporting a very dodgy basin haircut, but he was completely overshadowed by a fine hat-trick from Imre Varadi in a 4-0 home win. It was a good City side.

My next visit was supporting Norwich – another home win for Manchester City. Maine Road was never a happy hunting ground for the Canaries! My lasting memory of this visit in 1994 was of being amazed at the number of ticket touts outside the ground. I was astounded by their blatancy. I had never previously encountered such pro-active touting at a football match – especially when Norwich were the visitors!

Geoff Matthews

Six of the best

■ The 6-0 defeat of Norwich in the FA Cup fourth round (24th Jan 1981) was memorable because City scored six spectacular goals and all from different players. I was in the North Stand with my dad, a few rows behind Helen Turner and her infamous bell. Kevin Reeves set us on our way, and Gerry Gow added a second before the break. In the second half City ran riot with further goals from Mackenzie, Bennett, Power and finally Bobby McDonald, who powered home a header in the last minute. This was the match in which John Bond jumped down from the director's box to console his son Kevin and injured himself in the process. When the highlights were shown later, I saw myself on TV – another first! Our name was on the Cup or so we thought!

Five years later I was in the Kippax for the first game of the 1986-67 season, which pitted City against newly-promoted Wimbledon. After a goalless first half, Wimbledon took the lead just after the break, and I was thinking "Oh no!" There's always a surprise somewhere on the first day, and for a while it looked like it would be at Maine Road. Fortunately, an inspired substitution saved the day. Paul Simpson came on for Ian Brightwell and changed the game. Racing down the left wing, he tortured the Wimbledon defence and set up goals for Graham Baker (2) and Trevor Christie – all in the space of about ten minutes. It ended City 3 Wimbledon 1.

Richard Benson

Queue jumping

◼ At the time of the match with Sheffield Wednesday on 10th December 1983 I was spending the weekend with friends in Liverpool, so travelled across by train for the match. On the way to Lime Street station the bus I was on got stuck in a traffic jam, so I missed my intended train. Catching a later one, I didn't arrive at Maine Road until twenty to three. As usual, I got off the bus in Lloyd Street and made my way round behind the Platt Lane end down the alley to get to the Kippax. When I emerged from the alley I was horrified by what I saw. Stretching back from each turnstile was a massive queue, all the way across the car park. If I joined the back of one, I reckoned I'd be lucky to get in by half time. Then I noticed a couple of gates next to each other with no queue. At first I thought they were probably locked, but then I saw someone walk up to one and go through, so I went for a closer look. Over the gates was a sign: "Season Tickets Only". Phew! In all the scramble to get there on time, I'd forgotten I had a season ticket in my pocket. In previous games it hadn't really mattered which gate I went through, but attendances for those were all in the mid-twenties and I'd arrived at the stadium rather earlier. Today's gate turned out to be almost 42,000. It just shows how things have changed over 20 years, with crowds today being made up almost exclusively of season ticket holders.

The large attendance reflected the importance of the game. Both sides were chasing promotion. Wednesday were top, City were second and would go top with a 3-0 win. "We'll be top at five o'clock" sang the Kippax, and when the match started there looked to be every possibility they'd be right. After 10 minutes Kevin Bond's free kick deflected off a defender, who had run out of the defensive wall to close him down, and looped over goalkeeper Hodge into the net. City were dominating the play with Jim Tolmie in total control, and it was Tolmie who almost added a second, chipping over Hodge from the edge of the box. The ball floated agonisingly just over the post/bar angle, and it was the pivotal moment of the match. With 24 minutes gone, future Blue Imre Varadi got away down the right wing, but with nobody up in support he just hit the ball hopefully in the direction of the goal from somewhere in the region of 40 yards out. Too late did Alex Williams realise where it was going and tried in vain to reach it as it sailed over his head into the far corner of the net. You'd have thought there was a riot going on amongst the Wednesday fans standing on the corner terrace between Kippax and Platt Lane, such was the amount of thrashing around that greeted the goal, but of course it was just glee. City never quite recovered from conceding such a daft goal, and Wednesday gradually took control. With a quarter of the game remaining, Bond and Varadi tussled for control of a centre from the left. Bond lost the flight of the ball, it bounced off his back and fell nicely for Varadi to score. By now City had lost the initiative completely, and they couldn't recover it enough to force an equaliser. "We'll be top at five o'clock" was replaced by an uncomfortable feeling that even promotion might be difficult, never mind winning the division.

The Wednesday team, incidentally, contained future Blues Tony Cunningham and Gary Megson, in addition to Imre Varadi.

I don't think there was as much violence associated with football by this time as had been the case a few years earlier, but on this occasion I did see a small group of Sheffield fans try to start trouble at Piccadilly Station after the game. Fortunately the police were on hand to snuff it out quickly.

Simon Clarke

These pictures formed part of a special feature in a 1989 *Sunday Mirror Magazine* focussing on a typical Maine Road matchday, entitled 'Girls, Goals & Glory'. The baby being held by his father Alex Rees was named Alex Michael Clive Allen in honour of City's big summer signing. "They both arrived in August" was dad's logic.

There was little time for reflection in 1994 as the old
Kippax had to be replaced at speed. The stadium had
to be all seater by the start of the 1994-5 season,
while the club desperately needed to improve income
by developing the best corporate facilities possible.

Chapter Ten

All Seater

"I am happy to keep a low profile. There have been too many statements made from this club. I want us to be realistic and absolutely honest from now on. I know the fans will be sceptical, but they are entitled to be"

Chairman David Bernstein, October 1998

THE 1990s saw considerable ground development at Maine Road with first the building of the Umbro/Platt Lane Stand followed by the new Kippax Stand, but as the 1993-4 season began the general view was the Platt Lane Stand was a rather small-time construction, while plans for the new Kippax were unclear. Rumours had circulated how seats would be bolted onto the original terracing, while others suggested the stand would be built in phases with a second tier constructed at some future point. As with other issues connected with the club at the time there seemed to be an air of confusion.

During City's removal from Maine Road in June 2003 some plans were unearthed from August 1993 revealing the club's intentions. These show how the stand

would have housed two tiers with a total capacity of 10,035 (6602 on the lower tier, 3,386 on the top one and 47 spaces for disabled fans), however these figures were still being debated. Within a month the number of disabled spaces had been reduced by 16, while a further 123 seats had been squeezed in their place.

It was also suggested, as part of this plan, that most of the lower tier of the stand would make use of the original Kippax terracing. This would have set Maine Road back thirty years. As proved by the bench seating on the old Platt Lane Stand, seats on terracing designed for standing offered supporters exceptionally poor views. It also limited the amount of leg room.

Elsewhere, the plans included lots of areas marked for future development. These included toilets, bars, food

Below and right: A proposal for the redevelopment of Maine Road made in January 1994. The different colours helped highlight the different phases anticipated over a six year period. The plans were seriously considered and may have been progressed had the decision not been made to move to the new stadium. Note: the completion of the plan would have required the club to purchase and demolish houses on Carlton Avenue behind the North Stand.

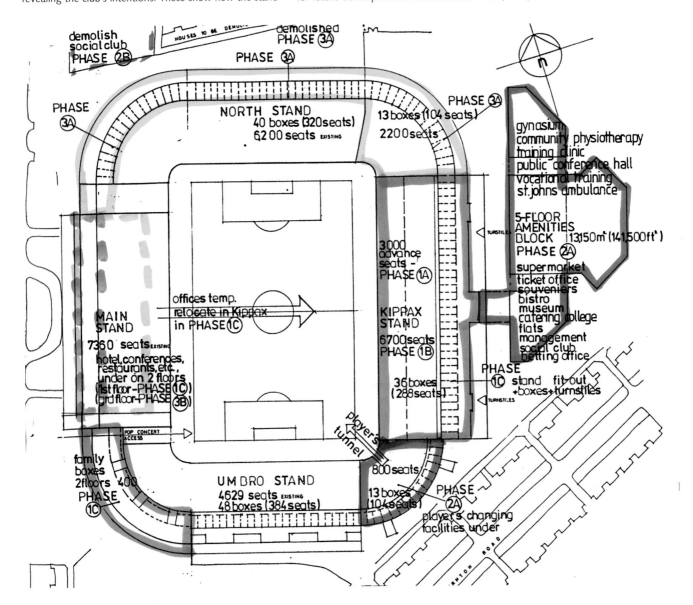

PROPOSED · STADIUM · DEVELOPMENT· ·MANCHESTER · CITY · FOOTBALL · CLUB · ·MAINE · ROAD·

Maine Memory

■ In 1995, my 13-year-old daughter Emma dislocated her knee in the week before City played Leeds United at home. We were left with the problem of how we were going to fit a leg in a full 'BLUE' plaster cast into a middle row seat - our normal season ticket position - in the Kippax. A phone call to the Ticket Office resulted in us being temporarily relocated in the Main Stand, with an end of aisle seat. Seeing Emma in plaster, Vince Miller, the pre-match announcer, invited us both up to the dressing room area after the game, where Franny Lee, the chairman, chatted to Emma and signed her plaster. He generally made a big fuss of her whilst Dad looked on open-mouthed in awe at the presence of one of his boyhood heroes.

Emma wrote to Franny to thank both him and the club for all their help while she had "her leg up". Shortly afterwards she received a personal reply from the Chairman, which is now framed and takes pride of place on her bedroom wall. Franny didn't have to do all this, but he obviously felt it important to look after young Blues fans. This is why we all feel that City is such a special club.

David Robinson

stalls, executive boxes, lifts, staircases, fire shutters, and even the main concourse area. It seems the entire stand was expected to consist of two tiers of tightly-packed seating, with all concourse areas blocked off, leaving supporters to use the old Kippax bar and toilet facilities.

All this strongly suggests the club could simply not afford to perform a sensible redevelopment of the ground.

The overall stand style and construction were to be similar to the Platt Lane Stand, with the stand including black, plum and two shades of Blue (Ocean and Solent) cladding.

While these plans were being made, the 1993-4 season was to prove one of the most difficult in the long history of the club. Early into the season the dismissal of Peter Reid as manager had led to demonstrations against Chairman Peter Swales. Supporters demanded change

and when former playing hero Francis Lee announced his intention to challenge the club's leadership they immediately backed his campaign.

Every home match became surreal. Francis Lee would move into the Directors' Box to the sound of cheers and applause and then Peter Swales would enter to widespread booing behind him. It was very much a pantomime atmosphere except this was far more serious than any Grimm fairy tale.

Sit-down protests, candlelight protests and demonstrations on the forecourt became the norm as Swales, Lee and their supporters fought out a takeover battle. Naturally this impacted on the pitch activity, but it also had an effect on the development of the stadium. While the takeover rumbled on, any plans for the Kippax took a back seat, although information did appear in the programme on what the new 'two-tier' stand might

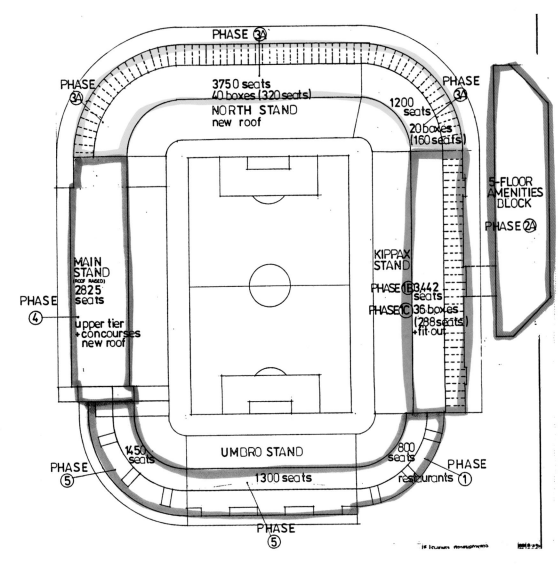

offer. To many, it simply looked as if a basic stand was to be constructed.

On the pitch there were also a few bizarre moments. The Ipswich match in January was abandoned after 39 minutes due to a waterlogged pitch. Understandably, as City were winning, the players were far from happy with this decision. Tony Coton certainly challenged it, while Kare Ingebrigtsen saw his only League goal for the Blues wiped from the records. He did find the net again five days later as Leicester were defeated 4-1 in the FA Cup, but this was another unusual match. Ingebrigtsen, who was widely viewed as one of club's fringe players, netted a hat-trick, while Alan Kernaghan, another man most fans struggled to accept, netted the other from 35 yards.

When Francis Lee's consortium eventually gained control of the club they had many issues to consider. Clearly, activities on the pitch had to be addressed quickly, and the Blues took steps to strengthen the squad. Uwe Rösler and Paul Walsh were brought in to help the fight against relegation and for the final weeks of the season City excited their followers.

Off the pitch Lee had two major issues to address – the redevelopment of the Kippax and generating more income for the club. Financially, the Blues were struggling. Income streams were limited with merchandising rights bringing in an annual payment rather than the depth of royalties enjoyed by other clubs, while corporate hospitality was also still relatively small time. The Platt Lane boxes had improved the situation enormously, but other than that City possessed one dining area – the Executive Suite – and a lounge for sponsors. There was also the Joe Mercer Suite – the club had already converted the Gym into a basic suite. Other sources of income had to be found if the club was to establish itself as one of the Premier League's elite.

Lee saw an immediate opportunity. The office space within the Main Stand had limited potential as modern offices but was in a prime position for corporate clients. Immediately, Lee and City's new Managing Director Colin Barlow came to the conclusion the club had to move its offices out of the ground and redevelop the entire space for restaurants and modern matchday facilities.

Maine Men Peter Swales

ROLE: Chairman

■ There are two distinct phases to the career of Peter Swales at Manchester City. During the first he was one of the most outgoing and popular footballing administrators the club had ever seen, while in the second he became public enemy number one as far as most fans were concerned.

During the Seventies, Swales travelled to supporters' meetings all over the world, encouraging fans with his openness and enthusiasm. Whereas most club chairmen were inaccessible figureheads, Swales was seen in a completely different light. He was open, and even allowed himself to be interviewed by some of his biggest critics – a move that always won him support in the early days. One national publication which liked to challenge the establishment was Foul, acclaimed as football's first serious fanzine. In one edition, published May 1974, Colin Shindler wrote a critical piece suggesting the appointment of Tony Book was misguided and also focused on the takeover battle which eventually led to Swales becoming Chairman. Shindler's comments focused on one of Swales' first public appearances: "The Chairman, Peter J Swales, in his mercifully few public utterances, makes Sooty seem like Albert Einstein. Appearing on Granada's Kick Off programme, the night of Allison's departure, Swales gave an interview of such outstanding incomprehension that even the urbane Gerald Sinstadt looked puzzled."

Shindler's criticism was unfair as media interest was new to Swales at this point, but the key issue here is that rather than avoid Foul, Swales willingly made himself available to its writers. In May 1975 Alan Stewart met with the City Chairman. The tone of the interview suggests Stewart wanted to find fault, but he was clearly impressed with the man. He asked him what role the Chairman has at a club like City. Swales replied: "It's up to me to appoint the right man to manage the club, and then create a mood, an atmosphere in the place in which he can do the job. Of course you make mistakes. Foul seems to think that Chairmen should be supermen who never make errors, but you've got the easy job. We're all human, and we often get things wrong. I made a mistake with Ron Saunders."

Swales' determination to meet his biggest critics during this period won him many admirers, and success in the 1976 League Cup final – under manager Tony Book – increased the glamour value of the Blues. By his pro-active involvement with the fans Swales helped lift City's average attendance to over 40,000 and ensured the club's place in the top four best-supported clubs. As the Seventies ended it seemed as if he could do no wrong, but a decade later supporters had become dejected following a lack of success.

They felt the Eighties should have seen the Blues challenge as one of Europe's top clubs but the decade was one of struggle. Perhaps because he had been so personable throughout his career Swales had become the figure on whom fans could focus their attention.

During the 1993-4 season he resigned from his role and then from the Board, and in May 1996 he died. By this point the Chairmanship of Francis Lee was coming under criticism. Perhaps, if circumstances had been different, the two men might have benefited from working together in 1994. It's possible a Board chaired by Francis Lee may have gained a great deal from having Peter Swales included in some way although most fans would probably not have accepted this.

Peter Swales was a true Blue with a passionate love of the club, and in terms of Maine Road's history he should be remembered as the man who developed the third Main Stand roof and the 'Umbro'/Platt Lane Stand. His Board also had a rolling programme of ground improvement works which saw wooden bench seating replaced in stages by plastic tip-up chairs.

Left: This unique 'team' picture taken in front of the main entrance in 1977 sees Peter Swales at the head of the City family. Pictured are team manager Tony Book and his squad, club directors and admin staff, as well as staff from ground and maintenance, coaching, scouting, medical, ticket office, social club, Junior Blues, Development Association, Souvenir Shop, kitchen and laundry.

Maine Memory

■ When my son, Stewart, was seven years old, and we still lived in Manchester (we live in Swindon now), I took him to his first Junior Blues Meeting. He was so excited to meet his hero Niall Quinn, and I must say if felt brilliant that the footballers made special efforts to come to the Sunday meetings.

We entered the raffle buying five tickets, and were really surprised to win the first ticket drawn. Our first meeting and a wonderful treat as well. I went from delight to horror to find that we also won the last prize out of the hat! The signed football. Faces turned to look at us. Many people had been going for years, and I'm sure they realised we were 'first-timers'. Nevertheless, my son was 'over the Blue Moon'.

Some years later we moved to Wootton Bassett, near Swindon. We had not long been in our new house when we had a fire. The football was lost in the fire. We were devastated. I wrote to Francis Lee and the Club was wonderful, sending Stewart a new signed football. We will never forget Maine Road and the warm welcome we always received there.

Gail McKay

This was a bold move and not too popular with staff at first. During the summer the club moved out - first to a business park off Princess Parkway then to a house on Hart Road, south of the ground, and finally into the former club shop and Social Club.

Throughout the summer of 1994 the office space was completely gutted and redeveloped. Out went the Boardroom – replaced by a smaller room on the other side of the reception - offices, and reception area, leaving the Sponsors' Suite (erected in the late 1970s) and the Executive Suite (original Players' Lounge and Billiard Room) and the kitchen more or less intact.

By the start of the new season this space was much more modern and impressive, although purists were disappointed to see many original features had been stripped from the stand. No one could argue, however, that change was needed and the new Boardroom Suite did prove very popular. As did the new reception area, which included a bust of former manager Joe Mercer, trophy cabinets and the club crest woven into the carpet.

The other key area requiring immediate activity was the redevelopment of the Kippax Stand. Due to Government legislation standing was no longer to be allowed at any Premier League venue, although it was possible to make a case for exemption if just cause could be established. City, along with newly promoted Newcastle, tried to put forward a case saying that plans put in place by the club prior to Lee's involvement were simply not appropriate. The capacity of Maine Road would be reduced to a ridiculous level once the stand was completed, while the actual construction would not be of the right quality.

City were also concerned that during the early months of the season the capacity of Maine Road would be less than 20,000 – an appallingly low figure for a club that had averaged over 27,000 in the three seasons prior to construction of the Platt Lane Stand.

Despite City's strong case their request was denied, although it was strange that Newcastle succeeded with theirs. The view was that City, having been a top-flight side since 1989, fully understood what was required and had more than sufficient time to plan. City's take-over was irrelevant as far as the authorities were concerned.

All of this led to frenetic activity by the new board. A better plan had to be created which allowed the club to increase its revenue, while also improving facilities for all Kippax attendees. The new stand could not be a shoddy affair. In addition, its construction, in the eyes of the new board, also had to be the first phase in what was eventually to become Maine Road's final development plan.

Maine Match 93/94

CITY v CHELSEA

DATE:	30th April 1994	
TYPE OF FIXTURE:	FA Premier League	
ATTENDANCE:	33,594	
RESULT:	City 2 Chelsea 2	
TEAMS & SCORERS:	CITY	CHELSEA
	Dibble	Kharine
	Hill	Clarke
	Edghill	Donaghy
	Vonk	Kjeldbjerg
	Brightwell D.	Johnsen
	Brightwell I.	Burley
	McMahon	Peacock (Hopkin)
	Rocastle	Wise
	Walsh 1	Spackman
	Rösler 1	Fleck 1
	Beagrie	Cascarino 1

■ This game marked the end of supporting City from the old Kippax terracing and as such will always be a significant moment in the stadium's history. The Kippax meant a great deal to many. The atmosphere was different from the other stands and, although people like to think of terracing as appealing mainly to men in their late 'teens and early twenties, this stand housed supporters of every age and sex. Elderly women would stand alongside teenage boys; young girls next to City's oldest male fans.

For some games the stand would be uncomfortably packed – Stoke 1934, Everton 1956 - while at others the space allowed supporters plenty of freedom. But one thing always remained and that was the surge down the two large exit tunnels at the end of a match. The tunnel closest to the away section was perhaps the busiest as this was usually the most densely-packed area of the stand. Supporters would charge to the tunnel in their rush to get to the match buses with some younger supporters running down the white side walling from their positions at the back and side – dangerous, but nothing compared to the occasions when supporters would hurl themselves off the parapet and be caught by those below!

The noise in the tunnels after most City wins was tremendous. The sound would echo loudly as songs of celebration rang out. Naturally, songs and chants would vary depending on the mood of the period, but the emotions felt by everyone as they marched through were of pride, passion and togetherness. After poor results the noise would still be heard, but instead either anger or resignation replaced pride – "We never win

Right: The final game in front of the Kippax terracing.

at home, and we never win away.... " – and during the eighties this would often lead to a rush to get onto the main forecourt and demonstrate.

Travelling through the tunnel, surrounded by echoing chanting, was an exhilarating experience. Supporters would slap the advertising board above the tunnel as they entered – it was something you just had to do – whilst trying to control their steps. The rush and crush would be so intense supporters would regularly be lifted off the ground. When this occurred you had no choice but to go with the flow in the same way a sea wave would wash a dinghy towards the beach.

Others would leave by the steps at the back of the stand. This was another Kippax experience lost when the stand was demolished. The old steps had been modified in the 1970s as a result of investigations into the Ibrox disaster. Originally there had been three main flights going from the top of the stand right down to the base, but by the late Seventies one of these had been blocked off completely, while the other two had been modified to ensure the crowd could not surge all the way down. For any Kippax regular this may have been safer, but that's not how most fans saw it. They would surge down the first half of the staircase, then hit the barriers designed to break up the flow. Some would occasionally topple over, pushed by their friends, while others would be forced against the fencing. People would eventually move around the barrier and carry on down. It's not known how many were injured by this 'safety' measure.

The final days of the Kippax were eagerly anticipated by fans but with the takeover and other problems the club had faced during the 1993-4 season it was inevitable they were not entirely ready for the planning necessary for widespread celebration. City supporter Mike Donaldson was one who felt something should mark the occasion: "I wrote to the club suggesting the 'Kippax Last Stand' and was eventually invited to the ground to meet a member of the Board and Gary James, a fellow fan who had also contacted the club with end of the Kippax ideas. I suppose my plan was to raise enthusiasm for the event then let the club get on with it. We certainly raised enthusiasm with the one Board member we met at the start, but were then asked to keep the whole thing secret for the time being. Incredibly, when another member of the club's management entered the room the subject would be changed until we were alone again.

"Gary and I probably met at Maine Road half a dozen times in planning the day, and then a week or so before the event we attended a meeting in the Club's old windowless Boardroom with the key people who would be involved on the day – we were made to feel as welcome as a Red on the Kippax. This was understandable as they had been excluded to some extent and were now expected to make it happen. I'd never heard so many excuses/reasons as to why things couldn't be done – maybe that was the reason our 'supportive Board member' hadn't involved them.

'We couldn't use the 10,000 balloons delivered to the club yesterday'. Lots of excuses for that one including 'the balloons are the wrong colour blue... they are more like Chelsea Blue and that will upset our fans'. I politely suggested we blew one up in the daylight to check this."

Despite the problems Mike and the other volunteer supporters, who on the day itself included members of the *King of the Kippax* team (they also produced special sweets for the day), City's community scheme, Ladies football team, and various other fans, performed an admirable job and made the event a major success.

A special programme was produced, again with supporters playing a key role, and a steel band performed on the pitch enhancing the proceedings. In truth though it was the fans again who generated the noise and the atmosphere.

Even the Chelsea supporters became involved. At one point a group of them dressed as Blues Brothers walked in front of the Kippax fence, and laid a wreath. It was a fitting gesture and much appreciated.

For another supporter, Michael Rennie, the day was an opportunity to create an unusual souvenir: "I have a rather unique item. It is an audio recording of events before the game. The best bit is the Kippax singing Blue Moon. There is a unity in the way it was sung at that moment that I have never heard since and the recording is absolutely perfectly clear. It brings tears to my eyes whenever I listen to it."

For another fan, Phill Gatenby, the Kippax was always a special place. For many years he has been a key figure behind SAFE [Standing Areas For Eastlands] – a group campaigning to allow safe standing at football grounds. These are his views on the old stand: "It is hard to believe the Kippax terrace has been gone for nine years. It seems like only a few seasons ago when it was given the send-off it deserved. Going to games as I did,

throughout the '80's and early 90's, it was obvious each ground had their own special 'end' that created the atmosphere that made attending a football match such a great occasion. I remember my first visit to Anfield, sat next to the Kop with my neck hairs sticking up whilst they sang their anthem 'You'll never walk alone' before the game. There was The North Bank at Highbury, The Holte End at Villa Park, The Shed (which it was!) at Stamford Bridge and, yes, the Stretford End at Old Trafford. And then there was The Kippax at Maine Road. Watching a game on TV, you recognised the stadium straight away by the 'ends' behind the goal. Watching a televised game today, you haven't a clue as to where the game is being played - Leicester, Southampton, Sunderland, Middlesbrough or Derby - all playing in identikit, soulless models.

"The Kippax was unique for two reasons. Firstly, after the North Stand was built in the early '70's, it became the only ground in the country with standing on one side only and secondly, it was situated along the length of the pitch and not behind one of the goals as traditionally sited. As a ten-year-old, my first visit to Maine Road was on The Kippax with my two elder brothers. Two of us managed to squeeze onto the bar that ran along the middle and sat with the other kids perched along it. How ironic that I actually sat down on The Kippax for my first game!

"My eldest brother somehow managed to bump into one of his teachers and stood with him. But that was the beauty of the terrace. You were free to wander around to find your mates in the same area each game, or to change position at half-time so you could always be at the end where City were attacking. One thing is for certain, I was hooked.

"Unfortunately, my trips to City over the next few years saw me in the North Stand, sat with my auntie and her boyfriend. My requests to watch from The Kippax were always denied, it being deemed 'too rough' for the likes of me. But once I reached sixteen and had left school with a job, The Kippax was mine! Of course, I am not sentimental enough to deny it wasn't rough. But again, The Kippax being so vast if you wanted the rough bits, you knew where to head. If you wanted quieter parts you had your place too. And the front was were all the parents with young kids went. As I said before, you moved around until you found a place that suited your style, your friends and your way of watching the game. Many friendships were forged on The Kippax. Even now, nine years on, going to games I still bump into Blues I used to stand near to and celebrate goals/suffer relegations with etc. I don't know many of their names, but a 'nod' or a 'hi ya' still get exchanged each time we pass.

"For two seasons, a few of us bought tickets in the old Platt Lane from 1981-83, I don't know why, we just did, but for cup games, we all headed for 'home' back into The Kippax. The pulling power was too strong. In the seats we were individuals. On the terrace, we were a part of something, something that's sadly missing from

grounds today. Of course, it could be argued that 'something missing' is hooliganism, and as mentioned yes, it did exist. But post-Hillsborough there were two major incidents of hooliganism at Maine Road whilst The Kippax was still there - and both of these incidents took place in seated areas (the North Stand against United '89 and from the Platt Lane Stand against Spurs in the cup '93).

"The Kippax and other terraces were also part of the class system that prevailed in football throughout the last century up until the last decade. The terrace was cheap. The Platt Lane was for Junior Blues and OAP's (those too young or too old to stand!). The North Stand is where your boss and his family went. And the Main Stand was where the businessmen and the wealthy sat. Generalisations I know, but you get the point. As we enter the new stadium, there are only two prices of entry. Behind both goals is one price and along both sides is another . The only exception to this - executive boxes apart - is the Family Stand. The last season ticket price for The Kippax terrace was £110. A season ticket for the equivalent seat to the lower Kippax is £460 if bought before the March 2003 deadline. A rise of 318% over a ten year period! My salary increase for this same period of time is 40% and I now also pay for my two daughters as well. Football for the masses?

"It's hard for me to write this and not bring politics into it. Yes we know why the all-seated requirements were brought in, we accepted something had to change. But by classing all terraces as the same and prohibiting standing completely was a knee-jerk reaction against a terrible disaster caused by a number of circumstances that individually occurred week in, week out for over one hundred years. Unfortunately, at Hillsborough, they all occurred at the same time with fatal consequences.

"So April 1994, was the last time City fans stood on The Kippax terrace to cheer their heroes on, but nine years on the fans still stand. The North Stand and lower Kippax near to the away fans spend most of the game stood up in a seated area - as do fans at each Premier League ground (with the exception of Middlesbrough's fans, but then not many of them turned up at Ayresome Park, so they never knew the culture of standing!). The authorities' attitude is to force fans to sit with threats, rather than looking at a practical solution to deal with the issue. You can take the terrace from the fans but you can't take the fans from the terrace. Having visited new and rebuilt stadiums in Germany (at Schalke, Hamburg and Bremen) I would love to have seen such standing areas as they have incorporated in our new stadium and have spent the last three years of my life trying to achieve that goal. But time and a lack of will by those in power have beaten me, though the campaign continues.

"It will be a wrench to leave Maine Road; there is no question about that. But for me not so much, as Maine Road has never been the same since The Kippax was demolished. I remember which spot on the terrace I stood on when we beat Everton in the quarter final of the FA Cup in '81, Charlton 5-1 for promotion in '85, Huddersfield 10-1 in '87. And, of course, United 5-1 in '89. The terrace may have gone, but the memories remain forever."

That game against Chelsea was less memorable than the events surrounding it. Prior to the match there had been an outside chance City could be relegated, causing some concern in the dressing room, however results went City's way and the 2-2 draw brought a satisfactory end to a difficult season.

The Flag

■ During the early 1990s Maine Road saw the arrival of a giant flag on the Kippax. It was bigger by half than any other flag ever seen at an English football ground. Former *Blue Print* contributor Rob Dunford remembers how it all began: "It was really Bill Borrows, who at the time was the editor of City fanzine *Blue Print*, who got it going. At the beginning of the '91-92 season, around £1,700 was spent at a fabric shop in Cheetham Hill, with three colours being chosen – sky blue, white and maroon. The banner was produced in a factory in Oldham and when fellow *Blue Print* contributors Frank Newton and Andy Webb went to collect it they suddenly realised the sheer size of it.

"The flag was a huge 40 metres long by 15 metres wide, and would not fit in the back of Andy's car! So he hastily arranged to borrow a

van. The aim was to have the flag on display at the November '91 derby but unforeseen problems arose at the ground. The flag was so heavy it needed at least eight people to carry it! So Frank went to the queues waiting to get in the Kippax, trying to persuade fans to come back to his vehicle and help carry a flag in. Eventually he managed to convince fans that he was genuine and the flag was carried into the ground via the turnstiles where it was passed through slowly as each carrier handed over their ticket stub.

"The sheer length and bulkiness of the flag was even used on a few occasions to smuggle in kids who were

hanging around the turnstiles attempting to jib their way in with an unsuspecting adult. A few layers were simply unwrapped and they folded themselves around and inside the flag, and were carried in past unsuspecting - and often bemused - stewards.

"At the derby game the flag was taken up the stairs and laid out on the back of the Kippax waiting for the right time to set it loose. Again, a large number of fans were needed to unroll it and while this was going on, a 'small flag' was on display and being passed about by the United fans. To the cries of 'What the ****ing hell is that?' from the Kippax, the biggest flag in the land was

passed over the heads of the fans on the biggest terrace in the land. The Reds' fans didn't know what had hit them and their 'handkerchief' was quickly withdrawn and kept out of sight for the remainder of the match. Excellent timing – but it was just pure coincidence! Again, pleas were made at the end of the game for fans to help carry the flag back to the van. This became easier the more it appeared as fans wanted to be seen with the flag.

"The flag made its TV debut before the infamous FA Cup game against Spurs in March 93, when the BBC gave it a good airing, but its appearances were having to be less frequent due to the sheer task of getting it to and from games. It was easily damaged and on average cost £150 from the *Blue Print* coffers to repair rips each time it was used. It was stored in Frank's damp cellar and by this time Phill Gatenby's Ford Escort Estate was just about able to take the weight and bulkiness to transport it around. The club was asked to find a home for the flag in the ground, but this was refused.

"The flag's farewell appearance was for the 'Kippax Last Stand' against Chelsea in April '94, the final game at which fans were able to stand at Maine Road. Its presence – for the first time in many months – added to the carnival atmosphere of a special occasion. In fact the club had actually requested the flag be present on the day, but when asked if they

would contribute to the repairs they refused! However, attempts were made to bring it out one more time for the match against QPR in May '95 – for the official opening of the new Kippax. The club announced plans to have the game designated as a 'Flag Day', but an enquiry made to bring the flag down the previous day was denied, and we were informed we couldn't bring it into the ground as the club's then safety officer declared it a 'fire hazard'! In retrospect the end of the terrace was a rather fitting end for the flag too. It was simply just too big to be passed around a seated area.

"By 1996, the flag was slowly rotting away in Frank's increasingly damp cellar and the decision was taken to dispose of it at the local council tip. It had become a victim of its own success and it is unlikely that a flag of its magnitude will ever be seen again in this country.

"It has, however, been recorded for prosperity and was featured excellently on Niall Quinn's video *The Will To Win* (Windmill Lane Pictures 1991). The footage shows it being taken from the derby game in '91. In more recent times, the club followed where the fans led by commendably producing the 'Eidos replica kit flag' in 1998/99 season. This 'official' demonstration towards enhancing matchday atmosphere gives further momentum to the concept of a dedicated 'songs and banners' section."

Above: When the roof came off the Kippax it was possible to stand and imagine just what it must have been like when the stadium first opened 70 years earlier... just briefly, until the bulldozers moved in to take away a piece of football history.

Below: With the Kippax gone, the view from the car park was that of three more modern roofs. Soon these stands would be dwarfed by a new structure towering up from behind the old perimeter wall.

The new Kippax was anticipated to hold around 10,000 spectators, leaving Maine Road's capacity at the 30,000 mark. This was far from sufficient for a club the size of City, so the board pursued other options.

After significant effort a plan was compiled which saw additional seating tiers added to the North, Platt Lane and Main Stands, while the Kippax would open as a three-tier stand containing corporate facilities unrivalled at any other footballing location. The design of each stand would fit within the overall pattern, and Maine Road would show a unity not seen since the 1920s.

The capacity was projected as a figure between 45,000 and 50,000.

Francis Lee was keen to see Maine Road develop: "By the time we took office we had a definite need to increase revenue and improve capacity. The Kippax had to be the biggest and best stand we could build, but time was against us. We looked at the plans of our predecessors and also looked at the most recent construction at the ground, the Platt Lane Stand. This stand was too small, and also possessed a number of areas where space was wasted – underneath the stand we discovered a void large enough for a good quality dining area which was just being used for storage. It was an incredible waste."

The void under the Platt Lane Stand was similar to a number of vacant areas planned for the new Kippax by Lee's predecessor. Lee found that particularly worrying and vowed to ensure every appropriate space would be utilised wherever possible: "Circumstances prevented us

from improving the Platt Lane void, but we were determined we wouldn't make a mistake like that in the new Kippax. We studied the plans and started to focus on what we could do to generate income and improve capacity. We created a three tier stand with improved catering and viewing for all fans, and also incorporated the top tier restaurant. The Millenium Suite was by far the best restaurant space at any ground in the north when it was constructed and the club took a major leap forward.

"Our plan was to then carry that same style and approach right around the ground, but we knew we'd have quite a few obstacles to overcome. Space was always going to be an issue at the North Stand end and at the corner between Platt Lane and the Kippax, but we were determined to make as much of the plan work as possible. We were also planning to build an amenities block on the Kippax car park and we started to look at the Social Club and club shop, so 1994 was a very busy year."

The demolition of the Kippax came first but Lee's plans hit their initial obstacle when it was revealed the stand had been built on waste earth, which in 1994 was viewed as needing specialist removal. It had been anticipated the earth could simply be used as landfill, but considerable extra costs were incurred as the club had to have the waste material removed to specialist sites.

By the start of the 1994 season the old Kippax had gone completely, meaning every area of original McAlpine terracing had now vanished. Only the base of

the Main Stand remained from 1923, although the exterior Kippax wall was still in place more or less as it first appeared.

The season opened with Maine Road's capacity down to less than 20,000, but the club planned to open up sections in stages throughout the season. As the capacity kept shifting, a casual glance at attendances throughout the 1994-5 season would suggest to a neutral City were poorly supported. Most stadium capacities are fixed for a significant part of the season and so it's easy to identify when the ground was full or not, but as Lee and Barlow were determined to open up as much of the Kippax as possible, game by game, it's not obvious to non-Blues that every game reached capacity. Occasionally just a few dozen additional seats were added so when one attendance was marginally higher than the previous match the impression may be the prior event did not sell out, but that was not the case.

By mid-season the capacity reached 25,000 and by mid-May had increased to almost 28,000. The highest attendance was 27,850 for the visit of QPR on 14th May, which included supporters on the bottom two tiers of the new Kippax. In fact a section of the second tier was used for the first time when Newcastle United visited in April.

During this time the supporters continued to generate news stories. The takeover battle had put fans on both the front and back pages, but then came the tale of the Platt Lane Chicken Man. During the first few seasons of the new Umbro/Platt Lane Stand a supporter brought an oven-ready chicken to a game. At one point he started swinging it around his head. This brought laughter from other areas of the stand, although those sitting closest to the Chicken Man were far from amused. After a series of complaints, and an official warning from

Above: With the old terracing removed, the new stand quickly begins to rise.

Top right: Seats are in place on the lower level of the Kippax and with the new season already underway, temporary floodlighting is in place.

Centre right: The upper level was partially occupied for the visit of Newcastle in April 1995.

Below: A late nineties photo shows the mixing of two eras as the Kippax stands proud on the other side of the old perimeter wall and turnstiles.

club was minimal. Then suddenly after the 1994-5 season ended, Brian Horton was dismissed and several weeks later was replaced by Alan Ball. Blues supporters felt let down by the appointment.

Naturally, all hoped the Ball appointment would prove a good one, but most feared the opposite. Sadly, his time at the club was one of struggle, although every so often there was a memorable moment, usually generated by the exciting Gio Kinkladze. One of the Georgian's brightest performances during this period came in a 2-1 victory over Southampton. He scored both goals that day but one in particular was incredible. Alan Hansen, on the BBC's *Match of the Day,* viewed it as pure genius while many City fans claim it's the greatest goal scored at Maine Road. For Kinkladze it was just one of many breathtaking moments.

The highest attendance of the 1995-6 relegation season was 31,436 for the visit of Liverpool on the final day. The ground was totally full (31,458 was the official capacity excluding segregation) and from that point on, despite extremely poor form, Maine Road was not equipped to deal with the number of supporters who wanted to see the Blues on a regular basis. Francis Lee: "We all knew the capacity was too small, but it was much better all-round than the original Kippax plans."

Had the 1993 Platt Lane Stand been developed with two tiers instead of one, ground capacity would have exceeded 35,000 by 1995 and shows how short-term planning with the Platt Lane created a long-term problem.

Lee's stadium plans continued to be viewed as the way forward although Manchester's bid for the 2000 Olympics brought suggestions that Maine Road's days were numbered. As early as the mid-1980s it had been proposed City might move to a new stadium. A group of key Manchester figures, led by Bob Scott, had first put together a plan to win the 1992 Olympics and suggested building a stadium west of Manchester at Dumplington, close to the Ship Canal.

In a late eighties newspaper article Peter Swales had been asked if City would move to the stadium and he said they would, providing conditions were right for the club.

Manchester failed to gain Britain's nomination – that went to Birmingham - but the seed was sown and a more concerted effort was made for the 1996 Olympics.

the club, the Chicken Man began bringing plastic or rubber chickens. When the atmosphere demanded he would begin swinging the poultry around his head. It was another surreal City sight.

Overall supporters were still very positive about the direction and development of the club at this point. They were behind Francis Lee and were delighted the club once again felt as if it belonged to the fans. For most of the eighties and nineties supporters felt their views had little or no influence. The fanzine culture had grown but, until the arrival of Francis Lee, their direct impact on the

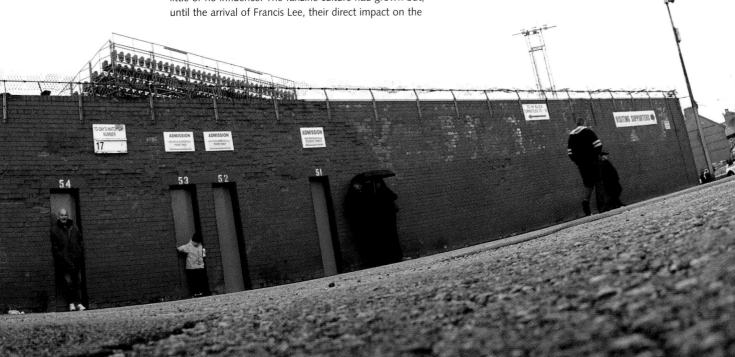

Maine Match 94/95

CITY v TOTTENHAM HOTSPUR

DATE:	22nd October 1994		
TYPE OF FIXTURE:	FA Premier League		
ATTENDANCE:	25,473		
RESULT:	City 5 Tottenham 2		
TEAMS & SCORERS:	CITY		TOTTENHAM
	Dibble		Walker
	Edghill		Kerslake
	Brightwell		Campbell
	Curle		Scott
	Phelan		Edinburgh
	Summerbee		Popescu
	Flitcroft	1	Dozzell
	Lomas	1	Dumitrescu 2
	Beagrie		Barmby
	Walsh	2	Klinsmann
	Quinn	1	Sheringham

■ The BBC *Match of the Day* cameras were at Maine Road for this classic encounter, as they always seem to be when a City-Spurs match makes national news. They were at Maine Road for the 1967 'Ballet On Ice' and also the 1993 FA Cup Quarter-final. Of course, they were also at Wembley for the 1981 final. The commentator in 1994 was John Motson: "This was a highly memorable Maine Road occasion and from my point of view there were several interesting features. The Kippax terracing had been demolished of course and already in its place was an uncovered seated area. All the supporters in that section were wearing plastic rain macs and it certainly made an interesting sight.

"Then of course the game itself saw some exquisite play. There were so many great moments that it's a little unfair to single out individual moments, suffice to say that both sides provided true entertainment that day and we at the BBC were privileged to witness the match. That night our producer took the opportunity to show scenes from City's famous victory in 1967 on the snow, and I know that delighted many viewers.

"Commentators hope the match they are to report on becomes a classic. Most never quite live up to that desire, but when they do it's a real pleasure to be able to commentate on it."

From a City perspective there was disappointment before this match as Uwe Rösler was unable to play. He was suffering with an injury sustained a month earlier and, although it was hoped he would return for this match against a Spurs side including fellow German Jurgen Klinsmann, City had to cope without him. In the end they didn't need him.

Paul Walsh, a very exciting player during this period, netted the first goal after 17 minutes, but Spurs equalised via a Dumitrescu penalty 13 minutes later. Despite this setback the Blues remained the dominant force and, a short while later, a City counter-attack led to another Blue goal. Steve Lomas passed out wide to Nicky Summerbee who then crossed to Walsh. The former Spurs man sent a powerful header at 'keeper Walker before Niall Quinn blasted home the rebound. Walsh scored a third five minutes later but, a minute into the second half, Klinsmann and Dumitrescu combined to make it 3-2 via a deflection off Keith Curle.

After about 52 minutes play Steve Lomas powered home a beautiful header to make it 4-2. Then with only ten minutes remaining Walsh made another superb run – it was a game for tremendous runs by the player. He passed four players before turning and crossing the ball to Flitcroft, who made it 5-2.

Manager Brian Horton simply but accurately stated: "You will not see a better game of soccer than that."

Below: Steve Lomas heads City's fourth goal against Spurs.

Manchester's bid was more successful but proved weak when it came down to physical venues. Almost everything was theory, as the committee's motto 'driving the dream' implied. By the time Manchester bid for the 2000 Olympics the velodrome was in place and a new stadium site in Bradford, east Manchester, had not only been found but also cleared.

From time to time it was suggested City would move, but nothing concrete had been agreed. It was felt none of this would occur until Manchester won the right to stage the Games. Cynics said it would never happen. For Francis Lee the redevelopment of Maine Road had to continue: "Completing the Kippax was a major step forwards but we still had so much more to do. The shop needed to be tackled and the rest of the ground plan progressed but then I was at a Premier League meeting and Sir John Hall started talking to me about the new Kippax. He complimented me on it and then said

Left: Following the development of the Kippax and Platt Lane, City erected two scoreboards. This one and another in the corner of Platt Lane closest to the Main Stand. This scoreboard was the third to appear in this location (there was a board here in the 1920s and another in the 1980s), but was the most shortlived. It was removed when temporary seating started to appear here in the late 1990s.

■ The 1995-6 season became City's worst since 1986-7, although the following couple of campaigns were even more depressing. At the time of this match everyone felt fairly optimistic about the Blues' chances of survival. Only one defeat – away at Everton – in their previous four matches set City up for this meeting with the League leaders.

To put the game into perspective it's worth noting Kevin Keegan's Newcastle had mounted a very entertaining – and refreshing – title challenge. They were six points clear with a game in hand over Manchester United and few expected City to achieve much in this game.

The Blues began brightly and after about fifteen minutes a Nigel Clough attempt was diverted into the goal by Niall Quinn. Georgi Kinkladze then started to perform at his best and enjoyed a number of blistering runs, but City failed to make the most of these chances and by half-time Newcastle had levelled.

Quinn headed home his second goal of the match but the Magpies equalised with only twenty minutes remaining. Six minutes later Uwe Rösler made it 3-2. Lomas fired a loose ball across the goalmouth and Rösler sneaked past a couple of defenders to force the ball home.

In the 81st minute City eased up and Newcastle scored their third equaliser of the game. The final nine minutes were frantic as both sides searched for a winner. Newcastle's Peacock appeared to handle in the penalty area and then in the game's final moments Keith Curle was headbutted by the Geordies' Colombian maverick Asprilla. That evening's *Match of The Day* focused on

Maine Match 95/96

CITY v NEWCASTLE UNITED

DATE:	24th February 1996	
TYPE OF FIXTURE:	FA Premier League	
ATTENDANCE:	31,115	
RESULT:	City 3 Newcastle United 3	
TEAMS & SCORERS:	CITY	NEWCASTLE

CITY		NEWCASTLE	
Immel		Srnicek	
Summerbee		Barton	
Hiley		Beresford	
Curle		Peacock	
Symons		Howey	
Clough		Albert	2
Lomas		Beardsley	
Brown		Clark	
Kinkladze		Ginola	
Quinn	2	Asprilla	1
Rösler	1	Ferdinand	

this incident (the player was later penalised by the authorities) and on the great skill of Kinkladze.

Although this game provided great entertainment and a draw against the league leaders, it's fair to say the result did neither side any favours. Newcastle ended the season as runners-up, while City's season became even more desperate.

Right: The game against Stoke in March 1997 was delayed by 45 minutes as a fire broke out in a room in the North Stand.

something like 'You know that great new stand of yours will be the last built at Maine Road'. He told me not to progress the further development of the ground because Manchester were to be given the Commonwealth Games and that City would move into the new stadium. How he knew I don't know, but the truth was that once

Manchester was awarded the Commonwealth Games a stadium had to be built and a tenant found to make it viable.

"City were the only viable tenants and with all the problems associated with developing Maine Road it started to make sense."

The prospect of the new stadium meant all plans for remodelling the other stands to match the Kippax were put on hold while discussions on a potential move were progressed. There was no let-up in City's restructure though as business opportunities were furthered; the Platt Lane training complex was redeveloped, and the Souvenir Shop was finally

Fans Committee

■ Ever since the takeover battle of 1993-4 the club has attempted to consult fans on a number of issues, but the methods chosen over the years have varied. When Francis Lee became Chairman he agreed to an election to appoint a supporters' representative to attend Board meetings and provide true supporter feedback. This was a great idea, however the concept failed.

The representative, King of the Kippax editor Dave Wallace, felt the club did not utilise him in the right way, while the Board seemed wary of allowing a fan to get too close to serious club issues. Nevertheless, it was still a major step forward and to the outside world appeared as if both Dave and the club were making real progress together.

Unfortunately, as time progressed Dave felt he was excluded – or at best not consulted – too often. The concept was eventually replaced with a Fans' Committee made up of representatives from both supporters' organisations and from others with a strong interest in the development of the club. Dave Wallace is an active member, while both the Club and the Committee have made it clear over the years that any supporter can become involved. This is not an 'exclusive' club.

In recent years the Committee have been involved with plans for the new stadium; Maine Road's End of an Era; the development of a club museum; and a whole host of everyday issues such as merchandising, segregation, policing, ticket allocations etc.

Although it has become the norm in recent years for football clubs to consult fans, it is fair to say most have done so following pressure from the Premier League and other bodies. City, however, have been at the forefront of supporter involvement and, although this does not go as far as many would like, it is still a clear indication the club understands it exists for the benefit of its supporters.

Maine Match 95/96

CITY v LIVERPOOL

DATE:	5th May 1996	
TYPE OF FIXTURE:	FA Premier League	
ATTENDANCE:	31,436	
RESULT:	City 2 Liverpool 2	
TEAMS &	CITY	LIVERPOOL
SCORERS:	Immel	James
	Summerbee	McAteer
	Brightwell	Wright
	Curle	Ruddock
	Symons 1	Babb
	Clough	Jones
	(Kavelashvili)	McManaman
	Lomas og	Redknapp
	Brown	(Kennedy)
	Kinkladze	Thomas
	Quinn (Phillips)	Rush 1
	Rösler 1	Fowler

■ The Luton relegation match of 1983 was a desperate and depressing one, however one aspect of that day most City fans recognise is the Blues were playing against a side fighting for survival, and therefore both teams had something to play for. This match against Liverpool ended with City relegated, but the entire circumstance and atmosphere of the day was markedly different to what occurred 13 years earlier.

For Liverpool the season was over. They had already finished third – no one could catch them, nor could they finish second – and also some of the Liverpool players appeared keen to see City remain in the top division.

The game has been covered extensively over the years, but it is important the key points are not forgotten. Firstly, pre-match, a minute's silence for former Chairman Peter Swales was impeccably observed. His untimely death was a shock, and the fact they paid great tribute to the man shows City fans recognised his love of the club and of football.

The supporters provided tremendous backing from the kick-off, but were let down within minutes as Liverpool took the lead through a series of mistakes that allowed them to race forward. City conceded a corner, and a half-hearted effort by Steve McManaman was sliced in by Lomas.

Later Ian Rush effortlessly made it 2-0. Effortlessly because he showed little interest in scoring and Liverpool were simply strolling around the pitch, but the Blues were ineffectual.

Eventually, with only twenty minutes remaining, City managed to fightback. Kinkladze was bundled over for a penalty and Rösler made it 2-1. Niall Quinn was substituted for Martin 'Buster' Phillips – a player Alan Ball predicted would be the first £10m footballer – who in the 78th minute latched on to a Summerbee corner and knocked the ball back for Kit Symons to fire home the equaliser. Everybody off the pitch celebrated, while many of the players seemed relieved, but this was not enough.

Niall Quinn: "We needed to win to stay up. It was another shambles. A wrong message was sent onto the pitch with five minutes to go. I'd already come off. I had a radio and knew that Southampton were winning elsewhere, so we needed to score. Alan Ball had a conflicting message and he was telling the lads to hold the ball up. I had to run down the sideline and scream at Steve Lomas we needed another goal. It made Alan Ball look bad, I suppose, but when you are bringing a great club down a division you can't worry about vanity."

Liverpool charged at the City players dawdling in the corner closest to the Family Stand and tried to open up play. It was all quite surreal, but at the same time desperately sad. The fans knew, Quinn knew, and Liverpool seemed to know a draw was not enough to ensure the Blues' survival.

Results elsewhere left City relegated on goal difference. Both Southampton and Coventry survived on exactly the same points as the Blues. Surely, if play had opened up properly an attack by the Blues against a disinterested Liverpool might have brought a goal. Time-wasting was a contributory factor behind City's relegation.

That evening Niall Quinn apologised to City supporters on *Match of The Day*. He had nothing to apologise for. For most, the man to blame was Alan Ball.

Maine Memory

■ City v QPR 2-2 - the final home game before relegation to Division Two. This game was the first time I took my daughter Emma to see City play. Kinky scored very early on - a great free kick - and we were in the Junior Blues Stand with a great view . Unfortunately, City shot themselves in the foot. A Jamie Pollock own goal, and a bizarre mix up, gave QPR a 2-1 lead. We came back and made it 2-2, but it was not good enough. I went to Stoke a week later to see the 5-2 win, but our fate was in the hands of others and City were doomed. Despite all this Emma enjoyed her first trip to Maine Road.

Alan Whitney

A selection of typical match day scenes around Maine Road at the turn of the new century.

brought back under the club's control with a new superstore replacing the Social Club in October 1997.

Sadly, events on the pitch did not match the success off it. In fact they took a major turn for the worst. The appointment of Alan Ball in 1995 was a huge disappointment and a year later the Blues were in Division One with scant hope of a return to the Premier League. But the demand to see City was still as great as ever and temporary seats were installed in the corner between the Kippax and the North Stand. The stand was nicknamed the Gene Kelly Stand during its first few months as, during one particularly wet match early in the season, City fans in the uncovered part became noted for 'Singing in the rain'.

Another stand was planned for the other Kippax corner but this area had always proved problematic with little space between the corner and houses on Thornton Road. Eventually seating was placed there but not before campaigns against Lee and his Board – 'Free The 30,000' led by Blue Dante Friend was the most publicised group – put a great deal of pressure on the club. Events on the pitch went from bad to worse and supporters felt absolutely devastated by City's performances.

In February 1998 during an appalling 1-0 defeat by Bury (the Bury scorer was City fan Paul Butler!), a fan walked onto the pitch and ripped up his season ticket in disgust. The action brought widespread applause as the miscreant was escorted away. Afterwards major shareholder David Makin criticised Lee on BBC GMR and then added: "The first thing I would do when Francis has gone is find that guy who has probably been barred for throwing his ticket away on the pitch and put him in the Directors' Box. It sums up how the fans feel."

In the following months matters came to a head as City were relegated to the third tier of English football for the first time ever. Francis Lee had already resigned as

Maine Match 98/99

CITY v STOKE CITY

DATE:	28th December 1998	
TYPE OF FIXTURE:	Football League Division Two (New)	
ATTENDANCE:	30,478	
RESULT:	City 2 Stoke 1	
TEAMS &	CITY	STOKE
SCORERS:	Weaver	Muggleton
	Crooks	Heath
	Edghill	Small
	Wiekens	Sigurdsson 1
	Vaughan	Robinson
	Horlock	Woods
	Brown	Kean
	Pollock	Kavanagh
	Taylor 1	(Oldfield)
	Bishop	Crowe
	(Goater)	Lightbourne
	Dickov 1	Forsyth (Wallace)

■ By Christmas 1998 City were in a desperate position. They had dropped to their lowest League position ever a week earlier and there was little optimism around the club. A 1-0 win at Wrexham on Boxing Day had lifted spirits a little and taken City from 12th place to 7th, but this was still the third tier of English football and promotion was vital to the long term survival of the club.

Steve Rigby remembers how important this match with Stoke really was: "One Maine Road memory I think a lot about is this game. City had lost away at York, just before Christmas, taking us as low as we had ever been in our history. We scraped a lucky win at Wrexham, but this game against Stoke was crucial. They were third in the League and we had to start gaining ground on the top teams if we were to have any chance of promotion.

"At half-time, City went in 0-1 down and you could feel the discontent start to build. The teams came out for the second half and after a few minutes a Stoke defender had the ball and the entire City team seemed to stand watching with their arms across their chests – like you see in the newsreels of old games!

"The crowd roared at them and I think it was Paul Dickov who then ran towards the defender. The Stoke player panicked and cleared the ball to a City man. 'That's it' the crowd shouted, 'come on, we can win it'. Joe Royle later claimed it was his paint-blistering half-time talk that turned things round but I didn't notice much difference in City's performance until the crowd started their encouragement.

"City went on to win 2-1 and hardly lost a game for the rest of the campaign. Everyone remembers the climax of the season at Wembley but, for me, if it hadn't been for those few seconds when the crowd could have got on the players' backs but instead got right behind them, we would never have been at Wembley in the first place.

"It's easy to enjoy venting your indignation when the players are not performing, but it's even more satisfying to get behind the team and then realise the crowd actually played a part in the victory."

City only lost two further matches that season – both ironically at Maine Road – and City's move into the play-offs was assured. As Steve suggests, it was this game above all other Maine Road matches that stopped the rot and allowed City to begin their journey back to the Premier League and European football.

Maine Memory

The Great Queue of '99

■ Back in 1955 City's progress to the FA Cup Final created huge problems for fans desperate to see this match. Enormous queues led to heavy criticism of the club and the following year City introduced the programme voucher scheme. This provided greater control over ticket distribution, and lasted until the 1980s. By 1999, season tickets, membership schemes, City Cards etc. meant the club had many different types of supporter to consider when allocating tickets for the Play-off Final. Unfortunately, the method chosen led to much criticism.

Basically, all supporters had to queue. No ifs, buts or maybes, queueing was the only opportunity to obtain a ticket you were entitled to.

Supporter David Lane remembers that time: "The sale of tickets for the play-off final of that year is an occasion I shall not forget. In many ways it summed up City supporters - the poor organisation that caused a massive queue; the acceptance of the situation; and the general good humour of the fans.

"I was in the queue for eleven hours. When I left home I had expected to be out for no more than a couple. However, I was about to have a unique experience, standing on my feet, shuffling forward with a group of - initially - total strangers, no food or drink with me, no idea when I would reach the head of the queue. I joined the queue behind the Platt Lane Stand and, like those around me, assumed we would move along in front of the Main Stand to the Ticket Office. As time went by there was a fear we would not reach there before the stated closing time. Stewards informed us the Ticket Office would remain open for an extra hour - it turned out to be more like an extra six!

"As my section of the queue progressed, we became aware the line went past the Ticket Office and around the back of the Kippax, before turning 180 degrees and returning inside the ground, beneath the North Stand, eventually sending us out again close to the Ticket Office. I can clearly remember the moment the reality of the situation hit us. One chap left the queue because he was getting married within the hour - I hope he made it! Another went off to phone his wife and never returned. Some distance ahead of me a fan was struggling along on crutches. I hope he made it to the end.

"By this time total strangers had ceased to be strangers. And this is what made the occasion so memorable. People from very different backgrounds, and with very different attitudes and values, but all with a common love of City slowly snaked around the ground demonstrating friendliness, kindness, humour and a "Let's make the best of it," attitude. While the queue was still outside the ground it was accepted it was all right to leave to ring your family, go to the chip shop (often taking "orders"), etc. and return to your place. Later, when 'imprisoned' inside the ground people shared sweets, chocolate and any other food they had. They also shared countless amusing stories of matches, travelling to games and the odd little quirks of many City fans. Still optimistic, many had rung home to families to say they would be late... but not how late. Another call was required, but we were now inside the ground, no nipping off to a call box.

"Mobile phones were not so common then. Those who had them were ringing home to say 'still in the queue' - it was getting on for 10pm by now. In another act of kindness those with mobiles were lending them to others. I remember borrowing one myself, and the owner refused to accept any money. As he allowed several people to use it, it could have cost him a considerable amount. Success at last, eventually eleven hours after joining the queue I had the tickets I had gone for."

Maine Men Francis Lee

ROLE: Player and Chairman

■ Francis Lee's position as one of City's greatest players is assured, but this profile details his influence in the redevelopment of Maine Road.

When Lee took control of the club during 1993-4, the Platt Lane Stand was less than a year old while the Kippax terracing had still to be demolished and replaced. He had to focus attention on ground developments.

His initial action was to plan a much grander Kippax Stand than his predecessor had aimed for, while also taking steps to improve the Main Stand's facilities. Lee: "John Dunkerley and Colin Barlow were key figures during this time. They put tremendous effort into the Main Stand, the Kippax and the redevelopment of the Platt Lane training complex. I don't think anyone can overestimate what we had to achieve during that period."

Lee certainly did aim for the best as far as the ground was concerned and, in most areas, he delivered. The only problem was the improvements to corporate facilities and the development of the Kippax Stand came at a time when performances on the pitch struggled. Critics point to the appointment of Alan Ball as being the first big mistake of Lee's reign. As with Peter Swales twenty years earlier, Lee's first managerial appointment did not deliver. The difference was that Swales' next acquisition (Tony Book) was successful.

Failure on the pitch ultimately led to Lee's resignation in 1998 but it has to be stressed that in terms of ground developments, and improvement in facilities off the pitch, Lee's time was hugely successful. Not since the development of the North Stand in the early Seventies, or indeed the ground in 1923, had the stadium improved so much for supporters of every type. Remember the Kippax carried better facilities for both corporate fans and 'old Kippax' regulars.

In addition to Maine Road's development, Lee was also the first City Chairman to pro-actively start discussions to move to the new stadium. By the time of his resignation he had already performed a great deal of negotiation on the club's behalf and had spoken with governing bodies for football, rugby and other sports. His aim was to make the new stadium a contender for every major team-sports event while ensuring City benefited too.

Since his resignation as Chairman he has continued to be a major shareholder and a keen supporter of the club. He is a regular attendee and enjoys watching City develop.

His time as Chairman ended with many fans critical of his reign – he had always said he would stand down if fans called for his head - however when the last match took place at Maine Road on 11th May 2003 he received a great ovation. Supporters voiced their appreciation of his time as a player and, potentially, recognised his contribution to the development of Maine Road. If only events on the pitch had been as successful as those off it.

Chairman and David Bernstein – previously a director brought on to the Board during Lee's reign – was his replacement. As far as Maine Road was concerned the prospect of future redevelopment was now completely dead.

City continued to ponder a move to the new stadium, but as Maine Road was by far the best ground in Division Two there was no desire to change anything in Moss Side. Focus had to be totally on events on the pitch.

The club continued to struggle for a while. In fact the position looked bleak in December as City lay in twelfth place, 15 points behind leaders Fulham and second-placed Walsall. In addition, the lowest Maine Road first team home crowd of 3,007 had witnessed a 2-1 defeat at the hands of Mansfield Town in the Auto Windscreens Shield. Tabloid stories suggested City fans had turned their backs on the club, but that was way off the mark. Maine Road's previous lowest first team crowd was 4,029 for the first Full Members' Cup match in 1986, but no-one then suggested fans had lost faith. In fact everything focused on the loyalty of those who did turn up for such a meaningless competition. Surely, from a fan's perspective the same was true in 1998? Promotion was the only objective but to say supporters had turned their backs on the club was an insult, especially as most League matches were a sell-out.

Fortunately, City's season started to turn around with a victory over Wrexham on Boxing Day 1998 being

Maine Memory

■ City were playing Bury. Me and my sister sat in the Kippax upper tier, watching the action unfold below. City were going through a rough patch, a surprise I know! The match was awful, the day was cold and murky, Bury were winning and the crowd were getting agitated. I looked around just as we were going out, wondering what the hell was going on.

Despite everything, it was great. I knew I was a Blue. I could sit through a match like that and still sense the optimism that lay ahead, as it always does at Maine Road. It's strange to have a home away from home, but Maine Road is Manchester. Stuck in the middle of a terraced-house jungle, it's raw and fashionable. I loved it, and still do. Now we are watching teams like Chelsea, Newcastle, and we've even tonked the unwashed. I'm going to miss this place. Every brick holds a memory of a certain kind, be it a first match, bad match, wonder goal, or favourite team. Theatre of dreams? Who wants to sit in a stadium and dream?
David Topping

Left: When Francis Lee became chairman he faced the problem of replacing the Kippax terracing.

Maine Match 99/00

CITY v BIRMINGHAM CITY

DATE:	28th April 2000	
TYPE OF FIXTURE:	Football League Division One (New)	
ATTENDANCE:	32,068	
RESULT:	City 1 Birmingham 0	
TEAMS & SCORERS:	CITY	BIRMINGHAM
	Weaver	Myhre
	Edghill	Rowett
	Prior	Holdsworth
	Jobson	Purse
	Tiatto	M.Johnson
	Whitley	McCarthy
	Wiekens	(A.Johnson)
	Horlock	Hughes
	(Pollock)	O'Connor
	Kennedy	Lazaridis
	(Granville)	Adebola
	Taylor 1	Furlong
	(Dickov)	(Ndlovu)
	Goater	

■ Promotion via the play-offs in 1999 set City off on a course fuelled by optimism and hope. The struggles of the Second Division and the memorable game at Wembley galvanised the team and, by the time of this match with Birmingham, the Blues felt anything was possible. Naturally, there had been a few setbacks along the way, but in the main, fans were delighted City were challenging for an automatic promotion place.

For supporter John Hamilton this was one of Maine Road's finest days: "I drove up from Hereford in the morning, stopping off in the Peak District, and then I parked up at Disley and boarded a train to Piccadilly. From there I walked down Oxford Road and eventually to Maine Road and the expectant throng.

"When I entered the Main Stand and climbed the stairs to the back row of HC block, just in front of the press box, I got the impression this was going to be a fantastic evening. The air of expectancy and the sheer noise from the crowd that evening were fantastic.

"In the first half the Goat went close, then the ball was crossed and 'Fat Bob' Taylor poked it home. Mass adulation and celebration as 'Fat Bob' celebrated with the first few rows of the Lower Kippax.

"In the second half Birmingham gave City a good game, and 'Fat Bob' was perhaps in his best form. He had a shot saved at the Platt Lane end. The Main Stand was shaking, such was the fervour. Then mass whistles from the crowd. We needed the victory. Could we hang on? Then the final whistle. Yes! Then with what seemed like 20,000 on the pitch and 'Rockin all over the World' and 'Moving on up' booming out of the tannoy, Maine Road was celebrating.

"As I walked back to Manchester there was a cacophony of car horns and many, many flags held aloft from sunroofs in celebration. It all seemed like a beautiful dream."

Another fan, Gary Knight, has similar memories from that night: "This 1-0 win over Birmingham virtually sealed our promotion. The match itself was a bit scrappy not a fluent City performance but the result all important. Big Bob Taylor smashed the winner home just before half time, but what I most remember was the raw emotion that evening. The support from all four stands was phenomenal; I was actually in J block of the Main Stand that evening, the only place I could get a ticket. I honestly believe with that support we could have beaten anyone that evening, even Real Madrid, such was the will to win."

An amazing victory over Blackburn in the next match ensured City's promotion to the Premier League.

Below: City fans swarm onto the pitch to celebrate a win that made promotion a distinct possibility.

Above: The temporary seating of the 'Gene Kelly Stand' would have looked more the part at the 18th green of The Open than it did on the Maine Road skyline.

Below: This Maine Road street sign didn't survive to the end of the stadium's days. It was stolen by souvenir hunters a year or so before City's final home game.

the first in an unbeaten run of twelve games. From then on City began to look like promotion contenders. One game saw City defeat Fulham 3-0 at Maine Road. For supporter Anthony Southern it was the most important result of the season: "I had not seen the Blues live for at least ten years, so me and my mate decided that City needed us. We thought we'd better get down to Maine Road and show our support. Fulham were top of the League and were easily the best side in the division. Also, Kevin Keegan was their manager.

"When the game started it was a really electric atmosphere, and when Goater scored after about 24 minutes it was like going to heaven. The crowd started singing 'Keegan, Keegan, what's the score?' Thinking now, I wonder what odds you would have got if you'd bet on him taking us into the Premiership? I believe that victory over Fulham changed our season. I've hardly missed a game since then. I'm glad I chose that day to resurrect my attendance at Maine Road."

City were promoted but still managed to do it the hard way, of course, with the Blues beating Gillingham in an amazing play-off final at Wembley in 1999.

Promotion was vital to long-term survival, and once it had been achieved serious moves could be made to plot the future. Naturally, the Premier League was the place to be, but reaching Division One at least allowed the club to plan. The biggest project, as far as Maine Road was concerned, was the move to the new stadium and at half-time in the opening match of the 1999-2000 season David Bernstein was joined on the pitch by council leader Richard Leese and Chief Executive Howard Bernstein for the official signing of the contract documentation confirming the move.

Maine Road was not forgotten though as additional temporary seating had now been installed in front of the scoreboard at the Kippax/Platt Lane corner, while the Gene Kelly stand was altered slightly with the addition of a couple of hundred seats early in the season. The increased capacity allowed City to reach an average attendance of 32,088 for the 1999-2000 promotion season – Maine Road's highest since the departure of Trevor Francis in 1982. City could only manage one season in the Premier League, and relegation brought an end to Joe Royle's managerial reign.

The arrival of Kevin Keegan as manager heralded a new era for the club but also meant Maine Road was nearing its end. However, some supporters were still making a first pilgrimage to the old stadium. Andy Noise: "As big a moment as your own first visit to Maine Road, is when you take your children for theirs. Born on the day Francis Lee resigned, I took my son, Jude Francis, to his on Feb 1st 2003. Was his highlight the atmosphere of a full house against West Bromwich Albion, a visit to the club shop, the fast food on the way to and from the game, the limitless sweets from Dad's pocket, the close proximity to legends like Anelka, Benarbia or a passing Schmeichel, or even celebrating your first goal? Not a chance. All were completely irrelevant compared to a half-time handshake from Moonchester!"

Success for Keegan and his squad came firstly with promotion as Division One Champions, and then in the following 2002-03 season City finished a respectable ninth and qualified for Europe via the Fair Play League. It was a great finale for Maine Road, and also a bright opening for City's return to East Manchester.

Maine Match 01/02

CITY v PORTSMOUTH

DATE:	21st April 2002	
TYPE OF FIXTURE:	Football League Division One (New)	
ATTENDANCE:	34,657	
RESULT:	City 3 Portsmouth 1	
TEAMS & SCORERS:	CITY	PORTSMOUTH
	Nash	Beasant
	Wright-Phillips	Pitt 1
	Jensen	(Brady)
	Dunne	Vincent
	Howey 1	Wilson
	Pearce	Primus
	Benarbia	Buxton
	Horlock	Summerbell
	Huckerby	Prosinecki
	Goater 1	Vine
	(Macken) 1	Harper
	Tiatto	(Cooper)
	(Berkovic)	Quashie

■ This was a day of celebration. City were already League Champions and, apart from a couple of weeks in February, had led the table since New Year's Day. The previous games at home to Barnsley and at Gillingham had seen City fans partying, but this day was so much better because, for the first time in many years, supporters knew exactly what to expect from their final home game.

Supporter John Lambert remembers the day: "I have been a City fan for over 30 years and like many of us have seen plenty of highs and lows. Living in Norfolk, when I get home from my ten-hour round trip I have often been greeted by my wife and daughter with the comment -- "You Must Be Mad! So, when it came to this match I thought I'd take them to see my beloved Blues. My wife has suffered, or is that enjoyed, the Maine Road experience a few times before, but for my ten-year-old daughter Chloe - who, like any child living outside Manchester, is in danger of becoming a closet Red - it was going to be a whole new experience.

"We set off from Norwich on a warm sunny day for April, and arrived outside Maine Road about an hour before kick-off. We walked Chloe round the ground. It was a carnival atmosphere like I had never seen before, and there were thousands of City fans everywhere. It appeared as though almost everyone had a flag and was singing -- even before the game had started. My daughter's eyes were like saucers as we walked up to our seats in the Main Stand. The result was 3-1 to the Blues, and she even heard the song her dad always sings in the bath - 'Feed the Goat and he will score'. At the end of the game the City team came back on the pitch and were presented with the League Championship trophy. Oh what a great day! Chloe's comment at the end was 'Daddy, is every game like this?' If only!"

The day also saw the final League match played by Stuart Pearce. The great England player had been a key

Above and left: Celebrations on and off the pitch as Maine Road's penultimate season closes with the return of the Football League championship trophy.

Below: Kevin Keegan repeated his achievements at Newcastle and Fulham by taking City back into the Premier League.

man with City throughout the season and this game, it was hoped, would see him score the 100th goal of his career. Throughout the match supporters urged him forward and almost every time the ball came anywhere near him they shouted 'shoot!' In the final minute City were awarded a penalty. Everyone knew Pearce would take it. Everybody waited for the celebration. Then Pearce blasted the ball into the Platt Lane Stand! He later admitted: "There is always a sting in the tail when Stuart Pearce does anything, and that penalty was comical. I have been psyched out by Dave Beasant!"

The goal would also have taken City to 109 in the season. This would have been a record, but with City's team celebrating their first significant piece of silverware since 1976 the statistic was not an issue. One worth recalling however is that Pearce's penalty was the last taken in a first team match at Maine Road. Co-incidentally, the first penalty taken at Maine Road back in August 1923 was also missed!

Maine Memory

■ As a City fan, it's impossible to truly get excited about an upcoming season. A certain Mr Royle would have us climbing the Premiership ladder with ease, winging our bandwagon through Europe, giant-killing, and slaying dragons en route. Giants and dragons don't exist of course and our exploits were destined for the humble First Division again - no fantasy about that. However, after the initial shock of Sir Joe being relieved of his place on the chipboard throne, an instalment was made in the form of Kevin Keegan.

Thoughts on England never really clouded the Maine Road faithful's view. In he strides sporting a Sky Blue old school Adidas top, playing us down but inadvertently playing us up too. "This team isn't good enough to get to the play-offs, never mind win the Championship" he hollered while sitting ruefully in eighth position. Whoosh - Masterstroke. Ali Bernabia in and they're off.

This City team charmed, teased, oozed confidence, disposed of opposition, ran riot, dug in, excelled, boasted class, style and flair, with swagger verging on arrogant. Most importantly they won. On and on went the swashbuckling. You could see opposition teams running out on to the Maine Road pitch, heads hung, thinking "Hope it's only one or two we concede". Try three!

Records smashed here, there and everywhere, the Manchester Ship pulls in winning a trophy and a degree of pride. Keegan had the pride from the start it transpires. We took a little longer coming round. We did arrive though.

Keegan makes you believe. You try and stop yourself but you just can't help it.

Joel Perry

Supporters' Organisations

■ City are blessed with two major supporters' organisations – the Official Supporters' Club and the Centenary Supporters' Association. The Supporters' Club can trace its roots back to 1949, while the Centenary Association was first formed during the Boardroom battles of 1993-4. Back then a number of branches broke away from the main organisation through disgruntlement at the support of Peter Swales and the existing Board. They called themselves the Independent Supporters' Association at the time as members felt a supporters' organisation should represent fans and not the Board. Other branches chose to remain and pointed to the strong support the Supporters' Club had always received from Peter Swales.

Clearly this was a very difficult period for all supporters and caused strong feelings of resentment, however once Francis Lee gained control of the club he tried to bring the two organisations together. Dave Wallace, who had been elected the club's first 'fan on the board', was given the task of trying to pull the factions together to form one official organisation. Unfortunately, the divisions were so great at that time the ultimate aim could not be achieved, nevertheless he did get the organisations talking and in the years since the two groups have worked together. It appears, however, they will always remain separate entities because of the problems encountered back in 1993-4.

By the summer of 2003 the Official Club boasted seventy branches while the Centenary Association had around thirty.

City did have a supporters' organisation before 1949. According to various sources a supporter called Bob Roden was a key figure with an organisation that seems to have existed during the early years of the Twentieth Century, however there are no details of how popular this organisation was, or of its main role. It seems, more than anything else, it was simply a group of supporters who liked to socialise and travel to games together - essentially, the same aims most modern day branches follow.

Ever since the Fifties the Supporters' Club have tried to support the main football club. This has varied from the presentation of radios and clocks to the club in the fifties, to sponsorship of

matches in the eighties. During this time the view of the Supporters' Club has always been each group should form their own local branch under the guidance of the umbrella organisation. This means each branch can follow its own aims while also taking part in the main organisation's activities.

Competitions such as cribbage, darts, bowling, football and the like have been organised over the years while the Seventies and Eighties saw the Supporters' Club organise other events, such as the annual banner competition. Branches would be encouraged to create their own banner and then parade around the pitch prior to a match.

Then there was the Miss Manchester City competition. This would no doubt be regarded as politically incorrect today, but for a while during the Seventies it was viewed in a positive manner by all concerned.

Above and left: The annual banner parade prior to a match at Maine Road was a very popular event during the 1970s, as it clearly demonstrated the large volume of supporters branches in existence. Perhaps a similar show of Blue pride will appear at the new stadium.

Helen Turner Lady with the bell

■ Helen Turner was a familiar figure throughout Maine Road's final thirty years. As a supporter she could regularly be heard ringing her famous bell during games. Often the Kippax would chant 'Helen, Helen, ring your bell!' and she was delighted to respond.

In 1976 she managed to find her way onto the pitch for the post-match celebrations when City won the League Cup. Commentator Brian Moore spotted her and explained to television viewers who she was. Helen: "It was terrific being on the pitch. One of my proudest moments. Mike Doyle let me hold the cup for a bit and I remember all the City fans cheering me. It was really good."

For most of her time at the ground she'd watch from the North Stand end. Helen: "I used to sit behind the goal. Always the same seat. Everybody knew where Helen was, but then in the last few years I had to move to the Platt Lane Stand because I go to the game in a wheelchair these days. Years ago I used to stand at the Scoreboard End and I remember sneaking youngsters in under my coat. I always thought children should be encouraged to attend, so I'd go through the turnstile with one under my coat. No one ever noticed, and if they did they never challenged me!"

"My favourite player was probably Joe Corrigan. Big Joe. I used to give him a sprig of heather before each game but sometimes I couldn't get the heather locally. I remember travelling up to Gretna Green on the Friday before the match to get some for the next day. I don't think Joe knew I went as far as that, but I couldn't let him down. It became a bit of a tradition."

Helen was also a key figure for the City Supporters' Travel Club. She would always steward one of the supporters' coaches for away games and woe betide anyone who crossed her: "I liked to ensure good discipline. I didn't want any swearing or carrying on. I suppose I was responsible for all these lads, and I wondered what their mums would say if they got into bother or didn't eat properly. I also made sure they appreciated the driver. We always had a collection."

Over the years Helen has become recognisable to many supporters. Even in Maine Road's final season she would often be seen outside the Supporters' Club offices, sporting a blue wig, collecting for local charities and she attended the opening games at Eastlands in the North Stand corner.

Maine Memory

■ I'm a fanatic Blues fan and have been now for over 36 years. Through that time I've seen some brilliant matches and some great sights but the one that hit me the most was in 2002. We had just seen the Blues get their trophy for winning the First Division, and I was one of the lucky few in wheelchairs who had Ali Benarbia come up to them and shake their hand.

That's my best memory of Maine Road but on the way out of the ground all the fans were singing and chanting and everyone was in a great mood. I was wheeling myself up the incline in the Family Stand to get out of the ground when I saw this old guy. He was about 70ish and he was doing that dance that Eric Morecambe and Ernie Wise did at the end of every programme. That for me said it all. This guy was now in his element and could cope with anything that life had to offer at that moment! I suppose City can do this to all of us from time to time.

Gary Campbell

The first League game at the
City of Manchester Stadium,
seen from the corner of the
North and West Stands.

Chapter Eleven
City are Back!

"I have been greatly impressed by the statements in the daily papers as to the danger caused by overcrowding at your home matches, the number you have had to turn away, and the great risks which are run by the football-loving public when attending a match on the City ground."

A section of a letter from United President John Davies to City recognising the problems caused by City's vast support at Hyde Road, October 1920

THE move from Maine Road to the City of Manchester Stadium in 2003 brought back memories for some of City's older supporters of the club's pre-Maine Road days. The Blues had been founded in the east of the city and the new location occasioned some to suggest City were coming home.

The specific details of City's early history can be read in *Manchester: The Greatest City*, however it is worth reiterating that the Blues first came into being in 1880 as the St. Mark's Church side in West Gorton and, after a series of moves around the Gorton area and amalgamations, had grown to become Ardwick AFC by 1887.

Ardwick were an ambitious professional club and possessed a ground known by many supporters as Bennett Street, but officially named Hyde Road. The ground grew to house crowds in excess of 40,000 within 18 years, but initially the area on which it stood was little more than wasteland.

By the end of August 1887 the ground was ready. The club made a large public house, the Hyde Road Hotel, its headquarters. All the important meetings of the period were held there and, on match days, the hotel would serve as Ardwick's changing rooms.

In 1892 the Ardwick Blues became founder members of the Football League Second Division, and in 1894 the club reformed as Manchester City; club officials wanted a name that represented the whole of Manchester despite their presence in the east.

Inevitably the bulk of City's support did come from the east of the city, but when the Blues became the first Manchester side to gain promotion (1899) and then win the FA Cup (1904) they gained a following from all areas of the conurbation.

East Manchester had a lively sporting and leisure industry, although it must be stressed this area of the city was also very industrial. In the Ardwick/Gorton area the key sites for entertainment were City's ground and the Belle Vue Zoological and Pleasure Gardens both off Hyde Road. Further north, but still on the eastern side of the city lay Philips Park – opened on 22nd August 1846 and recognised as the first public park in Manchester. This park lies close to the site of the City of Manchester Stadium and has been a crucial area of greenery in the Bradford-Clayton-Newton Heath area of the city.

Another key leisure site close to Philips Park (named after Mark Philips who purchased 31 acres of land for £6,200 to create the park) was the Manchester United ground at Bank Street (close to the present day velodrome). This means the City Of Manchester Stadium

Left: Was this Ardwick or the first Manchester City team? This heavily touched up photo of the Blues in 1894 does show a few key City players - Bob Milarvie (front row, far right), and Canadian Walter Bowman (2nd row, 3rd from left), but the specific date is unknown. Chairman John Chapman (see Maine Men, page 268) appears second from the right on the back row. Incidentally, Bowman was the first overseas international to play in English League football.

Above: An Ardwick season ticket for the Boys' Stand at Hyde Road in 1892-93.

Maine Match 1892/93

ARDWICK v BOOTLE

DATE:	3rd September 1892	
TYPE OF FIXTURE:	Football League Division Two	
ATTENDANCE:	c.4,000	
RESULT:	Ardwick 7 Bootle 0	
TEAMS & SCORERS:	ARDWICK	BOOTLE

ARDWICK		BOOTLE
Douglas		McLaughlin
McVickers		Hutchinson
Robson		Arridge
Middleton		Neilson
Russell		Hughes
Hopkins		Grierson
Davies	3	Finlayson
Morris	2	Gallacher
Angus	1	Law
Weir	1	McLafferty
Milarvie		Montgomery

■ The first League match to take place at Hyde Road was against Bootle. Both sides had met during the previous season in the Alliance League, but for their first taste of League football the Ardwick footballing public felt slightly let down by the size of the opposition. Nevertheless this was still a defining moment in the history of the club and the crowd. Poor weather and a limited amount of shelter at Hyde Road helped keep the attendance down to around 4,000, even so those brave souls who stood and cheered their heroes on were rewarded with an excellent Ardwick performance.

The final result was a 7-0 Ardwick victory, putting the Mancunians right at the top of the very first Second Division table on 3rd September 1892. Hugh Morris scored the club's first goal in a League game at the ground, while Joe Davies netted the first League hat-trick. In addition, the home side were also awarded their first League penalty when Jack Angus was fouled. Ardwick's new captain Dave Russell, a former member of the Preston double-winning side of 1888-9, sent the penalty straight into McLaughlin's hands. Co-incidentally, both the first and last penalties taken in League games at Maine Road were also missed - Frank Roberts against Sheffield United in August 1923 and Stuart Pearce against Portsmouth in April 2002.

is closer to the ground where United first gained prominence than City's old ground at Hyde Road. There was even a pub called 'The United Hotel' on the corner of Ashton New Road, roughly where the junction of Ashton New Road and Alan Turing Way is today.

Clearly, the proximity of United's early ground to the new stadium is irrelevant to some extent, but it does show how East Manchester should be regarded as the birthplace of professional football in the city. For both clubs to have gained prominence while based there suggests the people of East Manchester were very supportive and keen on professional football. In the 1880s and '90s there had been football clubs all around Manchester, including a very popular side called West Manchester based in the Trafford area, however it was

only those in the East that developed to a national level. The west of the city was home to cricket at Old Trafford and further north horse-racing at the Manchester Racecourse (since demolished).

At Hyde Road, City became Manchester's premier sports club, and the Blues rapidly outgrew the ground. Improvements were made on a regular basis but it was clear City would have to move if they were ever to really capitalise on their popularity. A walk around the Hyde Road ground at the beginning of 1920 would have shown the 21-year-old Main Stand, with wooden dressing rooms behind; three ten-year-old multi-span roofs over the other sides; oddly-shaped terracing behind both goals; and a large banked terracing opposite the Main Stand. Behind the western goal terracing there was

also a small seated area called the Stone Yard Stand (as one would expect, named after the stoneyard behind that end of the ground).

The multi-span roofs provided the ground with an air of stand uniformity not matched until the Blues moved to the new City Of Manchester Stadium in 2003. The Stone Yard Stand (to the right of the Main Stand) roof possessed five spans built on six front and six back stanchions. As with the other three multi-spans this was merely placed over the irregular sectioned terracing and seating.

The Popular Side roof, opposite the Main Stand, was similar, although much larger individual spans were erected.

It's fair to say an air of mystery surrounds the Galloway end of the ground, to the left of the Main Stand. Here City possessed a corner section known to an entire generation as the 'Boys Stand', and behind the goal a larger, more typical section of terracing.

Incredibly, the Boys Stand had a railway loop line running between it and the pitch. This was necessary to carry boilers and machinery from the Galloway Boilerworks behind the stand, but it was also a major inconvenience. There surely cannot ever have been any other ground in the world with a railway line running through it! The stand was also positioned at an awkward angle to the pitch, and was not the most ideal viewing location. In fact, as a comparison, the 'Gene Kelly' temporary stand at Maine Road was as remote as the 'Boys Corner' at Hyde Road.

No clear photographs of this end of the ground exist post-1910 and it is extremely difficult to state with clarity how it all appeared. It's possible the entire end was roofed exactly as that at the Stone Yard side of the ground, i.e. a five span of equal sizes thrown across the terracing, however maps from the period suggest – and

only suggest – the Boys Stand and main section of the Galloway End were roofed separately.

In addition, some poor-quality surviving photographs from 1920 show all the metalwork for a multi-span roof at this end but there appears to be no

Below: A map from 1894 showing the railway loop line. The Boys' Stand was later erected in the shaded area north of the line.

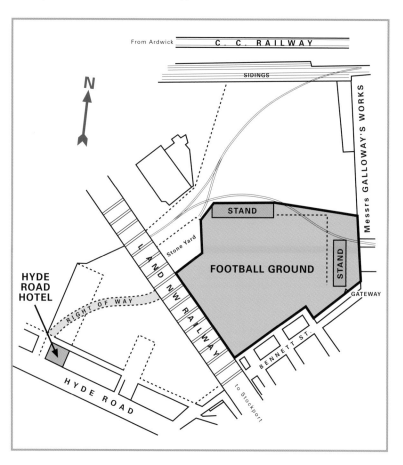

Left: Future Prime Minister Arthur Balfour poses for a photograph at the Hyde Road Main Stand in 1900. Although it's difficult to tell from this photograph, the Directors' Box (to the right of the Refreshment Bar sign) was decorated with bunting and material to give it a much grander feel than usual.

actual cover. Whether this was an accident that occurred later in City's history, or simply a trick of the light on the photograph, will never be known.

Multi-span roofs were unusual, even in 1910, but were essential at Hyde Road as they allowed spans of different lengths and depths to be developed if necessary, whereas a traditional single span roof - something like the old Kippax roof - would only really be able to cover a regular shaped area of terracing.

Hyde Road was probably the only ground in the world possessing three large roofs of this style. Sadly, this type of roof was relatively expensive to maintain.

Despite the modern day view that Hyde Road was dilapidated, it has to be stressed that in 1920 the buildings were relatively new. None of the seating areas were older than 21, while the terracing had all been modified over the years. The real problem with the ground was its size. Its absolute capacity was viewed as 40,000 (the ground reached this size in 1904), although this was surpassed on a regular basis. The City management always seemed to describe any capacity crowd as 40,000 regardless of how many additional fans actually attended!

Another major problem was access. The club could not open access on all sides and for many supporters entry was via a pathway at the side of the Hyde Road Hotel, under the railway arches and into the ground. According to the 18th August 1920 edition of the *Manchester Evening News:* "The approach from Hyde Road, over the croft, which in winter is oftener than not a sea of mud, has long been a thorn in the side of the club officials. Week after week thousands of enthusiasts have cheerfully plodded through the mire, and it was very evident that sooner or later something would have to be done to enable the club's supporters to witness matches without having to wander over ground which is frequently reminiscent of Flanders at its worst,"

It was no surprise the club had already taken steps to relocate and, importantly as far as officials were concerned, City's new ground was to remain in the East Manchester area. The Blues were moving to Belle Vue, or so everybody thought. The *Evening News:* "The future

Maine Match 1894/95

CITY v BURTON WANDERERS

DATE:	3rd September 1894	
TYPE OF FIXTURE:	Football League Division Two	
ATTENDANCE:	c.2,500	
RESULT:	City 1 Burton Wanderers 1	
TEAMS & SCORERS:	CITY	BURTON
	Williams	Brentnall
	Smith	Cunningham
	Dyer	Draper
	Mann	Haywood
	Jones	Ward
	Nash	Draycott
	Wallace	Moore
	Finnerhan	Brown
	Calvey	Capes (Adr) 1
	Sharples	Capes (Art)
	Little 1	Garfield

■ This first home game for Manchester City was important as it needed to demonstrate to the football world the Blues were a serious League outfit. Many thought City would be Ardwick in disguise but the club went to great lengths to show, despite the venue and much of the committee being the same, the club's outlook was different. This point was best demonstrated by the fact most of the squad had changed.

The team had already been defeated away from home, but the Hyde Road match was important to win over local support. In the end a 1-1 draw with Burton Wanderers reassured some but real interest in the newly-formed City side began five days later when Burslem Port Vale were defeated 4-1 in Hyde Road's next match.

Maine Memory

■ My father was a regular at Hyde Road and could remember all the early stars of the club. There's a cartoon of the City players stood around a cannon from about 1904. It includes Meredith with his toothpick and all the others except Billy Gillespie. The cartoon's called 'Getting ready for action' and Meredith has a bubble from his mouth and is asking 'Where's Gilly?' meaning Gillespie.

My father explained this because he said that the team would regularly get ready to go out for a match and suddenly realised there were only ten of them. Gilly Gillespie would always be in the pub!

Harry Bramble

Right: The 'Hornet Cartoon' referred to in Harry Bramble's Maine Memory (above).

APRIL 1, 1905.   THE ILLUSTRATED SPORTING AND DRAMATIC NEWS.   169

THE F.A. CUP SEMI-FINAL.—NEWCASTLE UNITED DEFEAT SHEFFIELD WEDNESDAY.

WON BY ONE GOAL TO NIL AT MANCHESTER, BEFORE 40,000 PEOPLE.

High kicking by Newcastle.   *Before the Sheffield goal.*

1. Taking the ball from a throw in.   *2. Sheffield pressing.*   *3. Good passing by Sheffield.*

Lawrence, the Newcastle United goalkeeper.   *Some good dribbling by the losers.*   *Lyall, the Sheffield Wednesday goalkeeper.*

I BALDWIN. 2 SMITH. 3 BUCHAN. 4 NORGROVE. 5 EADIE. 6 STEEL. 7 DAVIES. 8 DENNISON. 9 KELSO. 10 EVANS. 11 TAYLOR. 12 WHITTAKER.
13 HAMBLETT. 14 GRIEVE. 15 CHRISTIE. 16 CONLIN. 17 YOUNG. 18 BANKS. 19 STEWART. 20 THORNLEY. 21 FISHER. 22 DORSETT.

Above: The City team pose in front of the Main Stand at Hyde Road prior to the annual public practice match in August 1906. The numbers were not actually on the shirts - they were merely painted onto this photograph to help identify the players!

Left: Action from the 1905 FA Cup semi-final at Hyde Road between Newcastle United and Sheffield Wednesday, covered by the the Illustrated Sporting & Dramatic News. The Wednesday goalkeeper, Lyall, later joined City. The stand in the background of the photos marked 1 & 3 is the Galloway End, while the central photo on the bottom row shows fans sat on the pitch in front of the Popular Side. All other photos show the Main Stand in the background.

home of the Manchester City Football Club has been definitely settled. Mr. Mangnall, the secretary of the club, informs us that a long lease of the ground adjoining the Sports Ground at the Longsight end of Belle Vue, and inside the Gardens, has been secured, and with the space available it will be possible to erect an enclosure equal to any in the United Kingdom.

"The lease at Hyde Road expires, as a matter of fact, in December 1924, and by that date it is confidently expected that the new ground at Belle Vue, capable of holding over 100,000 spectators, will have been completed. Many years ago the view was expressed in the 'Evening News' that the famous Belle Vue pleasure gardens could provide a ground worthy of the City football club."

This news excited City's supporters. It was felt the club should remain in the east of the city and the prospect of a 100,000 capacity venue was very appealing, however some newspapers were not convinced the club could make such a leap forward and interviews were set up with manager Ernest Mangnall to find out more. The *Empire News* of 22nd August challenged Mangnall: "'I note' the interviewer ventured to remark, 'that you are having the roofs of your stands put in order, and that other improvements are being effected on your ground. Will it be long before you take up your new quarters at Belle Vue?' To this Mr. Mangnall replied that nothing definite could be said on that score at present. All he could say was that it was their intention to fix up their new quarters as soon as possible. They realised they were losing money by staying at their present ground."

The article went on to outline the plans, but it also

made note of City's popularity. The Blues were a tremendous attraction and Ernest Mangnall told the interviewer he was campaigning for supporters to be given excursion fares on the railway for away matches rather than the higher standard fare. Thinking about City's support he added that the club was popular with all Mancunians especially those involved with the war and the Blues had tried to help: "Never was there so much interest as there is now. Look at that stack of letters received at this office. These number many thousands, and the bulk of them have been replied to. I do not mention this in a spirit of boasting, but merely to show what was done in the way of providing footballs, cigarettes and other comforts for the boys who were fighting for our existence as a nation."

City's popularity continued to grow, and within two months the Blues were forced to consider hastening their move. Virtually every home game had seen large crowds packing the streets leading to the ground with many dissatisfied supporters. There was a very real concern that a good cup run or significant League campaign might lead to even greater crowd problems. Most northern newspapers focussed on City's position with each offering suggestions. The *Daily Dispatch* seemed the most interested: "The new home at Belle Vue cannot be available for a year or two at best, and meanwhile the club is carrying out its fixtures under conditions not merely of great discomfort but grave danger. Today I am in a position to set before the directors a proposal which I venture to think is one of the most interesting and important which has been mooted in the annals of Manchester football."

The *Dispatch* went on to suggest City move first

team fixtures to Old Trafford, with United moving reserve games to Hyde Road. The article considered how City would feel about a move: "No-one who understands football management, and what I may call the psychology of football directors, will imagine that the Manchester City management will, without serious thought, transfer their games to a rival ground several miles away, unique though is the opportunity provided. The objections to such a course, if not perhaps obvious to all, will readily be appreciated by many. But the advantages, as set off to the disadvantages, are very real.

"It is doubtful if Hyde Road will hold all who would wish to witness the least attractive of the City club's fixtures; it certainly is utterly unable to accommodate the crowds who flock to the ground on all big occasions. It is not merely disconcerting frequently to have to turn away thousands of supporters and to close the gates. It constitutes a very real danger to have a seething mass of enthusiasts, packed like sardines, inside, and thousands of disappointed people clamouring at the gates.

"The directors almost every time they have a home match, live in the shadow of a disaster which would do irreparable harm to the club, to the city, and to the game. Whatever may be the actual holding capacity of Hyde Road, the situation becomes difficult and dangerous as soon as 30,000 pass the turnstiles. A great deal might be written concerning the discomfort and inconvenience to which the crowd is subjected at Hyde Road even at the best of times. At the worst it is a menace to public safety, a possible death trap."

The comments make it crystal clear Hyde Road was simply too small for City. Unlike Maine Road in 2003, the club did not make matches all-ticket affairs, nor did they have a clear view on capacity. What they did have was a desire to let in as many fans as possible. On occasion this figure was too great for the ground, and yet the fans still came. They loved football the Hyde Road way.

On the day of the *Dispatch* article John Davies, Manchester United's President, sent a letter to City Chairman Lawrence Furniss making a formal offer to allow the Blues to play at Old Trafford. This caused considerable debate amongst most supporters against the move although the *Dispatch* claimed there were thousands of 'inarticulate' fans who would willingly move with the club to United's ground. It seemed an odd comment. The club listened to those who did come forward with views and by 13th October 1920 – two days after the suggestion had been made – Lawrence Furniss declined United's offer. The Blues were to soldier on, but then disaster struck.

Maine Men Jimmy Broad

ROLE: Trainer

■ Former boxing coach, athlete and St. Helens rugby player, Jimmy Broad is one of the club's forgotten heroes. For over forty years Broad was associated with the Blues but rarely has his involvement been properly recorded.

From the moment he was appointed Assistant Trainer in 1891 through to the move to Maine Road, Broad was a familiar face around the club. As the secretary-manager was often too involved with administrative matters in that period, the trainer's day-to-day activities were more consistent with responsibilities associated in the modern era with managers. For instance, all training was devised by the coaches and, in terms of influence on the team, Jimmy Broad fulfilled a role similar to Malcolm Allison while secretary-manager Tom Maley's role was perhaps closer to that of Joe Mercer.

Broad was a key figure throughout the club's time at Hyde Road, and was City's trainer when they won the FA Cup in 1904. During the cup run he told the press of his delight at working at Hyde Road: "It was a real pleasure to train that team. They were all as keen as mustard and always to be found together."

As well as coaching City to cup success in 1904, he was also a major influence behind promotion in 1899 and 1903, and City's appearance in the FA Cup semi-final in 1924. He had also been trainer to England on three occasions and for the Football League. By 1934 he was still a popular figure around Manchester.

At the time of the move to Maine Road in 1923 Broad was, along with Lawrence Furniss and Albert Alexander senior, one of the few remaining links with the 1890s. His great-granddaughter Karen Knowles has discussed his life with other family members: "My father was the grandson of Jimmy and, along with his brother Jim, attended all home games from an early age, while I have been attending Maine Road matches since the age of seven. Jimmy, was the trainer when City boasted the likes of Sandy Turnbull, Jimmy Bannister and Billy Meredith. He wasn't very tall and always wore a hat and carried a walking stick and, according to the family, he was very military looking.

"When he wasn't involved in football he travelled all around the world, and he wasn't without money. He was however a gambler. I suppose the most memorable thing my aunts and uncles remember is that he was the first person to use a rub on his players when they were injured. It was his own remedy and was called Broad's Embrication. Due to his gambling he got into debt and sold it to a chemist in Moss Side in order to pay off the debt. My uncle remembers as a child going to a chemist on Great Western Street where he saw a large display of Broad's Embrication in the window.

"He would go every Sunday to my grandad's for dinner where he would gather his six grandchildren around him and make them recite 'CONSTANTINOPLE' over and over again. When his grandchildren were good he would give them tuppence. He was also very strict.

"When his wife died he went to live in Wren Street in Gorton with his children. He was admitted into hospital with a serious illness but he couldn't stand it so he escaped! Not long after, about 1943, he died of pneumonia."

Broad was a true Blue. He loved City and even in his thirties (during the 1890s) turned out for the team in friendlies, testimonials and minor competition matches. He often used to tell a tale of appearing as outside-right in a match in South Wales when Billy Meredith played inside-right. The great Welsh player fed the ball to Broad and City's trainer scored.

Three of Jimmy's sons were on City's books – Wilf, who never managed a first team appearance; Tommy, who played for City from 1919 to 1921; and James Broad who played for the club in two spells between 1909 and 1913. Tommy was the more famous of the City players. Karen: "The local press at the time described Tommy as being of the 'tearaway class' who 'ran like a greyhound'. Tommy had a lot to offer and was still playing top class football at 38 years of age. He died in 1966. James Broad, better known as Jimmy, was one of English football's early exports and, at various times during his career, held coaching posts with Coruna, Las Palmas, Barcelona and Geneva. He began his career as a goalkeeper, but became one of the most dangerous and gifted attackers in the country after moving into the forward line, where he proved a clever player and a great finisher. It was said at the time he had 'feet like cannons', and would surely have gone on to great things had not the Great War intervened. He died in August 1963."

Jimmy Broad, City's popular trainer, was a key influence on the club from the age of 29 right through until his seventies.

Maine Men Lawrence Furniss

Below: Lawrence Furness.

ROLE: Player, Secretary-Manager, Chairman, and President

■ It's highly unlikely Manchester City would ever have achieved any form of success had it not been for Lawrence Furniss, one of the club's earliest figures. Furniss was the club's first manager, but his contribution to City and indeed Maine Road's history is so much more than that of a manager.

He first became involved with the club in the early 1880s as a player, probably at the age of 19. These were the days before the club had used the name Ardwick never mind Manchester City, and matches were often organised at short notice.

A leg injury brought a premature end to his career, but Furniss was an out and out Blue and wanted to stay involved. Like a Sunday football enthusiast, he helped organise fixtures and also searched for appropriate pitches and facilities. These formative years were exceptionally difficult for the club and it's clear that without the determination of Furniss and his colleagues the club could have folded on a number of occasions.

By 1887 Furniss was a key influence in the direction of the club and one of the major players behind the move to Hyde Road and the selection of the name Ardwick AFC. To Furniss, Hyde Road offered the club potential to establish themselves as a major force. It was an opportunity they could not miss.

Two years later, at the age of 27, he was named secretary-manager and under his direction the Blues won the Manchester Cup two years in succession and, on the back of these successes, were admitted as founder members of the Second Division.

His only League season in charge ended with the Blues finishing a creditable fifth, but Furniss stepped down to allow Joshua Parlby, an altogether much more public figure, to take on the lead role. Furniss was still younger than some of the club's players at this point.

A year later, when Ardwick was collapsing and City being created, Furniss became so involved in sorting out the financial problems he ended up paying off most of Ardwick's creditors from his own money. It cost him £70 – a substantial sum at the time – and as a result he had to delay his own wedding by three years while he raised enough cash to bale the club out. Consequently, City's very existence owes a great deal to the man.

Furniss continued to help the club develop however, and is recognised as the man who first spotted the potential of Billy Meredith – football's first major star. Legend has it that Furniss and another City official spent considerable time in Meredith's

home town of Chirk, Wales, buying the locals drinks in exchange for an opportunity to meet the player. At one point, so one story goes, the City men were thrown into a pond as the locals objected to the 'poaching' of their hero.

It is believed Furniss was a shareholder from the 1890s, although club records cannot prove this as the Hyde Road fire destroyed the first Shareholder Register. However, it is known he still held three shares in 1921 – the time he became Chairman (he had also been Chairman in 1916 for a while) – and that he purchased a further three in May 1923.

He first became a board member in 1903 but, as with most club officials, had to leave the board following investigations into the alleged bribe scandal. He rejoined the board a decade later, serving as chairman from 1921 to 1928. For many years the Blues had considered moving to Belle Vue, but the decision to develop Maine Road offered more potential. Just as the move to Hyde Road was seen as being vitally important for the club to establish itself, so was the Maine Road move viewed as an opportunity to push City forward.

As Chairman, Furniss ultimately made the decision to move, although he would have been first to admit it was a team decision with Ernest Mangnall, Wilf Wild, Albert Alexander senior and architect Charles Swain each playing their part.

According to some sources, it was actually suggested Maine Road should have been named after Furniss. Whether this was ever discussed at board level is debatable but it seems very likely Furniss would have refused such an accolade. He clearly was of the opinion the team was more important than any individual associated with the club.

By the time the Blues won the League Championship in 1937 Furniss was a very proud club President. He had watched the club grow from the equivalent of a Sunday pub team into League Champions in his lifetime. Not only that but his club were playing in the best stadium in the country.

Furniss was living in Mellor near Marple at this point. He had for many years been manager of The Roman Bridge Lakes Estate - a popular tourist attraction in its heyday - in that area.

Furniss died in 1941 after sixty years' active involvement with the club. He passed away at a house in Wilmslow Road, Fallowfield, where he was being nursed, but his main address was the Old Hall, Mellor, often referred to as Bottoms Hall. He was buried at St. Martin's Church in Marple and left three daughters. Understandably, as his death came during a crucial period of the Second World War it was largely ignored by the media and by supporters of the club. That's a shame, but no doubt Furniss himself would not have objected. Manchester City, and in particular Maine Road, was his legacy.

Left: This 1920 team picture shows trainer Jimmy Broad (2nd from left, back row) and his son Tommy (2nd left, front row). Tommy Johnson is 3rd from the right on the front row - this photograph belongs to his son, Alan.

Maine Memory

■ When the fire destroyed the Main Stand, United in their benign way offered the use of Old Trafford, but City politely refused saying 'Don't worry we'll have a grandstand!' and y'know we did! We had one built by the time we played United. It was made of tongue and groove and varnished. In fact you could still smell the varnish all over the ground. It was pretty rough, but it served its purpose, and as it was all new wood it must have been ten times stronger than the old stand.

As usual the band came out, formed a circle on the pitch and played all the popular songs of the day. Then they started playing 'I wouldn't leave my little wooden hut for you' and the crowd wasn't slow to notice that, and we all started laughing. Then the referee came on, blew his whistle at the band and told them to get off! So as they marched off they played 'Home Sweet Home' - very apt, very witty!

The late Harry Hughes (interviewed in 1996)

FOOTBALL HUMOUR.
"I Wouldn't Leave My Little Wooden Hut for You,"

There is no love lost between the two big Manchester football clubs, and the feeling has not been improved since the United first offered and then refused the City the free use of the Old Trafford ground for League matches.

Evidently a wag had been at work in the musical department prior to the match at Hyde-road yesterday, for just before the United team entered the field the band played with great pathos "I Wouldn't Leave My Little Wooden Hut For You," and followed by "Home, Sweet Home."

On Saturday 6th November at 11pm, fire wrecked the Main Stand, the club's offices, changing rooms and player facilities. Thousands were attracted to the ground to witness the blaze as it happened and the following morning the City directors and management considered their options. They approached United about their earlier offer and were shocked to discover the Reds demanded special terms. According to the *Athletic News* these were: "City should take the equivalent of last season's gate in the corresponding match and that the remainder should belong to the United. As gates have increased by 30 per cent at the very least in the First Division matches the Manchester City directors declined to entertain the proposal, and no wonder. Manchester United did not in our opinion manifest the much-vaunted League spirit.

RUSH TO HELP THE CITY.

Clearing the Debris at Hyde-road.

NIGHT AND DAY WORK.

By " THE PILOT."

Manchester City have entered upon the task of clearing and reconstructing the site of their grand stand, offices, and dressing-rooms with an energy which is an object-lesson to the housing experts. Immediately they decided that the revised offer of Manchester United was out of the question orders were given to two contractors and early yesterday morning a gang of 100 men set about the work of clearing the fire debris. A big crowd turned up at the ground offering their services, and a selected number of them were engaged and by night-time had progressed so rapidly that there is little doubt that excellent accommodation will be provided for Saturday's match against Huddersfield Town.

Work will proceed night and day, and the railway sidings of Galloway's works, which run alongside the ground, will enable train loads of cinders to be deposited for banking. Temporary offices and dressing-rooms are already in course of construction, and even if not ready for Saturday there is the alternative of rooms in Galloway's works, which contain excellent accommodation for the players and officials.

The Only Stand.

The only stand on the ground at present —the stoneyard stand—is being reseated, and will only hold about 250 people. Ticket holders, therefore, will greatly assist the club officials by reaching the ground early. When the old stand site is banked up there will be room for fully 5,000 more people than before the fire, but, of course, there will be no shelter from the weather. The volume of correspondence which has reached the City manager, Mr. J. E. Mangnall, does not contain one adverse criticism of the directors' decision to remain at Hyde-road. In fact the decision has given great satisfaction all round. Many people are asking why the United withdrew their offer of a month ago. If that offer was made in the best sporting spirit, as I feel sure it was, would it not have been gracious to repeat it under the changed conditions which entitled the City to deep sympathy? However, this is a matter for the United directors alone.

■ Welshman John Edward Chapman worked with Joshua Parlby during the 1893-4 season to create Manchester City from the ashes of Ardwick AFC. Due to considerable effort on his part, Manchester City became a credible offering and on the same day as Queen Victoria visited Manchester to open the Ship Canal, Chapman's City were accepted into the Football League. Secretary-Manager Joshua Parlby had made a great speech, but Chapman had also satisfied the League regarding details of the club's structure and finances.

For eight consecutive years Chapman was chairman, but his role also involved scouting, the signing of players and, with the support of his secretary-manager, the general day to day management of the club. One of Chapman's first major acts following the club's formation was to finalise the Billy Meredith transfer, while his period as chairman saw the Hyde Road ground develop at a good pace. The erection of the main stand and numerous other minor developments – such as the installation of turnstiles – brought Hyde Road into the twentieth century.

Chapman was a very popular figure in City's early history, but was not one for claiming credit. According to the *Umpire News* in 1904: "The name of John Chapman, as he is familiarly called, is known to most of the many thousands who claim to be numbered among the supporters of Manchester City, but it may safely be said that comparatively few are aware to what extent they are indebted to the gentleman who for so long presided over the destinies of the club. Though now a prosperous organisation, Manchester City has not always been in that happy position, and in the early years of its existence, when an effort was being made to get together a team worthy of representing a city like Manchester – a costly business – Chapman was always ready to furnish the sinews of war whenever necessary."

By 1902, however, Chapman was no longer felt to be the right man for the job. One director, famous newspaper baron Edward Hulton (his name lives on today with the Hulton-Getty photographic library), claimed Chapman was: "too kind hearted to run a football club". After standing down as Chairman, Chapman remained a key figure in City's development leading up to Cup success in 1904.

Outside of football Chapman was a publican, and at one time owned six public houses in the Ardwick area. He also became involved in politics and, with the support of the City players, stood for election as a Conservative councillor.

They missed a great opportunity to make the club popular by a fine sporting act.

"The followers of Manchester City have greater affection for the old club than ever. And they have formed a just opinion of their neighbours."

It seems United's terms were strongly criticised throughout the national press while the City management chose to forego moving for the time being and concentrate instead on ensuring Hyde Road could stage football again. Over a hundred volunteers arrived at the ground daily throughout the following week as a new stand was erected and dressing rooms constructed.

Further bad news followed. The *Athletic News*: "It is said that trouble never comes singly. After the club's grandstand had been burned down, an errant motor wagon smashed in the main gates, and the next day a runaway traction engine knocked down the entrances on the other side of the ground."

Despite these obstacles the club remained positive, while the work gained decent press coverage across the country. Over the following weeks reporters from other towns and cities travelled to Manchester simply to see how the club had recovered. The *Glasgow Evening Times* was very impressed when its reporter attended a match shortly after the fire: "Manchester City must have some good friends. They are of course the popular club in Manchester. It was surprising to find a fine new stand, estimated to hold 6,000 spectators, rising to the height of 25 tiers on the site of the old structure. In addition, extensive new terracing had been carried out, and new dressing rooms for both teams and offices had been

Maine Memory

■ My father told me an amusing story from his Hyde Road days. A member of the ground staff used to carry a notice board around the ground before games with team changes written in white chalk. One Saturday heavy rain washed away the chalk lettering – but the fellow continued his perambulation with a completely blank board! A board with chalked team changes was still used at Maine Road when I became a regular fan. There were groans and cheers from different sides of the ground as the board was carried past. One time snowballs were thrown at the board carrier, presumably because a team change didn't gain approval!
James Dowd

Right: Devastation after the Main Stand fire of 1920.

Below: This City group look delighted to have made the move to Maine Road. Included are Jimmy Broad (2nd left), Tommy Johnson (4th right), Frank Roberts (3rd right) and Billy Meredith (2nd right).

erected. Talk about the building of an American city!"

Inevitably, the need to move increased and City pushed forward with their plans. Week after week the press focussed on the situation and by May 1922 ideas were mooted that the club should make the new Belle Vue stadium a multi-function venue. Cycle tracks were suggested as many Mancunians viewed City's move as an opportunity to create a major stadium. Time after time the Blues responded by saying they wanted to focus on football. Then the club shocked everyone by revealing they would not be moving to Belle Vue after all, and that another site had been found at Maine Road.

The announcement ended all discussion about a multi-purpose venue, but also caused concern within East

Manchester. United had moved out and gone west over a decade earlier, and now City were leaving for south Manchester. When the Blues did move, another team - Manchester Central Football Club - was created with ambitions to join the League. Several bids for this MCFC who, incidentally played at the Belle Vue Athletics Stadium, to join the Third Division failed and inevitably the club collapsed.

Rugby, speedway, wrestling, boxing and greyhound racing all proved popular in the Belle Vue complex over the years, but as far as East Manchester was concerned professional football had completely disappeared from the area. It would be another eighty years before City would return East, but what a homecoming!

These two images are among the last taken of the Hyde Road Hotel - the birthplace of Manchester City Football Club. The scaffolding appeared in April 2001 and within a month the building had been demolished. Entry to the Hyde Road ground was possible to the left of the building. A pathway (marked 'Right of Way' on the map on page 262) led across a muddy 'croft' under railway arches and to the turnstiles.

Hyde Road Milestones

The Stone Yard end is in the background as Arthur Balfour joins Billy Meredith on the pitch during a visit in September 1900.

The Hyde Road ground had a 36-year life as City's first team home and during that time many significant games, ground developments and visits occurred. The attached offers an historical snapshot of the ground:

■ **1887** – Club Captain K. McKenzie suggests to the club wasteland close to Bennett Street and Hyde Road could become ground. Lawrence Furniss and Walter Chew agree lease with local railway company. Hyde Road Hotel becomes club headquarters and changing rooms.

■ **1888** – 1,000 seater stand erected and club's first paybox developed. The paybox cost £5 15s and helped gate money reach £213.

■ **1889** – Ardwick face Newton Heath (later Manchester United) in a floodlit match to raise funds for victims of the Hyde Coalmining disaster at Belle Vue. It is also known Ardwick faced League giants Preston North End in another floodlit match at Hyde Road around this time, although there is confusion over the exact date.

■ **1890** - £600 ground improvements made. Pitch returfed, new bars erected and a new entrance opened next door to the Hyde Road Hotel.

■ **1892** – The Cambridge Blue-shirted Ardwick become founder members of the Football League Second Division.

■ **1893** – Hyde Road stages the Football League Test Match (similar to modern day play-offs) between Notts County and Darwen. Darwen won 3-2. The selection of Hyde Road was a major honour for the Blues.

■ **1894** – Ardwick collapses and Manchester City is created in its place. First meeting of new club held at Hyde Road Hotel where decisions are made to play home games at Hyde Road, continue to wear Cambridge Blue and to create a club to represent the whole of Manchester.

■ **1896** – Ground improvements see the club erect dressing rooms, and a sign outside the Hyde Road Hotel proclaiming "The Headquarters of Manchester City Football Club". It is also believed the club purchased approximately four turnstiles from local company W.T. Ellison. These turnstiles were later moved to Maine Road and still in use during 2003. Other Ellison's and possibly 'Bailey's Quick Action' turnstiles would be erected in 1899.

■ **1897** – Hyde Road staged its first representative game when the Football League –

wearing white shirts and blue shorts – defeated the Irish League 8-1 before a 15,000 crowd. The League side included City men Charlie Williams and William 'Doc' Holmes.

■ **1898** – The 'Grand Stand Syndicate' is created to raise funds to erect a new stand. £1,500 was needed to purchase a stand used for the Fulham Pageant and transport it to Hyde Road for re-erection on the 'sixpence' side. This stand was erected the following year as the club's first major Main Stand.

■ **1899** – Promotion as Champions caused the Blues to investigate moving to the Belle Vue Zoological and Pleasure Gardens further along Hyde Road. They decided to erect the Fulham Pageant stand instead, and for the following 23 years the club would consider how to make a move to Belle Vue happen.

■ **1900** – Local MP and future Prime Minister Arthur Balfour visited Hyde Road for a game with Stoke.

■ **1904** – Cup winners City spent over £2,000 enlarging the stands, improving access and general all-round improvements to Hyde Road. This was a phenomenal figure – four times the amount Manchester United had spent on building a 1,000 seater stand only a couple of years

earlier. The Hyde Road capacity was raised to 40,000.

■ **1905** – Hyde Road hosted its only FA Cup Semi-final when Newcastle defeated Sheffield Wednesday. The club's ground improvements had made Hyde Road a major venue, and the following October the Football League beat the Irish League 4-0 in another inter-League match.

■ **1910** – Approximately £3,000 was spent on roofing the three uncovered sides of the ground. The newly refurbished ground held 35,000 under cover plus a further 4,000 uncovered. The newly opened Old Trafford only had covered accommodation for about a quarter of that figure. Interestingly, neither Old Trafford, nor indeed Maine Road, provided covered accommodation on all four sides until the 1970s. The £3,000 spend was only marginally less than Huddersfield Town had lavished on an entire new state of the art Main Stand the following close season.

■ **1913** – FA Cup tie with Sunderland abandoned when the crowd encroached onto the pitch. The stadium could no longer cope with the Blues huge suppor. Injuries became commonplace, while official crowds of 40,000 underestimate the actual number in attendance by several thousand game after game.

■ **1914** – Hyde Road used for stabling at various times during the Great War.

■ **1917** – The Club take over the ground lease from Chesters' Brewery at an annual rent of £500. Many felt Chesters' had too big an influence on ground matters, and the brewery had stood in the way of the club's move. Chesters had much to gain from City being at Hyde Road. Their public house, the Hyde Road Hotel, gained prestige from City's involvement, while Chesters owned retailing rights for the entire ground.

■ **1918** – The club seriously start to consider moving to Belle Vue again.

■ **1920** – King George V is the first reigning monarch to visit a provincial football ground when he watches City defeat Liverpool. The following November fire wrecks the Main Stand and the club speed up their search for a new home.

■ **1921** – City announce they have plans to move to a new 100,000 capacity ground at Belle Vue.

■ **1922** – City abandon the Belle Vue plans and announce they will move to a new 120,000 capacity ground on the Moss Side/Rusholme border.

■ **1923** – Hyde Road hosts its last game (a public practice match in August), and Maine Road opens.

■ **2001** – Hyde Road Hotel demolished.

The Popular Side, pictured during City's 2-0 win over Oldham in March 1913.

Turnstiles

■ First Ardwick then City's development as a professional football club led to a need to strengthen control over the admission of spectators and to raise income. In the 1890s football was becoming big business and its sudden growth came at a time when the turnstile business was starting to decline. The industry had grown during the middle of the nineteenth century as wealthier Victorians began to enjoy activities such as day trips to the seaside. This period saw the development of the pier industry with companies charging visitors an admission fee to enter the pier. Turnstiles were developed to control the crowds and generate income, and several companies were created to service this new demand. By the 1890s the number of new pier developments was reducing but the companies turned their attention to football.

Being a progressive club during this period, the Blues had already tried to control access and improve income by establishing 'pay boxes' during 1888, but entering the League in 1892 required better control. It's not clear exactly when the club first erected turnstiles, but it is known that by 1896 Hyde Road certainly possessed some. The club records were destroyed in the 1920 fire, but occasional comments in both the City Programme and the local and sporting press do make reference to ground improvements and new entrances. Piecing these comments together to provide cast-iron proof is difficult, however it is reasonable to assume City's main turnstile purchases were in 1896, 1898, 1904, and 1910. The club did open a new entrance in 1890, but it's debatable whether this would have housed any turnstiles.

Two main suppliers were used – W.T. Ellison and W.H. Bailey. Both were relatively local companies (Ellison's were from Irlam O' Th' Heights, Baileys were from Salford), and both were keen to advertise they had supplied turnstiles to Manchester City.

When City moved to Maine Road in 1923 club documents and newspaper articles mentioned that some turnstiles were taken to the new ground and re-erected in the exterior wall. It was never clear exactly how many were moved, however, an inspection of every turnstile in late 2002 has proved thirteen Ellison's turnstiles and two Bailey's were still in operation in the wall of the Kippax. Further examination identified that four of the Ellison's (turnstiles number 48, 59, 75 & 76) were marked as being made at 'Irlams o'th'heights' (sic), while the other nine were marked as being made at 'Salford'. Those marked 'Irlam' are believed to have been bought by the Blues in 1896, possibly earlier, while the others are possibly from 1904 or 1910.

The Main Stand turnstiles all appear to have been made by Bailey's or another company, Mayor, when the ground was originally built in 1923.

In May 2003 the Ellison's turnstiles were inspected by Ted Pearson, a recognised expert who has worked in the industry for most of his life. He is of the view the four 'Irlam' turnstile are extremely important finds: "Without a doubt these are fine examples of early turnstiles. In fact I'll go as far as saying these are among the oldest working examples of Ellison's turnstiles in the world. Looking at these I can see they are from an earlier period than most because they hadn't really developed all the mechanisms to stop lads from sneaking under. I would definitely say these are

from the mid-1890s and that there cannot be many other grounds with an example this old. Consider the history as well. Hyde Road staged a semi-final and other important games, while the King also visited the ground. Did he use a turnstile? If he did, he possibly used one of the Ellison's moved to Maine Road!"

It's unclear whether the King did use a turnstile, although it is known that future Prime Minister Arthur Balfour did when he visited in 1900.

The Ellison's Turnstiles were labelled 'Rush Preventive' and contained a counter hidden under the brass name plate. Bailey's followed a similar design but were named 'Bailey's Quick Action Turnstiles'. Both company's products proved very reliable over the years, although turnstile operators would regularly try to tamper with the counting mechanisms. Pearson: "Looking at your turnstiles I can see they've come in for a lot of tampering over the years. One or two of the counting mechanisms have cracked glass – a sure sign an operator thinks he can stop the machine counting which he can't of course – while some have tape (see photo above) on the arms of the turnstile. This is so that a turnstile operator knows

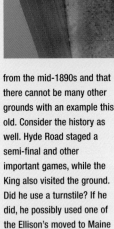

when a full turn has been made. Often they'd send someone in on half a turn and then the next would finish the turn. So they'd charge two people but only give the club one admission! Whenever you see tape on an old turnstile, one of the operators has tried a fiddle!"

Each Maine Road turnstile was also wired to an electric counting mechanism and, in more recent times, operators have disconnected the automatic counting cables, however the traditional counting mechanism has continued to work, and has allowed the club to identify fraudulent activity.

Since all-seater stadia and all-ticket matches, the ability to perform an activity of this kind without identification has reduced significantly. Stewards and other personnel can easily identify those without a legitimate seat.

City's move to the new stadium has allowed the club to consider improving the entry processes around the stadium, and the Blues have installed proximity card turnstiles. These allow each attendee to hold their admission card up to an electronic reader. The reader identifies a valid ticket and the attendee may move through the turnstile. The reader can also provide details on the type of attendee, for example a child

ticket, to allow club personnel to identify fraudulent use. Turnstiles of this type were trialled in the Platt Lane Family Stand during 2002-03.

Compared to the system employed by the original Hyde Road turnstiles this is a great innovation but will they still be in use in 107 years time, as Ellison's are? Ted Pearson: "Ellison's, Bailey's and the Mayor turnstiles housed around Maine Road were built to last. If City had decided to take all these turnstiles and re-erect them at the new stadium you'd find most of them still working in another eighty years! Those in the Kippax wall, and the Mayor in the Main Stand, require less maintenance than the ones in the North Stand and they're only thirty years old."

Interestingly, Ellison's boasted their turnstiles could admit up to 4,000 people per hour, or 3,000 if change had to be given. One hundred years later the Taylor Report recommended there should be enough turnstiles at each ground to admit the entire capacity within an hour at a rate of no more than 660 people per turnstile.

It is anticipated at least one of the Ellison's turnstiles from 1896 will be housed at the City of Manchester Stadium. This will then mean the turnstile has been sited at three major footballing venues.

Maine Memory

Right: A page from the 1989 book 'Maine Men to Banana Citizens' shows the idea of a new stadium was being suggested in the late 80's.

When news that City were considering a move to the stadium planned for the Commonwealth Games first became public, most were not entirely convinced it would happen. The club had often outlined major ground redevelopment plans only to see these collapse as the Blues hit problems. The 1972 plans to rebuild the Kippax were stopped the moment Eric Alexander handed over the Chairmanship to Peter Swales, while the 1982 ground redevelopment plans were shelved when relegation occurred. Surely the new stadium would need City to establish themselves as a European power?

In truth City's success or - more appropriately - failure had little impact on the plans. The Commonwealth Games were to be staged and a stadium built regardless of City's position but fans were apprehensive. Giving up Maine Road was significant in itself, but moving to a larger stadium when the club was potentially on a downward spiral would raise many, many issues.

The Games stadium was to be built in two phases with the first creating a 35,000-seater athletics stadium. The second stage would see the ground converted to a 48,000 capacity football stadium. These plans were announced during City's struggles of 1997-8 and, inevitably, many felt relegation to Division Two might kill off either the entire move or possibly the second phase. Fortunately, that was not the case and the stadium plans continued apace despite City's struggles.

In August 1999 City Chairman David Bernstein signed the legal documentation agreeing to the move, and the following December Prime Minister Tony Blair laid the first stone at the new stadium – the Government and various agencies had contributed a significant amount to the building's construction. From then on the stadium grew at a considerable pace.

In May 2002 visits to the stadium were organised by the club and it's fair to say most fans were delighted with

INTO THE NINETIES WITH THE OLYMPIC CITY BLUES

£100m site for Blues?

By Martyn Palmer

MANCHESTER CITY may quit its Maine Road soccer ground, it was revealed today.

The club could move to a new £100m all-seat stadium if Manchester wins its bid to stage the Olympics.

The shock plan is outlined in a document giving details of the city's 1992 Olympics hope.

If Manchester stages the games, organisers aim to build three new arenas alongside the Ship Canal — including a showpiece 60,000 all-seater Olympic stadium.

And City chairman Peter Swales has told the Manchester Olympic Bid Committee that he is interested in moving his club to the stadium afterwards.

Mr Swales said today: "If it all happens and the stadium is built, it is something we have got to be interested in.

But he added: "It is at a very early stage. We have spent a lot of money at Maine Road and the new stadium would have to be something pretty special to make us move.

"The Olympic Bid Committee have explained what they are trying to do and I think it is a very bold, adventurous plan to bring the games to Manchester."

The new stadium would be equipped as a ultra-modern sports arena with artificial turf and a closing roof to combat bad weather.

Bid Committee chairman Bob Scott confirmed: "I have spoken to Peter who thinks the stadium is an extremely interesting idea and would like to know more.

"He expressed an interest in moving City to what would be one of the finest stadiums in Europe, but we have not talked in detail."

The Manchester games would utilise land alongside the Ship Canal with three new arenas, the stadium, a velodrome and a swimming pool.

The games would cost between £365m and £415m

Comment: Page 6

Full details on Page 7

and would be self-funding. Most of the cash, between £300m and £350m, could come from TV rights sales.

The Bid Committee's document has been sent to the British Olympic Association who will choose between Manchester, Birmingham and London on July 12.

If Manchester wins it will be put to the International Olympic Commission and compete against Paris, Amsterdam, Barcelona, Belgrade, New Delhi and Brisbane. The IOC will decide on the 1992 venue next year.

Said Mr Scott : "This is not a one off. If we fail on July 12 we will try again.

"Manchester is an Olympic city and we are here to stay.

"It may be wrong to think we can get the games first time but we shall certainly try our best."

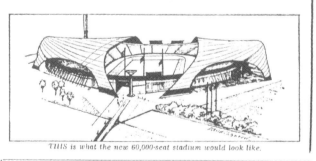

THIS is what the new 60,000-seat stadium would look like.

Above: Manchester is currently bidding to host the 1996 Olympic Games. During the City's unsuccessful bid for the 1992 Games Peter Swales stated that the Club would be interested in moving to the new "All-seater" stadium. Hopefully the 1990's will see a successful City side play at an improved Maine Road and re-establish the Club as the City's premier team.

what they saw. Typically supporters spoke of the venue as breathtaking, while former players Gary Owen and Mike Summerbee both likened it to an arena for gladiators.

The following July the Commonwealth Games were held there and proved very popular in spite of some initial national scepticism. As far as the world was concerned the Manchester Games were the best staged yet, and the stadium a fitting venue. Even when it rained during the final few days it seemed apt for Manchester, especially as all the city's leading dignitaries were caught in the centre of the stadium with the rain lashing down. Had that been the opening day scenario the media may have given a negative slant to the Games, but coming at the end the message was Manchester could achieve anything regardless of the weather or the obstacles.

The success of the Games led London to mount a bid for the 2012 Olympics – a move criticised by popular Manchester MP Graham Stringer who felt another provincial city should be given a chance - and encouraged Liverpool to successfully bid for European City of Culture – a move backed by Manchester. There were even calls for the stadium to remain an athletics venue, but in the main these came from other parts of the country and were not supported by the people of the north-west. Clearly, the feeling existed that the development of a major stadium, especially at a time when both Wembley and the proposed athletics stadium at Pickett's Lock seemed doomed, should be available for all sports but this overlooked the fact a stadium would not have been built at all had it not been for City's agreement to become anchor tenants. The stadium needed permanent usage and without City it would not have been developed.

The day after the Games ended, work commenced on converting the stadium to a football venue. The pitch was lowered and the lower tier and North Stand

Should we stay or should we go for it? **It's up to you!**

Looking to the future ... the dramatic new stadium design for Eastlands.

Manchester City supporters emerge this evening as key figures as the club considers a possible move to the state-of-the-art stadium at Eastlands.

Questionnaires handed to spectators at tonight's match, it is hoped, will bring opinions and suggestions club officials will take on board as they examine fully the implications of making a new start in Manchester's Commonwealth Games stadium in the year 2003.

Soundings are also being taken through the club's regular mailing list and through supporters' branches as City fulfil their promise to consult fans before reaching a legal commitment.

"We would only make this move to Eastlands if it is an exciting and proper long-term home with facilities that can take Manchester City into the new century," chairman David Bernstein assures supporters.

"The legally binding agreements have yet to be finalised and clearly before a final decision is made we are committed to consulting supporters," he added, explaining that 50,000 leaflets were to be distributed.

But the signs already are that supporters are strongly in favour of the move away from Maine Road which was 75 years old last month. A poll conducted by BBC GMR this week showed fans 11-1 in favour of the move to the £90 million stadium, which will be the centrepiece of a development known as SportCity.

Fans will be invited to study models of the stadium at three open days to be held at Platt Lane. These will take place on 22nd and 30th September and 1st October from 2pm to 7pm. The new stadium will accommodate between 45,000 and 50,000 seated spectators. Work will start on it next year and will be ready by the end of 2001, in good time for the Commonwealth Games which are held the following summer.

The attractions of a move are varied. The stadium is being designed for football. The running track for the Commonwealth Games will be removed and seating brought closer to the pitch to create an intimidating and suitable atmosphere.

The stadium will be dominated in colour by blue and designed as a proper home to MCFC. There will be extensive car parking and ease of access. Transport will be further improved by the extension of the Metrolink from the city centre to the stadium.

There will be no groundsharing. High quality hospitality will be available for at least 64 executive boxes.

Occupancy of the stadium by City will be secured by a long-term lease and City will manage and operate the stadium for all events.

A name has to be decided for the stadium but its choice will be subject to approval by the club. Maine Road transfers to the City Council as a consideration for the new stadium and City will then have no ongoing obligations.

Manager Joe Royle summed up the club's view when he emphasised: "City supporters are the best and they deserve the best. The new stadium is for them."

Please help the club by completing your questionnaire. YOUR opinions are important to us.

Questionnaires on the proposed new stadium can be deposited at a special collection point in the City Superstore.

City 41

constructed. In addition the club had to concentrate on the fitting-out of offices, lounges and other areas, plus facilities such as the ticket office, City Store, City Social (a café-bar) and the Manchester City Experience (a museum and tour planned to open late in the 2003-4 season).

Additional personnel were brought in to work alongside existing staff. Barry Pollen, Pete Bradshaw, Paul Kenyon and Clare Marsden were the key figures on the site during the 2002-03 season. Inevitably, the whole exercise required the close involvement of all directors, in particular Alistair Mackintosh and John Wardle. Of course former Managing Director Chris Bird and former Chairman David Bernstein had also dedicated

Above: This article in City's programme for the visit of Bournemouth in September 1998 gave fans the opportunity to have their say on a possible move. Remember, City were a Second Divison side then!

THE STADIUM THAT PUTS WEMBLEY TO SHAME

FACTFILE

Cost: £110m (inc. £15m cost of converting to soccer stadium for Manchester City), with £77m from Lottery funding

Height: 112ft (roof max)

Size: 38,000 square yards

Capacity: 38,000 seats with 54 corporate boxes and 1,000 toilets

Designed by: Arup Associates

■ Roof supported by 12 masts (210ft tall)
■ The roof weighs the same amount as two jumbo jets.
■ Roof design reflects sound back into the stadium to help reduce noise pollution.
■ Corners of the roof can be moved to regulate the amount of air that flows through the stadium.

EAST STAND

WEST STAND

Roof will be extended to cover all seating when the stadium becomes a football ground. The final capacity with the track removed will be 50,000.

■ There are 15 entrances – eight spiral ramps leading to the two upper tiers, four corner entrances, one away entrance plus two VIP entrances.

■ Coal mine on the site from 1757 until the mid 1960s. The stadium has been positioned away from the main coal shaft.

■ Site was also used as a gas works, dye works and iron works.

■ It took a year to clear the site before work could start on the stadium in January 2000

■ More than 3,000 people worked on the stadium, which was finished in March

■ 1,300,000 cubic feet of concrete was used in construction, which is the

equivalent to the same amount of water found in 28.8 Olympic size swimming pools or 480 average family size pools.

■ Total amount of concrete used weighs 70,800 tonnes.

■ 170 floodlight bulbs should each last approximately 33 football matches.

■ The Royal Box, where the Queen will sit during the opening and closing ceremonies, is in the middle of the West Stand.

■ Track is the same Mondo

cushion-backed rubber used at Stadium Australia during the 2000 Olympics.

■ There are nine lanes on the straight and eight around the 400-meter track.

■ After the Games the stadium will be Manchester City Football Club's home ground.

■ A prison at the stadium has three minimum-security cells and one maximum-security cell.

■ The changing rooms for the football seasons have blue floors with timber lockers and white tiling.

[Map showing: M66, M60, OLDHAM, STADIUM, A662, M602, MANCHESTER, M67, M60, 2 miles, M56, STOCKPORT]

Above: With nine days to go before the start of the Commonwealth Games in 2002 the *Daily Mirror* paid tribute to the new stadium.

considerable time to the new stadium and were certainly instrumental, along with Mackintosh and Wardle, for much of its construction.

By June 2003 the stadium grew near to completion; grass was beginning to show on the pitch while the fourth side was, to all intents and purposes, finished. To many visitors that's when the site started to become City's home as it finally gave the impression of being a true football stadium. Chairman John Wardle told the media: "Leaving Maine Road was a huge decision for Manchester City, but we have no doubt that the move to the City of Manchester Stadium is the right decision for this club. The increased capacity and superb new facilities the stadium will provide will put us amongst the elite of English football, and we are confident that in the City of Manchester Stadium we will have a home of which our fans can be proud."

Of course some East Manchester residents may just about remember City's former home in Ardwick, but for those who can't there remain a few surviving relics. As well as turnstiles located at Maine Road in 2002, sections of Hyde Road's multi-span roofs have been identified.

Some formed part of a factory building in Sale until its demolition in 1998, while the most visible and complete Hyde Road roof still exists at Halifax Town's Shay ground. It was purchased from the Blues when Maine Road was developed.

In addition, stonework from the old Hyde Road Hotel was obtained by the club when the old pub was demolished in 2001. It is anticipated some of this will be utilised at the new stadium at some point in the future.

With City's East Manchester heritage firmly established, the Blues moved to the new stadium during the Summer of 2003. The first game took place in August almost eighty years after Maine Road staged its first match. As with City's former home at Maine Road, the new stadium was the most modern in the country on its opening day. It was also the most awe-inspiring.

City of Manchester Milestones

■ **1986** – Plans are made for Manchester to bid for the 1992 Olympic Games. The bid ultimately fails but Peter Swales did confirm City's interest in moving to the new stadium if built. A subsequent bid for the 1996 Games receives good support but ultimately fails to Atlanta.

■ **1994** – The City Council begin clearing a site at Bradford, in the east of the city, in preparation for their bid for the 2000 Olympic Games. The bid fails.

■ **1995** – Manchester is awarded the 2002 Commonwealth Games and receives backing from the Government and other bodies to erect a new stadium.

■ **1997** – In August Francis Lee announced City were seriously considering a move to the new Commonwealth Games stadium. The Council were planning to erect a venue with around 60,000 seats.

■ **1998** – Manchester City Council announced it would build a £90m stadium for the Commonwealth Games. Situated a mile from the city centre, the Council stated it would be built in two phases with 21,000 covered seats for the Games, rising to 48,000 for future use as a football venue. City, subject to approval from fans, would move in at the start of the 2003-4 season.

Tony Blair

■ **1999** – Prime Minister Tony Blair lays the first stone of the new stadium.

■ **2000** – By October the exit towers start to appear as the stadium begins to rise.

■ **2001** – City present models and plans to supporters and answer specific concerns.

■ **2002** – The Commonwealth Games are held at a magnificent venue. The Queen and Prince Phillip attend the opening and closing ceremonies. The day after the games end, building work to transform the stadium into City's home commences.

■ **2003** – City open the completed City of Manchester Stadium with a 2-1 friendly win against Barcelona. In the first competitive game the Blues beat TNS Llansantffraid of Wales 5-0 in the Qualifying Round of the UEFA Cup whilst the opening League match sees a 1-1 draw with Portsmouth. The West Stand will be known as The Joe Mercer Stand.

A model of the new stadium went on display.

Above: Ali Benarbia leads City out for the opening game.
Right: David Sommeil celebrates City's first League goal.

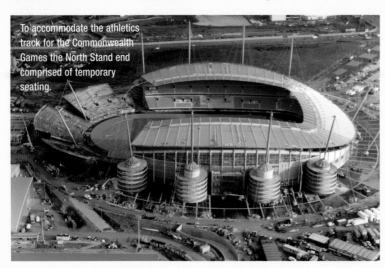

To accommodate the athletics track for the Commonwealth Games the North Stand end comprised of temporary seating.

Above: A sign of the times - City's presence inside the new stadium started with office moves during June 2003.

■ The first competitive match at the City Of Manchester Stadium in Eastlands had been eagerly anticipated since 1999 when David Bernstein signed the official documentation confirming City would move there in 2003. Back in 1999, with the Blues recently promoted from Division Two, no one could have anticipated the opening match would be a UEFA Cup tie.

City had qualified for the UEFA Cup via the Fair Play League, and had drawn Welsh side TNS from Llansantffraid ym Mechain – a village with a population of around 700. Inevitably most neutrals felt the match would be one sided, especially as City had defeated Barcelona in the match to open the stadium a few days earlier, and the full time score of 5-0 did suggest an annihilation, however it didn't quite start like that.

Plucky defending from the Welsh side, who incidentally contained more Englishmen than the Blues, restricted true goalscoring opportunities but in the fourteenth minute debutant Trevor Sinclair netted the first competitive goal in the new stadium. The former West Ham man sent a perfectly placed volley through a crowd of players and into the net at the South Stand end of the stadium. Sinclair, a £2.25m summer signing, had also scored against Barcelona, although Nicolas Anelka was the first to score in that match. City fans now expected the avalanche of goals predicted, but the half ended 1-0.

Five minutes into the second half a low shot by Wright-Phillips beat goalkeeper Doherty, and then nine minutes later Jihai Sun headed the third. In the 74th minute Sommeil diverted home an effort by Joey Barton, and then three minutes from time Anelka made it 5-0. The final two goals came after Paulo Wanchope, coming on as substitute for Robbie Fowler, was given a fantastic reception by the Sportcity crowd.

Afterwards Keegan told the media: "You look at the

Below: The teams line up for national anthems before the first competitive game at the new stadium.

Maine Match 2003/04

CITY v TOTAL NETWORK SOLUTIONS

DATE:	14th August 2003	
TYPE OF FIXTURE:	UEFA Cup Qualifying Round First Leg	
ATTENDANCE:	34,103	
RESULT:	City 5 TNS 0	
TEAMS & SCORERS:	CITY	TNS
	Seaman	Doherty
	Sun 1	Naylor
REFEREE:	Sommeil 1	Taylor
Alexey Tiumin	Distin	Aggrey
(Russia)	Tarnat (Tiatto)	King
	Wright-Phillips 1	Bridgewater (Wood)
	Bosvelt (Barton)	Leah
	Berkovic	Brabin
	Sinclair 1	Davies
	Anelka 1	Ruscoe
	Fowler (Wanchope)	Ward (Toner)

final score and it looks like a sound beating, but 1-0 at half-time wasn't too comfortable. They put ten men behind the ball and they made life difficult for us for a long time, but, in the end, our class told."

It was important the first competitive match ended in a victory and afterwards most of the talk was of the stadium and how it compared to Maine Road. It was clear to all in attendance that the City Of Manchester Stadium was considerably better in every department. Those with initial doubts about the move could see the difference in quality. Clearly Maine Road – and most other Premier League venues – had been surpassed but the old ground would never be forgotten.

The first chance to see floodlit football at the City of Manchester Stadium.

Above: Trevor Sinclair scores the first 'competitive' goal (left) and Jihai Sun heads the third (centre pictures). Sinclair is also seen in action (far right).

There were a few quibbles on the night. Some supporters had difficulty parking; some – most notably those on the front row – found their view was not as perfect as they had been led to believe; many others complained about the lack of a scoreboard. There were also ticketing issues. Clearly, these issues had to be dealt with and the club made it clear they would listen to any complainants and see how they could help resolve their issue.

As far as the scoreboard was concerned though, it was incredible how much of a furore its absence created, especially as the club already had plans in place to have one erected in time for the opening League match. It's worth noting that eighty years earlier Maine Road opened without most of the refreshment bars and other supporter facilities promised. Back then the aim was to open the stadium and worry about the rest later and, it may sound surprising today, few supporters complained. In fact every newspaper focused on the positives.

The attendance for the UEFA match was limited due to licensing restrictions but even with tight control over ticket sales and all other administrative issues, the crowd was still one of the highest recorded for a UEFA qualifying round match and stood at a shade less than the final capacity of Maine Road.

The first League fixture at Eastlands followed on 23rd August – 116 years to the day after Ardwick AFC was created and set up home at Hyde Road less than a mile from the new stadium – was watched by a crowd of 46,238. Sadly, the game did not go to plan as the visitors Portsmouth took the lead via a goal from Ayegbeni in the 24th minute, but the final ten minutes saw a determined City bombard the visitors goal. With only seven seconds of normal time remaining, according to the new scoreboard, Sommeil netted the equaliser. Frantic play followed but the opening League game ended 1-1. Interestingly, two days later the Blues led the table after defeating Blackburn 3-2 with another late goal. It was the first time City had led the top tier since the creation of the Premier League.

Already, the new stadium was being seen by some as the catalyst, but others believed the transformation had come about following the arrival of Kevin Keegan in 2001. Those with slightly longer memories talked of David Bernstein, John Wardle, Chris Bird, Alistair Mackintosh, and the other directors who helped breathe new life into the club in 1999.

A First Time for Everything...

Above: The impressive main entrance at the City of Manchester Stadium.

Left: Goalscoring firsts at Eastlands for Nicolas Anelka (top, with first substitute Eyal Berkovic); Trevor Sinclair in the UEFA Cup (centre) and David Sommeil's late equaliser v Portsmouth (bottom).

For the record, here's a list of some City of Manchester Stadium firsts...

First GAME	City 2 Barcelona 1, Friendly Match, Sunday 10th August 2003
First TOUCH	Robbie Fowler (kicked-off)
First GOAL	Nicolas Anelka, 34 mins v Barcelona (at the North Stand end of the ground)
First VISITING SCORER	Javier Pedro Saviola (Barcelona), 58 mins
First SUBSTITUTION	Eyal Berkovic for Ali Benarbia, 25 mins v Barcelona
First REFEREE	Mark Halsey
First COMPETITIVE GAME	City 5 Total Network Solutions FC 0, UEFA Cup Qualifying Round First leg Thursday 14th August 2003
First COMPETITIVE GOAL	Trevor Sinclair, 14 mins v Total Network Solutions FC
First YELLOW CARD	Gary Brabin (TNS) 90 mins, Unsporting Behaviour
First LEAGUE GAME	City 1 Portsmouth 1, FA Barclaycard Premiership, Saturday 23rd August 2003
First LEAGUE GOAL	Yakubu Ayegbini (Portsmouth), 24 mins
First LEAGUE GOAL FOR CITY	David Sommeil, 90 mins v Portsmouth
First VISITING TEAM TO WIN	Arsenal (1-2), Sunday 31st August 2003
First OWN GOAL	Bisan Lauren (Arsenal), 10 mins
First LEAGUE WIN FOR CITY	v Aston Villa (4-1), Sunday 14th September 2003
First PENALTY	Nicolas Anelka v Thomas Sorensen (Aston Villa) - scored, 48 mins
First HAT-TRICK	Nicolas Anelka v Aston Villa, 46 mins (penalty), 68 mins (penalty), 83 mins

No red cards at the time of going to print (up to 14.9.03)

Match Programmes

■ The history of City's programme could almost fill a book in its own right, however it's worth considering its role and importance here. Although it's difficult to identify what publications, team lists etc. were created during the 1880s and early 1890s, it is known that "The Official Programme" did exist from the start of the 1898-9 season. This was a combined publication for City, Newton Heath and the Salford and Broughton Rangers Rugby Clubs. It combined news and line-ups with general team gossip and sold for one penny. Its second edition is believed to be the first programme ever produced for a Manchester derby.

How popular this publication was isn't known, but in 1899 the club produced its own programme. *The City Program* (sic) provided similar information to the earlier publication but was the first to focus solely on the Blues and their opponents. It is believed it was known as the *'Blue & White'* as, by the time it had reached its seventh volume in 1906, each page was headed with the words 'Blue and White', while the cover remained *The City Program*.

By the time City moved to Maine Road, the programme had been officially named the *Blue and White*, and cost two pence. That first Maine Road edition became a collector's item, but in the main programmes were considered in a similar light to newspapers throughout football's first sixty years or so; they provided information on the club and the game, but were not viewed with any consideration for their long term value. In fact to most of the population they were pretty irrelevant. Libraries, including those in Manchester, saw no value in storing copies, while supporters would throw them away once fully read. Even the club didn't retain copies. This is a major shame as the information they provided, particularly prior to the 1940s, gives considerable insight on the way the Blues developed.

A programme from 1904, for example, details ground developments at Hyde Road, while those during World War Two give a true feeling for how the game carried on despite the wider situation.

As well as a means of receiving information, the programme would often be used to provide shelter from the rain – supporters would open it up and place it over their heads - in the days before roofing became established over the main terracing at Maine Road. Although as its importance started to grow some would rather get wet than risk their programme being damaged.

It's difficult to pinpoint exactly when collecting programmes became a pastime for City supporters, but it is clear the first to consider saving them were children. By the late 1930s, comics such as the *Dandy* and *Hotspur* started to appear and many of these would contain stories which ran over several issues. The *Dandy*, although it was mainly a humorous comic, carried the tale of a sheep dog called 'Black Bob' and boys would save each issue to allow them to keep the entire serial together. This perhaps led to a desire to collect other publications of importance to boys and inevitably programmes began to be saved. Football programmes meant something. They immediately transported younger supporters back to the day and allowed them to relive their first game, or their most enjoyable match.

These same supporters then kept hold of their programmes for as long as they could. Dennis Chapman: "I purchased my first programme during the war and

Below: Programmes from the 1950s and 60s show Maine Road on the cover. The 1906 Hyde Road issue (bottom left) was headed 'City Program' whilst 'The Blue and White' is from 1934.

Above: For the front cover of Maine Road's final match programme a photograph was set up of Kevin Keegan looking out of the players' tunnel towards the Kippax Stand, a re-make of a famous picture of Joe Mercer taken in the late 1960s and reproduced on the back cover. The idea of recreating the scene with Keegan, complete with discarded bucket, was suggested by the programme's graphic designer Trevor Hartley. The souvenir programme was a 100-page special issue.

Right: The A4-sized souvenir programme produced for the opening game at the City of Manchester Stadium. The programme for the first competitive game, a UEFA Cup tie with TNS, is already proving a collectors' item.

made sure I filed it away with my own comments on the match. I've continued to do this for every game I've been to. I'm not a football programme collector in the modern sense – I wouldn't try to find a copy of every City programme produced – but I do collect programmes for all games I've attended. The programmes mean something to me personally, and I think that's the best part really. Collecting a publication simply because it's there may interest some, but does the actual publication mean anything to your own life? To me every game means something and therefore the corresponding programme is special."

By the 1960s programme-collecting was a popular pastime for many supporters although, interestingly, some television shows from the period included the throwing away of football programmes and comics as a sign of a young male settling down to married life. So the perception that football programmes were a symbol of childish activity persisted. Of course, since the sixties programmes have become big business with many Maine Road issues proving extremely popular, particularly those from the twenties and thirties.

Throughout the fifties and sixties programmes were relatively dull, but the following decade City's programmes became more colourful and interesting. This was probably due to the editorship of Paul Doherty – in the sixties he had produced the club's first fanzine style magazine *Out of the Blues* – and, apart from paper shortages around 1973, it seemed to improve year after year. By the end of the eighties, the fanzine movement had forced clubs to breathe new life into their official publications and City turned their programme into a more glossy publication.

During Maine Road's final decade, Polar Publishing began working with City to create an informative,

colourful, popular publication with a mix of information, imagery, history and entertaining articles.

Of course Maine Road's final programme was also the most expensive ever produced for a football match at the ground. For a fee of £5 purchasers bought a 100-page, soft-backed souvenir booklet. It was a fitting tribute to the stadium.

The view down Maine Road
prior to the final League game
at the stadium.

Chapter Twelve
Statistics and Records

Hyde Road Facts & Figures

■ **Highest Official Attendance:** 41,709 v Sunderland, F.A. Cup Second Round on 1st February 1913

■ **Highest League Attendance:** 26th March 1921 v Burnley. This Attendance was recorded as c.40,000, however the actual attendance was probably somewhere in the region of 50 to 55,000, as fans had smashed down gates to get in. Most capacity attendances at Hyde Road were recorded as either 40,000 or 45,000. This match with Burnley was probably the highest crowd ever housed at Hyde Road.

■ **Highest Average Attendance:** c.31,020, 1920-21 season

■ **Lowest Average Attendance:** c.3,000, 1892-3 season

■ **First Football League game:** 3rd September 1892 v Bootle (City won 7-0, attendance c.4,000)

■ **Last Football League game:** 28th April 1923 v Newcastle United (game ended goalless, attendance c.20,000)

■ **Opening game:** 10th September 1887, Ardwick v Salford AFC. Salford failed to appear and the crowd of 5,000 were entertained by a band hired specifically to mark the occasion instead.

■ **First actual game played at Hyde Road:** 17th September 1887, Ardwick v Hooley Hill (Denton). Ardwick won 4-2.

■ **First FA Cup game:** 4th October 1890 v Liverpool Stanley (12-0 victory)

■ **Last FA Cup game:** 7th January 1922 v Darlington (3-1 victory)

■ **First Floodlit Match:** Anecdotal evidence suggests Ardwick played a floodlit friendly against Preston North End during the 1889-90 season however specific details have yet to be confirmed. The Blues did play a match under lights against Newton Heath at the Belle Vue Athletics Ground in February 1889 which for many years was believed to be the first floodlit match in Manchester. It is likely the match with Preston occurred around this time or possibly earlier.

■ **Most important game staged at Hyde Road:** 25th March 1905 Newcastle United v Sheffield Wednesday (Newcastle won 1-0, attendance c.40,000). Also staged inter-League matches, and Test Matches.

■ **First City Football League goal at Hyde Road:** Hugh Morris, 3rd September 1892 v Bootle

■ **Last City Football League goal at Hyde Road:** Frank Roberts, 14th April 1923 v Nottingham Forest

■ **First League penalty:** Dave Russell, 3rd September 1892 v Bootle (Missed)

■ **Highest League Score at Hyde Road:** 11-3 v Lincoln City, 23rd March 1895

■ **Highest FA Cup Score at Hyde Road:** 12-0 v Liverpool Stanley, 4th October 1890

■ **Most Goals in a Game at Hyde Road:** 5 Fred Williams v Darwen 18/2/1899 (City won this League match 10-0)

■ **Record Aggregate Support (League & FA Cup) in Season:** 651,420, 1920-21 (22 games)

■ **Top Wartime Attendance for a City Match:** 35,000, City v Manchester United, 18th April 1919

■ **Hyde Road Progressive Capacity:**
1887 – 4,000
1888 – 7,000
1891 – 10,000
1892 – 20,000
1896 – 25,000
1899 – 30,000
1904 – 40,000
1910 – 40,000 (covered accommodation for 35,000)
1920 – 45,000 (improvements after November fire increased capacity but reduced cover and seats)
1921 – 40,000

Below: Action from City's game with Tottenham at Hyde Road in January 1914, which City won 2-1. It is the only known photograph taken of the Main Stand during a City game. Built around 1899 the stand was destroyed by fire in 1920.

What's in a Name?

■ As the importance of Maine Road developed over the years many fans chose to use the name in other ways. A football team, Maine Road FC, was formed in 1955 by a group of supporters and began playing at Hough End, close to the old stadium. Over the years the club has grown, moved upwards through the local non-League scene and developed a fine reputation of its own. It is a worthy home for the name.

The name Maine Road has been seen connected with many other buildings and companies over the years from the Maine Road Joke Shop to the Maine Road Fast Food Bar. There is even a Maine Road School of Motoring in Calderdale, West Yorkshire.

Below: He didn't know it at the time, but Darren Huckerby's 87th minute winner against Crewe in October 2002 was the last League Cup goal to be scored at Maine Road. Liverpool's Danny Murphy scored the last FA Cup goal, from the penalty spot, whilst City's last Maine Road goal in that competition came a year earlier from Kevin Horlock against Swindon.

Maine Road Facts & Figures

■ **Highest Attendance:** 84,569 v Stoke City, F.A. Cup Sixth Round on 3rd March 1934

■ **Highest League Attendance:** 83,260, Manchester United v Arsenal on 17th January 1948 (Joe Mercer played for Arsenal in this match). The attendance has often been quoted as 82,950 or 81,962 but the largest of the three figures is the one returned by United in 1948. This is the record crowd for any League game, and is also Manchester United's record home crowd in all competitions.

■ **Highest League Attendance involving City:** 79,491 v Arsenal, 23rd February 1935

■ **Highest League Cup Attendance involving City:** 55,799 v United, 3rd December 1969

■ **Lowest League Attendance:** 8,015 v Swindon Town, 16th January 1965.
** *See note below on City v Forest, 13th February 1924.*

■ **Lowest FA Cup Attendance:** 8,595 v Darlington, 15th December 1998.

■ **Lowest League Cup Attendance:** 8,265 v Carlisle United, 25th September 1963.

■ **Lowest Official Attendance for a Competitive Game:** 3,007 v Mansfield Town, 8th December 1998, Auto-Windscreens Shield.

City v Forest, 13th February 1924. In Maine Road's first season this 3-1 defeat by Nottingham Forest was played in front of an exceptionally poor crowd. Some records suggest a figure around 3,000, however the actual attendance is unclear. The game was played in appalling weather on a Wednesday afternoon and according to one newspaper: "It had the effect of frightening away the half-holiday people to such an extent that at the start there were not more than 2,000 spectators present – an attendance that fell many thousands below the previous worst gate of the season."

Another report suggested the attendance doubled by half-time, but what the final figure became is open to debate. It is highly likely this is the actual lowest League crowd at Maine Road and potentially the lowest crowd for any first-team fixture at the ground.

■ *United's lowest League attendance since February 1935 was also recorded at City's venue: 8,456 v Stoke on 5th February 1947.*

■ **Highest Average Attendance:** 42,725, 1947-8 season.
Note: in previous analysis, including that contained within this book's sister publication *Manchester: The Greatest City*, the 1947-8 season average has been calculated at a figure of between 40,000 and 41,000, however extensive research for this book, and by Brian Tabner for his work *Football Through The Turnstiles*, has considered the figures officially presented to the League and other clubs. This has resulted in an average of League attendances officially recorded by the Football League of 42,725.

The next highest average is 41,687 during 1977-78 season. This has usually been recorded as City's record.

■ **Lowest Average Attendance:** 14,753, 1964-5 season

■ **Record Aggregate (League & FA Cup) Support in Season:** 1,064,525 (24 games), 1947-8

■ **Top Wartime Attendance for a City Match:** 62,144, Manchester United v City. 6th April 1946; 60,000, City v Blackpool, 22nd April 1944

■ **Maine Road Progressive Capacity:**

1923	84,000	1973	52,600
1931	86,000	1989	48,500
1935	88,000	1992	39,359
1946	84,000	1995	31,458
1953	76,500	1997	32,147
1957	77,000	1999	34,026
1963	64,000	2000	34,421
1972	54,500	2002	35,150

■ **First Friendly:** 28th April 1924 v Glentoran (7-2 victory)

■ **First Floodlit Match:** 14th October 1953 v Hearts (6-3 victory)

■ **First League Game:** 25th August 1923 v Sheffield United (City won 2-1, attendance 58,159)

■ **Last League Game:** 11th May 2003 v Southampton (a 1-0 defeat, attendance 34,957)

■ **First FA Cup Game:** 12th January 1924 v Nottingham Forest (2-1 victory)

■ **Last FA Cup Game:** 5th January 2003 v Liverpool (1-0 defeat)

■ **First League Cup Game:** 18th October 1960 v Stockport County (3-0 victory)

■ **Last League Cup Game:** 1st October 2002 v Crewe Alexandra (3-2 victory)

■ **First European tie involving City to be played at Maine Road:** 18th September 1968 v Fenerbahce (no score draw in European Cup)

■ **Last European tie involving City to be played at Maine Road:** 7th March 1979 v Borussia Monchengladbach (1-1 draw in UEFA Cup)

■ **Most important game staged at Maine Road:** There have been many important matches staged at the Maine Road stadium, obviously City themselves have featured in some pretty significant games over the years but there have also been internationals, cup semi-finals, and even finals held there. Possibly the most significant or memorable international was England's 8-0 demolition of Scotland on 16th October 1943. England also faced Ireland at Maine Road in the first World Cup qualifying match held in England in 1949. Another important international from a stadium perspective was the England v Scotland game (24th August 1946) in aid of the Bolton Disaster Fund .

Various F.A. Cup semi-finals have been held at Maine Road over the years, but the most significant domestic game was the all-Merseyside League Cup Final replay on 28th March 1984.

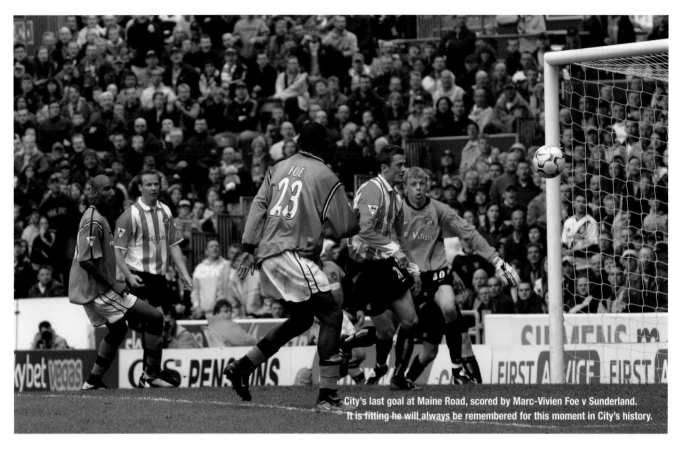

City's last goal at Maine Road, scored by Marc-Vivien Foe v Sunderland. It is fitting he will always be remembered for this moment in City's history.

The Maine Road Record

Competition	P	W	D	L	F	A	Pts
FA Premier League	120	41	37	42	160	151	160
Old Div One	1046	552	244	250	1988	1312	1415
Old Div Two	255	163	50	42	451	282	426
New Div One	92	54	15	23	173	87	177
New Div Two	23	13	6	4	38	14	45
Total League Games	**1536**	**823**	**352**	**361**	**2810**	**1846**	**2223**
Play-off Games	1	1	0	0	1	0	-
FA Cup*	101	62	20	19	227	107	-
FL Cup	81	53	16	12	186	67	-
European Cup	1	0	0	1	1	2	-
ECWC	8	7	0	1	19	2	-
UEFA Cup	7	4	3	0	16	7	-
Anglo-Italian	1	0	1	0	2	2	-
Texaco	2	1	1	0	4	3	-
Anglo-Scottish	1	1	0	0	3	1	-
Auto Windscreens Shield	1	0	0	1	1	2	-
Full Members Cup	9	6	1	2	22	10	-
FA Charity Shield	4	2	0	2	8	3	-
Full Competitive Total	**1753**	**960**	**394**	**399**	**3300**	**2052**	**2223**

* Incl 2 in 1945/46

Figures used refer to all competitive City home games at Maine Road from 1923-24 to 1938-39 and from 1946-47 to 2002-03.

The FA Cup figures DO include the two games played in 1945-46 as they are official Cup ties.

The following abandoned games are NOT included: 28/11/36 v Brentford (D1); 7/1/56 v Blackpool (FAC3); 15/2/58 v Birmingham (D1); 27/8/60 v Manchester Utd (D1); 8/9/65 v Norwich City (D2); 1/2/69 v Newcastle Utd (D1); 3/1/94 v Ipswich Town (PL); 12/12/00 v Ipswich Town (FLC5).

Three other games played at Maine Road but NOT included as City were the AWAY team: 7/4/48 v Manchester Utd 1-1 (D1) and 22/1/49 v Manchester Utd 0-0 (D1) as Old Trafford not in use due to War damage. Also 4/1/75 v Newcastle Utd 0-2 (FAC3) when Newcastle were drawn at home but the FA ordered it played at Maine Road following crowd trouble at St James Park during 1973-74 season.

Selected Maine Road Milestones

1922 – City announce their intention to build a 120,000 capacity stadium on the border of Rusholme and Moss Side
1923 – Stadium opened
1931 – Platt Lane Corner built
1935 – Platt Lane Stand erected
1939 – Maine Road development abandoned with outbreak of war
1953 – First floodlights erected
1957 – Kippax roof built and terracing squared off. Additional floodlighting developed on both Main Stand and Kippax roofs
1963 – Platt Lane benches installed
1964 – New floodlight towers erected
1966 – Social Club opened
1967 – New Main Stand roof
1971 – North Stand terraces opened
1972 – North Stand becomes seated stand
1973 – Planned redevelopment of the Kippax terracing abandoned
1981 – £6m redevelopment plan unveiled
1982 – £1m Main Stand roof built
1983 – Redevelopment plan put on hold
1993 – New 'Umbro' Stand opens behind southern goal, later renamed Platt Lane Stand
1994 – The last terraced area, the Kippax, is demolished
1995 – Three-tier Kippax Stand opened by Bert Trautmann
2003 – Maine Road stages its final game and reverts to council ownership

Above: Glyn Pardoe (left) youngest debutant and Colin Bell - most goals.

Events at Maine Road

■ Maine Road has been used for many events over the years. Naturally, football has been the most frequent event at the stadium, but home games have been played at the ground for a variety of clubs including England, The Football League, Manchester United, Stockport County, Altrincham, Northwich Victoria, and even Newcastle United (against City!).

It's worth noting that as far as neutral games are concerned only Sheffield Wednesday have played significant neutral games, in their case FA Cup semi-finals, at both Maine Road and Hyde Road.

Other events staged at the ground include professional tennis, Rugby League, Rugby Union-League exhibition matches, concerts, religious festivals, and the filming of several films/TV shows.

The stadium has also been the finish point for the Manchester City 10K race which during the mid-80s was a regular event. Runners would follow a 10km track along various roads in the area with a finish behind the Kippax Stand. When they crossed the line they were presented with a medal, bearing the City badge, and a Mars bar!

■ **First City League Goal at Maine Road:** Horace Barnes, 25th August 1923 v Sheffield United

■ **Last City League Goal:** Marc-Vivien Foe, 21st April 2003 v Sunderland

■ **Last League Goal:** Michael Svensson (Southampton), 11th May 2003

■ **First League Penalty:** Frank Roberts, 25th August 1923 v Sheffield United (missed)

■ **Last League Penalty:** Stuart Pearce, 21st April 2002 v Portsmouth (missed)

■ **Most League Goals in a Season at Maine Road:** 70 in 1927-8

■ **Most FA Cup Goals in a Season at Maine Road:** 19 in 1925-6

■ **Most League Cup Goals in a Season at Maine Road:** 10 in 1969-70

■ **Highest League Score at Maine Road:** 10-1 v Huddersfield Town, 7th November 1987

■ **Highest FA Cup Score at Maine Road:** 11-4 v Crystal Palace, 20th February 1926

■ **Highest League Cup Score at Maine Road:** 7-1 v Notts County, 19th August 1998

■ **Lowest League Goals in a Season at Maine Road:** 20 in 2000-01

■ **Most League Visits:** Arsenal (56)

■ **Most FA Cup Visits:** Leicester City (6)

■ **Most League Cup Visits:** Blackpool (7)

■ **Most Goals in a League Game at Maine Road:**
5 Tommy Browell v Burnley 24/10/25; George Smith v Newport County 14/6/47

■ **Most Goals in a FA Cup Game at Maine Road:** 5 Frank Roberts v Crystal Palace 20/2/26

■ **Most Goals in a League Cup Game at Maine Road:** 4 Dennis Tueart v Notts County 29/10/80

■ **Most Maine Road Appearances:** 340 plus one as substitute, Alan Oakes

■ **Most Goals at Maine Road in a City Career:** 107, Colin Bell; 106, Eric Brook

■ **Youngest City Player to appear at Maine Road:** 15 years & 314 days, Glyn Pardoe (11/4/61 v Birmingham City)

■ **Oldest City Player to appear at Maine Road:** 49 years & 238 days, Billy Meredith (22/3/1924 v Preston North End)

■ **First City Player to make his debut at Maine Road:** Alex Donaldson (25/8/23 v Sheffield United)

■ **Last City Player to make his debut at Maine Road:** Robbie Fowler (1/2/03 v West Bromwich Albion)

Above: Alan Oakes played more games at Maine Road than any other player, and returned to say farewell at the final game in 2003.

Stuart Pearce took, and missed, Maine Road's last penalty!

Home Attendance Records

The following table provides a season by season account of City's attendance information. To try and provide as complete a record as possible, the wartime seasons have also been included, although the peculiarities of football at the time should be fully understood before making assumptions as to how these compare to regular seasons.

For all attendances pre World War Two and many in the immediate post war period, it should be remembered these are in the main estimates based on newspaper reports from the period; the records of other clubs/the Football League; and other sources where possible. These have frequently been rounded and often excluded the total number of season tickets and complimentary tickets. In fact research for this book has proved some of these only include supporters who paid on the day. Wherever possible an attempt has been made to ensure these are the total number of spectators, including season ticket holders, however City's own records are exceptionally poor in this area. These attendances should not be taken as 100% accurate, they are merely an indication of City's pulling power. This table also includes the period when the Blues were Ardwick AFC (prior to 1894/5).

Please note it is extremely difficult to calculate the actual attendance for the vast majority of games played at Hyde Road. It is known the stadium held attendances in excess of 40,000 on several occasions, however club records and other sources rarely state attendances above that figure. It is widely assumed the capacity of City's old ground was 40,000 even though it is known there were several thousand more present for major fixtures (eg. Burnley 1920).

When comparing the annual figures it is worth remembering the capacity of Maine Road reduced dramatically after the Hillsborough disaster in 1989, and other ground developments, eg. the seating of the North Stand in 1972, also had a major effect on City's capacity. In addition, the redevelopment of the Kippax in the mid-90s reduced the capacity to approximately 30,000 – the lowest for a City venue for ninety years. The capacity of Maine Road did improve slightly during its final seasons, however City's pulling power remained severely restricted. Had the ground been able to hold around 48,000 during its final decade, City's average attendance throughout this period would undoubtedly have been over 40,000.

The table shows typical attendance information such as highest, average, lowest etc., but also includes the relative attendance position for the entire League. For example, in 1894-5 City were the 14th best supported club in football and then in 1927-8 they were the best supported club throughout the League, not simply the division they were in. Also included is the Highest Attendance for the division City were playing in. These figures provide a good overall impression of how high or low City's attendances actually were (where the two figures are equal City were the best supported side in that division). Simply looking coldly at City's attendance detail without considering the national picture would not give a fair reflection on the club's overall pulling power. It's interesting to note that City have rarely fallen out of the top ten best supported clubs nationally, and even in recent seasons the capacity of Maine Road restricted City's final attendance placing.

ATTENDANCE POSITION = City's average home League attendance in relation to rest of League
HIGHEST IN DIVISION = Highest average of all clubs

Season	Lge	Average Home League Attendance	Attendance Position	Highest in Division	Highest Home League Attendance	Lowest Home League Attendance	Highest Home Cup Attendance
1890-91	-	-	-	-	-	-	4,000 v Liverpool Stanley 4/10/90
1891-92	Alliance	6,800	-	-	12,000 v Lincoln City 28/11/91	4,000 v Small Heath 2/1/92	-
1892-93	FL Div2	3,000	18	3,600	6,000 v Small Heath 22/10/92 v Darwen 17/12/92	1,000 v Grimsby Town 30/1/93	2,000 v Fleetwood Rangers 5/10/92
1893-94	FL Div2	4,000	18	3,500	6,000 v Liverpool 16/9/93	1,000 v Burton Swifts 11/9/93	-
1894-95	FL Div2	6,000	14	6,400	14,000 v Newton Heath 3/11/94	2,000 v Lincoln City 23/3/95 (record score at Hyde Road)	-
1895-96	FL Div2	10,000	3	10,000	30,000 v Liverpool 3/4/96	2,000 v Loughborough Town 24/2/96	-
1896-97	FL Div2	8,000	8	8,075	20,000 v Newton Heath 3/10/96	1,000 v Walsall 6/1/97	-
1897-98	FL Div2	8,000	11	11,600	20,000 v Burnley 20/11/97	2,000 v Lincoln City 24/1/98	6,000 v Wigan County 29/1/98
1898-99	FL Div2	10,000	7	10,000	25,000 v Newton Heath 26/12/98	4,000 v Loughborough T. 17/12/98	-
1899-00	FL Div1	16,000	3	19,825	25,000 v Newcastle Utd 14/10/99 v Liverpool 28/10/99	3,000 v Sheffield United 25/12/00	22,000 v Aston Villa 27/1/00
1900-1	FL Div1	18,300	2	18,700	23,000 v Bury 5/1/01 v West Bromwich Albion 5/4/01	8,000 v Blackburn Rovers 19/1/01	-
1901-2	FL Div1	17,000	3	19,175	25,000 v Sheffield Wednesday 28/3/02	7,000 v Bury 5/4/02	16,000 v Nottingham Forest 8/2/02
1902-3	FL Div2	16,000	3	16,000	30,000 v Manchester United 10/4/03	8,000 v Blackpool 11/4/03	-
1903-4	FL Div1	20,000	2	20,350	30,000 v Aston Villa 17/10/03 v Middlesbrough 1/1/04	8,000 v Sheffield Wed. 28/11/03	35,000 v Middlesbrough 5/3/04
1904-5	FL Div1	20,000	3	21,250	40,000 v Newcastle Utd 28/1/05 v Everton 21/4/05	8,000 v Aston Villa 9/11/04	39,000 v Bolton Wanderers 18/2/05
1905-6	FL Div1	18,000	5	21,850	38,000 v Bolton W 25/11/05	3,000 v Sunderland 21/4/06	-
1906-7	FL Div1	22,150	3	33,650	40,000 v Manchester United 1/12/06	8,000 v Middlesbrough 2/1/07	30,000 v Blackburn Rovers 16/1/07
1907-8	FL Div1	23,000	3	30,850	40,000 v Manchester United 18/4/08	2,500 v Bristol City 21/4/98	25,000 v Fulham 22/2/08
1908-9	FL Div1	20,000	6	28,425	40,000 v Manchester United 19/9/09	3,000 v Nottingham F. 13/4/09	20,000 v Tottenham Hotspur 16/1/09
1909-10	FL Div2	18,275	8	18,275	40,000 v Oldham Athletic 26/3/10	8,000 v Clapton Orient 13/4/10	-
1910-11	FL Div1	26,000	1	26,000	40,000 v Liverpool 24/9/10 v Manchester United 21/1/11	12,000 v Bradford City 5/11/10	-
1911-12	FL Div1	24,625	3	26,400	40,000 v Blackburn Rovers 2/12/11	10,000 v Tottenham H. 5/4/12	45,000 v Oldham Athletic 3/2/12
1912-13	FL Div1	24,000	4	32,100	40,000 v Newcastle United 12/10/12	15,000 v Derby County 26/4/13	41,709 v Sunderland 1/2/13 (abandoned)
1913-14	FL Div1	27,000	3	37,900	40,000 v Blackburn Rovers 11/10/13 v Manchester United 6/12/13	15,000 v West Brom. A. 25/3/14	36,256 v Tottenham Hotspur 31/1/14

ATTENDANCE POSITION = City's average home League attendance in relation to rest of League
HIGHEST IN DIVISION = Highest average of all clubs

Season	Lge	Average Home League Attendance	Attendance Position	Highest in Division	Highest Home League Attendance	Lowest Home League Attendance	Highest Home Cup Attendance
1914-15	FL Div1	21,000	1	21,000	40,000 v Oldham Athletic 5/4/15	7,000 v Bradford P.A. 19/12/14	32,000 v Chelsea 20/2/15
1915-16	War Lge	10,600	-	-	24,000 v Everton 22/4/16	3,000 v Liverpool 11/12/15	-
1916-17	War Lge	10,000	-	-	15,000 v Manchester United 21/4/17	3,000 v Port Vale 31/3/17	-
1917-18	War Lge	12,200	-	-	20,000 v Manchester United 29/9/17 v Stoke 3/11/17	8,000 v Burnley 15/12/17	-
1918-19	War Lge	15,700	-	-	35,000 v Manchester United 18/4/19	10,000 v Southport V. 14/12/19	-
1919-20	FL Div1	25,240	11	42,860	40,000 v Liverpool 27/3/20	15,000 v Derby County 22/11/19	25,878 v Clapton Orient 10/1/20
1920-21	FL Div1	31,020	12	41,100	40,000 v Burnley 26/3/21	18,000 v Newcastle United 2/3/21	-
1921-22	FL Div1	25,000	12	37,160	35,000 v Birmingham City 14/4/22 v Bolton W 3/12/21, Oldham A 8/10/21 v Blackburn R 24/9/21, Aston Villa 27/8/21	12,000 v Sheffield United 8/4/22	23,686 v Darlington 7/1/22
1922-23	FL Div1	24,000	11	32,875	40,000 v Liverpool 17/3/23	14,000 v Nottingham F. 14/4/23	-
1923-24	FL Div1	27,400	6	30,710	[1] 58,159 v Sheffield Utd 25/8/23	3,000 v Nottingham F., 13/2/24	76,166 v Cardiff City 12/3/24 (FAC)
1924-25	FL Div1	29,000	3	30,250	50,000 v Huddersfield Town 18/10/24	12,000 v Sheffield Utd, 23/2/25	-
1925-26	FL Div1	32,000	2	31,614	[2] 62,994 v Manchester United 12/9/25	[3] 11,393 v Everton 19/9/25	74,789 v Huddersfield T. 30/1/26 (FAC)
1926-27	FL Div2	30,848	3	30,848	49,384 v Bradford City 7/5/27	12,000 v South Shields 27/11/26	-
1927-28	FL Div2	37,468	1	37,468	60,000 v Fulham 6/4/28	20,000 v Notts County 24/12/27 v Wolves 31/12/27	73,668 v Stoke City 18/2/28 (FAC)
1928-29	FL Div1	31,715	1	31,715	61,007 v Manchester United 1/9/28	15,000 v Newcastle Utd 10/11/28 v Cardiff City 24/11/28	-
1929-30	FL Div1	33,339	2	35,537	70,000 v Aston Villa 26/12/29	[4] 19,868 v Blackburn Rovers 26/4/29	61,574 v Hull City 15/2/30 (FAC)
1930-31	FL Div1	26,849	5	37,106	56,750 v Arsenal 25/12/30	14,739 v Derby County 31/1/31	-
1931-32	FL Div1	24,173	7	40,547	46,756 v Arsenal 19/9/31	[5] 15,153 v Derby County 9/9/31	62,641 v Derby County 13/2/32
1932-33	FL Div1	24,254	8	41,958	36,542 v Arsenal 10/9/32	8,428 v Blackburn Rovers 8/10/32	52,085 v Walsall 28/1/33 (FAC)
1933-34	FL Div1	30,058	4	40,750	60,401 v Arsenal 20/1/34	14,000 v Newcastle Utd 21/3/34	84,569 v Stoke City 3/3/34
1934-35	FL Div1	34,824	2	46,252	79,491 v Arsenal 23/2/35	15,000 v Wolves 4/5/35	-
1935-36	FL Div1	33,577	4	41,960	45,000 v Sunderland 4/1/36	12,498 v Blackburn Rovers 19/2/36	65,978 v Luton Town 25/1/36
1936-37	FL Div1	35,872	3	43,353	74,918 v Arsenal 10/4/37	15,000 v Preston 12/12/36	39,135 v Accrington Stanley 30/1/37
1937-38	FL Div1	32,670	4	44,045	53,328 v Bolton W 15/4/38	16,396 v Middlesbrough 9/3/38	71,937 v Bury 22/1/38
1938-39	FL Div2	31,291	6	32,693	47,998 v Tottenham H 5/11/38	12,258 v Chesterfield 29/4/39	-
1939-40	War Lge	4,100	-	-	21,596 v Manchester United 27/4/40	1,300 v Crewe A 13/5/40	-
1940-41	War Lge	4,000	-	-	15,304 v Preston NE 29/3/41	1,000 v Blackpool 18/1/41	-
1941-42	War Lge	4,900	-	-	14,715 v Wolves 2/5/42	2,000 (Numerous recorded)	-
1942-43	War Lge	10,900	-	-	53,204 v Blackpool 10/4/43	2,500 v Tranmere Rovers 12/12/42	-
1943-44	War Lge	14,200	-	-	60,000 v Blackpool 15/4/44	3,000 v Chester 27/11/43	-
1944-45	War Lge	15,400	-	-	30,000 v Everton 4/11/44	5,000 v Bury 2/12/44	-
1945-46	War Lge	24,000	-	-	50,440 v Manchester United 13/4/46	6,662 v Barnsley 13/3/46	19,589 v Barrow 5/1/46 (FAC)
1946-47	FL Div2	39,283	2	49,379	67,672 v Burnley 10/5/47	22,210 v Barnsley 14/12/46	39,355 v Bolton 29/1/47
1947-48	FL Div1	42,725	8	54,982	78,000 v Manchester United 20/9/47	18,393 v Preston 21/4/48	67,494 v Preston 7/2/48
1948-49	FL Div1	38,699	12	53,839	64,502 v Manchester United 11/9/48	16,502 v Sheffield Utd 5/3/49	-
1949-50	FL Div1	39,381	12	49,001	63,704 v Manchester United 31/12/49	20,000 v Liverpool 29/3/49	53,213 v Derby 7/1/50
1950-51	FL Div2	35,016	13	35,016	45,693 v Hull City 28/10/50	10,000 v Swansea T 14/3/51	-
1951-52	FL Div1	38,302	9	51,134	57,566 v Preston NE 13/10/51	13,842 v West Brom 5/4/52	54,497 v Wolves 12/1/52
1952-53	FL Div1	34,663	11	49,191	56,140 v Manchester United 30/8/52	13,562 v Stoke 20/12/52	38,411 v Luton 31/1/53

NOTES:

[1] The figure of 58,159 was released to the press in the days immediately after the match as the total attendance including season ticket holders; 56,993 are believed to have paid for admission on the day, while a figure of 60,000 has also been recorded on occasion. 58,159 has been used here as it is the figure released by the club.

[2] The Manchester derby was officially recorded as being watched by 66,000 including season ticket holders, however 62,994 represents an accurate figure of those who paid on the day. This situation is also true for many of the other figures quoted, including the 1926-7 Bradford crowd which is known to have been over 50,000 when season ticket holders are included.

[3] Some sources incorrectly claim the lowest attendance during 1925-6 was 7,000 for the visit of Sheffield Utd on 26/10/25, however this attendance was actually 14,053.

[4] A figure of 10,000 has been recorded for the visit of Leicester on 14/12/29. This is clearly an estimate and seems uncharacteristically low when compared to other attendances for this period, therefore the lowest known attendance has been recorded instead.

[5] Some sources quote the City v Sheffield Wednesday game on 30/4/32 as having an attendance of 15,000. The actual crowd for that match was 16,322.

ATTENDANCE POSITION = City's average home League attendance in relation to rest of League
HIGHEST IN DIVISION = Highest average of all clubs

Season	Lge	Average Home League Attendance	Attendance Position	Highest in Division	Highest Home League Attendance	Lowest Home League Attendance	Highest Home Cup Attendance
1953-54	FL Div1	30,155	16	50,278	53,097 v Manchester United 5/9/53	[6] 10,841 v Tottenham 17/3/54	50,576 v Tottenham 30/1/54
1954-55	FL Div1	35,217	10	48,260	60,611 v Sunderland 9/4/55	13,648 v Leicester City 15/1/54	74,723 v Manchester Utd 29/1/55 (FAC)
1955-56	FL Div1	32,198	11	42,768	63,925 v Blackpool 24/9/55	13,998 v Charlton 21/3/56	76,129 v Everton 3/3/56 (FAC)
1956-57	FL Div1	30,005	14	45,481	63,872 v Manchester United 2/2/57	19,731 v Bolton 25/12/56	46,988 v Newcastle 9/1/57 (FAC)
1957-58	FL Div1	32,765	10	46,073	70,483 v Manchester United 28/12/57	20,912 v Everton 7/12/57	-
1958-59	FL Div1	32,568	10	53,258	62,812 v Manchester United 27/9/58	16,405 v Blackburn 29/11/58	35,840 v Grimsby 24/1/59 (FAC)
1959-60	FL Div1	35,637	8	47,948	65,981 v Burnley 2/5/60	19,653 v Blackpool 9/3/60	42,065 v Southampton 9/1/60 (FAC)
1960-61	FL Div1	29,409	9	53,124	50,479 v Manchester United 4/3/61	18,252 v Nottm Forest 17/12/60	39,035 v Cardiff 11/1/61 (FAC)
1961-62	FL Div1	25,626	13	45,576	49,959 v Manchester United 10/2/62	15,971 v Blackpool 2/12/61	-
1962-63	FL Div1	24,683	15	51,603	52,424 v Manchester United 15/5/63	12,789 v Fulham 29/3/63	41,575 v Bury 13/3/63 (FAC)
1963-64	FL Div2	18,201	28	41,262	31,136 v Sunderland 18/1/64	8,053 v Middlesbrough 17/3/64	16,894 v Stoke 5/2/64 (FLC)
1964-65	FL Div2	14,753	34	35,659	22,299 v Bury 26/12/64	8,015 v Swindon 16/1/65	16,131 v Shrewsbury 9/1/65 (FAC)
1965-66	FL Div2	27,739	10	27,739	47,171 v Huddersfield Town 1/1/66	16,202 v Leyton Orient 11/12/65	63,034 v Everton 26/3/66
1966-67	FL Div1	31,209	11	53,854	62,983 v Manchester United 21/1/67	20,104 v Southampton 17/12/66	47,075 v Ipswich Town 11/3/67
1967-68	FL Div1	37,223	6	57,552	62,942 v Manchester United 30/9/67	22,002 v Southampton 30/8/67	51,009 v Leicester City 17/2/68
1968-69	FL Div1	33,750	9	51,169	63,052 v Manchester United 17/8/68	20,108 v Newcastle United 5/5/69	60,844 v Newcastle United 29/1/69
1969-70	FL Div1	33,930	10	49,862	63,013 v Manchester United 15/11/69	22,006 v Sunderland 4/4/70	-
1970-71	FL Div1	31,041	9	45,602	43,636 v Manchester United 5/5/71	17,975 v Liverpool 26/4/71	46,212 v Wigan Athletic 2/1/71
1971-72	FL Div1	38,573	6	47,687	63,326 v Manchester United 6/11/71	25,677 v West Bromwich Albion 1/3/72	42,620 v Middlesbrough 15/1/72
1972-73	FL Div1	32,351	7	48,623	52,050 v Manchester United 18/11/72	23,973 v Chelsea 27/3/73	54,478 v Sunderland 24/2/73
1973-74	FL Div1	30,756	7	42,712	51,331 v Manchester United 13/3/74	21,590 v Newcastle United 27/3/74	-
1974-75	FL Div1	32,898	6	45,966	45,194 v Liverpool 14/9/74	24,047 v Carlisle United 19/3/75	37,625 v Newcastle United 4/1/75 (City were the away team)
1975-76	FL Div1	34,281	4	54,750	50,439 v Liverpool 19/4/76	27,256 v Coventry City 13/12/75	26,863 v Hartlepool United 3/1/76
1976-77	FL Div1	40,058	3	53,710	50,020 v Liverpool 29/12/76	32,227 v Coventry City 18/12/76	38,195 v West Bromwich Albion 8/1/77

NOTE:
[6] For most seasons during the forties to sixties a low attendance is recorded that appears totally out of character for both the position of the Blues, the loyalty of City's support, and the stature of the opponents. This game against Tottenham is a typical blip, as is the 1948 match with Preston. Many historians have simply believed these low attendances are as a result of poor form, apathy, or general disloyalty of supporters. The truth, however, is somewhat different. These games were played on mid-week afternoons and many Blues would have been working. Games could not be played under floodlights during this period, and so clubs were forced to play during the afternoon or early evening to ensure good light. This fact must not be ignored when considering attendance data.

ATTENDANCE POSITION = City's average home League attendance in relation to rest of League
HIGHEST IN DIVISION = Highest average of all clubs

Season	Lge	Average Home League Attendance	Attendance Position	Highest in Division	Highest Home League Attendance	Lowest Home League Attendance	Highest Home Cup Attendance
1977-78	FL Div1	41,687	3	51,860	50,856 v Manchester United 10/9/77	32,412 v Coventry City 25/4/78	-
1978-79	FL Div1	36,203	4	46,430	46,710 v Liverpool 26/8/78	27,366 v Birmingham City 1/5/79	26,029 v Rotherham United 15/1/79
1979-80	FL Div1	35,272	3	51,608	50,067 v Manchester United 10/11/79	27,667 v Derby County 15/12/79	-
1980-81	FL Div1	33,587	4	45,071	50,114 v Manchester United 21/2/81	26,144 v Leicester City 31/3/81	52,532 v Everton 11/3/81
1981-82	FL Div1	34,063	4	44,571	52,037 v Manchester United 10/10/81	24,443 v Notts County 5/5/82	31,547 v Cardiff City 2/1/82
1982-83	FL Div1	26,789	4	41,552	45,400 v Manchester United 5/3/83	20,615 v Brighton & HA 18/12/82	22,356 v Sunderland 12/1/83
1983-84	FL Div2	25,604	6	29,811	41,862 v Sheffield Wednesday 10/12/83	19,147 v Charlton Athletic 31/3/84	-
1984-85	FL Div2	24,220	8	24,220	47,285 v Charlton Athletic 11/5/85	20,047 v Cardiff City 30/3/85	-
1985-86	FL Div1	24,229	4	46,321	48,773 v Manchester United 14/9/85	18,899 v Watford 15/3/86	31,632 v Watford 25/1/86
1986-87	FL Div1	21,922	8	40,594	35,336 v Liverpool 17/1/87	17,507 v Luton 21/2/87	-
1987-88	FL Div2	19,471	12	20,272	30,153 v Leeds United 26/12/87	15,172 v Reading 4/4/88	44,047 v Liverpool 13/3/88
1988-89	FL Div2	23,500	6	23,500	40,070 v Chelsea 18/3/89	16,033 v Brighton & HA 17/9/88	23,838 v Leicester City 7/1/89
1989-90	FL Div1	27,975	5	39,077	43,246 v Manchester United 23/9/89	23,354 v Aston Villa 22/10/89	25,038 v Millwall 6/1/89
1990-91	FL Div1	27,874	6	43,218	39,194 v Sunderland 11/5/91	20,404 v Luton Town 5/3/91	-
1991-92	FL Div1	27,691	7	44,984	38,180 v Manchester United 16/11/91	21,437 v QPR 14/12/91	-
1992-93	FA Prem	24,698	8	37,004	37,136 v Manchester United 20/3/93	19,524 v Wimbledon 21/4/93	34,050 v Tottenham Hotspur 7/3/93
1993-94	FA Prem	26,709	9	44,244	35,155 v Manchester United 7/11/94	20,513 v Everton 8/12/93	22,613 v Leicester City 8/1/94
1994-95	FA Prem	22,725	13	43,681	27,850 v QPR 14/5/95	19,150 v West Ham United 24/8/94	21,177 v Aston Villa 28/1/95
1995-96	FA Prem	27,869	10	41,700	31,436 v Liverpool 5/5/96	20,078 v Blackburn Rovers 2/3/96	22,419 v Coventry City 14/2/96
1996-97	FL Div1	26,753	11	26,753	30,729 v Oldham Athletic 8/3/97	23,079 v Oxford United 13/11/96	30,462 v Middlesbrough 15/2/97
1997-98	FL Div1	28,196	14	33,492	32,040 v QPR 25/4/98	24,058 v Charlton Athletic 28/1/98	26,495 v West Ham United 25/1/98
1998-99	FL Div2	28,261	13	28,261	32,471 v York City 8/5/99	24,291 v Walsall 2/9/98	11,106 v Halifax Town 13/11/98
1999-0	FL Div1	32,088	11	32,088	33,027 v Blackburn Rovers 23/10/99	30,057 v Fulham 16/1/00	29,240 v Leeds United 9/1/00
2000-1	FA Prem	34,058	10	67,544	34,629 v Liverpool 31/1/01	32,053 v Middlesbrough 17/9/00	24,637 v Coventry City 27/1/01
2001-2	FL Div1	33,059	11	33,059	34,657 v Portsmouth 21/4/02	30,238 v Millwall 30/1/02	21,581 v Swindon Town 5/1/02
2002-3	FA Prem	34,564	11	67,630	35,131 v Liverpool 28/9/02	33,260 v Fulham 29/2/03	28,586 v Liverpool 5/1/03

PROGRESSIVE ATTENDANCE RECORDS FOR CITY'S LEAGUE VENUES

c.4,000	3/9/1892	Bootle
c.6,000	22/10/1892	Small Heath
c.14,000	3/11/1894	Newton Heath
c.20,000	7/12/1895	Newton Heath
c.30,000	3/4/1896	Liverpool
c.35,000	5/3/1904	Middlesbrough (FAC)
c.40,000	28/1/1905	Newcastle
41,709	1/2/1913	Sunderland (FAC – abandoned)
58,159	25/8/1923	Sheffield United
76,166	8/3/1924	Cardiff City (FAC)
84,569	3/3/1934	Stoke City (FAC)

ATTENDANCES - MAINE ROAD'S LAST

84,000 plus	84,569, 3/3/1934, City v Stoke City (FAC)
80,000 plus	81,565, 12/2/1949, United v Yeovil Town (FAC)
76,000 plus	76,129, 3/3/1956, City v Everton (FAC)
70,000 plus	74,135, 26/3/1960, Blackburn Rovers v Sheffield Wednesday (FAC)
65,000 plus	65,981, 2/5/1960, City v Burnley (League)
60,000 plus	63,326, 6/11/1971, City v United (League)
54,000 plus	54,478, 24/2/1973, City v Sunderland (FAC)
50,000 plus	52,037, 10/10/1981, City v United (League)
48,000 plus	48,773, 14/9/1985, City v United (League)
44,000 plus	44,047, 13/3/1988, City v Liverpool (FAC)
40,000 plus	43,246, 23/9/1989, City v United (League)
39,000 plus	39,194, 11/5/1991, City v Sunderland (League)
38,000 plus	38,180, 16/11/1991, City v United (League)
36,000 plus	37,136, 20/3/1993, City v United (League)
35,000 plus	35,131, 28/9/2002, City v Liverpool (League)

AVERAGE LEAGUE & FA CUP ATTENDANCES ERA BY ERA:

1892 – 1900	8,172 (122 games)
1900 – 1910	19,427 (190 games)
1910 – 1915	24,852 (103 games)
1919 – 1923*	26,280 (86 games)
1923 – 1930	33,083 (158 games)
1930 – 1939	32,007 (202 games)
1946 – 1950	40,671 (90 games)
1950 – 1960	34,518 (221 games)
1960 – 1970	28,810 (226 games)
1970 – 1980	35,540 (219 games, excludes Newcastle United 'away' FAC game played at Maine Rd in 1975)
1980 – 1990	26,502 (225 games)
1990 – 2000*	27,110 (228 games)
2000 – 2003*	33,258 (65 games)

All-time Hyde Road FA Cup & League Average: 18,978
All-time Maine Road FA Cup & League Average: 31,568

The relatively low capacity of first Hyde Road and then Maine Road during the periods 1919 – 1930 and 1990 – 2003 seriously restricted City's attendances.

Images, Memories & Subscribers

A Special Place
in Our Hearts

Club photographer Ed Garvey took a walk around Maine Road to preserve various images for when memories fade.

These scenes can be found on the following pages: around Maine Road (page 298, 300, 310, 318); the Laundry Room (page 302); the Boot Room (page 303); the Dressing Rooms (page 304); hospitality at Maine Road (page 308); the Press area and TV interview room (page 312); the Boiler Room and groundsman's machinery (page 314); the Players' Tunnel (page 316).

Subscribers

No	Subscriber name	Memorable Maine Road game/event	Fave part of Maine Road
1	Bernard Halford	Newport County 14.6.47 (5-1)	Old Kippax
2	John Wardle	Manchester United 9.11.02 (3-1)	North Stand
3	Alistair Mackintosh	Manchester United 9.11.02 (3-1)	Directors' Box on 9.11.02!
4	Gary James	Manchester United 23.9.89 (5-1)	Old Kippax
5	David Bernstein		
6	Chris Bird		
7	Bryan Bodek		
8	Ashley Lewis		
9	Dennis Tueart		
10	Kevin Keegan		
11	Eric Alexander	Newport County 14.6.47 (5-1)	Kippax gangways/steps!
12	Sidney Rose		
13	Norah Mercer		
14	Heidi James	Manchester United 23.9.89 (5-1)	Main Stand
15	Michael James	Southampton 11.5.2003 (0-1)	Main Stand
16	Anna James	Newcastle United 24.08.02 (1-0)	New Platt Lane
17	Ed Garvey	Charlton Athletic 11.5.85 (5-1)	Rose's Room
18	Noel Bayley	Manchester United 23.9.89 (5-1)	Old Kippax
19	Dave Wallace	Everton 3.3.56 FAC 6 (2-1)	Old Kippax
20	Dennis Chapman, Nantwich	Leeds United 30.04.38 (6-2) my first game	Open Kippax 1938-69 & Main Stand 1970-2003
21	Brian Whitehouse, Castle Vale, Birmingham	Coventry City 22.11.80 (3-0)	Old Kippax
22	Lionel Major, Moelfre, Anglesey	Newcastle United 26.12.77 (4-0)	Old Kippax
23	William Walsh, Heaton, Bolton	Portsmouth 21.4.02 (3-1)	North Stand
24	Roni, Saul, Nathan & Barry Foy, Failsworth	Marriage of Elenni Foy & Peter Murray 31.5.03	Main Stand
25	Gareth Edwards, Lytham St Annes	Manchester United 23.9.89 (5-1)	Old Kippax
26	Stephen White, Denton, Manchester	Manchester United 23.9.89 (5-1)	Old Kippax
27	Nick Keeling, Thornton Cleveleys	Newcastle United 24.08.02 (1-0)	Old Kippax
28	Daniel McGowan, Ashton-under-Lyne	Bolton Wanderers 29.3.80 (2-2)	Old Kippax
29	Colin MacBean, Chapel-en-le-Frith	Manchester United 23.9.89 (5-1)	Block I, Main Stand
30	Nigel & Julie MacBean, Haughton, Darlington	Derby County 10.04.76 (4-3)	Block I, Main Stand
31	Helen Wood, Hazel Grove, Stockport	Manchester United 23.9.89 (5-1)	My seat, Main Stand
32	Gary Dickson, Sheffield	Manchester United 23.9.89 (5-1)	Old Kippax
33	John Collins, Sale	Portsmouth 21.4.02 (3-1)	Old Kippax
34	Timothy Cosgrove, Blackley, Manchester	Manchester United 6.11.71 (3-3)	Old Kippax
35	Sean & Jane Riley, Chadderton, Lancs	Barnsley, 6.4.02 (5-1)	Old Kippax & North Stand
36	Joseph Taylor, Norden, Lancs	Portsmouth 21.4.02 (3-1)	Kippax
37	Katie Margaret Bailey, Bredbury	Manchester United 23.9.89 (5-1)	Old Kippax
38	Brian Bailey, Bredbury	Birmingham City 28.4.2000 (1-0)	New Kippax
39	Paul Brian Bailey, Bredbury	Manchester United 23.9.89 (5-1)	Old Kippax
40	Gareth Jones, Sowerby, Thirsk, N.Yorks	Manchester United 23.9.89 (5-1)	Old Kippax
41	Graeme Wallis, Ashton-under-Lyne	Coventry City 16.1.74, FL Cup 5 rep (4-2)	Old Kippax
42	Emma Tamara Taylor, Rochdale	Wigan Athletic 17.5.99, P/off leg 2 (1-0)	Old & New Kippax
43	Richard J Booth, Waltham Chase, Hampshire	Portsmouth 21.4.02 (3-1)	North Stand
44	David Flatley, Rochdale	Manchester United 23.9.89 (5-1)	Old Kippax
45	David Bambrough, Fulwell, Sunderland	Sunderland 23.8.2000 (4-2)	Old Kippax
46	Rob Dunford, Swinton, Manchester	Blackpool, 8.8.98 - proved fans' loyalty	Old Kippax, halfway line
47	Ross Griffin, Chesterfield	Manchester United 23.9.89 (5-1)	Block D Main Stand
48	Carl Sharp, Levenshulme	Portsmouth 21.4.02 (3-1)	Old Kippax
49	Peter Loughlin, Leyland, Preston	Blackburn 30.1.93 (3-2)	Old Kippax
50	Mark Poyzer, Melton Mowbray, Leics	Newcastle United 26.12.77 (4-0)	Old Kippax
51	Peter Wilkinson, Bramhall, Stockport	Tottenham Hotspur 9.12.67 (4-1)	Main Stand
52	John Cunningham, Bishop Wilton, York	Arsenal 4.3.77 (2-0)	Old Kippax
53	Stuart Priestley, Gatley, Cheshire	Manchester United 23.9.89 (5-1)	Old Kippax
54	Neville Evans, Aberystwyth	Tottenham Hotspur 25.2.61 (0-1)	Kippax
55	Steve Bainbridge, Whaley Bridge, High Peak	Charlton Athletic 11.5.85 (5-1)	Old Kippax
56	Roland Griffin, Sale, Cheshire	Manchester United 15.11.69 (4-0)	Old Kippax
57	Steve Reed, Cinderford, Gloucestershire	Manchester United 23.9.89 (5-1)	Old Kippax
58	Wayne Prior, Chelmsford, Essex	Newcastle United 26.12.77 (4-0)	Old Kippax
59	Maurice Edward Cummings, Heaton Mersey	Manchester United 29.1.55 FAC4 (2-0)	Old Uncovered Popular Side
60	Paul Simon Bowring, Bollington, Macclesfield	Burnley 25.11.67 (4-2)	Old Kippax
61	Gavin N Childs, Manchester M14	Manchester United 23.9.89 (5-1)	Old Kippax
62	D.J. Musker, Romiley, Stockport	Manchester United 19.9.59 (3-0)	Kippax
63	David Taaffe, Salford, Manchester	Manchester United 23.9.89 (5-1)	Old Kippax
64	Terry Broderick, Heywood, Lancs	Tottenham Hotspur 9.12.67 (4-1)	New Kippax
65	Paul McGovern, Audenshaw, Manchester	Manchester United 23.9.89 (5-1)	Old Kippax
66	Sharif Mohammed, Didsbury, Manchester	Tottenham Hotspur 9.12.67 (4-1)	Old Kippax
67	S H Rigby, Chorlton, Manchester	Wolverhampton Wanderers 28.12.81 (2-1)	Old Kippax
68	Dave Djordjevic, Longridge, Preston	AC Milan 6.12.78 Rd 3, leg 2 (3-0)	Top, Halfway line Old Kippax
69	Dane Djordjevic, Clowne, Chesterfield	Schalke 04, 15.4.70 ECWC s/f leg 2 (5-1)	H Centre Main Stand
70	Stephen Robert Hather, Lazonby, Penrith	Manchester United 23.9.89 (5-1)	Old Kippax
71	Katie Jane Hather, Lazonby, Penrith	Barnsley 6.4.02 (5-1)	North Stand
72	Sophie Elizabeth Hather, Lazonby, Penrith	Norwich City 13.1.02 (3-1)	North Stand
73	Gwyn Calder-Williams, Armathwaite, Cumbria	Barnsley 6.4.02 (5-1)	North Stand
74	Bart Ganley, Cheadle, Cheshire	Tottenham Hotspur 9.12.67 (4-1)	North Kippax
75	David Shaw, Whinfield, Darlington	Portsmouth 21.4.02 (3-1)	New Kippax
76	William Garnett, Royton, Oldham	Manchester United 23.9.89 (5-1)	Old Kippax
	James Garnett, Royton, Oldham	Manchester United 9.11.02 (3-1)	New Kippax
77	Andrew Davenport, Levenshulme, Manchester	Manchester United 23.9.89 (5-1)	Main Stand
78	Graham Elliott, Glossop	Manchester United 23.9.89 (5-1)	Old Kippax
79	Ged Jepson, Didsbury, Manchester	Tottenham Hotspur 9.12.67 (4-1)	Old Kippax
80	John Jepson, Canada	Sunderland 11.5.91 (3-2)	Old Kippax
81	Peter Cordingley, Marple, Stockport	Barnsley 6.4.02 (5-1)	Old Kippax

"I have belted out victory hymns and roared in wonder at moments of genius"

I knew it was right, immediately, instinctively. It was the smell, the unique cocktail of cigar smoke, horses, sweat and beer. It assailed the senses in the street outside, in those dark, mysterious, inner-city alleys where the graffiti both chilled and excited me. It was the noise, the shouting, the aggression and the hope. The air shimmered sometimes under those naked floodlights as they pierced the night and pointed the way. The place seemed to hold the ghosts of dreams; some alive, others shattered.

On my first trip I witnessed shocking, full-scale fighting including a spectacular police charge. Scenes like that live with a wide-eyed seven year old forever. In the Platt Lane Stand, a true, traditional football stand with low roof, rust and a rabble, I counted the lighter flashes, gasped at the language, marvelled at the passion. At first I would just gape at the sheer enormity of such a spectacle, watching the crowd and listening to the singing. At night in bed I used to draw Maine Road and imagine the surging on the Kippax when we scored and the roar which sometimes filled the whole arena like thunder.

As I got older I started to watch and understand the football with the help of my Dad. He was the real reason I worshipped at this famous place. Unlike most, I was not born into a family of blues. My Dad was a good footballer and cricketer himself in those hazy seventies days, but he still found time to patiently take me to grounds around the North West: Burnley, Blackburn, Leeds, Everton, United, Oldham and Bury to name a few. But Maine Road immediately felt like a womb. I loved just being with my Dad, my hero. I pestered him with questions and listened to his stories in awe. If he decreed a player was "useless" or "couldn't pass water", then that became gospel for me. City brought us together. Even now, twenty five years on, we sit together, just me and him, absorbed in the spectacle. We drink Bovril at half time enjoying each other's company. It would break the magic of tradition if I told him the truth – I would rather drink spit. All the glory, the nightmares, the emotion, the passion, the fury; we have shared and loved it all together.

And there has been glory at this historic theatre. The Cup run in 1981 and Big Mal's return for Palace. The Charlton victory for promotion in 85, my first game in the Kippax. The derby victories, the Keegan era, the epic promotion 'do-or-dies'. And there has been heartbreak too, along with spirit-sapping mundanity. I have been in Maine Road when the reality of the club's predicament has seeped over the crowd like mustard gas. When the team have been booed off ferociously by a venomous crowd. And I have crept home sickened, seeing no light at the end of the tunnel.

But I have danced on the pitch as victory rushed through my body; pure, mainlined Class A glory. I have hugged sweaty scallies on the Kippax. I have belted out victory hymns and roared in wonder at

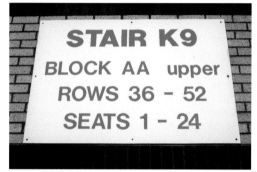

No	Subscriber name	Memorable Maine Road game/event	Fave part of Maine Road
82	Alan Rainford, Marple, Stockport	Liverpool 24.8.66 (2-1)	Old Kippax
83	Robert Dickson, Bury	Liverpool 24.8.66 (2-1)	Old Kippax
84	Stephen Welch, Salford, Manchester	My first game, c.1968 & the start of a great friendship	Old Kippax
85	Tony Dove, Hockley, Essex	Too many to mention!!!	Old Kippax
86	Andy Spragg, Manchester	Portsmouth 21.4.02 (3-1)	North Stand
87	John Read, Denton, Manchester	Portsmouth 21.4.02 (3-1)	North Stand
88	Stephen White, Swinton, Manchester	Manchester United 23.9.89 (5-1)	Old Kippax
89	John Smith, Tottington, Bury	Mike Summerbee Testimonial 1975	Old Scoreboard End
90	Graham Shawcross, Codsall, Wolverhampton	Tottenham Hotspur 9.12.67 (4-1)	Old Platt Lane
91	Joe Ziemniak, Diggle, Oldham	Manchester United 9.11.02 (3-1)	Main Stand
92	Moira Ziemniak, Diggle, Oldham	Manchester United 15.11.69 (4-0)	Scoreboard End
93	Mark Chung, Trawden, Colne	Middlesbrough 21.1.76 FLC s/f 2 (4-0)	Old Kippax
94	George Allen Hather, Seddons Farm, Bury	Manchester United 23.9.89 (5-1)	North Stand
95	Chris Astbury, Market Drayton, Shropshire	Tottenham Hotspur 22.10.94 (5-2)	
		Manchester Utd 23.9.89 (5-1), Charlton 11.5.85 (5-1)	Old Kippax
96	David John Smith, Peel Green, Eccles	Schalke 04, 15.4.70 ECWC s/f leg 2 (5-1)	North Stand
97	Mike Marycz, Barnton, Northwich	Schalke 04, 15.4.70 ECWC s/f leg 2 (5-1)	Old Kippax
98	Peter Hill, Beddington, Surrey	Portsmouth 21.4.02 (3-1)	Kippax
99	David Hall, Failsworth, Manchester	Tottenham Hotspur 9.12.67 (4-1)	Upper Tier, New Kippax
100	Barry Gate, Radcliffe, Manchester	Liverpool 24.8.66 (2-1)	Claremont
101	Ian Clarke, Lutton, Ivybridge, Devon	Everton 19.11.66 (1-0)	North Stand
102	David Bracegirdle, Westbrook, Warrington	Schalke 04, 15.4.70 ECWC s/f leg 2 (5-1)	Old Kippax
103	Pete Welch, Rhosddu, Wrexham	Manchester United 23.9.89 (5-1)	Old Kippax
104	Walter Irwin-Carruthers, Meltham, Holmfirth	West Ham United 17.8.74 (4-0)	Old Kippax
105	Richard Chorlton, Little Hulton, Worsley	Manchester United 15.11.69 (4-0)	Old Kippax
106	Paul Pheby, Ashton-under-Lyne	Manchester United 23.9.89 (5-1)	Old Kippax
107	Andrew Syme, Denton, Manchester	Newcastle United 26.12.77 (4-0)	Old Kippax
108	Paul Mackle, Salford	Southampton 16.12.72 (2-1)	Old Platt Lane
109	David & Walter Butler, Pilling, Preston	Manchester United 23.9.89 (5-1)	Old Kippax
110	Richard Bracha, Manchester	Huddersfield Town 7.11.87 (10-1)	Old Kippax
111	Christopher J Walsh, Burnage, Manchester	Manchester United 29.1.55 FAC4 (2-0)	Old Kippax
112	In memory of Arthur Walker	Portsmouth 21.4.02 (3-1)	Old Kippax
113	Alan Bates, Clitheroe, Lancs	Manchester United 23.9.89 (5-1)	Main Stand
114	Simon J Clarke, Wollaston, Northants	Liverpool 21.8.91 (2-1)	Old Kippax
115	David J Bowestead, Midsomer Norton	Grimsby Town 28.12.99 (2-1)	Main Stand
116	Sandra McCarthy, Rochdale	Manchester United 23.9.89 (5-1)	North Stand
117	Chris Cullen, Walton on Thames, Surrey	Newcastle United 26.12.77 (4-0)	Old Kippax
118	David Quest, Cheadle Hulme	Manchester United 23.9.89 (5-1)	Old Kippax
119	David Allan Phillips, Blackley	Manchester United 23.9.89 (5-1)	Old Kippax
120	Craig Gatley, Higher Blackley	Manchester United 23.9.89 (5-1)	Kippax, Standing
121	David Fleming, Ashton-under-Lyne	Manchester United 23.9.89 (5-1)	New North Stand
122	Paul Brady, Altrincham	Schalke 04, 15.4.70 ECWC s/f leg 2 (5-1)	Old Kippax
123	David John Henry Owen Howl, Runcorn	Tottenham Hotspur 9.12.67 (4-1)	Old Platt Lane
124	Simon Taylor, Highbury, London	Tottenham Hotspur 22.10.80 (3-1)	Old Kippax
125	Anthony Jackson, Gorton, Manchester	Sunderland 11.5.91 (3-2)	Old Kippax
126	Apollon Wujuklidis, Anderton, Northwich	Everton 9.12.2000 (5-0)	Old Kippax
127	Rick Potter, Bramhall, Cheshire	Sunderland 23.8.2000 (4-2)	The Pitch
128	Andrew Devlin, Longsight, Manchester	Huddersfield Town 7.11.87 (10-1)	Old Kippax
129	Graham L. Aldred, Marple Bridge	Manchester United 23.9.89 (5-1)	Old Kippax
130	Norman John Cooper, North Watford	Newcastle United 26.12.77 (4-0)	Old Kippax
131	John Leigh, Hazel Grove	Huddersfield Town 7.11.87 (10-1)	Standing, Old Kippax
132	Andrew Cleaver, Teddington, Middlesex	Wigan Athletic 17.5.99, P-O leg 2 (1-0)	New Kippax
133	Alexandra M Hamilton, Hazel Grove	Manchester United 23.9.89 (5-1)	Old Kippax
134	Geoff Eckersley, Twyford, Berkshire	Tottenham Hotspur 9.12.67 (4-1)	New Kippax, Lower
135	Andrew Sandford, Bury	Tottenham Hotspur 22.10.94 (5-2)	Old Kippax
136	Lee Goddard, Tottington, Bury	Tottenham Hotspur 22.10.94 (5-2)	Old Kippax
137	Mark Goddard, Bury	Tottenham Hotspur 22.10.94 (5-2)	Old Kippax
138	Norman Thornton, Sutton Coldfield	Huddersfield Town 15.9.37 (3-2) - my first game	Popular Side
139	Philip A Bellamy, Marple Bridge	Tottenham Hotspur 9.12.67 (4-1)	Old Kippax
140	Andrew Lavelle, Failsworth, Manchester	Portsmouth 21.4.02 (3-1)	North Stand, T Block
141	D G Broadstock, Irlam, Manchester	Everton 31.8.02 (3-1)	Old Kippax
142	Chick Cheetham, Northville, Bristol	Newcastle United 24.8.02 (1-0)	Kippax
143	Phil Cheetham, South Shore, Blackpool	Newcastle United 24.8.02 (1-0)	Kippax
144	Steve & Paula Bennett, Culcheth, Warrington	Manchester United 23.9.89 (5-1)	Main Stand
145	Ray Gillespie, Chelford, Cheshire	Newcastle United 26.12.77 (4-0)	Old Kippax
146	Dave, Paul & Jack Henshaw, Audenshaw	Barnsley 6.4.2002 (5-1)	GGL Block, Kippax Stand
147	Barry D Duck, Droylsden, Manchester	Portsmouth 21.4.02 (3-1)	Kippax Stand
148	Gary Tinker, Middleton, Manchester	Schalke 04, 15.4.70 ECWC s/f leg 2 (5-1)	Kippax Stand
149	Alun Rees, Gatley, Cheshire	Huddersfield Town 7.11.87 (10-1)	Old Kippax
150	Terry O'Sullivan, Middleton, Manchester	Tottenham Hotspur 9.12.67 (4-1)	Old Kippax
151	Paul A Taylor, Buxton, Derbyshire	Schalke 04, 15.4.70 ECWC s/f leg 2 (5-1)	New Kippax
152	N Ford, Stalybridge	Tottenham Hotspur 9.12.67 (4-1)	Middle of the Old Kippax
153	Daniel Clarke, Chadderton	Manchester United 9.11.02 (3-1)	North Stand
154	Joseph Gregory, aged 2, Chadderton	-	The Pitch
155	Frederick Rodney Genders, Macclesfield	Tottenham Hotspur 9.12.67 (4-1)	Old Kippax
156	Paul Simon Jenkinson, Eastleigh, Hants	Charlton Athletic 11.5.85 (5-1)	Old Kippax Terrace
157	Jon Buchan, Aston Pigott, Shropshire	Manchester United 23.9.89 (5-1)	Old Kippax
158	Andrew Smith, Denton, Manchester	AC Milan 6.12.78 UEFA Cup Rd 3, leg 2 (3-0)	Old Platt Lane
159	Anthony J Sudworth, Appley Bridge, Wigan	Charlton Athletic 11.5.85 (5-1)	Old Kippax
160	Barbara, Dave, Kelly & Lee Moreton, Caldicot, Monmouthshire	Every game, good or bad!	Our seats in Main Stand
161	Michael Kelly, Whalley Range, Manchester	Manchester United 23.9.89 (5-1)	Old Kippax
162	Kevin J Rochford, Crumpsall, Manchester	Portsmouth 21.4.02 (3-1)	Open corner, Old Kippax
163	John Renshaw, Chorlton, Manchester		
164	Martin Britton, Manchester	Gillingham Play-off Final @ Wembley 30.5.99 (3-2)	
165	Paul Wharton, Newton Heath, Manchester	Newcastle United 26.12.77 (4-0)	Old Kippax
166	John Geary, Heywood, Lancs	Preston North End 31.3.61 (2-3) my first match	Kippax Wall
167	R G Thomas, Euxton, Chorley	Tottenham Hotspur 9.12.67 (4-1)	Old Kippax
168	John Duffy, Cheadle Hulme	Manchester United 23.9.89 (5-1)	Old Kippax

No	Subscriber name	Memorable Maine Road game/event	Fave part of Maine Road
169	Steve Thompson, Worcester	Chelsea 30.4.94 (2-2)	Old Kippax
170	E King, Hadfield, Glossop	Manchester United 23.9.89 (5-1)	Old Kippax
171	Kenneth Doodson, Smithybridge, Littleborough	Schalke 04, 15.4.70 ECWC s/f leg 2 (5-1)	Kippax Stand
172	Christopher Powner, Crumpsall, Manchester	Manchester United 23.9.89 (5-1)	Main Stand
173	David C Lancaster, Blackpool		Old Kippax
174	Julian Cooke, Hertford	Newcastle United 26.12.77 (4-0)	Old Kippax
175	Phillip Burgess, Flixton, Manchester	Manchester United 23.9.89 (5-1)	Old Kippax
176	Graham Dyson, Astley, Tyldesley, M/cr	Everton FAC 6 rep 11.3.81 (3-1)	Old Kippax
177	Robert Lees, Cheadle Hulme, Cheshire	Tottenham Hotspur 9.12.67 (4-1)	Old Kippax
178	Clifford Lea, Stretford, Manchester	Tottenham Hotspur 9.12.67 (4-1)	Old Kippax
179	David Stead, Davyhulme, Manchester	Manchester United 23.9.89 (5-1)	Main Stand
180	Geoffrey Milne, Shrewsbury	Tottenham Hotspur 9.12.67 (4-1)	Old Kippax
181	Dennis Reilly, Davyhulme, Manchester	Manchester United 23.9.89 (5-1)	Old Kippax
182	Jo Couchman, York	Wolverhampton Wanderers 29.1.72 (5-2)	Main Stand
183	Andrew Thompson, Kimnel Bay, Rhyl	Huddersfield Town 7.11.87 (10-1)	Old Kippax
184	David Smith, Wistaston, Crewe	Schalke 04, 15.4.70 ECWC s/f leg 2 (5-1)	Old Platt Lane
185	Mark Dickman, Disley, Stockport	Huddersfield Town 7.11.87 (10-1)	Block D Main Stand
186	David Dickman, Disley, Stockport	Leicester City 29.4.59 (3-1)	Old Scoreboard End
187	Andrew Dickman, Disley, Stockport	Manchester United 23.9.89 (5-1)	North Stand
188	Colin Norton, Tadley, Basingstoke	Newcastle United 24.2.96 (3-3)	-
189	Ian David Ford, Clacton on Sea, Essex	Ipswich Town 27.10.99 (1-0)	Main Stand
190	John Crick, Wythenshawe, Manchester	Everton 3.3.56 FAC 6 (2-1)	Old Scoreboard End
191	Steve Crick, Wythenshawe, Manchester	Newcastle United (a) 11.5.68 (4-3)	Old Scoreboard End
192	Matthew Welch, Nantwich, Cheshire	Portsmouth 21.4.02 (3-1)	Gene Kelly Stand in the rain
193	Steve & Pauline Lambert, Westwood, Wiltshire	Barnsley 6.4.2001 (5-1)	Main Stand
194	Paul Amos, Glossop	Charlton Athletic 11.5.85 (5-1)	Old Kippax
195	Mike Phillips, Wrelton, Pickering, N.Yorks	Manchester United 9.11.02 (3-1)	Old Kippax
196	Matt Bewley, Leeds	Wigan Athletic Play-off s/f 15.5.99 (1-0)	Old Kippax
197	Stephen Mellon, Tyldesley, Manchester	Everton FAC s/f @ Villa Park (1-0)	Old Platt Lane
198	Christopher R Thomas, Edgeley, Stockport	Manchester United 23.9.89 (5-1)	Old Kippax
199	Graham Boyle, Warrington	Schalke 04, 15.4.70 ECWC s/f leg 2 (5-1)	Old Scoreboard End
200	Paul Scott, Blackburn	Blackburn Rovers 17.9.83 (6-0)	Old Kippax
201	Jay Cleary, Croydon, Surrey	Atletico Bilbao ECWC 1 leg 2, 1.10.69 (3-0)	Old Platt Lane
202	Neil Doody, Worthing, West Sussex	Manchester United 9.11.02 (3-1)	Main Stand
203	Alistair Stewart Lord, Great Sankey, Warrington	Manchester United 23.9.89 (5-1)	Upper Tier, Kippax
204	John Richards, Flixton, Urmston, M/cr	Tottenham Hotspur 9.12.67 (4-1)	Old Scoreboard End
205	Julian Wood, Harrow, Middlesex	Liverpool 29.10.78 (3-1)	Old Kippax
206	Iain Richardson, Braddan, Isle of Man	Manchester United 23.9.89 (5-1)	Old Kippax
207	Lee Williams, Sale, Cheshire	Manchester United 23.9.89 (5-1)	Old Kippax
208	Anthony J Gill, West Kensington, London	Manchester United 9.11.02 (3-1)	Main Stand
209	Dennis Hyde, Surbiton, Surrey	West Bromwich Albion Charity Shield 9.8.69 (6-1)	Old Kippax
210	Dean Gatiss, Sale, Cheshire	Manchester United 9.11.02 (3-1)	Old Kippax
211	Anthony Modsley, Dalton-in-Furness, Cumbria	Manchester United 23.9.89 (5-1)	Old Kippax
212	Mike P Strul, Rishworth, Calderdale	Ipswich Town FAC s/f 11.4.81 (1-0)	Main Stand, Block B, Row 1, Seat 17
213	Robert Knott, Northampton	Manchester United 23.9.89 (5-1)	Old Kippax
214	Alan White, Peterborough	Millwall 30.01.02 (2-0)	North Stand
215	Darren Seymour Jones, Urmston, Manchester	Every single match!	Kippax Stand
216	Calum Jarvis, Whitefield, Manchester	Manchester United 9.11.02 (3-1)	North Stand
217	Andy Wragg, Mansfield Woodhouse, Notts	Liverpool 29.10.77 (3-1)	Old Kippax - magic!
218	Geoffrey Mason, Denton, Manchester	Manchester United 23.9.89 (5-1)	Old Scoreboard End
219	Terence Philip Howse, Shirebrook, Mansfield	Manchester United 23.9.89 (5-1)	Old Kippax
220	Peter Hosie, Boothstown, Worsley, M/cr	Manchester United 23.9.89 (5-1)	New Platt Lane
221	Liam Hosie, Boothstown, Worsley, M/cr	Manchester United 23.9.89 (5-1)	New Platt Lane
222	Graham Bowker, Chadderton, Oldham	Manchester United 23.9.89 (5-1)	Old Kippax
223	Mike Frimston, Audenshaw, Manchester	Manchester United 9.11.02 (3-1)	Old Kippax
224	Richard Simon Aston, Holcombe Brook, Bury	Manchester United 10.11.79 (2-0)	Old Scoreboard End
225	Steinar Sel, Bryne, Norway	Manchester United 9.11.02 (3-1)	Old Kippax
226	Rev. John Serjeant, Chorlton, Manchester	Manchester United 23.9.89 (5-1)	Old Kippax
227	Alan Williams, Bethel, Caernarfon	Manchester United 9.11.02 (3-1)	New Kippax
228	Brian Wood, Cheadle, Cheshire	Manchester United 9.11.02 (3-1)	Main Stand
229	Stephen Topping, St Helens	Gillingham Play-off Final @ Wembley 30.5.99 (3-2)	North Stand
230	Ted Knott, Droylsden, Manchester	Wolverhampton Wanderers 5.9.59 (4-6)	Platt Lane
231	Peter S Wilson, Sutton St. Nicholas, Hereford	Manchester United 23.9.89 (5-1)	New Kippax, Lower
232	Richard Zieme, Whitefield, Manchester	Man. United 23.9.89 (5-1) & 9.11.02 (3-1)	Kippax Upper
233	Stephen Toovey, Marple Bridge, Stockport	Manchester United 9.11.02 (3-1)	Main Stand
234	John Green, Little Hulton, Worsley, M/cr	Manchester United 23.9.89 (5-1)	Kippax Upper AA
235	Gary Carruthers, Addingham, Ilkley	Manchester United 9.11.02 (3-1)	North Stand
236	Mike Sheldon, Droylsden, Manchester	Manchester United 23.9.89 (5-1)	Old Kippax
237	Peter Tierney, Handforth, Cheshire	AC Milan 6.12.78 UEFA Cup Rd 3, leg 2 (3-0)	Old Platt Lane
238	Albert J Sutton, Cheadle Hulme, Cheshire	Liverpool 14.1.81 FL Cup s/f 1 (0-1)	Centre line, Old Kippax
239	Stephen J Callaghan, Warrington	Schalke 04, 15.4.70 ECWC s/f leg 2 (5-1)	Centre line, Old Kippax
240	H. Norman M. Jones, Holywell, Flintshire	Manchester United 23.9.89 (5-1)	Kippax
241	Brian Spridgens, Brymore School, Somerset	Burnley 29.12.01 (5-1)	Kippax
242	Paul Campbell, Simmondley, Glossop	Newcastle United FL Cup Final 28.2.76 (2-1)	Lower Kippax AA
243	John C Malone, Huddersfield	Charlton Athletic 11.5.85 (5-1)	Old Kippax
244	Ian R Mason, Tottington, Bury	Manchester United 23.9.89 (5-1)	North Stand
245	Richard Fox, Burnham, Slough	Manchester United 9.11.02 (3-1)	Old Kippax
246	Mark Goodman, Royton, Oldham	Barnsley, 6.4.02 (5-1)	Main Stand
247	Roy Flanagan, Goostrey, Cheshire	Huddersfield Town 7.11.87 (10-1)	Old Kippax
248	Dave Beresford, Denton, Manchester	Tottenham Hotspur 9.12.67 (4-1)	Old Kippax
249	John Royle, Barnton, Northwich,Cheshire	Coventry City FL Cup Rd 5 rep 16.1.74 (4-2)	Old Kippax
250	George 'Jud' Nixon, Woodhouse Park, M/cr	Manchester United 23.9.89 (5-1)	Old Kippax
251	Jason & Ian Allcroft, Stalybridge, Cheshire	Manchester United 23.9.89 (5-1)	Old Kippax
252	Graham Green, Thornton Cleveleys	Manchester United 23.9.89 (5-1)	New Platt Lane
253	John Entwistle, Chadderton, Oldham	Manchester United 9.11.02 (3-1)	Main Stand
254	Bill Smith, Old Trafford, Manchester	Newcastle United FL Cup Final 28.2.76 (2-1)	Old Kippax
255	Andrew Smallwood, Sale, Cheshire	Manchester United 23.9.89 (5-1)	Old Kippax

moments of genius. Those are the moments which will always define the Old Lady for me.

Maine Road will always hold a special place in my heart. It sits like a church in an area where the streets suggest lawlessness and poverty. The local pubs became part of my routine and many hazy evenings have drifted away toasting famous victories and relighting the memory of legends. That feeling of nervous anticipation as I walk down Claremont Road, past the police horses and merchandise sellers, will never die in me. The increase in adrenaline as I walk around the North Stand and the forecourt buzzes with life and anxiety still quickens my pace. Although I have been in every part of the ground, the Main Stand has always felt special to me because it still reeks of memories of the past. It feels like the club's real heart and soul, with cushioned seats on crumbling concrete. It takes me back to a golden time when I was innocent and my Dad was Superman.

Progress is inevitable, and no-one can deny that the move to the City of Manchester Stadium presents a unique and wonderful opportunity for Manchester City to enter a new era. The club's figureheads of David Bernstein and Kevin Keegan have filled the supporters with a hope that seemed unthinkable a short time ago. I will be eternally grateful to the Gods of football that the last few years at Maine Road have left us with a legacy of pride and achievement. But part of me will die when we leave and the Old Lady sleeps forever. A huge part of my past will be consigned to the soft-focus of memory forever. When my tears flow, as they surely will, at the last game, they will be for the happy times I have spent with my Dad, but also for the loss of a loved one.

Rest In Peace, Old Lady. You will never be forgotten.

Paul Cahill

No	Subscriber name	Memorable Maine Road game/event	Fave part of Maine Road
256	Dave Massey, Sale, Cheshire	Coventry City 16.1.74, FL Cup 5 rep (4-2)	Old Kippax
257	Mark, Michael & Anthony Grimshaw, Walkden	Southampton 11.05.03 (0-1)	Old Scoreboard End
258	David Crozier, Hyde, Cheshire	Manchester United 9.11.02 (3-1)	
259	Christopher Jinks, Marsden, Huddersfield	Charlton Athletic 11.5.85 (5-1)	Old Kippax
260	George Curwen, Hale, Cheshire	Manchester United 23.9.89 (5-1)	Old Kippax
261	Simon Edwards, Scissett, Huddersfield	Manchester United 23.9.89 (5-1)	Old Kippax
262	'Sykesy', Bury	Chelsea 26.11.77 (6-2)	Old Kippax
263	Robert B Smith, Melbourne, Derbyshire	Manchester United 23.9.89 (5-1)	H Block, Main Stand
264	Gary Johnston, Catterick, Richmond	Manchester United 9.11.02 (3-1)	Old Kippax
265	Paul Kaminski, Downham Market, Norfolk	Manchester United 9.11.02 (3-1)	North Stand
266	Alan Platt, Failsworth, Manchester	Wigan Athletic 17.5.99, P-O leg 2 (1-0)	Old Kippax
267	Eric Heaton, Bingley, West Yorkshire	Charlton Athletic 11.5.85 (5-1)	Old Kippax
268	I Emmott, Eastburn, Keighley	Manchester Utd v Bradford P.A. 29.1.49 FA Cup 4 (1-1)	Old Platt Lane
269	Mark Jones, Springhead, Oldham	Manchester United 9.11.02 (3-1)	New Kippax
270	Bill Shannon, Ascot, Berkshire	Manchester United 15.11.69 (4-0)	Old North Stand (pre-seats!)
271	Ian Frank Handford, RAF Benson	Manchester United 23.9.89 (5-1)	North Stand
272	Paul, James & Edie Carlin, Tunstall, Tyne & Wear	Manchester United 9.11.02 (3-1)	Old Kippax
273	Damian Welsh, Manchester	Everton FAC 6 rep 11.3.81 (3-1)	
274	Simon Thomas, Atherton, Manchester	Manchester United 9.11.02 (3-1)	Old Kippax
275	David Alison, Lowgill, Kendal, Cumbria	Wolves 20.4.55 (2-0), my first match!	Old Kippax
276	Jane James, Middleton, Manchester	Manchester United 9.11.02 (3-1)	Centenary Suite, Kippax Stand
277	Alek Adamski, St John's Wood, London	Newcastle 26.12.77 (4-0)	Main Stand
278	Harry Hunt, West Timperley, Altrincham	Newcastle United 24.2.66 (3-3)	Main Stand
279	Bennett Harold Kushner, Nailsea, Bristol	Tottenham Hotspur 9.12.67 (4-1)	Old Kippax
280	Stuart Bain, Wythenshawe, Manchester	Manchester United 9.11.02 (3-1)	North Stand
281	Steven Parrott, Royton, Oldham	Manchester United 9.11.02 (3-1)	North Stand
282	Peter Kavanagh, Denton, Manchester	Manchester United 9.11.02 (3-1)	Main Stand
283	Colin Woolley, Sheffield	Manchester United 9.11.02 (3-1)	New Kippax
284	Andrew Philip Jackson, Silkstone, Barnsley	Manchester United 9.11.02 (3-1)	Old Kippax
285	Jim Burrows, Didsbury, Manchester	Manchester United 6.11.71 (3-3)	Scoreboard End
286	Raymond Guyatt, Malvern, Worcestershire	Manchester United 18.11.72 (3-0)	North Stand
287	Maurice Edward Cummings, Heaton Mersey	Manchester United 29.1.55 FA Cup Rd 4 (2-0)	Old Kippax
288	Andrew Worthington, Aspull, Wigan	Manchester United 23.9.89 (5-1)	Old Kippax
289	David Murray, Whitegate, Northwich	Manchester United 9.11.02 (3-1)	Old Kippax
290	Kevin Cullen, Stevenage, Herts	Manchester United 9.11.02 (3-1)	Old Kippax
291	Andrew James Norman, Salford, Manchester	Manchester United 9.11.02 (3-1)	Main Stand
292	Kevin Sutcliffe, Catsfield, East Sussex	Manchester United 23.9.89 (5-1)	Old Kippax
293	Neil A Shaw, Whaley Bridge, High Peak	Chelsea 17.4.71 (1-1)	Kippax Lower
294	Stephen Marsden, Sale, Cheshire	Charlton Athletic 11.5.85 (5-1)	Old Kippax
295	Kevin Moore, Wilmslow, Cheshire	Newcastle United (a) 11.5.68 (4-3)	Old Kippax
296	Sebastian Hankin, Standish, Wigan	Birmingham City 10.10.2001 FL Cup 3 (6-0)	Family Stand
297	David Noakes, Sale, Cheshire	Tottenham Hotspur 9.12.67 (4-1)	Old Kippax
298	Rachel Zöe McDonald, Preston, Lancs	Newcastle United 26.12.77 (4-0)	Old Kippax
299	Andy Howell, Chelmsford, Essex	Charlton Athletic 11.5.85 (5-1)	Kippax Lower
300	Simon Wells, Walton-on-the-hill, Staffs	Newcastle United 26.12.77 (4-0)	Main Stand
301	Barry Evans, Crumpsall, Manchester	Coventry City FL Cup Rd 5 rep 16.1.74 (4-2)	Old Kippax
302	Ian 'Wilf' Smallwood, Brooklands, Sale	Manchester United 23.9.89 (5-1)	Old Kippax
303	Don Price, Prestwich, Manchester	Charlton Athletic 11.5.85 (5-1)	Old Kippax, nr halfway line
304	R G F Brooke, Cheltenham, Glos	Manchester United 9.11.02 (3-1)	Main Stand
305	Joe Carroll, Minane Bridge, Co.Cork, Eire	Manchester United 23.9.89 (5-1)	Old Kippax, standing
306	David Mumby, Cleethorpes, Lincs		
307	Bill Lyno, Rhyl		Old Kippax
308	Keith Farnell, Ripon, North Yorkshire	Birmingham City 15.9.01 (3-0)	Kippax Lower
309	Martin Hurst, Bramhall, Stockport	Tottenham Hotspur 9.12.67 (4-1)	Old Kippax
310	Chris Keeling-Roberts, Marple, Stockport	Manchester United 9.11.02 (3-1)	Kippax Lower, back row
311	Raymond Walmsley, Flixton, Urmston, M/cr	Manchester United 9.11.02 (3-1)	Old Kippax, halfway line
312	David Bell, Nantwich	Manchester United 12.11.75 FL Cup Rd 4 (4-0)	Kippax
313	John Wildes, Droylsden, Manchester	Manchester United 9.11.02 (3-1)	Old Kippax
314	P G Barnes, Elmley Castle, Pershore, Worcs	AC Milan 6.12.78 UEFA Cup Rd 3, leg 2 (3-0)	Platt Lane
315	M G Barnes, Childswickham, Evesham		
316	Peter Stephen Glinka, Heaton Mersey, Stockport	Manchester United 23.9.89 (5-1)	Old Kippax
317	Chris Smith, Carrbrook, Stalybridge	Manchester United 23.9.89 (5-1)	Old Kippax
318	Neil Greenwood, Middleton, Manchester	Manchester United 9.11.02 (3-1)	Kippax
319	Les & Alan Whitney, Trafford Park	Tottenham Hotspur 9.12.67 (4-1)	Corner of the Kippax
320	Chris Palmer, Tottinghton, Bury	Charlton Athletic 11.5.85 (5-1)	Old Kippax, back left
321	Steve Clarke, Blackley, Manchester	Manchester United 12.11.75 FL Cup Rd 4 (4-0)	Old Kippax
322	Alan Ivanoski, Davyhume, Manchester	Tottenham Hotspur 9.12.67 (4-1)	Old Kippax
323	Colin Winward, Failsworth, Manchester	Manchester United 9.11.02 (3-1)	Old Kippax
324	Duncan Wilde, Newton, Hyde, Cheshire	Nottingham Forest 26.10.68 (3-3)	Platt Lane
325	Michael Vickerstaff, Macclesfield	Huddersfield Town 7.11.87 (10-1)	Old Platt Lane
326	Roger W Reade, Bessacarr, Doncaster	Schalke 04, 15.4.70 ECWC s/f leg 2 (5-1)	Old Platt Lane
327	Stuart Radcliffe, Warrington	Manchester United 9.11.02 (3-1)	Platt Lane
328	John Hamilton, Little Birch, Hereford	Birmingham City 28.4.2000 (1-0)	Main Stand, HC area
329	Mark Walker, Macclesfield	Newcastle United 24.2.96 (3-3)	Kippx Terrace
330	Michael Waggett, Cheadle Heath, Stockport	Manchester United 15.11.69 (4-0)	Old Kippax
331	E J G Williams, New Mills, High Peak	Manchester United 23.9.89 (5-1)	Old Kippax
332	Joan Potts, Wilmslow, Cheshire	Manchester United 23.9.89 (5-1)	Old Kippax
333	Ian Potter, North Luffenham, Rutland	Chalton Athletic 30.10.65 (0-0)	Old Kipax, halfway line
334	Adrian Keeble, Acomb Park, York	Manchester United 6.11.71 (3-3)	Old Kippax
335	Ged Bergin, Holgate, York	Wigan Athletic p/off leg 2, 19.5.99 (1-0)	New Kippax
336	Gary Pelham, Lingwood, Norwich	Manchester United 9.11.02 (3-1)	North Stand
337	Jonathan M Eastwood, Ackworth, Pontefract	Manchester United 23.9.89 (5-1)	North Stand
338	Dan Cundill, Cheadle Hulme, Stockport	Manchester United 23.9.89 (5-1)	Old Kippax
339	Patricia Williams, Little Eaton, Derby	Tottenham Hotspur 9.12.67 (4-1)	New Kippax
340	Gareth Austin, Wrexham	Manchester United 9.11.02 (3-1)	New Kippax
341	Dylan Austin, Rhuthun	Manchester United 9.11.02 (3-1)	New Kippax
342	Alun Thomas, Corwen	Manchester United 9.11.02 (3-1)	New Kippax
343	Saul Slater, Oldham	Manchester United 9.11.02 (3-1)	HH Uncovered

No	Subscriber name	Memorable Maine Road game/event	Fave part of Maine Road
344	Ivan Slater, Oldham	Manchester United 9.11.02 (3-1)	HH Uncovered
345	Steven Wilcock, Westminster Park, Chester	Tottenham Hotspur 22.10.94 (5-2)	Old Kippax
346	David Burton, Radcliffe, Manchester	Manchester United 23.9.89 (5-1)	Old Kippax
347	Owen McNeill, Romiley, Stockport	Manchester United 9.11.02 (3-1)	Scoreboard End
348	Don Parrish, Borras Park, Wrexham	Manchester United 9.11.02 (3-1)	Main Stand
349	John W Lewis, Wincham, Northwich	Manchester United 9.11.02 (3-1)	Main Stand
350	Rachel Heap, Heald Green	Manchester United 9.11.02 (3-1)	Main Stand
351	Thomas Owen, Northwich	Manchester United 9.11.02 (3-1)	Main Stand
352	Anthony Peter & Richard Bailey, Sandbach	Bolton Wanderers 30.11.02 (2-0)	Main Stand
353	Bryn Rigby, Manchester	Many!	Scoreboard End
354	Gary Rigby, Manchester		
355	Mark Rigby, Manchester		
356	Paul Doherty, Moston, Manchester	Manchester United 9.11.02 (3-1)	North Stand
357	Alan Hillyard, Brandlesholme, Bury	Manchester United 9.11.02 (3-1)	Kippax Lower
358	Eric Jones, Adlington, Chorley	Too many great memories since 1933!	Main Stand Block C
359	Denis Houlston, Levenshulme, Manchester	Stoke City 3.3.34 FAC Rd 6 (1-0)	Old Kippax
360	Nick Jefferson, Macclesfield	Everton 11.3.81 FAC Rd 6 rep (1-0)	Old Kippax
361	David A Jones, Nelson, South Wales	Manchester United 9.11.02 (3-1)	New Kippax
362	Dave Simpson, Queensland, Australia	Manchester United 23.9.89 (5-1)	Old Kippax
363	Marshall Kendrick, Crewe	Manchester United 9.11.02 (3-1)	Old Kippax
364	Richard Park, Bolton-by-Bowland, Lancs	Manchester United 9.11.02 (3-1)	Main Stand
365	David French, Whitchurch, Hampshire	Manchester United 9.11.02 (3-1)	Old Kippax
366	Richard Paul Cochran, Amblecote, Stourbridge	Manchester United 23.9.89 (5-1)	Main Stand
367	Alan Lambert, Chapel-en-le-Frith	Manchester United 9.11.02 (3-1)	New Kippax
368	Pete Lambert, Malcoff, Chapel-en-le-Frith	Leeds United 7.11.92 (4-0)	Old Kippax
369	Jim Lambert, Malcoff, Chapel-en-le-Frith	Manchester United 9.11.02 (3-1)	Old Kippax
370	Keith F Kirkman, Potton, Sandy, Beds	Everton 7.12.57 (6-2)	Old Kippax
371	Graham Smith, St Asaph, North Wales	Manchester United 25.9.54 (3-2)	Old Kippax
372	Graham Dalal, Bromsgrove, Worcs	Manchester United 23.9.89 (5-1)	Old Kippax
373	Andrew Collis, Sale, Cheshire	Manchester United 9.11.02 (3-1)	Main Stand
374	John Harris, East Goscote, Leicester	Manchester United 9.11.02 (3-1)	New Kippax
375	Dennis William Sissons, Offerton, Cheshire	Manchester United 9.11.02 (3-1)	New Kippax
376	William Harold Sissons, Offerton, Cheshire	Manchester United 9.11.02 (3-1)	New Kippax
377	John & Alice Shepard, Cheadle Hulme	Tottenham Hotspur 9.12.67 (4-1)	Old Kippax
378	Julian Richard N Carter, Cranage, Cheshire	Manchester United 9.11.02 (3-1)	North Stand
379	Ian Coffey, Northwich, Cheshire	Manchester United 9.11.02 (3-1)	Old Kippax
380	Maria Hanway (now Dean), Gosport, Hants	Manchester United 23.9.89 (5-1)	Old Kippax
381	Jean M Thackeray, Droylsden, Manchester	Manchester United 23.9.89 (5-1)	Old Kippax
382	Adrian Barclay, Droylsden, Manchester	Manchester United 9.11.02 (3-1)	Old Kippax
383	Mark Andrew, Whaley Bridge, High Peak	Manchester United 9.11.02 (3-1)	Old Kippax
384	David Connor, Denton, Manchester	Nottingham Forest 2.9.67 (2-0)	Old Kippax
385	Robert Jones, Whalley Range, Manchester	Manchester United 9.11.02 (3-1)	'New' Platt Lane
386	Geoffrey W Rothband, Didsbury, Manchester	Sheffield Wednesday 24.4.37 (4-1)	Old Kippax
387	David M Rothband, St Clement, Jersey	Leicester City FAC 3 28.1.67 (2-1)	Corner Old Platt Lane & Main Stand
388	Nigel J L Rothband, Stanmore, Middlesex	Manchester United 15.11.69 (4-0)	Old Kippax
389	Jim Critchley, Lowton, Warrington	Tottenham Hotspur 9.12.67 (4-1)	Old Kippax
390	Manfred Wojtas, Allerton, Bradford	Manchester United 23.9.89 (5-1)	Old Kippax
391	Christopher Lees, Scarborough, N.Yorks	Queens Park Rangers 14.5.95 (2-3)	Platt Lane
392	Kevin Sutcliffe, Loughborough, Leics	Queens Park Rangers 11.2.78 (2-1)	Platt Lane
393	Jonathan Poole, Valby, Denmark	Charlton Athletic 11.5.85 (5-1)	Old Kippax
394	G Richard Parkinson, Congleton, Cheshire	Sheffield Wednesday 20.10.62 (3-2)	Old Kippax
395	Michael Milne, Southport	Middlesbrough 11.4.77 (1-0) - first match!	Old Kippax
396	Emma Styche, Davenport, Stockport	Manchester United 23.9.89 (5-1)	Platt Lane, Block X, Row 20, Seat 74
397	Gavin Coyle, Dukinfield, Tameside	Derby County 20.4.91 (2-1)	Old Kippax, Windy Corner!
398	Paul Heaps, Dobcross, Saddleworth	Notts County 18.1.95 FAC 3 rep (5-2)	Kippax
399	David Bell, Formby, Lancs	Manchester United 23.9.89 (5-1)	Old Kippax
400	Graham Ward, Congleton, Cheshire	Manchester United 9.11.02 (3-1)	'New' Platt Lane
401	Leonard Ward Glynn, Salterforth, Lancs	Tottenham Hotspur 9.12.67 (4-1)	Main Stand
402	Andrew Cotton, Blackpool	Manchester United 23.9.89 (5-1)	Old Kippax
403	Tony McCardle, Wythenshawe, Manchester	Tottenham Hotspur 9.12.67 (4-1)	Old Kippax
404	Tony Prada, Westgate, Morecambe	Newcastle United 26.12.77 (4-0)	Old Kippax
405	Neil Palamountain, Bare, Morecambe	Manchester United 9.11.02 (3-1)	Old Kippax
406	John Marson, Worcester	Manchester United 9.11.02 (3-1)	Old Kippax, Windy Corner!
407	Neil Collis, Birch Vale, High Peak	Manchester United 9.11.02 (3-1)	Main Stand
408	John, Darren & Matthew Anderson, Co Down	Leeds United 7.11.92 (4-0) & Man Utd 9.11.02	N Block, North Stand
409	Jamie Potter (3 yrs) & dad Stephen, Davyhulme	Aston Villa 26.12.02 (3-1)	My dad's knee
410	Paul Mansfield, Hyde, Cheshire	Manchester United 9.11.02 (3-1)	North Stand
411	Jeremy Hutton, Bury, Lancs	Middlesbrough 21.1.76 FLC s/f 2 (4-0)	Old Kippax
412	Christopher Anthony Taylor, Milnrow, Rochdale	Manchester United 23.9.89 (5-1)	Old Kippax
413	Jeremy Randall, Beckenham, Kent	Manchester United 9.11.02 (3-1)	Main Stand
414	Mark Emmerson, Offerton, Stockport	Middlesbrough 21.1.76 FLC s/f 2 (4-0)	Old Kippax
415	Colin Byrne, Harrogate, N Yorkshire	Newcastle United 26.12.77 (4-0)	Old Kippax
416	Mark Chidgey, West Ewell, Epsom, Surrey	Charlton Athletic 11.5.85 (5-1)	Old Kippax
417	John Pickup, Chadderton, Lancs	Tottenham Hotspur 9.12.67 (4-1)	Old Kippax
418	S D Urmson, Woodhouse Park, Manchester		
419	John A Ingham, Ashton-under-Lyne	West Ham United 13.4.68 (3-0)	Back of Old Kippax
420	Stephen H Locke, Chorlton, Manchester	Manchester United 9.11.02 (3-1)	North Stand
421	Robert Bonar, Compstall, Stockport	Tottenham Hotspur 9.12.67 (4-1)	H Block, Main Stand
422	Paul Chapman, Barnard Castle, Co Durham	Manchester United 9.11.02 (3-1)	Main Stand
423	Stephen Astles, Northwich, Cheshire	Manchester United 6.11.71 (3-3)	Old Kippax
424	Colin Sinnott, New Tupton, Chesterfield	Tottenham Hotspur 9.12.67 (4-1)	Old Kippax
425	Richard Lawson, South Godstone, Surrey	Manchester United 23.9.89 (5-1)	Old Kippax
426	Peter & Lynn Barnard, Heaton Mersey	Manchester United 9.11.02 (3-1)	Main Stand
427	Mark Sandford, Gillingham, Kent	Huddersfield Town 7.11.87 (10-1)	Old Kippax
428	Paul Bradbury, London SE25	Manchester United 23.9.89 (5-1)	Old Kippax
429	Steve Blood, Hollywood, Birmingham	West Ham United 2.10.76 (4-2)	Old Kippax

No	Subscriber name	Memorable Maine Road game/event	Fave part of Maine Road
430	Barry MacLennan, Inverness	Norwich City 13.1.02 (3-1)	North Stand
431	Keith Casson, Uppermill, Oldham	FAC s/f rep March 1946, Derby Co v Birmingham C. (4-0)	Att: 80,407
432	Angus Neely, Wilderspool, Warrington	Huddersfield Town 7.11.87 (10-1)	Old Kippax
433	Richard J Sewell, Brighouse, West Yorks	Middlesbrough 21.1.76 FLC s/f 2 (4-0)	Old Kippax
434	Tony Breslin, Altrincham, Cheshire	Manchester United 23.9.89 (5-1)	Old Kippax
435	Nicholas Fisher, Wakefield	Manchester United 9.11.02 (3-1)	North Stand
436	Peter Drayton, Lidgate, Newmarket	Manchester United 23.9.89 (5-1)	
437	Mark Burton, Bury St Edmunds, Suffolk	West Bromwich Albion 5.9.70 (4-1)	Old Kippax
438	Andy Cooke, Loughbrickland, Co Down	Manchester United 9.11.02 (3-1)	Main Stand
439	David McFarlane, Coleraine, Co Londonderry	Everton 27.8.94 (4-0)	Main Stand
440	David Parr, Lurgan, Co Armagh	Manchester United 23.9.89 (5-1)	North Stand (my first seat)
441	Justin English, Whittlesey, Peterborough	Fulham 16.1.2000 (4-0)	Main Stand
442	Martin G Short, Colne, Lancs	Manchester United 23.9.89 (5-1)	Old Kippax
443	Nigel Tungate, Lichfield, Staffs		
444	Tony Ricketts, Withington, Manchester	Tottenham Hotspur 9.12.67 (4-1)	Main Stand
445	Michael Ricketts, East Didsbury, Manchester	Manchester United 23.9.89 (5-1)	Main Stand
446	Alan Spencer, Twickenham, Middx	Manchester United 9.11.02 (3-1)	Old Kippax
447	Andy Fecitt, Sale, Cheshire	Manchester United 23.9.89 (5-1)	Old Kippax
448	Daniel Crouchman. Sawbridgeworth, Herts	Manchester United 9.11.02 (3-1)	North Stand
449	John Phillips, Flixton, Urmston	Manchester United 23.9.89 (5-1)	Old Kippax
450	Gary Hankinson, Howley, Warrington	Charlton Athletic 11.5.85 (5-1)	Old Kippax
451	Donald Ireland, Sydney, Australia	Tottenham Hotspur 9.12.67 (4-1)	N67, H Block
452	Gillian Cooke, Culcheth, Warrington	Wolverhampton Wanderers 29.1.72 (5-2)	Main Stand
453	Happy 40th Birthday! Nick Mason, Witney, Oxon	Manchester United 9.11.02 (3-1)	North Stand
454	Sgt Karl Auger, BFPO 31	Wigan Athletic 17.5.99, P/off leg 2 (1-0)	Old Kippax
455	John W Hoyland, Redditch, Worcs	Manchester United 9.11.02 (3-1)	Main Stand
456	Happy 50th Birthday to Ken Nuttall of Bacup	Blackburn Rovers 7.5.2000 (4-1)	North Stand
457	Allen P Blakeley, Ladybridge, Bolton	Schalke 04, 15.4.70 ECWC s/f leg 2 (5-1)	Old Kippax
458	Karen Skeen, Stockton on Tees	Manchester United 23.9.89 (5-1)	Old Kippax - unsheltered
459	Keith Sargeant, Northwich, Cheshire	Manchester United 23.9.89 (5-1)	Old Kippax - unsheltered
460	Louise Deeks, Appleton, Warrington	Charlton Athletic 11.5.85 (5-1)	Main Stand
461	Mark Griffiths, Levenshulme, Manchester	Manchester United 9.11.02 (3-1)	Old Kippax
462	Andrew Leach, Letchworth, Herts	Charlton Athletic 11.5.85 (5-1)	Old Kippax
463	Peter Ellis, Bradshaw, Bolton	Tottenham Hotspur 9.12.67 (4-1)	Old Kippax
464	Bill & Mike Astbury, Winsford, Cheshire	Tottenham Hotspur 9.12.67 (4-1)	Platt Lane
465	Neil Glover, Sawtry, Huntingdon	Manchester United 23.9.89 (5-1)	Old Kippax
466	Paul Shepherd, Baswich, Stafford	Manchester United 9.11.02 (3-1)	Gene Kelly, 'Singin' in the Rain' Stand
467	Glyn & Abigail Cooke, Holmfirth, W Yorks	Manchester United 9.11.02 (3-1)	Old Kippax
468	Helen C Thowfeek, Sale, Cheshire	Manchester United 9.11.02 (3-1)	New Kippax
469	Carl S Frier, Chorlton, Manchester	Chelsea 18.3.89 (2-3)	Old Kippax
470	Ian Donnelly, Swinton, Manchester	Manchester United 23.9.89 (5-1)	Old Platt Lane
471	John Burfield, North Cheam, Sutton, Surrey	Wigan Athletic 17.5.99, P/off leg 2 (1-0)	Old Kippax
472	Ron Sharrock, Heywood, Lancs	Tottenham Hotspur 9.12.67 (4-1)	Old Kippax
473	Shaun David Read, Ebberston, Scarborough	Charlton Athletic 11.5.85 (5-1)	Old Kippax
474	Steven & Carl McCarthy, Oldham	Manchester United 23.9.89 (5-1)	New Kippax
475	Matthew Calloway, Markyate, St Albans	Manchester United 9.11.02 (3-1)	Old Kippax
476	Alan Cruse, Clapham, Bedford	Manchester United 9.11.02 (3-1)	Old Kippax
477	Stephen Spurgeon, Taverham, Norwich	Huddersfield Town 7.11.87 (10-1)	Main Stand
478	Richard Crabtree, Penwortham, Preston	Manchester United 23.9.89 (5-1)	Old Kippax
479	Russell Brewer, Malvern, Worcs	Portsmouth 21.4.02 (3-1)	Old Kippax
480	Peter Eadon, Whittle-le-Woods, Chorley	Manchester United 9.11.02 (3-1)	North Stand
481	Colin Taylor, Newton-le-Willows	Manchester United 9.11.02 (3-1)	Platt Lane End
482	Tony Crook, Chadderton, Oldham	Manchester United 6.11.71 (3-3)	New Kippax, Upper Tier
483	Peter, Joseph & James Garside, Stalybridge	Manchester United 9.11.02 (3-1)	Old Kippax
484	Peter Roberts, Greenfield, Oldham	Manchester United 23.9.89 (5-1)	Old Platt Lane
485	Anthony Southern, Abbey Hey, Gorton	Fulham 16.1.99 (3-0)	North Stand
486	John Renshaw, Partington, Manchester	Tottenham Hotspur 9.12.67 (4-1)	Old Kippax
487	Barry Heap, Sharston, Wythenshawe	Manchester Utd (5-1), Barnsley (5-1), Portsmouth (3-1)	Old Kippax
488	Christian Reddiough, Keighley, W Yorks	Norwich City 24.1.81 (6-0) - my City debut!	Main Stand
489	Stephen Elam, Cheadle Hulme, Cheshire	Manchester United 9.11.02 (3-1)	Old Kippax
490	Kieran Ray, Whalley Range, Manchester	Manchester United 9.11.02 (3-1)	Family Stand
491	Simon Callaghan, Allostock, Knutsford	Manchester United 9.11.02 (3-1)	Old Kippax
492	Samuel Andrew Shooter, Weymouth, Dorset	Manchester United 23.9.89 (5-1)	Old Kippax
493	Ken Sykes, Wellingborough, Northants	Charlton Athletic 11.5.85 (5-1)	Old Kippax
494	Ian Penney, Hazel Grove, Stockport	Schalke 04, 15.4.70 ECWC s/f leg 2 (5-1)	Main Stand
495	Mark Vincent Dolan, Frodsham, Cheshire	Everton FAC 6 rep 11.3.81 (3-1)	Old Kippax
496	Andrew J Wright, Stamford Bridge, E Yorks	Manchester United 5.03.83 (1-2)	Old Kippax
497	Kenneth Frank Wright, Wilberfoss, E Yorks		
498	Simon Plevin, Stalybridge	Manchester United 9.11.02 (3-1)	Main Stand
499	Mark Smith, Stalybridge	Manchester United 9.11.02 (3-1)	Main Stand
500	Margaret Nussey, Denton, Manchester	Manchester United 9.11.02 (3-1)	Old Kippax
501	Mark Shore, Sale, Cheshire		Old Kippax
502	Martyn Jackson, North Hykeham, Lincoln	Manchester United 9.11.02 (3-1)	Old Kippax
503	Keith Shuttleworth, Hazel Grove, Stockport	Manchester United (a) 12.4.72 (City won 3-1)	Old Kippax
504	Ian Shuttleworth, Edgeley, Stockport	Manchester United 9.11.02 (3-1)	New Kippax
505	Jeff Cohen, Nottingham	Tottenham Hotspur 9.12.67 (4-1)	
506	Jeff Cohen, Nottingham	International XI 15.4.64 - Bert Trautmann's Testimonial (5-4)	
507	David Kennerley, Mere, Cheshire	Manchester United 23.9.89 (5-1)	New Kippax - Upper
508	Glyn Williams, Appleton, Warrington	Manchester United 23.9.89 (5-1)	North Stand
509	Maxwell McLean, Shipley, Bradford	Manchester United 9.11.02 (3-1)	Old Kippax
510	Richard Peter Billinge, Edgeley, Stockport	Charlton Athletic 11.5.85 (5-1)	Old Kippax
511	Christopher Edwards, Levenshulme, Manchester	Tottenham Hotspur 22.10.94 (5-2)	Old Kippax
512	Neil King, Offerton, Stockport	Manchester United 23.9.89 (5-1)	Old Kippax
513	David Brooks, Wokingham, Berkshire	Wigan Athletic 17.5.99, P/off leg 2 (1-0)	New Kippax
514	Roger Brooks, Wokingham, Berkshire	Manchester United 12.11.75 FL Cup Rd 4 (4-0)	Old Kippax
515	Anthony Rimmer, Bury, Lancs	Charlton Athletic 11.5.85 (5-1)	New Kippax - GG Lower
516	Noel McPhillips, Sale, Cheshire	Manchester United 9.11.02 (3-1)	Old Kippax

No	Subscriber name	Memorable Maine Road game/event	Fave part of Maine Road
517	Kevin Esplin, Heydon, Royston, Herts	Blackburn Rovers 7.5.2000 (4-1)	Old Scoreboard End
518	Simon Harrop, Cheadle Hulme, Cheshire	Manchester United 23.9.89 (5-1)	Old Kippax
519	Nick Stickler, Harrogate	Leeds United 11.1.03 (2-1)	North Stand
520	Lisa Pimlott, Dukinfield, Cheshire	Manchester United 9.11.02 (3-1)	Main Stand
521	Philip Neale, Eccleshill, Bradford	Leeds United 30.1.71 (0-2)	Main Stand
522	Rachel Hicklin, Didsbury, Manchester	Manchester United 23.9.89 (5-1)	Old Kippax
523	Martin Parrin, Wisbech St Mary, Cambs	Manchester United 9.11.02 (3-1)	North Stand
524	Matthew Joseph Coyne, Blackley, Manchester	Wigan Athletic 17.5.99, P/off leg 2 (1-0)	Old Kippax, now Nth Stand
525	Simon Howard, Newquay, Cornwall	Norwich City 13.1.02 (3-1)	North Stand
526	Peter Leckenby, Whitefield, Manchester	Tottenham Hotspur 3.3.62 (6-2)	Old Kippax
527	Roderick Hall, Denton, Manchester	Manchester United 23.9.89 (5-1)	Old Kippax
528	Paul Hesten, St Helier, Jersey	Manchester United 9.11.02 (3-1)	Old Kippax
529	Philip J S Lockett, London N6	Tottenham Hotspur 16.9.72 (2-1)	Platt Lane
530	Steve Casson, Chorltonville, Manchester	Tottenham Hotspur 9.12.67 (4-1)	Old Kippax
531	Phil Gallier, Admaston, Telford	Liverpool 21.8.91 (2-1)	Old Kippax
532	Michael John Wild, Marple, Stockport	Tottenham Hotspur 9.12.67 (4-1)	Old Kippax
533	W R Jung, Hutton Rudby, Yarm	Barnsley, 6.4.02 (5-1)	Old Platt Lane - standing
534	Jack Blenkharn, Sale, Cheshire	Blackburn Rovers 15.9.02 (2-2)	North Stand
535	Chris Rogers, Brighton	Ipswich Town 1.4.78 (2-1)	Kippax
536	Pat Kenny, Weston, Limerick	Manchester United 23.9.89 (5-1)	Old Kippax
537	Marc Hampshire, New Mills, High Peak	Manchester United 23.9.89 (5-1)	Old Kippax
538	John Bogg (now Cooper), Hastings, E Sussex		
539	Stephen Bull, Tytherington, Macclesfield	Newcastle United 26.12.77 (4-0)	Main Stand
540	Mark Foster, Sale, Cheshire	Manchester United 23.9.89 (5-1)	New Kippax - Lower Tier
541	Richard Moullin, Les Petite Nouettes, Guernsey	Manchester United 9.11.02 (3-1)	Main Stand
542	Steve Bunker, Bury, Lancs	Manchester United 23.9.89 (5-1)	Main Stand
543	Jamie Plevin, Stalybridge, Cheshire	Manchester United 9.11.02 (3-1)	Main Stand
544	Paulette Kersh, Lymm, Cheshire	Gillingham Play-off Final @ Wembley 30.5.99 (3-2)	Old Kippax
545	Philip Graham, Telford, Shropshire	Manchester United 15.11.69 (4-0)	Old Kippax
546	Richard Mullen, Ellon, Aberdeenshire	Manchester United 9.11.02 (3-1)	New Kippax
547	Richard Donlan, Hazel Grove, Stockport	Charlton Athletic 11.5.85 (5-1)	Old Kippax
548	Steve Jackson, Chadderton, Oldham	Huddersfield Town 7.11.87 (10-1)	Old Kippax
549	Daevid Warren, Alresford, Hampshire	Manchester United 9.11.02 (3-1)	New Kippax
550	Dr. Chris Davies, Hale, Altrincham	Manchester United 9.11.02 (3-1)	North Stand
551	Gordon Hollingsworth, Blackley, Manchester	Liverpool 18.2.56 FAC 5 (0-0)	Old Kippax
552	Sean Gibson, Moulton, Northwich, Cheshire	Tottenham Hotspur 22.10.94 (5-2)	Old Kippax
553	Paul Stanton, New Mills, High Peak	Manchester United 9.11.02 (3-1)	New Kippax
554	Bob Gregg, South Reddish, Stockport	Manchester United 23.9.89 (5-1)	Old Kippax
555	Mark Goodison, Bradford	Bradford City 16.12.01 (3-1)	North Stand
556	Paul Richardson, Poynton, Stockport	Huddersfield Town 9.11.02 (3-1)	Kippax CCU/R42/S77
557	Michael Richardson, Poynton, Stockport	Manchester United 9.11.02 (3-1)	Kippax CCU/R42/S78
558	Katherine Richardson, Poynton, Stockport	Manchester United 9.11.02 (3-1)	Kippax CCU/R42/S79
559	Ashley Norman Reece, Swinton, Manchester	Manchester United 9.11.02 (3-1)	New Kippax
560	Stephen Cruise, Sale Moor, Cheshire	Tottenham Hotspur 9.12.67 (4-1)	Main Stand
561	Andrew Mark Butler, Bramhall, Stockport	Manchester United 23.9.89 (5-1)	Old Kippax
562	Will Linsdell, Croydon, Surrey	Charlton Athletic 11.5.85 (5-1)	Old Kippax
563	Kenneth Edwards, Northwich, Cheshire	West Bromwich Albion 1.2.58 (4-1)	Top corner, Nth Stand & Kippax
564	Rob, Tony, Hannah, William & Daniel Rotheram	Manchester United 23.9.89 (5-1)	Old Kippax
565	Vincent Andrew Costello, Reddish, Stockport	Manchester United 9.11.02 (3-1)	Main Stand
566	Graham Leese, Hazel Grove, Stockport		Kippax
567	Arthur Campbell, Clydebank, Glasgow	Newcastle United 26.12.77 (4-0)	Old Kippax
568	Steve Chivers, Barnes, London	Charlton Athletic 11.5.85 (5-1)	Main Stand
569	Marc Riley, Sale, Cheshire	Manchester United 9.11.02 (3-1)	Kippax
570	Kevin Dillon, Withington, Manchester	Manchester United 23.9.89 (5-1)	North Stand
571	Brian Southworth, Timperley, Cheshire	Newcastle United 26.12.77 (4-0)	Old Kippax
572	Bob Fidler, Bramhall, Stockport	Manchester United 9.11.02 (3-1)	Main Stand
573	Brian Lowndes, Irlam, Manchester	Schalke 04, 15.4.70 ECWC s/f leg 2 (5-1)	Old Kippax
574	Peter O'Grady, Heaton Moor	Tottenham Hotspur 9.12.67 (4-1)	Old Kippax
575	Martin Reid, Bolton	Wigan Athletic 17.5.99, P/off leg 2 (1-0)	New Kippax
576	Anne O'Grady, Astley, Manchester	Manchester United 9.11.02 (3-1)	Old Kippax
577	Mark Leigh, Mayford, Surrey	Chelsea 30.4.94 (2-2)	Old Kippax
578	Richard Plumb, Marcham, Oxon	Manchester United 9.11.02 (3-1)	Kippax
579	Paul Bridgman, Up Hatherley, Cheltenham	Watford, 11.8.2001 (3-0)	New Kippax
580	G J Moores, Hyde, Cheshire	Manchester United 15.11.69 (4-0)	Old Scoreboard End
581	David Knight, Parkside, Hereford	Sunderland 11.5.91 (3-2)	Main Stand
582	Ian Parkinson, Altrincham	Schalke 04, 15.4.70 ECWC s/f leg 2 (5-1)	Old Platt Lane
583	George Kittos, Haslingden, Lancs	Newcastle United 26.12.77 (4-0)	Old Kippax
584	Kozo Matsuzawa, Preston	Norwich City 13.1.02 (3-1)	New Kippax
585	Luca & Bruno Ewings, Sale, Cheshire	Manchester United 23.9.89 (5-1)	Old Kippax
586	A S Potts, Wilmslow, Cheshire	Manchester United 9.11.02 (3-1)	Old Kippax
587	Alan Jones, Worsley, Manchester	Manchester United 9.11.02 (3-1)	Old Kippax
588	Bob Storie, Cowdenbeath	West Bromwich Albion Charity Shield 9.8.69 (6-1)	Old Kippax
589	Angela Wrench, Moorside, Oldham	Manchester United 23.9.89 (5-1)	Old Kippax
590	Stephen Foster, St Helens	Portsmouth 21.4.02 (3-1)	North Stand
591	Paul Francis Hodge, Lowton, Cheshire	Manchester United 23.9.89 (5-1)	Old Kippax
592	Mark Squire, Stoke Mandeville, Bucks	Manchester United 9.11.02 (3-1)	New Kippax
593	John Hazleton, Ruislip Manor, Middlesex	Manchester United 15.11.69 (4-0)	Old Kippax
594	David McNeil, Skellingthorpe (ex-Wythenshawe)	Manchester United 9.11.02 (3-1)	Scoreboard End
595	Phil Rutter, Frodsham, Cheshire	Portsmouth 21.4.02 (3-1)	North Stand
596	Ron Smith, Congleton, Cheshire	Huddersfield Town 7.11.87 (10-1)	North Stand
597	Michael Smith, London SE1	Chelsea 26.11.77 (6-2)	Old Kippax
598	Dave Smith, Slains, Ellon, Aberdeenshire	Newcastle United 26.12.77 (4-0)	Old Kippax
599	Stephen Alan Hilton, Davyhulme, Manchester	Charlton Athletic 11.5.85 (5-1)	Old Platt Lane
600	Steve 'Jonah' Jones, Withington, Manchester	Manchester Utd 23.9.89 (5-1)	Main Stand
601	Adam Mumford, Witney, Oxon	Stoke City 28.12.98 (2-1)	Old Kippax
602	Paul Millward, Didsbury, Manchester	Tottenham Hotspur 9.12.67 (4-1)	Old Kippax
603	Neil Wain, Romiley, Stockport	Tottenham Hotspur 9.12.67 (4-1)	Old Kippax
604	Gareth Humphreys, Tremadog, Porthmadog	Manchester United 9.11.02 (3-1)	North Stand

Maine Memory

Holidays and match days spent on Wansford Street

■ Leaving Maine Road is the final closing of the door on the first half of my life. My dad is a Moss Side lad born and bred. The reason for his lifelong devotion to City is immediately clear when you ask him his birthplace. He entered the world in the front bedroom of a house on Wansford Street, one of the many rows of terraced streets that wedge between Maine Road and Lloyd Street. If you were to look out of that same bedroom window to your left you would immediately see City's Ticket Office. Behind it the North Stand disappears on one side and the brown brick of the Main Stand sits on the other with the forecourt dividing the club from the street. Dad's mother, my grandmother, was a proudly independent woman, her resolve strengthened over the years as she single-handedly brought up my dad. My grandad was killed in the war when Dad was just a few months old.

Maine Road became my dad's playground. He grew up playing football on the vast forecourt outside the Main Stand, clocking the players arriving and leaving for training. As per many youngsters of this era, my dad can lay claim to have played in a jumpers-for-goalposts match alongside Bert Trautmann who would gladly participate with the scraggy kids in their all-day matches. Some things don't change though. When my dad wanted to obtain autographs of the players the best place to catch the team at their most amenable was outside the Parkside pub, just down the road from the ground. Naturally my dad progressed from sneaking into the ground at three-quarter time to becoming a regular attendee.

Eventually Dad met my mum and got married, and a job offer took him reluctantly away from Manchester to live and work in Huntingdon, which is where my sister and I were born. Much to my future embarrassment, as it has been the cause of much mickey-taking off my mates, I can't claim to be a born and bred Mancunian. I think I should also tell you that I usually retort with "I was conceived in Manchester" but that is a lie. I started the first three years of my life, 1968-1971, living in exile, if it's possible to commence your life as an exile. Both Mum and Dad were unhappy living down south though, despite the perks my dad had earned as a result of migrating. Through perfect comic timing Dad ensured that one of only two breaks he has ever had away from Maine Road (he had to work for a couple of years on Saturdays, therefore missing City 5 United 1) coincided with City's greatest-ever period of success. Getting to games became almost impossible, though he does tell a good story about going to the League Cup Final of 1970. My dad knew if the game went to extra-time he would miss the last train back to Huntingdon and faced the dilemma of either leaving early or staying to see the outcome. Sure enough the game went to extra time, and Dad had a monumental journey back to Huntingdon. Mum was suffering. When she was pregnant with me she had a craving for Vimto which, back in the late sixties, was still very much a northern preserve not seen in southern grocery stores. Along with other necessities missed

MANCHESTER CITY FOOTBALL CLUB

NOTICE TO MATCH OFFICIALS

PLEASE NOTE THE EMERGENCY PROCEDURES THAT WE ADOPT IN THE STADIUM ARE AS FOLLOWS:

IN CASE OF FIRE OR THE FIRE ALARM SYSTEM BEING ACTIVATED.
A TWO-TONE CHIME WILL BE ACTIVATED FOLLOWED BY A CODED MESSAGE, "STAFF ANNOUNCEMENT, MR. BANKS IS IN ......OF THE......STAND."

MATCH OFFICIALS DO NOT NEED TO TAKE ANY ACTION AT THIS STAGE

WHEN THE EMERGENCY IS OVER THE FOLLOWING CODED MESSAGE WILL BE BROADCAST;

"STAFF ANNOUNCEMENT, MR BANKS HAS NOW LEFT THE GROUND"

IN THE EVENT OF A BOMB ALERT
THE BLUE FLASHING LIGHT WHICH IS DIRECTLY ABOVE THE PLAYERS TUNNEL WILL BE ACTIVATED.

MATCH OFFICIALS DO NOT NEED TO TAKE ANY ACTION AT THIS STAGE.

IN THE UNLIKELY EVENT OF AN EVACUATION, THE FOLLOWING PROCEDURE WILL APPLY;

A POLICE OFFICER OR SENIOR STEWARD SITUATED IN THE PLAYERS TUNNEL AREA WILL:

1. NOTIFY THE FOURTH OFFICIAL THAT AN EVACUATION IS IMMINENT

2. ENSURE THAT THE FOURTH OFFICIAL ATTRACTS THE ATTENTION OF THE REFEREE IMMEDIATLEY

3. INFORM THE REFEREE OF THE EVACUATION.

THE REFEREE MUST ENSURE THAT HIS OFFICIALS AND THE PLAYERS LEAVE THE PITCH AS QUICKLY AS POSSIBLE AS DIRECTED BY THE POLICE OFFICER/SENIOR STEWARD.

A STEWARD WILL BE ASSIGNED TO REMAIN WITH THE OFFICIALS UNTIL THE EVACUATION IS COMPLETE AND TO KEEP THEM APPRAISED OF THE SITUATION.

PETER FLETCHER
STADIUM AND SAFETY MANAGER

No	Subscriber name	Memorable Maine Road game/event	Fave part of Maine Road
605	Gerard Townley, Ajax, Ontario, Canada	Newport County 14.6.47 (5-1)	Platt Lane
606	John Clancy, Charlton Kings, Cheltenham	Tottenham Hotspur 22.10.94 (5-2)	Main Stand, by the tunnel
607	Dion Mulvey, Partington, Manchester	Manchester United 9.11.02 (3-1)	North Stand
608	John A Oldham, Bramhall, Cheshire	Manchester United 9.11.02 (3-1)	Kippax
609	Keith Wade, Tudhoe Village, Spennymoor	Manchester United 9.11.02 (3-1)	Old Kippax
610	Alastair Monks, Chorltonville, Manchester	Manchester United 9.11.02 (3-1)	Family Stand
611	Thomas Smith, Elton, Bury	Stoke City 3.3.34 FAC Rd 6 (1-0)	Platt Lane
612	Paul Glover, Lisburn, Northern Ireland		
613	Ken Tudor, Furness Vale, High Peak	Schalke 04, 15.4.70 ECWC s/f leg 2 (5-1)	Old & New Kippax
614	In Memory of Stuart Burrows		
615	Emma Louise Faraday, East Dulwich, London	Manchester United 9.11.02 (3-1)	Upper Tier, New Kippax
616	Mark Lacy, Offerton, Stockport	Manchester United 23.9.89 (5-1)	Old Kippax
617	Karen Gillespie, Heaton Norris, Stockport	Manchester United 23.9.89 (5-1)	Platt Lane
618	Frode Knapstad, Flaktveit, Norway	Manchester United 9.11.02 (3-1)	New Kippax
619	Gavin Lee Wells, Little Lever, Bolton	Gillingham Play-off Final @ Wembley 30.5.99 (3-2)	Old Kippax
620	Rodger Howarth, Norden, Rochdale	Manchester United 12.11.75 FL Cup Rd 4 (4-0)	North Stand
	In memory of Joseph Howarth	Newcastle United 26.12.77 (4-0)	Claremont Road End
621	David Dalton-Leggett, Mudford Sock, Yeovil	Tottenham Hotspur 9.12.67 (4-1)	
622	Keith Platts, Heaton, Moor, Stockport	Tottenham Hotspur 9.12.67 (4-1)	Old Platt Lane
623	Chris O'Donnell, Chorlton, Manchester	Middlesbrough 21.1.76 FLC s/f 2 (4-0)	Old Kippax - windy corner
624	Tim Dunphy, East Horsley, Surrey	Wigan Athletic 17.5.99, P/off leg 2 (1-0)	Old Kippax
625	Peter Chappell, Urmston, Manchester	Schalke 04, 15.4.70 ECWC s/f leg 2 (5-1)	Main Stand, H Block Centre
626	Steve Crooks, Sandy, Bedfordshire	Manchester United 12.11.75 FL Cup Rd 4 (4-0)	Old Kippax
627	Paul Sproston, Leftwich, Northwich	Manchester United 23.9.89 (5-1)	Old Kippax
628	Lee Gordon, Orford, Warrington	Manchester United 23.9.89 (5-1)	Old Kippax
629	Kevin Cannon, Middleton, Manchester	Schalke 04, 15.4.70 ECWC s/f leg 2 (5-1)	Main Stand
630	David Aston, Newell Green, Wythenshawe	Manchester United 9.11.02 (3-1)	North Stand
631	Darren Chiappori, Lepton, Huddersfield	Manchester United 23.9.89 (5-1)	Old Platt Lane
632	Julian Hardiman, Musbury, Devon	Southampton 16.3.96 (2-1)	Main Stand, H Block
633	Kevin Webb, Eton Wick, Windsor	Charlton Athletic 11.5.85 (5-1)	Main Stand
634	Andrew McConnell, Offerton, Stockport	Middlesbrough 21.1.76 FLC s/f 2 (4-0)	Old Kippax
635	Malcolm Seatree, Timperley, Altrincham	Charlton Athletic 11.5.85 (5-1)	Old Kippax
636	Christopher John Owen, Crewe	Manchester United 9.11.02 (3-1)	Kippax
637	Sidney Blain, Hollins, Bury	All games!	Old Scoreboard End
638	Mark Barratt, Bristol	Manchester United 9.11.02 (3-1)	New Platt Lane
639	Mark Worthington, Hyde, Cheshire	Manchester United 23.9.89 (5-1)	Old Kippax
640	Trevor Jones, Chorlton, Manchester	Leyton Orient 26.8.64 (6-0)	Kippax
641	Shaun Horan, Bury	Manchester United 9.11.02 (3-1)	Old Kippax
642	Yvette Cregan, Bollington, Cheshire	Manchester United 9.11.02 (3-1)	North Stand
643	Yvette Cregan, Bollington, Cheshire		
644	Yvette Cregan, Bollington, Cheshire		
645	Nigel Gregory, Macclesfield, Cheshire	Watford, 11.8.2001 (3-0)	Old Kippax Terrace
646	Ralph Thompson, Kenilworth, Warwickshire	Manchester United 23.9.89 (5-1)	Old Kippax
647	Mark Lunn, Belfast	Charlton Athletic 11.5.85 (5-1)	Old Kippax
648	Brian Cunliffe, Withington,. Manchester	Wolverhampton Wanderers Reserves 8.4.69 (3-1)	Old Platt Lane
649	Christopher Wellens, Middleton, Manchester	Manchester United 23.9.89 (5-1)	New Kippax
650	Martin Conlon, Timperley, Cheshire	Any time we beat Manchester United!	Old Kippax
651	Alan Schofield, Droylsden, Manchester	Manchester United 9.11.02 (3-1)	Old Kippax
652	Colin Binder, Middleton, Manchester	Manchester United 9.11.02 (3-1)	Old Kippax
653	John A Hooper, Lymm, Cheshire	Manchester United 9.11.02 (3-1)	North Stand
654	Mike Taylor, Bishops Stortford, Herts	Manchester United 23.9.89 (5-1)	Old Kippax
655	Hugh Sharrard, Thame, Oxfordshire	Manchester United 23.9.89 (5-1)	Old Kippax
656	Peter Barnett, Ellesmere Port	Manchester United 9.11.02 (3-1)	Main Stand
657	Ian M Barnett, Clayton-le-Woods	Manchester United 9.11.02 (3-1)	Main Stand
658	Steven D Barnett, Ellesmere Port	Manchester United 9.11.02 (3-1)	Main Stand
659	Lee Armitage, South Reddish, Stockport	Manchester United 9.11.02 (3-1)	North Stand
660	Mark Donlan, Ashton-in-Makerfield, Wigan	Manchester United 9.11.02 (3-1)	Platt Lane
661	Louise Williams, Wigan	Manchester United 9.11.02 (3-1)	Platt Lane
662	James Donlan, Wigan	Manchester United 9.11.02 (3-1)	Platt Lane
663	Lee James Wellens, Middleton, Manchester	Manchester United 9.11.02 (3-1)	New Kippax
664	Gordon Spotten, Stretford, Manchester	Charlton Athletic 11.5.85 (5-1)	Old Kippax - Windy Corner
665	Ian Philip Skitt, Leigh, Lancs	Ipswich Town 2.12.72 (1-1)	Old Kippax
		(Colin Bell threw a signed football into the crowd & Ian caught it!)	
666	Roy Skitt, Atherton, Manchester	Gillingham Play-off Final @ Wembley 30.5.99 (3-2)	North Stand
667	David Bennett, Little Hulton, Manchester	Derby County 20.4.91 (2-1)	North Stand
668	Colin James, Wilmslow, Cheshire	Newcastle United 24.08.02 (1-0)	Kippax
669	Nigel Capes, Reddish, Stockport	Newcastle United 26.12.77 (4-0)	Old Scoreboard End
670	Graham Johnson, Guisborough, N Yorks	Leicester City 29.4.59 (3-1)	Old Kippax
671	Chris Keogh, Birchgrove, Swansea	Charlton Athletic 11.5.85 (5-1)	Main Stand
672	Neil Morgan, Handforth, Cheshire	Coventry City 16.1.74, FL Cup 5 rep (4-2)	Old Kippax
673	George Bernard Maltby, Heald Green, Cheadle	Bert Trautmann Testimonial 15.4.64 (5-4)	North Stand
674	Joshua Clegg, Failsworth, Manchester	Manchester United 9.11.02 (3-1)	North Stand
675	Kevin Hancock, Buxworth, High Peak	Manchester United 23.9.89 (5-1)	Old Kippax
676	Duncan Baines, Blackpool	Charlton Athletic 11.5.85 (5-1)	Old Kippax
677	Jeremy Barber, Fleet, Hampshire	Manchester United 9.11.02 (3-1)	New Kippax
678	Graham S Bohanna, Moston, Manchester	Manchester United 9.11.02 (3-1)	North Stand
679	Graeme Stuart, Morecambe, Lancs	Manchester United 23.9.89 (5-1)	Old Kippax
680	Mike Watkins, Macclesfield, Cheshire	Southampton 16.3.96 (2-1) - Kinkladze's solo goal	Old Kippax
681	Andrew Jepson, New Mills, High Peak	City Yth v Man U Yth 1.5.95 Lancs FAYC s/f (2-0)	Old Kippax
682	Raymond Jolly, Ashton-under-Lyne	Manchester United 23.9.89 (5-1)	Main Stand 'A'
683	Carl Heald, Blackley, Manchester	Manchester United 23.9.89 (5-1)	Old Kippax
684	Owen Dyce, Moston, Manchester	Manchester United 23.9.89 (5-1)	Old Kippax
685	Phil Platt, Mottram, Hyde	Manchester United 6.11.71 (3-3)	Old Kippax
686	David Alldred, Chorlton, Manchester	Charlton Athletic 11.5.85 (5-1)	North Stand
687	Des Owens, Kersal Vale, Salford	Huddersfield Town 7.11.87 (10-1)	Old Platt Lane
688	Paul Ellison, Ormskirk, Lancs	Manchester United 9.11.02 (3-1)	Old Kippax
689	Darren Arnold, Radcliffe, Manchester	Manchester United 23.9.89 (5-1)	North Stand
690	Paul Healey, Leigh, Lancs	Manchester United 23.9.89 (5-1)	Old Kippax

No	Subscriber name	Memorable Maine Road game/event	Fave part of Maine Road
691	Nick Gledhill, Meltham, Holmfirth, Yorks	Charlton Athletic 11.5.85 (5-1)	Old Kippax
692	Yvonne Ardern, Davenport, Stockport	Manchester United 9.11.02 (3-1)	Lower Kippax
693	Stewart MacKinnon, Marple, Cheshire	Manchester United 23.9.89 (5-1)	New Kippax
694	Inez McKee, Burnage, Manchester	Sheffield United 25.8.54 (5-2)	New Kippax
695	Gary Davies, Heaton Norris, Stockport	Newcastle United 26.12.77 (4-0)	Kippax
696	Edward Burke, Cheadle Hulme, Cheshire	Tottenham Hotspur 9.12.67 (4-1)	Old Scoreboard End
697	Geoff Thomas, Davenham, Northwich	Tottenham Hotspur 9.12.67 (4-1)	Old Kippax
698	Richard John Swallow, Thirsk, N Yorks	Chelsea 18.3.89 (2-3)	Old Kippax
699	Peter Pheasey, Chapel-en-le-Frith	Manchester United 9.11.02 (3-1)	New Platt Lane
700	Lee & Sarah Redford, Houndstone, Yeovil	Everton 9.12.2000 (5-0)	North Stand
701	Andrew Grundy, Bamford, Rochdale	Charlton Athletic 11.5.85 (5-1)	Old Platt Lane
702	Gordon Maher, Northern Moor, Manchester	Manchester United 9.11.02 (3-1)	Old Kippax
703	Robert Gillespie, Prestwich, Manchester	Manchester United 23.9.89 (5-1)	Old Kippax
704	Dave Chantler, Davyhulme, Manchester	Manchester United 23.9.89 (5-1)	Old & New Kippax
705	Kevin Gorton, Urmston, Manchester	Manchester United 23.9.89 (5-1)	Old Kippax
706	David Hamer, Woolston, Warrington	Manchester United 23.9.89 (5-1)	Old Kippax
707	Jonathan O'Rourke, Oswaldtwistle, Lancs	AC Milan 6.12.78 UEFAC Rd 3, leg 2 (3-0)	Old Kippax
708	Bill Dawson, Stalybridge, Cheshire	Everton 29.4.68 (2-0)	Main Stand
709	Jonathan & Joanne Davis, Edgeley, Stockport	Manchester United 23.9.89 (5-1)	Old Kippax
710	Jonathan Selcoe, Poulton Le Fylde	Leicester City FAC Final 26.3.69 (1-0)	Main Stand, Block C
711	Peter Flanagan, Cheadle, Cheshire	Manchester United 23.9.89 (5-1)	Old Kippax
712	Gerald Flanagan, Ashtead, Surrey	Aston Villa 25.4.59 (0-0)	Old Kippax
713	Brendan Flanagan, Toronto, Canada	SK Lierse 26.11.69 ECWC Rd 2, leg 2 (5-0)	Old Kippax
714	Tom McMullen, Solihull, W Midlands	Manchester United 9.11.02 (3-1)	New Platt Lane
715	Tim McCormick, Droylsden, Manchester	Tottenham Hotspur 9.12.67 (4-1)	Old Kippax
716	D L Worthing, Marple, Cheshire	Manchester United 29.1.55 FAC 4 (2-0)	Old Scoreboard End
717	John Pearson, Redwood City, California		
718	Nigel Cadman, Daventry, Northants	Manchester United 23.9.89 (5-1)	Old Kippax
719	Charlie Cadman, Daventry, Northants		
720	Denis Le Clere, Crewe	Manchester United 9.11.02 (3-1)	Main Stand
721	Mrs R Evans, Heald Green, Cheadle	Portsmouth 21.4.02 (3-1)	North Stand
722	Maldwyn Jones, Talwrn, Llangefni, Anglesey	Portsmouth 21.4.02 (3-1)	Old Kippax
723	Andrew Showman, Cheadle, Cheshire	Birmingham City 28.4.2000 (1-0)	North Stand
724	Christopher O'Boyle, Withington, Manchester	Southampton 25.9.71 (3-0)	Old Kippax
725	Kevin Penny, St Brelade, Jersey	Manchester United 3.12.69 FLC s/f leg 1 (2-1)	Old Kippax
726	Kevin Penny, St Brelade, Jersey		
727	Noel Halliday, Openshaw, Manchester	Manchester United 18.11.72 (3-0)	Old Kippax
728	Leon Halliday, Openshaw, Manchester	Manchester United 9.11.02 (3-1)	New Kippax
729	Carl Brookes, Brighton	Manchester United 23.9.89 (5-1)	Old Kippax
730	John Cornelly, Warrington	Ipswich Town FAC s/f 11.4.81 (1-0)	Old Kippax
731	David Leach, Bramhall, Stockport	Manchester United 23.9.89 (5-1)	North Stand, Block N
732	Ian Leach, Bramhall, Stockport	Manchester United 23.9.89 (5-1)	North Stand, Block N
733	Adrian Wilson, Woodhouse Park, Manchester	Newcastle United 26.12.77 (4-0)	Old Kippax
734	Michael Thomson, Swinton, Manchester	Charlton Athletic 11.5.85 (5-1)	Old Kippax
735	Ken Callaghan, Elland, W Yorks	Tottenham Hotspur 22.10.94 (5-2)	Old Kippax
736	Daniel Bowen, Stretford, Manchester	Manchester United 9.11.02 (3-1)	New Platt Lane
737	Stuart Hargreaves, Stalybridge	Manchester United 23.9.89 (5-1)	Halfway line, Old Kippax
738	Chris Hayes, Fallowfield, Manchester	Huddersfield Town 7.11.87 (10-1)	Old Kippax
739	Michael Colquhoun, Manchester	Manchester United 23.9.89 (5-1)	Main Stand
740	Ken Gibson, Middleton, Manchester	Manchester United 12.11.75 FL Cup Rd 4 (4-0)	Main Stand
741	Gordon Irvine, Droylsden, Manchester	Manchester United 9.11.02 (3-1)	North Stand
742	Malcolm Whipday, Swinton, Manchester	Manchester United 9.11.02 (3-1)	New Kippax
743	Ralph James Davidson, Milnrow, Rochdale	Schalke 04, 15.4.70 ECWC s/f leg 2 (5-1)	Old Kippax
744	David Linton, Swinton, Manchester	Manchester United 9.11.02 (3-1)	New Kippax
745	Paul O'Grady, Chorley, Lancs	Manchester United 23.9.89 (5-1)	Old Kippax
746	Gary Knight, Sothall, Sheffield	Birmingham City 28.4.2000 (1-0)	Old Kippax
747	Steve Denton, Marple, Cheshire	Manchester United 23.9.89 (5-1)	Old Kippax
748	Steve Marshall, Brockhill, Redditch, Worcs	Millwall 30.01.02 (2-0)	Old Kippax
749	D Rogerson, Newton, Chester	Wigan Athletic 17.5.99, P/off leg 2 (1-0)	Kippax
750	Joshua Lewis, Bramhall, Stockport	Gillingham Play-off Final @ Wembley 30.5.99 (3-2)	Main Stand
751	Steve Laws, Milnrow, Rochdale	Manchester United 23.9.89 (5-1)	Old Kippax
752	Stephen Crook, Fallowfield, Manchester	Manchester United 23.9.89 (5-1)	Old Kippax
753	Gary Pickles, Denton, Manchester	Manchester United 23.9.89 (5-1)	Old Kippax
754	John Hughes, Whitefield, Manchester	Huddersfield Town 7.11.87 (10-1)	Old Kippax
755	Robbie MacKinnon, Marple Bridge, Cheshire	Derby County 20.4.91 (2-1)	Old Kippax
756	Paul Diggett, Cheadle, Cheshire	Manchester United 23.9.89 (5-1)	Old Kippax
757	Richard Barlow, Brockhall Village, Old Langho	Manchester United 9.11.02 (3-1)	New Kippax, FF Upper
758	Chris Griffiths, Stretford, Manchester	Portsmouth 21.4.02 (3-1)	Kippax
759	Mark D Sanders, Rainow, Macclesfield	Schalke 04, 15.4.70 ECWC s/f leg 2 (5-1)	Old Kippax
760	Janice Lancaster, Manchester M11	Manchester United 9.11.02 (3-1)	Platt Lane
761	Richard Oldham, Blackley, Manchester		Kippax
762	Michael Carr, Rhodes, Middleton, M/cr	Manchester United 23.9.89 (5-1)	Old Kippax
763	Benjamin Evans, Cheadle Hulme	Manchester United 9.11.02 (3-1)	Main Stand
764	Derek Potter, Fearnhead, Warrington	Tottenham Hotspur 3.3.62 (6-2)	Main Stand, C Block 765
765	Robert L Blair, Firswood, Old Trafford	Manchester United 9.11.02 (3-1)	North Stand
766	Les McDonald, Unsworth, Bury	Schalke 04, 15.4.70 ECWC s/f leg 2 (5-1)	Old Kippax
767	Steve Worthington, Timperley, Cheshire	Manchester United 23.9.89 (5-1)	Old Kippax
768	Dave Miller, Edgeley, Stockport	Atletico Bilbao 1.10.69 ECWC Rd 1 leg 2 (3-0)	Old Kippax
769	Neil Mather, Davenport, Stockport	Portsmouth 21.4.02 (3-1)	Old Kippax
770	Mark Gray, Eaglescliffe, Stockton-on-Tees	Birmingham City 28.4.2000 (1-0)	Players' Entrance
771	Nicholas Smith, Heaton Moor, Stockport	Nottingham Forest 6.4.91 (3-1)	Kippax
772	Graham Sydney Bates, Northwich	Gillingham Play-off Final @ Wembley 30.5.99 (3-2)	Old Kippax
773	Chris Hulme, Marple, Stockport	Manchester United 23.9.89 (5-1)	Old Kippax
774	Neil Keating, Wythenshawe, Manchester	Manchester United 23.9.89 (5-1)	Old Kippax
775	Abbie Roberts, Blackpool	Manchester United 23.9.89 (5-1)	Old Kippax
776	Philip Wood, Peak Dale, Buxton	Manchester United 23.9.89 (5-1)	Old Kippax
777	Linda Anderson, Heaviley, Stockport	Tottenham Hotspur 9.12.67 (4-1)	Old Kippax
778	Graham Corless, Victoria Park, Manchester	Fenerbahce 18.9.68 EC Rd 1, leg 1 (0-0)	Old Kippax

(they mentioned northern bread was superior) and homesickness looming, they took the decision to return to Manchester.

Temporarily we moved in with my grandma whilst Mum and Dad pondered their next move. I have my earliest childhood memories of this era. City were in the process of building the North Stand at the time, and I recall being fascinated, as a three-year-old would be, by the building site at the bottom of my grandma's street. I can even remember the words "Kennedy Construction" emblazoned on the vehicles, which I find strange, as I couldn't read at the time. To this day whenever I see a Kennedy van on the road I'm transported back to that era. Back in the Maine Road routine my dad happily went back to watch City regularly, taking my mum along too as Grandma looked after us. Occasionally Mum brags to me she saw Lee, Summerbee, and Bell (pre serious injury) on a regular basis but I never had the opportunity on account of my tender age. Shortly after my parents settled in Rochdale, where they still reside to this day.

In 1976 Dad decided it was about time I showed an interest in football. Fearing I might be lured to support an undesirable club he wanted to get me into Maine Road at an impressionable age. My first actual football memory was of a Sunday afternoon and my dad getting all excited watching highlights of the previous day's League Cup Final. "Watch this! Watch this!" he bellowed as he knew the moment Dennis Tueart scored a memorable Wembley winner was beckoning. The following season he decided to set me on the path I would never deviate from. Money was still tight for my dad and he wanted to test the water to see how interested I would be, so I started off going to reserve games. I can't recall much of these, except for asking the usual daft questions: 'Dad, when the goalkeepers aren't playing, do they have to look after the goal posts as well?' and Peter Barnes scoring a memorable goal on a rare second team sojourn. "He'll play for England one day that lad" my dad surmised. When just a year later he did I thought my dad was a footballing sage. By January 1977 Dad decided I was ready for the first team, and we embarked upon a routine that didn't alter greatly for 16 years.

I can still recall those early visits to Maine Road with great sentiment. It helps that the team was fabulous. My first league game was against Leicester; we won 5-0, Brian Kidd scoring four. I can still reel off the twelve playing for City that day. We sat in the North Stand. I recall the expanse of heads stretching up and down the stand in front of me and behind me. And the noise, nothing I'd ever heard before. I found it so very exciting and according to my dad made a fair bit of my own, yet I don't recall this. I was hooked, and looked forward to my visits to Maine Road every fortnight.

The routine was to stay with me identically almost until I was into my thirties. Depending upon circumstances I'd catch the 123 bus from town and jump off at the top of Wansford Street on Lloyd Street or I'd drive in with Dad, arriving at my grandma's around 1pm. She would place two old chairs directly outside her house to reserve a parking spot for my dad. When in the car my dad muttered unfailingly for 16 years "Your Grandma thinks I drive a Mini" as he negotiated all manner of vehicles (most humorously one of those big old Volvos) into the

Welcome to
Manchester City Football Club

Entrance for:
Millennium Suite

Welcome to
Manchester City Football Club

Entrance for:
Centenary Suite
100 Club
Manchester Lounge

No	Subscriber name	Memorable Maine Road game/event	Fave part of Maine Road
779	David Shorter, Failsworth, Manchester	Middlesbrough 21.1.76 FLC s/f 2 (4-0)	Old Kippax
780	Stephen Pierce, Bury	Charlton Athletic 11.5.85 (5-1)	Old & New Kippax
781	Deane McKillop, Peterborough	Manchester United 23.9.89 (5-1)	North Stand
782	Alan Lockett, Wythenshawe, Manchester	Newcastle United 26.12.77 (4-0)	Old Kippax
783	Simon M Bennett, Cheadle Hulme	Manchester United 23.9.89 (5-1)	North Stand, Block K
784	Steve Wright, East Bowling, Bradford	Manchester United 23.9.89 (5-1)	Old Kippax
785	W K Gregg, Burnage, Manchester	Manchester United 9.11.02 (3-1)	Kippax Lower
786	Tim Smith, Sandbach, Cheshire	Manchester United 23.9.89 (5-1)	Old Kippax
787	David Jacobs, London N12	Tottenham Hotspur 9.12.67 (4-1)	Old Platt Lane @ 3/6d a seat!
788	Terence Rowling, Stalybridge, Cheshire	Manchester United 23.9.89 (5-1)	Old Kippax
789	Matt Dawson, Hale Barns, Cheshire	Ipswich Town FAC s/f 11.4.81 (1-0)	Old Kippax
790	John Gillespie, Eagley, Bolton	Newcastle United 26.12.77 (4-0)	Old Kippax
791	Joseph Rankin, Bramhall, Cheshire	Manchester United 9.11.02 (3-1)	New Kippax
792	Alec Rankin, Bramhall, Cheshire	Charlton Athletic 11.5.85 (5-1)	Old Kippax
793	Andrew J Powell, Sale, Cheshire	Tottenham Hotspur 22.10.94 (5-2)	Kippax, unseated
794	Martin Grundy, Buxton, Derbyshire	Tottenham Hotspur 22.10.94 (5-2)	Old Kippax
795	Alison Barham, Droylsden, Manchester	Manchester United 9.11.02 (3-1)	Old Kippax
796	Guy Rayner, Sheffield	AC Milan 6.12.78 Rd 3, leg 2 (3-0)	Old Kippax
797	Neil Fitzgerald, Salford, Manchester	Newcastle United 26.12.77 (4-0)	Old Kippax
798	John Fitzgerald, Salford, Manchester	Wigan Athletic 17.5.99, P/off leg 2 (1-0)	North Stand
799	Andrew Harris, Leicester	Manchester United 9.11.02 (3-1)	New Kippax, GG Lower
800	Ian Reeves, Chelmsford, Essex	Charlton Athletic 11.5.85 (5-1)	Old Kippax
801	Iain Macintosh, Wilmslow, Cheshire	Manchester United 9.11.02 (3-1)	Kippax - BBL R27, S54
802	Ray Chadfield, Whitchurch, Shropshire	Scunthorpe United 26.12.63 (8-1)	Old Kippax
803	Phil Brown, Hambleton, Poulton-le-Fylde	Charlton Athletic 11.5.85 (5-1)	Old Kippax
804	Gavin James Miller, Rothwell, Leeds	AC Milan 6.12.78 Rd 3, leg 2 (3-0)	Old Kippax
805	Robert Sloan, Milnrow, Rochdale	Tottenham Hotspur 3.3.62 (6-2)	Scoreboard End
806	Graeme Brock, Marple, Cheshire	Manchester United 6.11.71 (3-3)	Old Kippax
807	Peter Aidan Vallom, Feltham, Middlesex	Manchester United 12.11.75 FL Cup Rd 4 (4-0)	North Stand
808	Stuart Allan, Knutsford, Cheshire	Tottenham Hotspur 3.3.62 (6-2)	Old Kippax
809	Paul Holt, Winsford, Cheshire	Huddersfield Town 7.11.87 (10-1)	Old Kippax
810	Martin Taylor, Accrington, Lancs	Manchester United 23.9.89 (5-1)	Old Kippax
811	David Fawcett, Wrangle, Boston, Lincs	Manchester United 23.9.89 (5-1)	Old Kippax
812	David Fawcett		
813	Alan & Emma Whitney, Stafford	Manchester United 9.11.02 (3-1)	North Stand
814	David Woodcock, Bramhall, Stockport	Tottenham Hotspur 3.3.62 (6-2)	Old Kippax
815	Michael Woodcock, Davenport, Stockport	Manchester United 23.9.89 (5-1)	Old Kippax
816	Philip Woodcock, Davenport, Stockport	Manchester United 23.9.89 (5-1)	Old Kippax
817	Barry Thompson, Alkrington, Manchester	Sunderland 2.4.56 (4-2)	Kippax
818	Graham Thompson, Alkrington, Manchester	Manchester United 23.9.89 (5-1)	Kippax
819	Robert & Vicki Redpath, Cheadle Hulme	Manchester United 23.9.89 (5-1)	Kippax
820	Ken Bridgeman, Sherston, Malmesbury, Wilts	Manchester United 9.11.02 (3-1)	Old & New Kippax
821	Dave Lathrope, Darley Bridge, Matlock	Tottenham Hotspur 9.12.67 (4-1)	Old Kippax
822	M & J Taylor, Chorley, Lancs	Manchester United 23.9.89 (5-1)	New Kippax
823	Mark Bent, Urmston, Manchester	Huddersfield Town 7.11.87 (10-1)	Main Stand - my seat!
824	Roger Alan Davison, Poynton, Cheshire	Newcastle United 24.2.96 (3-3)	Old Kippax
825	Jeff Cheetham, Cottam, Preston	Newcastle United 26.12.77 (4-0)	Old Kippax
826	Paul Smith, Dukinfield, Cheshire	Tottenham Hotspur 9.12.67 (4-1)	Old Kippax
827	Andy Brack, Glossop, Derbyshire	Charlton Athletic 11.5.85 (5-1)	Old Kippax
828	Vincent Regan, Cheadle, Cheshire	Tottenham Hotspur 9.12.67 (4-1)	Old Kippax
829	John Whatmough, Littleborough, Lancs	Everton FAC 6 rep 11.3.81 (3-1)	Old Kippax, next to Nth Stand
830	Andrew Shaw, Bowdon, Cheshire	Schalke 04, 15.4.70 ECWC s/f leg 2 (5-1)	The Boardroom Suite!
831	Nigel Gaskill, Reddish, Stockport	Middlesbrough 21.1.76 FLC s/f 2 (4-0)	Old Kippax
832	Will Smith, Northenden, Manchester	Blackburn Rovers (a) 7.5.2000 (4-1)	Old Platt Lane
833	David L T Edge, Cheadle Hulme, Cheshire	Tottenham Hotspur 9.12.67 (4-1)	Old Kippax
834	Tush, Swinton, Manchester	Blackburn Rovers (a) 7.5.2000 (4-1)	Old Kippax
835	Lynne Wilbraham, Audenshaw, Manchester	Manchester United 23.9.89 (5-1)	Old Kippax
836	Alan Perrin, Goostrey, Cheshire	Tottenham Hotspur 9.12.67 (4-1)	Kippax
837	S Jones, Heaton Chapel, Stockport	Wolverhampton Wanderers (a) 1.4.2002 (2-0)	New Platt Lane
838	Lee Townley, Reddish, Stockport	Manchester United 9.11.02 (3-1)	North Stand
839	Peter Starbuck, Cilcain, Mold	Manchester United 9.11.02 (3-1)	Old Kippax
840	Carol Darvill, Bramhall, Cheshire	Man Utd 23.9.89 (5-1) & Man Utd 9.11.02 (3-1)!	Old Kippax
841	Steve Fullen, Failsworth, Manchester	Manchester United 23.9.89 (5-1)	Old Kippax
842	Michael Kay, Horwich, Bolton	Manchester United 23.9.89 (5-1)	Block D, Main Stand
843	Richard Barcoe, Droylsden, Manchester	Manchester United 23.9.89 (5-1)	Old Kippax
844	Paul Derbyshire, Eccles, Manchester	Charlton Athletic 11.5.85 (5-1)	Old Kippax
845	Philip Crompton, Penn, Bucks	Schalke 04, 15.4.70 ECWC s/f leg 2 (5-1)	Old Kippax
846	Derek Crompton, Stratford-on-Avon	Tottenham Hotspur 9.12.67 (4-1)	Old Kippax
847	Nigel McLoughlin, Heaton Chapel	Manchester United 23.9.89 (5-1)	Old Kippax, near away tunnel
848	Kevin Leather, Offerton, Stockport	Manchester United 23.9.89 (5-1)	Old Kippax
849	Kevin Doyle, Higher Blackley, Manchester	J Hart Testimonial 1.5.74 (3-1)	Kippax
850	Philip Stear, Stretford, Manchester	Manchester United 9.11.02 (3-1)	Old Kippax
851	Neil Slinger, Droylsden, Manchester	Manchester United 9.11.02 (3-1)	Old Kippax
852	Gary Higham, Gorton, Manchester	Manchester United 9.11.02 (3-1)	Old Kippax
853	Dr Alan Jacob, Cheadle Hulme, Cheshire	Manchester United 9.11.02 (3-1)	New Kippax
854	Graham Royle, Cheadle, Cheshire	Tottenham Hotspur 3.3.62 (6-2)	Old Kippax, windy corner
855	Marshall McMahon, Castleton, Rochdale	Man Utd 23.9.89 (5-1) & Man Utd 9.11.02 (3-1)	Old Kippax
856	James Dowd, Prestbury, Macclesfield	Everton 3.3.56 FAC 6 (2-1)	Main Stand
857	D Brian Cooper, Cottam, Preston	Tottenham Hotspur 3.3.62 (6-2)	H Block, Main Stand
858	Russell A Chadwick, Romiley, Cheshire	Manchester United 23.9.89 (5-1)	Old Kippax
859	I Howarth, Manchester M20	Manchester United 23.9.89 (5-1)	Centre, back of Main Stand
860	Fiona White, Calcot, Reading	Portsmouth 21.4.02 (3-1)	Centre, back of Main Stand
861	Julian Howarth, London W5	Crystal Palace 2.5.81 (1-1)	Centre, back of Main Stand
862	Ian Walker, Swythamley, Cheshire	Middlesbrough 21.1.76 FLC s/f 2 (4-0)	Old Kippax
863	David Rigney, Bradford-on-Avon, Wilts	Charlton Athletic 11.5.85 (5-1)	Old Kippax
864	Anthony Watkin, Knighton, Powys	Manchester United 9.11.02 (3-1)	Kippax Lower
865	Hazel J Wheeler, Withington, Manchester	Arsenal 6.2.54 (0-0)	Old Scoreboard End
866	Lyndon Wheeler, Withington, Manchester	Manchester United 23.9.89 (5-1)	Old Kippax

minute space my grandma had reserved. Meanwhile Gran would juggle cooking a roast dinner with sitting hawk-like at her front window, ready to pounce on anybody cheeky or daring enough to try and pinch Dad's reserved spot. Once safely parked the dinner awaited us; roast meat, potatoes, Yorkshire puddings. I lost count of the number of envious City fans passing by the window as we tucked into the feast which was followed by Grandma's speciality - all manner of homemade cakes, pies and fancies that I eagerly binged on.

Later in life when Grandma became a great-grandmother she was known as 'Grandma Cakes' by the latest additions to the family. Along with the greatest cup of tea I've ever tasted, my match day routine was dissimilar to the traditional one but greatly enjoyed by me. After the game we'd head back to my grandma's; she would open the door to us and if City had won she'd be wearing a massive City rosette with "Well done City!" written upon it. We'd also have more cake and tea, dissecting the day's results firstly on TV and then on the radio allowing the traditional traffic jams to die away before heading back to Rochdale. During the winter months the warm fire was also a reviver at 5pm. It also killed us in May and August, as Gran always seemed to presume, whatever the weather, we'd need to return from the match to a fire pumping heat to its full capacity!

My mum and dad started their own business in 1979. Consequently as they became busier, I was packed off to stay at my grandma's during school holidays. I loved these times, as suddenly my dad's childhood playground became my own. Times had changed, naturally over the 20 years since Dad hung around the ground. I managed to get involved in games of football on the same forecourt, though there were no players willing to join in with us. Target practice took place on the shutters of the club's ticket office, and a peculiar game with a golf ball was played - the objective to hit the security mesh at the top of the Kippax walls. The mesh looked like a steamboat paddle and rotated, the idea being that if you put your hand on it hoping to gain free access into the ground your hand slid away from the wall preventing you obtaining a foothold. However if you chucked a golf ball at it the mesh would rapidly spin, hurling the golf ball at great speed in a random direction, sometimes causing you to duck or run for your life. Often a turnstile door in the Main Stand would be left open as workmen would be coming and going and some new acquaintances of mine and I would sneak in to have a nosey around. I can recall the dark inhospitable old Main Stand roof conjuring a gloomy dark night, staring out onto the pitch while the contrasting daylight beamed down onto the green. The arena appeared to be illuminated. The quiet stands surrounding the pitch uncharacteristically silent, unnaturally so, I would stare in awe at this wondrous site until groundsman Stan Gibson would realise we were there and chase us out of the ground. Nobody hung around when Stan was on the warpath!

Living around Maine Road during the holidays was frequently eventful. I always carried my autograph book or a scrap of paper with a pen to ensure I never missed an opportunity to get a personality to sign. This led to me duplicating most of the players many times over as I repeatedly obtained the signature of any player I bumped into regardless of the number of

THE JOE MERCER SUITE

Officially opened by
Mrs Norah Mercer
on Tuesday 24th August, 1993

This Suite was built
with the aid of funds from the
Professional Footballers Association
for use in the
Football and Community Programme.

No	Subscriber name	Memorable Maine Road game/event	Fave part of Maine Road
867	Adam Radford, Stretford, Manchester	Manchester United 23.9.89 (5-1)	North Stand
868	Nick & Jordan Clarke, South Hykeham, Lincs	Manchester United 9.11.02 (3-1)	Kippax Lower, R12, S165
869	Derek Newton, Bredbury, Stockport	Manchester United 23.9.89 (5-1)	
870	James Alan Rose, Gorton Manchester	Manchester United 15.11.69 (4-0)	Old Kippax
871	Kevin Rose, Lincoln	Manchester United 23.9.89 (5-1)	North Stand
872	John Lambert, Ashby St Mary, Norfolk	Manchester United 9.11.02 (3-1)	Main Stand
873	David Ward, Great Moor, Stockport	Manchester United 9.11.02 (3-1)	Frank Swift Bar, Main Stand
874	Nigel Childs, Impington, Cambridge	Manchester United 9.11.02 (3-1)	Kippax
875	Ian Derbyshire, Higher Bebington, Wirral	Manchester United 9.11.02 (3-1)	New Kippax
876	Richard Nowotarski, Cheadle Hulme	Manchester United 9.11.02 (3-1)	Old Kippax
877	Sharon Marsland, Blackpool	Tottenham Hotspur 22.10.94 (5-2)	Kippax
878	John Grundy, Southport	Manchester United 9.11.02 (3-1)	New Kippax, Lower
879	Scott I McIlvanney, Newton, Hyde	Manchester United 9.11.02 (3-1)	New Kippax
880	Ian D McIlvanney, Denton, Manchester	Newcastle United 26.12.77 (4-0)	Old Kippax
881	Alf Warburton, Holyhead, Anglesey	Too many to mention!	Old Kippax
882	Paul Clinton, Cheadle Heath, Stockport	Manchester United 9.11.02 (3-1)	New Kippax
883	Mark Savage, Kingsmead, Northwich	Everton FAC 6 rep 11.3.81 (3-1)	North Stand
884	W R G Borrows, Vauxhall, London	Huddersfield Town 7.11.87 (10-1)	Old Kippax
885	Frank & Lynne Upton, Horton, Northampton	Manchester United 9.11.02 (3-1)	Main Stand, C Block
886	James Davies, Newton, Hyde	Wigan Athletic 17.5.99, P/off leg 2 (1-0)	North Stand
887	Robert Seabright, Helsby, Cheshire	Manchester United 23.9.89 (5-1)	Old Kippax
888	Andrew Cummings, Mile End, Stockport	Manchester United 23.9.89 (5-1)	Old Kippax
889	Arthur Sutton, Macclesfield	Manchester United 9.11.02 (3-1)	Old Kippax
890	David Griffiths, Morley, Leeds	Manchester United 23.9.89 (5-1)	Old Kippax- The Singing End
891	Geoff Perkins, Sale, Cheshire	Tottenham Hotspur 9.12.67 (4-1)	Kippax Upper
892	John Swales, Radcliffe, Manchester	Tottenham Hotspur 9.12.67 (4-1)	Old Kippax
893	Adam, Cathy & Savannah Heelis, Gee Cross	Huddersfield Town 7.11.87 (10-1)	Old Kippax
894	John Norbury, Hyde, Cheshire	Charlton Athletic 11.5.85 (5-1)	Old Kippax
895	Dean Robinson, Cheadle Hulme, Stockport	Norwich City 16.8.75 (3-0)	Old Platt Lane
896	Andy Herbert, Ruislip Manor, Middlesex	Manchester United 23.9.89 (5-1)	Old Kippax
897	Olivia & Peter Kay, Chorley, Lancs	AC Milan 6.12.78 UEFA Cup Rd 3, leg 2 (3-0)	Old Kippax
898	Ian Kay, Sheffield	Sheffield United 26.12.92 (2-0)	New Kippax
899	Stephen James Shaw, Glossop, Derbyshire	Derby County 20.4.91 (2-1)	U Block, North Stand
900	Tony Davies, Coedpoeth, Wrexham	Manchester United 9.11.02 (3-1)	New Platt Lane
901	Gordon Booth, East Didsbury, Manchester	Tottenham Hotspur 9.12.67 (4-1)	Old Kippax
902	Nigel Homer, Burton upon Trent	Manchester United 9.11.02 (3-1)	Old Kippax
903	Andrew Bramwell Hardicre, Failsworth, M/cr	Newcastle United 26.12.77 (4-0)	Old Kippax
904	Archie Paul Fox, Abbeymead, Gloucester	Sheffield United 21.8.99 (6-0)	New Kippax Lower
905	John Whiting, South Reddish, Stockport	Manchester United 23.9.89 (5-1)	Old Platt Lane
906	Steve Newell, Reabrook, Shrewsbury	Manchester United 9.11.02 (3-1)	Old Kippax
907	Bob Ollerenshaw, Hazel Grove, Stockport	Tottenham Hotspur 1.3.68 FAC Rd 6 (1-0)	Main Stand
908	Darren Ratcliffe, Enfield, Middlesex	Newcastle United 26.12.77 (4-0)	Main Stand
909	Andrew Brookfield, Davyhulme, Manchester	Manchester United 23.9.89 (5-1)	My seat, Main Stand
910	Jim Norris, Goosnargh, Preston	Manchester United 23.9.89 (5-1)	Old Kippax
911	Andrew Clarke, Gatley, Cheadle	Charlton Athletic 11.5.85 (5-1)	Old Platt Lane
912	Alan Coe, Reddish, Stockport	Huddersfield Town 7.11.87 (10-1)	Old Kippax
913	Helen Wiles, Boothstown, Worsley, M/cr	Sunderland 23.8.2000 (4-2)	Old Kippax
914	Mike & Tom Nolan, Urmston, Manchester	Manchester United 9.11.02 (3-1)	New Kippax
915	Jason Blue & Ethan Blue King, Denton, M/cr	Manchester United 23.9.89 (5-1)	Kippax
916	Chris Schilling, Heald Green, Cheadle	Huddersfield Town 7.11.87 (10-1)	New Kippax
917	Bernard McAlinden, Davyhulme, Manchester	Everton 3.3.56 FAC 6 (2-1)	Main Stand
918	Mark Speake, Preston	Manchester United 23.9.89 (5-1)	Old Kippax
919	Anne Woods-Maher, Fallowfield, Manchester	Huddersfield Town 7.11.87 (10-1)	Old Platt Lane
920	Roger Whitworth, Middleton, Manchester	West Bromwich Albion 1.2.58 (4-1)	Old Kippax
921	Stephen Chilton, Offerton, Stockport	Manchester United 9.11.02 (3-1)	New Kippax
922	Jason Marbeck, Horbury, Wakefield	Arsenal 12.2.77 (1-0)	Kippax standing, next to away fans
923	Phil Hale, Black Notley, Essex		Old Kippax
924	Gordon Labrey, New Mills, High Peak	Charlton Athletic 11.5.85 (5-1)	My time in the Directors' Box!
925	Sean Grovestock, Boothstown, Worsley, M/cr	Charlton Athletic 11.5.85 (5-1)	Old Kippax
926	Michael Anthony Barnett, Barrow, Chester	Tottenham Hotspur 9.12.67 (4-1)	Old Kippax
927	Symon McGrath, Tytherington, Macclesfield	Manchester United 9.11.02 (3-1)	North Stand
928	Mark O'Halloran, Astley, Manchester	Everton FAC 6 rep 11.3.81 (3-1)	Old Kippax
929	Paul Jones, Littleborough, Lancs	Everton FAC 6 rep 11.3.81 (3-1)	Old Kippax
930	Colin Murray, Kingsmead, Northwich	Manchester United 9.11.02 (3-1)	Old & New Kippax
931	Peter North, Droylsden, Manchester	West Ham United 14.1.78 (3-2) my first match!	My seat in New Kippax
932	James Albert Shaw, Cheadle Hulme	Coventry City 22.9.79 (3-0)	North Stand
933	Phil Knowles, Denton, Manchester	Sunderland 27.8.66 (1-0) - first match!	Old Kippax
934	Colin Walker, Denton, Manchester		
935	Phil Fallon, East Didsbury, Manchester	Manchester United 6.11.71 (3-3)	Old Kippax
936	Derek J Price, Bramhall, Stockport	Manchester United 23.9.89 (5-1)	Main Stand
937	Bill Bailey, Chorley, Lancs	Stoke City 3.3.34 FAC 6 (1-0)	Old Kippax
938	Tony Ball, Kendal, Cumbria (late Prestwich)	Everton 3.3.56 FAC 6 (2-1) day my first son born!	Old Scoreboard End
939	Paul Threlfall, Heaton Chapel, Stockport	Newcastle United 26.12.77 (4-0)	Old Kippax
940	Tony Mottram, Sale,Cheshire	Everton 3.3.56 FAC 6 (2-1)	Block H, Main Stand
941	Andrew Harris, Watford, Herts	Charlton Athletic 11.5.85 (5-1)	Block C, Main Stand
942	Pam Stevenson, Denton, Manchester	Portsmouth 21.4.02 (3-1)	Old Kippax
943	Peter Wilkinson, Diggle, Oldham	Huddersfield Town 1.1.66 (2-0)	Old Kippax
944	John Foster, Haxby, York	Manchester United 9.11.02 (3-1)	Main Stand
945	Lisa Aronoffsky, Prestwich, Manchester	Manchester United 23.9.89 (5-1)	Main Stand
946	Paul Rowlands, Norwich	Blackburn Rovers 7.5.2000 (4-1)	New Kippax
947	Ian Morgan, Cockermouth, Cumbria	Tottenham Hotspur 22.10.94 (5-2)	Old Kippax
948	Blaine Nathan Stewart, Altrincham	Manchester United 9.11.02 (3-1)	'New' North Stand
949	Danny Wayne Hadfield, Altrincham	Manchester United 23.9.89 (5-1)	Old Kippax
950	Carl Chambers, Sprotbrough, Doncaster	Middlesbrough 7.11.82 (3-2) my first game!	Old Kippax
951	Damian Duffy, Denton, Manchester	Manchester United 9.11.02 (3-1)	Block R, North Stand
952	Frank Curley, Littleborough, Lancs	Portsmouth 21.4.02 (3-1)	Old Kippax
953	Dave & Paul Bailey, Crudwell, Wiltshire	International XI 15.4.64 - B. Trautmann's Test. (5-4)	Claremont Road End

No	Subscriber name	Memorable Maine Road game/event	Fave part of Maine Road
954	John Stockley, Marple, Stockport	Manchester United 23.9.89 (5-1)	Old Kippax
955	Paul Stockley, Boston, Massachussetts, USA	Manchester United 23.9.89 (5-1)	Old Kippax
956	James Walker, Marple, Stockport	Manchester United 23.9.89 (5-1)	Old Kippax
957	Barry Walker, Marple, Stockport	Manchester United 23.9.89 (5-1)	
958	Ken Ball, Altrincham, Cheshire	AC Milan 6.12.78 Rd 3, leg 2 (3-0)	Old Kippax
959	Kent O'Sullivan, Denton, Manchester	Newcastle United 29.1.69 FAC Rd 4 rep (2-0)	Old Kippax
960	Chris Morris, Burton upon Trent (Boothstown)	Sheffield United 19.1.91 (2-0) first match in the Kippax	Old Kippax
961	Eddie Nevill, Burgess Hill, West Sussex	Stoke City 3.3.34 FAC 6 (1-0)	Block A, Main Stand
962	Bernard Healey, Newton Heath, Manchester	Newcastle United 26.12.77 (4-0)	North Stand
963	C Bowker, Heaton Chapel, Stockport	Manchester United 29.1.55 FAC4 (2-0)	Old Kippax
964	Simon Maguire, Alwoodley, Leeds	Manchester United 23.9.89 (5-1)	Old Kippax
965	Andrew Maguire, West Didsbury, Manchester	Manchester United 23.9.89 (5-1)	North Stand
966	Mark McCormick, Middleton, Manchester	Manchester United 23.9.89 (5-1)	Old Kippax
967	Mrs B Hughes, Cheadle Hulme, Cheshire	Manchester United 9.11.02 (3-1)	Kippax Lower
968	Mrs L Smith, Sale, Cheshire	Portsmouth 21.4.02 (3-1)	Kippax Lower
969	B Peters, Audenshaw, Manchester	Birmingham City 25.12.50 (3-1)	Platt Lane
970	Rob Sullivan, Beverley, East Yorkshire	Manchester United 9.11.02 (3-1)	North Stand
971	Darren Milnes, Cheadle Hulme, Cheshire	Manchester United 23.9.89 (5-1)	Main Stand
972	Gary Critchley, Chadderton, Oldham	Manchester United 9.11.02 (3-1)	Old Kippax
973	Julie Marsden, Hillstown, Chesterfield	Manchester United 9.11.02 (3-1)	Main Stand
974	Michael Fletcher, Heywood, Lancs	Manchester United 9.11.02 (3-1)	Old Kippax
975	Rick Eagles, Beeston, Nottinghamshire	West Bromwich Albion 25.3.2000 (2-1)	Kippax Lower
976	Colin Redmayne, Crooklands, Cumbria	Manchester United 9.11.02 (3-1)	Block C, Main Stand
977	Steven Redmayne, Crooklands, Cumbria	Manchester United 9.11.02 (3-1)	Block C, Main Stand
978	Graham Chapman, Sedgewick, Cumbria	Manchester United 23.9.89 (5-1)	Old Kippax
979	Neill & Matt Buckley, Tollerton, Notts	Schalke 04, 15.4.70 ECWC s/f leg 2 (5-1)	Corner Nth Stand/Kippax
980	Barry & Liz Neild, Sharston, Manchester	Manchester United 9.11.02 (3-1)	Main Stand
981	David Lawrence, Standish, Wigan	Schalke 04, 15.4.70 ECWC s/f leg 2 (5-1)	Old Kippax
982	Geoff Clowes, Heaton Chapel, Stockport	Manchester United 12.11.75 FL Cup Rd 4 (4-0)	Old Kippax
983	Steve Coe, Lowton, Warrington	Manchester United 23.9.89 (5-1)	Main Stand
984	Diane Robinson, Heald Green, Cheadle	Middlesbrough 21.1.76 FLC s/f 2 (4-0)	K Block, North Stand
985	Scott Turton, Harefield, Middlesex	Wigan Athletic 17.5.99, P/off leg 2 (1-0)	New Kippax
986	Howard Jones, Lytham St Annes	Tottenham Hotspur 3.3.62 (6-2)	Old Kippax
987	Barry Wright, Urmston, Manchester	Tottenham Hotspur 9.12.67 (4-1)	Old Scoreboard End, behind goal
988	Gary Hassall, Hyde, Cheshire	Manchester United 9.11.02 (3-1)	Old Kippax
989	Alan Bradshaw, Didsbury, Manchester	Widzew Lodz 14.9.77 UEFA Rd 1, leg 1 (2-2)	Old Kippax
990	Lee Simmonds, Stalybridge, Cheshire	Leicester City 4.11.2000 (0-1) my 21st!	Platt Lane
991	Eddie Walsh, Grappenhall, Warrington	Everton FAC 6 rep 11.3.81 (3-1)	Old Platt Lane, Y5
992	Gary Griffiths, Crumpsall, Manchester	Manchester United 12.11.75 FL Cup Rd 4 (4-0)	North Stand
993	J D Whittney, Filey, N Yorkshire	Just being there 1955/56 - 1977/78	Block B, Row 5, Seat 765-767
994	Nick Naylor, Hammersmith, London	AC Milan 6.12.78 Rd 3, leg 2 (3-0)	Old Kippax
995	Peter Mason, Greenmount, Bury	Manchester United 23.9.89 (5-1)	Old Kippax
996	Mark Brandreth, Walton, Warrington	Huddersfield Town 7.11.87 (10-1)	Old Pie-crust Corner in Kippax
997	Roman Filipowski, Stockton Heath, Warrington	Manchester United 23.9.89 (5-1)	Old Kippax
998	Russell Brine, Offerton, Stockport	Manchester United 23.9.89 (5-1)	Old Kippax
999	Graham Southgate, Rochdale	International XI 15.4.64 - Bert Trautmann's Testimonial (5-4)	Old Kippax
1000	Graham Southgate, Rochdale		
1001	Deborah Darbyshire, Rusholme, Manchester	Manchester United 23.9.89 (5-1)	Old Kippax
1002	Chris Thyer, Woodthorpe, York	Charlton Athletic 11.5.85 (5-1)	Old Kippax
1003	Simon Kerr, Plas Newton, Chester	Manchester United 23.9.89 (5-1)	Old Kippax
1004	David Tooth, Bollington, Macclesfield	Tottenham Hotspur 9.12.67 (4-1)	Block C, Main Stand
1005	Deborah Page, Chorlton-cum-Hardy, M/cr	Portsmouth 21.4.02 (3-1)	New Kippax, Lower
1006	Paul & Peta Jones, Droylsden, Manchester	Manchester United 9.11.02 (3-1)	New Platt Lane
1007	Mark Whelan, Buxton, Derbyshire	Manchester United 23.9.89 (5-1)	Old Kippax
1008	David Williams, Alwoodley, Leeds	Newcastle United 26.12.77 (4-0)	Old Kippax, prior to roof
1009	Anthony Tapper, Failsworth, Manchester	Manchester United 23.9.89 (5-1)	Old Kippax
1010	John Martin, Heaton Moor, Stockport	Tottenham Hotspur 9.12.67 (4-1)	Old Kippax
1011	Tim Jorgensson, Heaton Moor, Stockport	Manchester United 9.11.02 (3-1)	Kippax
1012	David Stones, Cheadle Hulme, Cheshire	Portsmouth 21.4.02 (3-1)	Platt Lane
1013	David McKee, Heaton Chapel, Stockport	Wigan Athletic 17.5.99, P/off leg 2 (1-0)	Kippax
1014	Brandon Alexander Thompson, Middleton, M/cr	Manchester United 9.11.02 (3-1)	Family Stand
1015	Brian Tongue, Gorton, Manchester	Manchester United 23.9.89 (5-1)	Old Kippax
1016	Barbara Mary George, Swinton, Manchester	Manchester United 9.11.02 (3-1)	Block K, R19, Seat 21 Nth Std
1017	Max George, Swinton, Manchester	Manchester United 9.11.02 (3-1)	Block K, R19, Seat 22 Nth Std
1018	Jack George, Swinton, Manchester	Manchester United 9.11.02 (3-1)	Block K, R19, Seat 23 Nth Std
1019	Andy Partington, Stalybridge	Manchester United 9.11.02 (3-1)	North Stand
1020	Alan Chappell, Stalybridge	West Bromwich Albion 3.8.68 Charity Shield (6-1)	Old Kippax
1021	Wayne Penny, Haydock, Merseyside	Manchester United 9.11.02 (3-1)	Old Kippax
1022	Nicola Dulson, Stretford, Manchester	Manchester United 9.11.02 (3-1)	Old & New Kippax
1023	Sebastian Earley, Heaton Chapel, Stockport	Manchester United 9.11.02 (3-1)	
1024	John E Deakin, Huyton, Liverpool	Middlesbrough 21.1.76 (4-0)	Old Kippax
1025	Anthony Preston, Cheadle Hulme, Cheshire	Manchester United 23.9.89 (5-1)	Old Kippax
1026	Sheila Pawson, Blackley, Manchester	Portsmouth 21.4.02 (3-1)	New Kippax
1027	Yvonne Salt, Rochdale	Tottenham Hotspur 3.3.62 (6-2)	Old Kippax
1028	Anthony Salt, Rochdale	Manchester United 23.9.89 (5-1)	New Kippax
1029	Martyn Bean, Chichester, Sussex	Queens Park Rangers 25.4.98 (2-2)	North Stand
1030	Paul Seery, Heaton Norris, Stockport	Manchester United 12.11.75 FL Cup Rd 4 (4-0)	Old Kippax
1031	Alan Jones, Timperley, Cheshire	Manchester United 23.9.89 (5-1)	Old Kippax
1032	M Paterson, Drax, Nr Selby, N Yorkshire	Manchester United 9.11.02 (3-1)	North Stand
1033	David Mason, Offerton, Stockport	Charlton Athletic 11.5.85 (5-1)	Old Kippax
1034	Ruth Woodhead, Heaton Moor, Stockport	Charlton Athletic 11.5.85 (5-1)	Old Kippax corner next to Nth Std
1035	Gary Griffin, Biddulph, Cheshire	Wigan Athletic 17.5.99, P/off leg 2 (1-0)	New Kippax
1036	Mark Gilligan, Royton, Oldham	Charlton Athletic 11.5.85 (5-1)	Old Kippax
1037	R J Derbyshire, Rumney, Cardiff	Newcastle United (a) 11.5.68 (4-3)	Old Kippax
1038	Richard Hale, Hyde, Cheshire	Norwich City 24.1.81 FAC 4 (6-0)	Old Kippax
1039	Paul Ramsbottom, Hyde, Cheshire	Manchester United 23.9.89 (5-1)	Old Kippax

times I'd previously procured it. Indeed, looking back on the autograph book I can surmise that after arriving in England eccentric Yugoslav Dragoslav Stepanovic must have been dossing down at Maine Road for a spell, judging by the number of times he signed my book. He always seemed to be hanging around. Kevin Reeves signed a couple of times, and also gave me a bruised backside when, in a rush leaving training one afternoon, he collided with me and I hit the ground. He did have the decency to stop, apologise, and get me back on my feet. The scariest moment was the time I encountered Joe Corrigan in a fearsome mood. After one training session Nicky Reid and Tommy Caton emerged from the players' entrance midway through a squabble. Nicky wanted a lift home, Tommy was having none of it. So desperate was Nicky that he climbed onto the bonnet of Tommy's Ford Capri. Tommy stubbornly drove off at speed, leaving Nicky clinging on for dear life. As I witnessed this Joe came storming out of the players' entrance screaming and swearing about how stupid and irresponsible they'd been. I was still a little chubby geek aged 11 or 12, the sight of a clearly furious 6ft 4 Joe Corrigan was too much to behold, and I ran back to Grandma's, worried he might have a go at me for not trying to stop them. One of my 'holiday friends' told me he had seen Nicky still clinging on for his life a mile down the road on Lloyd Street!

Around this time City were in decline and the quality of the players brought in was clearly poorer than the ones they replaced. This was neatly summed up for me in the unpaid employment I always embarked on down at the Platt Lane training ground. I'd follow behind the players who would walk from the dressing rooms at Maine Road to do their morning's work at the training complex a few hundred yards down the road. I would position myself behind the goal but on the outside of the training complex, so that when City did their shooting practice I was in the ideal place to retrieve all of the badly-hit shots that skied the perimeter fence into my direction. This happened a little too often for me to feel optimistic about the club's situation.

Eventually I became old enough to look after myself during school holidays so my trips to Maine Road narrowed down to matchdays, or to when visiting my grandma. However the same old routine that I loved so much was still adhered to. This was a golden age for me of going to the match, even though the football on offer wasn't always the greatest. Another happy period was my two years as a student at Manchester Poly. There were a number of lads in my class into football but separated from their own clubs they adopted City as their second club and stood on the Kippax with me. The conversation in class centred on football because of this, and City was the main focus. So much so that one of the girls in the class, fed up with hearing so much about City, asked if she could come along. She was from Harrogate, and I considered her a bit posh, her dad being a "huntin', shootin', fishin'" kind of guy who believed all football fans were hooligans. She couldn't tell him she was going to the game because he would have forbidden it. I still remember her first game fondly, as it was a real stinker. Charlton, January 1990, a relegation clash that we lost, and Howard Kendall took some fierce stick for the first (but not the

No	Subscriber name	Memorable Maine Road game/event	Fave part of Maine Road
1040	Neil Herd, Hampton Hargate, Peterborough	Portsmouth 21.4.02 (3-1)	New Kippax
1041	Phil Simpson, Copenhagen, Denmark	Derby County 20.4.91 (2-1)	Old Kippax
1042	Martin Waters, Ramsbottom, Lancs	Manchester United 23.9.89 (5-1)	Old Kippax
1043	Janice Pickup, Wilmslow, Cheshire	Manchester United 9.11.02 (3-1)	Block B Main Stand
1044	Tommy Muir, Cheadle, Cheshire	Schalke 04, 15.4.70 ECWC s/f leg 2 (5-1)	Every square inch!
1045	Joyce Maddocks, Bramhall, Stockport	Newcastle United 26.12.77 (4-0)	Main Stand with John
1046	Phil Holme, Portadown, Co Armagh	Manchester United 23.9.89 (5-1)	Old Kippax
1047	Graham Dorrian, Ordsall, Manchester	Manchester United 23.9.89 (5-1)	Old Kippax
1048	Pete Roberts, Eastbourne, East Sussex	Wigan Athletic 17.5.99, P/off leg 2 (1-0)	New Kippax
1049	Frank Pegg, Adelaide, Australia	Manchester United 9.11.02 (3-1)	Old Kippax
1050	Pat Barber, Droylsden, Manchester	West Ham United 17.8.74 (4-0)	North Stand
1051	John Wragg, Burnage, Manchester	Manchester United 6.11.71 (3-3)	Old Kippax
1052	Andrew Whelan, Buxton, Derbyshire	Manchester United 9.11.02 (3-1)	Kippax Stand
1053	Ken Pritchard, Heaton Norris, Stockport	Manchester United 9.11.02 (3-1)	Old Kippax
1054	Robert Moska, Halifax	Manchester United 9.11.02 (3-1)	Old Kippax
1055	Eddie Pepper, Beckenham, Kent	Middlesbrough 22.10.83 (2-1) - my first visit to Maine Road	Old Kippax
1056	J Nerney, Edgeley, Stockport	Tottenham Hotspur 3.3.62 (6-2)	Old Kippax
1057	John Logan Petch, Gatley, Cheadle	Manchester United 6.11.71 (3-3)	Main Stand
1058	Peter Hilton, Wythenshawe, Manchester	Manchester United 9.11.02 (3-1)	Old Kippax
1059	Roger Herring, Didsbury, Manchester	Manchester United 23.9.89 (5-1)	Old Kippax
1060	Anthony Tomlinson, Great Harwood, Blackburn	Manchester United 23.9.89 (5-1)	North Stand
1061	Neil Scott, Denton, Manchester	Everton FAC 6 rep 11.3.81 (3-1)	Old Kippax
1062	Simon Oxley, Cheadle Hulme, Cheshire	Tottenham Hotspur 9.12.67 (4-1)	Kippax
1063	John Chadwick, Appley Bridge, Wigan	Tottenham Hotspur 22.10.94 (5-2)	Old Kippax
1064	Brian Field, Withington, Manchester	Huddersfield Town 7.11.87 (10-1)	Old Platt Lane
1065	Paul McKay, Hadfield, Glossop	Huddersfield Town 7.11.87 (10-1)	North Stand
1066	Danny Liam Prosser, Llysfaen, Colwyn Bay	Manchester United 9.11.02 (3-1)	New Platt Lane
1067	Christopher & Jason Clarke, Sale, Cheshire	Everton FAC 6 rep 11.3.81 (3-1)	Main Stand
1068	Leslie Dawson Fitzsimmons, Didsbury, M/cr	Chelsea 8.12.56 (5-4)	Main Stand
1069	Barry Jenkinson, Pensarn, Abergele	Tottenham Hotspur 9.12.67 (4-1)	Block C, Main Stand
1070	Anthony McGowan, Urmston, Manchester	Manchester United 23.9.89 (5-1)	Old Kippax
1071	Paul England, Royton, Oldham	Tottenham Hotspur 9.12.67 (4-1)	Main Stand
1072	Jack Bumby, Crantock, Newquay Cornwall	Tottenham Hotspur 3.3.62 (6-2)	Old Kippax
1073	Donna King, New Mills, High Peak	Manchester United 9.11.02 (3-1)	Back of the opposition's net!
1074	Des Webb, Droylsden, Manchester	Manchester United 9.11.02 (3-1)	Kippax
1075	Chris Scholes, Mossley, Ashton-under-Lyne	Tottenham Hotspur 9.12.67 (4-1)	Old Kippax
1076	Michael Henneberry, Killaloe, Co Clare	West Ham United 21.10.72 (4-3)	Main Stand
1077	Nick Armstrong, Brookbottom, High Peak	Manchester United 23.9.89 (5-1)	Kippax Stand
1078	Les J Bibby, Middleton, Manchester	Tottenham Hotspur 9.12.67 (4-1)	Old Kippax
1079	Colin St John, Hastings, East Sussex	Newcastle United 26.12.77 (4-0)	North Stand
1080	Andy Mason, Mickleover, Derbyshire	Manchester United 23.9.89 (5-1)	Kippax Stand
1081	Robert Heslop, New Moston, Manchester	Wolverhampton Wanderers 29.1.72 (5-2)	Old Kippax
1082	Steve Reid, Carrbrook, Stalybridge	Manchester United 9.11.02 (3-1)	Kippax
1083	May Cooper, Prestwich	Manchester United 9.11.02 (3-1)	Kippax
1084	Richard Kwai Thompson, Walkden, Manchester	Manchester United 23.9.89 (5-1)	Old Kippax
1085	Phil, Robert & Johnny Goldstone, Leeds	Manchester United 9.11.02 (3-1)	Main Stand
1086	Joe Murchan, Irlam, Manchester	Charlton Athletic 11.5.85 (5-1)	Old Kippax
1087	Brian Evans, Irlam, Manchester	Charlton Athletic 11.5.85 (5-1)	Old Kippax
1088	W George Renshaw, Colwyn Bay	Sheffield United 25.8.54 (5-2)	Old Kippax
1089	Barbara Smith, Kidderminster, Worcs	Cardiff City 16.3.57 (4-1)	Old Kippax
1090	Suzanne Buckley, Dagenham, Essex	Huddersfield Town 7.11.87 (10-1)	Old Family Stand
1091	Helen Thomas, Sale, Cheshire	Manchester United 9.11.02 (3-1)	Old Family Stand
1092	Paul & Alyson King, Little Holtby, Northallerton	Our wedding day at Maine Road - 2.5.98	New Kippax
1093	John P Birchall, Crumpsall, Manchester	Manchester United 23.9.89 (5-1)	Old Kippax
1094	Will Plumb, Heaton Mersey, Stockport	Tottenham Hotspur 9.12.67 (4-1)	Standing in Old North Stand
1095	David John Flynn, Neath, Glamorgan	Manchester United 9.11.02 (3-1)	Main Stand
1096	Dave Vickers, Rhos-on-Sea, Gwynedd	Manchester United 23.9.89 (5-1)	Platt Lane Stand
1097	Gareth Roberts, Bedale, Yorkshire	Derby County 20.4.91 (2-1)	Pitch view from Main Stand
1098	Paul Rowan, Boothstown, Manchester	Manchester United 23.9.89 (5-1)	New Kippax
1099	David Hand, Heaton Mersey, Stockport	Newcastle United 26.12.77 (4-0)	Old Kippax
1100	Clifford Townley	Tottenham Hotspur 3.3.62 (6-2)	Old Kippax
1101	Baz Riley, Timperley, Cheshire	Newcastle United 26.12.77 (4-0)	Old Scoreboard End
1102	Paul Squire, Upton, Chester	Manchester United 23.9.89 (5-1)	Old Kippax
1103	John Arthur Holliday, Southampton	Manchester United 23.9.89 (5-1)	Old Kippax
1104	Mike Taylor, Audenshaw, Manchester	Manchester United 9.11.02 (3-1)	Old Scoreboard End
1105	Joe Radcliffe, Manchester	Manchester United 9.11.02 (3-1)	Main Stand
1106	Philip Radcliffe, Fernilee, Derbyshire	Manchester United 9.11.02 (3-1)	Main Stand
1107	Neil McCreavey, Gatley Cheshire	Manchester United 23.9.89 (5-1)	Old Kippax
1108	Jonathan McCreavey, Withington, Manchester	Manchester United 23.9.89 (5-1)	Old Kippax
1109	Michael Maguire, Oshawa, Canada	Manchester United 23.9.89 (5-1)	Old Kippax
1110	Nick Warmisham, Norton St Philip, Bath	Schalke 04, 15.4.70 ECWC s/f leg 2 (5-1)	Centre of Old Kippax
1111	Jason Warmisham, Norton St Philip. Bath	Bournemouth 6.5.89 (3-3)	Old Kippax
1112	Chris Williams, Stokenchurch, Bucks	Ipswich Town 5.3.67 FAC 5 (1-1)	Main Stand Block B
1113	Oliver C Williams, Stokenchurch, Bucks	Manchester United 9.11.02 (3-1)	Main Stand Block B
1114	Gerard Moran, Blackley, Manchester	Newcastle United 26.12.77 (4-0)	Old Kippax
1115	Liam Moran, Blackley, Manchester	Manchester United 9.11.02 (3-1)	North Stand
1116	Joanne Ratcliffe, East Malling, Kent	Manchester United 9.11.02 (3-1)	Main Stand
1117	Joanne Ratcliffe, East Malling, Kent	Manchester United 9.11.02 (3-1)	Main Stand
1118	Mike Burkey, Prestwich, Manchester	Manchester United 23.9.89 (5-1)	Old Kippax
1119	Mike Burkey, Prestwich, Manchester	Manchester United 23.9.89 (5-1)	Old Kippax
1120	John Egerton, Northwich, Cheshire	Portsmouth 21.4.02 (3-1)	Old Kippax
1121	Colin Earley, Kathmandu, Nepal	Manchester United 23.9.89 (5-1)	Old Kippax
1122	David Dunkerley, Gee Cross, Hyde	Manchester United 23.9.89 (5-1)	Main Stand Block B
1123	Geoffrey Glynn, Whitefield, Manchester	Watford 4.9.82 (1-0)	Old Kippax
1124	Colin MacDonald, Kirksmeaton, Yorkshire	Manchester United 9.11.02 (3-1)	Old Kippax
1125	Karen Foulkes, Dukinfield, Cheshire	Birmingham City 28.4.2000 (1-0)	Main Stand
1126	Craig Atkinson, Grimsargh, Preston	Birmingham City 28.4.2000 (1-0)	Windy Corner, Old Kippax
1127	Neil Starkey, Flixton, Manchester	Manchester United 23.9.89 (5-1)	Old Kippax

last.) time that day. Amazingly she was immediately smitten. The noise, the passion, the desperation in the Kippax as we urged our team on really struck a chord with her. Next season she became a season ticket holder and, on entering a long-term relationship, turned her future husband into a blue. Even now, despite motherhood, work commitments and finance ultimately turning her into an infrequent visitor to Maine Road, she still remains strongly committed to the cause.

In addition, my grandma always loved the extensive brotherhood we created in her house on a match day. Privileged friends would be offered the opportunity to share the roast dinner with us; all my City supporting mates who wanted to stand with us on the Kippax would meet at Gran's for a pre-match brew and slice of cake and then afterwards troop back there for a warm-up. Often after the brew we'd travel into town and have a Manchester night out. This was the beauty of going to the match in those days; people could just show up on the doorstep, otherwise we always stood on the same spot on the Kippax so latecomers could still locate us quickly. A mate of mine from my Poly days, before all-seater stadia were even dreamt of, once summed it up for me: "Steve, if ever I lose contact with you and want to get back in touch, I'll just head for the half-way line, first barrier up, of the Kippax and you'll be there."

Things can't stand still forever though, and in 1993 I felt the first visible sign that things were changing. Initially it was the decision to introduce residents' parking to Wansford Street. This irritated us as we had to park on a car park and then rescue the car prior to locking up, meaning we generally had to rush away from my grandma's a little earlier on a Saturday evening. This was only a minor worry though in comparison. My grandma wasn't getting any younger, and her legs were evidently causing her a lot of pain. My dad told her she should start taking it easier when we visited; cups of tea would be enough and we'd bring a takeaway with us and eat it there, saving her the hassle of cooking a large meal. Stubborn and proud, she continued to make her own roast dinner whilst we looked on jealously with our pie and chips!

There was no doubt about it, she was finding things harder. The advent of all-seater stadia killed off the large posse travelling to her house, which probably was a good thing though she preferred a lively Saturday afternoon, she was that kind of person. With tickets having to be secured up front, my mates turning up on spec dwindled away. We were back to just me and my dad. There was one notable addition a couple of years later, my nephew Aaron, Dad's first grandson, obtaining a seat in the Kippax with the two of us when he was old enough in 1998. What a first season he had watching the blues regularly - Second Division football and a trip to Wembley!

Grandma continued to shuffl painfully around her house but talking to her became difficult as her hearing deteriorated. Still she bravely battled on, always cheerful, enjoying the regular visits from us that I had equally enjoyed since 1977. She continued to brew up the greatest cup of tea I'd ever tasted, and whilst the cakes weren't as regular, she still baked and it was a treat we enjoyed from time to time. In March 2001 she passed away. It was hard letting all my mates know, many were as upset as I was. Visiting

No	Subscriber name	Memorable Maine Road game/event	Fave part of Maine Road
1128	Sean O'Connor, Chichester, W.Sussex	Manchester United 9.11.02 (3-1)	Old Kippax
1129	Mark Kidd, Davyhulme, Manchester	Manchester United 23.9.89 (5-1)	Old Kippax
1130	Gary Webster, Denton, Manchester	Manchester United 9.11.02 (3-1)	Main Stand
1131	Sean & Lee Daley, Swinton, Manchester		Main Stand
1132	C P Cheshire, Norley, Frodsham	Schalke 04, 15.4.70 ECWC s/f leg 2 (5-1)	Old Platt Lane
1133	Tania Worsley, Pewsey, Wiltshire	Charlton Athletic 11.5.85 (5-1)	Old Kippax
1134	David A Clough, Macclesfield	Wigan Athletic 17.5.99, P/off leg 2 (1-0)	New Kippax
1135	Reg Duff, Prestatyn, Denbighshire	Tottenham Hotspur 3.3.62 (6-2)	Old Kippax
1136	Paul Ellison, Bramhall, Stockport	Manchester United 12.11.75 FL Cup Rd 4 (4-0)	Old Kippax
1137	Adrian Whitehurst, Moston, Manchester	Manchester United 23.9.89 (5-1)	Old Kippax
1138	Barry & Julia Macklin, Marple Bridge	Tottenham Hotspur 9.12.67 (4-1)	Old Kippax
1139	Toby Nolan-Shaw, Wardle, Rochdale	Blackpool 8.8.98 (3-0) my first game	Main Stand
1140	David Connolly, Baguley, Manchester	AC Milan 6.12.78 Rd 3, leg 2 (3-0)	Kippax
1141	David P Turner, Macclesfield	Manchester United 9.11.02 (3-1)	Old Kippax
1142	David A Barnes, Bury, Lancs	Gillingham Play-off Final @ Wembley 30.5.99 (3-2)	Kippax
1143	Dean King, Wigan	Manchester United 23.9.89 (5-1)	New Main Stand
1144	Tony Parke, Ashton-under-Lyne	Manchester United 9.11.02 (3-1)	Platt Lane
1145	Adrian Furness, Ripponden, Halifax	Manchester United 23.9.89 (5-1)	Old Kippax
1146	Alan Barber, Ashton-under-Lyne	Manchester United 23.9.89 (5-1)	Main Stand
1147	Michael Barber, Ashton-under-Lyne	Manchester United 23.9.89 (5-1)	Main Stand
1148	P D Whittaker, Clifton, Nr Swinton	Manchester United 23.9.89 (5-1)	Old Kippax
1149	Alan David Bedford, Heald Green	Schalke 04, 15.4.70 ECWC s/f leg 2 (5-1)	Old Kippax
1150	Michael Bruce, Newport, South Wales	Manchester United 23.9.89 (5-1)	Old Platt Lane
1151	Andrew Vaughan, Sale, Cheshire	Huddersfield Town 7.11.87 (10-1)	Old Kippax
1152	John Francis Cornelly, Huddersfield	Huddersfield Town 7.11.87 (10-1)	Old Kippax
1153	Trevor Bowles, Exeter, Devon	Manchester United 23.9.89 (5-1)	Main Stand
1154	Keith Gooch, Cranleigh, Surrey	Tottenham Hotspur 9.12.67 (4-1)	Old Kippax
1155	David Marsden, Stalybridge	Manchester United 9.11.02 (3-1)	Old Kippax
1156	Darren Barker, Taunton, Somerset	Juventus 15.9.76 UEFA Cup (1-0)	Old Kippax
1157	Glynn Heselwood, Knutsford, Cheshire	Newcastle United 24.08.02 (1-0)	Old Kippax
1158	Phil Gibbons, Bollington, Macclesfield	Manchester United 6.11.71 (3-3)	Old Kippax
1159	Tony Georgiou, Hastings	Bolton Wanderers 3.3.79 (2-1)	Kippax
1160	Trevor Francis, Bidford on Avon	Manchester United 9.11.02 (3-1)	Old Kippax
1161	Lisa Smith, Warwick	Manchester United 9.11.02 (3-1)	Old Kippax
1162	Lee & Alan Betney, Alkrington, Middleton	Tottenham Hotspur 9.12.67 (4-1)	Scoreboard end, Old Kippax
1163	Phil Pollard, Manchester	Tottenham Hotspur 9.12.67 (4-1)	Old Kippax
1164	Steve & Ashley Kay, Failsworth	Every Maine Road match was magical!	17th step, Old Kippax
1165	Lee Campbell, Blackley, Manchester	Manchester United 9.11.02 (3-1)	New Kippax
1166	Andrew Terence William Taylor, Knutsford	Manchester United 9.11.02 (3-1)	Old Kippax
1167	Chris Young, Harrogate	Beating Leeds or Manchester United!	Main Stand
1168	Stav of Nottinghamshire	Manchester United 9.11.02 (3-1)	North Stand Block S
1169	Dave Bennett, Kent	Manchester United 23.9.89 (5-1)	Old Kippax
1170	Ian L G Niven, Didsbury, Manchester	Southampton 18.5.66 (0-0)	Boys' Corner!
1171	Ian Stuart Niven, Davenport, Stockport	Charlton Athletic 11.5.85 (5-1)	Main Office, Main Stand
1172	Ian Andrew Niven, Davenport	Manchester United 23.9.89 (5-1)	Window 8, Ticket Office
1173	Bill Witter, Manchester	Manchester United 9.11.02 (3-1)	New Platt Lane
1174	Glenn Brock, Southampton	Manchester United 9.11.02 (3-1)	Old Kippax
1175	Mike Lord, Little Baddow, Essex	Middlesbrough 21.1.76 FLC s/f 2 (4-0)	North Stand
1176	F E Hillier, Droylsden, Manchester	Newcastle United 9.1.57 FAC 3 rep (4-5)	Old Kippax
1177	Gemma Kristen Williams, Macclesfield	Everton 9.12.2000 (5-0)	Kippax Upper
1178	Dominic James Williams, Macclesfield	Wimbledon 29.9.01 (0-4)	Kippax Upper
1179	Chelsea Tensel, Heywood	Gillingham Play-off Final @ Wembley 30.5.99 (3-2)	Platt Lane
1180	Ashley Tensel, Heywood	Manchester United 9.11.02 (3-1)	Platt Lane
1181	Michael H Lancaster, Blackpool	Tottenham Hotspur 9.12.67 (4-1)	Platt Lane
1182	Stuart H Renshaw, Davenport, Stockport	Tottenham Hotspur 3.3.62 (6-2)	Main Stand
1183	Chris Openshaw, Flixton, Urmston, M/cr	Leeds United 31.8.74 (2-1)	Main Stand
1184	Fred Isherwood, Chinley, Derbyshire	Manchester United 9.11.02 (3-1)	Old Kippax
1185	Wayne Jenkins, Fallings Park, Wolverhampton	Manchester United 9.11.02 (3-1)	Old Kippax
1186	Graham Smith, Nantwich, Cheshire	Manchester United 23.9.89 (5-1)	Old Kippax
1187	Steve Crompton, Downend, Bristol	Newcastle United 26.12.77 (4-0)	Blockl B/C Main Stand
1188	Ian Stuart Fletcher, Fairfield, Buxton	Middlesbrough 21.1.76 FLC s/f 2 (4-0)	New Kippax
1189	Frank O'Neill, Newton, Hyde, Tameside	Manchester United 12.11.75 FL Cup Rd 4 (4-0)	Old Kippax
1190	Eddie Briggs, Hattersley, Hyde	Bury 14.5.68 Friendly (4-2)	Old Kippax
1191	David Bardsley, Dukinfield, Cheshire	Manchester United 23.9.89 (5-1)	New Platt Lane
1192	Margaret Stringer, Warrington	Manchester United 9.11.02 (3-1)	New Kippax
1193	Christopher Connor, East Didsbury, M/cr	Manchester United 9.11.02 (3-1)	Kippax
1194	Michael E Fleming, Hadfield, Glossop	Manchester United 23.9.89 (5-1)	Kippax
1195	Peter Thomson, Lichfield, Staffs	Manchester United 23.9.89 (5-1)	North Stand
1196	Frazer Allen Jones, Llanrhaedr, Denbigh	Leeds United 7.11.92 (4-0)	Main Stand
1197	Steven Blackmore, Miles Platting, Manchester	Newcastle United 26.12.77 (4-0)	Old Kippax
1198	Jayne Price, Ansdell, Lytham	Newcastle United 26.12.77 (4-0)	Old Platt Lane
1199	Edward Varley, Stretford, Manchester	Stoke City 3.3.34 FAC Rd 6 (1-0)	Main Stand
1200	Jed Cutmore, Hertford	Manchester United 9.11.02 (3-1)	Old Kippax
1201	Colin Cline, Sharston, Wythenshawe, M/cr	Manchester United 9.11.02 (3-1)	North Stand
1202	Bryn Wooller, Heald Green, Cheshire	Tottenham Hotspur 9.12.67 (4-1)	Old Kippax
1203	Angela Lane, East Didsbury, Manchester	Manchester United 9.11.02 (3-1)	Main Stand
1204	Mrs M E Galbraith, Hale, Altrincham	Manchester United 9.11.02 (3-1)	Old Kippax
1205	Kenneth Fisher, Rhyl, Denbighshire	West Bromwich Albion 3.8.68 Charity Shield (6-1)	Old Kippax
1206	Stuart Ewing, Bishopsteignton, Devon	Manchester United 23.9.89 (5-1)	Old Kippax
1207	Colin Connor Turner, Swinton, Manchester	Manchester United 9.11.02 (3-1)	Platt Lane
1208	Neil Woodhead, Newton Heath, Manchester	Schalke 04, 15.4.70 ECWC s/f leg 2 (5-1)	North Stand
1209	Lyndon Day, Heysham, Lancs	Manchester United 9.11.02 (3-1)	Old Kippax
1210	Mike Wilson, Offerton, Stockport	Schalke 04, 15.4.70 ECWC s/f leg 2 (5-1)	Old Kippax
1211	Michael Warren, Redding, Connecticut, USA	Wolverhampton Wanderers 28.12.81 (2-1)	Old Kippax
1212	Ricky King, St Andrew, Guernsey, C.I.	Manchester United 9.11.02 (3-1)	Old Kippax
1213	Jeremy Harrison, West Molesey, Surrey	Manchester United 23.9.89 (5-1)	Main Stand
1214	Brian K Raine, Southport	Manchester United 30.8.52 (2-1)	Old Kippax
1215	Samantha Myers, Kingswood, Warrington	Manchester United 9.11.02 (3-1)	Kippax

No	Subscriber name	Memorable Maine Road game/event	Fave part of Maine Road
1216	Ian Drew, Portsmouth	Manchester United 9.11.02 (3-1)	BBL Row 24 Seat 46
1217	Keith Roberts, Whitefield, Manchester	Manchester United 23.9.89 (5-1)	Old Kippax
1218	In memory of Arthur Roberts 1930-1991	Manchester United 12.11.75 FL Cup Rd 4 (4-0)	'The Popular Side'
1219	Shaun, Leanne, Steven & Ellen Crowley	Manchester United 23.9.89 (5-1)	Old Kippax
1220	Laura Cookson, Flixton, Manchester	Manchester United 9.11.02 (3-1)	New Platt Lane
1221	John Garry Cookson, Flixton, Manchester	Manchester United 9.11.02 (3-1)	New Platt Lane
1222	Michael Plummer, East Ham, London		Kippax
1223	Bill Bolger, East Ham, London		Kippax
1224	Harold & Sheila Tapley, Didsbury, Manchester	Chelsea 11.1.69 (4-1)	Main Stand, Block B, Row W, S14/15
1225	Geoff Griffiths, Denton, Manchester	Newcastle United 26.12.77 (4-0)	Kippax
1226	Steve Trinick, Heaton Mersey, Stockport	Newcastle United 26.12.77 (4-0)	Platt Lane
1227	In loving memory of Mandy Eastaugh	Manchester United 23.9.89 (5-1)	Main Stand, H left
1228	Phil Warrender, Cheadle Hulme, Cheshire	Manchester United 23.9.89 (5-1)	Upper tier, New Kippax
1229	Eric J Broad, Guiseley, Leeds	Manchester United 23.9.89 (5-1)	Old Kippax
1230	Christopher Cash, Weston-super-Mare	Schalke 04, 15.4.70 ECWC s/f leg 2 (5-1)	Old Kippax
1231	Joan I Brown, Wilmslow, Cheshire	The whole front & No.221 Maine Road - I lived there!	
1232	Edwin Humphrys, Worsley, Manchester	As a child -over tunnel on the old Kippax, as an adult - New Kippax	
1233	Graham Humphrys, Worsley, Manchester		
1234	David Edwards, Balerno, Mid-Lothian	Norwich City 12.2.2000 (3-1)	Main Stand
1235	Phil & Lucy Connor, New Moston, Manchester	Manchester United 9.11.02 (3-1)	Old & New Kippax
1236	James & Emma Breslin, Failsworth, Manchester	Manchester United 9.11.02 (3-1)	New Kippax
1237	Gareth Owen, Aberystwyth	Leeds United 12.11.77 (2-3)	Old Kippax
1238	Jessica B L McMahon, Newnham, Cambridge	West Ham United 27.4.03 (0-1)	Old Kippax & Main Stand
1239	Steve Buckley, Crewe	Everton FAC 6 rep 11.3.81 (3-1)	Old Kippax
	Linda Moseley, Crewe	Preston North End 10.2.02 (3-2)	New Kippax
1240	Adam Buckley, Crewe	Manchester United 9.11.02 (3-1)	North Stand
1241	Clive, Lee & David Gwilliam, Newquay, Cornwall	Manchester United 9.11.02 (3-1)	Old Kippax
1242	Michael J Hawley, Poulton-le-Fylde	Schalke 04, 15.4.70 ECWC s/f leg 2 (5-1)	Old Kippax
1243	Garry Lippett, Openshaw, Manchester	West Bromwich Albion 14.3.81 (2-1)	Old Kippax
1244	Michael Relph, Chorlton, Manchester	Burnley 22.12.73 (2-0)	Old Platt Lane
1245	A Wainwright, Denton, Manchester	Manchester United 15.11.69 (4-0)	Kippax
1246	Chris Diggle, Dukinfield, Cheshire	Manchester United 9.11.02 (3-1)	Kippax Lower
1247	John Hodkinson, Greengates, Bradford	Manchester United 23.9.89 (5-1)	Singers' Corner, Old Kippax
1248	David Brown, Kingsdown, Kent	Everton 3.3.56 FAC 6 (2-1)	Old Kippax
1249	Roger Melvyn Ince, Tottington, Bury	Manchester United 9.11.02 (3-1)	Old Kippax
1250	Emily & Frank Street, Kirkham, Preston	Manchester United 9.11.02 (3-1)	New Kippax
1251	Neil Street & Wendy Lucas, Southport	Manchester United 23.9.89 (5-1)	Old Kippax
1252	T Rogers, Littleport, Ely, Cambs	Manchester United 9.11.02 (3-1)	Kippax
1253	Keith J Russell, Wolverhampton	Huddersfield Town 7.11.87 (10-1)	Old Kippax
1254	Alan Lawrence, Weymouth	Manchester United 23.9.89 (5-1)	North Stand
1255	Adrian Brodkin, London N2	Tottenham Hotspur 9.12.67 (4-1)	Frank Swift Bar, Main Stand
1256	Sam McEwen, Prestatyn	Blackburn 15.9.02 (2-2)	Family Stand
1257	Michael Duff, Prestatyn	AC Milan 6.12.78 Rd 3, leg 2 (3-0)	Platt Lane
1258	Stephen Wilson, Ovenden, Halifax	Chelsea 30.04.94 (2-2)	Old Kippax
1259	Stephen McCardle, Bury	Manchester United 9.11.02 (3-1)	Main Stand
1260	Paul E Leese, Kidsgrove, Stoke on Trent	Leeds United 7.1.78 FAC 3 (2-1)	Old Kippax
1261	Ade Evans, Elworth, Sandbach	Watford, 11.8.2001 (3-0)	Old Kippax
1262	Alan Phillips, Withington, Manchester	Manchester United 23.9.89 (5-1)	Old Kippax
1263	David O'Neill, Sale, Cheshire	Tottenham Hotspur 22.10.94 (5-2)	J Block
1264	Stafford Waters, Maxwell Park, Glasgow	Tottenham Hotspur 9.12.67 (4-1)	Old Kippax
1265	Terence Fletcher, Batley, W Yorkshire	Manchester United 23.9.89 (5-1)	Old Kippax
1266	Pamela E Harrison, Wrexham	Bert Trautmann's Testimonial 15.4.64 (5-4)	Claremont Road End
1267	Dave Pearson, Buxton, Derbyshire	Tottenham Hotspur 9.12.67 (4-1)	North Stand
1268	Geoffrey Addy, Glossop, Derbyshire	Newcastle United 26.12.77 (4-0)	Old Platt Lane
1269	Paul O'Keefe, Wythenshawe, Manchester	Manchester United 9.11.02 (3-1)	Old Kippax
1270	Clive Graham, Prestwich, Manchester	Charlton Athletic 11.5.85 (5-1)	Old Kippax
1271	Happy 40th (17th July) Graham Perry, Prestwich	Manchester United 23.9.89 (5-1)	North Stand
1272	Walter Scott, Bury, Lancs	Manchester United 9.11.02 (3-1)	Old Kippax
1273	Michael Lambert, Urmston, Manchester		
1274	John Carroll, Gorton, Manchester	Newcastle United 26.12.77 (4-0)	Old Kippax
1275	James McHugh, New Zealand (ex Manchester)	Manchester United 23.9.89 (5-1)	Old Kippax
1276	Harvey Slifkin, Ashton-under-Lyne	Manchester United 12.11.75 FLC 4 (4-0)	
1277	Mark Barrowclough, Hazel Grove, Stockport	Charlton Athletic 11.5.85 (5-1)	Old Kippax
1278	Anton Boddy, Retford, Notts	Birmingham City 28.4.2000 (1-0)	Old Kippax
1279	Pauline Yates, Castleton, Rochdale	Manchester United 23.9.89 (5-1)	Main Stand
1280	Christopher Yates, Castleton, Rochdale	Manchester United 23.9.89 (5-1)	Old Kippax
1281	Ronald Frederick Cook, Buxton	Schalke 04, 15.4.70 ECWC s/f leg 2 (5-1)	Scoreboard End
1282	Bryan P Charnley, Great Sankey, Warrington	Manchester United 15.11.69 (4-0)	Old Kippax
1283	David Gerard Mullahey, Stretford, Manchester	Manchester United 12.11.75 FLC 4 (4-0)	New Kippax
1284	Paul Newton, Port St Mary, Isle of Man	Middlesbrough 21.1.76 FLC s/f 2 (4-0)	North Stand
1285	Gary Stapleton, Horsham, Sussex	Atletico Bilbao ECWC 1 leg 2, 1.10.69 (3-0)	Old Kippax
1286	John Davies, Wythenshawe, Manchester	Schalke 04, 15.4.70 ECWC s/f leg 2 (5-1)	Old Kippax
1287	Paul Hughes, Connahs Quay, Flintshire	Manchester United 9.11.02 (3-1)	North Stand
1288	Mike Ronayne, Wythenshawe, Manchester	Manchester United 23.9.89 (5-1)	Old Kippax
1289	Diane & Michael Dillon, Newton, Hyde	Manchester United 9.11.02 (3-1)	Old Kippax
1290	Lee Caulfield, Godley, Hyde	Schalke 04, 15.4.70 ECWC s/f leg 2 (5-1)	Old Kippax
1291	Dominic Moran, Epsom, Surrey	Manchester United 9.11.02 (3-1)	Main Stand
1292	Simon Newby, London N2	Manchester United 9.11.02 (3-1)	Old Kippax
1293	Peter Williams, Northenden	Manchester United 9.11.02 (3-1)	
1294	Daniel Mackinnon, Timperley, b.11th January 2003		
1295	Sophie Mackinnon, Timperley, b. 11th January 2003		
1296	Ben Mackinnon, b. 1st August 2002		
1297	Mark Blackford, Swinton, Manchester	Manchester United 23.9.89 (5-1)	Old Kippax
1298	Stewart Richardson, Wibsey, Bradford	Huddersfield Town 7.11.87 (10-1)	Old Platt Lane
1299	Colin Ducker, West Walton, Cambs	Barnsley, 6.4.02 (5-1)	Platt Lane
1300	Tony Bennett, Moulton, Northwich	Manchester United 9.11.02 (3-1)	Old Kippax
1301	Glyn Edwards, Poynton, Cheshire	Manchester United 23.9.89 (5-1)	Platt Lane

City involved going to the match with me at some stage of their lives therefore my gran had become a little part of their City folklore, as much as she was a major part of mine. The first game after she died was a hard one. I can't recall who we played that day despite it being so recent, and despite the fact my life revolves along a soundtrack of City results I just can't revive this in my memory. My dad was clearly upset about her loss too. But what I remember most that day was the strange feeling of alienation. All I knew about going to Maine Road involved visiting Grandma before and after the game. We couldn't adjust to arriving at the ground a little later, or having to disappear straight from Maine Road without loitering. All this had gone, 24 years of watching City and it was no longer the same.

When it was announced City were moving to the stadium I was greatly in favour. Maine Road has served us well. However the possibility we could develop it into a stadium of the future was unlikely - due to a number of reasons such as poor planning/development by previous regimes, residents' issues, and the fact the council had an opportunity to shoehorn us into the new stadium by blocking any new planning requests. Understandably, they quite rightly didn't want the Commonwealth Games stadium to become a white elephant.

I have tried to write this next paragraph many times but it keeps coming out in my eyes as cold and heartless. I apologise if this is how it sounds to you reading this because my intentions are good. When City do move to the new stadium I'm glad Grandma won't be around to see it because I think it would be upsetting for her not to be involved any more. It would be like the party was happening someplace else, and she wasn't invited. After all, she has 25 years of family tradition, watching me take my first steps to Maine Road as an intrigued 8-year-old. She watched me grow up, become a husband and father.

I look forward to the day my children accompany me regularly to the match and I feel a sadness that they will never feel the unique experience of going to matches at Maine Road the way I did. They'll never consider Maine Road as part of their heritage, or birthright, the way I do.

Steve Heald

No	Subscriber name	Memorable Maine Road game/event	Fave part of Maine Road
1302	David Ibbotson, Manchester	Manchester United 23.9.89 (5-1)	Old Kippax
1303	Mark & Ros Paulson, Turton, Bolton	Manchester United 9.11.02 (3-1)	Main Stand
1304	Susan Maaz, Ettington, Stratford on Avon	Newcastle United 28.2.76 FLC final (2-1)	Old Platt Lane
1305	Jason Concar, Sale Moor, Cheshire	Charlton Athletic 11.5.85 (5-1)	Old Kippax
1306	George Hadfield, Droylsden, Manchester	Tottenham Hotspur 9.12.67 (4-1)	Old Kippax
1307	Liam Tilston, Widnes, Cheshire	Manchester United 9.11.02 (3-1) My birthday!	North Stand
1308	Neil Bluey Faulkner, Kendal, Cumbria	Manchester United 23.9.89 (5-1)	Main Stand
1309	Keith Gatley, Burnage, Manchester	Manchester United 9.11.02 (3-1)	Old Kippax
1310	Martin Scott Smith & Andrew McDonald	Manchester United 9.11.02 (3-1)	North Stand
1311	B A Midgley, Kearsley, Bolton	Manchester United 23.9.89 (5-1)	Main Stand
1312	Patrick R Ruse, Kingsbridge, South Devon	Charlton Athletic 11.5.85 (5-1)	Old Kippax
1313	Gary Mitchell, Clayton Bridge, Manchester	Manchester United 23.9.89 (5-1)	Old Kippax
1314	M McGee, Gorton, Manchester		
1315	Steve Briggs, Rawtenstall, Lancs	Manchester United 9.11.02 (3-1)	Old Kippax
1316	Ian Bowden, Wavertree, Liverpool	Manchester United 23.9.89 (5-1)	Old Kippax
1317	Howard Barnett, Heworth, York	Everton 29.4.68 (2-0)	Old Kippax
1318	Asa Fitton, Hasland, Chesterfield	Crewe Alexandra 8.4.2000 (4-0)	Kippax Lower
1319	Alan Rowbotham, Droylsden, Manchester	Newcastle United 26.12.77 (4-0)	Old Kippax
1320	Andy Bell, Denton, Manchester	Tottenham Hotspur 22.10.94 (5-2)	Old Kippax
1321	Michael Glynn, Whitefield, Manchester	Charlton Athletic 11.5.85 (5-1)	Old Kippax
1322	Joe Farquhar & Mother & late Father, Oldham	Manchester United 9.11.02 (3-1)	Main Stand
1323	The Burrows Family of Timperley	Tottenham Hotspur 9.12.67 (4-1)	Old Kippax
1324	The Souch Family of Copmanthorpe, York	Manchester United 9.11.02 (3-1)	Main Stand
1325	Ian Surrey, Bolton	Manchester United 23.9.89 (5-1)	New Kippax
1326	Eddie Brownhill, Cheadle Hulme, Cheshire	Tottenham Hotspur 9.12.67 (4-1)	Old Kippax
1327	The England Family of Radcliffe, Manchester	Manchester United 9.11.02 (3-1)	Old Kippax Corner
1328	Martin Duddridge, Halifax	Newcastle United 26.12.77 (4-0)	Old Kippax
1329	Mike Shaughnessy, Sale, Cheshire	Manchester United 23.9.89 (5-1)	New Kippax Upper
1330	Suey Ross, Manchester	Norwich City 16.8.75 (3-0) My first game	Kippax Lower GG, R8, S190
1331	David Ross, Prestwich, Manchester	Manchester United 12.11.75 FL Cup Rd 4 (4-0)	North Stand
1332	Christopher Pannell, Fallowfield, Manchester	Newcastle United 26.12.77 (4-0)	Old Kippax
1333	Jo-Ann Cundill, Stockport	Manchester United 9.11.02 (3-1)	Old Kippax
1334	Tom Casey, Old Trafford, Manchester	Manchester United 23.9.89 (5-1)	Old Kippax
1335	The Franklin Family of Blackley	All of them, all magic!	
1336	Keith, Helen & Emma Hargreaves, Denton	Middlesbrough 21.1.76 FLC s/f 2 (4-0)	Old Kippax
1337	Peter, Kate & Dave McDonough, Bramhall	Manchester United 9.11.02 (3-1)	New Kippax
1338	Trevor Makings, Glossop, in memory of Harold	Newcastle Utd 29.1.69 FAC Rd 4 rep(2-0)	Kippax standing, halfway line
1339	Ron Robinson, Manchester	Tottenham Hotspur 9.12.67 (4-1)	Old Kippax
1340	Patrick O'Sullivan, Urmston, Manchester	Manchester United 9.11.02 (3-1)	New Platt Lane
1341	Bernard O'Sullivan, Offerton, Stockport	Manchester United 9.11.02 (3-1)	New Platt Lane
1342	Karl Cross, Blackburn	Everton FAC 6 rep 11.3.81 (3-1)	Main Stand
1343	Anthony J Garlick, Fitton-Hill, Oldham	Middlesbrough 21.1.76 FLC s/f 2 (4-0)	Old Kippax
1344	David G Lapham, Stockport	Manchester United 23.9.89 (5-1)	Old Kippax
1345	Garry Lee Lapham, Stockport	Huddersfield Town 7.11.87 (10-1)	New Kippax
1346	Andrew Dean, Stockport	Manchester United 23.9.89 (5-1)	Old Kippax
1347	Jason Pott, Tiverton, Devon	Manchester United 23.9.89 (5-1)	Old Kippax
1348	Richard Mulhearn, Cheetham, Manchester	AC Milan 6.12.78 Rd 3, leg 2 (3-0)	Platt Lane, behind goal
1349	Robert Hitchens, Wilnecote, Tamworth	Wigan Athletic 17.5.99, P/off leg 2 (1-0)	Kippax
1350	Peter Moore, Sale, Cheshire	Manchester United 6.11.71 (3-3)	Main Stand
1351	Jack Bache, Prestwich, Manchester	Manchester United 9.11.02 (3-1)	Old Kippax
1352	G Wrend, Atherton, Manchester	Manchester United 23.9.89 (5-1)	Old Kippax
1353	John Lea, Hazel Grove, Stockport	Tottenham Hotspur 7.5.77 (5-0)	1970s North Stand
1354	Kevin Fowles, Brooklands, Manchester	Manchester United 23.9.89 (5-1)	Old Kippax
1355	J P Goodall, Darlington, Co Durham	Wigan Athletic 17.5.99, P/off leg 2 (1-0)	Old Kippax
1356	David Tomes, St Mary, Jersey C.I.	Southampton 11.5.03 (0-1)	New Kippax
1357	Howard Croft, Bury, Lancs	Tottenham Hotspur 9.12.67 (4-1)	Old Kippax
1358	Mick Grayson, Woodhouse, Sheffield		
1359	Gaz Ridings, Blues Brothers Birchwood	Manchester United 23.9.89 (5-1)	Old Kippax
1360	Ian Bowie, Denton, Manchester	Tottenham Hotspur 9.12.67 (4-1)	Old Kippax
1361	Ken Mills, Flixton, Manchester	Manchester United 9.11.02 (3-1)	Umbro & Kippax Stands
1362	Bernard Griffin, Millom, Cumbria	Manchester United 9.11.02 (3-1)	Kippax
1363	Michael Beattie, Houghton, Carlisle	Manchester United 9.11.02 (3-1)	Platt Lane
1364	John Arthur Tyson, Stretford, Manchester	Manchester United 23.9.89 (5-1)	Old Kippax
1365	Trevor Goddard, Warnham, W Sussex	Birmingham City 28.4.2000 (1-0)	Kippax
1366	Bernard Berman, Prestwich, Manchester	Manchester United 23.9.89 (5-1)	Old Scoreboard End
1367	Eric Chadwick, Droylsden, Manchester	Manchester United 9.1.37 (1-0)	Main Std, Block C, Row J, seat 33
1368	William Rowe, Tytherington, Macclesfield	Manchester United 9.11.02 (3-1)	Main Stand
1369	Mark Chadwick, Cheadle, Cheshire	Manchester United 23.9.89 (5-1)	Main Stand
1370	R J Chadwick	Charlton Athletic 11.5.85 (5-1)	Main Std, Block C, Row J, seat 32
1371	Bartley Ramsay, Lucan, Co Dublin	Manchester United 23.9.89 (5-1)	Old Kippax
1372	Dave Bradley, Ashton-under-Lyne	Wigan Athletic 17.5.99, P/off leg 2 (1-0)	Old Kippax
1373	Alan Bradley, Ashton-under-Lyne	Newcastle United 26.12.77 (4-0)	Old Kippax
1374	Paul Thompson, Whaley Bridge	Stockport County 7.12.99 (1-2), 10-1 & 5-1	Old Kippax, 40/Social clubs
1375	Greg Hughes, in memory of Harry Hughes	Newcastle United 26.12.77 (4-0)	Old Kippax
1376	Stephen Coope, Great Moor, Stockport	Manchester United 9.11.02 (3-1)	New Kippax
1377	Nigel & Chris Scott, Bredbury, Stockport	Manchester United 9.11.02 (3-1)	North Stand
1378	Gordon & Howard Slack, Claydon, Ipswich	Tottenham Hotspur 9.12.67 (4-1)	Old Kippax
1379	Ian Sutton, Davyhulme, Manchester	Derby County 20.4.91 (2-1)	Old Kippax
1380	Alistair Hay, Radcliffe, Manchester	Middlesbrough 21.1.76 FLC s/f 2 (4-0)	Old Kippax
1381	David W Homer, Stretford, Lancs	Tottenham Hotspur 9.12.67 (4-1)	B Block, Main Stand
1382	Stephen & Thomas Willis, Stalybridge	Manchester United 9.11.02 (3-1)	Old Kippax
1383	David Wayne Mitchell, Leigh, Lancs	West Ham United 25.1.98 FAC 4 (1-2)	Old Kippax
1384	Graham & Siobhan Brine, Offerton, Stockport	Manchester United 23.9.89 (5-1)	New Kippax
1385	Paul Goodwin, Heaton Chapel, Stockport	Barnsley 6.4.2002 (5-1)	Old Kippax
1386	T Hardicre, Poynton, Cheshire	Manchester United 3.12.69 FLC s/f (2-1)	Kippax
1387	Francis Carr, Miles Platting, Manchester	Every one!	M Block, North Stand
1388	Neil Whiting, Heywood, Lancs	Any City victory!	Kippax Street terrace
1389	Debbie Williams, Stretford, Manchester	Manchester United 9.11.02 (3-1)	Old Kippax

No	Subscriber name	Memorable Maine Road game/event	Fave part of Maine Road
1390	David Gaskill, Southport	Wigan Athletic 17.5.99, P/off leg 2 (1-0)	North Stand
1391	Tony Whiting, Primrose Hill, Huddersfield	Manchester United 23.9.89 (5-1)	Kippax Street terrace
1392	David Williams, Cleckheaton, Yorkshire	Charlton Athletic 11.5.85 (5-1)	Old Kippax
1393	Dawn Morris, Stretford, Manchester	Huddersfield Town 7.11.87 (10-1)	Old Kippax
1394	Ian Floyd, Chadderton, Oldham	Schalke 04, 15.4.70 ECWC s/f leg 2 (5-1)	Main Stand
1395	Kevin Brookes, Leigh (ex Wythenshawe)	Manchester United 23.9.89 (5-1)	Old Kippax
1396	Andrew Leslie & Dr Leslie Thomas Cookson	Manchester United 9.11.02 (3-1)	Old Kippax
1397	Richard, George, John & Robert Coulson	Manchester United 9.11.02 (3-1)	Main Stand
1398	Graham Palmer, Appleton, Warrington	Norwich City 24.1.81 (6-0)	Old Kippax
1399	John W Bourne, Jumbleholes, Accrington	Tottenham Hotspur 9.12.67 (4-1)	Old Kippax
1400	Malc Blinston, Leigh, Grtr Manchester	Manchester United 9.11.02 (3-1)	Old Kippax
1401	Anthony Nolan, New Moston, Manchester	Manchester United 23.9.89 (5-1)	New Kippax
1402	Michael Gibson, Rochdale	West Ham United 21.3.70 (1-5)	Kippax
1403	Mark Derbyshire, Stepping Hill, Stockport	Manchester United 23.9.89 (5-1)	Old Kippax
1404	Tony Sloan, Bluntisham, Cambs	Manchester United 6.11.71 (3-3)	North Stand
1405	Paul Kinder, Denton, Manchester	Manchester United 23.9.89 (5-1)	Old Kippax
1406	Gary Lewis, Woodhouses, Manchester	Manchester United 9.11.02 (3-1)	Old Kippax
1407	Ian Wilson, Kings Sutton, Oxfordshire	Tottenham Hotspur 9.12.67 (4-1)	Main Stand, nr Directors' Box
1408	Iain & Gary Barnes, Lostock, Bolton	Manchester United 9.11.02 (3-1)	New Kippax
1409	Tommy Bird, Lymm, Cheshire	Manchester United 9.11.02 (3-1)	Old Kippax
1410	Sally Davenport, Steve, Kate & Alex Robinson	Manchester United 23.9.89 (5-1)	Main Stand
1411	Tony Berry, Archer Park, Middleton	Manchester United 23.9.89 (5-1)	Main Stand
1412	Tim Whitworth, Mansfield, Notts	Manchester United 9.11.02 (3-1)	Main Stand
1413	Neil Looker, Irwell Vale, Lancs	Manchester United 23.9.89 (5-1)	Old Kippax
1414	Joan Grimley, Prestwich, Manchester	Manchester United 9.11.02 (3-1)	North Stand
1415	Kevin Pearce, Burnage, Manchester	Manchester United 9.11.02 (3-1)	Old Kippax
1416	Paul & Frances Monk, Caton, Lancs	Manchester United 23.9.89 (5-1)	Old Kippax
1417	Mark Kershaw, Westhoughton, Bolton	Manchester United 9.11.02 (3-1)	North Stand
1418	Tony Hudson, Chorlton, Manchester		
1419	Nigel Bardsley, Bowdon, Altrincham	Manchester United 9.11.02 (3-1)	Old Kippax
1420	Lee & George Edwards, Salford	Manchester United 23.9.89 (5-1)	New Platt Lane
1421	Alan Burge, Burwell, Cambs	CambridgeUnited 17.12.83(0-0)	Away End
1422	Greg Kelly, Renfrew, Scotland	Manchester United 9.11.02 (3-1), Denis Law, that back-heel	Old Kippax
1423	Mark Helsby, Davyhulme, Manchester	Kippax Last Stand	Main Stand
1424	David Helsby, Davyhulme, Manchester	Newcastle United 26.12.77 (4-0)	North Stand
1425	Helen Botterill, Wakefield	Barnsley, 6.4.02 (5-1)	Main Stand
1426	Tom Hickson, Sale, Cheshire	Any City victory!	Old Platt Lane
1427	Gordon & Ben Hyslop, Bramhall, Cheshire	Tottenham Hotspur 9.12.67 (4-1)	Old Kippax
1428	David O'Brien, Millom, Cumbria	Manchester United 9.11.02 (3-1)	Old Kippax
1429	John Rawnsley, Pudsey, W Yorkshire		
1430	Simon Tebbit, Otford, Kent	Any victory over Manchester United	New Platt Lane
1431	Simon, Mel & Dylan Malkin, Clayton Le Moors	Manchester United 9.11.02 (3-1)	Main Stand
1432	James Richard Shuffleton, Waterthorpe, Sheffield	Tottenham Hotspur 9.12.67 (4-1)	Old Kippax
1433	Dee & Bev Brocklehurst, Buxworth, High Peak	Manchester United 9.11.02 (3-1)	Kippax Upper
1434	Jim Brocklehurst, Buxworth, High Peak	Tottenham Hotspur 9.12.67 (4-1)	1970s North Stand
1435	Dee Brocklehurst, Buxworth, High Peak	Wolverhampton Wanderers 8.9.71 FLC 2 (4-3)	Kippax Upper CC
1436	Adrian Leeming, Denton, Manchester	Manchester United 9.11.02 (3-1)	New Kippax
1437	Mr & Mrs Offiler, Grimsby	Manchester United 9.11.02 (3-1)	North Stand
1438	Richard Woodward, West Cuddington, Cheshire	Manchester United 9.11.02 (3-1)	North Stand
1439	Stephen Booth, Littleborough, Lancs	Schalke 04, 15.4.70 ECWC s/f leg 2 (5-1)	Old Kippax
1440	Steven Boden, Appleton Thorn, Warrington	Manchester United 23.9.89 (5-1)	Old Kippax
1441	Paul Chapman, Poynton, Cheshire	Charlton Athletic 11.5.85 (5-1)	New Kippax
1442	Des Burns, Cheadle Hulme, Cheshire	Manchester United 23.9.89 (5-1)	Old Kippax
1443	Danny Feely, Newton Heath, Manchester	Charlton Athletic 11.5.85 (5-1)	Kippax
1444	Gavin Feely, Winshill, Burton on Trent	Charlton Athletic 11.5.85 (5-1)	Kippax
1445	Paul Kielty, Abbey Hey, Gorton, M/cr	Manchester United 23.9.89 (5-1)	Old Kippax
1446	Peter John Conroy, Radcliffe, Manchester	Tottenham Hotspur 9.12.67 (4-1)	Old Kippax
1447	Matt, Jade & Jack, the Davey Family, Exeter	Leeds United 11.1.2003 (2-1)	North Stand
1448	Mark Arrundale, Dukinfield, Cheshire	Manchester United 9.11.02 (3-1)	Old Kippax
1449	Gary Plant, Kingsmead, Northwich	Manchester United 23.9.89 (5-1)	Old Kippax
1450	Joyce Ryles, Cadishead, Manchester	Manchester United 9.11.02 (3-1)	Kippax
1451	Alan Hughes, Bolton	Manchester United 6.11.71 (3-3)	Old Kippax
1452	Peter Williams, Wetherby, W Yorkshire	Newcastle United 26.12.77 (4-0)	Scoreboard End
1453	Norma Hargreaves, in memory of John	All of them!	Old Kippax
1454	Christopher Maguire, Burghfield, Reading		Kippax
1455	Mike Puncher, Dorchester, Dorset	Manchester United 23.9.89 (5-1)	Old Kippax
1456	Dermot Griffin, Millom, Cumbria	All the games!	Old Kippax
1457	Derek Miller, Blackley, Manchester	Manchester United 15.11.69 (4-0)	Old Kippax
1458	Brian Rogerson, ex Stockport, now St Ives	Newcastle United 26.12.77 (4-0)	Old Kippax
1459	Chris Simon, Walthamstow, London	Manchester United 9.11.02 (3-1)	Old Kippax
1460	David Steele, Carlisle		
1461	Nicola Gage, Poynton, Cheshire	Manchester United 9.11.02 (3-1)	North Stand
1462	Darren Wood, Poynton, Cheshire	Manchester United 9.11.02 (3-1)	North Stand
1463	Keith Saville, Denton, Manchester	Charlton Athletic 11.5.85 (5-1)	Old Kippax
1464	Don Bryce, Hale Barns, Cheshire	Manchester United 23.9.89 (5-1)	Old Kippax
1465	Mark Kershaw, Poynton, Cheshire	Derby County 10.04.76 (4-3)	Old Kippax
1466	Terence Henry Chadwick, Wigan	Newcastle United 24.2.96 (3-3)	Old Kippax
1467	Brian Stimpson, Fallowfield, Manchester	Tottenham Hotspur 9.12.67 (4-1)	Old Kippax
1468	Andrew Hesford, Withington, Manchester	Manchester United 23.9.89 (5-1)	Old Kippax
1469	Robert Saxon, Woodley, Stockport	Manchester United 23.9.89 (5-1)	New Kippax
1470	Stuart Brereton, Pennington, Leigh	Manchester United 9.11.02 (3-1)	Old Kippax
1471	Julie Brannan, Heaton Chapel, Stockport	Charlton Athletic 11.5.85 (5-1)	New Kippax
1472	Steven Wilson, Newton Heath, Manchester	Manchester United 9.11.02 (3-1)	Kippax
1473	In memory of Arnold Cookson	Any City match	North Stand
1474	Brian, Tom, Paul & Rosemary Gratton, E.Didsbury	Manchester United 9.11.02 (3-1)	Old Scoreboard End
1475	Raymond Thompson, Kinmel Bay, Conwy	Everton FAC 6 rep 11.3.81 (3-1)	Old Kippax
1476	John Russell Jamieson, Lytham St Annes	Wolverhampton Wanderers 28.3.53 (3-1)	Old Kippax
1477	Mrs Ellen Smith, Droylsden, Manchester	Manchester United 9.11.02 (3-1)	Old Kippax

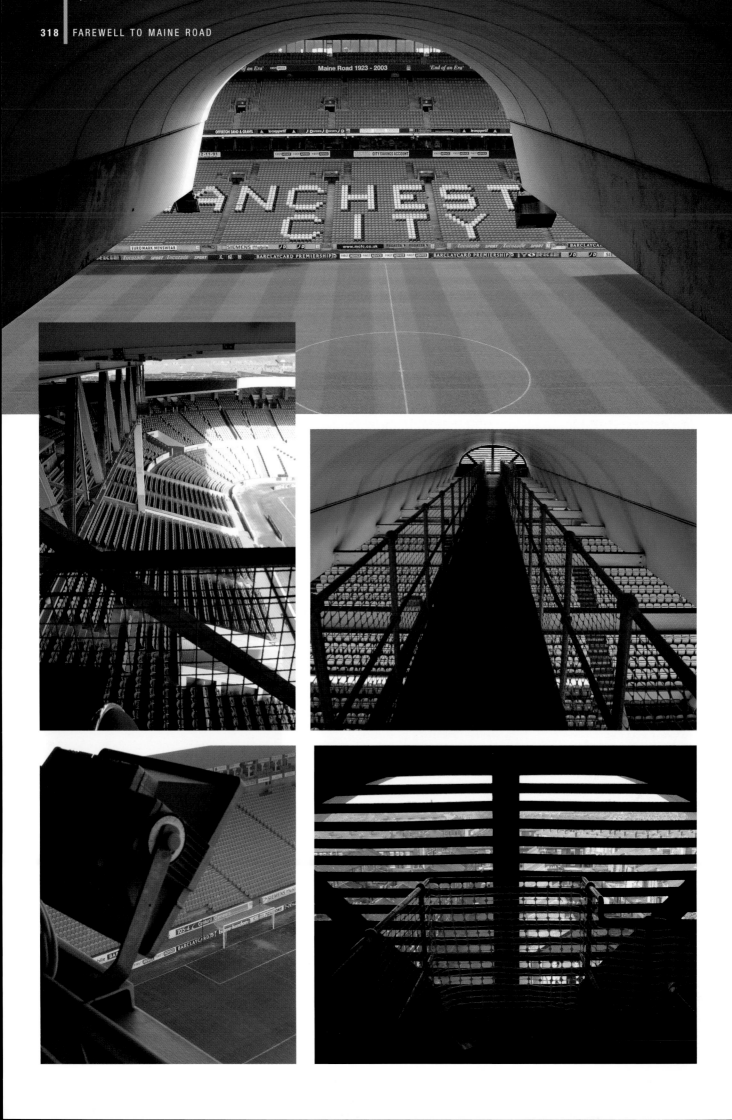

No	Subscriber name	Memorable Maine Road game/event	Fave part of Maine Road
1478	Iain McConnell, Renfrew, Scotland	Manchester United 9.11.02 (3-1)	Kippax
1479	Doug Jervis, Wythenshawe, Manchester	Manchester United 9.11.02 (3-1)	Platt Lane
1480	Doug Jervis, Wythenshawe, Manchester	Manchester United 9.11.02 (3-1)	Platt Lane
1481	Doug Jervis, Wythenshawe, Manchester	Manchester United 9.11.02 (3-1)	Platt Lane
1482	Doug Jervis, Wythenshawe, Manchester	Manchester United 9.11.02 (3-1)	Platt Lane
1483	Paul Davey, Brooklands, Manchester	Manchester United 9.11.02 (3-1)	Old Kippax
1484	Berny Lawton, Heaton Mersey, Stockport	Charlton Athletic 11.5.85 (5-1)	Old Kippax
1485	Paul Jackson, Aylesbury, Bucks	Arsenal 17.2.71 FAC 5 (1-3)	Old Kippax
1486	Tom Albert Sellers, Prague	Manchester United 23.9.89 (5-1)	Old Kippax
1487	Roy Clarke, Sale, Cheshire	Everton 3.3.56 FAC 6 (2-1)	Old Kippax
1488	Tony Higgs, Bradshaw, Bolton	Manchester United 23.9.89 (5-1)	Old Kippax
1489	Ian J Stuchbury, Cotham,Cambs	Manchester United 9.11.02 (3-1)	Old Kippax
1490	The Revd Canon Dr D C Gray, Stamford	The 1969 Season	Old Kippax Corner
1491	Francis Edward Hillier, Droylsden, Manchester	Newcastle United 9.1.57 FAC 3 rep (4-5)	North Stand
1492	Colin Heath, Droylsden, Manchester	Norwich City 13.01.2002 (3-1)	North Stand
1493	Steven A Boyd, Didsbury, Manchester	Newcastle United 26.12.77 (4-0)	Main Stand
1494	In Memory of John Powell	All Wins!	Main Stand
1495	Teresa Francis, Heckington, Sleaford	Manchester United 9.11.02 (3-1)	New Platt Lane
1496	Mike Mills, Marton, Middlesbrough	Sheffield United 21.8.99 (6-0)	Kippax
1497	John Watson, Bollington, Macclesfield	Portsmouth 28.4.34 FAC Final (2-1)	Platt Lane
1498	Andrew Wright, Coventry	Manchester United 9.11.02 (3-1)	Kippax
1499	Trevor Wright, Kenilworth	Manchester United 9.11.02 (3-1)	Kippax
1500	Revd. Jeremy James Frost, Shawbirch, Telford	Manchester United 9.11.02 (3-1)	Top of the Kippax
1501	Graeme Bullen, Denton, Manchester	Manchester United 9.11.02 (3-1)	Kippax
1502	Matt Cunliffe, Surbiton, Surrey	Manchester United 21.2.81 (1-0)	Old Kippax
1503	Peter Dunn, Keynsham, Bristol	Wolverhampton Wanderers 23.8.47 (4-3)	Behind the goal
1504	Ian Rodger, Durham,		Old Kippax
1505	Adam Rodger, North Harrow		Main Stand
1506	David Priestley, Howick, Auckland, New Zealand		Kippax
1507	Tony Drinkwater, Royton, Oldham	Tottenham Hotspur 9.12.67 (4-1)	Old Kippax
1508	Colin McAndry, Urmston, Manchester	Manchester United 9.11.02 (3-1)	Platt Lane Block X
1509	Martin McNelis, Govan, Glasgow		
1510	Kevin Greene, Great Moor, Stockport	Manchester United 23.9.89 (5-1)	Old Kippax
1511	Andrew Waldon, Withington, Manchester	Huddersfield Town 7.11.87 (10-1)	Windy corner, Old Kippax
1512	Gerald Toon, Leicester	Leicester City 25.1.95 (0-1)	Main Stand
1513	Julian Baskcomb, Melton Mowbray, Leics	Tottenham Hotspur 16.9.72 (2-1)	North Stand
1514	In memory of George C H Revill, ex Levenshulme		

Maine Memory

"Maine Road all to myself"

■ Young lads sometimes get asked by their dads if they want to go to his place of work and I was no exception but this dad's workplace was just that little bit different. Some Sundays a trip to Maine Road would be on the agenda. You would enter the stadium in those days through a little side door next to the present day main entrance which was the actual players' entrance. That's when the tingle of excitement would start. Turning right the smell of liniment would fill the air and I would follow my dad through the main changing room which was just an open expanse of wood panelling, nothing special really and then into a second room where there were showers, a sauna and the biggest square bath you could imagine. The final doorway opened up into the treatment room and usually there would be at least a couple of the players we would have been hero-worshipping the day before in for some sort of physio. At the time meeting players became quite normal, if that happened today even at my slightly more mature 34 years I would be totally awestruck. But they never seemed to act like prima donnas and were nothing other than regular people. Most would say hello and in those days one or two might even have popped round your house occasionally. But the real reason I was at Maine Road was purely self-indulgent. All I wanted was to get the nod, leg it to the ball cupboard - money must have been tight in those days because they all looked knackered - then walk down the tunnel tentatively peering out to see if anyone was about. Head down running out onto the pitch was an adrenaline rush; I'd usually head towards the North Stand goal. I was Denis Tueart or Peter Barnes, providing my own commentary as I dribbled past five men rounding the goalkeeper and sticking it in the top corner of what was to this 9 or 10-year-old the biggest set of nets ever seen (how do they miss every week?). Then run the whole length of the pitch to take the acclaim of a totally empty Kippax. But that didn't matter. To me there were 25,000 on that terrace, this was heaven, and the only place I wanted to be. To have the run of Maine Road all to myself was very special, the best playground in the world and in the late '70's it was a great place to be around. To me a truly family atmosphere was created and thanks to my father it's something I'll never forget.

Tony Book Jnr

Left: In July 2003 the hammer came down on Maine Road as the City Council asked the club to work with them to auction off a few souvenirs. Many fans attended simply to buy their old seat.

Below: Room with a View - if you knew where to look it was possible to catch a glimpse of the new stadium from a window on a staircase at the back of the Kippax Stand.
Club photographer Ed Garvey used a powerful lens to capture this rare image during Maine Road's final days.